THE THREE MEANINGS

The
Three Meanings

PRAYER
FAITH
SERVICE

HARRY EMERSON FOSDICK

Garden City Books

GARDEN CITY, NEW YORK

THE MEANING OF PRAYER

THE MEANING OF
PRAYER

HARRY EMERSON FOSDICK

*Author of "The Manhood of the Master," "The Meaning of Service,"
"The Meaning of Faith," etc.*

Garden City Books
GARDEN CITY, NEW YORK

PRINTED IN THE UNITED STATES OF AMERICA

To
FLORENCE WHITNEY FOSDICK

Preface

TO NEW EDITION

Thirty-five years ago, I wrote this little book on Prayer, never dreaming that a long generation afterward I should be asked for a preface to a new edition.

The book started with my own personal questions about prayer to which I was seeking an honest answer. To my congregation in Montclair, New Jersey, I presented in a series of sermons—undertaken, I recall, with much misgiving—such insight as I had into prayer's meaning; and then in mid-week conferences we discussed together the problems and difficulties which Christians face in praying. Urged to write a book on the subject, I demurred. No considerable audience, I thought, would be interested.

Because the subject was so vital to me personally, however, I could not finally put the suggestion aside. One summer, in an empty Maine coast cottage close by the sea, with a rough table and chair as the only furniture, I immured myself, day after day, as in a monastic cell, to write this book. Sending the manuscript to my friend, Mr. Frederick M. Harris of Association Press, who had constantly encouraged me, I recall saying that I foresaw no wide demand for such a book and that if two thousand copies were disposed of the publishers could count themselves fortunate.

I am told now that the book has been circulated in at least eighteen different languages; that of the four English editions, published in the United States, Great Britain, Australia, and India, about half a million copies have been sold; and that a new edition is called for here. Such an unexpected welcome for an unpretentious book like this could have come only from persons who were being helped to pray, and for that I am deeply grateful.

"Prayer is the soul of religion"—so I wrote in the original preface to this book—"and failure there is not a superficial lack for the supply of which the spiritual life leisurely can wait. Failure in prayer is the loss of religion itself in its inward and dynamic aspect of fellowship with the Eternal. Only a theoretical deity is left to any man who has ceased to commune with God, and a theoretical deity saves no man from sin and disheartenment and fills no life with a sense of divine commission. Such vital consequences require a living God who actually deals with men."

In these troubled times that message is especially relevant to human need. We face one of the most critical eras in history, with public problems of immense import confronting us and with personal problems inevitably accentuated. I wrote this book when the first world war was beginning in Europe. Certainly its central message is not less pertinent today—vital Christianity must mean access to resources of power greater than our own. If this book can still help any to make the transforming discovery of these resources, I shall be thankful.

HARRY EMERSON FOSDICK

Boothbay Harbor, Maine
July 15, 1949

Preface

This little book has been written in the hope that it may help to clarify a subject which is puzzling many minds. Prayer is the soul of religion, and failure there is not a superficial lack for the supply of which the spiritual life leisurely can wait. Failure in prayer is the loss of religion itself in its inward and dynamic aspect of fellowship with the Eternal. Only a theoretical deity is left to any man who has ceased to commune with God, and a theoretical deity saves no man from sin and disheartenment and fills no life with a sense of divine commission. Such vital consequences require a living God who actually deals with men.

In endeavoring to clear away the difficulties that hamper fellowship with this living God, the book has used the Scripture as the basis of its thought. But the passages of Scripture quoted are not employed as proof texts to establish an opinion; they are uniformly used as descriptions of an experience which men have actually had with God. In a study such as this, the Bible is the invaluable laboratory manual which records all phases of man's life with God and God's dealing with man.

A debt of gratitude is due to many books and many friends consulted by the author. In particular, Professor George Albert Coe, Ph.D., of the Union Theological Seminary, New York City, and Mr. Frederick M. Harris, of Association Press, have given generously of their time and counsel.

Each chapter is divided into three sections: Daily Readings, Comment for the Week, and Suggestions for Thought and Discussion. This arrangement for daily devotional reading—"The Morning Watch," for intensive study, and for study group discussion, has met such wide acceptance in my previous book that it has been continued here.

Special acknowledgment is gladly made to the following: to the Pilgrim Press for permission to use selections from Dr. Rauschenbusch's "Prayers of the Social Awakening"; to E. P. Dutton & Company for permission to use prayers from "A Chain of Prayers Across the Ages"; to the Rev. Samuel McComb and the publishers for permission to draw upon "A Book of Prayer," Copyright, 1912, Dodd, Mead & Company; to George W. Jacobs & Company for permission to make quotations from "The Communion of Prayer"; to Mrs. Mary W. Tileston for the use of "Prayers Ancient and Modern"; to Fleming H. Revell for permission to quote from Henry Ward Beecher's "Book of Public Prayer"; and to the author and publishers of W. E. Orchard's "The Temple," E. P. Dutton & Company.

H. E. F.

June 1, 1915

CONTENTS

CONTENTS

THE MEANING OF PRAYER

CHAPTER I

The Naturalness of Prayer

DAILY READINGS

First Day, First Week

Samuel Johnson once was asked what the strongest argument for prayer was, and he replied, "Sir, there is no argument for prayer." One need only read Johnson's own petitions, such as the one below, to see that he did not mean by this to declare prayer irrational; he meant to stress the fact that praying is first of all a native tendency. It is a practice like breathing or eating in this respect, that men engage in it because they are human, and *afterward* argue about it as best they can. As Carlyle stated it in a letter to a friend: "Prayer is and remains the native and deepest impulse of the soul of man." Consider this universal tendency to pray as revealed in "Solomon's prayer" at the dedication of the temple:

Moreover concerning the foreigner, that is not of thy people Israel, when he shall come from a far country for thy great name's sake, and thy mighty hand, and thine outstretched arm; when they shall come and pray toward this house; then hear thou from heaven, even from thy dwelling place, and do according to all that the foreigner calleth to thee for; that all the peoples of the earth may know thy name, and fear thee, as doth thy people Israel, and that they may know that this house which I have built is called by thy name.—II Chron. 6:32, 33.

Note how this prayer takes for granted that any stranger coming from anywhere on earth is likely to be a praying man. Let us say to ourselves on this first day of our study, that in dealing with prayer we are dealing, as this Scripture suggests, with a natural function of human life.

> "All souls that struggle and aspire,
>   All hearts of prayer, by thee are lit;
>   And, dim or clear, thy tongues of fire
>   On dusky tribes and twilight centuries sit."

O Lord, in whose hands are life and death, by whose power I am sustained, and by whose mercy I am spared, look down upon me with pity. Forgive me that I have until now so much neglected the duty which Thou hast assigned to me, and suffered the days and hours of which I must give account to pass away without any endeavor to accomplish Thy will. Make me to remember, O God, that every day is Thy gift, and ought to be used according to Thy command. Grant me, therefore, so to repent of my negligence, that I may obtain mercy from Thee, and pass the time which Thou shalt yet allow me in diligent performance of Thy commands, through Jesus Christ. Amen.—Samuel Johnson (1709-1784).

Second Day, First Week

Epictetus was a non-Christian philosopher and yet listen to him: "When thou hast shut thy door and darkened thy room, say not to thyself that thou art alone. God is in thy room." Read now Paul's appreciation of this hunger for God and this sense of his presence which are to be found among all peoples.

Ye men of Athens, in all things I perceive that ye are very religious. For as I passed along, and observed the objects of your worship, I found also an altar with this inscription, "To an Unknown God." What therefore ye worship in ignorance, this I set forth unto you. The God that made the world and all things therein, he, being Lord of heaven and earth, dwelleth not in temples made with hands; neither is he served by men's hands, as though he needed anything, seeing he himself giveth to all life, and breath, and all things; and he made of one every nation of men to dwell on all the face of the earth, having determined their appointed seasons, and the bounds of their habitation; that they should seek God, if haply, they might feel after him and find him, though he is not far from each one of us; for in him we live, and move, and have our being; as certain even of your own poets have said, For we are also his offspring.—Acts 17:22-28.

Consider the meaning of the fact that prayer and worship are thus universal; that all peoples do "seek God, if haply, they might feel after him and find him." It is said that an ignorant African woman, after hearing her first Christian sermon, remarked to her neighbor, "There! I always told you that there ought to be a God like that." Somewhere in every man there is the capacity for worship and prayer, for the apprehension of God and the love of him. Is not this the distinctive quality of man and the noblest faculty which he possesses? How then are we treating this best of our endowments?

O Lord our God, grant us grace to desire Thee with our whole heart; that so desiring we may seek and find Thee; and so finding Thee may love Thee; and loving Thee, may hate those sins from which Thou hast redeemed us. Amen. —Anselm (1033-1109).

Third Day, First Week

Prayer has been greatly discredited in the minds of many by its use during war. Men have felt the absurdity of praying on opposite sides of a battle, of making God a tribal leader in heaven, to give victory, as Zeus and Apollo used to do, to their favorites. Let us grant all the narrow, bitter, irrational elements that thus appear in prayer during a war, but let us not be blind to the meaning of this momentous fact: *whenever in national life a time of great stress comes, men, however sceptical, feel the impulse to pray.* How natural is Hezekiah's cry in the siege of Jerusalem!

O Jehovah, the God of Israel, that sittest above the cherubim, thou art the God, even thou alone, of all the kingdoms of the earth; thou hast made heaven and earth. Incline thine ear, O Jehovah, and hear; open thine eyes, O Jehovah, and see; and hear the words of Sennacherib, wherewith he hath sent him to defy the living God. Of a truth, Jehovah, the kings of Assyria have laid waste the nations and their lands, and have cast their gods into the fire; for they were no gods but the work of men's hands, wood and stone; therefore they have destroyed them. Now therefore, O Jehovah our God, save thou us, I beseech thee, out of his hand, that all the

**kingdoms of the earth may know that thou Jehovah art God alone.
—II Kings 19:15-19.**

Consider now the same tendency to pray in a crisis, which appears
in the European war. Here is a passage from a Scotchman's letter,
describing the infidel in his town, who never went to church, but
who now sits in the kirk, and is moved to tears when he hears the
minister pray for the king's forces, and for the bereaved at home:
"It was then that my friend stifled a sob. There was Something after
all, Something greater than cosmic forces, greater than law—with
an eye to pity and an arm to save. There was God. My friend's son
was with the famous regiment that was swaying to and fro, grap-
pling with destiny. He was helpless—and there was only God to
appeal to. There comes an hour in life when the heart realizes that
instinct is mightier far than logic. With us in the parish churches of
Scotland the great thing is the sermon. But today it is different; the
great thing now is prayer." So always a crisis shakes loose the tendency to pray.

*O Lord God of Hosts, grant to those who have gone forth to fight
our battles by land or sea, protection in danger, patience in suffering, and moderation in victory. Look with compassion on the
sick, the wounded, and the captives; sanctify to them their trials,
and turn their hearts unto Thee. For Thy dear Son's sake, O Lord,
pardon and receive the dying; have mercy upon the widow and
fatherless, and comfort all who mourn. O gracious Father, who
makest wars to cease in all the world, restore to us, Thy people,
speedily the blessing of peace, and grant that our present troubles
may be overruled to Thy glory, in the extension of the Redeemer's
Kingdom, and the union of all nations in Thy faith, fear, and love.
Hear, O Lord, and answer us; for Jesus Christ's sake. Amen.—*
E. Hawkins (1789-1882).

Fourth Day, First Week

H. Clay Trumbull tells us that a soldier in the Civil War, wounded
in a terrific battle at Fort Wagner, was asked by an army chaplain,
"Do you ever pray?" "Sometimes," was the answer; "I prayed last
Saturday night, when we were in that fight at Wagner. I guess
everybody prayed *there*." Consider how inevitably the impulse to

pray asserts itself whenever critical danger comes suddenly upon any life. In view of this, read the Psalmist's description of a storm at sea:

They that go down to the sea in ships,
That do business in great waters;
These see the works of Jehovah,
And his wonders in the deep.
For he commandeth, and raiseth the stormy wind,
Which lifteth up the waves thereof.
They mount up to the heavens, they go down again to the depths:
Their soul melteth away because of trouble.
They reel to and fro, and stagger like a drunken man,
And are at their wits' end.
Then they cry unto Jehovah in their trouble.

—Psalm 107:23-28.

Remember those times in your experience or observation when either you or someone else has been thrown back by an emergency upon this natural tendency to pray in a crisis. Consider what it means that this impulse to pray is not simply age-long and universal; that it also is exhibited in every one of us—at least occasionally. How natural as well as how noble is this prayer of Bishop Ridley during the imprisonment that preceded his burning at the stake!

O Heavenly Father, the Father of all wisdom, understanding, and true strength, I beseech Thee, for Thy only Son our Savior Christ's sake, look mercifully upon me, wretched creature, and send Thine Holy Spirit into my breast; that not only I may understand according to Thy wisdom, how this temptation is to be borne off, and with what answer it is to be beaten back; but also, when I must join to fight in the field for the glory of Thy name, that then I, being strengthened with the defence of Thy right hand, may manfully stand in the confession of Thy faith, and of Thy truth, and may continue in the same unto the end of my life, through the same our Lord Jesus Christ. Amen.—Bishop Ridley (1500-1555).

Fifth Day, First Week

The instinctive turning of the heart to a "Power not ourselves" is often felt, not alone in crises of peril, but in the presence of great *responsibility,* for which a man unaided feels inadequate. Despite Solomon's shallowness of life, there were times when something finer and deeper was revealed in him than his deeds would have suggested. When he first realized that the new responsibility of kingship was upon him, how elevated the spirit of his impulsive prayer!

And now, O Jehovah my God, thou hast made thy servant king instead of David my father: and I am but a little child; I know not how to go out or come in. And thy servant is in the midst of thy people which thou hast chosen, a great people, that cannot be numbered nor counted for multitude. Give thy servant therefore an understanding heart to judge thy people, that I may discern between good and evil; for who is able to judge this thy great people? —I Kings 3:7-9.

As a companionpiece with this cry of Solomon, see Lincoln's revealing words: "I have been driven many times to my knees by the overwhelming conviction that I had nowhere else to go; my own wisdom and that of all around me seemed insufficient for the day." Whenever a man faces tasks for which he feels inadequate and upon whose accomplishment much depends, he naturally turns to prayer. Let us imagine ourselves in Luther's place, burdened with new and crushing responsibilities, and facing powerful enemies, when he cried:

O Thou, my God! Do Thou, my God, stand by me, against all the world's wisdom and reason. Oh, do it! Thou must do it! Yea, Thou alone must do it! Not mine, but Thine, is the cause. For my own self, I have nothing to do with these great and earthly lords. I would prefer to have peaceful days, and to be out of this turmoil. But Thine, O Lord, is this cause; it is righteous and eternal. Stand by me, Thou true Eternal God! In no man do I trust. All that is of the flesh and savours of the flesh is here of no account. God, O God! dost Thou not hear me, O my God? Art Thou dead? No. Thou canst not die; Thou art only hiding Thyself. Hast Thou chosen me for this work? I ask Thee how I may be sure of this, if it be Thy will; for I would never have thought, in all my life, of undertaking aught against such great lords. Stand by me, O God, in the Name of Thy dear Son, Jesus Christ, who shall be my Defence and Shelter, yea, my Mighty Fortress, through the might and strength of Thy Holy Spirit. God help me. Amen.—Martin Luther (1483-1546).

Sixth Day, First Week

And when Daniel knew that the writing was signed, he went into his house (now his windows were open in his chamber toward Jerusalem); and he kneeled upon his knees three times a day, and prayed, and gave thanks before his God, as he did aforetime.— Daniel 6:10.

We are evidently dealing here with a new element in prayer, not apparent in our previous discussion. *Prayer, to Daniel, was not simply an impulsive cry of need, wrung from him by sudden crises or by overwhelming responsibilities.* Daniel had done with the impulse to pray what all wise people do with the impulse to eat. They do not neglect it until imperious hunger demands it to save their lives or until special work absolutely forces them to it. They rather recognize eating as a normal need of human beings, to be met regularly. So Daniel not only prayed in emergencies of peril and responsibility; he prayed three times a day. How many of us leave the instinct of prayer dormant until a crisis calls it into activity! "Jehovah, in *trouble* have they visited thee; they poured out a prayer *when thy chastening was upon them*" (Isaiah 26:16). Consider how inadequate such a use of prayer is.

I am forced, good Father, to seek Thee daily, and Thou offerest Thyself daily to be found: whensoever I seek, I find Thee, in my house, in the fields, in the temple, and in the highway. Whatsoever I do, Thou art with me; whether I eat or drink, whether I write or work, go to ride, read, meditate, or pray, Thou art ever with me; wheresoever I am, or whatsoever I do, I feel some measure of Thy mercies and love. If I be oppressed, Thou defendest me: if I be envied, Thou guardest me; if I hunger, Thou feedest me; whatsoever I want Thou givest me. O continue this Thy loving-kindness towards me for ever, that all the world may see Thy power, Thy mercy, and Thy love, wherein Thou hast not failed me, and even my enemies shall see that Thy mercies endure forever.—J. Norden (1548-1625).

Seventh Day, First Week

For this cause I bow my knees unto the Father, from whom every family in heaven and on earth is named, that he would grant you, according to the riches of his glory, that ye may be strengthened with power through his Spirit in the inward man; that Christ may dwell in your hearts through faith; to the end that ye, being rooted and grounded in love, may be strong to apprehend with all the saints what is the breadth and length and height and depth, and to know the love of Christ which passeth knowledge, that ye may be filled unto all the fulness of God.—Eph. 3:14-19.

Compare praying like this with the spasmodic cry of occasional need and see how great the difference is. Here prayer has risen into an elevated demand on life, unselfish and constant. It gathers up the powers of the soul in a constraining desire for God's blessing on the one who prays and on all men. What starts in the pagan as an unregulated and fitful impulse has become in Paul an intelligent, persevering, and well-directed habit. As power of thought confused and weak in an Australian aboriginal, becomes in a Newton capable of grasping laws that hold the stars together, so prayer may begin in the race or in the individual as an erratic and ineffective impulse, but may grow to be a dependable and saving power. Consider how much you understand this latent force in your own life and how effectively you are using it.

O God, Thou art Life, Wisdom, Truth, Bounty, and Blessedness, the Eternal, the only true Good! My God and my Lord, Thou art my hope and my heart's joy. I confess, with thanksgiving, that Thou hast made me in Thine image, that I may direct all my thoughts to Thee, and love Thee. Lord, make me to know Thee aright, that I may more and more love, and enjoy, and possess Thee. And since, in the life here below, I cannot fully attain this blessedness, let it at least grow in me day by day, until it all be fulfilled at last in the life to come. Here be the knowledge of Thee increased, and there let it be perfected. Here let my love to Thee grow, and there let it ripen; that my joy being here great in hope, may there in fruition be made perfect. Amen.—Anselm (1033-1109).

COMMENT FOR THE WEEK

I

When any one undertakes to study the meaning and to cultivate the habit of prayer, it is well for him to understand from the beginning that he is dealing with a natural function of his life and not with an artificial addition. Raising palm trees in Greenland would be an unnatural proceeding. They never were intended to grow there, and never can grow there save under stress of artificial forcing. The culture of prayer would be just as strained a procedure, were it not true that the tendency to pray is native to us, that prayer is indigenous in us, that we *do* pray, one way or another, even though fitfully and without effect, and that men always have prayed and always will pray. The definition of man as a "praying animal," while not comprehensive, is certainly correct. *The culture of prayer, therefore, is not importing an alien, but is training a native citizen of the soul.* Professor William James of Harvard was thinking of this when he wrote: "We hear in these days of scientific enlightenment a great deal of discussion about the efficacy of prayer; and many reasons are given us why we should not pray, whilst others are given us why we should. But in all this very little is said of the reason why we do pray. . . . The reason why we do pray is simply that we cannot help praying."

Our justification for calling prayer natural may be found, in part, in the *universality* of it. In some form or other, it is found everywhere, in all ages and among all peoples. The most discouraging circumstances do not crush it, and theories of the universe directly antagonistic do not prevent it. Buddhism, a religion theoretically without a God, ought logically to exclude prayer; but in countries where Buddhism is dominant, prayer is present. Confucius, a good deal of an agnostic, urged his disciples not to have much to do with the gods; and today Confucius is himself a god and millions worship him. *Before the tendency to pray all barriers go down.*

The traveler climbs the foothills of the Himalayas, and among the Khonds of North India hears the prayer: "O Lord, we know not what is good for us. Thou knowest what it is. For it we pray." The archeologist goes back among the Aztec ruins and reads their prayer in affliction: "O merciful Lord, let this chastisement with which thou hast visited us, give us freedom from evil and from folly." The historian finds the Greek world typical of all ancient civilizations at least in this, that prayer is everywhere. Xenophon begins each day's march with prayer; Pericles begins every address with prayer; the greatest of Greek orations, Demosthenes' "On the Crown," and the greatest of Greek poems, "The Iliad," are opened with prayer. When from the superstitious habits of the populace one turns to the most elevated and philosophic spirits to see what they will say, he hears Plato, "Every man of sense before beginning an important work will ask help of the gods." And turning from Plato's preaching to his practice, he reads this beautiful petition, "King Zeus, grant us the good whether we pray for it or not, but evil keep from us, though we pray for it."

If today one crosses the borders of Christianity into Mohammedanism, not only will he find formal prayer five times daily, when the muezzin calls, but he will read descriptions of prayer like this from a Sufi—"There are three degrees in prayer. The first is when it is only spoken by the lips. The second is when with difficulty, by a resolute effort, the soul succeeds in fixing its thought on divine things. The third is when the soul finds it hard to turn away from God." And if from all others, one looks to the Hebrew people, with what unanimous ascription do they say, "O thou that hearest prayer, unto thee shall all flesh come" (Psa. 65:2) A man is cutting himself off from one of the elemental functions of human life when he denies in himself the tendency to pray.

II

Moreover, justification for calling prayer natural is found in the fact that *mankind never outgrows prayer*. Both the practice and the theory of it have proved infinitely adaptable to all stages of culture. In its lowest forms, among the most savage peoples, prayer and magic were indistinguishable. To pray then was to use charms that compelled the assent of the gods. And from such pagan beginnings to Jesus in the Garden or a modern scientist upon his knees, prayer, like all other primary functions, has proved capable of unlimited development. It has not been crushed but has been lifted into finer forms by spiritual and intellectual advance. It has shaped its course like a river, to the banks of each generation's thought; but it has flowed on, fed from fountains that changing banks do not affect. Nowhere is this more plain than in the Bible. Compare the dying prayer of Samson, as he wound his arms around the sustaining pillars of the Philistine dining hall and cried: "O Lord Jehovah, remember me, I pray thee, and strengthen me, I pray thee, only this once, O God, that I may be at once avenged of the Philistines for my two eyes" (Judges 16:28); with the dying prayer of Stephen, as he was being stoned, "Lord, lay not this sin to their charge" (Acts

7:60). Both are prayers, but they come from two ages between which the revelation of God and the meaning of prayer had infinitely widened.

Both in the Scripture and out of it, the quality of prayer is suited to the breadth or narrowness of view, the generosity or bitterness of spirit, which the generation or the individual possesses. As Sabatier puts it, *"The history of prayer is the history of religion."* At one end of the scale,

> "In even savage bosoms
> There are longings, yearnings, strivings
> For the good they comprehend not;
> And their feeble hands and helpless,
> Groping blindly in the darkness,
> Touch God's right hand in that darkness
> And are lifted up and strengthened."

At the other end of the scale, Coleridge says, "The act of praying is the very highest energy of which the human mind is capable"; and President Harper of the University of Chicago, on his death-bed prays: "May there be for me a life beyond this life; and in that life may there be work to do, tasks to accomplish. If in any way a soul has been injured or a friend hurt, may the harm be overcome, if it is possible." The human soul never outgrows prayer. At their lowest, men pray crudely, ignorantly, bitterly; at their best, men pray intelligently, spiritually, magnanimously. *Prayer is not only universal in extent; it is infinite in quality.* A man may well give himself to the deepening and purifying of his prayer, for it is as natural in human life as thought.

III

The naturalness of prayer is further seen in the fact that *prayer is latent in the life of every one of us.* At first the experience of some may seem to gainsay this. They have given up praying. They get on very well without it, and when they are entirely candid they confess that they disbelieve in it. But they must also confess that their disbelief lies in their *opinions* and not in their *impulses.* When some overwhelming need comes upon them, their impulse is still to pray.

Modern scepticism has done all that it could to make prayer unreasonable. It has viewed the world as a machine, regular as an automaton, uncontrollable as sunrise. It has made whatever God there is a prisoner in the laws of his own world, powerless to assist his children. It has denied everything that makes prayer possible; and yet men, having believed all that sceptical thought says, still have their times of prayer. Like water in an artesian well, walled up by modern concrete, prayer still seeps through, it breaks out; nature is stronger than artifice, and streams flowing underground in our lives insist on finding vent. Sometimes a crisis of personal danger lets loose this hidden impulse. "I hadn't prayed in ten years," the writer heard a railroad man exclaim when his train had just escaped a wreck; "but I prayed *then*." Sometimes a crushing responsibility makes men pray almost in spite of themselves. General Kodoma, of the Japanese army during the Russian war, used to retire each morning for an hour of prayer. When asked the reason, he answered: "When a man has done everything in his power, there remains nothing but the help of the gods." Anything—peril, responsibility, anxiety, grief—that shakes us out of our mere opinions, down into our native impulses, is likely to make us pray.

This is true of whole populations as well as of individuals. Shall not a war like the appalling conflict in Europe make men doubt God and disbelieve all good news of him that they have heard? Only of far distant spectators is any such reaction true. In the midst of the crisis itself, where the burdens of sacrifice are being borne and super-human endurance, courage, and selflessness are required, the reaction of men, as all observers note, is accurately described in Cardinal Mercier's famous pastoral letter: "Men long unaccustomed to prayer are turning again to God. Within the army, within the civil world, in public, and within the individual conscience there is prayer. Nor is that prayer today a word learned by rote, uttered lightly by the lip; it surges from the troubled heart, it takes the form at the feet of God of the very sacrifice of life." Whether in the individual or in society, great shocks that loosen the foundations of human life and let the primal tendencies surge up, always set free the pent fountains of prayer. *In the most sceptical man or generation prayer is always underground, waiting.* Henry Ward Beecher was giving us something more than a whimsical simile when he said: "I pray on the principle that the wine knocks the cork out of a bottle. There is an inward fermentation and there must be a vent." Even Comte, with his system of religion that utterly banished God, soul, and immortality, prescribed for his disciples two hours of prayer daily, because he recognized the act itself as one of the elemental functions of human nature.

Whether, therefore, we consider the universality of prayer, or its infinite adaptability to all stages of culture and intelligence, or the fact that it is latent in every one of us, we come to the same conclusion: praying is a natural activity of human life. We may only note in passing the patent argument here for the truth of religion. *Can it be that all men, in all ages and all lands, have been engaged in "talking forever to a silent world from which no answer comes"?* If we can be sure of anything, is it not this—that wherever a human function has persisted, unwearied by time, uncrushed by disappointment, rising to noblest form and finest use in the noblest and finest souls, that function corresponds with some Reality? Hunger never could have persisted without food, nor breathing without air, nor intellectual life without truth, nor prayer without God. Burke said that it was difficult to press an indictment against a nation. It is far more difficult to sustain a charge against all mankind.

IV

From this argument which the naturalness of prayer suggests, we press on, however, to a matter more immediate to our purpose. The fact that prayer is one of our native tendencies accounts for one peril in our use of it. *We let prayer be merely a tendency, and therefore spasmodic, occasional, untrained.* A tragedy is always present in any fine function of human nature that is left undisciplined. The impulse to love is universal; but left to be merely an impulse, it is brutal and fleshly. The love that inspires our noblest poems and is celebrated in our greatest music, that builds Christian homes and makes family life beautiful, is a primal impulse trained and elevated, become intelligent, disciplined, and consecrated. The tendency to think is universal, but left as such, it is but the wayward and futile intellect of savages. Their powers of thinking are stagnant, called into activity by accident, not well understood, carefully trained, and intelligently exercised. So prayer left to spasmodic use is a futile thing. In the one hundred and seventh Psalm, a marvelous description of a storm at sea ends with a verse which reveals the nature of impulsive prayer: "They . . . are at their wits' end. Then they cry unto Jehovah" (Psalm 107:27, 28). When prayer is left untrained, men pray only when they have reached their wits' end. In moments of extreme physical danger, men who never make a daily friend of God, cry to him in their need. "He that will learn to pray," says George Herbert, pithily, "let him go to sea"; and Shakespeare in the "Tempest," knowing human nature as the Psalmist knew it, has the sailors, when the storm breaks, cry: "All lost! To prayers! To prayers! All lost!" In extreme moral danger, also, where pleasant dalliance with evil has run out into the unbreakable habit of evil, men almost always pray. And in death how naturally men think of God! So Dame Quickly says of the dying Falstaff: "Now I, to comfort him, bid him a' should not think of God. I hoped there was no need to trouble himself with any such thoughts yet!"

Prayer, left as an undisciplined impulse, inevitably sinks into such a spasmodic and frantic use. "When my soul fainted within me, I remembered Jehovah" (Jonah 2:7). Like the old Greek dramatists, men hopelessly tangle the plot of their lives, until at the end, with a dilemma insoluble by human ingenuity and power, they swing a god from the wings by machinery to disentangle the desperate situation. They use prayer as a *deus-ex-machina,* a last resort when they are in extremity. In one way or another, how many of us must accuse ourselves of this fitful use of prayer! One of the supreme powers of our lives is left to the control of impulse and accident, its nature unstudied, and its exercise untrained.

V

The baneful effect of this spasmodic use of prayer is easily seen. *For one thing it utterly neglects all Christian conceptions of God and goes back to the pagan thought of him. God becomes nothing more than a power to be occasionally called in to our help.* This is the conception of an Indian woman bowing at an idol's shrine. Her god is power, mysterious and masterful, whose help she seeks in her emergencies. When, therefore, we pray as she does, fitfully running to God in occasional crises, we are going back in substance, if not in form, to paganism. We deserve Luther's rebuke in his sermon on praying to the saints: "We honor them and call upon them only when we have a pain in our legs or our heads, or when our pockets are empty." But the best of humanity have traveled a long way from such an idea of deity. The Christian God desires to be to every one an inward and abiding friend, a purifying presence in daily life, the One whose moral purpose continually restrains and whose love up-

holds. Above all advances made in human life none is so significant
as this advance in the thought of God. We have moved from rum-
bling oxcarts to limited express trains, from mud huts to cathedrals,
from tom-toms to orchestras. If we neglected these gains, we should
rightly be regarded as strange anachronisms. Yet in our treatment of
God how often are we ancient pagans born after our time! We are
examples of religious reversal to type. We are misdated A. D. instead
of B. C. when we use God as a power to be occasionally summoned
to our aid.

Consider a new parable of a father and his two sons. One son
looked upon his father as a last resort in critical need. He never
came to him for friendly conference, never sought his advice, in
little difficulties never was comforted by his help. He did not make
his father his confidant. He went to college and wrote home only
when he wanted money. He fell into disgrace, and called on his
father only when he needed legal aid. He ran his life with utter disregard of his father's character or purpose, and turned to him only
when in desperate straits. The other son saw in his father's love the
supreme motive of his life. He was moved by daily gratitude so that
to be well-pleasing to his father was his joy and his ideal. His father
was his friend. He confided in him, was advised by him, kept close
to him, and in *his* crises came to his father with a naturalness born
of long habit, like Jesus, who having prayed without ceasing, now at
last bows in Gethsemane. *Is there any doubt as to which is the
nobler sonship? And is not the former type a true picture of our
relationship with God when we leave prayer to be a merely instinctive and untrained cry of need?*

VI

*For another thing, this use of prayer as merely a spasmodic cry
out of an occasional crisis, makes it utterly selfish.* We think of God
solely with reference to our own emergencies. We never remember
the Most High except when we wish him to run an errand for us.
Our prayer does not concern itself with the fulfilment of his great
purposes in us and in the world, and does not relate itself to a life
devoted to his will. In utter selfishness we forget God until it occurs
to us that we may get something from him.

Some men treat God in this respect as others treat their country.
That regard for native land which in some has inspired heroic and

sacrificial deeds, appears in others in the disguise of utter selfishness. Consider a man who does nothing whatever for his country; is not interested in her problems; is careless of the franchise, evades every public responsibility, and even dodges taxes. One would suppose that this man never thought of his country at all. Upon the contrary, there are occasions when he thinks of her at once. When his person or property is attacked and his rights invaded, this same man will appeal clamorously to the government for protection. He reserves every thought of his country for the hours of personal crisis. His relationship with his government is exhausted in spasmodic cries for help. *He furnishes a true parallel to that ignoble type of religion, in which prayer, left fitful and undisciplined, is nothing more than an occasional, selfish demand on God.*

VII

The shame of leaving thus uncultivated one of the noblest functions of man's spirit is emphasized when we face the testimony of the masters in prayer concerning its possibilities. What the power of thought can mean must be seen in the thinkers; what prayer can do must be seen in the pray-ers. Whenever *they* speak, language seems to them inadequate to describe the saving and empowering influences of habitual prayer. As in our Christian songs, where we leave the more superficial differences of opinion and go down into the essential spirit of worship, Catholics and Protestants, Jews and Gentiles, men of every shade of special belief and sectarian alliance are authors of the hymns we all sing, so in prayer men of opposite opinions agree as one. Luther, the Protestant, is alien at how many points from St. Bernard the Catholic, and yet says Luther—"In the faith wherein St. Bernard prays, do I pray also." Not only does a liberal philosopher, Sabatier, say, "Prayer is religion in act; that is, prayer is real religion"; and a conservative theologian, Hartmann, say, "God has given to real prayer the power to shape the future for men and the world"; and a Catholic poet, Francis Thompson, say, "Prayer is the very sword of the saints": even Professor Tyndall, the scientist, who was regarded by the Christians of his generation as the most aggressive antagonist of prayer, says: "It is not my habit of mind to think otherwise than solemnly of the feelings which prompt to prayer. Often unreasonable, even contemptible, in its purer forms prayer hints at disciplines which few of us can neglect without moral loss." If there is any element in human life to whose inestimable value we have abundant testimony, it is prayer; and to leave misunderstood and untrained a power capable of such high uses is a spiritual tragedy.

This, then, is the summary of the matter. Deep in every one of us lies the tendency to pray. If we allow it to remain merely a tendency, it becomes nothing but a selfish, unintelligent, occasional cry of need. But understood and disciplined, it reveals possibilities whose limits never have been found.

SUGGESTIONS FOR THOUGHT AND DISCUSSION

How far can prayer be said to be natural to all peoples in all times?

Are the following exercises forms of prayer?
An African throwing a stone on the votive pile along the roadside.
A Buddhist using a prayer wheel.
A Thibetan tying a prayer flag to a tree.
An Indian Fakir lying on a bed of spikes.
An American nailing a horse shoe over the door for good luck.

How far can superstitious prayers, growing out of ignorance, of mysterious happenings and attempts to propitiate some unknown mighty power, be said to be proof of the universality of prayer?

How far can Paul's statement in regard to the men of Athens being very religious be duplicated in non-Christian countries today?

To what degree is crying out for help in time of great trouble a proof that prayer is natural? Was Stephen's prayer as natural as Samson's? Compare Hezekiah's prayer at the siege of Jerusalem with prayer in modern wars. Is the Psalmist's description of a man praying in a storm at sea proof of the naturalness of prayer?

Is prayer more natural to some types of individuals and races than others? Is it more natural to women than men?

In the sense that you use the word "prayer," do all men pray?

How far is the universality of prayer a proof of its reality?

What effect has lack of control and training upon fine natural tendencies?

Is love involuntary, or can a man control and develop his love instinct?

To what degree is the instinct to pray capable of development and direction?

Wherein do untrained natural prayer instincts fall short? Why are the prayers of a Christian often really pagan in character?

What were the distinctive elements in Daniel's prayer? in the prayer of Ephesians 3:14-19?

Can spasmodic and untrained prayer be unselfish?

How can prayer be trained? What determines the limit of the development of prayer in any individual? For instance, what process is necessary to develop the turning of a prayer wheel into a prayer like Stephen's?

CHAPTER II

Prayer as Communion with God

DAILY READINGS

First Day, Second Week

The thought of prayer as a natural function in human life ought to be of this practical service to us: it should keep us from yielding too easily to disbelief or discouragement when we have difficulty with prayer in our individual experience. At least, so one of the psalmists felt.

> My God, my God, why hast thou forsaken me?
> Why art thou so far from helping me, and from the words of my
> groaning?
> O my God, I cry in the daytime, but thou answerest not;
> And in the night season, and am not silent.
> But thou art holy,
> O thou that inhabitest the praises of Israel.
> Our fathers trusted in thee:
> They trusted, and thou didst deliver them.
> They cried unto thee, and were delivered:
> They trusted in thee, and were not put to shame.
> —Psalm 22:1-5.

Note the three troubles which this psalmist has been having with prayer. He cannot make God seem real to him; his prayer brings him no relief in his difficulties; and even persistency in prayer accomplishes nothing. Then he remembers that prayer is not something with which he, for the first time in history, is experimenting. "Our fathers trusted in thee . . . and thou didst deliver them." He sees that the accumulating testimony of his fathers in all ages bears witness to the power of prayer. He therefore sensibly concludes that he would better not pit a few months of individual failure in praying against the general experience of the race. In view of what prayer has meant to all peoples, *he sees that probably the trouble is with himself and not with prayer.* He sets himself therefore to understand prayer if he can, and in the 22nd verse of the Psalm, he begins the recital of the victorious outcome: "I will declare thy name unto my brethren: In the midst of the assembly will I praise thee." May God make us as sensible as this psalmist and give us as real a triumph!

O God, who art, and wast, and art to come, before whose face the generations rise and pass away; age after age the living seek Thee, and find that of Thy faithfulness there is no end. Our fathers in their pilgrimage walked by Thy guidance, and rested on Thy compassion; still to their children be Thou the cloud by day, the fire by night. In our manifold temptations, Thou alone knowest and are ever nigh: in sorrow, Thy pity revives the fainting soul; in our prosperity and ease, it is Thy Spirit only that can wean us from our pride and keep us low. O Thou sole Source of peace and righteousness! take now the veil from every heart; and join us in one communion with Thy prophets and saints who have trusted in Thee, and were not ashamed. Not of our worthiness, but of Thy tender mercy, hear our prayer. Amen.—James Martineau (1805-1900).

Second Day, Second Week

Let us consider this week some of the practical reasons for our failure to make the most out of our power to pray. To that end read these verses representing two aspects of the Master's life:

We must work the works of him that sent me, while it is day: the night cometh, when no man can work.—John 9:4.

In the morning, a great while before day, he rose up and went out, and departed into a desert place, and there prayed.—Mark 1:35.

Which of these two emphases in the Christian life do we appreciate the better? Is it not clear that all the characteristic enthusiasms of our day cluster around work? In the churches, service is the popular note, and the favorite hymns are "The Son of God goes forth to war," "Soldiers of Christ arise," and their kind. Our failure in prayer is partly due to the prevailing temper of our generation, which in its splendid enthusiasm for work has neglected that culture of prayer, on which in the end the finest quality of spirit and the deepest resources of power must depend. Is not this one reason why keen observers note that our generation is marked by practical efficiency and spiritual shallowness? May we not hope to keep in ourselves the best gains of this efficient age and at the same time recover the "practice of the presence of God"?

Almighty Father, enter Thou our hearts, and so fill us with Thy love, that, forsaking all evil desires, we may embrace Thee, our only good. Show unto us, for Thy mercies' sake, O Lord our God, what Thou art unto us. Say unto our souls, I am thy salvation. So speak that we may hear. Our hearts are before Thee; open Thou our ears; let us hasten after Thy voice, and take hold on Thee. Hide not Thy face from us, we beseech Thee, O Lord. Enlarge Thou the narrowness of our souls, that Thou mayest enter in. Repair the ruinous mansions, that Thou mayest dwell there. Hear us, O Heavenly Father, for the sake of Thine only Son, Jesus Christ, our Lord, who liveth and reigneth with Thee and the Holy Spirit, now and for ever. Amen.—St. Augustine (354-430).

Third Day, Second Week

Failure to cultivate our power of prayer goes back in many to childish ideas of prayer's meaning, which, never altogether outgrown, hamper us and make our praying seem unreasonable and futile. There are some who still think of prayer in terms of childish supplications to a divine Santa Claus. Let us note the two aspects of truth set forth in these two passages:

And he sat down, and called the twelve; and he saith unto them, If any man would be first, he shall be last of all, and servant of all. And he took a little child, and set him in the midst of them: and taking him in his arms, he said unto them, Whosoever shall receive one of such little children in my name, receiveth me: and whosoever receiveth me, receiveth not me, but him that sent me.—Mark 9:35-37.

When I was a child, I spake as a child, I felt as a child, I thought as a child: now that I am become a man, I have put away childish things.—I Cor. 13:11.

When Christ sets as our ideal the childlike qualities of sincerity and humility, he is not asking us to be *childish*. Many foolish prayers are offered by the well-meaning but unintelligent with the excuse that they are childlike in their simple trust. But we are grown-up children, and have an obligation to exercise our intelligence, to outgrow infantile ideas of prayer that belittle it, and to enlarge our conceptions of the significance which fellowship with God may have for life. To pray to God as though he were Santa Claus is *childish;* but a man may still be *childlike* in his faith and range up into another sort of praying:

> "Thou Life within my life, than self more near,
> Thou Veiled Presence infinitely clear;
> From all illusive shows of sense I flee
> To find my center and my rest in Thee."

O Heavenly Father, the Author and Fountain of all truth, the bottomless Sea of all understanding, send, we beseech Thee, Thy Holy Spirit into our hearts, and lighten our understandings with the beams of Thy heavenly grace. We ask this, O merciful Father, for Thy dear Son, our Saviour, Jesus Christ's sake. Amen.—Bishop Ridley (1500-1555).

Fourth Day, Second Week

Childishness in prayer is chiefly evidenced in an overweening desire to beg *things* from God, and a corresponding failure to desire above all else the *friendship of God himself*. The same growth ought to take place in our relationship with God which occurs in a normal fellowship between a child and his parents. At first the child wants the parents' gifts, and thinks of the parents largely in terms of the things which they do for his comfort and pleasure. He is not able yet to appreciate the value of the parents' personalities. A sure sign of wholesome maturity, however, is found in the child's deepening understanding of the parents themselves—his increasing delight in their friendship, thankfulness for their care, acceptance of their ideals, reliance on their counsel, and joy in their approval. The child grows through desiring things from his parents into love of his parents, for their own sakes.

A certain man had two sons: and the younger of them said to his father, Father, give me the portion of thy substance that falleth to me. And he divided unto them his living. And not many days after, the younger son gathered all together and took his journey into a far country; and there he wasted his substance with riotous living. . . . But when he came to himself he said, How many hired servants of my father's have bread enough and to spare, and I perish here with hunger! I will arise and go to my father, and will say unto him, Father, I have sinned against heaven, and in thy sight: I am no more worthy to be called thy son: make me as one of thy hired servants.—Luke 15:11-13, 17-19.

Note the change of prayer from *"Give me"* to *"Make me."* Whether through experience of sin or sorrow or hard practical struggle we come to a real maturity, we always tend to grow out of crying to God "Give me" into the deeper prayer "Make me." In a word we cease valuing God merely because of the things he may give, and we come into the love of God himself and the desire to be made over by him.

Grant me, O most loving Lord, to rest in Thee above all creatures, above all health and beauty, above all glory and honor, above all power and dignity, above all knowledge and subtilty, above all riches and art, above all fame and praise, above all sweetness and comfort, above all hope and promise, above all gifts and favors that Thou canst give and impart to us, above all jubilee that the mind of man can receive and feel; finally, above angels and archangels, and above all the heavenly host, above all things visible and invisible, and above all that Thou art not, O my God. It is too small and unsatisfying, whatsoever Thou bestowest on me apart from Thee, or revealest to me, or promisest, whilst Thou art not seen, and not fully obtained. For surely my heart cannot truly rest, nor be entirely contented, unless it rest in Thee. Amen.—Thomas à Kempis (1379-1471).

Fifth Day, Second Week

Prayer has failed in some because it has always appeared to them as an *obligation rather than a privilege.* When they think of it they

think of a duty to be done. Contrast with this the glowing words of
the sixty-third Psalm:

O God, thou art my God; earnestly will I seek thee: . . .
Because thy lovingkindness is better than life,
My lips shall praise thee. . . .
My soul shall be satisfied as with marrow and fatness;
And my mouth shall praise thee with joyful lips;
When I remember thee upon my bed,
And meditate on thee in the night-watches.
For thou hast been my help,
And in the shadow of thy wings will I rejoice.
My soul followeth hard after thee:
Thy right hand upholdeth me.—Psalm 63:1, 3, 5-8.

Prayer here is not a burden to be borne, an obligation to be fulfilled, something that is due to God and must be paid. Prayer is a
privilege; like friendship and family love and laughter, great books,
great music, and great art, it is one of life's opportunities to be
grasped thankfully and used gladly. The man who misses the deep
meanings of prayer has not so much refused an obligation; he has
robbed himself of life's supreme privilege—friendship with God.

*O Thou divine Spirit that, in all events of life, art knocking at the
door of my heart, help me to respond to Thee. I would not be driven
blindly as the stars over their courses. I would not be made to work
out Thy will unwillingly, to fulfil Thy law unintelligently, to obey
Thy mandates unsympathetically. I would take the events of my life
as good and perfect gifts from Thee; I would receive even the sorrows of life as disguised gifts from Thee. I would have my heart open
at all times to receive—at morning, noon, and night; in spring, and
summer, and winter. Whether Thou comest to me in sunshine or in
rain, I would take Thee into my heart joyfully. Thou art Thyself
more than the sunshine, Thou art Thyself compensation for the rain;
it is Thee and not Thy gifts I crave; knock, and I shall open unto
Thee. Amen.*—George Matheson.

Sixth Day, Second Week

I exhort therefore, first of all, that supplications, prayers, intercessions, thanksgivings, be made for all men; for kings and all that

are in high place; that we may lead a tranquil and quiet life in all godliness and gravity. This is good and acceptable in the sight of God our Saviour; who would have all men to be saved, and come to the knowledge of the truth. For there is one God, one mediator also between God and men, himself man, Christ Jesus. . . . I desire therefore that the men pray in every place, lifting up holy hands, without wrath and disputing.—I Tim. 2:1-5, 8.

Our failure to think of prayer as a privilege may be partly due to the fact that we can pray any time, "in every place." The door of prayer is open so continuously that we fail to avail ourselves of an opportunity which is always there. There are plenty of people in London who never have seen the inside of Westminster Abbey, partly because they could go there any day. Consider then the aptness of Austin Phelps' illustration: "In the vestibule of St. Peter's, at Rome, is a doorway, which is walled up and marked with a cross. It is opened but four times in a century. On Christmas Eve, once in twenty-five years, the Pope approaches it in princely state, with the retinue of cardinals in attendance, and begins the demolition of the door, by striking it three times with a silver hammer. When the passage is opened, the multitude pass into the nave of the cathedral, and up to the altar, by an avenue which the majority of them never entered thus before, and never will enter thus again. Imagine that the way to the Throne of Grace were like the Porta Sancta, inaccessible, save once in a quarter of a century. Conceive that it were now ten years since you, or I, or any other sinner, had been *permitted* to pray: and that fifteen long years must drag themselves away, before we could venture again to approach God; and that, at the most, we could not hope to pray more than two or three times in a lifetime! With what solicitude we should wait for the coming of that Holy Day!" It may be that through sheer negligence and the deceiving influence of good but weak intentions, we are missing one of life's great privileges, because it is so commonplace.

O Lord, keep me sensitive to the grace that is round about me. May the familiar not become neglected! May I see Thy goodness in my daily bread, and may the comfort of my home take my thoughts to the mercy seat of God!—J. H. Jowett.

Seventh Day, Second Week

Another practical reason for failure in prayer is found in *impatience*. We have made a few fitful and hurried attempts at praying and seeing no good consequence have impatiently called the practice worthless and have quit it. Suppose that a man should similarly make a dash at friendship and after throwing off a few trial conversations should dogmatically conclude that there was nothing in friendship after all. But friendship is not really tested in so dashing and occasional a way; friendship is rather a life to be lived, habitually, persistently—and its results are cumulative with the years. So prayer is a *cumulative life of friendship with God*.

And it came to pass, as he was praying in a certain place, that when he ceased, one of his disciples said unto him, Lord, teach us to pray, even as John also taught his disciples. And he said unto them, When ye pray, say, Father, Hallowed be thy name. Thy kingdom come. Give us day by day our daily bread. And forgive us our sins; for we ourselves also forgive every one that is indebted to us. And bring us not into temptation.—Luke 11:1-4.

Note that when the disciples heard Jesus pray they became aware that praying like his was nothing that they could happen on, or drift into, or dash off in a moment of special inspiration. Such praying was a lesson to be learned by assiduous practice. "It is a great art to commune with God," said Thomas à Kempis. We would not expect to take a try at a violin once in a while and yet make much of it. But see how we treat this finer instrument of prayer!

Which of these seven practical causes of failure, considered this week, apply to you?—pitting a little individual failure against the experience of the race; welcoming the emphasis on work to the exclusion of the emphasis on prayer; thinking of prayer childishly until it has seemed irrational; valuing God less than the things he may give until prayer has looked mean; regarding prayer as an obligation rather than a privilege; neglecting prayer because it is so familiar an opportunity; impatience with praying after a few, fitful trials.

Come, O Lord, in much mercy down into my soul, and take possession and dwell there. A homely mansion, I confess, for so glorious a Majesty, but such as Thou art fitting up for the reception of Thee,

*by holy and fervent desires of Thine own inspiring. Enter then, and
adorn, and make it such as Thou canst inhabit, since it is the work
of Thy hands. Give me Thine own self, without which, though Thou
shouldst give me all that ever Thou hast made, yet could not my
desires be satisfied. Let my soul ever seek Thee, and let me persist in
seeking, till I have found, and am in full possession of Thee. Amen.*—
St. Augustine (354-430).

COMMENT FOR THE WEEK

I

When a man begins to make earnest with prayer, desiring to see
what can be done with it in his life, he finds that one of the first
necessities is a fairly clear idea of what praying means. In most lives,
behind all theoretical perplexities about this problem, there lies a
practical experience with prayer that is very disconcerting.

When we were little children prayer was vividly real. We prayed
with a naive confidence that we should obtain the things for which
we asked. It made but little difference what the things were; for
prayer was an Aladdin's lamp by rubbing which we summoned the
angels of God to do our bidding, prayer was a blank check signed
by the Almighty which we could fill in at will and present to the
universe to be cashed. Such a conception of prayer is picturesquely
revealed in the confession which Robertson of Brighton, the great
English preacher, gives us in a paragraph about his childhood. "I
remember when a very, very young boy," he says, "going out shooting with my father, and praying, as often as the dogs came to a point,
that he might kill the bird. As he did not always do this, and as
sometimes there would occur false points, my heart got bewildered.
I believe I began to doubt sometimes the efficacy of prayer, sometimes the lawfulness of field sports. Once, too, I recollect when I was
taken up with nine other boys at school to be unjustly punished, I
prayed to escape the shame. The master previously to flogging all
the others, said to me, to the great bewilderment of the whole school:
'Little boy, I excuse you: I have particular reasons for it,' and in
fact, I was never flogged during the three years I was at that school.
That incident settled my mind for a long time; only I doubt whether
it did me any good, for prayer became a charm. I fancied myself
the favorite of the Invisible. I knew that I carried about a talisman

unknown to others which would save me from all harm. It did not make me better; it simply gave me security, as the Jew felt safe in being the descendant of Abraham, or went into battle under the protection of the Ark, sinning no less all the time."

Many of us can look back to some such experience as this with prayer; but, as with Robertson, serious doubts soon disturbed our simple-hearted trust. How often we rubbed this magic lamp, and no angels came! How steadily our faith in its efficacy gave place to doubt and then to confident denial! As experience increased, we relied not on prayer but on foresight, work, money, and shrewdness to obtain our desires. Frederick Douglass said that in the days of his slavery he used often to pray for freedom, but that his prayer was not answered until it got down into his own heels and he ran away. In that type of prayer we come increasingly to believe; but where then, is the old trust that used to look for gifts from heaven? Indeed, when in anguish we have cried for things on which the worth and joy of life seemed utterly to depend, our faith has been staggered by the impotence of our petition and the seeming indifference of God. We have entered into Tennyson's crushing doubt:

"O mother, praying God will save
Thy sailor,—while thy head is bow'd,
His heavy-shotted hammock-shroud
Drops in his vast and wandering grave."

II

This practical disappointment with prayer as a means of getting things leads in most men to one of two conclusions: either a man gives over praying altogether; or else, continuing to pray, he seeks a new motive for doing so to take the place of his old expectation of definite results from God. Men used to put flowers on graves because they thought that the departed spirits enjoyed the odor. Although that superstition long has been overpassed, we still put flowers on graves; but we have supplied a motive of sentiment in place of the old realistic reason.

So men who learned to pray in childlike expectation of getting precisely what they asked, are disillusioned by disappointment; but they continue prayer, with a new motive. "Never mind if you do not obtain your requests," men say in this second stage of their experience with prayer; "remember that it does *you* good to pray. The act itself enlarges your sympathies, quiets your mind, sweetens your disposition, widens the perspective of your thought. Give up all idea that some one does anything for you when you pray, but remember that you can do a great deal for yourself. In prayer we soothe our own spirits, calm our own anxieties, purify our own thoughts. Prayer is a helpful soliloquy; a comforting monologue; a noble form of auto-suggestion." So men returning disappointed from prayer as a means of obtaining definite requests, try to content themselves with prayer as *the reflex action of their own minds.* This is prayer's meaning, as they see it, put into an ancient parable: Two boys were sent into the fields to dig for hidden treasure, where all day they toiled in vain; and at evening, coming weary and disappointed home, they were met by their father. "After all," he said to comfort them, "you did get something—*the digging itself was good exercise.*"

How many today think thus of prayer as a form of spiritual gymnastics—what Horace Bushnell called "mere dumb-bell exercise!" They lift the dumb-bell of intercessory prayer, not because they think it helps their friends, but because it strengthens the fiber of their own sympathy. They lift the dumb-bell of prayer for strength in temptation not because God helps them, but because the act itself steadies them. Prayer to them is one form of menticulture. But this kind of prayer is not likely to persist long. A thoughtful man balks at continuing to cry "O God," simply to improve the quality of his own voice. He shrinks from the process which Charles Kingsley describes in a letter as "Praying to oneself to change oneself; by which I mean the common method of trying by prayer to excite oneself into a state, a frame, an experience." Or if he does indulge in such spiritual exercise, he must call what he is doing by its right name; it is meditation, it is soliloquy, but it is not prayer. When a man indulges in this occasional self-communion for spiritual discipline; when no sense of fellowship with God is left in his soliloquies to remind one of Jesus' great confession, "I am not alone, but I and my Father" (John 8:16), his meditation can be called prayer only in the qualified phrase of one of the parables, where a man "stood and prayed . . . *with himself*" (Luke 18:11).

Is not this a typical experience of modern men? They find themselves impaled, as they think, upon the horns of a dilemma. *"Either,"* they say, *"prayer is an effective way of getting things by begging, or else prayer is merely the reflex action of a man's own mind."* But the *dilemma is false.* Prayer may involve something of both, but the heart of prayer is neither the one nor the other. The essential nature of prayer lies in a realm higher than either, where all that is false in both is transcended and all that is true is emphasized.

To Jesus, for example, the meaning of prayer was not that God would give him whatever he asked. God did not. That sustained and passionate petition where the Master thrice returned with blood-stained face, to cry, "Let this cup pass" (Matt. 26:39), had "No" for an answer. Neither did prayer mean to Jesus merely the reflex action of his own mind. Jesus prayed with such power that the one thing which his disciples asked him to teach them was how to pray (Luke 11:1); he prayed with such conscious joy that at times the very fashion of his countenance was changed with the glory of it (Luke 9:28, 29). Can you imagine him upon his knees then *talking to himself?* Was he merely catching the rebound of his own words? *Surely, when the Master prayed, he met somebody.* His life was impinged on by another Life. He felt "a Presence that disturbed him with the joy of elevated thoughts." His prayer was not monologue, but dialogue; not soliloquy, but friendship. *For prayer is neither chiefly begging for things, nor is it merely self-communion; it is that loftiest experience within the reach of any soul, communion with God.*

Of course, this does not answer all questions about prayer, nor exhaust all its meaning. Definite petition has its important place, and later we must consider it. *But at the beginning of our study, the thought of prayer as communion with God puts the center of the matter where it ought to be.* The great gift of God in prayer is himself, and whatever else he gives is incidental and secondary. Let us, then, consider in particular the significance which this truth has for our idea of praying.

III

For one thing, the thought of prayer as communion with God makes praying an *habitual attitude,* and not simply an *occasional act.* It is continuous fellowship with God, not a spasmodic demand for his gifts. Many people associate prayer exclusively with some special posture, such as kneeling, and with the verbal utterance of their particular wants. They often are disturbed because this act gives them no help, because it issues in no perceptible result at all.

But even a casual acquaintance with the biographies of praying men makes clear that praying is to them a very different thing from saying prayers. One who all her life had identified with prayer certain appointed acts of devotion, properly timed and decently performed, exclaimed "Prayer has entirely left my life"; yet when asked whether she never was conscious of an unseen Presence in fellowship with whom she found peace and strength, she answered, "I could not live without *that!*" Well, that *is* prayer—"not a mechanical repetition of verbal forms," as A. C. Benson puts it, "but a strong and secret uplifting of the heart to the Father of all."

Let any of the spiritual seers describe the innermost meaning of prayer to them, and always this habitual attitude of secret communion lies at the heart of the matter; they are seeking God himself, rather than his outward gifts. As Horace Bushnell says: "I fell into the habit of talking with God on every occasion. I talk myself asleep at night, and open the morning talking with him"; and Jeremy Taylor describes his praying as "making frequent colloquies and short discoursings between God and his own soul"; and Sir Thomas Browne, the famous physician, says, "I have resolved to pray more and to pray always, to pray in all places where quietness inviteth, in the house, on the highway, and on the street; and to know no street or passage in this city that may not witness that I have not forgotten God." Ask a monk like Brother Lawrence what praying means to him; and he answers, "That we should establish ourselves in a sense of God's presence, by continually conversing with Him"; and ask the question of so different a man as Carlyle, and the reply springs from the same idea, "Prayer is the aspiration of our poor, struggling, heavy-laden soul toward its Eternal Father, and with or without words, ought not to become impossible, nor, I persuade myself, need it ever."

To be sure, this habitual attitude is helped, not hindered, by occasional acts of devotion. Patriotism should extend over all the year, but that end is encouraged and not halted by special anniversaries like Independence Day; gratitude should be a continuous attitude, but all the months are thankfuller because of Thanksgiving Day; "Remember the week day to keep it holy" is a great commandment, but the experience of the race is clear that to keep one day each week uniquely sacred makes all days sacreder. So if all hours are to be in some degree God-conscious, some hours should be deliberately so. The biographies of praying men reveal regularity as

well as spontaneity. One would expect John Wesley to undertake
anything methodically, and prayer is no exception. In addition to
his voluminous Journal, Wesley kept diaries, scores of which have
been preserved, and on the first page of each this vow is found:
"I resolve, *Deo juvante,* (1) to devote an hour morning and evening
to private prayer, no pretense, no excuse whatsoever; and (2)
to converse κατὰ θεόν (face to face with God), no lightness, no
εὐτραπελία (facetiousness)." The greatest praying has generally
meant habitual communion with God that expressed itself in occasional acts, and occasional acts that deepened habitual communion;
but whatever the method, alike the basis and the end of all was abiding fellowship with God.

> "There is a viewless, cloistered room,
>   As high as heaven, as fair as day,
> Where, though my feet may join the throng,
>   My soul can enter in, and pray.
>
> One hearkening, even, cannot know
>   When I have crossed the threshold o'er;
> For He alone, who hears my prayer,
>   Has heard the shutting of the door."

IV

For another thing, the thought of prayer as communion with God
relieves us from the pressure of many intellectual difficulties. To pray
for detailed gifts from God, to ask him in the realm where the laws
of nature reign to serve us in this particular, or to refrain in that—
this sort of entreaty raises puzzling questions that baffle thought. To
commune with God, however, is not only prayer in its deepest meaning; it is prayer in its simplest, most intelligible form. Here, at least,
we can confidently deal with reality in prayer, undisturbed by the
problems that often confuse us. For the standard objections to prayer
—the reign of natural law making answer impossible, the goodness
and wisdom of God making changes in his plans undesirable—need
not trouble us here. When a man sits in fellowship with his friend,
neither begging for things, nor trying to content himself with soliloquy, but gaining the inspiration, vision, peace, and joy which friendship brings through mutual communion, he does not fear the reign

of law. *The law of friendship is communion, and prayer is the fulfilling of the law.* So fellowship in the spirit may be free and unencumbered, theoretical perplexities may be left far behind; and we may range out into a transforming experience of the divine friendship, when we learn that prayer is not beggary, it is not soliloquy, it is communion with God.

This interpretation of the innermost nature of prayer as the search of the soul for God rather than for his gifts, has, to some, a modern sound, as though it were new—invented, perhaps, to put the possibility of praying out of reach of this generation's special difficulties. But to call this view modern is to betray ignorance of what the choicest people of God in all centuries have meant by praying. Recall St. Augustine's entreaty in the fourth century, "Give me thine own self, without whom, though thou shouldst give me all that ever thou hadst made, yet could not my desires be satisfied." Recall Thomas à Kempis in the fifteenth century, praying, "It is too small and unsatisfactory, whatsoever thou bestowest on me, apart from thyself." And then recall George Matheson in the nineteenth century: "Whether thou comest in sunshine or in rain, I would take thee into my heart joyfully. Thou art thyself more than the sunshine; thou art thyself compensation for the rain. It is thee and not thy gifts I crave." This view of prayer is neither peculiarly modern nor ancient; it is the common property of all Christian seers who have penetrated to the heart of praying. The intellectual puzzles are found in the fringes of prayer; prayer at its center is as simple and as profound as friendship.

v

The inevitable effect of this sort of communion is that God becomes real. *Only to one who prays can God make himself vivid.* Robertson of Brighton has already described for us his crude ideas of prayer in his boyhood. Listen to him, however, as at the age of twenty-five he writes: "It seems to me now that I can always see, in uncertainty, the leading of God's hand after prayer, when everything seems to be made clear and plain before the eyes. In two or three instances I have had evidence of this which I cannot for a moment doubt." An experience like this makes God vivid, but to many people God is only a vague Being in whom they dimly believe but with whom they have no dealings. They have heard of him in

the home from childhood and never have entirely escaped the influence of their early teaching about him; they have heard of him
in the church and find it difficult to doubt what everywhere, always,
and by all has been believed concerning him; they have heard of him
from the philosophers, and when a scientist like Sir Oliver Lodge
says, "Atheism is so absurd that I do not know how to put it into
words," they see no reason to dispute. But all this is like the voice
of many astronomers saying that there are rings about Saturn. Men
believe it who never saw the rings. They believe it, but the rings
have no influence upon their lives. They believe it, but they have no
personal dealings with the object of their faith. So men think that
God is, but they never have *met him*. They never have come into
that personal experience of communion with God which says: *"I
had heard of thee by the hearing of the ear; but now mine eye seeth
thee."* (Job 42:5).

Nothing is real to us except those things with which we habitually
deal. Men say that they do not pray because to them God is not real,
but a truer statement generally would be that God is not real because they do not pray. *Granted a belief that God is, the practice
of prayer is necessary to make God not merely an idea held in the
mind but a Presence recognized in the life.* In an exclamation that
came from the heart of personal religion, the Psalmist cried, "O
God, thou art *my* God" (Psalm 63:1). To stand afar off and say "O
God," is neither difficult nor searching. We do it when we give intellectual assent to a creed that calls God "Infinite in being and perfection; almighty, most wise, most holy, most free, most absolute;
working all things according to the counsel of his own immutable
and most righteous will." In such a way to say, "O God," is easy,
but it is an inward and searching matter to say, "O God, thou art
my God." The first is theology, the second is religion; the first involves only opinion, the second involves vital experience; the first
can be reached by thought, the second must be reached by prayer;
the first leaves God afar off, the second alone makes him real. To
be sure, all Christian service where we consciously ally ourselves with
God's purpose, and all insight into history where we see God's providence at work, help to make God real to us; but there is an inward
certainty of God that can come only from personal communion with
God. *"God,"* said Emerson, *"enters by a private door into every individual."*

One day in Paris, a religious procession carrying a crucifix passed

Voltaire and a friend. Voltaire, who was generally regarded as an infidel, lifted his hat. "What!" the friend exclaimed, "are you reconciled with God?" And Voltaire with fine irony replied: *"We salute, but we do not speak."* That phrase is a true description of many men's relationship with God. They believe that God is; they cannot explain the universe without him; they are theists, but they maintain no personal relationships with him. They salute, but they do not speak. They believe in the church, and, especially in sensitive moments when some experience has subdued them to reverence, they are moved by the dignity and exaltation of the church's services, but they have no personal fellowship with God. They salute, but they do not speak.

When men complain, then, that God is not real to them, the reply is fair: How *can* God be real to some of us? What conditions have we fulfilled that would make anybody real? Those earthly friendships have most vivid reality and deepest meaning for us, where a constant sense of spiritual fellowship is refreshed occasionally by special reunions. The curtain that divides us from the thought of our friend is never altogether closed, but at times soul talks with soul in conscious fellowship. The friend grows real. We enter into new thankfulness for him, new appreciation of him, new intimacy with him. No friendship can sustain the neglect of such communion. Even God grows unreal, ceases to be our Unseen Friend and dwindles into a cold hypothesis to explain the world, when we forget communion.

Jude expressed a deep insight into the necessities of the spiritual life, when he said: *"Keep yourselves in the love of God"* (vs. 21).

SUGGESTIONS FOR THOUGHT AND DISCUSSION

What are the primary practical difficulties in prayer?

Why does a child lose confidence in prayer if it is not literally answered?

How far do men continue to pray who believe in prayer as spiritual exercise?

What difficulties in prayer are set forth in Psalm 22:1-5? How far are these typical?

In your experience, what have been the chief practical difficulties in praying?

If no petition were ever answered, would it still be worth while to pray?

What light does the Bible throw upon these practical difficulties?

What was the difference in the prayer of the prodigal on leaving and returning home?

What was the essential element in prayer in the experience of Jesus? Did Jesus receive everything he prayed for? Why did Jesus pray?

Why did the disciples ask Jesus to teach them to pray?

Why is communion with God the central idea of prayer?

What is the greatest gift that any friend gives another? What is the essence of any personal relationship? Is this true of relationship with God?

How does communion with God differ from the experience of human friendship?

What effect upon the prayer life has the experience of prayer as communion with God?

What is necessary for the maintenance of communion with God?

CHAPTER III

God's Care for the Individual

DAILY READINGS

First Day, Third Week

Perhaps the greatest single difficulty in maintaining the habit of prayer is our tendency to make of it a *pious form* and not a *vital transaction*. We begin by trying to pray and end by saying prayers. To urge ourselves to a practice that has thus become a stereotyped and lifeless form is futile. Nobody ever succeeds in praying as a *tour de force;* but if the act of prayer can be seen as the great Christians have seen it—a vital and sustaining friendship with a God who cares for every one of us—praying will cease being a form and become a force and a privilege. Note the vitality of prayer as the Psalmist has experienced it:

My soul, wait thou in silence for God only;
For my expectation is from him.
He only is my rock and my salvation:
He is my high tower; I shall not be moved.
With God is my salvation and my glory:
The rock of my strength, and my refuge, is in God.
Trust in him at all times, ye people;
Pour out your heart before him:
God is a refuge for us.—Psalm 62:5-8.

In confirmation of this same experience in our own day, consider the testimony of Sir Wilfred Grenfell: "The privilege of prayer to me is one of the most cherished possessions, because faith and experience alike convince me that God himself sees and answers, and his

answers I never venture to criticise. It is only my part to ask. It is
entirely his to give or withhold, as he knows is best. If it were otherwise, I would not dare to pray at all. In the quiet of home, in the
heat of life and strife, in the face of death, the privilege of speech
with God is inestimable. I value it more because it calls for nothing
that the wayfaring man, though a fool, cannot give—that is, the
simplest expression to his simplest desire. When I can neither see,
nor hear, nor speak, still I can pray so that God can hear. When I
finally pass through the valley of the shadow of death, I expect to
pass through it in conversation with him."

*O Lord, renew our spirits and draw our hearts unto Thyself that
our work may not be to us a burden, but a delight; and give us such
a mighty love to Thee as may sweeten all our obedience. Oh, let us
not serve Thee with the spirit of bondage as slaves, but with the
cheerfulness and gladness of children, delighting ourselves in Thee
and rejoicing in Thy work. Amen.*—Benjamin Jenks (1646-1724).

Second Day, Third Week

One of the root reasons why prayer becomes merely a pious form
is that while people believe in God in a general and vague fashion,
*they do not vividly grasp the idea that God cares for and is dealing
with every one of us.*

How think ye? If any man have a hundred sheep, and one of
them be gone astray, doth he not leave the ninety and nine, and
go unto the mountains, and seek that which goeth astray? And if so
be that he find it, verily I say unto you, he rejoiceth over it more
than over the ninety and nine which have not gone astray. Even
so it is not the will of your Father who is in heaven, that one of
these little ones should perish.—Matt. 18:12-14.

A man may hold true this individual care of God for each of his
children, and still may not practice habitual prayer, but it is difficult
to see how anyone can practice habitual prayer if he does not hold
for true that God loves every one of us. Who can continue praying,
in any Christian sense, to a God that does not care? *For prayer, at
least, a God who does not care, does not count.* Haeckel, the materialist, has displaced the Creator by a primal substance which he

solemnly crowns Emperor of the universe under the title of "Mobile Cosmic Ether." Can we imagine anyone finding vital and sustaining help in supplications addressed to such an object, or are vast congregations likely to be stirred in adoration, praying, "O Mobile Cosmic Ether, hallowed be thy name!" Why not? Is not the reason simply this, that the God to whom real prayer is made must care for us as a race and as individuals?

Almighty God, the refuge of all that are distressed, grant unto us that, in all trouble of this our mortal life, we may flee to the knowledge of Thy lovingkindness and tender mercy; that so, sheltering ourselves therein, the storms of life may pass over us, and not shake the peace of God that is within us. Whatsoever this life may bring us, grant that it may never take from us the full faith that Thou art our Father. Grant us Thy light, that we may have life, through Jesus Christ our Lord. Amen.—George Dawson (1821-1876).

Third Day, Third Week

Are not two sparrows sold for a penny? and not one of them shall fall on the ground without your Father: but the very hairs of your head are all numbered. Fear not therefore: ye are of more value than any sparrows.—Matt. 10:29-31.

Let us face again today that formality in prayer that comes from a failure to grasp the individual love of God. There are real difficulties for the mind to face when it tries to believe that God so cares for each of us, but perhaps even greater for most people is the difficulty that the *imagination* faces. In this vast universe how can we picture God as caring for every individual thing, even to stricken sparrows and to the hairs of our head? Consider, however, the scientific truth of gravitation, that the whole earth rises to meet a child's ball, just as truly as the ball falls to meet the earth, and that only the lack of sensitiveness in our instruments prevents us from measuring the earth's ascent as it responds to the pull of the child's toy. Can we imagine that? Is it not unimaginable, though plainly true? And if in a gravitate system a whole planet moves to meet a tossed ball, we ought not to dismiss, for reasons of weak imagination, the truth that in a love-system of persons, the Eternal God responds to each child's approach. As Kipling sings:

"Who clears the grounding berg,
And guides the grinding floe,
He hears the cry of the little kit fox,
And the lemming on the snow."

*O Thou good omnipotent, who so carest for every one of us, as if
Thou caredst for him alone; and so for all, as if all were but one!
Blessed is the man who loveth Thee, and his friend in Thee, and his
enemy for Thee. I behold how some things pass away that others
may replace them, but Thou dost never depart. O God, my Father,
supremely good, Beauty of all things beautiful, to Thee will I intrust
whatsoever I have received from Thee, and so shall I lose nothing.
Thou madest me for Thyself, and my heart is restless until it repose
in Thee. Amen.*—St. Augustine (354-430).

Fourth Day, Third Week

**Neither for these only do I pray, but for them also that believe
on me through their word; that they may all be one; even as thou,
Father, art in me, and I in thee, that they also may be in us: that
the world may believe that thou didst send me. And the glory which
thou hast given me I have given unto them; that they may be one,
even as we are one; I in them, and thou in me, that they may be
perfected into one; that the world may know that thou didst send
me, and lovedst them, even as thou lovedst me.—John 17:20-23.**

It is easy to think that God's love centered about the Master, but
consider what it would mean for prayer vitally to believe that God
so cares for each of us—*"lovedst them, even as thou lovedst me!"*
As Silvester Horne puts it in his Yale lectures: "What is the Gospel?
—It is contained in a verse of one of the greatest Christian hymns:

'Were the whole realm of Nature mine,
That were a present far too small!
Love so amazing, so Divine,
Demands my soul!——'

That is to say that my soul is a greater and bigger thing than the
whole realm of nature. Do you believe it? I agree it is the most
romantic of all beliefs. It affirms that the soul of every forced laborer
on the Amazon is of more value than all the mines of Johannesburg,
all the diamonds of Kimberley, all the millions of all the magnates of

America. It affirms that in God's sight all the suns and stars that people infinite space, are of inferior worth to one human spirit dwelling, it may be, in the degraded body of some victim of drink or lust, some member of the gutter population of a great city who has descended to his doom by means of the multiplied temptations with which our so-called society environs him. It is a romantic creed. But if it is not true Christianity itself is false." *Has your failure in prayer been due to your failure in apprehending for yourself this heart of the Gospel?*

O God, mercifully grant unto us that the fire of Thy love may burn up in us all things that displease Thee, and make us meet for Thy heavenly Kingdom.—Roman Breviary.

Fifth Day, Third Week

For we have not a high priest that cannot be touched with the feeling of our infirmities; but one that hath been in all points tempted like as we are, yet without sin. Let us therefore draw near with boldness unto the throne of grace, that we may receive mercy, and may find grace to help us in time of need.—Hebrews 4:15, 16.

Note the sequence of thought in these verses: first, the revelation in Christ of a God who cares; and second, resultant confidence in the reality of prayer. In contrast with this reality of prayer to those who apprehend the personal love of God, consider how many people know prayer only as an *inherited bit of propriety*. Prayer to them is a formality because it is a practice taught in infancy, and maintained by force of habit as a tradition. It is not vital. It does not mean "Grace to help us in time of need." They are true to George Eliot's description of Hetty in Adam Bede: "Hetty was one of those numerous people who have had god-fathers and god-mothers, learned their catechism, been confirmed, and gone to church every Sunday, and yet for any practical result of strength in life, or trust in death, have never appropriated a single Christian idea or Christian feeling." Over against such a futile form of religion consider a vital prayer like this of Thomas à Kempis, founded on the thought of God's individual love.

Ah, Lord God, Thou holy Lover of my soul, when Thou comest into my soul, all that is within me shall rejoice. Thou art my Glory

*and the exultation of my heart; Thou art my Hope and Refuge in
the day of my trouble. Set me free from all evil passions, and heal
my heart of all inordinate affections; that, being inwardly cured
and thoroughly cleansed, I may be made fit to love, courageous to
suffer, steady to persevere. Nothing is sweeter than Love, nothing
more courageous, nothing fuller nor better in heaven and earth;
because Love is born of God, and cannot rest but in God, above all
created things. Let me love Thee more than myself, nor love myself
but for Thee. Amen.*—Thomas à Kempis (1379-1471).

Sixth Day, Third Week

To many people prayer is a pious practice rather than a vital
transaction, not so much because it is an inherited bit of propriety,
but because it is looked upon as a *good work which wins merit* in the
eyes of God. Men think of prayer as a safe practice to indulge in if
they are to keep on good terms with God. They go through it as a
courtier might observe the rituals of obeisance that please the king
and the neglect of which might get a careless man into trouble.
Prayer to many is a safety appliance, like a lightning-rod, upward
raised lest the Eternal God, seeing their neglect, fall foul of them.
It is founded on fear. They conceive that the saying of prayer is a
measure of protection which they would better attend to. *What a
pitiful misunderstanding of prayer!* Prayer is not a "good work" in
return for which a blessing is given, as men buy and sell over the
counter. Our pious practices are as useless as a Tibetan prayer
wheel, unless at the heart of them all is conscious fellowship with the
Father who cares.

Listen to Isaiah's expression of God's contempt for formal worship
without spiritual meaning:

**What unto me is the multitude of your sacrifices? saith Jehovah:
I have had enough of the burnt-offerings of rams, and the fat of fed
beasts; and I delight not in the blood of bullocks, or of lambs, or
of he-goats. When ye come to appear before me, who hath required
this at your hand, to trample my courts? Bring no more vain oblations; incense is an abomination unto me; new moon and sabbath,
the calling of assemblies,—I cannot away with iniquity and the
solemn meeting. Your new moons and your appointed feasts my
soul hateth; they are a trouble unto me; I am weary of bearing**

them. And when ye spread forth your hands, I will hide mine eyes from you; yea, when ye make many prayers, I will not hear: your hands are full of blood.—Isaiah 1:11-15.

Most loving Lord, give me a childlike love of Thee, which may cast out all fear. Amen.—E. B. Pusey (1800-1882).

Seventh Day, Third Week

For as many as are led by the Spirit of God, these are sons of God. For ye received not the spirit of bondage again unto fear; but ye received the spirit of adoption, whereby we cry, Abba, Father. The Spirit himself beareth witness with our spirit, that we are children of God: and if children, then heirs; heirs of God, and joint-heirs with Christ.—Romans 8:14-17.

In the light of this passage how impossible to think of saying prayers as merely a pious practice. Prayer seen in the light of this Christian truth becomes at once the *claiming of our sonship, the appropriation of our heritage.* All through the New Testament the reader is conscious that wealth is waiting to be claimed. "Unsearchable riches of Christ," "Rich toward God," "Heirs of God," phrases such as these suggest the sense of spiritual wealth in which the first Christians rejoiced. They had found an Eldorado in the Gospel that God loved every son of man. Now, prayer is the active appropriation of this wealth. Of how many of us is it true that friendship with God is an *unclaimed heritage!* We have the title-deeds in our church membership, but we do not have the spiritual riches in our lives. *In our prayers we are not appropriating our faith that God really does care.*

Grant me, even me, my dearest Lord, to know Thee, and love Thee, and rejoice in Thee. And, if I cannot do these perfectly in this life, let me at least advance to higher degrees every day, till I can come to do them in perfection. Let the knowledge of Thee increase in me here, that it may be full hereafter. Let the love of Thee grow every day more and more here, that it may be perfect hereafter; that my joy may be great in itself, and full in Thee. I know, O God, that Thou art a God of truth; O make good Thy gracious promises to me, that my joy may be full. Amen.—St. Augustine (354-430).

COMMENT FOR THE WEEK

When a man, making earnest with prayer, sets himself to practice communion with God, he is likely to awaken with a start some day to a disturbing reflection. "This thing that I am doing," he well may say, "presupposes that the Almighty God takes a personal interest in me. I am taking for granted when I pray that the Eternal is specially solicitous on my behalf. Praying may seem a simple matter, but on what an enormous assumption does it rest!" Now, this reflection accords entirely with the facts. Prayer does involve confidence that God takes interest in the individual who prays. The fact, for example, that the Bible is preeminently a book of prayer, involves of necessity the companion fact that the God of the Bible cares for individuals. He knows all the stars by name (Psalm 147:4); he numbers the hairs of our heads (Matt. 10:30); of all the sparrows "not one of them is forgotten in the sight of God" (Luke 12:6). John is expressing his thought of God as well as his interpretation of Christ when he says, "He calleth his own sheep by name" (John 10:3). God is like a shepherd who misses even one lost from his flock, a housewife who seeks for a single coin, a father who grieves for one boy gone wrong (Luke 15). Of all the children in the world, says Jesus, "It is not the will of your Father . . . that *one of these* little ones should perish" (Matt. 18:14). Throughout the Bible, and especially in the New Testament, God is not a king dealing with men in masses. He is no Napoleon, who, warned by Metternich that a campaign would cost a million men, said, "What are a million men to me?" God is a father, and the essence of fatherhood is individual care for the children. For all that there are so many of us, as St. Augustine said, *"He loves us every one as though there were but one of us to love."* That is the message of the Book, and it underlies the possibility of vital prayer.

This truth that God cares for every one of us is easy to speak about, beautiful to contemplate, but hard to believe. How *can* God care for each of us? We know the heart of Jesus well enough to understand that he loved every one he met. But *God?* How can we make it real to ourselves that he who sustains the milky way, who holds Orion and the Pleiades in his leash, knows us by name?

II

For one thing, we seem too small and insignificant for him to know. If God cares for each of us, that presupposes in us a degree of value and importance surpassing imagination; and as one considers the vastness of the physical universe, it seems almost unbelievable that individual men can be worth so much. Even the Psalmist felt the wonder of man's worth in such a world, when he cried: "When I consider thy heavens, the work of thy fingers, the moon and the stars, which thou hast ordained; what is man, that thou art mindful of him? And the son of man, that thou visitest him?" (Psalm 8:3, 4). The Psalmist, however, never saw more than 6,000 stars on the clearest night when he looked at the sky from the heights of Zion. We today can see 100,000,000 of them through our telescopes; and when we put a photographic plate, instead of our eyes, at the orifice of the instrument, we obtain indications of multitudes more. When, therefore, a modern psalmist like Tennyson thinks of man's possible value in so great a universe, he feels the terrific urge of doubt; he gathers all the activities of mankind, our wars, politics, arts and sciences, and cries,

"What is it all but a trouble of ants in the gleam of a million million of suns?"

How in the face of this new knowledge of the universe can we pray in the confidence that God knows and cares for each one of us?

Many a man's faith is undone and his prayers stopped by this appalling contrast between the size of the world and his own smallness. The *microscope,* however, should counteract a little the disheartening influence of the *telescope.* It is evident that the Power which cares for the stars cares for all things with utter disregard of size. Inside any common pin as marvelous activity is going on as ever was present among the stars. Here are electrons so many and so small that the race in a million years could not count them, and yet not one electron touches another. In comparison with their size they are as far apart as the planets of a solar system. Endlessly they revolve about each other, and no one ever slips by an infinitesimal degree from the control of law. Not strong reason but weak imagination leads us to be terrified by the mere size of the universe into the thought that God cannot care for us. So far as physical nature has any testimony to bear on the matter at all, she says, "There is nothing too great for the Creator to accomplish, and nothing too small for him to attend to. The microscopic world is his, as well as the stars."

The real answer to our doubt, however, comes not from physical nature at all, but from spiritual insight. We are so small that God cannot care for every one of us? *But surely, we ourselves are not accustomed to judge comparative value by size.* As children we may have chosen a penny rather than a dime because the penny was larger; but as maturity arrives, that basis of choice is outgrown. The dearest possessions of the human race—diamonds and little children, for example—are rather notable for their comparative smallness. A mother's love for her baby is not a matter of pounds and ounces. When one believes in God at all, the consequence is plain. God must have at least our spiritual insight to perceive the difference between *size* and *worth*. Mere bulk cannot deceive him. He must know where in all his universe the real values lie.

As to where the real values *do* lie, the thoughtful of all races have unanimously agreed that they are found inside personality, not outside of it. Tennyson's word is a summary of the best thought of all time:

"For tho' the Giant Ages heave the hill
And break the shore, and evermore
Make and break, and work their will—
Tho' world on world in myriad myriads roll
Round us, each with different powers,
And other forms of life than ours,
What know we greater than the soul?"

The thinker is of nobler worth than any external thing that he can think about; the seer is more wonderful than all he sees; and righteousness, friendship, generosity, courage, wisdom, love, functions of personality, all of them, are, so far as *value* goes, worth more than infinite galaxies of stars. No star ever knew that it was even being gazed upon. No star ever felt God's hand upon it, or was moved by gratitude for its creation, preservation, and all the blessings of this life. As an astronomer watches the unconscious heavens, does not God know, as we do, that the man, with his powers of vision, intellect, volition, and character, is far more marvelous than all the stars he sees? We may as well deny God's existence altogether, as, granting his existence, affirm that he is enamoured by hugeness, in love with avoirdupois, and blind to spiritual values. To gain the whole world and lose a soul would be a poor bargain for God as well as for man. *Personality is the one infinitely valuable treasure in the universe.* If God is, he cares; if he cares, he cares for personality. "For Jehovah's portion is his people" (Deut. 32:9).

III

The difficulty which many experience in trying to conceive of God's individual care, is complicated by the fact that not only are we small, but *there are countless multitudes of us.* With so many people, how can God know us all by name? This difficulty is one of the commonest stumbling blocks to prayer, and yet its mere statement ought to be its sufficient refutation. Could anything be more plainly an attempt to make God in man's image than this suggestion that his powers may be inadequate to his responsibilities? "It is hard for us to keep individual interest in many people," we are saying, "therefore it must be hard for God." This crude and childish imposition of our human limitations on God, this fear that he will find it trying to remember so many, springs not from good reason but from immature thoughtlessness.

"There was an old woman, who lived in a shoe;
 She had so many children, she didn't know what to do."

Is that nursery rhyme to represent our picture of God?

We may help ourselves to the conception of God's individual care, which is essential to all vital and earnest praying, by noting that knowledge, when it moves out toward omniscience, always breaks up vague masses into individual units, and cares for each of them. When an ignoramus goes into a library, he can see only long rows of books, almost indistinguishable as units. But when the librarian comes, the student and lover of books, he knows each one by name. Each volume has its special associations; he knows the edition, the value, the contents, the author, the purpose. He takes down one book after another, revealing his individual appreciation of each. *The more he knows, as a librarian, the less he sees books in the mass; the more he knows them one by one.*

Increasing knowledge is always thus not *extensive* only but *intensive.* The average man returns from seeing the turbines at Niagara, with a vague impression of enormous masses moving at tremendous speed. But the engineer? He knows every bolt and screw, every lever and piston; he knows the particular details of secret bearing and balanced strain; he pokes his wrench around dark corners for hidden bolts that the spectator never guessed were there. The more he knows, as an engineer, the more he sees the details and not the bulk. *Ignorance sees things in mass; knowledge breaks all masses up into units and knows each one; omniscience perfectly understands and cares for every most minute detail.*

Consider then the meaning of God's knowledge of men. When a stranger thinks of China he imagines a vague multitude, with faces that look all alike. When a missionary thinks of China, the vague multitude is shaken loose in one spot, and individuals there stand out, separately known and loved. When God thinks of China, he knows every one of the Chinese by name. He does for humanity what a librarian does for his books, or an engineer for his turbines. We stand, every one, separate in his thought. He lifts us up from the obscurity of our littleness; he picks us out from the multitude of our fellows; he gives to our lives the dignity of his individual care. The Eternal God calls us every one by name. He is not the God of mankind in the mass; he is the God of *Abraham,* of *Isaac,* and of *Jacob!* All great pray-ers have lived in the power of this individual relationship with God. They have said with the Psalmist,

> "*I* will give thanks in the *great assembly:*
> *I* will praise thee among *much people.*"
> (Psalm 35:18.)

IV

So important is the vital apprehension of this truth that we may well approach it from another angle. When one believes in God at all, he must believe that God has a purpose for the universe as a whole. The seers have uttered this faith in scores of figures, but no one of them is adequate to express the full meaning of this confidence that creation means something, has a goal, is not a blind accident, but a wise plan. "Nothing walks with aimless feet," says Tennyson. "There are no accidents with God," says Longfellow. All who believe in God must somehow share this faith. For them there is a divine purpose that "binds in one book the scattered leaves of all the universe." Indeed, most men *do* believe this. The contrary position makes life too empty and futile to be easily tolerable. If there is

no purpose in creation at all, if it came from nowhere, is going nowhere, and means nothing, then the world is like a busy seamstress
sewing on a machine with no thread in it. The centuries move like
cloths beneath the biting needle, but no thread binds them. Nothing
is being done. The years will pass; the machine will wear out; the
scrap-heap will claim it; but there will be nothing to show for all its
toil. That is the world without divine purpose; and because such an
outlook on life makes it utterly vain and futile, most men do believe
in "one far-off divine event, toward which the whole creation
moves." They believe that there is a thread of divine purpose in this
machine of the universe and that it binds the separate centuries
together.

As soon as we speak of this general purpose of God, however, an
inevitable corollary faces us. *Can God have a purpose for the whole
and not for the parts?* Can an architect thoroughly plan a house
without planning the details? Shall he stand upon the site and say in
a vague and sweeping way, "Let there be a house"? But, if you ask
him about the chimney angles and the window frames, shall he
answer, "There is no plan for them"? Rather planning a house consists in arranging the parts. And when we turn from dealing with
things to deal with persons, each one so individual and unique, how
much more clear the truth is! *No father can love his family in general, without loving the several members of it in particular.* So God
can neither care nor plan for his world as a whole, without caring
and planning for each of the individuals that make his world. The
faith of the Bible, in the individual knowledge, love, and purpose of
God for each of us is not mere sentiment. It is the inevitable corollary of theism. No man can think through the meaning of belief in
God without coming to it. Purpose for the universe and purpose for
each life are two aspects of the same thing and they mutually involve
each other. You can as easily find a shield with only one side as a
purpose that concerns the whole and not the parts. Here, too, God
calls us every one by name. As an Indian poet sings,

"The subtle anklets that ring on the feet of an insect when it moves
    are heard of Him."

Whether, therefore, we consider the fact that God must care for
value rather than for size; or the fact that knowledge, as it grows,
always breaks up masses into units and understands each one of

the fact that no love and purpose in general can fail to
~~~ particular parts, we come to the same conclusion: God's
care for us is not only a reasonable, it is an inevitable
corollary of our faith. Of course, God numbers the hairs of our
heads! Just that sort of thing infinite knowledge necessarily implies.
Of course, the Scripture cries in a passage, quoted by Jesus, "All of
you sons of the Most High!" (Psalm 82:6). Just that *must* be said
when the fatherhood of God is believed at all. Of course, it is not
God's will that "one of these little ones should perish" (Matt.
18:14). How could he care for all and not for each? Of course, Jesus
says, "Having shut thy door, pray to thy Father who is in secret"
(Matt. 6:6). For trust in God's individual love, if it have normal
growth, must always flower out in prayer.

V

*Indeed, prayer is the personal appropriation of this faith that God
cares for each of us.* When a man really prays he no longer leaves his
thought of God's individual care as a theory, held in his mind, beautiful but ineffective. He now avails himself of the truth which he
sees; he thrusts his life out upon it; he enters into that fellowship
with God of which the creed is the theory, and prayer is the practice.
It is one thing to think that a man is your friend; it is another thing
actively to enter into friendly relations with him. So some men
merely believe that God is, and that he cares for them; but some
richly profit by their faith, so acting upon it in prayer that vague
belief about God passes over into transforming relationship with
him. Belief by itself is a map of the unvisited land of God's care;
prayer is actually traveling the country. The tragedy of the Church
is to be found in the thousands who fondle their credal maps, on
which are marked the roadways of God's friendship, but who do not
travel. They would resent any sceptical doubt about God's love for
every individual, but they do not in habitual reliance and communion take advantage of the faith they hold. They miss the daily
guidance, the consciousness of divine resource, the sustaining sense
of God's presence, which can come only to those who both believe
that God cares for each, and who in habitual communion with him
are making earnest with their faith.

When, therefore, we have satisfied our minds of God's individual
care, we have arrived at the beginning, not at the end of the matter.

Now comes the vital and searching task of laying hold on the *experience* of that care, in whose existence we believe. We must pass from thought into spiritual activity, from the "industrious squirrel work of the brain" into an adventure of the soul in the practice of prayer. The Gospel offers a great privilege; prayer appropriates it. In Calvin's vivid figure, "Prayer *digs out* those treasures which the Gospel of the Lord discovers to our faith."

SUGGESTIONS FOR THOUGHT AND DISCUSSION

What makes prayer a pious form rather than a vital transaction?

What gave vitality to the Psalmist's prayer?
What is the difference between a Buddhist turning a prayer wheel and a Christian praying?
What merit is there in praying?

What is the estimate of the value of the individual in the Christian religion?

What was Jesus' view as set forth in the Daily Readings?
What place has the individual had in the history of the Church?
How does the Christian religion differ from other religions in its estimate of the worth of the individual?

How far are Christians justified in basing their confidence in prayer on God's care for the individual?

Is the possibility of prayer dependent upon God's care for the individual?
To what extent is prayer futile if God does not care for us?
What are your chief difficulties in a belief that God cares for each individual? To what extent do you feel these difficulties make prayer impossible?
How far is it reasonable to think that God cares for us?

What difference will it make in my prayers if I really believe God cares for me as an individual?

CHAPTER IV

Prayer and the Goodness of God

DAILY READINGS

First Day, Fourth Week

And there came near unto him James and John, the sons of
Zebedee, saying unto him, Teacher, we would that thou shouldest
do for us whatsoever we shall ask of thee. And he said unto them,
What would ye that I should do for you? And they said unto him,
Grant unto us that we may sit, one on thy right hand, and one on
thy left hand, in thy glory. But Jesus said unto them, Ye know not
what ye ask. Are ye able to drink the cup that I drink? or to be
baptized with the baptism that I am baptized with?—Mark 10:35-
38.

Of all misconceptions of prayer, none is more common than the
idea that it is a way of *getting God to do our will.* Note the request
which James and John made of our Lord: they wanted him to put
himself at their disposal; they wished their will for themselves to be
in absolute control, with the Master as aider and abettor of it.
Prayer to God, so conceived, is simply self-will, expecting the Almighty to back it up and give it right-of-way. Consider how often
our praying is thus our demand on God that he shall do exactly
what we want; and then in contrast, note this *real* prayer of D. L.
Moody:

*Use me then, my Saviour, for whatever purpose, and in whatever
way, Thou mayest require. Here is my poor heart, an empty vessel;
fill it with Thy grace. Here is my sinful and troubled soul; quicken
it and refresh it with Thy love. Take my heart for Thine abode; my*

mouth to spread abroad the glory of Thy name; my love and all my powers, for the advancement of Thy believing people; and never suffer the steadfastness and confidence of my faith to abate—that so at all times I may be enabled from the heart to say, "Jesus needs me, and I Him."—D. L. Moody.

Second Day, Fourth Week

The trouble with many folk is that they *believe in only a part of God.* They believe in his *love,* and thinking of that alone they are led into entreating him as though he might be coaxed and wheedled into giving them what they want. They argue that because he is benign and kindly he will give in to a child's entreaty and do what the child happens to desire. They do not really believe in God's *wisdom*—his knowledge of what is best for all of us, and in his *will*—his plan for the character and the career of each of us. When anyone believes in the whole of God, is sure that he has a wise and a good purpose for every child of his, and for all the world, prayer inevitably becomes not the endeavor to get God to do our will, but the endeavor to open our lives to God so that *God can do in us what he wants to do.* Consider, in the light of this truth, the prayer of the Master in Gethsemane:

Then cometh Jesus with them unto a place called Gethsemane, and saith unto his disciples, Sit ye here, while I go yonder and pray. And he took with him Peter and the two sons of Zebedee, and began to be sorrowful and sore troubled. Then saith he unto them, My soul is exceeding sorrowful, even unto death: abide ye here, and watch with me. And he went forward a little, and fell on his face, and prayed, saying, My Father, if it be possible, let this cup pass away from me: nevertheless, not as I will, but as thou wilt. And he cometh unto the disciples, and findeth them sleeping, and saith unto Peter, What, could ye not watch with me one hour? Watch and pray, that ye enter not into temptation: the spirit indeed is willing, but the flesh is weak. Again a second time he went away, and prayed, saying, My Father, if this cannot pass away, except I drink it, thy will be done. And he came again and found them sleeping, for their eyes were heavy. And he left them again, and went away, and prayed a third time, saying again the same words.—Matt. 26:36-44.

*O Lord, Thou knowest what is best for us, let this or that be done,
as Thou shalt please. Give what Thou wilt, and how much Thou
wilt, and when Thou wilt. Deal with me as Thou thinkest good, and
as best pleaseth Thee. Set me where Thou wilt, and deal with me
in all things just as Thou wilt. Behold, I am Thy servant, prepared
for all things; for I desire not to live unto myself, but unto Thee;
and Oh, that I could do it worthily and perfectly! Amen.*—Thomas
à Kempis (1379-1471).

Third Day, Fourth Week

*Let us this week consider particularly the ways in which the
practice of prayer opens our lives to God so that his will can be
done in and through us.* For one thing, prayer, as we now are thinking of it, involves *solitude,* where the voice of God has a chance to
be heard.

**And when ye pray, ye shall not be as the hypocrites: for they love
to stand and pray in the synagogues and in the corners of the streets,
that they may be seen of men. Verily I say unto you, They have received their reward. But thou, when thou prayest, enter into thine
inner chamber, and having shut thy door, pray to thy Father who
is in secret, and thy Father who seeth in secret shall recompense
thee.—Matt. 6:5, 6.**

Consider the testimony of different sorts of men to the value of
occasional solitude in the midst of a busy life. Says Walter Savage
Landor, the poet, "Solitude is the ante-chamber of God; only one
step more, and you can be in his immediate presence. Goethe says,
"No one can produce anything important unless he isolates himself."
"Chinese" Gordon writes to his sister, "Getting quiet does one good
—it is impossible to hear God's voice in a whirl of visits—you must
be more or less in the 'desert' to use the scales of the sanctuary, to
see and weigh the true value of things and sayings." And an anonymous epigram hits off the important truth, "He is a wonderful man
who can thread a needle while at cudgels in a crowd." *How much
time, away from the distractions of business, and the strife of
tongues, are we giving to the enriching use of solitude?*

*O God, by whom the meek are guided in judgment, and light
riseth up in darkness for the godly; grant us, in all our doubts and*

*uncertainties, the grace to ask what Thou wouldest have us to do;
that the spirit of Wisdom may save us from all false choices, and
that in Thy light we may see light, and in Thy straight path may not
stumble, through Jesus Christ our Lord. Amen.*—William Bright.

Fourth Day, Fourth Week

Prayer opens our lives to the guidance of God because by its very
nature *it encourages the receptive mood.* The dominant mood today
is active; but some things never come into life until a man is receptive. That a boy should run many errands for his father and should
be faithful and energetic in doing it is of great importance; but the
most far-reaching consequences in that boy's life are likely to come
from some quiet hour, when he sits with his father, and has his eyes
opened to a new *idea of life,* which the father never could give him
in his more active moods. God's trouble to get people to listen is set
forth in the eighty-first Psalm:

Hear, O my people, and I will testify unto thee:
But my people hearkened not to my voice;
And Israel would none of me.
So I let them go after the stubbornness of their heart,
That they might walk in their own counsels.
Oh that my people would hearken unto me.

—Psalm 81:8, 11-13.

*Lord, I know not what I ought to ask of Thee; Thou only knowest
what I need; Thou lovest me better than I know how to love myself.
O Father! give to Thy child that which he himself knows not how
to ask. I dare not ask either for crosses or consolations: I simply
present myself before Thee, I open my heart to Thee. Behold my
needs which I know not myself; see and do according to Thy tender
mercy. Smite, or heal; depress me, or raise me up: I adore all Thy
purposes without knowing them; I am silent; I offer myself in sacrifice: I yield myself to Thee; I would have no other desire than to
accomplish Thy will. Teach me to pray. Pray Thyself in me. Amen.*
—François de la Mothe Fénelon (1651-1715).

Fifth Day, Fourth Week

Jesus therefore answered them, and said, My teaching is not
mine, but his that sent me. If any man willeth to do his will, he shall

know of the teaching, whether it is of God, or whether I speak from
myself. He that speaketh from himself seeketh his own glory: but he
that seeketh the glory of him that sent me, the same is true, and no
unrighteousness is in him.—John 7:16-18.

Prayer opens our lives to God so that his will can be done in and
through us, because in true prayer we habitually put ourselves into
the attitude of *willingness to do whatever God wills*. If a young man
says, "I am willing to be a lawyer, but not a business man; I am
willing to be a physician, but not a medical missionary," he will
never discover what God really wants him to be. He must hand God
a *carte blanche* to be filled in as God wills, and there must be no
provisos and reservations to limit the guidance of God. If a man of
whose wisdom and motives we are suspicious asks us to do what he
is about to demand, we may well say, "Tell me what you expect and
I will tell you whether or not I will do it." But we may not take that
attitude toward God; we may not distrust his wisdom, or his love, or
his power to see us through what he demands. We must be willing
to do whatever he wills. True prayer is deliberately putting ourselves
at God's disposal.

*O Lord, let me not henceforth desire health or life, except to
spend them for Thee, with Thee, and in Thee. Thou alone knowest
what is good for me; do, therefore, what seemeth Thee best. Give to
me, or take from me; conform my will to Thine; and grant that,
with humble and perfect submission, and in holy confidence, I may
receive the orders of Thine eternal Providence; and may equally
adore all that comes to me from Thee; through Jesus Christ our
Lord. Amen.*—Blaise Pascal (1623-1662).

Sixth Day, Fourth Week

And Jehovah spake unto Moses face to face, as a man speaketh
unto his friend.—Exodus 33:11.

And the scripture was fulfilled which saith, And Abraham believed God, and it was reckoned unto him for righteousness; and he
was called the friend of God.—James 2:23.

The most transforming influences in life are *personal friendships*.
Everyone who meets us influences us, but friendship opens the heart
to the ideas, ideals, and spiritual quality of another life, until we

are susceptible to everything that the friend is and sensitive to everything that he thinks. Desdemona describes the natural effect of close friendship:

> "My heart's subdued
> Even to the very quality of my lord."

Consider then what persistent fellowship with God will mean in changing life's quality and tone. Henry Drummond said, "Ten minutes spent in Christ's society every day; aye, two minutes, if it be face to face and heart to heart, will make the whole life different." In how many people is the fine quality which all feel and none can describe, the result of this inner fellowship! Some things cannot be bought or earned or achieved; they must be *caught*, they are transmitted by contact as fragrance is. Perhaps the greatest consequence of prayer is just this atmosphere which the life carries away with it, as Moses came with shining face from the communion of his heart with God. *True prayer is habitually putting oneself under God's influence.*

We rejoice that in all time men have found a refuge in Thee, and that prayer is the voice of love, the voice of pleading, and the voice of thanksgiving. Our souls overflow toward Thee like a cup when full; nor can we forbear; nor shall we search to see if our prayers have been registered, or whether of the things asked we have received much, or more, or anything. That we have had permission to feel ourselves in Thy presence, to take upon ourselves something of the light of Thy countenance, to have a consciousness that Thy thoughts are upon us, to experience the inspiration of the Holy Spirit in any measure—this is an answer to prayer transcending all things that we can think of. We are glad that we can glorify Thee, that we can rejoice Thee, that it does make a difference to Thee what we do, and that Thou dost enfold us in a consciousness of Thy sympathy with us, of how much Thou art to us, and of what we are to Thee. —Henry Ward Beecher.

Seventh Day, Fourth Week

Yet thou hast not called upon me, O Jacob; but thou hast been weary of me, O Israel.—Isaiah 43:22.

And there is none that calleth upon thy name, that stirreth up himself to take hold of thee; for thou hast hid thy face from us, and hast consumed us by means of our iniquities.—Isaiah 64:7.

Consider the reasonableness of the prophet's vehement condemnation of prayerlessness, in view of this week's truth. Take out of life solitude where God's voice can be heard, the receptive mood that welcomes guidance, the willingness to do whatever God wills that puts itself habitually at God's disposal, and the fellowship that gives God's secret influence its opportunity; and what can God do with any life? Two very young girls were discussing prayer. Said one: "I am not going to pray again for two weeks." After an interval of shocked silence, the other exclaimed: "Poor God!" Does not this exclamation reveal a true philosophy of prayer? *Think of the things God wants to give to and do through our lives, and consider how the prayerless, unreceptive heart blockades his will.*

Almighty God, and most merciful Father, give us, we beseech Thee, that grace that we may duly examine the inmost of our hearts, and our most secret thoughts, how we stand before Thee; and that we may henceforward never be drawn to do anything that may dishonor Thy name: but may persevere in all good purposes, and in Thy Holy service, unto our life's end; and grant that we may now this present day, seeing it is as good as nothing that we have done hitherto, perfectly begin to walk before Thee, as becometh those that are called to an inheritance of light in Christ. Amen.—George Hickes (1642-1715).

COMMENT FOR THE WEEK

I

Strangely enough, when we have convinced ourselves of the individual love and care of God, we do not so much evade difficulty as encounter it; for we find ourselves running straight into the arms of one of the commonest perplexities concerning prayer. God is all wise and all good; why should we urge on him our erring and ignorant desires? He knows what we need; why tell him? His love purposes the best for us; why beseech him? Why should we, weak and fallible mortals, urge the good God to work good in the world? Is not

Rousseau speaking sound sense when he says: "I bless God, but I pray not. Why should I ask of him that he would change for me the course of things?—I who ought to love, above all, the order established by his wisdom and maintained by his Providence, shall I wish that order to be dissolved on my account?"

This objection to prayer is the stronger because reverence and humility before God seem to be involved in it. "We will take whatever God sends," says the objector, "we will pray for nothing. We trust him perfectly. Can we in our ignorance suggest to him any excellent thing of which he has not thought or which he has forgotten, or can we in our weakness cajole him to do something which he has purposed otherwise? Rather 'Let him do what seemeth him good!' " This sort of speech has the ring of sincere faith. It comes from a strong and glad belief in the providence of God. *The man shrinks from prayer because it seems silly and presumptuous for ignorance to instruct perfect wisdom, for human evil to attempt the persuasion of perfect love to do good.*

It is interesting, then, to discover that the Master's life of urgent prayer was founded on these very ideas which now are used as arguments against prayer. No one, before or since, has believed quite so strongly as he did in the wisdom and love of God. Did they seem to him, then, reasons for abandoning prayer? *On the contrary, the love and wisdom of God were the foundations of his prayer.* In God's goodness he saw a solid reason for praying: "If ye then, being evil, know how to give good gifts unto your children, how much more shall your Father . . . give good things to them that ask him?" (Matt. 7:11). In God's wisdom he found assuring confidence, when he prayed. "Your Father knoweth what things ye have need of, before ye ask him" (Matt. 6:8). Just *because* of God's perfect knowledge and love, the Master seems to say, pray with confidence. Do not think that you can add to God's information about your need or can inspire in him an increased good-will by your petition. You cannot. He knows your need in advance and is more willing to give than you are to take. But one thing you can do. You can open the way for God to do what he wants to do. Prayer cannot change God's purpose, but prayer can release it. God cannot do for the man with the closed heart what he can do for the man with the open heart. You can give God a chance to work his will in and for and through you. *Prayer is simply giving the wise and good God an opportunity to do what his wisdom and love want done.*

II

This point of view is the distinguishing element in the Christian conception of prayer, and to understand it, is of the utmost importance.

The argument that because God is infinitely good and wise, prayer is a superfluity, rests on two fallacies. The first is the idea that praying is an attempt to secure from God by begging, something which God had not at all intended, or had intended otherwise. But Christian prayer is never that. The African savage beats his fetish when a petition is unanswered. He endeavors to make his god his slave. His one idea is to get what he wants. Christian prayer is giving God an opportunity to do what *he* wants, what he has been trying in vain, perhaps for years, to do in our lives, hindered by our unreadiness, our lack of receptivity, our closed hearts and unresponsive minds. God stands over many lives, like the Master over Jerusalem, saying, "How oft would I . . . and *ye* would not" (Matt. 23:37). True prayer changes that. It opens the door to the will of God. It does not change God's plan, but it does give God's plan gang-way. It is not begging from God; it is cooperation with God. In the luminous words of Archbishop Trench: *"We must not conceive of prayer as an overcoming of God's reluctance, but as a laying hold of his highest willingness."*

The other fallacy underlying the thought that the wisdom and love of God make praying superfluous is the idea that God can do all he wills without any help from us. But he cannot. *The experience of the race is clear that some things God never can do until he finds a man who prays.* Indeed, Meister Eckhart, the mystic, puts the truth with extreme boldness: "God can as little do without us, as we without him." If at first this seems a wild statement, we may well consider in how many ways God's will depends on man's cooperation. God himself cannot do some things unless men *think*. He never blazons his truth on the sky that men may find it without seeking. Only when men gird the loins of their minds and undiscourageably give themselves to intellectual toil, will God reveal to them the truth, even about the physical world. And God himself cannot do some things unless men *work*. Will a man say that when God wants bridges and tunnels, wants the lightnings harnessed and cathedrals built, he will do the work himself? That is an absurd and idle fatalism. God stores the hills with marble, but he never built a Parthenon; he fills the mountains with ore, but he never made a needle or a locomotive. Only when *men* work can some things be done. Recall the words of Stradivarius, maker of violins, as George Eliot interprets him:

> "When any master holds
> 'Twixt chin and hand a violin of mine,
> He will be glad that Stradivari lived,
> Made violins, and made them of the best
> . . . For while God gives them skill
> I give them instruments to play upon,
> God choosing me to help Him.
> . . . If my hand slacked
> I should rob God—since He is fullest good—
> Leaving a blank instead of violins.
> . . . He could not make
> Antonio Stradivari's violins
> Without Antonio."

Now if God has left some things contingent on man's *thinking* and *working* why may he not have left some things contingent on man's *praying?* The testimony of the great souls is a clear affirmative to this: some things never without thinking; some things never without working; some things never without praying! *Prayer is one of the three forms of man's cooperation with God.*

The fact, therefore, that God is all-wise and all-good, is no more reason for abandoning prayer than for abandoning thought and work. At their best, none of them is an endeavor to get anything against the will of God, and all of them alike are necessary to make the will of God dominant in human life. Who would dream of saying, God is all wise, he knows best; he is all good and will give the best; why, therefore, should I either think or work? But that is just as sensible as to say, If God is good, why should I pray? *We pray for the same reason that we work and think, because only so can the wise and good God get some things done which he wants done.*

Indeed, there is a deal of nonsense talked about resignation to God's will as the *only* attitude in prayer. Not resignation to God's will, but cooperation with God's will is the truer expression of a Christian attitude. *We are not resigned anywhere else.* We find an arid desert and, so far from being resigned, we irrigate it until it blossoms like a garden. We find a thorny cactus, and commission Luther Burbank as speedily as possible to make of it a thornless plant for food. We find social evils like slavery, and from Moses to Lincoln all that are best among us are willing to surrender life rather than rest content with wrong. Resignation in the presence of things evil or imperfect is sin; and all the heroes of the race have been so far discontented and unresigned that Blake's challenge has been kindred to their resolution,

> "I will not cease from mental fight,
> Nor shall my sword sleep in my hand,
> Till we have built Jerusalem
> In England's green and pleasant land."

This unresigned attitude, inseparable from nobility of character, is not rebellion against God but cooperation with God. Men act on the assumption that the present situation may be temporarily God's will, but that he has put them in it so that they may fight their way out to a situation that is ultimately his will. To this end they *think* and *work* and *pray*. Resignation is in all three only in the sense that by all three men are endeavoring to open doors for the free passage of God's hindered will. They do not *submit* to God's purpose; they *assert* it. Prayer, like the other two, when it is at its best, never says, Thy will be *changed*, but it says tremendously, Thy will be *done!*

III

That we may clearly perceive God's inability to accomplish his will until men cooperate in prayer, we may note, for one thing, that unless men pray there are some things which God cannot *say* to them. One of our strongest misconceptions concerning prayer is that it consists chiefly in our *talking* to God, whereas the best part of prayer is our *listening* to God. Sometimes in the Scripture a prayer of urgent and definite petition rises, "Oh that I might have my request; And that God would grant me the thing that I long for!" (Job 6:8); but another sort of prayer is very frequently indicated: "Speak; for thy servant heareth" (I Sam. 3:10); "My soul, wait thou in silence for God only; For my expectation is from him" (Psalm 62:5); "I will hear what God Jehovah will speak" (Psalm 85:8); or in Luther's version of Psalm 37:7, "Be silent to God and

let him mold thee." Without such openheartedness to God, some
things which he wills never can be done.

Madame de Staël, after a two hours' visit in which she had talked
continuously, is said to have remarked at parting, "What a delightful
conversation we have had!" Too many prayers are conducted on
that plan. The ironical remark of Savonarola that the saints of his
day were "so busy talking to God that they could not hearken to
him," is applicable to us at least to this extent: *we seldom listen*. We
hammer so busily that the architect cannot discuss the plans with us.
We are so preoccupied with the activities of sailing, that we do not
take our bearings from the sky. When the Spirit stands at the door
and knocks, the bustle of the household tasks drowns the sound of
his knocking. God has a hard time even to get in a word edgewise;
and in lives so conducted, there are some things which God himself,
with all his wisdom and good-will, cannot do. Even a casual study
of the effective servants of the world reveals how much of their
vision and stimulus came in quiet and receptive hours. Prayer gave
God his opportunity to speak, for prayer is the listening ear.

IV

The dependence of God's will upon the cooperation of men's
prayer may be further seen in the fact that until men pray there are
some things which God cannot *give* to them. One of the most disconcerting verses in Scripture tells us that God is more willing to
give to us than fathers are to give to their children (Matt. 7:11).
To some this seems mere sentiment, an exaggerated statement, made
in a poetic hour. To others, who have cried in vain for things that
appeared certainly good, it seems mockery. If God is willing to give,
why doesn't he? What hinders him? How can he be willing to give,
when, being omnipotent, he still withholds? Even a superficial observation of human life, however, could supply the answer. *Giving
is not a simple matter. It is always a dual transaction in which the
recipient is as important a factor as the giver.*

No suffering on earth is more tragic than great love hindered in
its desire to bestow. If a father wishes to give his son an education,
why doesn't he? If he sees the need, has the means, is willing, even
anxious to bestow, what hinders him? In how many cases is the
answer clear: the boy has no genuine desire, no earnest prayer for
the blessing which the father would give. The father is helpless. He

must wait, his love pent, his willingness checkmated, until a prayer, however faint, rises in the boy's heart. The finest gifts cannot be dropped into another's life like stones in a basket. They must be *taken* or else they cannot be *given*. Jesus was thinking of the two factors involved when he said to the Samaritan woman, "If thou knewest the *gift of* God, . . . thou wouldest have *asked*" (John 4:10). The receptive heart is the absolute pre-requisite of all great gifts, and God himself cannot bestow his best on men unless they pray.

Whenever, therefore, we pray intent chiefly on what *we* want, we are likely to be disappointed. But when we pray, intent chiefly on what God wants to give us—perhaps fortitude to bear the trouble which we wish to evade, or patience to wait for the blessing which we demand now, or leadership down a road of service from which we are asking release—we need never be disappointed. Men who come to God not to *dictate* but to *receive* have approached prayer from the right angle. They have seen that prayer is giving God an opportunity to bestow what he is more willing to give than we are to welcome. Prayer is the taking hand. As a sixteenth century mystic said, "Prayer is not to ask what we wish of God, but what God wishes of us."

v

The dependence of God on the cooperation of men's prayer may be further seen in the fact that until men pray there are some things which God cannot *do through them*. Many today, in spite of the busyness, wealth, and efficient organization of our Christian work, bemoan the lack of real power. "What is the matter?" says the practical man. "Have we not taken our time, money, talents and given them in many consecrated and unselfish ways to the service of God? Why, with so many working for God, is not more done?" The answer is written plainly in history. The souls who have ushered in new eras of spiritual life have never been content with *working for God*. They have made it their ideal to *let God work through them*. A scientist has figured that the farmer's toil is five per cent of the energy expended in producing a crop of wheat. The other ninety-five per cent is the universe taking advantage of the chance which the farmer gave it. So these greater servants of God have not thought chiefly of what they could do for God, but of what God could do through them if they gave him opportunity. To be pliable in the hands of God was their first aim. Never to be unresponsive to his will for them was their supreme concern. They said, therefore, with Thomas Hooker, *"Prayer is my chief work, and it is by means of it that I carry on the rest."*

No one can walk through the pages of Scripture, or of Christian biography, with these greater servants of the Kingdom without feeling their power. They are God-possessed. Their characteristic quality is found in Jesus: Not my words, my Father's; not my deeds, his; he that believeth on me, believeth not on me but on him that sent me (John 14:24; 9:4; 5:24). The secret of their lives is like the secret of the Nile: they are the channel of unseen resources. The ideal of such living is deeper than working for God. To release the Eternal Purpose through their lives into the world; to be made a vehicle for power which they do not create but can transmit—this is their ideal. They pray because theirs is the sublime ambition of the German mystic, *"I would fain be to the Eternal Goodness what his own hand is to a man."*

Only through men who take this attitude can God do his choicest work. A life that utterly lacks this attitude, wants the elements of power. When, therefore, a man prays, intent chiefly on what *he* wishes done, his prayer is a failure; but when he prays in order that he may release through his life what God wishes done, he has discovered the great secret. Through him, habitually praying, God can do what else would be impossible. He is one of God's open doors into the world.

VI

We have, then, two fundamentally opposed ideas of prayer: one, that by begging we may change the will of God and curry favor or win gifts by coaxing; the other, that prayer is offering God the opportunity to say to us, give to us, and do through us what he wills. Only the second is Christian. At once we see that the second, no less than the first, and in a way far truer, makes prayer not a form but a force. Prayer really does things. *It cannot change God's intention, but it does change God's action.* God had long intended Isaiah to be his prophet. When Isaiah said, "Here am I, send me," he did not alter in the least the divine purpose, but he did release it. God could *do* then what before he could not. God had long intended that

Africa should be evangelized. When Livingstone cried, "O God, help me to paint this dark continent white," he did not alter God's intention, but he did alter God's action. Power broke loose that before had been pent; the cooperation of a man's prayer, backed by his life, opened a way for the divine purpose. There was an invasion of the world by God through Livingstone. No one can set clear limits to this release of divine power which the effectual prayer of a righteous man can accomplish. Pentecost is typical: "When they had prayed, the place was shaken wherein they were gathered together; and they were all filled with the Holy Spirit, and they spake the word of God with boldness" (Acts 4:31).

SUGGESTIONS FOR THOUGHT AND DISCUSSION

If God is all-wise and all-good, what is the use of praying?

Can prayer change God's plans? If not, what is the use of praying?

How far are God's plans dependent upon individuals?

Can God's purpose be stopped by the failure of an individual to cooperate?

If God is in any way dependent upon the cooperation of individuals, is this inconsistent with his sovereign power and wisdom?

What light do the experiences recorded in the Bible throw upon the problem of prayer and the goodness of God?

In what respect did the request of James and John differ from true prayer?

Why did his belief in the goodness of God give Jesus confidence to pray?

What is the difference in emphasis between the prayer recorded in the eighty-first Psalm and Jesus' comment on the prayer of the hypocrites on the street corners?

In his Gethsemane prayer, what was Jesus' attitude to the will of God?

What place has prayer in the life of every man in finding and doing God's will?

CHAPTER V

Hindrances and Difficulties

DAILY READINGS

First Day, Fifth Week

Howbeit what things were gain to me, these have I counted loss for Christ. Yea verily, and I count all things to be loss for the excellency of the knowledge of Christ Jesus my Lord: for whom I suffered the loss of all things, and do count them but refuse, that I may gain Christ, and be found in him.—Phil. 3:7-9.

We have been speaking of the privilege of prayer, the supreme opportunity of friendship with God kept vital by deliberate communion, and we may well stop now to count the cost. Paul is typical of all Christian seers in discovering that the "excellency of the knowledge of Christ Jesus" is not arrived at without counting some things loss. *It does cost to win a life that really can pray.* Vasari says that Raphael used to wear a candle in a pasteboard cap, so that, while he was painting, his shadow would not fall upon his work. Many a man's prayers are spoiled by his own shadow. There are things in his life which must be given up if ever he is truly to pray. He must wear on his forehead the candle of renunciation for his work's sake. Consider the evil attitudes, cherished sins, bad tempers in your life that make praying in any deep and earnest way a difficult undertaking.

O Lord, come quickly and reign on Thy throne, for now oft-times something rises up within me, and tries to take possession of Thy throne; pride, covetousness, uncleanness, and sloth want to be my kings; and then evil-speaking, anger, hatred, and the whole train of vices join with me in warring against myself, and try to reign over me. I resist them, I cry out against them, and say, "I have no other king than Christ." O King of Peace, come and reign in me, for I will have no king but Thee! Amen.—St. Bernard (1091-1153).

Second Day, Fifth Week

In nothing be anxious; but in everything by prayer and supplication with thanksgiving let your requests be made known unto God. And the peace of God, which passeth all understanding, shall guard your hearts and your thoughts in Christ Jesus. Finally, brethren, whatsoever things are true, whatsoever things are honorable, whatsoever things are just, whatsoever things are pure, whatsoever things are lovely, whatsoever things are of good report; if there be any virtue, and if there be any praise, think on these things.—Phil. 4:6-8.

This connection of verses on great praying and right thinking is not accidental. A man cannot habitually indulge in mean, perverse, or abominable thoughts and suddenly come out of them into unimpeded communion with God. An automobile can be shifted from "low" to "high" with a stroke of the hand, but not so a man's mind. Real praying costs *habitual self-discipline in thinking*—the pure in heart see God. Sherwood Eddy says that the great Madras Young Men's Christian Association building was held up for months, after the site was chosen, the plans drawn, and the money provided, because two shanty-owners would not let go their hold on a little ground in the center of the plot. What is the name of that shanty in your mind which is holding up the great building of character and service for which God has the plans and the means ready?

Most Merciful Father, who orderest the wills and affections of men; inspire in the heart of this Thy servant holy wishes and aspirations, that all base imaginings and sinful broodings may be cast out. Spirit of purity and grace, cleanse the thoughts of his heart and bring his whole being into captivity to the law of Christ. So direct and control his mind that he may ever think on whatsoever things are true and pure and lovely. Let no corrupt thought get dominion over him. Enter Thou into the house of his soul. Enlarge and renew it and consecrate it to Thyself, that he may love Thee with all his

*mind and serve Thee with all his might. Free him from the fascina-
tions of false pleasures and the allurements of debasing desires. Fill
his eyes with the eternal beauty of goodness, that vice and sin may
appear as they really are, the last shame and despair of life. Keep
him outwardly in his body and inwardly in his soul, and constrain
him to reverential obedience to the laws Thou hast ordained for
both. Sustain him in health of body that he may the better control
the motions of thought, and repel the assaults of passion. We ask it
for Thy Son our Saviour's sake. Amen.*—Samuel McComb.

Third Day, Fifth Week

**Be not rash with thy mouth, and let not thy heart be hasty to
utter anything before God; for God is in heaven, and thou upon
earth: therefore let thy words be few.—Eccl. 5:2.**

Successful prayer involves not only the general preparation of
good living and right thinking; it often costs *special preparation.*
The mood may not be right; an irritated or anxious temper may be
in the way; the preoccupation of business may still be straining our
minds so that if we pray, only a small fraction of us is engaged in it—
a dozen different exigencies may make special preparation an absolute necessity for real prayer. Consider with what rash hastiness,
unprepared thoughts, preoccupied minds, and unexamined lives we
often rush into God's presence and out again. Dr. South puts the
matter with brusque directness, "None but the careless and the confident would rush rudely into the presence of a great man; and shall
we in our applications to the great God, take that to be religion
which the common reason of mankind will not allow to be manners?"

*Slay utterly, Oh Lord, and cast down the sin which does so easily
beset us; bridle the unholy affection; stay the unlawful thought;
chasten the temper; regulate the spirit; correct the tongue; bend the
will and the worship of our souls to Thee, and so sanctify and
subdue the whole inward man, that setting up Thy throne in our
hearts, to the dethronement of all our idols, and the things of earth
we hold too dear, Thou mayest reign there alone in the fulness of
Thy grace, and the consolations of Thy presence, till the time arrives
when we shall reign with Thee in glory. Amen.*—Richard S. Brooke
(1835-1893).

Fourth Day, Fifth Week

O Jehovah, the God of my salvation,
I have cried day and night before thee.
Let my prayer enter into thy presence;
Incline thine ear unto my cry.
For my soul is full of troubles . . .
Unto thee, O Jehovah, have I cried;
And in the morning shall my prayer come before thee.
Jehovah, why castest thou off my soul?
Why hidest thou thy face from me?

—Psalm 88:1-3, 13, 14.

Such an experience as finds voice in this Psalm suggests at once that at times prayer costs *persistence in the face of difficulties*. The unreality of God, the difficulty of holding the mind to the act of prayer, the wayward mood, the disappointment of the spirit at praying which rings hollow and gives no result—all these difficulties men of prayer have known. Read the diary of Benjamin Jowett, the great Master of Balliol, "Nothing makes one more conscious of poverty and shallowness of character than difficulty in praying or attending to prayer. Any thoughts about self, thoughts of evil, daydreams, love fancies, easily find an abode in the mind. But the thought of God and of right and truth will not stay there, except with a very few persons. I fail to understand my own nature in this particular. There is nothing which at a distance I seem to desire more than the knowledge of God, the ideal, the universal; and yet for two minutes I cannot keep my mind upon them. But I read a great work of fiction, and can hardly take my mind from it. If I had any real love of God, would not my mind dwell upon him?"

Gracious Father, who givest the hunger of desire, and satisfiest our hunger with good things; quicken the heart of Thy servant who mourns because he cannot speak to Thee, nor hear Thee speak to him. Refresh, we beseech Thee, the dulness and dryness of his inner life. Grant him perseverance that he may never abandon the effort to pray, even though it brings for a time no comfort or joy. Enlarge his soul's desires that he may be drawn unto Thee. Send forth Thy Spirit into his heart to help his infirmities; to give him freedom of

utterance, and warmth of feeling. Let him muse upon Thy good-
ness; upon the blessings with which Thou hast strewn his path; upon
the mystery of the world, and the shame of sin, and the sadness of
death,—until the fire kindles and the heart melts in prayer and
praise and supplication.

Lord, teach him to pray the prayer that relieves the burdened
spirit, and brings Thy blessing, which maketh rich and addeth no
sorrow. Hear us, for Jesus' sake. Amen.—Samuel McComb.

Fifth Day, Fifth Week

Give ear to my words, O Jehovah,
Consider my meditation.
Hearken unto the voice of my cry, my King, and my God;
For unto thee do I pray.
O Jehovah, in the morning shalt thou hear my voice;
In the morning will I order my prayer unto thee, and will keep
    watch.—Psalm 5:1-3.

Probably most people are so constituted by nature and are so
preoccupied by business that some such arrangement as is suggested
in this Psalm about regularity is essential to a successful life of
prayer. To be sure, Alice Freeman Palmer, first President of Wellesley, has this written of her in her husband's story of her life, "God
was her steady companion, so naturally a part of her hourly thought
that she attached little consequence to specific occasions of intercourse. . . . She had no fixed times of prayer." But before any one
presumes on such a record of fine living with God, minus regularity
of prayer, he would better examine his own character with some
scrutiny. *The chances are in most lives that the keeping of the
"morning watch" will prove to be one of the most salutary agencies
within the control of the will.* This will cost, as regularity always
costs, a persistent determination not to surrender to adverse circumstances or wayward moods. But consider what it would mean each
morning to put the life at God's disposal in some such way as
Thomas à Kempis does in this prayer:

Lord, work in my heart a true Faith, a purifying Hope, and an
unfeigned Love towards Thee; give me a full Trust on Thee, Zeal
for Thee, Reverence of all things that relate to Thee; make me fear-

ful to offend Thee, Thankful for Thy Mercies, Humble under Thy Corrections, Devout in Thy Service, and sorrowful for my Sins; and Grant that in all things I may behave myself so, as befits a Creature to his Creator, a Servant to his Lord: . . . make me Diligent in all my Duties, watchful against all Temptations, perfectly Pure and Temperate, and so Moderate in Thy most Lawful Enjoyments, that they may never become a Snare to me; make me also, O Lord, to be so affected towards my Neighbour that I never transgress that Royal Law of Thine, of Loving him as myself; grant me exactly to perform all parts of Justice; yielding to all whatsoever by any kind of Right becomes their due, and give me such Mercy and Compassion, that I may never fail to do all Acts of Charity to all men, whether Friends or Enemies, according to Thy Command and Example. Amen.— Thomas à Kempis (1379-1471).

Sixth Day, Fifth Week

And after six days Jesus taketh with him Peter, and James, and John, and bringeth them up into a high mountain apart by themselves: and he was transfigured before them; and his garments became glistening, exceeding white, so as no fuller on earth can whiten them. And there appeared unto them Elijah with Moses: and they were talking with Jesus. And Peter answereth and saith to Jesus, Rabbi, it is good for us to be here: and let us make three tabernacles; one for thee, and one for Moses, and one for Elijah.—Mark 9:2-5.

How natural for Peter to desire to remain in such a glowing experience! But he could not; it was one of those elevated hours, that cannot be continuous, but that can reveal outlooks which make all the dusty traveling afterward more meaningful. Once in a while our moods go up a mountain and have a great experience, returning cleansed, exhilarated and reassured. We must cherish such hours, believe in the validity of their witness to God's presence with us, gain confidence from their testimony to our sonship with him, and keep the reassuring memory of life's meaning as we saw it then. But we must not refuse another sort of praying, less ecstatic and glowing, more quiet and commonplace. We must not cherish false expectations, demanding transfigured hours continually. Gethsemane is also prayer and many a lesser time when the soul inwardly steadies itself on God and trusts where it cannot see. *Successful praying costs this sort of patience with commonplace hours.* Said Fénelon: "Do not be discouraged at your faults; bear with yourself in correcting them, as you would with your neighbor. Accustom yourself gradually to carry prayer into all your daily occupations. Speak, move, work in peace, as if you were in prayer."

O God, Thou hast found us, and not we Thee. At times we but dimly discern Thee; the dismal mists of earth obscure Thy glory. Yet in other and more blessed moments, Thou dost rise upon our souls, and we know Thee as the Light of all our seeing, the Life of all that is not dead within us, the Bringer of health and cure, the Revealer of peace and truth. We will not doubt our better moments, for in them Thou dost speak to us. We rejoice that Thou hast created us in Thine image. Thy love has stirred us into being, has endowed us with spiritual substance. In the intellect, whose thoughts wander through eternity; in the conscience that bears witness to Thy eternal righteousness; in the affections that make life sweet, and reach forth to Thee, O Lover of Mankind—in these, we are made heirs to the riches of Thy grace.—Samuel McComb.

Seventh Day, Fifth Week

Hold not thy peace, O God of my praise;
For the mouth of the wicked and the mouth of deceit have they
    opened against me:
They have spoken unto me with a lying tongue.
They have compassed me about also with words of hatred
And fought against me without a cause.
For my love they are my adversaries:
But I give myself unto prayer.—Psalm 109:1-4.

Such things as these true prayer is likely to cost: a good life, right thinking, special preparations of the mind, persistence through difficulties, regularity, and patience with commonplace hours. But a life that has learned the secret of real praying is worth all that it costs. As the Psalmist says, it is *worth giving ourselves to.* Consider Luther's great description of such a life: "Therefore, where there is a Christian, there is also the Holy Spirit, and he does nothing else save pray continually. For even if the mouth be not always moving and uttering words, yet the heart goes on beating unceasingly with cries like these, Ah! dear Father, may thy name be hallowed, may thy Kingdom come, and thy will be done. And whenever there come sorer buffetings and trials and needs, then the aspiration and supplication increase, even audibly, so that you cannot find a Christian man who does not pray; just as you cannot find a living man without a pulse that never stands still, but beats and beats on continually of itself, although the man may sleep or do anything else, so being all unconscious of this pulse."

Let us today make Archbishop Trench's sonnet our prayer

"If we with earnest effort could succeed
    To make our life one long connected prayer,
    As lives of some perhaps have been and are;
If, never leaving thee, we had no need
Our wandering spirits back again to lead
    Into thy presence, but continue there,
    Like angels standing on the highest stair
Of the sapphire throne,—this were to pray indeed.

But if distractions manifold prevail,
And if in this we must confess we fail,
Grant us to keep at least a prompt desire,
    Continual readiness for prayer and praise,
An altar heaped and waiting to take fire
    With the least spark, and leap into a blaze."

COMMENT FOR THE WEEK

I

A critic with discriminating insight has objected to Voltaire's writings on the ground that nothing could possibly be quite so clear as Voltaire makes it. A book on prayer readily runs into danger of the same criticism. For, like every other vital experience, prayer in practice meets obstacles that a theoretical discussion too easily glosses over and forgets. Even when prayer is defined as communion with God, and our thought of it is thereby freed from many embarrassments, as a kite escapes the trees and bushes when one flies it high, there remain practical difficulties which perplex many who sincerely try to pray.

For example, real communion involves the vivid consciousness that someone is present, with whom we are enjoying fellowship. Now a man may believe that God is, may desire earnestly to speak with him, and may not doubt in theory the possibility of such communion; but in practice he may utterly fail to feel the presence of God. In spite of his best efforts he may seem to himself to be talking into empty space. The sense of futility—such as comes to one who finds that he has been speaking in the dark to nobody, when he supposed a friend was in the room—may so confuse him that, theory or no theory, prayer becomes practically valueless. He cries with Job, not in a spirit of scepticism, but in great perplexity and in genuine desire for the divine fellowship, "Behold, I go forward, but he is not there; And backward, but I cannot perceive him" (Job 23:8). The practice of God's presence is not so simple as words sometimes make it seem.

One obvious reason for this sense of God's unreality, which often makes helpful prayer impossible, lies of course in *character*. Isaiah was dealing with a universal truth when he said: "Your iniquities have separated between you and your God, and your sins have hid his face from you" (Isaiah 59:2). One has only to consider that frivolous American who in the Rembrandt room of the Amsterdam Gallery looked lackadaisically around and asked: "I wonder if there is anything here worth seeing"; one has only to recall the women who climbed an Alpine height on an autumn day, when the riot of color in the valley sobered into the green of the pines upon the heights, and over all stood the crests of eternal snow, and who inquired in the full sight of all this, "We heard there was a view up here; where is it?" to see that there is a spiritual qualification for every experience, and that without it nothing fine and beautiful can ever be real to any one. "Mr. Turner," a man once said to the artist, "I never see any sunsets like yours." And the artist answered grimly, "No, sir. Don't you wish you could?" How clearly then must the sense of God's reality be a progressive and often laborious achievement of the spirit! It is not a matter to be taken for granted, as though any one could saunter into God's presence at any time, in any mood, with any sort of life behind him, and at once perceive God there.

Let some debauché from the dens of a city walk into a company

where men are chivalrous and women pure, and how much will the
debauché understand of his new environment? Stone walls are not
so impenetrable as the veil of moral difference between the clean
and unclean. So spiritual alienation between God and man makes
fellowship impossible. Of all the evils that most surely work this
malign result in man's communion with the Father, the Master
specially noted two: *impurity*—"Blessed are the pure in heart, for
they shall see God"; and *vindictiveness,* the unbrotherly spirit that
will not forgive nor seek to be forgiven—"If therefore thou art
offering thy gift before the altar, and there rememberest that thy
brother hath ought against thee, leave there thy gift before the altar,
and go thy way, first be reconciled to thy brother, and then come
and offer thy gift" (Matt. 5:23, 24). *No one can be wrong with man
and right with God.* In Coleridge's "Ancient Mariner," one of the
most vivid pictures of sin's consequences ever drawn, the effect of
lovelessness on prayer is put into a rememberable verse:

> "I looked to heaven and tried to pray,
> But or ever a prayer had gush't,
> A wicked whisper came and made
> My heart as dry as dust."

Most of us have experienced that stanza's truth. The harboring of
a grudge, the subtle wish for another's harm, the envy that corrupts
the heart, even if it find no expression in word or deed—such attitudes always prove impassable barriers to spontaneous prayer.
When, therefore, any one encounters the practical difficulty that
arises from the sense of God's unreality, he may well search his life
for sinister habits of thought, for cherished evils dimly recognized
as wrong but unsurrendered, for lax carelessness in conduct or
deliberate infidelity to conscience, for sins whose commission he de-
plores, but whose results he still clings to and desires, and above all
for selfishness that hinders loving and so breaks the connections that
bind us to God and one another.

II

The sense of God's unreality, however, does not necessarily imply
a wicked life. There are other reasons which often hinder men from
a vivid consciousness of God. All of us, for example, have *moods* in

which the vision of God grows dim. Our life is not built on a level so
that we can maintain a constant elevation of spirit. We have
mountains and valleys, emotional ups and downs; and, as with our
Lord, the radiant experience of transfiguration is succeeded by an
hour of bitterness when the soul cries, "My God, my God, why hast
thou forsaken me?" (Matt. 27:46). Cowper tells us that in prayer
he had known such exaltation that he thought he would die from excess of joy; but at another time, asked for some hymns for a new
hymnal, he wrote in answer, "How can you ask of me such a service?
I seem to myself to be banished to a remoteness from God's
presence, in comparison with which the distance from the East to
the West is vicinity, is cohesion." Of course we cannot always pray
with the same intensity and conscious satisfaction. "I pray more
heartily at some times than at others," says Tolstoi; and even
Bunyan had his familiar difficulties: "O, the starting holes that the
heart hath in the time of prayer! None knows how many by-ways
the heart hath and back lanes to slip away from the presence of
God." The first step in dealing with this familiar experience is to
recognize its naturalness and therefore to go through it undismayed.
When Paul said to Timothy, "Be urgent in season, out of season,"
he was giving that advice which a wise experience always gives to
immaturity: Make up your mind in advance to keep your course
steady, *when you feel like it and when you don't.* This difficulty of
moods has been met by all God's people. The biography of any
spiritual leader contains passages such as this, from one of Hugh
Latimer's letters to his fellow-martyr, Ridley: "Pardon me and pray
for me; pray for me, I say. For I am sometimes so fearful, that I
would creep into a mouse-hole; sometimes God doth visit me again
with his comfort. So he cometh and goeth."

*A man who surrenders to these variable moods is doomed to in-
efficiency.* He is like a ship that drifts as the tides run and the winds
blow, and does not hold its course through them and in spite of
them. Matthew Arnold goes to the pith of the problem, so far as
duty-doing is concerned:

> "tasks in hours of insight willed
> Can be in hours of gloom fulfilled."

And the same attitude is necessary in the life of prayer. Of course
we cannot always pray with the same sense of God's nearness, the

same warmth of conscious fellowship with him. Plotinus said that
he had *really* prayed only four times in his life. Lowell, in his
"Cathedral," writes,

> "I that still pray at morning and at eve . . .
> Thrice in my life perhaps have truly prayed,
> Thrice, stirred below my conscious self, have felt
> That perfect disenthralment which is God."

The heights of fellowship with God are not often reached—even the
record of Jesus' life contains only one Transfiguration—but this
does not mean that the value of prayer is only thus occasional. As
Dean Goulburn put it, *"When you cannot pray as you would, pray
as you can."* A man does not deny the existence of the sun because
it is a cloudy day, nor cease to count on the sun to serve him and his.
Moods are the clouds in our spiritual skies. A man must not over-
emphasize their importance. Surely he should not on account of
them cease to trust the God who is temporarily obscured by them.

Moreover, a man need not passively allow his moods to become
chronic. Many a life, like an old-fashioned well, has latent resources
of living water underneath, but the pump needs priming. Into a
man's prayerless mood let a little living water from some one else's
prayer be poured, and water from the nether wells of the man's own
soul may flow again. For such a purpose, collections of prayers like
the Bishop of Ripon's "The Communion of Prayer" or Tileston's
"Great Souls at Prayer" are useful; and books of devotion such as
St. Augustine's "Confessions." They often prime the pump. Indeed,
prayer itself is a great conqueror of perverse moods. You are not in
the spirit of prayer and therefore will refuse to pray until your mood
chances to be congenial? But clearly Dr. Forsyth's comparison is
apt: "Sometimes when you need rest most you are too restless to lie
down and take it. Then compel yourself to lie down and to lie still.
Often in ten minutes the compulsion fades into consent and you
sleep, and rise a new man . . . So if you are averse to pray, pray
the more."

III

Deeper than the difficulty of passing moods lies the problem of
those who *habitually* fail to feel the presence of God. In many cases

the trouble is *temperamental*. Some men seem by their native constitution to be specially designed for religion. They are geniuses in
the realm of spirit, as a Beethoven is in music or a Raphael in art.
The unseen is real to them; they are immediately aware of its
presence, sensitive to its meaning, responsive to its appeal. When they
speak of prayer their vivid experience of God demands for its expression poetry rather than prose. "Orison," they cry with Mech-
thild of Magdeburg, "draws the great God into the small heart; it
drives the hungry soul out to the full God. It brings together two
lovers, God and the soul, into a joyful room." To temperaments of
this quality the practice of God's presence is as spontaneous as any
human love and quite as real.

But what of one who is not thus gifted? He is perhaps of a
practical temperament, a man of action rather than of meditation.
Even in human relationships he is not demonstrative, and is more
given to revealing his loyalty and affection by concrete deeds of
service than by radiant hours of communion. He stands perplexed
before the exalted moods of the mystic. He cannot so strain himself
as to reach them. He feels out of his element when he reads about
them. When he prays he reaches no heights of conscious fellowship
with God. During the singing of a hymn like "Sweet Hour of
Prayer" he feels as unresponsive to the experience from which the
hymn arose as Dean Stanley would have felt to the music. The Dean
could not recognize even the national anthem save by the fact that
the people all arose at the first bar. What shall be said to a man who
thus believes in God and tries to do his will, but who is not warmly
conscious of fellowship with him in prayer? Something surely must
be said, for if prayer is so interpreted that it is left as the possession
of those only who are of the emotional and mystic temperament,
many of the most useful folk on earth, in whom practical and intellectual interests are supreme—the thinkers and the workers—will
feel themselves excluded from the possibility of praying.

We touch here one of the most crucial matters in our study of
prayer. *Every man must be allowed to pray in his own way.* It is far
from being true that the most valuable temperament in religion is
the mystical. God needs us all. Some are phlegmatic—stolid, patient,
undemonstrative; some are choleric—high-spirited, nervous, passionate; some are sanguine—hopeful, cheerful, light-hearted; some
are somber and serious. Even this time-honored classification of the
temperaments is not exhaustive. There are as many temperaments

as there are men, and each has his own problems and his peculiar way of expressing the spirit of Christ. The first step in useful living for many folk is the recognition of God's purpose in making us on such unique and individual plans. He evidently likes us better that way. John makes a better John than Peter ever could have been, and Peter a more useful Peter than was possible to John. We are so used to school examinations where the whole class must submit to the same tests of excellence that we forget how surely in the moral life we shall have individual tests. Each man is being tried in a private examination. He is not expected to be a Christian in any other man's way. As in Emerson's parable of the mountain and the squirrel, he can be undismayed by the special excellence of another, and can say as the squirrel did to the mountain,

"If I cannot carry forests on my back,
Neither can you crack a nut."

Now this general principle has its special application to prayer. *Nothing could be more intensely individual than the prayers of the Bible.* Nobody tries to commune with God in any one else's way. Some pray kneeling, like Paul (Acts 20:36); some standing, like Jeremiah (Jer. 18:20); some sitting, like David (II Sam. 7:18); some prostrate, like Jesus (Matt. 26:39). Some pray silently, like Hannah (I Sam. 1:13); some aloud, like Ezekiel (Ezek. 11:13). Some pray in the temple (II Kings 19:14); some in bed (Psalm 63:6), in the fields (Gen. 24:11, 12), on the hillside (Gen. 28:18-20), on the battlefield (I Sam. 7:5), by a riverside (Acts 16:13), on the seashore (Acts 21:5), in the privacy of the chamber (Matt. 6:6). Moreover all sorts of temperaments are found at prayer; practical leaders like Nehemiah, who in a silent ejaculation of the spirit seeks God's help before he speaks to the king (Neh. 1:3, 5); poets like the writer of the twenty-seventh Psalm, who love communion with God; men of melancholy mind like Jeremiah, "Hast thou utterly rejected Judah? hath thy soul loathed Zion?" (Jer. 14:19); and men of radiant spirit like Isaiah, "Jehovah, even Jehovah, is my strength and song; and he is become my salvation" (Isaiah 12:2). *There are as many different ways of praying as there are different individuals.* Consider the prayer of St. Augustine: "Let my soul take refuge from the crowding turmoil of worldly thoughts beneath the shadow of thy wings; let my heart, this sea of restless

waves, find peace in thee, O God." And then in contrast consider
the prayer of Lord Ashley, before he charged at the battle of Edge
Hill: "O Lord, thou knowest how busy I must be this day. If I forget thee, do not thou forget me."

We need always to remember, therefore, that there is no one
mould of prayer into which our communion with God must be run.
Let each man pray as best he can. Let no man make himself the
slave of another's methods. Professor George Albert Coe has put a
valuable truth into a few succinct sentences: "The tendency . . . is
to create an impression that the more valuable forms of prayer are
reserved for a special class of persons. This impression, too, is unconsciously fostered by the adulation that is bestowed upon men,
often young men, who cultivate a particular type of prayer, and
talk a great deal about it. What we need more than almost anything
else is to cultivate in timid souls that tend to self-distrust, in critical
souls that think before they assert, and in active souls that prefer
giving to receiving, a robust respect for their own natural types of
prayer."

IV

If we are to deal adequately, however, with the trouble which
some habitually and all of us occasionally have in realizing the
presence of God, we must do more than tell each man to pray
as he can. There are prevalent attitudes among people who try
to pray that make the consciousness of God's presence well-nigh impossible. We may note as the first of these that *vague groping after a
God outside of us which so often ends in the futile feeling of having
talked to empty space.* Many men, in their earnest desire to enter
fully into the Christian experience, strain after a realization of God's
presence as though by some violence and stress of the will it could be
attained. Their souls are mortars, their petitions bombs; they ex-
plode themselves toward heaven, and save for the echo of their own
outburst they hear no answer whatever. Madame Guyon records
that just this was her perplexity until a Franciscan friar gave her this
suggestive advice: "Madame, you are seeking *without* that which
you have *within.* Accustom yourself to seek God in your own heart,
and you will find him." This counsel is wise and practical. The
presence of God can be *experienced* only within our own hearts. *All
the best in us is God in us.* Generally, if not always, it is quite im-

possible to distinguish between the voice of God and the voice of our own best conscience and ideals. They are not to be distinguished. What we call conscience and ideals *are* God's voice, mediated to us through our own finest endowments.

This does not mean that these voices of God, mediated to us through our best, are infallible. It does mean that God in them is trying to speak to us according to our capacity to understand. If our windows are soiled, the sun's rays are hindered; but that fact is no denial of the truth that whatever light does come through our windows comes from the sun. So God is compelled to minister his blessing to us through our own capacities to receive and appropriate. *No man should ever grope outside of his best self to find God. He should always seek the God who is speaking to him in his best self.*

During a dry season in the New Hebrides, John G. Paton the missionary awakened the derision of the natives by digging for water. They said water always came down from heaven, not up through the earth. But Paton revealed a larger truth than they had seen before by discovering to them that heaven could give them water through their own land. So men insist on waiting for God to send them blessing in some supernormal way, when all the while he is giving them abundant supply if they would only learn to retreat into the fertile places of their own spirits where, as Jesus said, the wells of living waters seek to rise. We need to learn Eckhart's lesson, "God is nearer to me than I am to myself; he is just as near to wood and stone, but they do not know it." We need to understand the word attributed to Albert the Great, "To mount to God is to enter into one's self. For he who inwardly entereth and intimately penetrateth into himself gets above and beyond himself and truly mounts up to God." And in learning the meaning of words like these, we shall be coming into the spirit of many a Scripture passage: "If we love one another, God *abideth in us*" (I John 4:12); "We are a temple of the living God; even as God said, I will *dwell in them*" (II Cor. 6:16); "If any man . . . open the door, I will *come in* to him, and will sup with him, and he with me" (Rev. 3:20); "The water that I shall give him shall become *in him* a well of water" (John 4:14).

Any one, therefore, troubled by the seeming unreality of God may well imitate the Psalmist who begins his psalm by saying, "I will cry unto God," and who in the sixth verse says, "I commune with mine own heart" (Psalm 77). The two verses are not in conflict. The only way any one can commune with God is *through* his own heart. Indeed, we may call those psychologists to witness who discover in the spirit's life the transforming influences of which we have been speaking, and who ascribe them to the "subconscious." Powers of joy and peace, influences that renovate character, change disposition, and inspire service, do appear in human life, they say, but these effects which the New Testament attributes to the Holy Spirit, they ascribe to the "subconscious." There should be no permanent misunderstanding here. The tides that come into New York Harbor come through the Narrows, but they do not start there. You never can get at the secret of the inflow from the sea, which makes the sailing of great ships possible, by saying that the presence of the Narrows explains it. The tides come *through* the Narrows, not *from* them. So we cannot solve the mystery of that divine help which great souls know by giving names to substations in our own minds. We must go deeper and farther than that. *God himself is trying through our best to find a channel for his Spirit.*

v

The consideration of this vague groping after a God outside of us, leads us to a matter even more important. The elemental trouble with the prayers of those who fail to find God real is often the very fact that they are *seeking for God*. No one is prepared to experience the presence of God until he sees that *God is seeking for him*. Paul describes the pagan world as seeking God, "if haply they might feel after him and find him" (Acts 17:27) ; and many a Christian in this regard is a pagan still. We have turned the parables of Jesus in the fifteenth Chapter of Luke quite upside down. According to our attitude in prayer, the shepherd is lost, and the sheep have gone out on the tempest-driven mountainside to hunt for him. But not so the Master! To him the sheep are wandering, and the shepherd with undiscourageable persistency is seeking them. Without this thought of God as initiating the search, so that our finding of him is simply our response to his quest for us, the endeavor of any man to seek God is of all enterprises the most hopeless. How can the finite discover the Infinite unless the Infinite desires to be found? How can man break up into an experience of God unless God is seeking to reach down into friendship with man? *The deepest necessity of a fruitful life of prayer is the recognition that God's search for men is prior to any man's search for God.* In the words of one of Faber's hymns,

> " 'Tis rather God who seeks for us
> Than we who seek for him."

Now the search of God for man has always been believed by Christians, but by many it has become a historical matter. God *did* seek for man in Christ. This fundamental truth is of the utmost importance for prayer. For, as a matter of fact, whenever a Christian prays he prays to the God whose love for us Christ revealed, and to the knowledge of whom we never should have come without Christ. As Fichte put it, "All who since Jesus have come into union with God have come unto union with God *through him.*" But this belief in God's search for man in Christ is not sufficient for prayer. *God is forever seeking each man.* The promptings of conscience, the lure of fine ideals, the demands of friendship, the suggestions of good books, the calls to service, every noble impulse in hours when

> "The spirit's true endowments
> Stand out plainly from the false ones,"

are all the approach of God to us. Prayer is not groping after him. Prayer is opening the life up to him. The prayerless heart is fleeing from God. Finding God is really letting God find us; for our search for him is simply surrender to his search for us. When the truth of this is clearly seen, prayer becomes real. There is no more talking into empty space, no more fumbling in the dark to lay hold on him. We go into the secret place and there let every fine and ennobling influence which God is sending to us have free play. We let him speak to us through our best thoughts, our clearest spiritual visions, our finest conscience. We no longer endeavor to escape. We find him as run-away children, weary of their escapade, find their father. *They consent to be found by him.*

> "I said, 'I will find God,' and forth I went
>   To seek Him in the clearness of the sky,
>   But over me stood unendurably
>   Only a pitiless, sapphire firmament
> Ringing the world, blank splendour; yet intent
>   Still to find God, 'I will go seek,' said I,
>   'His way upon the waters,' and drew nigh
> An ocean marge, weed-strewn and foam-besprent;

And the waves dashed on idle sand and stone,
  And very vacant was the long, blue sea;
But in the evening as I sat alone,
My window open to the vanishing day,
Dear God! I could not choose but kneel and pray,
  And it sufficed that I was found of Thee."[1]

SUGGESTIONS FOR THOUGHT AND DISCUSSION

Why do most people find it hard to pray?

In how far are the types of hindrances which prevent communion with God peculiar to the "realm of religion"?

What is necessary to be able to enjoy a sunset, a painting, or a musical symphony? Can any but a technical expert really enjoy these? To what extent do these conclusions apply to enjoying communion with God?

Can a man without an appreciation of nature, art and intellectual integrity fully commune with God? How far is the completeness of such communion dependent upon the range of human interests and experiences?

In the light of the above questions, to what extent are "spiritual" qualifications essential only to "religious" experiences?

How do the hindrances to human friendship differ from the hindrances to communion with God?

In the light of Jesus' teachings, what are the principal hindrances to prayer in the realm of character?

Where first shall we look for hindrances to communion with God?

What dependence is to be placed upon "favorable moods"?

In the general enterprises of human life, how much allowance is made for favorable moods?

How far is special application necessary if advantage is to be taken of such moods? What is the relation of favorable moods to prayer? What light does the Transfiguration throw on this?

[1]Edward Dowden.

*What relation has a man's temperament to his ability to achieve
reality in prayer?*

How far is reality in prayer possible to people with other than a
mystical temperament? What proportion of prayers recorded in the
Bible are the prayers of mystics? What proportion in later history?

To what degree must the form of prayer be determined by the
type of personality? What answer would the Bible record of prayers
suggest?

What prevalent attitudes among the people make the consciousness of God's presence well-nigh impossible? How can these attitudes
be overcome?

*How can the hindrances to prayer in the life of any particular in-
dividual be overcome?*

CHAPTER VI

Prayer and the Reign of Law

DAILY READINGS

First Day, Sixth Week

The heavens declare the glory of God;
And the firmament showeth his handiwork.
Day unto day uttereth speech,
And night unto night showeth knowledge.
There is no speech nor language;
Their voice is not heard.
Their line is gone out through all the earth,
And their words to the end of the world.
In them hath he set a tabernacle for the sun,
Which is as a bridegroom coming out of his chamber,
And rejoiceth as a strong man to run his course.
His going forth is from the end of the heavens,
And his circuit unto the ends of it;
And there is nothing hid from the heat thereof.
—Psalm 19:1-6.

Consider the ease with which the Psalmist here ascribes all the activities of the heavens to the direct influence of God. The idea of natural law has not gotten between him and the Creator; whenever the sun comes up or the stars appear he feels that God is doing it. Now it may still be true, as Mr. Chesterton remarks, that each morning God says to the sun, "Get up, do it again!" but it is difficult for most people to imagine that. The sun seems to *run itself by law;* everything seems to run itself, so that in the modern mind this psalm is unconsciously changed until it reads, "The heavens declare the

glory of *law*." In the weekly comment we shall consider the unreasonableness of this negation of religious faith which our modern
scientific knowledge has caused in many, but in the daily readings
let us note *the ways in which our new information about natural
law practically affects us*. Does it not, as we have today suggested,
seem to push God away off? The world looks like a great machine,
self-running and self-regulating, with God a very distant Sustainer,
if he is anywhere at all. Thomas Hood put the feeling into a familiar
verse:

> "I remember, I remember
>   The fir-trees dark and high;
> I used to think their slender tops
>   Were close against the sky.
> It was a childish ignorance,
>   But now 'tis little joy
> To know I'm farther off from heaven
>   Than when I was a boy."

*O God, we thank Thee for this universe, our great home; for its
vastness and its riches, and for the manifoldness of the life which
teems upon it and of which we are part. We praise Thee for the
arching sky and the blessed winds, for the driving clouds and the
constellations on high. We praise Thee for the salt sea and the running water, for the everlasting hills, for the trees, and for the grass
under our feet. We thank Thee for our senses by which we can see
the splendor of the morning, and hear the jubilant songs of love, and
smell the breath of the springtime. Grant us, we pray Thee, a heart
wide open to all this joy and beauty, and save our souls from being
so steeped in care or so darkened by passion that we pass heedless
and unseeing when even the thornbush by the wayside is aflame with
the glory of God.*—Walter Rauschenbusch.

Second Day, Sixth Week

O Jehovah, thou hast searched me, and known me.
Thou knowest my downsitting and mine uprising;
Thou understandest my thought afar off.
Thou searchest out my path and my lying down,
And art acquainted with all my ways.

For there is not a word in my tongue,
But, lo, O Jehovah, thou knowest it altogether.
Thou hast beset me behind and before,
And laid thy hand upon me.
Such knowledge is too wonderful for me;
It is high, I cannot attain unto it.
Whither shall I go from thy Spirit?
Or whither shall I flee from thy presence?
If I ascend up into heaven, thou art there;
If I make my bed in Sheol, behold, thou art there.
If I take the wings of the morning,
And dwell in the uttermost parts of the sea;
Even there shall thy hand lead me.—Psalm 139:1-10.

In contrast with this Psalmist's sense of God's immediate presence, the reign of law not only seems to push God away off; it pushes him away back into history. He becomes nothing more than a hypothesis to explain how the universe happened to exist in the first place. In President Faunce's figure, men think of God as an engineer who started this locomotive of a world, pulled the throttle wide open, and then leaped from the cab; and the world has been running its own unguided course ever since on the rails of law.

This does not simply make impossible the spiritual faith which glows in our Scripture passage; it violates every canon of sound thinking. It is childish. It is on a par with the belief of the Piedmontese peasant, of whom Benjamin Constant tells. He thought that the world was made by a God who had died before his work was completed. Consider whether your prayers have been hindered by the subtle influence of this idea of God. Before men can really pray, God must be seen as the present *living* God—whose ways of action we partially have plotted and called laws.

O Lord, our God, we desire to feel Thee near us in spirit and in body at this time. We know that in Thee we live and move and have our being, but we are cast down and easily disquieted, and we wander in many a sad wilderness where we lose the conscious experience of Thy presence. Yet the deepest yearning of our hearts is unto Thee. As the hart panteth after the waterbrooks, so pant our souls after Thee, O God. Nothing less than Thyself can still the hunger, or quench the thirst with which Thou hast inspired us.

*Power of our souls! enter Thou into them and fit them for Thyself,
making them pure with Christ's purity, loving and lovable with His
love.*—Samuel McComb.

Third Day, Sixth Week

And in like manner the Spirit also helpeth our infirmity: for we
know not how to pray as we ought; but the Spirit himself maketh
intercession for us with groanings which cannot be uttered; and he
that searcheth the hearts knoweth what is the mind of the Spirit,
because he maketh intercession for the saints according to the will
of God. And we know that to them that love God all things work
together for good, even to them that are called according to his
purpose.—Romans 8:26-28.

Note the connection of thought here between *prayer,* and *belief in
the controlling providence of God* that makes all things work together for good to those that love him. Is not this connection vital?
Unless God's providence does control, so that he is now at work in
the world shaping events and moulding men, what is the use of
praying? But just here is one of our modern perplexities. *The reign
of law seems to rule out the activity of Providence.* When we were
children, many of us doubtless prayed as Florence Nightingale said
she did. "When I was young," she writes, "I could not understand
what people meant by 'their thoughts wandering in prayer.' I asked
for what I really wished, and really wished for what I asked. And
my thoughts wandered no more than those of a mother would
wander, who was supplicating her Sovereign for her son's reprieve
from execution. . . . I liked the morning service much better than
the afternoon, because we asked for more things. . . . I was always
miserable if I was not at church when the Litany was said. How ill-
natured it is, if you believe in prayer, not to ask for everybody what
they want. . . . I could not pray for George IV. I thought the
people very good who prayed for him, and wondered whether he
could have been much worse if he had not been prayed for. William
IV I prayed for a little. But when Victoria came to the throne, I
prayed for her in a rapture of feeling and my thoughts never
wandered."

What is it that has changed this childlike spirit in our prayers? Is
it not our increasing knowledge of the reign of natural law? So

Miss Nightingale came to say in contrast with her childhood's point of view, "God's scheme for us is not that he should give us what we ask for, but that mankind should obtain it for mankind." Consider the people whom you know who have altogether given up praying for this same reason.

Almighty God, of Thy fulness grant to us who need so much, who lack so much, who have so little, wisdom and strength. Bring our wills unto Thine. Lift our understandings into Thy heavenly light; that we thereby beholding those things which are right, and being drawn by Thy love, may bring our will and our understanding together to Thy service, until at last, body and soul and spirit may be all Thine, and Thou be our Father and our Eternal Friend. Amen. George Dawson (1821-1876).

Fourth Day, Sixth Week

Bless Jehovah, O my soul.
O Jehovah, my God, thou art very great;
Thou art clothed with honor and majesty:
Who coveredst thyself with light as with a garment;
Who stretchest out the heavens like a curtain;
Who layeth the beams of his chambers in the waters;
Who maketh the clouds his chariot;
Who walketh upon the wings of the wind;
Who maketh winds his messengers;
Flames of fire his ministers;
Who laid the foundations of the earth,
That it should not be moved for ever.
Thou coveredst it with the deep as with a vesture;
The waters stood above the mountains.
At thy rebuke they fled;
At the voice of thy thunder they hasted away
(The mountains rose, the valleys sank down)
Unto the place which thou hadst founded for them.
Thou hast set a bound that they may not pass over;
That they turn not again to cover the earth.
He sendeth forth springs into the valleys;
They run among the mountains;
They give drink to every beast of the field;

The wild asses quench their thirst.
By them the birds of the heavens have their habitation;
They sing among the branches.—Psalm 104:1-12.

Read the entire Psalm, a glowing expression of faith in the controlling presence of God in his world. Now in our day many are troubled in their endeavor to share such a faith, because the reign of law suggests that any help from God would involve a *miracle*, an intervention in the regular, natural order. How can God shape the course of nature and human history without *interfering with law?* But consider that what we call a miracle need not involve at all a break in any law. Plant a pebble and a seed side by side. The law of the pebble is to lie dead; the law of the seed is to grow. If therefore the pebble could see the seed sprouting, how certainly it would lift its pebble hands in astonishment and cry, "A miracle!" But no law is broken there. There and everywhere else, what is called miracle is not a rupture of law; *it is the fulfilling of a larger and higher law than we have yet understood.* God's providence never has and never does involve breaking his laws; it means that we are as little acquainted with all the resources of the spiritual universe as a pebble is with the resources of a plant, and that God guides the course of events by means of laws, some of which are known to us and some unknown. Remember that natural law is nothing but man's statement of how things regularly happen, *so far as he has been able to observe them.* What looks like a miracle to man is no miracle to God. To him it is as natural as sunrise.

O Lord God, in whom we live, and move, and have our being, open our eyes that we may behold Thy Fatherly presence ever about us. Draw our hearts to Thee with the power of Thy love. Teach us to be anxious for nothing, and when we have done what Thou hast given us to do, help us, O God our Saviour, to leave the issue to Thy wisdom. Take from us all doubt and mistrust. Lift our thoughts up to Thee in heaven, and make us to know that all things are possible to us through Thy Son our Redeemer. Amen.—Bishop Westcott.

Fifth Day, Sixth Week

It is he that sitteth above the circle of the earth, and the inhabitants thereof are as grasshoppers; that stretcheth out the heavens

as a curtain, and spreadeth them out as a tent to dwell in; that bringeth princes to nothing; that maketh the judges of the earth as vanity. Yea, they have not been planted; yea, they have not been sown; yea, their stock hath not taken root in the earth: moreover he bloweth upon them, and they wither, and the whirlwind taketh them away as stubble. To whom then will ye liken me, that I should be equal to him? saith the Holy One. Lift up your eyes on high, and see who hath created these, that bringeth out their host by number; he calleth them all by name; by the greatness of his might, and for that he is strong in power, not one is lacking.—Isaiah 40:22-26.

The central trouble in the religious thinking of many people lies here: *the new knowledge of the universe has made their childish thoughts of God inadequate, and instead of getting a worthier and larger idea of God to meet the new need, they give up all vital thought about God whatsoever.* We can feel Isaiah in this fortieth chapter reaching out for as great a conception of God as he can compass, because the situation demands it. Our modern situation calls for the same outreach of mind. This is the truth behind Sam Foss's poem:

"A boy was born 'mid little things,
    Between a little world and sky,
And dreamed not of the cosmic rings
    'Round which the circling planets fly.

"He lived in little works and thoughts,
    Where little ventures grow and plod,
And paced and ploughed his little plots,
    And prayed unto his little God.

"But, as the mighty system grew,
    His faith grew faint with many scars;
The cosmos widened in his view,
    But God was lost among his stars.

"Another boy in lowly days,
    As he, to little things was born,
But gathered lore in woodland ways,
    And from the glory of the morn.

"As wider skies broke on his view,
   God greatened in his growing mind;
Each year he dreamed his God anew,
   And left his older God behind.

"He saw the boundless scheme dilate,
   In star and blossom, sky and clod;
And, as the universe grew great,
   He dreamed for it a greater God."

O God our Father, who dost exhort us to pray, and who dost grant what we ask, if only, when we ask, we live a better life; hear me, who am trembling in this darkness, and stretch forth Thy hand unto me; hold forth Thy light before me; recall me from my wanderings; and, Thou being my Guide, may I be restored to myself and to Thee, through Jesus Christ. Amen.—St. Augustine (354-430).

Sixth Day, Sixth Week

For though the fig-tree shall not flourish,
Neither shall fruit be in the vines;
The labor of the olive shall fail,
And the fields shall yield no food;
The flock shall be cut off from the fold,
And there shall be no herd in the stalls:
Yet I will rejoice in Jehovah,
I will joy in the God of my salvation.
                 —Habakkuk 3:17, 18.

We have noted five effects that knowledge of the reign of law has on modern minds: it pushes God away off; pushes him away back; makes his special help seem impossible; suggests that any providential aid would involve a miracle; and finally makes our immature, childish ideas of him inadequate. But now supposing that all of these were overcome, and that like Habakkuk, a man believed thoroughly in the providential control of a living God in his world—note the lack of presumption with which he uses his faith. The forces of nature are in the hands of God, but the prophet does not immodestly demand that they shall be used in accordance with human desire. It may even be that they bring dire trouble on him, as the seventeenth verse pictures; yet he does not doubt the guidance of God in the world. Consider the importance of this attitude for prayer. Belief in God's providence is not to be confused with the arrogant assumption that that providence must be exercised as we wish. One summer in England when the clergy were vehemently praying for dry weather, Charles Kingsley refused to do so. "How do we know," he said in a sermon, "that in praying God to take away these rains, we are not asking him to send the cholera in the year to come? I am of opinion that we are . . . Now, perhaps you may understand better why I said that I was afraid of being presumptuous in praying for fine weather."

O Thou, who givest liberally, unto all men and upbraidest not, give to this, Thy servant, the desire of his heart. Thou knowest his inward and outward state. Whatever it be that holds him back from self-surrender, unto Thee, grant that it may be taken out of the way, that there may be a free and open intercourse between him and Thee. May he be willing to trust where he cannot prove; willing to believe his better moments in spite of all that contradicts them. Open his eyes to see Thee as Thou art, infinitely real, infinitely gracious, infinitely good. Speak to him in the daily witness of earth and sky; in the goodness and tender mercy of human hearts; above all, in the words and works of Thy perfect Son in whom Thou hast spoken the "everlasting yea" that puts to flight our every care. Take from him all dread of evils that may never happen. Grant him the victory over every besetting doubt; and patience while any darkness remains, that he may glorify Thee, through Jesus Christ our Lord. Amen.—Samuel McComb.

Seventh Day, Sixth Week

I will give thee thanks with my whole heart:
Before the gods will I sing praises unto thee.
I will worship toward thy holy temple,
And give thanks unto thy name for thy lovingkindness and for thy
    truth:
For thou hast magnified thy word above all thy name.
In the day that I called thou answeredst me,
Thou didst encourage me with strength in my soul . . .
Though I walk in the midst of trouble, thou wilt revive me;

Thou wilt stretch forth thy hand against the wrath of mine enemies,
And thy right hand will save me.
Jehovah will perfect that which concerneth me:
Thy lovingkindness, O Jehovah, endureth for ever.

—Psalm 138:1-3, 7, 8.

Note the joyful certainty with which this Psalmist testifies to the effect of prayer on his own life. With all the puzzles that perplex our thought when we try to pray that God will change outward circumstances, this inward realm where prayer is continually efficacious remains undisturbed. Read thoughtfully this testimony from Henry M. Stanley, the African explorer: "To relate a little of the instances in my life wherein I have been grateful for the delicate monitions of an inner voice, recalling me, as it were, to 'my true self,' it would be difficult for me to do their importance justice. I, for one, must not, dare not, say that prayers are inefficacious. Where I have been earnest, I have been answered. . . . In the conduct of the various expeditions into Africa, prayer for patience has enabled me to view my savage opponents in a humorous light; sometimes with infinite compassion for their madness. . . . Without prayer for it, I doubt that I could have endured the flourish of the spears when they were but half-a-dozen paces off. . . . On all my expeditions prayer made me stronger, morally and mentally, than any of my non-praying companions. It did not blind my eyes, or dull my mind, or close my ears; but, on the contrary, it gave me confidence. It did more; it gave me joy and pride in my work, and lifted me hopefully over the one thousand five hundred miles of forest tracks, eager to face the day's perils and fatigues."

Eternal God, lead us into the blessedness of the mystery of communion with Thee. Bow our spirits in deepest reverence before Thee, yet uplift us into a sense of kinship. Send the spirit of Thy Son into our hearts, crying "Abba Father," that all unworthy fear may be banished by the gladness of Thy perfect love. Thy love is like the luminous heaven, receiving only to purify the foulest breath of earth. Thy gentleness is like the sun, seeking to cheer and warm the chilled hearts of men. Touch us, O our Father, with a feeling of Thy great realities, for though our thought about Thee is better than our words, our experience of Thee is better than our thought.— Samuel McComb.

COMMENT FOR THE WEEK

I

One element in communion with God has so far been kept in the background of our discussion. Prayer is conversation, but generally it is not merely conversation for conversation's sake. Sometimes we talk with our friends for the sheer joy of talking, but sometimes we talk because we want something. So communion with God is commonly motivated by desire; *the element of petition belongs by nature to the tendency which has led all men to pray.* Now, as soon as petition enters into a man's prayers, he is likely to run against an obstacle that seems very formidable. He comes face to face with the reign of law, as modern knowledge has revealed it.

In a world where there is a cause for every effect and an effect for every cause, where each event is intermeshed with every other and all move by inevitable consequence from what has gone before, it seems absurd to expect God to change anything in answer to our call. Men feel this when they consider the vastness of the universe throughout which the unbroken reign of law obtains. If the ring upon a girl's finger be taken as the orbit of the earth, 180,000,000 miles in diameter, the nearest star is one and a half miles away; the mass of the heavenly bodies scores of hundreds of miles beyond that, and throughout the whole expanse law is absolute. Or if one looks at near-by things to rest his thought from such iron regularity, he finds no comfort there. Of all snow-crystals that ever fell, there have been no angles of crystallization in their filaments except 60° and 120°. The wind is as obedient to law as is a falling stone; the temperature of the air is as much a creature of cause and effect as is the rising sun; and the rays of radium, infinitesimally minute and so swift that one could encompass the earth thrice in a single second and still have time to spare, are as regular in their law-abiding ways as an eclipse.

Indeed, if one look within himself, in hope of evading law, he fails. The mind's operations too are controlled by laws, and the psychologists are plotting them with increasing accuracy. The conviction irresistibly claims our assent that nothing happens anywhere contrary to law. The conditions which cause an Aurora Borealis are not fully known, but no one doubts that the conditions exist, and

that if they fail by the least degree an Aurora cannot be conjured
up by all the prayers of all the saints on earth. Definite petition to
God in such a world seems absurd. To many even communion with
God grows difficult, so lost is he in the maze of law. Job's cry
gains strength a thousand fold today—"O that I knew where I might
find him!" (Job 23:3). As for the demand that we continue to pray
without understanding, self-respect rebels. Otway's words in "Venice
Preserved," though written in 1682, have a contemporary ring in
them:

> "You want to lead
> My reason blindfold like a hampered lion,
> Check'd of his noble vigour—then, when baited
> Down to obedient tameness, may it couch
> And show strange tricks which you call signs of faith."

In this special difficulty men are often disappointed because the
Bible does not directly help. Dr. McFadyen clearly states the truth
of the matter—"Just as the Bible assumes the existence of God, so
it also assumes the naturalness of prayer. It does not answer, and,
for the most part does not even raise the problems which bear so
heavily upon educated men today." In the Bible there is no difficulty in the way of fleece on the same night becoming both wet and
dry (Judges 6:37ff); the sun may stop or proceed (Josh. 10:13),
the shadow on the sun dial go forwards or backwards (Isaiah 38:8);
the axe head may sink or float (II Kings 6:5ff); and the prison
doors may open without human help (Acts 5:19). *Like all people
of the generations during which the Bible was being written, the
writers of Scripture for the most part described events in terms of
miracle and not of law.*

But this biblical assumption that prayer is entirely natural, and
this description of the results of prayer in terms of miracle, rather
increase than allay the perplexity of many Christians. "This world
of the Bible is not our world," they cry in doubt. "Show us a single
place in the world in which *we* live, where we cannot depend for
certain on nature's regularity. We predict sunrise and sunset to the
second and they never fail. We plot the course of the planets and
they are never late. The achievements of our modern world rest on
the discovery that we can rely on the same things happening under
the same conditions, always and everywhere. When we figure strain

on a bridge we know that the laws of mechanics will not shift over-
night. Indeed, the marvel of our present age is symbolized by the
English astronomers, going out to Africa to study an eclipse, and
standing at last on the veldt beside their instruments. 'Now,' said
one, watch in hand, 'if we have made no mistake in our calculations,
the eclipse should begin at once.' On the instant the shadow of the
moon pushed its edge over the rim of the sun! What is the use of
praying in a world like that?—'Stern as fate, absolute as tyranny,
merciless as death; too vast to praise, too inexorable to propitiate;
it has no ear for prayer, no heart for sympathy, no arm to save.' "

No one needs to travel far to discover men whose religious thinking has stumbled over this difficulty. It is, therefore, important thus
early in our discussion to see clearly that *natural law is not at all
what superficial thinking makes it appear to be.* Dealing with the
reign of law is like going through the Simplon tunnel. Go a little
way and one has darkness and imprisonment. Go a little further
and one has light, liberty, and the far stretches of the Italian hills.
The classic word of Bacon is nowhere more true than here—"This
I dare affirm in knowledge of nature that a little natural philosophy,
and the first entrance into it, doth dispose the opinion to atheism,
but on the other side, much natural philosophy and wading deep
into it, will bring about men's minds to religion."

II

We may approach this deeper truth about "natural philosophy"
by remarking that the man who believes in nature's inexorable regularity immune from personal control, ought not to expect, under
ordinary circumstances, to see water flow up hill. As a matter of
fact, however, he can see it any day. Reservoirs are built among the
mountains or pumping stations are established and water runs up
hill and down dale with equal facility and seeks the topmost stories
of the tallest buildings. And this is the important secret there revealed—*Persons cannot violate the law of gravitation, but they can
use the law-abiding force of gravitation to do what, without their
cooperation, never would occur.*

So ordinarily a heavy substance will not float upon a lighter one.
But every day iron steamships plow the sea, and heavier-than-air
machines navigate the sky. Here too is revealed the fact that persons
while they can never break nor change laws, can utilize, manipulate,

and combine the forces which laws control to do what those forces by themselves would not accomplish. The insight which takes from the heart of religion all fear of the reign of law is this: *Personality, even in ourselves, how much more in God, is the master and not merely the slave of all law-abiding forces.* As Huxley put it, "The organized and highly developed sciences and arts of the present day have endowed man with a command over the course of non-human nature greater than that once attributed to the magicians."

This truth underlies all our modern material accomplishments. If an engineer proposed to bridge a stream, who would say to him: "It is impossible. The laws of nature forbid hanging iron over air"? He could answer: "I am not merely the slave of nature but in part its master. Nature can be *used* as well *as obeyed.*" And if one insisted to the contrary, claiming that natural laws are inviolable, the engineer's reply is evident: "The inviolability of natural laws is the beauty of them. They are trusty servants. They can be depended on. They are unwavering yesterday, today, and forever. And if you will watch, you will see me say to this force, come, and it will come; to this force, go, and it will go; and I, a person, will manipulate and utilize the law-abiding energies of nature, making infinitely varied combinations of invariable procedures, until millions of men shall cross this river on my bridge."

III

So important is it clearly to see the truth that personality, even in ourselves, can work the most unexpected results, not by violating laws, but by using knowledge of them, that we may well approach it from another angle. When men are dismayed by the inflexibility of law, they are thinking of cause and effect as forming a rigid system in whose established order no break can come. Now, we may not enter here into the philosophy of causation, but it is worth noting that in practical experience we seem to be dealing with *two kinds of cause.* When the atmospheric pressure makes the wind blow that is one sort; when a man sails by that same wind, skilfully tacking until he reaches his destination, that is another. In one case we have absolutely predetermined procedure; in the other we have a personal will serving a personal purpose by utilizing the predetermined procedure. These two kinds of cause seem everywhere to be at work. When the snow falls on the walk, its removal may be effected by *natural causes,* the sunshine or the rain. But its removal may also be effected by *personal causes.* A man with an ideal and a shovel may put his shovel at the service of his ideal and clear the walk. Personal causation is everywhere in evidence and when the reign of cause and effect seems rigid and merciless, it is because we forget how pliable law-abiding forces are in the hands of personality.[1]

Strange that we should forget it! All our human achievements are illustrations of this truth. Natural causes cannot explain St. Paul's Cathedral. Gravitation never cried to his brethren, the forces of nature, "Come, let us conspire to build a temple to God." The cause of St. Paul's Cathedral is personality utilizing its knowledge of laws. Natural causation cannot explain the sonatas of Beethoven. Nothing could be more mathematically exact than the laws of sound-vibration, but all great music bears witness to the power of personality when it uses its privilege of manipulating law-abiding sounds. Natural causation may explain the straits of Gibraltar but it cannot explain the Panama Canal. Personal cause alone can account for that.

> "A man went down to Panama
>   Where many a man had died,
>   To slit the sliding mountains
>   And lift the eternal tide.
>   A man stood up in Panama,
>   And the mountains stood aside."

One of the most liberating conceptions that can come to any mind is this perception that *law-abiding forces can be made the servants of personal will.* The only possibility of denying this truth lies in a theory of absolute determinism that makes the whole world a material machine with personality a helpless cog in the wheels. Grant, even in the least degree, what experience asserts and the greatest philosophies confirm, the truth of individual initiative; and we have a new element in the reign of cause and effect—namely personal causation. *Continually we are projecting personal cause into the realm of natural causes.* And when one deeply considers this, he sees what we call natural cause may not be *impersonal* cause at all, *that our limited control of universal forces may be a counterpart*

---

[1]One of the best philosophic statements of this truth will be found in Prof. G. H. Palmer's "The Problem of Freedom."

of God's unlimited control. Then all cause would be personal, and all procedure that we call natural would be God's regular ways of acting. Neither with God nor man do cause and effect make an iron system in which personality is enslaved. Rather they present to personality a reliable instrument through which personal freedom is continually expressed.

IV

Many of the arguments against prayer, based on the reign of law, bear with exactly the same force against any request made of an earthly friend. God cannot answer prayer because he cannot interfere with the reign of law? Let us see! A child falls from an open window and, badly hurt, calls to his father. Will the father regret his inability to help because the reign of law prevents? On the contrary, the father will set about using his knowledge of the reign of law as speedily as possible. He lifts the child from the ground although gravitation by itself would have kept the child there. He calls up the hospital by telephone and in that act uses a combination of natural forces, put together by personal will, so wonderful that the thought of it may well make even a modern man gasp. The ambulance clangs down the street, representing a utilization of nature where knowledge of hundreds of invariable mechanical, physical, and chemical laws has been utilized. The surgeon projects personal will against the dead set and certainly fatal outcome of natural causation, and the child is saved. *How many laws did that father violate? Not one, but he utilized knowledge of so many that no man can count them, and he employed that knowledge as the instrument of his love in the service of his child.*

Whether, therefore, we consider the ways in which men subject natural processes to their will; or the ways in which personal cause controls natural causes; or the ways in which we answer requests, not by violating laws but by using our knowledge of them, we come to the same conclusion: personality can control the universal forces to serve personal ends. Scientific laws are human statements and increasingly true statements of nature's invariable procedures, but the procedures are always pliable in the hands of human intelligence and will. *Do we mean to say that God is less free than we are? Are we, the creatures, in so large measure masters of law-abiding forces and is he, the Creator, a slave to them? Are the universal powers plastic and usable in our hands, and in his hands stiff and rigid? The whole analogy of human experience suggests that the world is not governed by law; that it is governed by God according to law. He providentially utilizes, manipulates, and combines his own invariable ways of acting to serve his own eternal purposes.*

V

Our fundamental fallacy about God is our thought of him as an artificer, now far-off, who has left this machine of his running by its own laws, and who cannot do anything with it except by intervention. Let us banish so primitive a picture of God, so childish a conception of the universe! He is not far-off. He is the Indwelling Presence in the World, as our life is in our bodies, controlling all. He is the immanent and eternal Creator, and the laws, some known to us, some unknown, are his ways of doing things. He is not a prisoner caught in the mechanism of his own world; he is not reduced to the impotency of Louis Philippe, "I reign, but I do not govern." He is free, more free than we can guess, to use the forces he has ordained. *Providence is possible.* A youth can deflect a brook's course from one channel to another. God can do with any life and with the course of history, what we do with a brook. The laws are all in his leash. Says Jesus, "Not a sparrow shall fall on the ground without your Father" (Matt. 10:29).

While the Bible, therefore, does not deal with the modern problem of natural law, in its reference to prayer, we still may share with the Bible that utter confidence in the power and willingness and liberty of God to help his children, which makes the Scriptures radiant with trust and hope. When the Bible says, "God hath spoken once, twice have I heard this, that power belongeth unto God" (Psalm 62:11); or "Jehovah is my strength and my shield; my heart hath trusted in him, and I am helped" (Psalm 28:7); or "To them that love God all things work together for good" (Rom. 8:28)—it is saying nothing that the most thorough believer in the reign of law may not say too. There are many prayers that God *must not* answer, but there are no good prayers which God *cannot* answer. He is the master of all laws, known to us and unknown. When God utilizes his knowledge of his own laws, who can say in advance what may happen? God is free, so far as the mere possibilities are concerned, to answer any petition whatsoever; and if a prayer is left unanswered it is not because the reign of law prevents. *It is because there are vast realms where God must not substitute our wish for his plan.*

VI

This last statement deserves emphasis. We may prefer to have the sun rise earlier, or to have a dozen colors in the spectrum, or to think without association of ideas, or to sin and not suffer; but we may as well spare our pains. *God does not remake his world for the asking, not because he cannot, but because he must not.* It may be convenient for us to substitute rain for sunshine or sunshine for rain, but we are likely to be vainly substituting presumption for faith when we try to control the weather. As the old rabbis put it: A mother had two sons, one a gardener and the other a potter. Said the gardener, "O mother, pray God for rain to water my plants." Said the potter, "O mother, pray God for sunshine to dry my pots." Now the mother loved them equally well. Shall she pray for rain or sun? Nay, she would best leave it in the hands of God.

When entire confidence has been established, therefore, in the power and liberty of God to utilize any force at any time, a due humility will restrain us from making a presumptuous application of this truth to prayer. Within the realm of personal relationships the effect of prayer is so clear that our faith in prayer's efficacy has assured ground in experience, but the power of prayer to affect the objective processes of nature is incapable of scientific demonstration. We never can so completely isolate an event, like a change in the weather, as to prove that nothing but our prayer could have caused it. To be sure no man can draw a clear boundary, saying, "Within this we may expect God to use his laws in answer to our prayers, and without we may look for nothing of the kind." Professor Browne's word is sane and helpful: *"To pray about everything, in submission to God's will, would be both more human and more Christian than a scrupulous limitation of our prayers to what we might think permissible subjects of petition."*

But it must be obvious that we should never presumptuously demand the use of natural forces in the objective world to serve our personal purpose, and then confidently expect our prayer to work the change. Before sun and rain, as Jesus said, the just and unjust seem to fare alike (Matt. 5:45). Lyman Beecher's public claim that

the burning of an unorthodox church was due to the special judgment of God on false doctrine was shown to be perilous, as well as
untrue, when the next week Lyman Beecher's church burned down.
The forces of the external world are in the hands of God to do with
them as he wishes, but that does not necessarily mean that he must
do with them as we wish. God must not surrender his sovereignty
on demand. It is far better that man should learn the discipline of
law than be exempt for the asking. Prayer distinctly is *not* "a machine warranted by the theologians to make God do what his clients
want!"

In all our praying therefore, we need to remember the distinction, to use Trumbull's phrases, between *"faith in prayer"* and
"prayer in faith." Faith in prayer may be presumptuous and clamorous; it may present ultimatums to the Almighty demanding his
acquiescence; it may try to make of prayer a magic demand on
God. But prayer in faith asks everything in entire submission to
the will of God. It desires never to force its wish on the Eternal
Purpose but always to align its wish with the Eternal Purpose. It
pleads passionately for its needs; but it closes its petition, as the
Master did, "Thy will be done." Prayer in faith rejoices in God's
sovereignty, is confident that all forces are in his leash, and that
to those who love him all things work together for good. Prayer thus
becomes meaningful because God is free to do what he will in his
world; but prayer does not on that account become presumptuous
as though God must do what *we* will in his world.

VII

There is a realm, however, where none need be hesitant in expecting answer to prayer. *Prayer is the law of personal relationships.*
It is important to see clearly that all laws do not apply in all realms.
Gravitation for example is not universal; it obtains without exception in the objective physical world, but it does not range up into
the personal, spiritual world. We come there into a new realm where
we deal with realities that cannot be caught in test-tubes, measured
by yardsticks, or weighed in scales. In that new realm new laws are
at work. Gravitation cannot break up into the world of spirit, although spirit can break down and use the force of gravitation. Laws
are thus arranged in regimes. When one leaves the inorganic world
for the organic, he leaves behind him laws that are now no longer

applicable; when he leaves the world of plants for the world of men, he moves up to laws that do not concern plants but do apply to men; and in this higher realm where men deal with one another and with God, there are conditions of communion, laws of fellowship and prayer. One cannot imagine Jesus asking for an objective change in the physical world, without entire willingness to submit to a negative answer; but when he goes up into the mountain alone to commune with God, he goes with absolute assurance that the strength and peace and vision which he needs will come. Personal relationship is the unique realm of prayer. As one reads the great prayers of the church he sees that in this realm supremely the people of God have prayed with confidence, have expected answer and have not been disappointed.

> "Lord, what a change within us one short hour
> Spent in Thy presence will avail to make!
> What heavy burdens from our bosoms take;
> What parched grounds refresh, as with a shower!
> We kneel, and all around us seems to lower;
> We rise, and all the distant and the near
> Stands forth in sunny outline, brave and clear!
> We kneel, how weak! we rise, how full of power!
> Why, therefore, should we do ourselves this wrong,
> Or others, that we are not always strong;
> That we are ever overborne with care;
> That we should ever weak or heartless be,
> Anxious or troubled, when with us is prayer,
> And joy and strength and courage are with Thee?"

SUGGESTIONS FOR THOUGHT AND DISCUSSION

If things are going to happen in any case according to fixed law, what is the use of petitioning for change?

What effect does knowledge of the reign of law have upon a man's attitude toward prayer?

How far can personal volition control the operation of natural forces?

What is the difference between violating a natural law and using a law-abiding force to accomplish something which would not have happened in the ordinary course of nature?

How far is the injection of a personal will into the operation of natural laws a violation of such laws?

To what degree is the Psalmist's faith in the controlling presence of God in his world justified?

How far could parents meet the need of their children if they were bound rigidly by the reign of law?

To what extent is doubt about the possibility of answer to prayer due to the belief that it violates law, and to what extent to lack of understanding of the operation of law?

How far is confidence in God's control of natural forces inconsistent with a belief in the reliability of law?

To what extent does the reign of law prevent the answer to prayer?

Are there any prayers which God cannot answer?

How far is the Bible's confidence in the power and willingness and liberty of God to help his children justified?

How do you think God's plans for the world affect his response to individual prayers?

What is the difference between law in the realm of nature and law in the personal, spiritual world?

What is the difference between faith in prayer and prayer in faith?

CHAPTER VII

Unanswered Prayer

DAILY READINGS

First Day, Seventh Week

Complaint about unanswered prayer is nothing new. Consider this cry of distress with which Habakkuk opens his book:

The burden which Habakkuk the prophet did see. O Jehovah, how long shall I cry, and thou wilt not hear? I cry out unto thee of violence, and thou wilt not save. Why dost thou show me iniquity, and look upon perverseness? for destruction and violence are before me; and there is strife, and contention riseth up. Therefore the law is slacked, and justice doth never go forth; for the wicked doth compass about the righteous; therefore justice goeth forth perverted. . . . Thou that art of purer eyes than to behold evil, and that canst not look on perverseness, wherefore lookest thou upon them that deal treacherously, and holdest thy peace when the wicked swalloweth up the man that is more righteous than he?—Habakkuk 1:1-4, 13.

The weekly comment will take up the reasons for such an experience as is revealed here, but in the daily readings let us consider the *unreasonableness of allowing such experiences to cause the abandoning of prayer.* For one thing, unanswered petition ought not to cause the abandonment of all praying because much of the greatest praying is not petition at all. Even the pagans in their polytheism have occasionally perceived this truth; as, for example, in an ancient book, De Mysteriis Aegyptorum, "Prayer is not a means of inducing the gods to change the course of things, but their own gift of communion with themselves, the blessing of the living gods upon their children." When one turns to Christian experience he finds this aspect of prayer everywhere magnified and exalted. When Tennyson described prayer's meaning for his life he said, "Prayer is like opening a sluice between the great ocean and our little channels, when the sea gathers itself together and flows in at full tide." Consider how entirely this realm of prayer lies outside the disappointments of denied petition for changed circumstances.

Father, I thank Thee for Thy mercies which are new every morning. For the gift of sleep; for health and strength; for the vision of another day with its fresh opportunities of work and service; for all these and more than these, I thank Thee. Before looking on the face of men I would look on Thee, who art the health of my countenance and my God. Not without Thy guidance would I go forth to meet the duties and tasks of the day. Strengthen me so that in all my work I may be faithful; amid trials, courageous; in suffering, patient; under disappointment, full of hope in Thee. Grant this for Thy goodness' sake. Amen.—Samuel McComb.

Second Day, Seventh Week

How precious also are thy thoughts unto me, O God!
How great is the sum of them!
If I should count them, they are more in number than the sand:
When I awake, I am still with thee. . . .
Search me, O God, and know my heart:
Try me, and know my thoughts;
And see if there be any wicked way in me,
And lead me in the way everlasting.
                                   —Psalm 139:17, 18, 23, 24.

Consider the Psalmist's use of prayer as an opening of the heart to God's search, a means of restandardizing the life and aligning it continually with God's will. Should any number of disappointed petitions for external things blind our eyes to this transforming use of prayer? A typical result of Quintin Hogg's work for boys in London was seen in Jem Nicholls, a reclaimed lad of the streets. When Jem was asked, after Mr. Hogg's death, how the fight for character was coming on, he said, "I have a bit of trouble in keeping straight, but I thank God all is well. You see, I carry a photo of 'Q. H.' with me always, and whenever I am tempted, I take it out and his look is a wonderful help, and by the grace of God I am able to overcome all." Prayer can be in our lives this sort of cleansing and empowering look at our Lord. It sets us right, reestablishes our standards, confirms our best resolves. After all, is not this what we most want prayer for? Are we not showing poor judgment when we surrender this kind of praying because other kinds do not always seem effective?

Almighty God, who by Thy grace and providence hast brought my great and crying sins to light, I most humbly beseech Thee to continue Thy grace and mercy to me, that my conscience being now awakened, I may call my ways to remembrance, and confess, and bewail and abhor all the sins of my life past. And, O merciful God, give me true repentance for them, even that repentance to which Thou hast promised mercy and pardon, that even the consequences of my wrongdoing may bring a blessing to me, and that in all I may find mercy at Thy hands, through the merits and mediation of our Lord Jesus Christ. Amen.—Bishop Thos. Wilson (1663-1755).

Third Day, Seventh Week

Seek ye Jehovah while he may be found; call ye upon him while he is near: let the wicked forsake his way, and the unrighteous man his thoughts; and let him return unto Jehovah, and he will have mercy upon him; and to our God, for he will abundantly pardon. For my thoughts are not your thoughts, neither are your ways my ways, saith Jehovah. For as the heavens are higher than the earth, so are my ways higher than your ways, and my thoughts than your thoughts. For as the rain cometh down and the snow from heaven, and returneth not thither, but watereth the earth, and maketh it bring forth and bud, and giveth seed to the sower and bread to the eater; so shall my word be that goeth forth out of my mouth: it shall not return unto me void, but it shall accomplish that which I please, and it shall prosper in the thing whereto I sent it.—Isaiah **55:6-11.**

To make unanswered petition an excuse for abandoning all prayer is clearly unreasonable when we stop to consider how utterly unfitted we are to substitute our wish for God's will, and what appalling results would follow if all our requests were answered. Think over the faith in God's providence, superior wisdom, and mercy which Isaiah here makes the basis of prayer. Is it not clear that our clamorous demands that this kind of God should *please us*, justify Longfellow in his table-talk in breaking out into this indignant and somewhat exaggerated reproof: "What discord should we bring into the universe if our prayers were all answered! Then *we* should govern the world and not God. And do you think we should govern it better? It gives me only pain when I hear the long, wearisome petitions of men asking for they know not what. As frightened women clutch at the reins when there is danger, so do we grasp at God's government with our prayers. Thanksgiving with a full heart—and the rest silence and submission to the divine will!"

Thou hast called us to Thyself, most merciful Father, with love and with promises abundant; and we are witnesses that it is not in vain that we drew near to Thee. We bear witness to Thy faithfulness. Thy promises are Yea and Amen. Thy blessings are exceeding abundant more than we know or think. We thank Thee for the privilege of prayer, and for Thine answers to prayer; and we rejoice that Thou dost not answer according to our petitions. We are blind, and are constantly seeking things which are not best for us. If Thou didst grant all our desires according to our requests, we should be ruined. In dealing with our little children we give them, not the things which they ask for, but the things which we judge to be best for them; and Thou, our Father, art by Thy providence overruling our ignorance and our headlong mistakes, and are doing for us, not so much the things that we request of Thee as the things that we should ask; and we are, day by day, saved from peril and from ruin by Thy better knowledge and by Thy careful love. Amen.—Henry Ward Beecher.

Fourth Day, Seventh Week

Yet a further reason for the way we let denied petition break our faith in prayer is that we fail to see how often God answers our prayers in ways that we do not expect and, it may be, do not like. Consider Paul's experience, in the one petition that, so far as we have record, he ever offered for his own individual need:

And by reason of the exceeding greatness of the revelations, that I should not be exalted overmuch, there was given to me a thorn in the flesh, a messenger of Satan to buffet me, that I should not be exalted overmuch. Concerning this thing I besought the Lord thrice, that it might depart from me. And he hath said unto me, My grace is sufficient for thee: for my power is made perfect in weakness. Most gladly therefore will I rather glory in my weaknesses, that the power of Christ may rest upon me.—II Cor. 12:7-9.

How often do God's replies thus come to us in disguise, so that we, lacking Paul's insight, do not recognize them. Henry Ward Beecher stated with characteristic humor what is often a very serious truth in the practice of prayer. "A woman," he said, "prays for patience and God sends her a green cook." That is, we seek for a *thing*, and God gives us a *chance*. When our answers come so, they are likely neither to be recognized nor welcomed. The old Olney Hymns contain two stanzas that are applicable to not a little experience with prayer:

"I asked the Lord that I might grow,
  In faith, and love and ev'ry grace,
Might more of his salvation know,
  And seek more earnestly his face.

"Twas he who taught me thus to pray,
  And he I know has answered prayer,
But it has been in such a way
  As almost drove me to despair."

O God, forgive the poverty, the pettiness, Lord, the childish folly of our prayers. Listen, not to our words, but to the groanings that cannot be uttered; hearken, not to our petitions, but to the crying of our need. So often we pray for that which is already ours, neglected and unappropriated; so often for that which never can be ours; so often for that which we must win ourselves; and then labour endlessly for that which can only come to us in prayer.

How often we have prayed for the coming of Thy kingdom, yet when it has sought to come through us we have sometimes barred the way; we have wanted it without in others, but not in our own hearts. We feel it is we who stand between man's need and Thee; between ourselves and what we might be; and we have no trust in our own strength, or loyalty, or courage.

O give us to love Thy will, and seek Thy kingdom first of all. Sweep away our fears, our compromise, our weakness, lest at last we be found fighting against Thee. Amen.—W. E. Orchard.

Fifth Day, Seventh Week

But if any of you lacketh wisdom, let him ask of God, who giveth to all liberally and upbraideth not; and it shall be given him. But let him ask in faith, nothing doubting: for he that doubteth is like the surge of the sea driven by the wind and tossed. For let not that man think that he shall receive anything of the Lord; a double-minded man, unstable in all his ways.—James 1:5-8.

Our petitions seem to us to be denied and we give up praying in discouragement, when the fact may be that God is suggesting to us all the time ways in which we could answer our own requests. Many a man asks for a *thing,* and God's answer is *wisdom sufficient to get the thing.* Dean Bosworth puts it clearly: "Almost all the petitions a disciple ever has occasion to make to his Father can be answered without recourse to the so-called laws of nature, *if God has power to put a thought into the mind of man.* Suppose that the disciple wants work or money. If his Father has power to put an appropriate suggestion into his mind, or into some other man's mind, or into the minds of both, the prayer can be answered. And this can be done by means of, and not in spite of, the laws of mental action. We are able to put thoughts into each other's minds by means of words, and science seems to be surely demonstrating the fact that there are other ways of doing it. Jesus simply assumes that God has so made the human mind that it is capable of an interchange of thought with himself, its Heavenly Father."

O Thou, who art the true Sun of the world, ever rising, and never going down; who, by Thy most wholesome appearing and sight dost nourish, and gladden all things, in heaven and earth; we beseech Thee mercifully to shine into our hearts, that the night and darkness of sin, and the mists of error on every side, being driven away, by the brightness of Thy shining within our hearts, we may all our life walk without stumbling, as in the day-time, and, being pure and clean from the works of darkness, may abound in all good works which Thou hast prepared for us to walk in. Amen.—Erasmus (1467-1536).

Sixth Day, Seventh Week

And he spake a parable unto them to the end that they ought always to pray, and not to faint; saying, There was in a city a judge, who feared not God, and regarded not man: and there was a widow in that city; and she came oft unto him, saying, Avenge me of mine adversary. And he would not for a while: but afterward he said within himself, Though I fear not God, nor regard man; yet because this widow troubleth me, I will avenge her, lest she wear me out by her continual coming. And the Lord said, Hear what the unrighteous judge saith. And shall not God avenge his elect, that cry to him day and night, and yet he is longsuffering over them? I say unto you, that he will avenge them speedily. Nevertheless, when the Son of man cometh, shall he find faith on the earth?—Luke 18:1-8.

Men often call their petitions unanswered because in their impatience they do not give God time. Remember that in this parable the judge stands *in contrast* with God, not in similarity with him, and that the lesson is: If it was worth while waiting persistently upon the unjust judge, how much more surely worth while to wait patiently on the fatherly God! Many of our greatest desires demand time, patience, persistent search, long waiting as conditions of their fulfillment. Our petitions sometimes are unanswered only because we too soon give them up as unanswered. Spurgeon put the case strongly: "It may be your prayer is like a ship, which, when it goes on a very long voyage, does not come home laden so soon; but when it does come home, it has a richer freight. Mere 'coasters' will bring you coals, or such like ordinary things; but they that go afar to Tarshish return with gold and ivory. Coasting prayers, such as we pray every day, bring us many necessaries, but there are great prayers, which, like the old Spanish galleons, cross the main ocean, and are longer out of sight, but come home deep laden with a golden freight."

O Merciful God, fill our hearts, we pray Thee, with the graces of Thy Holy Spirit, with love, joy, peace, long-suffering, gentleness, goodness, faith, meekness, temperance. Teach us to love those who hate us; to pray for those who despitefully use us; that we may be the children of Thee, our Father, who makest Thy sun to shine on

the evil and on the good, and sendest rain on the just and on the
unjust.—Anselm (1033-1109).

Seventh Day, Seventh Week

Beloved, think it not strange concerning the fiery trial among you, which cometh upon you to prove you, as though a strange thing happened unto you: but insomuch as ye are partakers of Christ's sufferings, rejoice; that at the revelation of his glory also ye may rejoice with exceeding great joy. If ye are reproached for the name of Christ, blessed are ye; because the Spirit of glory and the Spirit of God resteth upon you. For let none of you suffer as a murderer, or a thief, or an evildoer, or as a meddler in other men's matters: but if a man suffer as a Christian, let him not be ashamed; but let him glorify God in this name. . . . Wherefore let them also that suffer according to the will of God commit their souls in well-doing unto a faithful Creator.—I Peter 4:12-16, 19.

Note the serious situation reflected in this Scripture, the suffering endured, the "fiery trial" to be faced, and consider the spirit of prayer in the last verse, where "as to a faithful Creator" they commit their souls. Some people make an unreasonable surrender of their praying, because they have been disappointed in getting their desires, and suppose that the great pray-ers have estimated the value of prayer in terms of the trouble out of which it saved them. On the contrary, many a saint has prayed his best for changed circumstances and then has committed his soul "as to a faithful Creator," although the outward trouble still was there. "Chinese" Gordon was a great believer in prayer; he said that he "prayed his boats up the Nile"; but he also has left on record this statement: "I think all prayer for temporalities must be made in subjection to God's will, with this reservation—if it falls in with his great scheme. The person who prays must be ready to have his request denied, if it runs counter to God's rule, which is dictated by infinite wisdom."

O Father, who hast ordained that we be set within a scheme of circumstance, and that in stern conflict we should find our strength and triumph over all; withhold not from us the courage by which alone we can conquer. Still our tongues of their weak complainings, steel our hearts against all fear, and in joyfully accepting the condi-

tions of our earthly pilgrimage may we come to possess our souls and achieve our purposed destiny.

It has pleased Thee to hide from us a perfect knowledge, yet Thou callest for a perfect trust in Thee. We cannot see to-morrow, we know not the way that we take, darkness hangs about our path and mystery meets us at every turn. Yet Thou hast shut us up to final faith in goodness, justice, truth; that loving these for themselves alone, we may find the love that passeth knowledge, and look upon Thy face.

O suffer us not for any terror of darkness or from any torment of mind to sin against our souls, or to fail at last of Thee. Amen.— W. E. Orchard.

COMMENT FOR THE WEEK

I

To a beginner in the high art of praying the Bible is often a very disheartening book. Its characters appear at first sight to enjoy the uninterrupted experience of answered prayer. The refrain of the Psalmist seems typical: "Thou hast given him his heart's desire, thou hast not withholden the request of his lips" (Psalm 21:2). If the Bible, however, knew no other experience with prayer than the enjoyment of successful petition, it would be a book utterly inadequate to meet our needs. One of the sorest trials of our faith is petition unanswered. It is worth our notice, therefore, that the Bible itself records the experience of ungranted prayer. Even in the Psalms one finds not alone jubilant gratitude over petitions won but despondent sorrow over petitions denied. "O my God, I cry in the day-time, but thou answerest not; and in the night season, and am not silent" (Psalm 22:2).

Indeed, upon examination, the Bible turns out to be full of unanswered prayers. Moses prays to enter the Promised Land, but dies on Nebo's top, his request refused. In the midst of national calamity the patriot lifts his Lamentation, "Thou hast covered thyself with a cloud, so that no prayer can pass through" (Lam. 3:44); and the prophet Habakkuk in his despondency exclaims, "O Jehovah, how long shall I cry, and thou wilt not hear?" (Hab. 1:2). Paul prays thrice that a vexatious, physical handicap, a "thorn in the flesh," which hinders his missionary labors, may be removed; but for the rest of his life he is compelled to make the best of it and to let it make the best of him. (II Cor. 12:9). Even the Master in the Garden prays for release from the appalling cup, but goes out to drink it to the dregs.

Not only do we meet in the Scriptures such outstanding examples of unanswered prayer; we find as well whole classes of men whose petitions are on principle denied. In the first chapter of Isaiah men are praying and God is speaking to them, "When ye make many prayers, I will not hear: your hands are full of blood" (Isaiah 1:15). In the fourth chapter of James' Epistle men are praying, and the Apostle says, "Ye ask, and receive not, because ye ask amiss, that ye may spend it in your pleasures" (James 4:3). Throughout the Old Testament the reader runs continually on verses such as these: "What is the hope of the godless? . . . Will God hear *his* cry?" (Job 27:8, 9); "Pray not thou for this people, neither lift up a cry or prayer for them; for I will not hear them in the time that they cry unto me" (Jer. 11:14); "If I regard iniquity in my heart, the Lord will not hear me" (Psalm 66:18). Even in the Gospels, Jesus, the supreme believer in prayer, tells his disciples that if a man does not forgive his enemies, even his own prayer for God's pardon will be disregarded (Matt. 6:15). *The Bible is full of unanswered prayer.* We have here no monotonous, unreal record of petitions always granted. This book is no stranger to that complaint which, more than any puzzle over theory, makes confident prayer difficult: "I cry unto thee, and thou dost not answer me: I stand up, and thou gazest at me" (Job 30:20).

II

In dealing with this problem we should emphasize the truth before maintained that petition is by no means the only form of prayer. Even though a man never asked God for anything, he still could pray. Indeed, the value of prayer is made to hinge too often upon the granting of minor material requests. God is reduced to the office of a village charity organization doling out small supplies to improvident applicants. This conception of prayer's use and value is infinitely removed from the elevated thought of Scripture. When we listen there in the places where men pray, we hear, for example: "Bless Jehovah, O my soul; and all that is within me, bless his holy name" (Psalm 103:1). It is the prayer of *adoration*. Or we hear the cry of a great statesman, remaking a ruined nation, "O my God, I am ashamed and blush to lift up my face to thee, my God; for our iniquities are increased over our head, and our guiltiness is grown up unto the heavens" (Ezra 9:6). It is the prayer of *confession*. We hear a grateful Psalmist pray: "I will extol thee, O Jehovah; for thou hast raised me up . . . O Jehovah my God, I will give thanks unto thee for ever" (Psalm 30:1, 12). It is the prayer of *thanksgiving*. We hear the vow: "Teach me, O Jehovah, the way of thy statutes; and I shall keep it unto the end. Give me understanding, and I shall keep thy law; yea, I shall observe it with my whole heart" (Psalm 119:33, 34). It is the prayer of *consecration*. And often, a voice like this is heard: "How precious also are thy thoughts unto me, O God! How great is the sum of them! . . . When I awake, I am still with thee" (Psalm 139:17, 18). It is the prayer of *communion*. Adoration, confession, thanksgiving, consecration, communion—these are the great prayers of the Book as they are of the soul. *Petition is only one province in the vast Kingdom of Prayer. Whatever our difficulties there, the wide ranges of prayer are not closed to us.*

Nevertheless this province of petition is important. It is not the whole of prayer, but it is the original form of prayer and never can be nor ought to be outgrown. Men cannot be content simply to praise God, confess to him, thank him, make vows of devotion, and enjoy communion with him. Men have desires, all the way from the long-sought coming of the Kingdom to the welfare of their loved ones and the prosperity of their daily business, to whose furtherance they instinctively call the help of any god in whom they really believe. "Thy will be done on earth as it is in heaven," and "Give us this day our daily bread," are both petitions; and they belong in the Lord's Prayer, together with "Hallowed be thy name." Petition, in its lower forms, trying to make God a mere means to serve some selfish, external end, is the result of ignorant, unspiritual immaturity. But petitions that well up out of mankind's deep desires for real good, are an integral part of prayer. They are to the whole domain what the thirteen original states are to America; not the whole of it, nor the major portion of it, but the primary nucleus of it and the initial influence in it.

Moreover, the Bible, with all its emphasis upon the other aspects of prayer, uses words very explicit, sweeping, and confident about petition: "Call unto me, and I will answer thee" (Jer. 33:3); "Ask, and it shall be given you" (Matt. 7:7); "All things, whatsoever ye shall ask in prayer, believing, ye shall receive" (Matt. 21:22); "All things whatsoever ye pray and ask for, believe that ye receive them, and ye shall have them" (Mark 11:24); "If two of you shall agree on earth as touching anything that they shall ask, it shall be done for them of my Father" (Matt. 18:19). What expectations such words awaken! And what a puzzling, baffling obstacle to active faith is the repeated denial of our requests! What is the use of proving that prayer *can* bring results if our experience shows that it *does* not?

III

One obvious reason for our unanswered petitions is, of course, *the ignorance of our asking*. Piety is no guarantee of wisdom. One has but to consider the spectacle of all sorts and conditions of men at prayer, voicing to God their various and often contradictory desires; praying vehemently on opposite sides of the same war; some even praying, like the Bourbon king, that they may be allowed to sin once more; and almost all of us praying in ignorance of our profoundest needs, to see that many petitions *must* be denied. Indeed, instead of calling prayers unanswered, it is far truer to recognize that "No" is as real an answer as "Yes," and often far more kind. When one considers the partialness of our knowledge, the narrowness of our outlook, our little skill in tracing the far-off consequences of our desire, he sees how often God must speak to us, as Jesus did to the ambitious woman, "Ye know not what ye ask" (Matt. 20:22). This suggestion is no special pleading, superficially to evade a difficulty. Rabindranath Tagore, the Bengali poet, was not constructing a Christian apologetic, but was stating a profound human experience, when he wrote:

"My desires are many and my cry is pitiful, but ever didst thou save me by hard refusals; and this strong mercy has been wrought into my life through and through."

This suggestion gains force when we perceive that often, *if God granted the form of our petition, he would deny the substance of our desire*. In one of the most impressive passages in his "Confessions," St. Augustine pictures his mother, Monica, praying all one night, in a sea-side chapel on the north African coast, that God would not let her son sail for Italy. She wanted Augustine to be a

Christian. She could not endure losing him from her influence. If under her care, he still was far from being Christ's, what would he be in Italy, home of licentiousness and splendor, of manifold and alluring temptations? And even while she prayed there passionately for her son's retention at home, he sailed, by the grace of God, for Italy, where, persuaded by Ambrose, he became a Christian in the very place from which his mother's prayers would have kept him. The form of her petition was denied; the substance of her desire was granted. As St. Augustine himself puts it: "Thou, in the depth of thy counsels, hearing the main point of her desire, regardedst not what she *then asked,* that thou mightest make me what she *ever desired.*" It would be a sorry world for all of us, if our unwise petitions did not often have "No" for their answer.

IV

Another plain reason for our denied requests is that *we continually try to make prayer a substitute for intelligence and work.* We have already seen that there are three chief ways in which men cooperate with God: thinking, working, and praying. *Now, no one of these three can ever take the place of another.* Each has its peculiar realm. No human mind may be acute and penetrating enough exactly to trace the boundaries, but it is clear that the boundaries must be there. When our petitions cross over into the realms where results must be achieved, not by asking, but by working and thinking, the petitions cannot be granted.

There are prayers, for example, which attempt to achieve by supplication what can be achieved only by effective *thinking.* Consider what this world would become if everything could be accomplished by prayer. What if men could sail their ships as well by prayer alone as by knowledge of the science of navigation; could swing their bridges as firmly by petition only as by studying engineering laws; could light their houses, send their messages, and work out their philosophies by mere entreaty? Is it not clear that if, as in fairy-tales, we had the power of omnipotent wishing conferred upon us, we never would use our intelligence at all? If life is to mean development and discipline, some things must be impossible until men think, no matter how hard men pray. If a boy asks his father to work out his arithmetic lesson because he wishes to play, will the father do it? The father loves the boy; he could work out the lesson, but he must not. The boy's prayer must never be made a substitute for his intellectual discipline. The father, in answer to the boy's request, may encourage him, assist him, stand by him and see him through; but the father must not do for the boy anything that the boy can possibly do for himself. Harsh though at times it may seem, God surely must require us as individuals and as a race to endure the discipline of painful enterprise and struggle, rather than find an easy relief by asking.

There are prayers, also, which attempt to accomplish by supplication what can be accomplished only by *work*. In one of the most dramatic scenes of the Exodus, where the Israelites are caught with the unfordable Red Sea in front and the pursuing Egyptians behind, Moses goes apart to pray. The reply which he receives from Jehovah is startling. It is nothing less than a rebuke for having prayed: "Wherefore criest thou unto me? speak unto the children of Israel, that they go forward" (Ex. 14:15). It is as though God were saying, "I have everything prepared for your aggressive action. I have done the last thing that I can do, until you resolutely take advantage of it. It is your move! You cannot obtain by prayer what comes only as the reward of work." Such a rebuke many of our prayers deserve. We forget the proverb: "If wishes were horses, beggars would ride."

When one studies the great servants of the Kingdom at prayer, he always finds in them this sturdy common-sense. If ever an enterprise was begun, continued, and ended in prayer, it was Nehemiah's reconstruction of the Hebrew commonwealth; but Nehemiah always *combined* prayer and work, without *confusing* them: "I prayed unto the God of heaven. *And* I said unto the king" (Neh. 2:4, 5); "We made our prayer unto our God, *and* set a watch against them day and night" (Neh. 4:9); "Remember the Lord . . . *and* fight" (Neh. 4:14). So Cromwell prayed, but when he faced a weak and flaccid piety that made prayer a substitute for practical devotion, he put his feeling into a phrase as hard as his bullets: "Trust God and keep your powder dry." Such men have understood that God has *three* ways of accomplishing his will through men, not *one* way only. "Pray to God," said Spurgeon, "but keep the hammer going."

V

Still another reason for ungranted petition may be noted: *we are not ready for the reception of the gift which we desire.* The trouble is not with the petition but with us who offer it. We need not be wilfully wicked. We may simply lack that eager readiness to receive which voices itself in earnest, persistent prayer. The note of Jacob's wrestling with the angel, "I will not let thee go, except thou bless me" (Gen. 32:26), is lacking in our supplication. We are lackadaisical in our desires and therefore are not importunate in our prayers.

At first it may be surprising, in view of all that has been said about the individual love of God, that we should insist on importunity in prayer. If God is good and wishes to give us the best, why must we clamor long after a real good, eagerly and patiently and with importunity seeking it?

At this point many of Jesus' sayings are difficult to understand. He clearly insisted on importunate prayer. "He spake a parable unto them to the end that they ought always to pray, and not to faint" (Luke 18:1), and the parable recorded a woman's tiresome, reiterated petitioning of a judge until he cried in despair, "I will avenge her, lest she wear me out by her continual coming." He who believed so fully in the utter willingness and power of God to help, even illustrated prayer by a man's arousal of a sleepy neighbor and his pestering persistence in calling for bread until "because of his importunity" he won his request (Luke 11:5f). We must allow for the picturesque exaggeration in these vivid parables; we must remember that they were supposed to illustrate only one aspect of prayer, not the whole of it; we must balance these passages by Jesus' own condemnation of those who think they shall be "heard for their much speaking": but we must not thin out, until we lose it, the obvious meaning here. Jesus was insisting on tireless praying. He said prayer was seeking (Luke 11:9); and if one considers what intellectual search means, as when Copernicus questioned the heavens year after year to discover the truth, or what geographical search means, as when Peary tried undiscourageably for the Pole, he catches at least a faint idea of the Master's thought of prayer as an unwearied seeking after spiritual good. "For twenty-four years," said Peary, "sleeping or awake, to place the Stars and Stripes on the Pole had been my dream." That is the spirit of seeking, and that, the Master said, is the spirit of prayer.

The necessity of this sort of prayer is not difficult to understand. Boys on Hallowe'en ring bells and run. So, many of us pray. But any one who has serious business will wait for an answer to his summons and if need be, will ring again. The patient waiting, the reiterated demand are an expression and a test of our earnestness. When we said that both *"No"* and *"Yes"* were real answers to prayers, we did not exhaust the possibilities. There is another answer which God continually gives us—*"Wait."* For nearly two thousand years the church has been praying "that they may all be one." God never has said "No" to that, nor yet has he said "Yes." He has said "Wait." Since Jesus taught them first to pray, "Thy kingdom come," his disciples have lifted that supplication century after century; and "Lo! Thy church is praying yet, a thousand years the same." Great prayers such as these are not affairs of "Yes" or "No"; they reach over ages and bind together the aspirations of God's noblest sons; they are an eager, patient, persistent search after good.

Now compare with such undiscourageable prayers our individual spasms of petition. Our requests spurt up like intermittent geysers; we cry out and fall back again. We are not in earnest. "Easiness of desire," said Jeremy Taylor, "is a great enemy to the success of a good man's prayer. It must be an intent, zealous, busy, operative prayer. For consider what a huge indecency it is that a man should speak to God for a thing that he values not. Our prayers upbraid our spirits when we beg tamely for those things for which we ought to die." This, then, is the rationale of importunity in prayer, not that it is needed to coax God, but that it is needed alike to express and by expressing to deepen our eager readiness for the good we seek. *Some things God cannot give to a man until the man has prepared and proved his spirit by persistent prayer.* Such praying cleans the house, cleanses the windows, hangs the curtains, sets the table, opens the door, until God says, "Lo! The house is ready. Now may the guest come in."

VI

As we step, then, from the wider domain of prayer into the special province of petition, we can see three comprehensive reasons for denied request: *the ignorance of our asking, our use of prayer in fields where it does not belong,* and *the unreadiness of our own lives to receive the good we seek.* There are many people who have a thoughtless and unauthorized belief in the power of prayer to get things for themselves. They forget the searching condition put on all petition, that it must be in Christ's name (John 14:13; 16:23, 24,

26). No hurried addition of "For Jesus' sake" appended to a prayer can satisfy this deep and spiritual demand. Petition must be in accordance with the divine will and in harmony with Christ's spirit; it must be wise in itself and must come from a life persistent in its desires and unselfish in its purposes, before that law of prayer can be satisfied. To pray in Christ's name is nothing less than the acceptance of St. Augustine's attitude when he cried: "O Lord, grant that I may do thy will as if it were my will; so that thou mayest do my will as if it were thy will." Prayer is not magic, and it is a fortunate thing for us that Trumbull's word is true, alike to Scripture and experience, that so far as petition is concerned "Prayer is not to be depended on, but God is!"

There is one sense, however, in which answer to prayer can always be depended on, if a man has kept his life at all in harmony with God. *Even when God cannot answer affirmatively the man's petition he can answer the man.* Paul's petition for relief from his physical distress was not affirmatively answered, but Paul was answered. He went out from that denied request, thrice repeated, with a reply from God that put fortitude and courage into him: "My grace is sufficient for thee: for my power is made perfect in weakness" (II Cor. 12:9). God always answers true prayer in one of two ways— "No good prayer ever comes weeping home." For either he changes the circumstances or he supplies sufficient power to overcome them; he answers either the petition or the man. As Luther put it, "A Christian knows that he is not refused what he has prayed for, and finds, in fact, that he is helped in all troubles . . . and that God gives him power to bear his troubles and to overcome them: which is just the same thing as taking his trouble away from him, and making it no longer misfortune or distress, seeing it has been overcome."

This truth explains such amazing statements as Adoniram Judson, for example, made at the close of his life: "I never prayed sincerely and earnestly for anything, but it came; at some time—no matter at how distant a day—somehow, in some shape—probably the last I should have devised—it came." But Judson had prayed for entrance into India and had been compelled to go to Burmah; he had prayed for his wife's life, and had buried both her and his two children; he had prayed for release from the King of Ava's prison and had lain there months, chained and miserable. Scores of Judson's petitions had gone without an affirmative answer. But *Judson* always had been answered. He had been upheld, guided, reenforced; unforeseen doors had opened through the very trials he sought to avoid; and the deep desires of his life were being accomplished not in his way but beyond his way. He meant by his assertion of the unfailing power of prayer what Paul meant when he cried, "My God shall supply every need" (Phil. 4:19). Yes, even the Master faced denied petition. "Let the cup pass," was a cry that could not be granted. But Jesus himself was greatly answered in the Garden. The request was denied, but as our Lord goes out to face Pilate and the cross, with a loyalty to his Cause that no temptation can relax, a steadiness that no suffering can shake, a magnanimity that neither nails nor spear nor gibe can embitter, who can measure what in prayer has been done for the Man?

SUGGESTIONS FOR THOUGHT AND DISCUSSION

Why are prayers unanswered?

What would happen if all petitions were granted?

If the course of events were decided alone in accordance with the petitions to God by men, what kind of a world would it be?

To what extent would any individual be willing to have his prayers answered?

What is the effect upon personal character of a religion that substitutes begging for honest work?

Under what circumstances do you think God would grant a petition for definite help in securing something which a man might get by his own intellect and work?

To what extent is it possible for a man's "petition" to be denied and his "prayer" still to be answered?

If we ask God for something in how far is it an answer to this petition to be given the opportunity and direction to answer the petition for ourselves?

In response to his petition to be relieved from "the thorn in the flesh," which do you think presented the greater value to Paul—the granting of his actual petition or the answer which he received?

If all petitions were unanswered, would it still be worth while to pray?

Why are answers to prayer deferred?

What prerequisites does a wise father require of his sons before granting them their share of the inheritance? What light does this throw upon the answer to a petition being deferred by God?

Why did Jesus suggest the necessity of importunity in prayer?

What does the New Testament mean when it speaks of praying "in Christ's name"?

What is the difference between "answering a petition" and "answering a man"? Have any of my prayers really been unanswered?

CHAPTER VIII

Prayer as Dominant Desire

DAILY READINGS

First Day, Eighth Week

And God hath set some in the church, first apostles, secondly prophets, thirdly teachers, then miracles, then gifts of healings, helps, governments, divers kinds of tongues. Are all apostles? are all prophets? are all teachers, are all workers of miracles? have all gifts of healings? do all speak with tongues? do all interpret? But desire earnestly the greater gifts. And moreover a most excellent way show I unto you. If I speak with the tongues of men and of angels, but have not love, I am become sounding brass, or a clanging cymbal.—I Cor. 12:28-13:1.

Note the unfortunate break in this great passage made by a new chapter's beginning. The thirteenth chapter on love should always be read as an explanation of the verse in the twelfth chapter, "Desire earnestly the greater gifts."

Many reasons for unreality in prayer we have noted, such as perversity of mood, or failure to grasp the individual love of God, or wilful alienation of the life in sin. With one of the deepest troubles in our praying, however, we have not dealt. *Our prayers are often unreal because they do not represent what in our inward hearts we sincerely crave.* We ask God for the "greater gifts" which we do not "desire earnestly." For example we pray against some *evil habit* in our lives, while at the same time we refuse to give up the practices that make the habit easy, or the companionships in which the habit thrives. We go through the form of entreating God to save us from the sin, but we do not want the answer enough to burn the bridges across which the sin continually comes. Our petition is a lame and ineffective whim without driving power. Said "Chinese" Gordon: "I have been thinking over our feelings and how often it is that we are so very insincere even in prayer. . . . We pray for power to give up a certain habit, say evil speaking, and, at the moment of so praying, we have a thought of evil against some one, and we, as it were, whisper to that thought, 'By and by I will attend to you, not now,' and we go on praying against the very act we intend in our hearts to do. All this is insincere and dishonoring."

O God, whose Spirit searcheth all things, and whose love beareth all things, encourage us to draw near to Thee in sincerity and in truth. Save us from a worship of the lips while our hearts are far away. Save us from the useless labour of attempting to conceal ourselves from Thee who searchest the heart.

Enable us to lay aside all those cloaks and disguises which we wear in the light of day and here to bare ourselves, with all our weakness, disease and sin, naked to Thy sight.

Make us strong enough to bear the vision of the truth, and to have done with all falsehood, pretence, and hypocrisy, so that we may see things as they are, and fear no more.

Enable us to look upon the love which has borne with us and the heart that suffers for us. Help us to acknowledge our dependence on the purity that abides our uncleanness, the patience that forgives our faithlessness, the truth that forbears all our falsity and compromise. And may we have the grace of gratitude, and the desire to dedicate ourselves to Thee. Amen.—W. E. Orchard.

Second Day, Eighth Week

Therefore is the kingdom of heaven likened unto a certain king, who would make a reckoning with his servants. And when he had begun to reckon, one was brought unto him, that owed him ten thousand talents. . . . And the lord of that servant, being moved with compassion, released him, and forgave him the debt. But that servant went out, and found one of his fellow-servants, who owed him a hundred shillings: and he laid hold on him, and took him by the throat, saying, Pay what thou owest. So his fellow-servant fell down and besought him, saying, Have patience with me, and I will pay thee. And he would not: but went and cast him into prison, till he should pay that which was due. So when his fellow-servants saw what was done, they were exceeding sorry, and came and told unto their lord all that was done. Then his lord called him unto him, and saith to him, Thou wicked servant, I forgave thee all that debt, because thou besoughtest me: shouldest not thou also have had mercy on thy fellow-servant, even as I had mercy on thee? And his lord was wroth, and delivered him to the tormentors, till he should pay all that was due. So shall also my heavenly Father do unto you, if ye forgive not every one his brother from your hearts. —Matt. 18:23, 24, 27-35.

The unreality of our praying may be illustrated in our petitions for *forgiveness*. Nothing may be more superficial than a request for pardon; nothing can be more searching than a genuine experience of penitence. A boy who has sinned and faces the consequence may have a momentary spell of regret; he naturally wishes to have the slate wiped clean. But to be sincerely sorry for his evil itself, rather than for its consequences; to be ashamed of his failure, so that he feels himself a brother of all sinners, and like Richard Baxter, could say of a murderer going to execution, "There but for the grace of God goes Richard Baxter!"—how penetrating an experience is that! Consider this expression of penitence from Tagore, the Bengali poet:

"I came out alone on my way to my tryst. But who is this that follows me in the silent dark?
I move aside to avoid his presence, but I escape him not.
He makes the dust rise from the earth with his swagger; he adds his loud voice to every word that I utter.
He is my own little self, my lord, he knows no shame; but I am ashamed to come to thy door in his company."

A man so sincerely ashamed of himself will seek forgiveness and renewal, with a genuine desire that will make his supplications real, and by the very vividness of his own sense of guilt will find it impossible to be unforgiving to any other man. Read again today's Scripture, and consider the Master's insistence on that kind of genuineness in our prayers for pardon.

O Searcher of hearts, Thou knowest us better than we know ourselves, and seest the sins which our sinfulness hides from us. Yet even our own conscience beareth witness against us, that we often slumber on our appointed watch; that we walk not always lovingly with each other, and humbly with Thee; and we withhold that entire sacrifice of ourselves to Thy perfect will, without which we are not crucified with Christ, or sharers in His redemption. Oh, look upon our contrition, and lift up our weakness, and let the dayspring yet arise within our hearts, and bring us healing, strength, and joy. Day by day may we grow in faith, in self-denial, in charity, in heavenly-mindedness. And then, mingle us at last with the mighty host of Thy redeemed for evermore. Amen.—James Martineau (1805-1900).

Third Day, Eighth Week

Holy Father, keep them in thy name which thou hast given me, that they may be one, even as we are. While I was with them, I kept them in thy name which thou hast given me: and I guarded them, and not one of them perished, but the son of perdition; that the scripture might be fulfilled. But now I come to thee; and these things I speak in the world, that they may have my joy made full in themselves. I have given them thy word; and the world hated them, because they are not of the world, even as I am not of the world. I pray not that thou shouldest take them from the world, but that thou shouldest keep them from the evil one. They are not of the world, even as I am not of the world. Sanctify them in the truth: thy word is truth. As thou didst send me into the world, even so sent I them into the world. And for their sakes I sanctify myself, that they themselves also may be sanctified in truth. Neither for these only do I pray, but for them also that believe on me through their word; that they may all be one; even as thou, Father, art in me, and I in thee, that they also may be in us: that the world may believe that thou didst send me.—John 17:11-21.

Consider another way in which we pray insincerely. We go through the form of praying for our *friends*. It seems the right thing to do, and it gives us at least a momentary glow of unselfishness. But the prayer does not so rise from a controlling desire for our friends' good, that we can be counted on all that day to be thoughtful about their needs, sensitive to their feelings, generous to their faults, glad of their success, and helpful to our utmost in their service. We often do not really *care* enough about our friends, so that our supplication for them has vital meaning for us and, therefore, for God. As Nolan Rice Best has expressed it, "Like the supreme court of our land, the Supreme Court of heaven passes on no hypothetical matters; the petitioner must have a real case in order to obtain attention."

Think of the Master's love for his disciples, of the ways he revealed it, of the lengths to which he willingly went in being true to it. The reality of this intercessory prayer in John's seventeenth chapter goes back to the genuineness of the love out of which it came. The prayer actually represented what the Master sacrificially desired.

O blessed Lord and Saviour, who hast commanded us to love one another, grant us grace that, having received Thine undeserved bounty, we may love every man in Thee and for Thee. We implore Thy clemency for all; but especially for the friends whom Thy love has given to us. Love Thou them, O Thou fountain of love, and make them to love Thee with all their heart, with all their mind, and with all their soul, that those things only which are pleasing to Thee they may will, and speak, and do. And though our prayer is cold, because our charity is so little fervent, yet Thou art rich in mercy. Measure not to them Thy goodness by the dulness of our devotion; but as Thy kindness surpasseth all human affection, so let Thy hearing transcend our prayer. Do Thou to them what is expedient for them, according to Thy will, that they, being always and everywhere ruled and protected by Thee, may attain in the end to everlasting life; and to Thee, with the Father and the Holy Spirit, be all honour and praise for ever and ever. Amen.—Anselm (1033-1109).

Fourth Day, Eighth Week

If I have withheld the poor from their desire,
Or have caused the eyes of the widow to fail,
Or have eaten my morsel alone,
And the fatherless hath not eaten thereof. . . .
If I have seen any perish for want of clothing,
Or that the needy had no covering;
If his loins have not blessed me,
And if he hath not been warmed with the fleece of my sheep;
If I have lifted up my hand against the fatherless,
Because I saw my help in the gate:
Then let my shoulder fall from the shoulder-blade,
And mine arm be broken from the bone.—Job 31:16-22.

When a man can take words like these on his lips, as a description of his own life, he is prepared sincerely to pray for the *poor*. We often emphasize the fact that prayer is a powerful builder of character; but the other side of the truth is important, that *great character is essential to great praying.* A man with a small, mean, self-indulgent life cannot genuinely offer a noble prayer. This is the meaning of the saying that it is easy to commit the Lord's Prayer to memory, but difficult to learn it by heart. In any man's entreaty, no matter how great the words, only that much is real which is the expression of his character, the inward quality and habitual desire of his life. When, therefore, pity leads us to ask God's mercy on the poor, the value of our praying depends on the controlling power of that good desire in our lives. Does the supplication come out of an inward devotion that is to us of serious concern? Can God see in our habitual, systematic care for the poor and support of the agencies that help them, the proof of our prayer's sincerity?

We beseech Thee, Lord and Master, to be our help and succour. Save those who are in tribulation; have mercy on the lonely; lift up the fallen; show Thyself unto the needy; heal the ungodly; convert the wanderers of Thy people; feed the hungry; raise up the weak; comfort the faint-hearted. Let all the peoples know that Thou art God alone, and Jesus Christ is Thy Son, and we are Thy people and the sheep of Thy pasture; for the sake of Christ Jesus. Amen.— St. Clement of Rome (90 A. D.).

Fifth Day, Eighth Week

Now there were at Antioch, in the church that was there, prophets and teachers, Barnabas, and Symeon that was called Niger, and Lucius of Cyrene, and Manaen the foster-brother of Herod the tetrarch, and Saul. And as they ministered to the Lord, and fasted, the Holy Spirit said, Separate me Barnabas and Saul for the work whereunto I have called them. Then, when they had fasted and prayed and laid their hands on them, they sent them away. So they, being sent forth by the Holy Spirit, went down to Seleucia; and from thence they sailed to Cyprus.—Acts 13:1-4.

Note how this first missionary tour of Paul and his companions was conceived in the spirit of prayer and furthered by prayer's

power. We too have prayed for *missions*. Perhaps we have personal
friends on the foreign field and that fact has quickened our sense of
obligations to pray for the Cause. But the plain fact often is that
while we are offering prayers, we are offering nothing else. We make
supplication a substitute for devotion. We do not give to missions
with any deep sense of stewardship, but rather treat the Cause of the
Kingdom as a charity, to which an occasional dole from our surplus
is sufficient. In our inmost desires we are not devotedly set on the
triumph of Christ's cause, so that we seek information about missions, make as generous gifts as we can, and put personal service into
strengthening the church as the "home base." In our petitions for
the missionaries, how often, as Friar Lawrence phrases it, we are
"fooling ourselves with trivial devotions."

*O great Lord of the harvest, send forth, we beseech Thee, labour-
ers into the harvest of the world, that the grain which is even now
ripe may not fall and perish through our neglect. Pour forth Thy
sanctifying Spirit on our fellow Christians abroad, and Thy convert-
ing grace on those who are living in darkness. Raise up, we beseech
Thee, a devout ministry among the native believers, that all Thy
people being knit together in one body, in love, Thy Church may
grow up into the measure of the stature of the fulness of Christ;
through Him who died, and rose again for us all, the same Jesus
Christ our Lord. Amen.*—Bishop Milman (1791-1868).

Sixth Day, Eighth Week

Pray for the peace of Jerusalem:
They shall prosper that love thee.
Peace be within thy walls,
And prosperity within thy palaces.
For my brethren and companions' sakes,
I will now say, Peace be within thee.
For the sake of the house of Jehovah our God
I will seek thy good.—Psalm 122:6-9.

In the time of a great war, nothing is more natural than prayer
for *peace*. But of all petitions that arise for peace, how many represent deep and transforming devotion of the life to the cause of
human brotherhood? Men pray for peace, and still retain and ex-

press those racial prejudices that are one of the most prolific causes of war. They ask for human brotherhood to come, but they are most unbrotherly to the foreigner within their own communities. Women piously frame petitions in behalf of the day when there shall be no "barbarian, Scythian, bondman, freeman; but Christ is all, and in all," but all the while they violate every Christian principle in their dealings with their servants, their social inferiors, or the aliens of their city. Their prayers are long-range dreams that do not touch their lives. And least of all do many of us, when we pray for peace, purge our own hearts of that rancor that lies behind all war. "Let all bitterness, and wrath, and anger, and clamor, and railing, be put away from you, with all malice: and be ye kind one to another, tender-hearted, forgiving each other, even as God also in Christ forgave you" (Eph. 4:31).

O Lord, since first the blood of Abel cried to Thee from the ground that drank it, this earth of Thine has been defiled with the blood of man shed by his brother's hand, and the centuries sob with the ceaseless horror of war. Ever the pride of kings and the covetousness of the strong have driven peaceful nations to slaughter. Ever the songs of the past and the pomp of armies have been used to inflame the passions of the people. Our spirit cries out to Thee in revolt against it, and we know that our righteous anger is answered by Thy holy wrath.

Break Thou the spell of the enchantments that make the nations drunk with the lust of battle and draw them on as willing tools of death. Grant us a quiet and steadfast mind when our own nation clamors for vengeance or aggression. Strengthen our sense of justice and our regard for the equal worth of other peoples and races. Grant to the rulers of nations faith in the possibility of peace through justice, and grant to the common people a new and stern enthusiasm for the cause of peace. Bless our soldiers and sailors for their swift obedience and their willingness to answer to the call of duty, but inspire them none the less with a hatred of war, and may they never for love of private glory or advancement provoke its coming. May our young men still rejoice to die for their country with the valor of their fathers, but teach our age nobler methods of matching our strength and more effective ways of giving our life for the flag.

O Thou strong Father of all nations, draw all Thy great family together with an increasing sense of our common blood and destiny,

*that peace may come on earth at last, and Thy sun may shed its
light rejoicing on a holy brotherhood of peoples.*—Walter Rauschenbusch.

Seventh Day, Eighth Week

And it came to pass after these things, that Naboth the Jezreelite
had a vineyard, which was in Jezreel, hard by the palace of Ahab
king of Samaria. And Ahab spake unto Naboth, saying, Give me
thy vineyard, that I may have it for a garden of herbs, because it is
near unto my house; and I will give thee for it a better vineyard
than it: or, if it seem good to thee, I will give thee the worth of it
in money. And Naboth said to Ahab, Jehovah forbid it me, that I
should give the inheritance of my fathers unto thee. And Ahab
came into his house heavy and displeased because of the word which
Naboth the Jezreelite had spoken to him; for he had said, I will not
give thee the inheritance of my fathers. And he laid him down upon
his bed, and turned away his face, and would eat no bread.—
I Kings 21:1-4.

Supposing that Ahab had said his prayers that night, would it
have made much difference what he said in praying? Imagine him
rehearsing some formal petitions learned in his childhood; *would
that have been his real prayer?* It is clear that Ahab's demand on
life that night was simply his covetous desire for Naboth's vineyard.
No formal, proper, pious supplication addressed to God could have
hidden from the divine insight this deeper fact, that what Ahab
really wanted was his neighbor's field. Consider how often God must
so look through our conventionally proper petitions, and in our
hearts perceive our unvoiced but controlling wants—sometimes as
mean, selfish, covetous as Ahab's. These are the deep *prayers* of our
lives—our hearts are set upon them—and God is not deceived when
we tell him in pious phrases that we wish his blessing. Let us consider
this week what our hearts really are set on, what are our chief ambitions and desires.

*O Eternal God, sanctify my body and soul, my thoughts and my
intentions, my words and actions, that whatsoever I shall think, or
speak, or do, may be by me designed for the glorification of Thy
Name, and by Thy blessing, it may be effective and successful in the
work of God, according as it can be capable. Lord, turn my necessi-*

*ties into virtue; the works of nature into the works of grace; by
making them orderly, regular, temperate; and let no pride or self-
seeking, no covetousness or revenge, no little ends and low imaginations, pollute my spirit, and unhallow any of my words and actions;
but let my body be a servant of my spirit, and both body and spirit
servants of Jesus; that, doing all things for Thy glory here, I may
be partaker of Thy glory hereafter, through Jesus Christ our Lord.
Amen.*—Jeremy Taylor (1613-1667).

COMMENT FOR THE WEEK

I

Hitherto we have spoken of prayer as a definitely religious act.
In using the word we thought of hearts bowed in the presence of
God; we thought of shut doors, bent knees, reverent spirits. *But in
this chapter we must sink down into that realm of human desire,
which, like an ocean under separate waves, lies beneath all specially
religious petitions.*

At least during the early portion of this chapter we must think of
prayer as quite separable from religion; we must ask not only what
our desires are when we bow before God, but what our dominant
aims are in daily business; what we are really after in our innermost
ambitions; what is our demand on life. Prayer, in this more inclusive
sense, is the settled craving of a man's heart, *good or bad,* his inward
love and determining desire. When the prodigal in Jesus' parable
said, "Father, give me the portion of thy substance that falleth to
me," he was in a real sense praying. His innermost ambition was
there expressed. His heart was set on gaining the means that in the
end would be his ruin. It was a prayer resolutely directed toward
evil, but it was prayer. In this sense, Columbus' search for America
was prayer; Edison's long attempt to find the secret of incandescence
was prayer; Paul's ambition to found Christian churches and Napoleon's ambition to rule Europe both were prayers. Not alone the
woman who pleads with the reluctant judge for justice, but the
prodigal seeking from his father the means of dissipation, is praying;
and any man who after money or fame or pleasure insistently directs
his course, has in his dominant desire the prayer that shapes his life.
We must accept for a while the fruitful definition which Mrs.
Browning gives us, "Every *wish,* with God, is a prayer."

II

One immediate result of this point of view is a clear perception that *everybody is praying.* Prayer regarded as a definite act of approach to God may be shut out from any life. But prayer regarded as desire, exercised in any realm and for anything, at once includes us all. In this general sense we pray without ceasing. We are hungerpoints in the universe; the elemental fact in every human life is desire. To a man who disclaims any act of prayer we may retort, "Your life *is* an organized prayer. Your body craves food, your mind craves knowledge, your affection craves friendship, your spirit craves peace and hope. You do not pray? Rather every stroke of work and every purposeful thought are endeavors to satisfy inward prayers."

Ordinarily prayer is regarded as the act of a man's best hours. *But in this deeper sense men pray in their worst hours too.* Prayer may be either heavenly or devilish. When we think of a man's dominant desire as in very truth his prayer, we see that Gehazi, with covetous eyes following Naaman to filch his wealth, is praying; that David, with licentious heart putting Uriah at the front of the battle, is praying; that the prodigal seeking the means of his own ruin is praying. None ever found heaven, here or anywhere, without prayer —the uplift of a settled desire after God and righteousness. And none ever found hell, here or anywhere, without prayer—the dead set and insistent craving of the heart after evil. In any group of men, you may not in this sense divide those who pray from those who do not. All are praying the prayer of dominant desire. The great question is: what are they after? what is their demand on life?

III

It is to be noted, also, that prayer in this sense is the inward measure of any man's quality. Living beings reveal their grade in the scale of existence by their wants. Inanimate things want nothing. Stones and clods are undisturbed by any sense of lack. The faintest glimmering of life, however, brings in the reign of want. Even in some one-celled amoeba rolling about in search of food, the presence of life means a hunger which is the rudiment of prayer. And from these dim beginnings of instinctive need to the spiritual demands of sage and saint, the extent and quality of a being's wants are a good measure of his life.

In the difference between a savage, wanting nothing but nakedness, a straw-hut, and raw food to content him, and one of us, demanding conveniences that lay tribute on the ends of the earth, our material progress can be measured. In the difference between an African dwarf, with no interests beyond his jungle's edge, and a modern scientist beating the wings of his enquiry against the uttermost bars of the universe, we can gauge our intellectual growth. In the difference between a pagan with his fetish, and Paul saying of his life with Christ, "I press on," our spiritual enlargement is measured. The greater a man is, the wider and deeper and finer are his desires. His prayer is the measure of him. What it takes to meet his need is the gauge of his size. Men come into life as they move into strange cities and at once begin praying. Some ask for the city's places of vulgar amusement or of vice; some for the best music and the finest art; some for low companionship, others for good friends; and some for the centers of social service and the temples of God. So each man prays and as he prays he reveals his quality. *No man can escape the prayer of dominant desire, nor evade the inevitable measurement of his life by his prayer.*

IV

This truth becomes very serious when we face a further development of it: *that the prayer of dominant desire always tends to attain its object.* This is true, in the first place, because a central craving organizes all the faculties of our lives about itself and sets mind and hands to do its bidding. Of the three ways in which men cooperate with God, working, thinking, and praying, a cursory view might suggest that praying is a somewhat superfluous addition; that, at least, the other two plainly belong first in importance. *On the contrary the prayer of dominant desire habitually precedes thought and work.* We think and labor because in our innermost heart we have prayed first, because some Desire is in us, calling to our minds, "Come, bring me this!" and ordering our hands, "Go bring me that!" Desire is the elemental force in human experience.

A man wants money. That is his real demand on life—his prayer. How his mind, then, puts on servile livery to wait on his dominant desire! How quick his wit becomes, how sinewy his thought in the

service of his prayer! Wherever men concentrate their wills, apply
their minds and submit to toil, back of this visible consequence is
dominant desire. If Bismarck stops at nothing in amalgamating the
German Empire, an ambition is in the saddle—"You may hang me,"
he said, "so long as the rope you do it with binds Germany to the
Prussian throne." And if Burns writes incomparable Scotch lyrics,
we must trace his labor back to his prayer:

> "E'en then a *wish* (I mind its pow'r),
> A wish that to my latest hour
> Shall strongly heave my breast,
> That I for poor auld Scotland's sake
> Some usefu' plan or book could make,
> Or sing a song at least."

Dominant desire gathers up the scattered faculties, concenters the
mind, nerves the will, and drives hard toward the issue. It always
tends to achieve its end. As John Burroughs put it, "If you have a
thing in mind, it is not long before you have it in hand."

This prayer of dominant desire, however, tends to achieve its
object, not merely because it concentrates the powers within the
man, but because *it calls into alliance with it forces from without the
man*. Wherever there is low pressure in the atmosphere, thither the
wind rushes to fill the need. So the cravings of men create low-
pressure areas and, from without, help blows in to the fulfilment of
their desires. This is easily illustrated in the social life, for in every
enterprise now on foot in the world, men are endeavoring to supply
other men's desires—churches to meet the desire for worship, saloons
to meet the craving for drink, schools to supply the thirst for knowledge. Behind every organization lies a craving. Human wants are the
open bays that call the sea of human effort in.

This truth is just as evident in the life of the individual. When a
man craves vicious pleasure, low companions inevitably drift to him
from every side; low books that pure minds pass unobserved, flow in
to satisfy his appetite. His prayer creates a call that is answered by
everything kindred to his want. As a whirlwind catches up the adja-
cent air into its vortex, so a man's desire calls in the congenial forces
of his environment. To the prodigal, doubtless, every evil influence
in the village came by spiritual gravitation to further his evil purpose, until at last his dominant desire *drew his father in*. The very

patrimony which was meant to be his blessing he used in furtherance of his controlling passion until it proved his curse. To translate the story at once into the terms of our experience with God, the universe itself responds to a man's insistent demands upon it. Even the forces of the spiritual world align themselves, however reluctantly, with a man's controlling prayer. He can create a back eddy in the river of God's will, and the very waters that would have helped him go straight on, will now swirl around his dominant desire.

Here, then, is one of the most revealing and startling aspects in which the meaning of prayer may be considered: *we all are praying the prayer of dominant desire, our quality is measured by it; and because it both engages in its service our inward powers and calls to its furtherance forces from without, it tends with certainty to achieve its end.*

v

When from this general consideration of prayer as desire, we move up to the more usual thought of prayer as the soul's definite approach to God, we gain outlooks on our subject that no other road so well affords. We see clearly that *many of the speeches addressed to God that we have called our prayers are not real prayers at all.* They are not our dominant desires. They do not express the inward set and determination of our lives. What we pray for in the closet is not the thing that daily we are seeking with undiscourageable craving. It is not difficult to pray with the *lips* for renewed character and serviceable life, for social justice and the triumph of the Gospel. The Bible shows us in many a familiar passage what we *ought* to pray for. The liturgies of the churches too are beautifully eloquent with prayers that welled up from sincerely aspiring hearts, and we readily can frame petitions that copy the letter of the churches' prayers. A man in this superficial sense may gain the trick of public supplication. His prayers are eloquent and beautiful, they are verbal aspiration after most worthy things. But as with "Solomon's Prayer" at the dedication of the temple, there is an appalling hiatus between the requests publicly made and the manifest desires of the man who prays. *Prayer that is not dominant desire is too weak to achieve anything.* Any loitering student can cheaply pray to be learned; any idler in the market place can pray to be rich; any irresolute dodger of duty can pray for a vigorous character. But such praying is not really prayer.

"Prayer is the *soul's sincere desire,*
Uttered or unexpressed,
The motion of a hidden *fire*
That trembles in the breast."

This perception of the nature of true prayer as dominant desire addressed to God, lights up two important matters. For one thing it adds a significant contribution to our thought on unanswered prayer. *It suggests that while a man's outward petition may be denied, his dominant desire, which is his real prayer, may be granted.* Parents for example pray for their children's character and usefulness. They ask that godliness and public-mindedness may make their sons and daughters men and women of spiritual distinction. Such supplications are eminently worthy; but too often, proper as they are, they do not represent the parents' dominant desire. The real wish that controls decisions, that creates the atmosphere of the home and shapes the character of the children, is the parents' ambition for the children's wealth or social success. There lies the family's masterful craving. Now as between the spoken prayer and the dominant desire, is there any question which will be answered? The fact is that the *real* prayer of that family tends inevitably to be answered. Many a man would have to confess that for all his denied petition, he had gotten what his heart was inwardly set upon. The controlling passion in any life draws an answer, sometimes with appalling certainty.

Men are given to complaining of unanswered prayer, but *the great disasters are due to answered prayers.* The trouble with men is that so often they *do* get what they want. When the prodigal in the far country came to himself, friends gone, reputation gone, willpower almost gone, to find himself poor, hungry, feeding swine, he was suffering from the consequence of an answered prayer, a dominant desire fulfilled. So Lot wanted Sodom, and got it; Ahab craved Naboth's vineyard, and seized it; Judas desired the thirty pieces, and obtained them. The Bible is full of answered prayers that ruined men. The power of dominant desire is terrific. Again and again in history we see the old truth come true: "He gave them their request, but sent leanness into their soul!" (Psalm 106:15).

"O Gracious Lord, how blind we are,
On our own ruin bent!
Make not thine answer to our prayer
Our bitterest punishment!

"For to importunate approach
Persistent in its wrong,
Thou grantest its deluded wish
To make thy warning strong."

VI

*This perception of the nature of prayer as dominant desire also
lights up one of the most notable causes of failure in praying—insincerity.* The Master laid reiterated emphasis upon sincerity in prayer.
He meant that the petition offered must be the genuine overflow of
inward desire. The fault of the Pharisees who prayed on the corners
was not that they were asking for unworthy things. Their petitions
were doubtless excellent, springing out of scriptural ideas and
couched in scriptural language. But the prayers did not represent
the inward and determining wishes of the men. The petitions were
not sincere. The lives of the Pharisees blatantly advertised that their
habitual ambitions did not tally with their occasional supplications.
When the Master bids us make prayer private, to think of God
when we pray as "the Father who seeth in secret," to use no futile
and repetitious formulas but to go at once to the pith of our want
(Matt. 6:5ff), he is making a plea for sincerity. Prayer to him is the
heart, with all its most genuine and worthy desires aflame, rising up
to lay hold on God. It is no affair of hasty words at the fag-end of
a day, no form observed in deference to custom, no sop to conscience to ease us from the sense of religious obligations unfulfilled.
Prayer is the central and determining force of a man's life. *Prayer is
dominant desire, calling God into alliance.*

The fact that we do not stand on street corners to perform our
devotions ought not to blind us to the subtle temptation by which,
even in private, we are led into theatrical, insincere praying. We
pray as we think we *ought* to. We ask for blessings that we feel are
properly to be asked for, graces that we *should* want, whether we do
or not. We mask ourselves behind an imaginary personage—ourselves disguised in court clothes and asking from God the things
which we presume God would like to be asked to give. We cry as St.
Augustine did, "O Lord, make me pure"; and then we hear our real
self add as his did, "but *not now!*" How much such praying there is
and how utterly ineffective! It is not real. We have not at the center
of our lives controlling desires so worthy that we can ask God to

further them and so earnest that our prayers are the spontaneous utterance of their urgency.

In the last chapter we spoke of such petitions as "Thy kingdom come," which for nearly twenty centuries has been the prayer of the church. But how many have *really* prayed it? In how many has it been the dominant desire? Economists describe what they call "effective demand." It is the demand of those who not only need commodities, but who are willing and able to pay the price. Only when a petition becomes an "effective demand" is it real prayer. When a man rehearses all the blessings he has prayed for himself and the world, he may well go on to ask whether he really wishes the prayers granted. Is he willing to pay the price? The great servants of the Kingdom in history always have been men of prayer and the implication is sometimes suggested that praying would make us similarly serviceable. But this essential element should never be forgotten, that the great servants of the Kingdom were men of powerful prayer because they were men of dominant desires for whose fulfilment they were willing to sacrifice anything. Paul, Carey, Livingstone, and all their spiritual kin praying for the triumph of Christ with all their hearts and hurling their lives after their prayers; St. Augustine at last *really* praying for purity, until the answer involved tearing loose the dearest ties of his past life—these are examples of costly praying which achieves results. This is not prayer called in to eke out what is lacking in an otherwise contented life; this is life centering in and swung round prayer like planets round the sun. Prayer becomes serious business when it becomes dominant desire. We stand there at life's center, at the springs of its motive and the sources of its power.

A cursory reading of the Beatitudes awakens surprise because prayer is not mentioned there. How could the Master sum up the benedictions of the spiritual life and omit prayer from his thought? Turn to them again, then, and read more deeply. The Master put prayer into the Beatitudes in one of the greatest descriptions to be found in the Bible: "Blessed are they that *hunger and thirst* after righteousness: for they shall be filled" (Matt. 5:6). Prayer is hunger and thirst. *Prayer is our demand on life, elevated, purified, and aware of a Divine Alliance.*

SUGGESTIONS FOR THOUGHT AND DISCUSSION

What is the relation between prayer and a person's dominant desires and purposes?

How far does prayer represent the real purpose and desire of the man?

When do the words spoken in prayer fail to represent the real prayers?

How far can a man's character be measured by his prayers?

What is the difference between outward petition and a dominant desire of a life?

What effect upon the answer to prayer has a person's dominant desire?

Can prayer which does not represent dominant desire be answered? Why or why not?

What made the difference in the prayer for forgiveness of the servant who owed ten thousand talents and the one who owed one hundred shillings? When has a person a right to expect an answer to a prayer for forgiveness?

How far was the first missionary tour of Paul the result of prayer? What is the difference between offering a prayer for missions and offering ourselves?

When is a nation's prayer for peace sincere? To what extent does prejudice against other classes and nations interfere with an effective prayer for peace?

When are we justified in praying for the poor? for our friends? for forgiveness? for world brotherhood? for missions?

Are all prayers representing dominant desire answered?

When is prayer sincere?

Why did the Master denounce the prayers of the Pharisees?

Why does lack of time for meditation make for insincerity in prayer?

When does a person really pray "Thy kingdom come"?

What is the relation of procrastination to the inefficacy of prayer?

What light do the Beatitudes throw upon the prerequisite of answered prayer?

What makes the difference between a petition addressed to God and a sincere prayer?

What makes for insincerity in prayer?

What is the relation of dominant desire to sincerity in prayer?

How can I make my prayers sincerely represent my dominant desires?

CHAPTER IX

Prayer as a Battlefield

DAILY READINGS

First Day, Ninth Week

Behold, thou desirest truth in the inward parts;
And in the hidden part thou wilt make me to know wisdom.
Purify me with hyssop, and I shall be clean:
Wash me, and I shall be whiter than snow.
Make me to hear joy and gladness,
That the bones which thou hast broken may rejoice.
Hide thy face from my sins,
And blot out all mine iniquities.
Create in me a clean heart, O God;
And renew a right spirit within me.
Cast me not away from thy presence;
And take not thy holy Spirit from me.
Restore unto me the joy of thy salvation;
And uphold me with a willing spirit.
Then will I teach transgressors thy ways;
And sinners shall be converted unto thee.—Psalm 51:6-13.

The Psalmist is praying here for a cleansed and empowered personality. The secret place where he first offered these entreaties must have been to him a battlefield. There took place those inner struggles on whose issue moral purity and power depend. *Prayer is the innermost form of the fight for character.* As Clement of Alexandria in the second century, put it, "The aim of prayer is to attain the habit of goodness, so as no longer merely to have the things that are good, but rather to be good," and in our generation George Meredith restates the same truth, "Who rises from his prayer a better man, his prayer is answered." *The profoundest need of the world is clean, strong, devoted personality.* We are poor there—not in material prosperity or organizing skill or intellectual ingenuity, but in radiant, infectious, convincing personality. The real poverty is poverty of character, and that is due in how large a measure to the lack of those spiritual disciplines and fellowships which are included in genuine prayer! Let us consider this week the service of prayer as an inner battlefield on which the issues of character are settled.

O God, make perfect my love toward Thee and to my Redeemer and Justifier; give me a true and unfeigned love to all virtue and godliness, and to all Thy chosen people wheresoever they be dispersed throughout all the world; increase in me strength and victory against all temptations and assaults of the flesh, the world, and the devil, that according to Thy promise I be never further proved or tempted than Thou wilt give me strength to overcome. Give me grace to keep a good conscience; give me a pure heart and mind, and renew a right spirit within me. Amen.—Christian Prayers (1556).

Second Day, Ninth Week

And at even, when the sun did set, they brought unto him all that were sick, and them that were possessed with demons. And all the city was gathered together at the door. And he healed many that were sick with divers diseases, and cast out many demons; and he suffered not the demons to speak, because they knew him. And in the morning, a great while before day, he rose up and went out, and departed into a desert place, and there prayed. And Simon and they that were with him followed after him; and they found him, and say unto him, All are seeking thee. And he saith unto them, Let us go elsewhere into the next towns, that I may preach there also; for to this end came I forth. And he went into their synagogues throughout all Galilee, preaching and casting out demons. —Mark 1:32-39.

Was not this solitary prayer of the Master a battle for courage and strength to go on? It came between the crushing labors of Capernaum and the preaching tour that lay ahead; it came at a time when the storm of the Pharisees' wrath was gathering. If the Master needed the courage that comes in solitary prayer, can we well dispense with it? Many lives would be incalculably strengthened, their tone would be changed from anxious timidity to power, if they would learn the secret of this inner fellowship. It is said that Napoleon before a great battle would stand alone in his tent, and one by one the marshals and commanders of his armies would enter, grasp his hand in silence, and go out again—fired with a new courage and resolute in a new willingness to die for France. Some such effect those souls have felt who have learned the secret of prayer's power.

O Thou, who art the ever-blessed God, the underlying Peace of the world, and who wouldst draw all men into the companionship of Thy joy; speak, we beseech Thee, to this Thy servant, for whom we pray. Take him by the hand and say unto him, "Fear not; for I am with thee. I have called thee by my name; thou art mine." Put such a spirit of trust within him that all fear and foreboding shall be cast out, and that right reason and calm assurance may rule his thoughts and impulses. Let quietness and confidence be his strength. Reveal to him the vision of a universe guided and governed by Thy wise and loving care; and show him that around and about him are Thy unseen and beneficent powers. Lift up his whole being into communion with Thy life and thought. Let him ever remember that Thou dost not give to any the spirit of fearfulness, but a spirit of power and love and self-mastery. In this faith, grant, O Lord, that he may summon the energies of his soul against the miseries that cast him down. Give him courage, confidence, an untroubled heart, and a love that loves all creatures, great and small, for Thy love's sake. Amen.—Samuel McComb.

Third Day, Ninth Week

Finally, be strong in the Lord, and in the strength of his might. Put on the whole armor of God, that ye may be able to stand against the wiles of the devil. For our wrestling is not against flesh and blood, but against the principalities, against the powers, against the world-rulers of this darkness, against the spiritual hosts of wickedness in the heavenly places. Wherefore take up the whole armor of God, that ye may be able to withstand in the evil day, and, having done all, to stand. Stand therefore, having girded your loins with truth, and having put on the breastplate of righteousness, and having shod your feet with the preparation of the gospel of peace; withal taking up the shield of faith, wherewith ye shall be able to quench all the fiery darts of the evil one. And take the helmet of salvation, and the sword of the Spirit, which is the sword of God: with all prayer and supplication praying at all seasons in the Spirit, and watching thereunto in all perseverance and supplication for all the saints.—Eph. 6:10-18.

Note the surprising conclusion of this warlike passage. The man is armed for conflict and then the climax reads "with all prayer . . . praying." To the Apostle prayer evidently has a warlike aspect. He is writing this passage in prison, where he needs *fortitude to endure.* In prayer he finds the battlefield where he fights his fears and gains enduring power that he may be able, "having done all, to stand." How many people weakly give way in the face of trouble, lose their spirit, fall into self-pity, and refuse to join that great succession of God's people who have proved by the way they handled their troubles, even more than by the way they handled their talents, what God can do for a man of faith! It is said that in a newly invented vacuum furnace everything in a log of wood that is destructible can be consumed, leaving only an irreducible minimum that man's skill is not yet great enough to burn. And we are told that that indestructible remainder is pure carbon, *every bit of which the tree took from the sunlight through the leaves.* Many may think of prayer as a strange way of gaining power to endure, but the indestructible elements of the soul, that cannot be crushed or consumed by adversity, do come from our spiritual fellowship with God.

Consider this prayer of Lady Jane Grey in her last imprisonment:

O Merciful God, be Thou now unto me a strong tower of defence, I humbly entreat Thee. Give me grace to await Thy leisure, and patiently to bear what Thou doest unto me; nothing doubting or mistrusting Thy goodness towards me; for Thou knowest what is good for me better than I do. Therefore do with me in all things what Thou wilt; only arm me, I beseech Thee, with Thine armour, that I may stand fast; above all things, taking to me the shield of faith; praying always that I may refer myself wholly to Thy will, abiding Thy pleasure, and comforting myself in those troubles which it shall please Thee to send me, seeing such troubles are

profitable for me; and I am assuredly persuaded that all Thou doest cannot but be well; and unto Thee be all honour and glory. Amen.
—Lady Jane Grey (1537-1554).

Fourth Day, Ninth Week

Then was Jesus led up of the Spirit into the wilderness to be tempted of the devil. And when he had fasted forty days and forty nights, he afterward hungered. And the tempter came and said unto him, If thou art the Son of God, command that these stones become bread. But he answered and said, It is written, Man shall not live by bread alone, but by every word that proceedeth out of the mouth of God. Then the devil taketh him into the holy city; and he set him on the pinnacle of the temple, and saith unto him, If thou art the Son of God, cast thyself down: for it is written,

He shall give his angels charge concerning thee:
and,

On their hands they shall bear thee up,
Lest haply thou dash thy foot against a stone.

Jesus said unto him, Again it is written, Thou shalt not make trial of the Lord thy God. Again, the devil taketh him unto an exceeding high mountain, and showeth him all the kingdoms of the world, and the glory of them; and he said unto him, All these things will I give thee, if thou wilt fall down and worship me. Then saith Jesus unto him, Get thee hence, Satan: for it is written, Thou shalt worship the Lord thy God, and him only shalt thou serve. Then the devil leaveth him; and behold, angels came and ministered unto him.—Matt. 4:1-11.

These verses are the record of an inward struggle in which the Master fought out the purpose of his life. The use of Scripture, the continual reference in Jesus' words to God and God's claims on men, indicate the atmosphere of devotion in which this battle was fought. *Do we deal with our temptations in this high way?* Consider our besetting sins—temper, passion, irreverence or whatever other form of self-will we may most easily fall into, and think of the ways the habitual use of inward prayer would help us. How an improper story or a mean judgment withers on our lips if a fine, high-minded personality happens to join the circle! And what a cleansing effect takes place in our lives if we grow accustomed to usher God upon the scene when uncleanness or ill-temper or self-will appears! Gradually but surely those feelings and thoughts which are not comfortable when God is present disappear. The life grows clear of those tempers and attitudes that make spontaneous prayer impossible. "The devil leaveth him."

O Thou, who proclaimest liberty to the captives, and the opening of the prisons to them that are bound; we rejoice that Thou hast brought the soul of this Thy servant out of prison that he might praise Thy name. Thou didst inspire him with pure desires. Thou didst rouse him again and again from despair and didst sustain him in the fight for freedom. And now we bless Thee that Thou hast crowned his efforts with success. Abide with him and in him that henceforth he may bear the fruits of good living. So fill him with love and holiness, with courage and trust, that through all the coming days temptation will lose its power. Let the dead past bury its dead. Go with him into the new world of joy and peace and health. Inspire him with the resolve to do something for Thy sake, to tell another imprisoned soul what great things Thou hast done that, if it please Thee, he may have a double joy. Hear our thanksgiving and bless us through Jesus Christ, our Lord. Amen.—Samuel McComb.

Fifth Day, Ninth Week

Is any among you suffering? let him pray. Is any cheerful? let him sing praise. Is any among you sick? let him call for the elders of the church; and let them pray over him, anointing him with oil in the name of the Lord: and the prayer of faith shall save him that is sick, and the Lord shall raise him up; and if he have committed sins, it shall be forgiven him. Confess therefore your sins one to another, and pray one for another, that ye may be healed. The supplication of a righteous man availeth much in its working.— James 5:13-16.

Never more than in our day has the wisdom of this ancient advice been clear. *Prayer is the inner battlefield where men often conquer most effectually the false worries, trivial anxieties, morbid humors and all the unwholesome specters of the mind that irritate the spirit and make the body ill.* There they learn Paul's lesson, "In nothing be anxious; but in everything by prayer and supplication with thanksgiving let your requests be made known unto God. And the peace of God, which passeth all understanding, shall guard your hearts and your thoughts in Christ Jesus" (Phil. 4:6, 7). Dr. Hyslop, Superintendent of Bethlehem Royal Hospital, at the annual meeting of the British Medical Association in 1905, said: "As an alienist, and one whose whole life has been concerned with the sufferings of the mind, I would state that of all hygienic measures to counteract disturbed, sleep-depressed spirits, and all the miserable sequels of a distressed mind, I would undoubtedly give the first place to the simple habit of prayer."

Ever Blessed God, whose word is, "Peace, peace to him that is far off and to him that is near," fulfil Thy promise to this Thy servant for whom we pray. Rescue him from the misery of groundless fears and restless anxieties. Take him more and more out of himself, that duty may be no longer a drudgery but a delight. Lead him into the secret of Thy peace which quiets every misgiving and fills the heart with joy and confidence. Save him from the shame and emptiness of a hurried life. Grant him to possess his soul in patience. Amid the storms and stress of life, let him hear a deeper voice assuring him that Thou livest and that all is well. Strengthen him to do his daily work in quietness and confidence, fearing no tomorrow, nor the evil that it brings, for Thou art with him. And this we ask for Jesus Christ's sake. Amen.—Samuel McComb.

Sixth Day, Ninth Week

And he went forward a little, and fell on his face, and prayed, saying, My Father, if it be possible, let this cup pass away from me: nevertheless, not as I will, but as thou wilt.—Matt. 26:39.

Again a second time he went away, and prayed, saying, My Father, if this cannot pass away, except I drink it, thy will be done. —Matt. 26:42.

And he said, Abba, Father, all things are possible unto thee; remove this cup from me: howbeit not what I will, but what thou wilt.—Mark 14:36.

Father, if thou be willing, remove this cup from me: nevertheless not my will, but thine, be done.—Luke 22:42.

Consider the battlefield of Gethsemane. Was there ever a more eventful engagement than that? *It was a struggle for clear vision to see and strength to do the will of God.* Peter Annet, an old Deist, used to say that praying men are like sailors who have cast anchor on a rock, and who imagine they are pulling the rock to themselves, when they are really pulling themselves to the rock. But that is a caricature of what praying men at their best think. The Master here was deliberately trying to pull himself to the rock. That was the objective of the struggle in the garden. The will of God was settled; he wanted clearly to see it and strongly to be apprehended by it, and he called God in to fight the narrower self will that opposed the larger devotion. What a deep experience such praying brings into any life that knows it! As Phillips Brooks exclaimed: "God's mercy seat is no mere stall set by the vulgar road side, where every careless passer-by may put an easy hand out to snatch any glittering blessing that catches his eye. It stands in the holiest of holies. We can come to it only through veils and by altars of purification. To enter into it, we must enter into God."

O God, who hast in mercy taught us how good it is to follow the holy desires which Thou manifoldly puttest into our hearts, and how bitter is the grief of falling short of whatever beauty our minds behold, strengthen us, we beseech Thee, to walk steadfastly throughout life in the better path which our hearts once chose; and give us wisdom to tread it prudently in Thy fear, as well as cheerfully in Thy love; so that, having been faithful to Thee all the days of our life here, we may be able hopefully to resign ourselves into Thy hands hereafter. Amen.—Rowland Williams (1818-1870).

Seventh Day, Ninth Week

And I said, O my God, I am ashamed and blush to lift up my face to thee, my God; for our iniquities are increased over our head, and our guiltiness is grown up unto the heavens. Since the days of our fathers we have been exceeding guilty unto this day; and for our iniquities have we, our kings, and our priests, been delivered into the hand of the kings of the lands, to the sword, to captivity, and to plunder, and to confusion of face, as it is this day. . . . And now, O our God, what shall we say after this? for we have forsaken thy commandments . . . And after all that is come upon us for our evil deeds, and for our great guilt, seeing that thou our God hast punished us less than our iniquities deserve, and hast given us such a remnant, shall we again break thy commandments . . . ? O Jehovah, the God of Israel, thou art righteous; for we are left a remnant that is escaped, as it is this day: behold, we are before thee in our guiltiness; for none can stand before thee because of this.— Ezra 9:6, 7, 10, 13-15.

See how plainly the concern with which this prayer is burdened is the character of the people. Ezra's interest as he prays is moral; he wants transformed life, cleansed personality, empowered manhood, social righteousness. This week we have been noting some special aspects of this central objective in prayer. We have seen how moral courage, fortitude, power in temptation, spiritual poise and clear vision of God's will, may all be won upon the inner battlefield of prayer. Consider the vitality that such a use of prayer puts into the religious life. It involves making God an actual partner in our moral struggle; it fills our religion with practical significance. Gladstone, in a letter to the Duchess of Sutherland, wrote: "There is one proposition which the experience of life burns into my soul; it is this, that a man should beware of letting his religion spoil his morality. In a thousand ways, some great, some small, but all subtle, we are daily tempted to that great sin." The sort of praying described in this chapter is the most efficient guard against that evil. It makes the center of religion a fight for character.

Strong Son of God, who was tried and tempted to the uttermost, yet without sin; be near me now with Thy strength and give me the victory over this evil desire that threatens to ruin me. I am weak, O Lord, and full of doubts and fears. There are moments when I am afraid of myself, when the world and the flesh and the devil seem more powerful than the forces of good. But now I look to Thee in whom dwelleth all the fulness of grace and might and redemption. Blessed Saviour! I take Thee afresh to be my Refuge, my Covert, my Defence, my strong Tower from the enemy. Hear me and bless me now and ever. Amen.—Samuel McComb.

COMMENT FOR THE WEEK

I

If we define praying as "Communion with God," we naturally think of it as fellowship with a friend, and so emphasize its peaceful aspect. When Robert Burns bewailed the fact that he could not "pour out his inmost soul without reserve to any human being without danger of one day repenting his confidence," he expressed a need which is met in the lives of those who habitually commune with God. Prayer means restfulness, quietude; men come from it saying,

"And I smiled to think God's greatness flowed around our incompleteness;
Round our restlessness, his rest."

As Jeremy Taylor described it, "Prayer is the peace of our spirit, the stillness of our thought, the evenness of our recollection."

Now, praying is all of this, but none can think of it as dominant desire without seeing that it is more. *Prayer is a battlefield.* When a man, hungering and thirsting after righteousness, calls God into alliance, he does so because he has a fight on his hands. He may have set his heart in dominant desire on goodness, but that desire meets enemies that must be beaten. "No man ever became a saint in his sleep." From without, the influences of the world assail his best ambitions; from within, the perverse inclinations of his own heart make war on his right resolutions. A fight is on in every aspiring life. Sometimes, like the captain of a ship in mid-sea with a tempest raging and his own crew in rebellion, a man must at once steady his course amid outward temptations, and hold a pistol at the head of his mutinous desires. No one in earnest about goodness has ever succeeded in describing the achievement of goodness except in terms of a fight. "The flesh lusteth against the Spirit, and the Spirit against the flesh," says Paul, "I buffet my body, and bring it into bondage."

In this moral battle, as in every other, *the decisive part of the engagement is not public and ostentatious; it is in secret.* Long before the armies clash in the open field, there has been a conflict in the general's office, where pro met con, and the determinations were reached that controlled each movement of the outward war. Even in law, "Cases are won in chambers." So, in the achievement of character there is a hidden battlefield on which the decisive conflicts of the world are waged. Behind the Master's public ministry, through which he moved with such amazing steadfastness, not to be deflected by bribes, nor halted by fears, nor discouraged by weariness, lay the battles in the desert where he fought out in prayer the controlling principles of his life. Behind his patience in Pilate's

Court, and his fidelity on Calvary, lay the battle in Gethsemane, where the whole problem was fought through and the issue settled before the face of God. All public consequences go back to secret conflicts. Napoleon sat for hours in silent thought before he ordered the Russian Campaign. Washington, praying at Valley Forge, was settling questions on which the independence of his country hung. We are deceived by the garish stage-settings of big scenes in history. The really great scenes are seldom evident. *The decisive battles of the world are hidden, and all the outward conflicts are but the echo and reverberation of that more real and inward war.*

To be sure, prayer, which at its best is thus a fight for character, can be perverted to the hurt of character. Because certain temperaments are so constituted that they can experience a high degree of tranquil peace, and sometimes ecstatic delight, in protracted communion with God, the exaggerations of the mystic are always possible. "I made many mistakes," said Madame Guyon, "through allowing myself to be too much taken up by my interior joys." Nothing so hurts genuine piety as that spurious piety which is expressed, at its extreme limit, in the words of the Blessed Angela of Fulginio, "In that time and by God's will there died my mother, who was a great hindrance unto me in following the way of God: my husband died likewise, and in a short time there also died all my children. And because I had commenced to follow the aforesaid Way, and had prayed God that he would rid me of them, I had great consolation of their deaths, albeit I did also feel some grief." The worst enemies of prayer are those who thus speak much of it and revel much in it, but whose lives exhibit in ordinary relationships little of the trustworthiness, the "plain devotedness to duty," the thoughtful generosity and large-heartedness, which are the proper fruits of real communion with God. Jesus himself called his enraptured disciples away from the Mount of Transfiguration, where they wished to prolong their glowing experience, and led them down to save a demoniac groveling in the valley (Matt. 17:2-18). He would be the first to rebuke us for praying, "Lord, Lord," and not doing the things which he says (Matt. 7:21). The real pray-ers, however, have not thus weltered in futile emotion, supposed to be induced by God; they have been warriors who on the inner battlefield fought out the issues of righteousness with God as their ally.

II

As one seeks in the biographies of praying men to discover in terms of actual experience what prayer as a battlefield has meant to them, *he sees that for one thing it has been the place where they reconquered faith and reestablished confidence in God and in themselves.* Professor Royce, of Harvard, has given us this testimony from a friend: "When things are too much for me, and I am down on my luck, and everything is dark, I go alone by myself, and I bury my head in my hands, I think hard that God must know it all and will see how matters really are, and understand me; and in just that way alone, by understanding me, will help me. And so I try to get myself together, and that, for me, is prayer." St. Francis, of Assisi, used to sit in prayer by the hour, with no spoken word except the occasional exclamation, "God." Doubts, it may be, had assailed his faith; the clamor of the flesh had dulled the voice of the spirit; practical perplexities had distracted his life; and he went out from all of these to take a reassuring look at the Eternal. He "got himself together," and came back—"things seen" a little more obscure, "things unseen" vivid. Of how many powerful lives is this the secret!

> "As torrents in summer
> Half-dried in their channels,
> Suddenly rise, though the
> Sky is still cloudless,
> For rain has been falling
> Far off at their fountains;
>
> "So hearts that are fainting
> Grow full to o'erflowing,
> And they that behold it
> Marvel, and know not
> That God at their fountains
> Far off has been raining!"

This sort of inward self-conquest to some may seem impractical. They feel about it as a man may feel, who, not understanding what astronomy has done for life, goes into an observatory and sees the astronomer studying the stars. That the world needs ploughs and looms and locomotives is as plain as a pike-staff; that the real wants of men are on the earth, not in the heavens, appears so obvious that this hard-headed man of common sense may wonder what use could be made of a star-gazing tube that looks away from earth and seeks the sky. But the fact is that the star-gazer sets the clock by which we time our simplest tasks; he made the almanac by which we measure all our days. We never caught a train, nor figured time on contracts, nor set ourselves to any common duty, that we did not put ourselves under obligation to the astronomer. Men never understood this earth until they looked away from it. It never was truly seen until it was seen in its infinite relationships. Galileo and Kepler and Copernicus did not idly dream in impractical aloofness from the needs of men: they rather fought out in their observatories a conflict for the truth that has remade the world. So prayer is an observatory. Even though our only solitude is that of the woman in the tenement who said, "I throw my apron over my head when I want solitude; it is all that I can get," prayer may still be our observatory; and there outlooks are attained that orient life aright, that reveal perspective and give proportion, so that the solitary conflict proves the redemption of every day's most common task.

III

The biographies of praying men show us also that *their struggles for right desire were fought out on the battlefield of prayer.* We said in the last chapter that prayer is real only when it voices an elevated and purified demand on life, calling God into alliance. But such praying requires in us the very thing we lack. Let a man try as he will to set his heart on righteousness, the course of that desire does not flow smoothly; it is impeded, sometimes halted, by landslides and cross-currents. The profoundest trouble in our characters is our wayward appetites. The old picture of a Judgment Day gains its terror not so much from thunder, lightning, shaken earth, and falling mountains, nor from anything that these may signify. What would cover us with unutterable shame is the fulfilment of the repeated scriptural threat, *All secret desires known* (Eccl. 12:14; Rom. 2:16; I Cor. 4:5). No one could endure that with equanimity. When one contemplates the possibility, he becomes aware that the deepest need in character is right desire.

Now, prayer has been the battlefield where the war against wrong desire has been fought out. George Adam Smith in a Dwight Hall talk at Yale suggested that no one had so frankly revealed this use of prayer as a battlefield for the conquest of desire as "Chinese" Gordon. A search of his letters to his sister reveals the truth of this. "I can say for my part," writes Gordon, "that backbiting and envy were my delight, and even now often lead me astray, but by dint of perseverance in prayer, God has given me the mastery to a *great degree;* I did not *wish to give it up,* so I besought him to give me *that wish;* he did so, and then I had the promise of his fulfilment." Even more vividly does Gordon put his use of prayer when he speaks of Agag—his figure for his own selfish ambition and pride: "My constant prayer is against Agag, who, of course, is here, and as insinuating as ever"; "I had a terrible struggle this morning with Agag"; "I had a terrible half-hour this morning, hewing Agag in pieces before the Lord."

Who can fail to see what Gordon meant? Some impurity was in him and he hauled it before the face of God and slew it there; some selfish ambition, counter to the will of God, he dragged up into the light and hewed in pieces before the Lord. Prayer is so often spoken of as the preparation for the fight of life that it is worth while to note how truly here prayer was the fight itself. Prayer, to Gordon, was no drill, where forms were observed that might add to the army's graces or even to its future efficiency; prayer was the actual battle between a wrong desire and a right one, with God called in as an ally. He went to prayer as to earnest business, saying with the Psalmist, "Lord, all my desire is before thee" (Psalm 38:9). Day by day he returned to cast down unholy passions and selfish aims and to confirm every true ambition in the sight of God. The very fountains of his life, the springs from which all action comes, were cleansed, until that injunction which Hartley Coleridge put into verse became the familiar prose of his daily living:

> "Whate'er is good to wish, ask that of heaven,
>   Though it be what thou canst not hope to see;
> Pray to be perfect though the material leaven
>   Forbid the spirit so on earth to be;
> But if for any wish thou dar'st not pray,
> Then pray to God to cast that wish away."

IV

The biographies of praying men show also that prayer was *the battlefield where they fought out the issue between the two conflicting motives that most master human life—the praise of the world, on the one side, and the approval of God on the other.* One distinguishing quality of superior souls is their capacity to discount the praise of men and to set their hearts singly upon pleasing God. We catch the note in Socrates before he drinks the hemlock, "We must obey not men, but God"; we hear it in Peter facing persecution, "We must obey God rather than men" (Acts 5:29). Such men were not so acutely aware of the public opinion of the earth as they were of the Public Opinion of the universe, in the sight of which they set themselves to stand clear and blameless. They lived as Milton sang of Abdiel:

> "This was all thy care—
> To stand approved in sight of God, though worlds
> Judged thee perverse."

At times the vividness with which such souls perceive the will of God for them, and the steadiness with which they do it, despite the condemnation of their fellows, lifts heroism to superhuman heights. Like the boy in school who pitched his best game of ball on the Saturday after his blind father died, because he said it was the first game that his father had ever watched him pitch, so these men live and work in the vivid consciousness of the "Father who seeth in secret." Their dominant motive is to satisfy him.

But such living as this costs a fight. God is not the only one whom we may try to please. Evil assumes its most seductive form when it appeals to this same motive—when some wrong-minded friend requests what good conscience cannot grant, or when popular taste sets the tone of living low and offers us praise if we will join the song. Sin in the abstract is hateful, but when it clothes itself in human flesh and waits to smile approval upon our compliance, it becomes tremendously attractive. Drink and impurity and all their ilk are horrible in theory, but dressed in the invitation of a friend, made alluringly incarnate in a person, what terrific fascination they may gain! Would Herod have slain John if the deed had not been pleasing to Herodias? Would Antipas have killed James and imprisoned Peter if he had not seen that "it pleased the Jews"? Would Charles IX have ordered the massacre of St. Bartholomew if his mother had not wanted it?

To be sure, there are times when to please God and to please some human friend are synonymous. From the time our only possible understanding of our duty was to deserve the approval of our parents, until now when the commendation of our worthy friends is life's highest earthly gratification, duty has assumed its most attractive form when it clothed itself in a person to be pleased. Stopford Brooke tells us that while gathering material for his life of Robertson of Brighton, he stepped into a Brighton bookstore and noticed a picture of Robertson upon the wall. "Yes," said the bookseller, "whenever I am tempted to do anything mean I look at that face, and it recalls me to my better self."

Many a living friend has so served us, and in the satisfaction of that friend's ideal for us we found duty no cold keeping of a law, but the warm pleasing of a person. Indeed, neither right nor wrong is often presented to our choice as an abstract proposition. They are almost always incarnate; they have faces and hands, and blood flows through them; they appeal to us with all the enticement that human flesh and a human voice can give. Because, therefore, to displease people causes us most acute unhappiness, and to win their approval is life's most poignant satisfaction, some of the severest battles in the moral life must be fought about this issue. If there is any commandment in Scripture most difficult of all to keep, it is this: "If thy brother, the son of thy mother, or thy son, or thy daughter, or the wife of thy bosom, or thy friend, that is as thine own soul, entice thee secretly, saying, Let us go and serve other gods, . . . thou shalt not consent unto him, nor hearken unto him" (Deut. 13:6, 8).

This conflict between the desire to please God and those who represent him, and to please the generation in which he lived was the central struggle of the Master's life, and he fought it out in prayer. We look at him now, across the centuries, and all his life seems singly set on pleasing God. To satisfy his Father was his motive, the possibility of doing it his joy, the consciousness of having done it his recompense. His great hours, such as his baptism and transfiguration, were blessed with the assurance that he was the beloved Son in whom God was well pleased; his idea of daily duty was defined in his own words, "I do always the things that are pleasing to him" (John 8:29); and when he thought of heaven and reward he dreamed of no golden streets and gates of pearl—he saw only his approving Father saying, "Well done, good and faithful servant." But even with the Master this life involved an inward war. To please God meant to displease his family, the leaders of his nation, the venerable fathers of his people's faith; it meant desertion by his friends and calumny from his enemies; it meant that he would be thought crazy by his household, a traitor by his nation, and a heretic by his church.

This great battle of the Master was waged in prayer, before ever its results were seen in public. In many a secret conflict the engagement was fought out, until in Gethsemane he "offered up prayers and supplications with strong crying and tears unto him that he was able to save him from death" (Heb. 5:7). That sort of praying is a real battle, not a dress parade. Jeremy Taylor may call prayer "the peace of our spirits, the stillness of our thoughts"; but when David Brainerd, colonial missionary to the Indians, comes out from one of his Gethsemanes, saying, "My joints were loosed; the sweat ran down my face and body as if it would dissolve," it is clear that Taylor's definition is inadequate. *Prayer is a fight for the power to see and the courage to do the will of God.* No man's life can altogether lack that struggle, if he is to achieve dependable integrity that cannot be bought or scared. The best guaranty of a character that is not for sale is this battlefield of prayer, where day by day the issue is settled that we shall live "not as pleasing men, but God who proveth our hearts" (I Thess. 2:4).

v

To the great pray-ers the practice of prayer has meant this vital struggle of which we have been speaking. On that secret battlefield faith and confidence have been reconquered, right desires have been confirmed, and men have gone from it to live "in the sight of God." When men say that they have *no time for praying,* they can hardly have seen the truth that prayer is this innermost, decisive business of life. The time involved in the deliberate practice of prayer may indeed be brief or long. Whitefield, the great companion of the Wesleys, used to lie all day prostrate in prayer, and Luther, in the crisis of his life, said, "I am so busy now that if I did not spend two

or three hours each day in prayer I could not get through the day."
But Spurgeon, quite as good a Christian, when speaking of prolonged prayer said, "I could not do it even if my eternity depended
upon it. Besides, if I go to the bank with a check, what do I wait
loafing around the premises for when I have got my money!" The
length of time is not the decisive matter in prayer. "We may pray
most when we say least," as St. Augustine remarked; "and we may
pray least when we say most." With many of us time must be
divided, as is the land of the United States. The little District given
to Congress for the Federal Government, would on any quantitative
basis be most ill-proportioned. Texas is 4,430 times as large as the
District of Columbia, and even Rhode Island would contain it
twenty times and over. So one, regarding the brief time that a
Christian spends in deliberate prayer, might cry out against such ill
proportion, seeing how business and recreation of necessity pre-
occupy so many hours. But is not the answer clear? In quantity the
little District is small, but it is preeminently powerful. *The government is there.* Nothing goes on in all these states utterly out of the
control and influence of that District. Its mandates are over the
commerce and legislation of all the states; and every mooted question, not elsewhere resolvable, is taken before its Supreme Court
for ultimate decision.

Granted then, that our spiritual District of Columbia must be
smaller in area than our State of Texas, have we done with that
inward District what our fathers did in the nation? Have we
solemnly chosen it and set it sacredly aside? Have we located there
the central government, so that all power issues thence and all
questions come back to it for settlement? Is it apparent to those who
know us best that we would rather any other place in our lives
should be taken by the enemy than this Capital of our Country, the
place of prayer?

SUGGESTIONS FOR THOUGHT AND DISCUSSION

*What determines whether a man's good intentions will issue in
action?*

Why do good intentions fail?
What are the enemies that oppose a man's dominant desires?
Upon what does their strength depend?

What happens to the man whose good intentions habitually fail to result in action?

What is the relative importance of time for preparation and execution in a successful achievement?

To what extent is a victory in a great public battle of life dependent upon previous victory in an unseen battle?

How far are right decisions in times of crisis dependent upon the controlling purpose of life? Where is this purpose determined?

What is the relation of secret prayer to public action?

What was the relation of the Master's habit of prayer to the controlling purpose of his life? What suggestions are given in the record of the temptations?

What place did Jesus give to time for prayer in the critical periods of his life?

What has been the relation of the prayers of praying men to their public action?

What great issues of life must be fought out in secret prayer?

Why does time for secret prayer give assurance of victory? What constitutes complete personal victory for a man in his life struggles? How far is it dependent on securing one's ends?

In these "prayers of preparation" what is the nature of the answer expected of God?

How far is it true that the longer the time spent in secret prayer the greater the victories in practical life?

CHAPTER X

Unselfishness in Prayer

DAILY READINGS

First Day, Tenth Week

And straightway he constrained the disciples to enter into the boat, and to go before him unto the other side, till he should send the multitudes away. And after he had sent the multitudes away, he went up into the mountain apart to pray: and when even was come, he was there alone.—Matt. 14:22, 23.

We are surely right in saying that the dominant motive of the Master's life was service. Yet we find him here sending away multitudes, some of whom he might never have another chance to address, and retiring into the solitude of the hills to pray. Was this selfish? Must we not suppose that he sent away the people, sought solitude, and gave himself to prayer, because he believed that by so doing he was rendering the largest service to others? Make real in your thought the truth of this; consider the increased power for usefulness that came to the Master in his prayer, the recovery from spiritual exhaustion and the fresh sense of God's companionship that he there secured. Are we not often shallow in our service and superficial in our influence, just because we do not escape the multitude long enough for the ministry of unselfish praying alone?

O Merciful Lord, who hast made of one Blood and redeemed by one Ransome all Nations of Men, let me never harden my heart against any that partake of the same Nature and Redemption with me, but grant me an Universal Charity towards all Men. Give me, O Thou Father of Compassions, such a tenderness and meltingness of Heart that I may be deeply affected with all the Miseries and Calamities outward or inward of my Brethren, and diligently keep them in Love: Grant that I may not only seek my own things, but also the things of others. O that this mind may be in us all, which was in the Lord Jesus, that we may love as Brethren, be Pitiful and Courteous, and endeavour heartily and vigorously to keep the Unity of the Spirit in the Bond of Peace, and the God of Grace, Mercy and Peace be with us all. Amen.—Thomas à Kempis (1379-1471).

Second Day, Tenth Week

And he said unto them, Which of you shall have a friend, and shall go unto him at midnight, and say to him, Friend, lend me three loaves; for a friend of mine is come to me from a journey, and I have nothing to set before him: and he from within shall answer and say, Trouble me not: the door is now shut, and my children with me in bed; I cannot rise and give thee? I say unto you, Though he will not rise and give him because he is his friend, yet because of his importunity he will arise and give him as many as he needeth. —Luke 11:5-8.

Notice the suggestive situation which the Master here describes. The one who prays is asking for bread, *not for his own sake, but for his friend's.* The need of another has made him feel the poverty of his own life; "I have nothing to set before him." How much such praying ought to be done!—by parents who feel their insufficiency in meeting their children's deepest needs, by friends who take seriously the fine possibilities of mutual service, by every teacher or minister or physician who deals intimately with human lives, by all in responsible positions in the social or political life of a community. Many of us, like the man in the parable, do not see how empty our cupboards are until a friend "comes to us from a journey," and then our barren uselessness, our ill-equipped spirits, our meager souls shame us. Such persistent importunity as this belongs rightfully to a man who is praying unselfishly—whose cry is motived by desire to have plenty to set before his friend.

Grant unto us, O Lord God, that we may love one another unfeignedly; for where love is, there art Thou; and he that loveth his brother is born of Thee, and dwelleth in Thee, and Thou in him..

And where brethren do glorify Thee with one accord, there dost Thou pour out Thy blessing upon them. Love us, therefore, O Lord, and shed Thy love into our hearts, that we may love Thee, and our brethren in Thee and for Thee, as all children to Thee, through Jesus Christ our Lord. Amen.—Anonymous (1578).

Third Day, Tenth Week

For as the body is one, and hath many members, and all the members of the body, being many, are one body; so also is Christ. For in one Spirit were we all baptized into one body, whether Jews or Greeks, whether bond or free; and were all made to drink of one Spirit. For the body is not one member, but many. If the foot shall say, Because I am not the hand, I am not of the body; it is not therefore not of the body. And if the ear shall say, Because I am not the eye, I am not of the body; it is not therefore not of the body. If the whole body were an eye, where were the hearing? If the whole were hearing, where were the smelling? But now hath God set the members each one of them in the body, even as it pleased him. And if they were all one member, where were the body? But now they are many members, but one body. And the eye cannot say to the hand, I have no need of thee: or again the head to the feet, I have no need of you. . . . And whether one member suffereth, all the members suffer with it; or one member is honored, all the members rejoice with it. Now ye are the body of Christ, and severally members thereof.—I Cor. 12:12-21, 26, 27.

Is not the truth which Paul here puts into his classic figure of body and members, the basic of intercessory prayer? *"No man is the whole of himself; his friends are the rest of him."* A man's bare individuality is like the piece of grit that gets into an oyster shell, but the pearl of his life is made by the relationships that are built up around it. Let a man endeavor to abstract from his life all the meaning that has come from friends, family, and social relationships, and he will soon see how very small his narrow self is, and how his true and greater self is inconceivable without the social body of which he is a member. "In such a kingdom," says Professor Jones of Haverford—"an organic fellowship of interrelated persons—prayer is as normal an activity as gravitation is in a world of matter. Personal spirits experience spiritual gravitations, soul reaches after soul, hearts draw toward each other. We are no longer in the net of blind fate, in the realm of impersonal force, we are in a love-system where the aspiration of one member heightens the entire group, and the need of one—even the least—draws upon the resources of the whole —even the Infinite. We are in actual Divine-human fellowship."

O God, Thou great Redeemer of mankind, our hearts are tender in the thought of Thee, for in all the afflictions of our race Thou hast been afflicted, and in the sufferings of Thy people it was Thy body that was crucified. Thou hast been wounded by our transgressions and bruised by our iniquities, and all our sins are laid at last on Thee. Amid the groaning of creation we behold Thy spirit in Travail till the sons of God shall be born in freedom and holiness.

We pray Thee, O Lord, for the graces of a pure and holy life, that we may no longer add to the dark weight of the world's sin that is laid upon Thee, but may share with Thee in Thy redemptive work. As we have thirsted with evil passions to the destruction of men, do Thou fill us now with hunger and thirst for justice that we may bear glad tidings to the poor and set at liberty all who are in the prison-house of want and sin. Lay Thy spirit upon us and inspire us with a passion of Christ-like love, that we may join our lives to the weak and oppressed and may strengthen their cause by bearing their sorrows. And if the evil that is threatened turns to smite us and if we must learn the dark malignity of sinful power, comfort us by the thought that thus we are bearing in our body the marks of Jesus, and that only those who share in His free sacrifice shall feel the plenitude of Thy life. Help us in patience to carry forward the eternal cross of Thy Christ, counting it joy if we, too, are sown as grains of wheat in the furrows of the world, for only by the agony of the righteous comes redemption.—Walter Rauschenbusch.

Fourth Day, Tenth Week

And in praying use not vain repetitions, as the Gentiles do: for they think that they shall be heard for their much speaking. Be not therefore like unto them: for your Father knoweth what things ye have need of, before ye ask him. After this manner therefore pray ye: Our Father who art in heaven, Hallowed be thy name. Thy kingdom come. Thy will be done, as in heaven, so on earth. Give us this day our daily bread. And forgive us our debts, as we also have forgiven our debtors. And bring us not into temptation, but deliver us from the evil one. For if ye forgive men their trespasses, your heavenly Father will also forgive you. But if ye forgive not men their trespasses, neither will your Father forgive your trespasses. —Matt. 6:7-15.

"When ye pray," said Jesus, "*say, Our*"—"*our* Father," "*our* daily bread," "*our* debts," "*our* debtors." Mark the fact that this prayer is not given simply for public use when many are praying together; it is directly related with the injunction to go into one's closet, shut the door, and pray in secret (Matt. 6:5, 6). Even when in solitude an individual is communing with God, he is to say not merely I and my, but our. The degree to which this social spirit in prayer will take possession of us depends on the vividness with which we perceive the intimate relationships that bind all men together, until each individual is seen not simply as a separate thread but as an inseparable element in the closely woven fabric of human life. "One man," said an old Latin proverb, "is no man at all!" To be sure, he is not. Rather every acquaintanceship is a live-wire connection between one life and another. Suppose that each one of us has a thousand acquaintances, and each one of those a thousand more, and so on over all the earth. Then we are completely intermeshed with one another. No two persons can be selected though one lived on Fifth Avenue, New York, and the other on the plains of Arabia, between whom, by many a circuitous route, live-wire connections might not conceivaby be traced by a mind sufficient for the task. Subtle influences run out from each and sooner or later come to all; no blessing and no disaster ever can be strictly private; common needs, common perils, and common possibilities bind all mankind together. "When ye pray, say, Our."

Once more a new day lies before us, our Father. As we go out among men to do our work, touching the hands and lives of our fellows, make us, we pray Thee, friends of all the world. Save us from blighting the fresh flower of any heart by the flare of sudden anger or secret hate. May we not bruise the rightful self-respect of any by contempt or malice. Help us to cheer the suffering by our sympathy, to freshen the drooping by our hopefulness, and to strengthen in all the wholesome sense of worth and the joy of life. Save us from the deadly poison of class-pride. Grant that we may look all men in the face with the eyes of a brother. If any one needs us, make us ready to yield our help ungrudgingly, unless higher duties claim us, and may we rejoice that we have it in us to be helpful to our fellow-men.—Walter Rauschenbusch.

Fifth Day, Tenth Week

Another parable set he before them, saying, The kingdom of heaven is like unto a grain of mustard seed, which a man took, and sowed in his field: which indeed is less than all seeds; but when it is grown, it is greater than the herbs, and becometh a tree, so that the birds of the heaven come and lodge in the branches thereof.—Matt. 13:31, 32.

The kingdom of heaven is like unto a treasure hidden in the field; which a man found, and hid; and in his joy he goeth and selleth all that he hath, and buyeth that field. Again, the kingdom of heaven is like unto a man that is a merchant seeking goodly pearls: and having found one pearl of great price, he went and sold all that he had, and bought it.—Matt. 13:44-46.

Read these words of the Master in the light of our thought about prayer as dominant desire. How plainly the petition, "Thy kingdom come" represented the controlling passion of Jesus! Prayer at its best always refuses the impossible task of separating the *I* from the *we,* and in its supplications gathers up the common needs of all mankind to carry them in earnest sympathy to God. It thanks God for communal blessings in which all share; it repents for communal sins in which every one of us who has thought selfishly or acted grossly has had some part; and it strives in earnest entreaty for social justice, international peace, the brotherhood of man, the triumph of Christ—every cause on which the welfare of all of us depends. As the Talmud puts it, "A prayer that makes not mention of the Kingdom is no prayer at all."

O Christ, Thou hast bidden us pray for the coming of Thy Father's kingdom, in which His righteous will shall be done on earth. We have treasured Thy words, but we have forgotten their meaning, and Thy great hope has grown dim in Thy Church. We bless Thee for the inspired souls of all ages who saw afar the shining city of God, and by faith left the profit of the present to follow their vision.

We rejoice that to-day the hope of these lonely hearts is becoming the clear faith of millions. Help us, O Lord, in the courage of faith to seize what has now come so near, that the glad day of God may dawn at last. As we have mastered Nature that we might gain wealth, help us now to master the social relations of mankind that we may gain justice and a world of brothers. For what shall it profit our nation if it gain numbers and riches, and lose the sense of the living God and the joy of human brotherhood?

Make us determined to live by truth and not by lies, to found our common life on the eternal foundations of righteousness and love, and no longer to prop the tottering house of wrong by legalized cruelty and force. Help us to make the welfare of all the supreme law of our land, that so our commonwealth may be built strong and secure on the love of all its citizens. Cast down the throne of Mammon who ever grinds the life of men, and set up Thy throne, O Christ, for Thou didst die that men might live. Show Thy erring children at last the way to the City of Love, and fulfil the longings of the prophets of humanity. Our Master, once more we make Thy faith our prayer: "Thy Kingdom Come! Thy will be done on earth!"—Walter Rauschenbusch.

Sixth Day, Tenth Week

Verily I say unto you, What things soever ye shall bind on earth shall be bound in heaven; and what things soever ye shall loose on earth shall be loosed in heaven. Again I say unto you, that if two of you shall agree on earth as touching anything that they shall ask, it shall be done for them of my Father who is in heaven.—Matt. 18:18, 19.

Jesus' words about praying *together* are quite as positive as his words about praying alone. We often quote this reference to "two or three," as though the contrast were between a few and a multitude; but in fact the contrast lies between social and solitary prayer. Christ means to stress the fact that he is especially present in a praying group. Praying *for* another, especially an unfriendly man, is a searching test of our relationship with him. But praying *with* another—how much more intimate and penetrating a test is that! If there is unforgiven grudge or impenitent unkindness or secret disloyalty, we cannot do it. As Jesus said, we must "agree." Prayer is a most effective cleanser of personal relationships when in the home, for example, people kneel amid the familiar scenes of daily life. The bitter word and the neglected kindness will quarrel with the mutual prayer; people must really be loyal to one another to pray well together. This is one of the fundamental reasons for public prayer, and in the family circle, the college group, or the church, the sincere and habitual practice of it will help any who genuinely catch its spirit to say Our—our blessings, our sins, our needs, and our Father.

Eternal, Holy, Almighty, whose name is Love; we are met in solemn company to seek Thy face, and in spirit and truth to worship Thy name. We come in deep humility, since Thou art so high and exalted, and because Thou beholdest the proud afar off. We come in tender penitence, for the contrite heart is Thy only dwelling. We come in the name and spirit of Jesus to make our wills one with Thine; to abandon our lonely and selfish walk for solemn communion with Thee, to put an end to sin by welcoming to our hearts Thy Holy Presence. Deeper than we have known, enter, Thou Maker of our souls; clearer than we have ever seen dawn Thy glory on our sight. Light the flame upon the altar, call forth the incense of prayer, waken the song of praise, and manifest Thyself to all. Amen.
—W. E. Orchard.

Seventh Day, Tenth Week

Simon, Simon, behold, Satan asked to have you, that he might sift you as wheat: I made supplication for thee, that thy faith fail not; and do thou, when once thou hast turned again, establish thy brethren. And he said unto him, Lord, with thee I am ready to go both to prison and to death. And he said, I tell thee, Peter, the cock shall not crow this day, until thou shalt thrice deny that thou knowest me.—Luke 22:31-34.

Ye have heard that it was said, Thou shalt love thy neighbor, and hate thine enemy: but I say unto you, Love your enemies, and pray for them that persecute you; that ye may be sons of your Father who is in heaven: for he maketh his sun to rise on the evil and the good, and sendeth rain on the just and the unjust.—Matt. 5:43-45.

Look through these two passages as through open windows into the habitual intercessions of the Master. We have been noting this week different forms which unselfish praying takes: praying for our own need that we may serve others better; pleading the common wants which belong to all of us; offering our entreaty for the coming Kingdom; and praying together in a social group. But in addition to these the Master prayed for individual people, both his enemies and his friends. His love was personal and concrete; when he prayed, he used names. Think of different tests by which we can measure the reality of love—such as willingness to render costly service or daily thoughtfulness in little matters. Consider then the quality and depth of love that are revealed by this further test—a care profound enough to express itself in sincere and habitual intercession. *When a man prays in secret for another, and does it genuinely, he must really care.* Put yourself in Peter's place and see what the revelation of the Master's love, expressed in secret intercession, must have meant to him. At the death of Robert McCheyne, the Scotch preacher, some one said, "Perhaps the heaviest blow to his brethren, his people, and the land, is the loss of his intercession."

Two or three days before Cromwell died, the Chronicler tells us, his heart was "carried out for God and his people—yea, indeed, for some who had added no little sorrow to him." This was his prayer:

Lord, though I am a miserable and wretched creature, I am in Covenant with Thee through grace. And I may, I will, come to Thee, for Thy People. Thou hast made me, though very unworthy, a mean instrument to do them some good, and Thee service; and many of them have set too high a value upon me, though others wish and would be glad of my death; Lord, however Thou dost dispose of me, continue and go on to do good for them. Give them consistency of judgment, one heart, and mutual love; and go on to deliver them, and with the work of reformation; and make the Name of Christ glorious in the world. Teach those who look too much on Thy instruments, to depend more upon Thyself. Pardon such as desire to trample upon the dust of a poor worm, for they are Thy People too. And pardon the folly of this short Prayer:—even for Jesus Christ's sake. And give us a good night, if it be Thy pleasure. Amen.—Oliver Cromwell (1599-1658).

COMMENT FOR THE WEEK

I

Of all forces in human life that go to the making of dominant desire, none is more powerful than love. Love in the family circle makes the mother's dominant desires center about the children, until no words can tell how cheap she holds her own life and how dear she holds theirs. In the nation such devotion makes patriots, consuming in them selfishness and fear, until they endure for their country's sake what they would never endure for their own. When one ranges through biography to see what desire has meant in men, he finds not only the sordid Ahab, the avaricious Judas, the licentious Herod, the ambitious Felix; he finds also men in whom devotion to people and to causes has made dominant desire utterly unselfish. A young lad named Müller, who was picked up from the river after the burning of the "General Slocum," bore this testimony: "My mother gave me a life preserver, that's how I got saved. I guess she didn't have none herself, 'cause they can't find her." Trace in this testimony the direction of that mother's dominant desire! So the controlling wants of the world's devotees, from mothers to martyrs, have been unselfish. Said Gordon in the Soudan, "I declare, if I could stop this slave traffic, I would willingly be shot this night." Cried John Knox, "God, give me Scotland, or I die!"

Indeed, what expression of dominant desire could be more natural than this prayer of Knox? The tendency to pray is shaked into action, not alone by crises of individual need, but by hours of masterful love. Men who do not pray for themselves will sometimes pray for others; fathers who do not think to ask God's grace on their own lives, find themselves exclaiming, "God bless my son!" If, as in Paul, vital trust in God is combined with devotion to a cause, the result is always urgent, intercessory prayer. "Unceasingly I make mention of you, always in my prayers" (Rom. 1:9); "Always in every supplication of mine on behalf of you all making my supplication with joy" (Phil. 1:4); "I . . . cease not to give thanks for you, making mention of you in my prayers" (Eph. I:15, 16)— these are windows through which we look into Paul's habitual intercession. He prays for the Jews—"My heart's desire and my sup-

plication to God is for them, that they may be saved" (Rom. 10:1);
for new converts—"To the end he may establish your hearts un-
blamable in holiness" (I Thess. 3:13); for the church—that they may
"walk worthily of the Lord unto all pleasing, bearing fruit in every
good work" (Col. 1:10). *When dominant desire becomes unselfish
the result is truly represented in these prayers of Paul.*

II

In considering the meaning of this sort of praying we may well
note, first, that *a man can pray unselfishly for himself.* Sir Edward
Burne-Jones put significant truth into his saying, "There is only one
religion: 'Make the most of your best for the sake of others' is the
catholic faith, which except a man believe faithfully he cannot be
saved." All that we have said about the service of prayer to individual character may be reaffirmed here as part of the unselfish
aspect of prayer's ministry. When the Master said, "I sanctify myself," he was not selfish. A very unselfish motive was behind his care
for his own life. *"For their sakes* I sanctify myself."

The vividness with which this motive in prayer will appeal to any
man depends on his clear perception of the *intimate ways in which
his friends' welfare and happiness depend on him.* Many a young
man, rebuked for an evil in his life, has answered in effect, "My
habits are my private affair." The reply which ought to be made to
such a statement is obvious: a private affair is precisely what your
habits are not. Your habits are the interest of everybody else. They
are as truly a matter of social concern, if not of social control, as is
the tariff, or the conflict between capital and labor. No man can
keep the consequences of any evil to himself. They seep through his
individual life, and run out into the community. When the Scripture
says, "Be sure your sin will find you out," it does not mean "will be
found out." It means what it says, "will find *you* out," track you
down, spoil your character, destroy your happiness, ruin your influence; and because it does that, it will find your friends out, will
tend to pull them down with you, will surely make goodness harder
for them, and within your family circle will roll upon those who love
you a burden of vicarious suffering. If a man *could* sin privately,
he might allow himself the ignoble self-indulgence. But he cannot.
Somebody else always is involved. The whole world is involved, for

the man has deprived the world of a good life and given it a bad life instead. Sinning, even in its most private forms, is putting poison into the public reservoir, and sooner or later everybody is the worse for the pollution.

A man then has the choice between two prayers. Either he will pray for his friends' sake and his family's, for the sake of the girl he may marry and the children he may beget, for the sake of the commonwealth and the Kingdom which he may help or hinder, that he may defeat his temptations and live a godly, righteous, and useful life; or else some day he will be driven to a petition of the sort which Shakespeare put on the lips of the Duke of Clarence:

> "O God! if my deep prayers cannot appease thee
> But thou wilt be avenged on my misdeeds,
> Yet execute thy wrath in *me alone!"*

The latter is always a hopeless request. God cannot grant it. *No man ever yet bore all the consequences of his own sin.* The cross is a universal fact—symbol of the suffering brought on those who have not done the wrong by those who have. To pray for one's life in the light of this fact is to pray unselfishly.

Moreover, even when the fight with definite sin does not occupy the center of attention, a man for his friends' sake may well pray against the emptiness and uselessness of his life, and may well seek power to be worth as much as possible to others. Unselfishness is clearly the motive of such a cry for blessing as we have in the sixty-seventh Psalm: "God be merciful unto *us,* and bless *us,* and cause his face to shine upon *us;* that thy way may be known upon earth, thy salvation among *all nations."* Wherever real friendship and devotion come, prayer takes on this quality. When Quintin Hogg, with his Polytechnic Institute on his heart, during his last illness, wrote, "I would that I could be of some use to my boys, instead of the barren, dried up old scarecrow that I am!" he revealed the inevitable result of true friendliness. His desire to be at his best was motivated by his love for "his boys." Here we face the real trouble with our prayers. *Not for lack of a satisfying philosophy do our prayers run dry, but for lack of love.* We do not care enough about people and causes to pray for ourselves on their account. Let any one be possessed by a genuine devotion, and necessarily he will rise toward that

union of love and prayer which Mrs. Browning put into rememberable words:

> "And when I sue
> God for myself he hears that name of thine
> And sees within my eyes, the tears of two."

III

Unselfishness in prayer, however, never has been and never can
be fully satisfied with praying for ourselves for others' sakes. It involves specifically praying for others, and the more deep and constraining the love, the more natural is the definite entreaty for God's
blessing upon our friends. The Master is our example here. The
prayers of Jesus verbally reported in the Gospels, are not many in
number and are few in words; but the indications of his habit of
intercession are abundant and convincing. He prays for the *children*—"Then were there brought unto him little children, that he
should lay his hands on them, and pray" (Matt. 19:13); for the
sick—when a blind man is to be healed, we find the Master "looking
up to heaven" (Mark 7:34); for his *disciples*—"Simon . . . I made
supplication for thee, that thy faith fail not" (Luke 22:31, 32); for
his *enemies*—"Father, forgive them; for they know not what they
do" (Luke 23:34); for *laborers* in the harvest, since he must have
practiced his own injunction—"Pray ye therefore the Lord of the
harvest, that he send forth laborers into his harvest" (Luke 10:2);
and for the *whole community* of his followers to the end of time—
"For them also that shall believe on me through their word" (John
17:20). That the most unselfish life ever lived would be unselfish in
prayer was to have been expected, and the evidence that he was so
is clear.

When one, endeavoring to catch the Master's spirit, considers
the various effects that may be expected from this kind of praying,
he sees immediately that such intercession sincerely and habitually
practiced, *will have notable result in the one who prays*. How much
experience with vicarious prayer is summed up in that revealing
verse with which the book of Job draws toward its close, "Jehovah
turned the captivity of Job, when he prayed for his friends" (Job
42:10). Such prayer does liberate. It carries a man out of himself;
it brings to mind the names and needs of many friends, making the

heart ready for service and the imagination apt to perceive ways of helping those else forgotten and neglected; it purges a man's spirit of vindictive moods and awakens every gracious and fraternal impulse. As William Law put it, "Intercession is the best arbitrator of all differences, the best promoter of true friendship, the best cure and preservative against all unkind tempers, all angry and haughty passions."

For another thing intercession will often have effect in the lives of those on whose behalf the prayer is made, if only for this reason, *that the knowledge that his friends are praying for him is one of the finest and most empowering influences that can surround any man.* For Peter to know that the Master was interceding for him was in itself what a source of sustenance and strength! They say that Luther when he felt particularly strong would exclaim, "I feel as if I were being prayed for"; and in illustration of the same truth, John G. Paton, the missionary to the New Hebrides, writes in his autobiography, "I have heard that in long after years the worst woman in the village of Torthorwald, then leading an immoral life but since changed by the grace of God, was known to declare that the only thing that kept her from despair and from the hell of the suicide, was when in the dark winter nights she crept close up underneath my father's window, and heard him pleading in family worship that God would convert the sinner from the error of wicked ways and polish him as a jewel for the Redeemer's crown. . . . 'I felt,' said she, 'that I was a burden on that good man's heart, and I knew that God would not disappoint *him*. That thought kept me.' "

Many lives have been kept by knowledge of intercessions continually offered for them; and one need know only a little of Christian leaders, with their urgent requests for the support of their friends' prayers, to see what encouragement they always have found in the assurance that supplications were offered on their behalf. Melanchthon here is typical, rejoicing over his accidental discovery that children were praying for the Reformation. Paul writes, "Brethren, pray for us" (I Thess. 5:25); "Ye also helping together on our behalf by your supplication" (II Cor. 1:11); "I beseech you, brethren, . . . that ye strive together with me in your prayers to God for me" (Rom. 15:30). Cromwell writes to his admirals at sea: "You have, as I verily believe and am persuaded, a plentiful stock of prayers going for you daily, sent up by the soberest and most approved ministers and Christians in this nation; and, notwithstanding some discour-

agements, very much wrestling of faith for you; which is to us and
I trust will be to you, a matter of great encouragement."

IV

In addition to these two effects, however, Christians have looked
to intercession for a far more vital consequence. When *trust in God
and love for men* co-exist in any life, prayer for others inevitably
follows. Deepening intimacy with God, by itself, may find expression
in quiet communion; enlarging love for men, alone, may utter itself
in serviceable deeds; but these two cannot live *together* in the same
life without sometimes combining in vicarious prayer. Now, such
prayer always has been offered, not as a formal expression of well-
wishing, but as a vital, creative contribution to God's good purposes
for men. The genuine intercessors, who in costly praying have thrown
their personal love alongside God's and have earnestly claimed blessings for their friends, have felt that they were not playing with a toy,
but that they were somehow using the creative power of personality
in opening ways for God to work his will. They have been convinced
that their intercessions wrought consequences for their friends.

In this generation, however, with its searching doubts, its honest
unwillingness to act without knowledge, its refusal even when faith
would be a comfort to accept faith without good reason, this projectile power of intercession has to many become dubious. One reason for this doubt lies in the inadequate way in which intercession
has been conceived and preached. To some people it seems to mean
that one person may persuade a thoughtless or unwilling God to do
something for another person. A popular analogy has tended to keep
alive this misconception. God in many ways, so runs the analogy,
refuses to work his will save as some man cooperates with him. The
home life suffers, the government becomes corrupt, the non-Christian
world goes unevangelized until men come to God's help. So intercessory prayer may be another way in which God waits for our
assistance. If he will not do some things for my friend until I *work*,
it may be that he will not do other things until I *pray*.

There is an element of truth in this analogy, but the limited
application of the comparison is clear. God cannot save my family
life without my cooperation, because he cannot take my place as
son or husband or father; he *must* work through me. He cannot
save the government without men, because he cannot take the

voter's place; he *must* work through the citizens. And in the evan-
gelizing of China, he cannot go as a missionary; he must find some
man to go. There is nothing artificial about this necessity of human
cooperation; it belongs to the nature of the case. But that God
should deliberately withhold from a man in China something that
he is free to give to him, and should continue to withhold it until
it occurs to me to ask him to bestow it, looks like an arbitrary proceeding. It argues imperfect goodness in God. No true father would
keep from one child a blessing that the child has a right to and that
the father is free to give, simply because he waits for another child
to ask for its bestowal. The trouble with such an idea of intercession
is not simply intellectual; it is moral. That one individual, myself,
should try to persuade another individual, God, to do for a third
individual, my friend, something which the second individual, God,
had not thought of, or was intending otherwise, or was arbitrarily
withholding until I asked to have it given, plainly involves a thought
of deity with pagan elements in it. And many people feeling this
have given up intercession as unreasonable.

V

This surrender of reality, however, because it is explained in an
inadequate form of thought, is never a solution of any problem.
With or without adequate interpretations of vicarious prayer, earnest
Christians in their intercessions are about a serious and reasonable
business, whose sources lie deep in the needs of human life. A clear
and rational belief in intercession must start with two truths: *first,
the Christian Gospel about God; and second, the intimate relationships that make the world of persons an organic whole.*

As to the first, the Christian God desires the welfare of all men
everywhere; his love is boundless in extent and individual in application; his purpose of good sweeps through creation, comprehend-
ing every child of his and laboring for a transformed society on
earth and in the heavens. This, as Paul says, is "the eternal purpose
which he purposed in Christ." Nothing that we ever dreamed of
good for any man or for the race has touched the garment's hem
of the good which he purposes and toward which he works. He is
not an individual after the fashion of a pagan deity, who, like Baal,
must be awakened from his sleep and besought to do good deeds for
men. Rather every dim and flickering desire our hearts ever have

known for mankind's good has been lighted at the central fire of his
eternal passion for the salvation of his children. As Whittier sang it:

> "All that I feel of pity thou hast known
> Before I was; my best is all thy own.
> From thy great heart of goodness mine but drew
> Wishes and prayers; but thou, O Lord, wilt do,
> In thine own time, by ways I cannot see,
> All that I feel when I am nearest thee!"

Such is the Christian God.

When men go up to such a God in vicarious prayer, their intercession must mean casting themselves in with the eternal purpose
of the Father for his children, "laying hold on God," not to call him
to ministry, as though he needed that, but to be *carried along with*
him in his desire for all men's good. Nothing is more wanted in the
world than such intercession. The title of Dr. Mott's address "Intercessors—the Primary Need," is clearly the statement of a fact. God
wants men to lay hold on him in inward prayer, aligning their dominant desires with his, until their intercession becomes the effective
ally of his will. As in an irrigation system, with its many reticulated
channels, the sluice-gate would not plead with the reservoir to remember its forgotten power of doing good, but rather, feeling the
urge of the ready water, would desire to be opened, that through
it the waiting stream might find an entrance into all the fields and
the will of the reservoir be done—so men should pray to God.

As to the second truth which underlies the reasonableness of intercession—*persons are not separate individuals merely, like grains of
sand in a bag, but, as Paul says, are "members one of another."*
The ganglia of a nervous system are hardly more intimately related
and more interdependent than are people in this closely reticulated
system of personal life. As Professor Everett once put it: "We ask the
leaf, are you complete in yourself? and the leaf answers, No, my life
is in the branches. We ask the branch, and the branch answers, No,
my life is in the trunk. We ask the trunk, and it answers, No, my life
is in the root. We ask the root, and it answers, No, my life is in the
trunk and the branches and the leaves. Keep the branches stripped
of leaves and I shall die. So it is with the great tree of being. Nothing is completely and merely individual." The more we know about
personality, the less possible it is to draw clear circles about each

of us, partitioning us off from one another. We all run into each other, like interflowing rivulets, with open channels, above ground and subterranean, connecting all of us. Even telepathy may prove to be true. So that if a man believes in God, in whom *all* live and move and have their being, there is no basis for denying the possibility that prayer may open ways of personal influence even at a distance. Personality, at its best, in its thinking and working is *creative,* and when in this love-system of persons, a soul throws in its dominant desire alongside God's, no one easily can set boundaries to that prayer's influence.

Indeed, there are certain aspects of intercessory praying where the consequences are plain. It is not a theory but a fact empirically demonstrable, that if in any community a large number of earnest Christians unite in unselfish praying for a revival of religious interest, that revival is sure to come. This can be tested anywhere at any time, if earnest men and women are there to do the praying. To say that this effect is simply psychological, is only another way of saying that God has so ordained psychological laws that vicarious praying by a group of earnest people does bring results. *So far from depreciating the value of intercession, this fact gives to it the stability of a universal law.* It names the conditions under which God does his most effective work through men. "For many years," says Dr. Mott, "it has been my practice in traveling among the nations to make a study of the sources of the spiritual movements which are doing most to vitalize and transform individuals and communities. At times it has been difficult to discover the hidden spring, but invariably where I have had the time and patience to do so, I have found it in an intercessory prayer-life of great reality."

While our minds are insufficient for the task of seeing to its end the explanation of intercession's power, our experience is clear that something creative is being done when in this unitary system of personal life human souls take on themselves God's burden for men, and in vicarious prayer throw themselves in with his sacrificial purpose. "Surely the man who joins himself with God," writes Professor Coe, "does not leave the universe just where it was before. All things are bound together into unity. I drop a pebble from my hand; it falls to earth, but the great earth rises to meet it. They seek a common center of gravity, determined by the mass of one as truly as by that of the other. You cannot change any one thing without changing something else also. The man who prays changes the center of gravity of the world of persons. Other persons will be different as well as himself, and he could not have produced this difference by any other means than this union of himself with God."

But no explanation, however reasonable, can do justice to the *experience* of vicarious praying. To feel that, we must turn to life. When a mother prays for her wayward son, no words can make clear the vivid reality of her supplications. Her love pours itself out in insistent demand that her boy must not be lost. She is sure of his value, with which no outward thing is worthy to be compared, and of his possibilities which no sin of his can ever make her doubt. She will not give him up. She follows him through his abandonment down to the gates of death; and if she loses him through death into the mystery beyond, she still prays on in secret, with intercessions which she may not dare to utter, that wherever in the moral universe he may be, God will reclaim him. As one considers such an experience of vicarious praying, he sees that it is not merely resignation to the will of God; it is urgent assertion of a great desire. She does not really think that she is persuading God to be good to her son, for the courage in her prayer is due to her certain faith that God also must wish that boy to be recovered from his sin. *She rather is taking on her heart the same burden that God has on his; is joining her demand with the divine desire. In this system of personal life which makes up the moral universe, she is taking her place alongside God in an urgent, creative outpouring of sacrificial love.*

Now, this mother does not know and cannot know just what she is accomplishing by her prayers. But we know that such mothers save their sons when all others fail. The mystery of prayer's projectile force is great, but the certainty of such prayer's influence, one way or another, in working redemption for needy lives, is greater still. It may be, as we have said, that God has so ordained the laws of human interrelationship that we can help one another not alone by our deeds but also directly by our *thoughts,* and that earnest prayer may be the exercise of this power in its highest terms. But whether that mother has ever argued out the theory or not, she still prays on. Her intercession is the utterance of her life; it is *love on its knees.*

VI

Let any man of prayerless life, or of a life in which prayer, an untrained tendency, is nothing more than an occasional cry of selfish need, consider himself in the light of this ideal of unselfish praying. To pray for himself for the sake of others, and to pray in vicarious entreaty for his friends, his enemies, and all mankind—this ministry he has denied. Let him not hide his real and inward lack of the intercessory *spirit* behind any confusion of mind about the *theory*. If a man honestly seeks the reason why a prayer like that of Moses is not easily conceivable upon his own lips, "Oh, this people have sinned a great sin. . . . Yet now, if thou wilt forgive their sin—and if not, blot me, I pray thee, out of thy book which thou hast written" (Ex. 32:31, 32), he sees that the difference between Moses and himself is mainly one of moral passion. We have no such high and commanding desires as Moses had; our wishes are lame and weak and petty compared with his; if every mental perplexity were overcome, we still should lack the spirit out of which such prayers spontaneously pour. Supposing that we knew exactly and held completely the Master's *theory* of prayer; is there any man for whom we *care enough* to pray as Jesus did for Peter? Is there any cause that could call from us his cry: "O Jerusalem, Jerusalem!"

The chief obstacles to intercession are moral. We live for what we can get; our dominant desires are selfish. The main current of us runs in the channel of our mean ambitions, and our thoughts of other people and of great causes are but occasional eddies on the surface of the stream. Even when we do succeed in praying for our friends, our country, or the Kingdom, we are often giving lip-service to conventionality; we are not expressing our urgent and continual demand on life. Our prayers are hypocrites. If the cause we pray for should suddenly take form and ask of us our share in the achievement of our own entreaty, we would dodge and run. All such intercession is clanging brass. "Our prayers must mean something to us," said Maltbie Babcock, "if they are to mean anything to God."

Before a man therefore blames his lack of intercession on intellectual perplexities, he well may ask whether, if all his questions were fully answered, he has the spirit that would pour itself out in vicarious praying. Is his heart really surcharged with pent devotion waiting to find vent in prayer as soon as the logic of intercession is made evident? Rather, it is highly probable that if his last interrogation point were laid low by a strong answer, he would intercede not one whit more than he does now. *Intercession is the result of generous devotion, not of logical analysis.* When such devotion comes into the life of any man who vitally believes in God, like a rising stream in a dry river bed it lifts the obstacles at whose removal he had tugged in vain, and floats them off. The unselfish prayer of dominant desire clears its own channel. We put our *lives* into other people and into great causes; and our prayers follow after, voicing our love, with theory or without it. We lay hold on God's alliance for the sake of the folk we care for and the aims we serve. We do it because love *makes* us, and we continue it because the validity of our praying is proved in our experience. St. Anthony spoke to the point, *"We pray as much as we desire, and we desire as much as we love."*

Of such intercession it is true,

> "More things are wrought by prayer
> Than this world dreams of. Wherefore, let thy voice
> Rise like a fountain for me night and day.
> For what are men better than sheep or goats
> That nourish a blind life within the brain,
> If, knowing God, they lift not hands of prayer
> Both for themselves and those who call them friend?
> For so the whole round earth is every way
> Bound by gold chains about the feet of God."

SUGGESTIONS FOR THOUGHT AND DISCUSSION

How far can a man say: "It is nobody else's concern, what I do"?

Is there a person so far away that no act of mine can touch him?
Is there anything which a person can ask for in prayer which concerns nobody but himself?
When can a person really pray the Lord's Prayer?

When is a prayer for personal needs an unselfish prayer?

What are the results of unselfish prayer?

What does prayer accomplish for the man who prays?
Why does the knowledge that others are praying for him help a man? How far is this a sufficient reason for unselfish prayer?
"Can prayer accomplish anything apart from the man who prays?" What kind of answers have we a right to expect?

Why is it necessary to intercede with a loving God for human needs?

What is really accomplished by intercessory prayer?

What place has reason and what place experiment in determining the results of prayer?

Why do men fail to practice intercession?

SELECTED BIBLIOGRAPHY

I. DISCUSSIONS OF VARIOUS ASPECTS OF PRAYER

"PRAYER. WHAT IT IS AND WHAT IT DOES," by Samuel McComb.
A brief but worthy treatment of the personal effects of habitual prayer.

"CONQUERING PRAYER," by L. Swetenham.
A valuable essay on the relationships between prayer and character.

"THE POWER OF PRAYER," by Forsythe and Greenwell.
Two brief essays of real insight from a deeply religious point of view.

"THE PSYCHOLOGY OF PRAYER," by Anna Louise Strong.
A Ph.D. thesis on the psychological aspects of prayer.

"THE PRAYERS OF THE BIBLE," by John Edgar McFadyen.
A stimulating treatment of the subject, with a topical catalogue of Scriptural prayers.

"THE CHRISTIAN DOCTRINE OF PRAYER," by James Freeman Clarke.
Somewhat out of date in many of its positions but still suggestive.

"THE DOUBLE SEARCH," by Rufus M. Jones.
Two vital essays on Atonement and Prayer—God's search for man and man's search for God.

"PRAYER, ITS NATURE AND SCOPE," by H. Clay Trumbull.
Written in a popular vein but with more than ordinary good sense.

"THE PLACE OF PRAYER IN THE CHRISTIAN RELIGION," by James M. Campbell.
One of the best studies of the New Testament passages on prayer.

"COMMUNION WITH GOD," by Wilhelm Herrman.
Solid theological reading after the German style and very rewarding.

II. DEVOTIONAL TREATMENT OF PRAYER

"THE STILL HOUR," by Austin Phelps.
   A well-known devotional classic.
"PRAYER AND ACTION," by E. E. Holmes.
   Written for Lenten reading in the Diocese of London and in
   parts very suggestive.
"WITH CHRIST IN THE SCHOOL OF PRAYER," by Andrew Murray.
   A well-known book of meditations on prayer.

III. COLLECTIONS OF PRAYERS

"PRAYERS, ANCIENT AND MODERN," by Mrs. Mary W. Tileston.
"THE COMMUNION OF PRAYER," by William Boyd Carpenter, Bishop
   of Ripon.
"PRAYERS OF THE SOCIAL AWAKENING," by Walter Rauschenbusch.
"A CHAIN OF PRAYERS ACROSS THE AGES," by S. F. Fox.
"THE TEMPLE," by W. E. Orchard.
"A BOOK OF PRAYERS," by Samuel McComb.
"A BOOK OF PUBLIC PRAYERS," by Henry Ward Beecher.

THE MEANING OF FAITH

THE MEANING OF

FAITH

HARRY EMERSON FOSDICK

Author of "The Manhood of the Master," "The Meaning of Prayer,"
"The Meaning of Service," etc.

Garden City Books

GARDEN CITY, NEW YORK

PRINTED IN THE UNITED STATES OF AMERICA

The Bible Text used in this volume is taken from the American Standard
Edition of the Revised Bible, copyright, 1901, by Thomas Nelson & Sons,
and is used by permission.

Preface

TO NEW EDITION

This book was written during the first world war—"the most terrific war," I called it, "men ever raged, when faith is sorely tried and deeply needed." I little thought that that "war to end war" would so utterly fail of its purpose, and that a second world war would issue in the futility and frustration of the most perilous and threatening generation in human history.

In this last half-century we have gone a long way from the optimism with which the century began. Then the doctrine of inevitable and automatic progress was affirmed, not so much by preachers as by supposedly hard-headed, realistic men of the world. Herbert Spencer foresaw inevitable progress toward perfection; Mark Twain wrote Walt Whitman that thirty years more would see mankind coming at last to full stature; and Swinburne grew lyrical:

> "Glory to man in the highest,
> For man is the master of things."

Such sentimental optimism has blown up in our faces now, and even if pessimism has not universally taken its place, many find faith difficult and scepticism and discouragement easy. Perhaps a new edition of this book, which is now being called for, may still meet a contemporary need, despite the fact that it was written thirty years ago.

There is no sectarianism in the book. I am not pleading for any denominational creed. I had in mind, when I wrote it, what has become more critically evident now, that this world is a battlefield of contending faiths. If one does not believe in democracy, one gives help by his defection to those who believe in totalitarianism. It is the believers who count, the men who verily have convictions to live by and die for. Seldom has the world seen such believers in doctrine as are the Communists. The central question of mankind has become

What do you believe? and for us one by one no question goes deeper. Said Thomas Carlyle: "The thing a man does practically lay to heart and know for certain concerning his vital relations to the mysterious Universe, and his duty and destiny there, *that* is in all cases the primary thing for him and creatively determines all the rest. *That* is his religion." This book was written as one man's testimony about *that*.

My indebtedness is widespread, as the text makes evident but to one person in particular, my friend, George Albert Coe, Ph.D., who still lives to receive my thanks for his careful reading of the manuscript a generation ago, my special gratitude belongs.

HARRY EMERSON FOSDICK

January 9, 1950.

Acknowledgments

Special acknowledgment is gladly made to the following: to E. P. Dutton & Company for permission to use prayers from "A Chain of Prayer Across the Ages" and from "The Temple," by W. E. Orchard, D.D.; to the Rev. Samuel McComb and the publishers for permission to quote from "A Book of Prayers," Copyright, 1912, Dodd, Mead & Company; to the American Unitarian Association for permission to draw upon "Prayers," by Theodore Parker; to the Pilgrim Press and the author for permission to use selections from "Prayers of the Social Awakening," by Dr. Rauschenbusch; to the Missionary Education Movement for permission to make quotations from "Thy Kingdom Come," by Ralph E. Diffendorfer; to Fleming H. Revell Co., for permission to make use of "A Book of Public Prayer," by Henry Ward Beecher; and to the publishers of James Martineau's "Prayers in the Congregation and in College," Longmans, Green & Co.

None of the above material should be reprinted without securing permission.

CONTENTS

THE MEANING OF FAITH

CHAPTER I

Faith and Life's Adventure

DAILY READINGS

Discussion about faith generally starts with faith's *reasonableness;* let us begin with faith's *inevitableness*. If it were possible somehow to live without faith, the whole subject might be treated merely as an affair of curious interest. But if faith is an unescapable necessity in every human life, then we must come to terms with it, understand it, and use it as intelligently as we can. *There are certain basic elements in man which make it impossible to live without faith.* Let us consider these, as they are suggested in the Epistle to the Hebrews, which, better than any other book in the Bible, presents faith as an unavoidable human attitude.

First Week, First Day

Now faith is assurance of things hoped for, a conviction of things not seen.—Heb. 11:1.

As Moffatt translates: "Now faith means we are confident of what we hope for, convinced of what we do not see." When faith is described in such general terms, its necessity in human life is evident. Man cannot live without faith, because he deals not only with a past which he may know and with a present which he can see, but with a *future in whose possibilities he must believe*. A man can no more avoid looking ahead when he lives his life than he can when he sails his boat, and in one case as in the other, his direction is determined by his thought about what lies before him, his "assurance of things hoped for." Now, this future into which continually we press our way can never be a matter of demonstrable knowledge.

We know only when we arrive, but meanwhile we believe; and our knowledge of what is and has been is not more necessary to our quest than our faith concerning what is yet to come. As Tennyson sings of faith in "The Ancient Sage":

> "She sees the Best that glimmers thro' the Worst,
> She feels the sun is hid but for a night,
> She spies the summer thro' the winter bud,
> She tastes the fruit before the blossom falls,
> She hears the lark within the songless egg,
> She finds the fountain where they wail'd 'Mirage'!"

However much a man may plan, therefore, to live without faith, he cannot do it. When one strips himself of all convictions about the future he stops living altogether, an active, eager, vigorous manhood is always proportionate to the scope and power of reasonable faith. The great spirits of the race have had the aspiring, progressive quality which the Scripture celebrates:

These all died in faith, not having received the promises, but having seen them and greeted them from afar, and having confessed that they were strangers and pilgrims on the earth. For they that say such things make it manifest that they are seeking after a country of their own. And if indeed they had been mindful of that country from which they went out, they would have had opportunity to return. But now they desire a better country, that is, a heavenly: wherefore God is not ashamed of them, to be called their God; for he hath prepared for them a city.—Heb. 11:13-16.

Almighty God, let Thy Spirit breathe upon us to quicken in us all humility, all holy desire, all living faith in Thee. When we meditate on the Eternal, we dare not think any manner of similitude; yet Thou art most real to us in the worship of the heart. When in the strife against sin we receive grace to help us in our time of need, then art Thou the Eternal Rock of our salvation. When amid our perplexities and searchings, the way of duty is made clear, then art Thou our Everlasting Light. When amid the storms of life we find peace and rest through submission, then art Thou the assured Refuge of our souls. So do Thou manifest Thyself unto us, O God!

Our Heavenly Father, we give Thee humble and hearty thanks for all the sacred traditions which have come down to us from the

*past—for the glorious memories of ancient days, concerning that
Divine light in which men have been conscious of Thy presence and
assured of Thy grace. But we would not content ourselves with memories. O Thou who art not the God of the dead, but the God of the
living, manifest Thyself unto us in a present communion. Reveal
Thyself unto us in the tokens of this passing time. Give us for ourselves to feel the authority of Thy law: give us for ourselves to realize the exceeding sinfulness of sin: give us for ourselves to understand the way of salvation through sacrifice. Teach us, by the Spirit
of Christ, the sacredness of common duties, the holiness of the ties
that bind us to our kind, the divinity of the still small voice within
that doth ever urge us in the way of righteousness. So shall our hearts
be renewed by faith; so shall we ever live in God. Amen.*—John
Hunter.

First Week, Second Day

By faith Abraham, when he was called, obeyed to go out unto a
place which he was to receive for an inheritance; and he went out,
not knowing whither he went. By faith he became a sojourner in
the land of promise, as in a land not his own, dwelling in tents, with
Isaac and Jacob, the heirs with him of the same promise: for he
looked for the city which hath the foundations, whose builder and
maker is God.—Heb. 11:8-10.

By faith Moses, when he was grown up, refused to be called the
son of Pharaoh's daughter; choosing rather to share ill treatment
with the people of God, than to enjoy the pleasures of sin for a
season; accounting the reproach of Christ greater riches than the
treasures of Egypt: for he looked unto the recompense of reward.
By faith he forsook Egypt, not fearing the wrath of the king: for he
endured, as seeing him who is invisible.—Heb. 11:24-27.

Man cannot live without faith because his relationship with the
future is an affair not alone of thought but also of action; *life is a
continuous adventure into the unknown.* Abraham and Moses pushing out into experiences whose issue they could not foresee are typical of all great lives that had adventured for God. "By faith" is the
first word necessary in every life like Luther's and Wesley's and
Carey's. By faith John Bright, when his reforms were hard bestead,
said: "If we can't win as fast as we wish, we know that our opponents can't in the long run win at all." By faith Gladstone, when the

Liberal cause was defeated, rose undaunted in Parliament, and said, "I appeal to time!" and by faith every one of us must undertake each plain day's work, if we are to do it well. Robert Louis Stevenson said that life is "an affair of cavalry," "a thing to be dashingly used and cheerfully hazarded." But so to deal with life demands faith. The more one sees what venturesome risks he takes every day, what labor and sacrifice he invests in hope of a worthy outcome, with what great causes he falls in love until at his best he is willing for their sakes to hazard fortune and happiness and life itself, the more he sees that the soul of robust and serviceable character is faith.

O God, who hast encompassed us with so much that is dark and perplexing, and yet hast set within us light enough to walk by; enable us to trust what Thou hast given us as sufficient for us, and steadfastly refuse to follow aught else; lest the light that is in us become as darkness and we wander from the way. May we be loyal to all the truth we know, and seek to discharge those duties which lay their commission on our conscience; so that we may come at length to perfect light in Thee, and find our wills in harmony with Thine.

Since Thou hast planted our feet in a world so full of chance and change that we know not what a day may bring forth, and hast curtained every day with night and rounded our little lives with sleep; grant that we may use with diligence our appointed span of time, working while it is called today, since the night cometh when no man can work; having our loins girt and our lamps alight, lest the cry at midnight find us sleeping and the door fast shut.

Since we are so feeble, faint, and foolish, leave us not to our own devices, not even when we pray Thee to; nor suffer us for any care to Thee or for any pain to us to walk our own unheeding way. Plant thorns about our feet, touch our hearts with fear, give us no rest apart from Thee, lest we lose our way and miss the happy gate. Amen.—W. E. Orchard.

First Week, Third Day

Man cannot live without faith because the prime requisite in life's adventure is *courage,* and the sustenance of courage is faith.

And what shall I more say? for the time will fail me if I tell of Gideon, Barak, Samson, Jephthah; of David and Samuel and the

prophets: who through faith subdued kingdoms, wrought righteousness, obtained promises, stopped the mouths of lions, quenched the power of fire, escaped the edge of the sword, from weakness were made strong, waxed mighty in war, turned to flight armies of aliens. Women received their dead by a resurrection: and others were tortured, not accepting their deliverance; that they might obtain a better resurrection: and others had trial of mockings and scourgings, yea, moreover of bonds and imprisonment: they were stoned, they were sawn asunder, they were tempted, they were slain with the sword: they went about in sheep-skins, in goat-skins; being destitute, afflicted, ill-treated (of whom the world was not worthy), wandering in deserts and mountains and caves, and the holes of the earth. And these all, having had witness borne to them through their faith, received not the promise, God having provided some better thing concerning us, that apart from us they should not be made perfect.—Heb. 11:32-40.

When in comparison with men and women of such admirable spirit, one thinks of weak personalities, that ravel out at the first strain, he sees that the difference lies in courage. *When a man loses heart he loses everything.* Now to keep one's heart in the midst of life's stress and to maintain an undiscourageable front in the face of its difficulties is not an achievement which springs from anything that a laboratory can demonstrate or that logic can confirm. It is an achievement of faith.

> "The virtue to exist by faith
> As soldiers live by courage."

Consider this account of Havelock, the great English general: "As he sat at dinner with his son on the evening of the 17th, his mind appeared for the first and last time to be affected with gloomy forebodings, as it dwelt on the probable annihilation of his brave men in a fruitless attempt to accomplish what was beyond their strength. After musing long in deep thought, his strong sense of duty and his confidence in the justice of his cause restored the buoyancy of his spirit; and he exclaimed, 'If the worst comes to the worst, we can but die with our swords in our hands!' " No man altogether escapes the need for such a spirit, and, as with Havelock and the Hebrew heroes, confidence in someone, faith in something, is that spirit's source.

O God, who hast sent us to school in this strange life of ours, and hast set us tasks which test all our courage, trust, and fidelity; may we not spend our days complaining at circumstance or fretting at discipline, but give ourselves to learn of life and to profit by every experience. Make us strong to endure.

We pray that when trials come upon us we may not shirk the issue or lose our faith in Thy goodness, but committing our souls unto Thee who knowest the way that we take, come forth as gold tried in the fire.

Grant by Thy grace that we may not be found wanting in the hour of crisis. When the battle is set, may we know on which side we ought to be, and when the day goes hard, cowards steal from the field, and heroes fall around the standard, may our place be found where the fight is fiercest. If we faint, may we not be faithless; if we fall, may it be while facing the foe. Amen.—W. E. Orchard.

First Week, Fourth Day

Man cannot live without faith, because the adventure of life demands not only courage to achieve but *patience to endure and wait*, and all untroubled patience is founded on faith. When the writer to the Hebrews speaks of those who "through faith and patience inherit the promises" (Heb. 6:12), he joins two things that in experience no man successfully can separate. By as much as we need patience, we need faith.

But call to remembrance the former days, in which, after ye were enlightened, ye endured a great conflict of sufferings; partly, being made a gazingstock both by reproaches and afflictions; and partly, becoming partakers with them that were so used. For ye both had compassion on them that were in bonds, and took joyfully the spoiling of your possessions, knowing that ye have for yourselves a better possession and an abiding one. Cast not away therefore your boldness, which hath great recompense of reward. For ye have need of patience, that, having done the will of God, ye may receive the promise.—Heb. 10:32-36.

The most difficult business in the world is *waiting*. There are times in every life when action, however laborious and sacrificial, would be an unspeakable relief; but to sit still because necessity constrains us, endeavoring to live out the admonition of the psalmist, "Rest in the Lord, and wait patiently for him," is prodigiously difficult. *No one can do it without some kind of faith.* "In your patience," said Jesus, "ye shall win your souls" (Luke 21:19), but such an achievement is no affair of logic or scientific demonstration; it is a venture of triumphant faith. The great believers have been the unwearied waiters: faith meant to them not controversial opinion, but sustaining power. As another has phrased it, "Our faculties of belief were not primarily given to us to make orthodoxies and heresies withal; they were given us to *live* by."

We beseech of Thee, O Lord our God, that Thou wilt grant to every one of us in Thy presence, this morning, the special mercies which he needs—strength where weakness prevails, and patience where courage has failed. Grant, we pray Thee, that those who need long-suffering may find themselves strangely upborne and sustained. Grant that those who wander in doubt and darkness may feel distilling upon their soul the sweet influence of faith. Grant that those who are heart-weary, and sick from hope deferred, may find the God of all salvation. Confirm goodness in those that are seeking it. Restore, we pray Thee, those who have wandered from the path of rectitude. Give every one honesty. May all transgressors of Thy law return to the Shepherd and Bishop of their souls with confession of sin, and earnest and sincere repentance. Amen.—Henry Ward Beecher.

First Week, Fifth Day

Man cannot live without faith because he exists in a universe, the complete explanation of which is forever beyond his grasp, so that *whatever he thinks about the total meaning of creation is fundamentally faith.*

By faith we understand that the worlds have been framed by the word of God, so that what is seen hath not been made out of things which appear.—Heb. 11:3.

Not only is this true, but if we think that there is *no* God, that also is faith; and if we hold that the basic reality is physical atoms, that is faith; and whatever anybody believes about the origin and destiny of life is faith. When Haeckel says that the creator is "Cosmic Ether," and when John says that "God is love," they both are making a leap of faith. This does not mean that faith can dispense with reason. In these studies we shall set ourselves to marshal the ample arguments that support man's faith in God. But when the utmost that argument can do has been achieved, the finite mind, dealing with the infinite reality, is forced to a sally of faith, a venture of confidence in Goodness at the heart of the world, not opposed to reason but surpassing reason. *Faith always sees more with her eye than logic can reach with her hand.* And especially when men come to the highest thought of life's meaning and believe in the Christian God, they face the fact which the writer to the Hebrews presents:

And without faith it is impossible to be well-pleasing unto him; for he that cometh to God must believe that he is, and that he is a rewarder of them that seek after him.—Heb. 11:6.

Indeed, in all stout conviction about the meaning of life there is a certain defiant note, refusing to surrender to small objections. Cried Stevenson, "I believe in an ultimate decency of things; ay, and if I woke in hell, should still believe it!"

O Thou Infinite Spirit, who needest no words for man to hold his converse with Thee, we would enter into Thy presence, we would reverence Thy power, we would worship Thy wisdom, we would adore Thy justice, we would be gladdened by Thy love, and blessed by our communion with Thee. We know that Thou needest no sacrifice at our hands, nor any offering at our lips; yet we live in Thy world, we taste Thy bounty, we breathe Thine air, and Thy power sustains us, Thy justice guides, Thy goodness preserves, and Thy love blesses us forever and ever. O Lord, we cannot fail to praise Thee, though we cannot praise Thee as we would. We bow our faces down before Thee with humble hearts, and in Thy presence would warm our spirits for a while, that the better we may be prepared for the duties of life, to endure its trials, to bear its crosses, and to triumph in its lasting joys. . . .

In times of darkness, when men fail before Thee, in days when men of high degree are a lie, and those of low degree are a vanity, teach us, O Lord, to be true before Thee, not a vanity, but soberness and manliness; and may we keep still our faith shining in the midst of darkness, the beacon-light to guide us over stormy seas to a home and haven at last. Father, give us strength for our daily duty, patience for our constant or unaccustomed cross, and in every time of trial give us the hope that sustains, the faith that wins the victory and obtains satisfaction and fulness of joy. Amen.—Theodore Parker.

First Week, Sixth Day

Man cannot live, lacking faith, because *without it life's richest experiences go unappropriated.* Opportunities for friendship lie all about us, but only by trustful self-giving can they be enjoyed; chances to serve good causes continually beckon us, but one must have faith to try; superior minds offer us their treasures, but to avail oneself of instruction from another involves teachable humility. A man without capacity to let himself go out to other men in friendly trust or to welcome new illumination on his thought with grateful faith would be shut out from the priceless treasures of humanity. A certain trustful openheartedness, a willingness to venture in personal relationship and in attempts at service is essential to a rich and fruitful life. And what is true of man's relationship with man is true of man's relationship with God. So Prof. William James, of Harvard, states the case: "Just as a man who in a company of gentlemen made no advances, asked a warrant for every concession, and believed no one's word without proof, would cut himself off by such churlishness from all the social rewards that a more trusting spirit would earn—so here, one should shut himself up in snarling logicality and try to make the gods extort his recognition willy-nilly, or not get it at all, might cut himself off forever from his only opportunity of making the gods' acquaintance." *Wherever in life great spiritual values await man's appropriation, only faith can appropriate them.*

Let us fear therefore, lest haply, a promise being left of entering into his rest, any one of you should seem to have come short of it. For indeed we have had good tidings preached unto us, even as also they: but the word of hearing did not profit them, because it was not united by faith with them that heard!—Heb. 4:1, 2.

O Infinite Source of life and health and joy! the very thought of Thee is so wonderful that in this thought we would rest and be still. Thou art Beauty and Grace and Truth and Power. Thou art the light of every heart that sees Thee, the life of every soul that loves Thee, the strength of every mind that seeks Thee. From our narrow and bounded world we would pass into Thy greater world. From

*our petty and miserable selves we would escape to Thee, to find in
Thee the power and the freedom of a larger life. . . . We recognize Thee in all the deeper experiences of the soul. When the conscience utters its warning voice, when the heart is tender and we
forgive those who have wronged us in word or deed, when we feel
ourselves upborne above time and place, and know ourselves citizens
of Thy everlasting Kingdom, we realize, O Lord, that these things,
while they are in us, are not of us. They are Thine, the work of Thy
Spirit brooding upon our souls.*

*Spirit of Holiness and Peace! Search all our motives; try the secret
places of our souls; set in the light any evil that may lurk within, and
lead us in the way everlasting. Amen.*—Samuel McComb.

First Week, Seventh Day

Man cannot live without faith, because in life's adventure the
central problem is *building character*. Now, character is not a product of logic, but of faith in ideals and of sacrificial devotion to them.
What *is* becomes only the starting point of a campaign for what
ought to be, and in the prosecution of that campaign what ought to
be must be believed in with passionate intensity. Faith of some sort,
therefore, is necessarily the dynamic of character; only limp and
ragged living is possible without faith; and the greatest characters
are girded by the most ample faith in God and goodness. The writer
to the Hebrews saw this intimate relationship between quality of
faith and quality of life, and challenged his readers to judge the
Christian faith by its consequence in character.

**Remember them that had the rule over you, men that spake unto
you the word of God; and considering the issue of their life, imitate
their faith.—Heb. 13:7.**

Such are the basic elements in human experience that make faith
necessary: we deal with a future, about which we must think, with
reference to which we must act, and adventuring into which we
need courage and patience; this venture of life takes place in a world
the meaning of which can be grasped only by a leap of faith; and
in this venture the best treasures of the spirit are obtainable only
through openheartedness, and character is possible only to men of
resolute conviction. Plainly the subject to whose study we are setting
ourselves is no affair of theoretical interest alone; it affects the deep-

est issues of life. No words could better summarize this vital idea of faith which the Epistle to the Hebrews presents than Hartley Coleridge's:

"Think not the faith by which the just shall live
Is a dead creed, a map correct of heaven,
Far less a feeling, fond and fugitive,
A thoughtless gift, withdrawn as soon as given.
It is an affirmation and an act
That bids eternal truth be present fact."

How great are the mercies, O Lord, our God, which Thou hast prepared for all that put their trust in Thee! . . . Thou hast comfort for those that are in affliction; Thou hast strength for those that are weak; . . . Thou hast all blessings that are needed, and standest ready to be all things to all, and in all. And yet, with bread enough and to spare, with raiment abundant, and with all medicine, how many are there that go hungry, and naked, and sick, and destitute of all things! We desire, O Lord, that Thou wilt, to all Thine other mercies, add that gift by which we shall trust in Thee—faith that works by love; faith that abides with us; faith that transforms material things, and gives them to us in their spiritual meanings; faith that illumines the world by a light that never sets, that shines brighter than the day, and that clears the night quite out of our experience. This is the portion that Thou hast provided for Thy people. We beseech of Thee, grant us this faith, that shall give us victory over the world and over ourselves; that shall make us valiant in all temptation and bring us off conquerors and more than conquerors through Him that loved us. Amen.—Henry Ward Beecher.

COMMENT FOR THE WEEK

I

When Donald Hankey, who died in the trenches in the Great War, said that "True religion is betting one's life that there is a God," he not only gave expression to his own virile Christianity, but he gave a good description of all effective faith whatsoever. Faith is holding reasonable convictions, in realms beyond the reach of final demonstration, and, as well, it is thrusting out one's life upon those convictions as though they were surely true. *Faith is vision plus valor*.

Our study may well begin by recognizing that, as it is exercised in the religious life, such faith is the supreme use of an attitude which we are employing in every other realm. No man can live without vision to see as true what as yet he cannot prove, or without valor to act on the basis of his insight. Our vocabulary in ordinary relationships, quite as much as in religion, is full of words involving faith. I believe, I feel sure, I am confident, I venture—such phrases express our common attitudes in work and thought. Each day we act on reasonable probabilities, hold convictions not yet verified, take risks whose outcome we cannot know, and trust people whom we have barely met. We may pride ourselves that our twentieth century's life is being built on scientifically demonstrable knowledge, but a swift review of any day's experience shows how indispensable is another attitude, without which our verifiable knowledge would be an unused instrument. In order to *live* we must have insight and daring. It is not alone the just who live by faith; lacking it, there is no real life anywhere.

To be sure, we may not leap from this general necessity of faith to the conclusion that therefore our religious beliefs are justified. Many men use faith in business and in social life who cannot find their way to convictions about God. But our desire to understand faith's meaning is quickened when we see how indispensable a place it holds, how tremendous an influence it wields, whether it be religiously applied or not. All sorts of human enterprise bear witness to its unescapable necessity. Haeckel, the biologist, describing science's method, says: "Scientific faith fills the gaps in our knowledge of natural laws with temporary hypotheses." Lincoln, the statesman, entreating the people, cries: "Let us have faith that right makes might and in that faith let us to the end dare to do our duty." Stevenson, the invalid, trying with fortitude to bear his trial, writes: "Whether on the first of January or the thirty-first of December, faith is a good word to end on." And the Master states the substance of religion in a single phrase: "Have faith in God" (Mark 11:22). Scientific procedure, social welfare, personal quality, religion—the applications of our subject are as wide as life. Vision and valor are the dynamic forces in all achievement, intellectual as well as moral, and as for man's spiritual values and satisfactions, "It is faith in something," as Oliver Wendell Holmes put it, "which makes life worth living."

II

One major reason for this necessary place of faith in our experience is clear. *Life is an adventure and adventure always demands insight and daring.* That "Chinese" Gordon, on his hazardous expedition into the Soudan, should be thrown back on undiscourageable faith in himself, in the justice of his cause, in the bravery of his men, and in God; that he should even speak of praying his boats up the Nile, seems to us natural; for some kind of faith is obviously necessary to any great adventure. But men often forget that all ordinary living is essentially adventurous and that by this fact the need of faith is woven into the texture of every human life. It is an amazing adventure to be born upon this wandering island in the sky and it is an adventure to leave it when death calls. To go to school, to make friends, to marry, to rear children, to face through life the swift changes of circumstance that no man can certainly predict an hour ahead, these are all adventures. Each new day is an hitherto unvisited country, which we enter, like Abraham leaving Ur for a strange land, "not knowing whither he went" (Heb. 11:8), and every New Year we begin a tour of exploration into a twelvemonth where no man's foot has ever walked before. If we all love tales of pioneers, it is because from the time we are weaned to the time we die, life is pioneering. Of course we cannot live by verifiable knowledge only. Imagine men, equipped with nothing but powers of logical demonstration, starting on such an enterprise as the title of Sebastian Cabot's joint stock company suggests: "Merchants Adventurers of England for the discovery of lands, territories, isles and seignories, unknown."

Indeed no knowledge of the sort that our scientific inductions can achieve ever will take from life this adventurous element. Scientific knowledge in these latter decades has grown incalculably; yet for all that, every child's life is a hazardous experiment, every boy choosing a calling takes his chances, every friendship is a risky exploration in the province of personality, and all devotion to moral causes is just as much a venturesome staking of life on insight and hope as it was when Garrison attacked slavery or Livingstone landed in Africa. To one who had acquired not only all extant but all possible knowledge, as truly as to any man who ever lived, life would be full of hazard still. He could not certainly know in advance the outcome of a single important decision of his life. He could not at any moment tell in what new, strange, challenging, or terrific situation the next hour might find him. With all his science, he must face each day, as Paul faced his journey to Rome, "not knowing the things that shall befall me there" (Acts 20:22).

The reason for this is obvious. Our systematized knowledge is the arrangement under laws of the experiences which we have already had. It furnishes invaluable aid in guiding the experiments and explorations which life continuously forces on us. In every enterprise, however, we must use not only legs to stand on, but tentacles as well with which to feel our way forward—intuitions, insights, hopes, unverified convictions, faith. We project our life forward as we build a cantilever bridge. Part of the structure is solidly bolted and thoroughly articulated in a system; but ever beyond this established portion we audaciously thrust out new beginnings in eager expectation that from the other side something will come to meet them. Without this no progress ever would be possible.

Every province of life illustrates this necessity of adventure. In *science,* the established body of facts and laws is only the civilized community of knowledge from whose frontiers new guesses and intuitions start. Says Sir Oliver Lodge about the great Newton: "He had an extraordinary faculty for guessing correctly, sometimes with no apparent data—as for instance, his intuition that the mean density of the earth was probably between five and six times that of water, while we now know it is really about five and one half." In *personal character,* our habits are basic, but our ideals in which, despite ourselves, we must believe, are pioneers that push out into new territory and call our habits after them to conquer the promised land. In *social advance,* some Edmund Burke, statesman of the first magnitude, basing his judgment on the established experience of the race, can call slavery an incurable evil and say that there is not the slightest hope that trade in slaves can be stopped; and yet within eighty-two years the race can feel its way forward to Lincoln's Emancipation Proclamation. As for *daily business,* adventurous daring is there the very nerve of enterprise. Says a modern newspaper man: "There are plenty of people to do the possible; you can hire them at forty dollars a month. The prizes are for those who perform the impossible. If a thing can be done, experience and skill can do it; if a thing cannot be done, only faith can do it." Great in human life is this adventurous element, and, therefore, great in human life is the necessity of faith. To chasten and discipline, to make reasonable and stable the faiths by which we live is a problem unsurpassed in importance for every man.

III

One result of special interest follows from this truth. It is commonly suspected that as mankind advances, the function of faith proportionately shrinks. It is even supposed that the place of faith in human life has sensibly diminished with our growing knowledge, and that Matthew Arnold told the truth:

> "The sea of faith
> Was once, too, at the full, and round earth's shore
> Lay like the folds of a bright girdle furl'd.
> But now I only hear
> Its melancholy, long, withdrawing roar,
> Retreating, to the breath
> Of the night-wind, down the vast edges drear
> And naked shingles of the world."

Accordingly by custom we call the mediæval centuries the "Age of Faith." But even a cursory comparison between the mediæval people and ourselves reveals that among the many differences that distinguish us from them, none is more marked than the diversity and range of our faiths. One considers in surprise the things which they did not believe. That the world would ever grow much better, that social abuses like political tyranny and slavery could be radically changed, that man could ever master nature by his inventions until her mighty forces were his servants, that the whole race could be reached for Christ, that war could be abolished and human brotherhood in some fair degree established, that common men could be trusted with responsibility for their own government or with freedom to worship God according to the dictates of their own consciences— none of these things did the mediæval folk believe. One of the most distinguishing characteristics of the so-called "Age of Faith" was its lack of faith. It lived in a static world; it was poor in possibilities except in heaven; it pitiably lacked those most certain signs of vital faith, the open mind eager for new truth and the ardent, vigorous life seeking new conquests. In comparison with such an age our generation's faiths are rich and manifold. To call our time an "Age of Doubt" because of its free spirit of critical inquiry, is seriously to misunderstand its major drift. Bunyan's Pilgrim found Doubting Castle kept by Giant Despair and his wife Diffidence and in any Doubting Castle these two always dwell. But who, considering our generation's life as a whole, would call it diffident or desperate? It is rather robust and confident; its social faiths, at least, are unprecedented in their sweep and certainty. Even the Great War is the occasion of such organized faith in a federated and fraternal world as mankind has never entertained before.

The truth is that with the progress of the race the adventure of life is elevated and enlarged, and in consequence faith grows not less but more necessary. *The faiths of a savage are meager compared with a modern man's.* The Australian bushman never dreams of laboring for social ideals even a few years ahead. What can he know of those superb faiths in economic justice and international brotherhood, which even in the face of overwhelming difficulty, master the best of modern men? The primitive mind was not curious enough to wonder whether the sun that rises in the morning was the same that set the night before. What could such a mind understand of modern science's faith in the universal regularity of law? Put a Moro head hunter beside Mr. Edison, and see how incalculable the difference between them, not simply in their knowledge, but in their faith as to what it is possible for humanity to do with nature! Or put a fetish worshipper from Africa beside Phillips Brooks and compare the faith of the one in his idol with the faith of the other in God. Faith does not dwindle as wisdom grows; vision and valor are not less important. *The difference between the twentieth century man and the savage is quite as much in the scope and quality of their faith as in the range and certainty of their knowledge.*

Faith, therefore is not a transient element in human life, to be evicted by growing science. For whatever life may *know,* life *is* adventure; and as the adventure widens its horizons, the demand for faith is correspondingly increased. If one tries to imagine the world with all faith gone—knowledge supposedly having usurped its place —he must conceive a world where no conscious life and effort remain at all. Take trust in testimony away from courts of law, and unsure experiments from the physician's practice; refuse the teacher his confidence in growing minds and the business man his right to ventures that involve uncertainty; abstract from civic reforms all faith in a better future, from science all unproved postulates, from society all mutual trust and from religion all belief in the Unseen, and life would become an "inane sand heap." A man who tries to live without faith will die of inertia. A society that makes the attempt will be paralyzed within an hour. The question is not whether or no we shall live by faith. The question is rather—By what faiths shall we live? What range and depth and quality shall they have? How reasonable and how assured shall they be?

IV

Among all the faiths which mankind has cherished and by which it has been helped in life's adventure, none have been more universally and more passionately held than those associated with religion. In the daring experiment of living, men naturally have sought by faith interpretation not only of life's details but of life itself—its origin, its meaning, and its destiny. Australian bushmen, unable to count above four on their fingers, have been heard discussing in their huts at night whence they came, whither they go, and who the gods are anyway. And when one turns to modern manhood in its finest exhibitions of intelligence and character, he sees that Professor Ladd, of Yale, speaks truly: "The call of the world of men today, which is most insistent and most intense, if not most loud and clamorous, is the call for a rehabilitation of religious faith."

For it does make a prodigious difference to the spirit of our adventure in this world, whether we think that God is good or on the other hand see the universe as Carlyle's terrific figure pictures it— "one huge, dead, immeasurable Steam-engine, rolling on, in its dead indifference, to grind me limb from limb." It does make a difference of quite incalculable magnitude whether we think that our minds and characters are an evanescent product of finely wrought matter which alone is real and permanent, or on the contrary with John believe that "Now are we children of God and it is not yet made manifest what we shall be" (I John 3:2).

How great a difference in life's adventure religious faith does make is better set forth by concrete example than by abstract argument. On the one side, how radiant the spirit of the venture as the New Testament depicts it! The stern, appealing love of God behind life, his good purpose through it, his victory ahead of it, and man a fellow worker, called into an unfinished world to bear a hand with

God in its completion—here is a game that indeed is worth the candle. On the other side is Bertrand Russell's candid disclosure of the consequences of his own scepticism: "Brief and powerless is man's life; on him and all his race the slow sure doom falls pitiless and dark. Blind to good and evil, reckless of destruction, omnipotent matter rolls on its relentless way; for Man condemned today to lose his dearest, tomorrow himself to pass through the gate of darkness, it remains only to cherish, ere yet the blow falls, the lofty thoughts that ennoble his little day—proudly defiant of the irresistible forces that tolerate for a moment his knowledge and his condemnation, to sustain alone, a weary but unyielding Atlas, the world that his own ideals have fashioned despite the trampling march of unconscious power."

Man's life, interpreted and motivated by religious faith, is glorious, but shorn of faith's interpretations life loses its highest meaning and its noblest hopes. Let us make this statement's truth convincing in detail.

When faith in God goes, man the thinker loses his greatest thought. Man's mind has ranged the universe, has woven atoms and stars into a texture of law; his conquering thoughts ride out into every unknown province of which they hear. But among all the ideas on which the mind of man has taken hold, incomparably the greatest is the idea of God. In sheer weight and range no other thought of man compares with that. Amid the crash of stars, the reign of law, the vicissitudes of human history, and the griefs that drive their ploughshares into human hearts, to gather up all existence into spiritual unity and to believe in God, is the sublimest venture of the human mind.

When faith in God goes, man the worker loses his greatest motive. Man masters nature until the forces that used to scare him now obey; in society he labors tirelessly that his children may have a better world. Wars come, destroying the achievements of ages; yet when war is over, man rebuilds his cities, recreates his commerce, dreams again his human brotherhoods, and toils on. Many motives, deep and shallow, fine and coarse, have sustained him in this tireless work, but when one seeks the fountain of profoundest hope in mankind's toil he finds it in religious faith. To believe that we do not stand alone, hopelessly pitted against the dead apathy of cosmic forces which in the end will crush us in some solar wreck and bring our work to naught; to believe that we are fellow-laborers with God, our human purposes comprehended in a Purpose, God behind us, within us, ahead of us—this incomparably has been the master-faith in man's greatest work.

When faith in God goes, man the sinner loses his strongest help. For man is a sinner. He tears his spiritual heritage to shreds in licentiousness and drink. He wallows in vice, wins by cruelty, violates love, is treacherous to trust. His sins clothe the world in lamentation. Yet in him is a protest that he cannot stifle. He is the only creature whom we know whose nature is divided against itself. He hates his sin even while he commits it. He repents, tries again, falls, rises, stumbles on—and in all his best hours cries out for saviorhood. No message short of religion has ever met man's need in this estate. That God himself is pledged to the victory of righteousness in men and in the world, that he cares, forgives, enters into man's struggle with transforming power, and crowns the long endeavor with triumphant character—such faith alone has been great enough to meet the needs of man the sinner.

When faith in God goes, man the sufferer loses his securest refuge. One who has walked with families through long illnesses where desperate prayers rise like a fountain day and night, who has seen strong men break down in health or lose the fortune of a lifetime, who has stood at children's graves and heard mothers cry, "How empty are my arms!" does not need long explication of life's tragic suffering. The staggering blows shatter the hopes of good and bad alike. Whether one's house be built on rock or sand, on both, as Jesus said, the rains descend and the floods come and the winds blow. In this experience of crushing trouble nothing but religious faith has been able to save men from despair or from stoical endurance of their fate. To face the loom of life and hopefully to lay oneself upon it, as though the dark threads were as necessary in the pattern as the light ones are, we must believe that there is a purpose running through the stern, forbidding process. What men have needed most of all in suffering, is not to know the explanation, but *to know that there is an explanation.* And religious faith alone gives confidence that human tragedy is not the meaningless sport of physical forces, making our life what Voltaire called it, "a bad joke," but is rather a school of discipline, the explanation of whose mysteries is in the heart of God. No one who has lived deeply can ever call such faith a "matter of words and names." To multitudes it is a matter of life and death.

When faith in God goes, man the lover loses his fairest vision.
When we say our worst about mankind, this redeeming truth remains, that each of us has some one for whose sake he willingly would die. The very love lyrics of the race are proof of this human quality, from homely folk songs like "John Anderson, My Jo, John" to great poetry like Mrs. Browning's sonnets. We call them secular, but they are ineffably sacred. And when one seeks the faith that has made these loves of men radiant with an illumination which man alone cannot create, he finds it in religion. Love is not a transient fragrance from matter finely organized—so men have dared believe; love is of kin with the Eternal, has there its source and ground and destiny; love is the very substance of reality. "God is love, and he that abideth in love, abideth in God, and God abideth in him" (I John 4:16). Man the lover is bereft of his finest insight and love's inner glory has departed, when that faith has gone.

When faith in God goes, man the mortal loses his only hope.
Man's nature, like a lighthouse, combines two elements. At the foundation of the beacon all is stone; as one lifts his eyes, all is stone still; but at the top is something new and wonderful. It is the thing for which the rock was piled. Its laws are not the laws of stone nor are its ways the same. For while the stolid rock stands fast, this miracle of light with speed incredible hurls itself out across the sea. Two worlds are here, the one cold and stationary, the other full of the marvel and mystery of fire. So man has in him a miracle which he cannot explain; he "feels that he is greater than he knows"; and he never has been able to believe that the mystery of spirit was given him in vain, had no reality from which it came, and no future beyond death. The finest thing ever said of Columbus is a remark of his own countryman, "The instinct of an unknown continent burned in him." That is the secret of Columbus' greatness. All the arguments by which he attempted to convince the doubters were but afterthoughts of this; all the labors by which he endeavored to make good his hopes were but its consequence. And if we ask of man why so universally he has believed in life to come, the answer leaps not superficially from the mind, but out of the basic intuitions of man's life. We know that something is now ours which ought not to die; the instinct of an unknown continent burns in us. But all the hopes, the motives, the horizons that immortality has given man must go, if faith in God departs. In a godless world man dies forever.

One, therefore, who is facing loss of faith may not regard it as a light affair. To be sure, some denials of religion, even a Christian must respect. Huxley, for example, at the death of his little boy, wanting to believe in immortality as only a father can whose son lies dead, yet, for all that, disbelieving, wrote to Charles Kingsley, "I have searched over the grounds of my belief, and if wife and child and name and fame were all to be lost to me one after another as the penalty, still I will not lie." One respects *that*. When George John Romanes turned his back for a while on the Christian faith, he wrote out of his agnosticism, "When at times I think, as think at times I must, of the appalling contrast between the hallowed glory of that creed which once was mine, and the lonely mystery of existence as now I find it—at such times I shall ever feel it impossible to avoid the sharpest pang of which my nature is susceptible." One respects *that*. But some discard religion from their life's adventure with no such serious understanding of the import of their denial. They are pert disbelievers. They toss faith facilely aside in a light mood. Such frivolous sceptics indict their own intelligence. Whoever discards religious faith should appoint a day of mourning for his soul, and put on sackcloth and ashes. He must take from his life the greatest thought that man the thinker ever had, the finest faith that man the worker ever leaned upon, the surest help that man the sinner ever found, the strongest reliance that man the sufferer ever trusted in, the loftiest vision that man the lover ever saw, and the only hope that man the mortal ever had. So he must deny his faith in God. Before one thus leaves himself bereft of the faith that makes life's adventure most worth while he well may do what Carlyle, under the figure of Teufelsdröckh, says that he did in his time of doubt: "In the silent night-watches, still darker in his heart than over sky and earth, he has cast himself before the All-seeing, and with audible prayers cried vehemently for Light."

v

If minimizing the importance of religious faith is unintelligent, so is avoiding some sort of decision about religious faith impossible. Most of those into whose hands these studies fall will grant readily faith's incalculable importance. Some, however, will be not helped but plunged into deeper trouble by their consent. For they feel themselves unable to decide about a matter which they acknowledge to be the most important in the world. Asked whether they believe in

God, they would reply with one of Victor Hugo's characters, "Yes—
No—Sometimes." They grant that to be steadily assured of God
would be an invaluable boon, but for themselves, how can they balance the opposing arguments and find their way to confidence? All
our studies are intended for the help of such, but at the beginning
one urgent truth may well be plainly put. However undecided they
may appear, men cannot altogether avoid decision on the main matters of religion. Life will not let them. For while the mind may hold
itself suspended between alternatives, the adventure of life goes on,
and men inevitably tend to live either as though the Christian God
were real or as though he were not.

Some questions allow a complete postponement of decision. As to
which of several theories about the Northern Lights may be true, a
man can hold his judgment in entire suspense. Life does not require
from him any action that depends on what he thinks of the Aurora
Borealis; and whether a man think one thing or another, no conceivable change would be the consequence in anything he said or
did. But there is another kind of question, where, however much the
mind may waver between opinions and may resolve on indecision,
life itself compels decision. A man cannot really be agnostic and
neutral on a question like the moral law of sexual purity, for, by an
irrevocable necessity, he has to act one way or another. He may stop
thinking, but he cannot stop living. With tremendous urgency the
adventure of life insistently goes on, and it never pauses for any man
to make up his mind on any question. Therefore while a man may
theoretically suspend his judgment as to the requirements of the
moral law, his life will be a loud, convincing advertisement to all
who know him that he has vitally decided. *A man can avoid making
up his mind, but he cannot avoid making up his life.*

Quite as truly, though, it may be, not quite as obviously, religious
questions belong to this second class. Not all questions that are called
religious belong there. With fatal pettiness religious men have reduced the great faiths to technicalities and some beliefs called religious a man may hold or not, with utter indifference to anything he
is or does. But on the basic attitudes of religion such as we have just
rehearsed, a man cannot be completely neutral, no matter how he
tries. Bernard Shaw's remark, "What a man believes may be ascer-
tained not from his creed, but from the assumptions on which he
habitually acts," should be taken to heart by any one trying to remain religiously neutral. For one cannot by any possibility avoid

"assumptions on which he habitually acts." He tends to undertake social service either as confident cooperation with God's purpose or as an endeavor to make one corner of an unpurposed world as decent as possible. He tends to follow his ideals, either as the voice of God calling him upward, or as the work of natural selection, adjusting him to a temporary environment. He tends to face suffering either hopefully as a school of moral discipline, in a world presided over by a Father, or grimly as a hardship in which there is no meaning. He tends to face death either as the supreme adventure, full of boundless hope, or as a final exit that leads nowhere. He may never consciously formulate his ideas on any of these matters, he may maintain an intellectual agnosticism, genuine and complete, but his living subtly involves the confession of some faith. "A man's action," said Emerson, "is only the picture-book of his creed." And the more thoughtful he is, the more he will be aware of that unescapable tendency to confess in his living an inward faith about life.

One practical result of this urgent truth is too frequently seen to be doubtful. *Those who in religion do not decide, thereby decide against religion.* Religious faith is a positive achievement, and he who does not deliberately choose it, loses it. A man who, rowing down Niagara River, debates within himself whether or not he will stop at Buffalo, and who cannot decide, thereby has decided. His irresolution has not for a moment interfered with the steady flow of the river, and if he but debate long enough concerning his stop at Buffalo, he will awake to discover that he has finally decided not to stop there. As much beyond the control of man's volition is the steady flow of life. It pauses for no man's indecision, and if one is irresolute about any positive, aspiring faith in any realm, his indecisiveness is decision of a most final sort.

This, then, is the summary of the matter. Life is a great adventure in which faith is indispensable; in this adventure faith in God presents the issues of transcendent import; and on these issues life itself continuously compels decision. Our obligation is obvious—since willy-nilly the decision must be made—to make it consciously, to reach it by reason, not by chance, by thinking, not by drifting. If a man is to be irreligious, let him at least know why, and not slip into this estate, as most irreligious men do, by careless living and frivolous thought. If a man is to be religious, let him have reason for his choice; let his faith be founded not on credulity and chance, but on real experience and reasonable thought. So his faith shall be good not only for domestic consumption, but for export too—clear in his own mind and convincing to his friends. The forms of thought shift with the centuries and old situations cannot be repeated in detail, but one crisis in its essential meaning is perennial: "Elijah came near unto all the people, and said, How long go ye limping between the two sides? if Jehovah be God follow him; but if Baal then follow him" (I Kings 18:21).

CHAPTER II

Faith a Road to Truth

DAILY READINGS

Many minds are prevented from even a fair consideration of religious faith by prejudices which spring, not from reasoned argument, but from practical experience. They are biased before argument has begun; they *feel* that faith means credulity, and that religious faith in particular is a surrender of reason. Before we positively present faith as an indispensable means of dealing with reality in any realm, let us, in the daily readings, consider some of the practical experiences and attitudes that thus prejudice men against religion.

Second Week, First Day

Many men are biased in advance by the *unwise treatment to which in their childhood they were subjected.* Paul pictures the home life of Timothy as ideal:

I thank God, whom I serve from my forefathers in a pure conscience, how unceasing is my remembrance of thee in my supplications, night and day longing to see thee, remembering thy tears, that I may be filled with joy; having been reminded of the unfeigned faith that is in thee; which dwelt first in thy grandmother Lois, and thy mother Eunice; and, I am persuaded, in thee also.—II Tim. 1:3-5.

"Unfeigned faith" is often thus a family heritage, handed down by vital contagion. But in many homes religion is not thus beautifully presented to the children; it is a hard and rigorous affair of dogma and restraint. "Oh, why," said a young professional man, whom Professor Coe quotes, "why did my parents try to equip me with a doctrinal system in childhood? I supposed that the whole system must be believed on pain of losing my religion altogether. And so, when I began to doubt some points, I felt obliged to throw all overboard. I have found my way back to positive religion, but by what a long and bitter struggle!" If, however, one has been so unfortunate as to be hardened in youth by unwise training, is it reasonable on that account forever to shut himself out from the most glorious experience of man? This complaint about mistreatment in youth is often an excuse, not a reason for irreligion. Says Phillips Brooks: "I have grown familiar to weariness with the self-excuse of men who say, 'Oh, if I had not had the terrors of the law so preached to me when I was a boy, if I had not been so confronted with the woes of hell and the awfulness of the judgment day, I should have been religious long ago.' My friends, I think I never hear a meaner or a falser speech than that. Men may believe it when they say it—I suppose they do—but it is not true. It is unmanly, I think. It is throwing on their teaching and their teachers, or their fathers and their mothers, the fault which belongs to their own neglect, because they have never taken up the earnest fight with sin and sought through every obstacle for truth and God. It has the essential vice of dogmatism about it, for it claims that a different *view* of God would have done for them that which no view of God can do, that which must be done, *under any system, any teaching,* by humility and penitence and struggle and self-sacrifice. Without these no teaching saves the soul. With these, under any teaching, the soul must find its Father."

O Thou, who didst lay the foundations of the earth amid the singing of the morning stars and the joyful shouts of the sons of God, lift up our little life into Thy gladness. Out of Thee, as out of an overflowing fountain of Love, wells forth eternally a stream of blessing upon every creature Thou hast made. If we have thought that Thou didst call into being this universe in order to win praise and honor for Thyself, rebuke the vain fancies of our foolish minds and show us that Thy glory is the joy of giving. We can give Thee nothing of our own. All that we have is Thine. Oh, then, help us to glorify Thee by striving to be like Thee. Make us just and pure and good as Thou art. May we be partakers of the Divine Nature, so that all that is truly human in us may be deepened, purified, and strengthened. And so may we be witnesses for Thee, lights of the world, reflecting Thy light.

Help us to make religion a thing so beautiful that all men may be won to surrender to its power. Let us manifest in our lives its sweetness and excellency, its free and ennobling spirit. Forbid that we should go up and down the world with melancholy looks and dejected visage, lest we should repel men from entering Thy Kingdom. Rather, may we walk in the freedom and joy of faith, and with Thy new song in our mouths, so that men looking on us may learn to trust and to love Thee. Amen.—Samuel McComb.

Second Week, Second Day

Many men are prejudiced against religion during their youthful *period of revolt against authority.* Listen to an ancient father talking with his sons:

Hear, my sons, the instruction of a father,
And attend to know understanding:
For I give you good doctrine;
Forsake ye not my law.
For I was a son unto my father,
Tender and only beloved in the sight of my mother.
And he taught me, and said unto me:
Let thy heart retain my words;
Keep my commandments, and live;
Get wisdom, get understanding;
Forget not, neither decline from the words of my mouth;
Forsake her not, and she will preserve thee;
Love her, and she will keep thee.
Wisdom is the principal thing; therefore get wisdom;
Yea, with all thy getting get understanding.
Exalt her, and she will promote thee;
She will bring thee to honor, when thou dost embrace her.
She will give to thy head a chaplet of grace;
A crown of beauty will she deliver to thee.

—Prov. 4:1-9.

No father can read this urgent, anxious plea without understanding the reason for its solicitude. Every boy comes to the time when he breaks away from parental authority and begins to take his life into his own hands. It is one of youth's great crises, and the spirit of it is sometimes harsh and rebellious. So Carlyle describes his own experience: "Such transitions are ever full of pain: thus the Eagle when he moults is sickly; and, to attain his new beak, must harshly dash-off the old one upon rocks." For religious faith this period of life is always critical. Stevenson in his revolt, when he called respectability "the deadliest gag and wet-blanket that can be laid on man," also became, as he said, "a youthful atheist." How many have traveled that road and stopped in the negation! Stevenson did not stop, and years afterward wrote of his progress: "Because I have reached Paris, I am not ashamed of having passed through Newhaven and Dieppe." Surely if anyone has been "a youthful atheist," it was an experience to be "passed through."

O God, we turn to Thee in the faith that Thou dost understand and art very merciful. Some of us are not sure concerning Thee; not sure what Thou art; not sure that Thou art at all. Yet there is something at work behind our minds, in times of stillness we hear it, like a distant song; there is something in the sky at evening-time; something in the face of man. We feel that round our incompleteness flows Thy greatness, round our restlessness Thy rest. Yet this is not enough.

We want a heart to speak to, a heart that understands; a friend to whom we can turn, a breast on which we may lean. O that we could find Thee! Yet could we ever think these things unless Thou hadst inspired us, could we ever want these things unless Thou Thyself wert very near?

Some of us know full well; but we are sore afraid. We dare not yield ourselves to Thee, for we fear what that might mean. Our foolish freedom, our feeble pleasures, our fatal self-indulgence suffice to hold us back from Thee, though Thou art our very life, and we so sick and needing Thee. Our freedom has proved false, our pleasures have long since lost their zest, our sins, oh how we hate them!

Come and deliver us, for we have lost all hope in ourselves. Amen.
—W. E. Orchard.

Second Week, Third Day

Some men—often the precocious, clever ones—are biased against religion because *in youth they accepted an immature philosophy of life and have never changed it.* The crust forms too soon on some minds, and if it forms during the period of youthful revolt, they are definitely prejudiced against religious truth. The difference between such folk and the great believers is not that the believers had no doubts, but that they did not fix their final thought of life until more mature experience had come. They fulfilled the admonition of a wise father to keep up a tireless search for truth:

My son, if thou wilt receive my words,
And lay up my commandments with thee;
So as to incline thine ear unto wisdom,
And apply thy heart to understanding;
Yea, if thou cry after discernment,
And lift up thy voice for understanding;
If thou seek her as silver,
And search for her as for hid treasures:
Then shalt thou understand the fear of Jehovah,
And find the knowledge of God.

—Prov. 2:1-5.

Mrs. Charles Kingsley, for example, says of her husband that at twenty "He was full of religious doubts; and his face, with its unsatisfied, hungering, and at times defiant look, bore witness to the state of his mind." At twenty-one Kingsley himself wrote: "You believe that you have a sustaining Hand to guide you along that path, an Invisible Protection and an unerring Guide. I, alas! have no stay for my weary steps, but that same abused and stupefied reason which has stumbled and wandered, and betrayed me a thousand times ere now, and is every moment ready to faint and to give up the unequal struggle." If Kingsley had framed his final philosophy then, what a loss to the world of an inspiring life transfigured by Christian faith! He cried after discernment, lifted up his voice for understanding, and he found the knowledge of God. Many a man ought to revise in the light of mature experience and thought a hasty irreligious guess at life's meaning which he made in youth.

O Father, we turn to Thee because we are sore vexed with our own thoughts. Our minds plague us with questionings we cannot answer; we are driven to voyage on strange seas of thought alone. Dost Thou disturb our minds with endless questioning, yet keep the answers hidden in Thy heart, so that away from Thee we should always be perplexed, and by thoughts derived from Thee be ever drawn to Thee? Surely, our God, it must be so.

But still more bitter and humbling, O Father, is our experience of failure, so frequent, tragic, and unpardonable. We have struggled on in vain, resolves are broken ere they pass our lips; we can see no hope of better things, we can never forgive ourselves; and after all our prayers our need remains and our sense of coming short but deepens. Yet, at least we know that we have failed, and how, if something higher than ourselves were not at work within?

Our desperate desires have driven us at last to Thee, conscious now, after all vain effort, that it is Thyself alone can satisfy, and now at peace to know that Thou it is who art desired, because Thou it is who dost desire within us. Beyond our need reveal Thyself, its cause and cure; in all desire teach us to discern Thy drawing near. Amen.—W. E. Orchard.

Second Week, Fourth Day

Men are often prejudiced against religion because *the churches which they happened to attend in youth urged on them an irrational faith.* Some men never recover from the idea that all religion everywhere must always be the same kind of religion against which in youth their good sense rose in revolt; they are in perpetual rebellion against religion as it was when they broke with it a generation ago. But if one thing more than another grows, expands, becomes in the intelligent and pure increasingly pure and intelligent, it is religion.

Consider an early Hebrew idea of God:

And it came to pass on the way at the lodging-place, that Jehovah met him, and sought to kill him. Then Zipporah took a flint, and cut off the foreskin of her son, and cast it at his feet; and she said, Surely a bridegroom of blood art thou to me. So he let him alone. Then she said, A bridegroom of blood art thou, because of the circumcision.—Exodus 4:24-26.

Over against so abhorrent a picture of a deity who would have committed murder, had not a mother swiftly circumcised her son, consider a later thought of God:

How think ye? if any man have a hundred sheep, and one of them be gone astray, doth he not leave the ninety and nine, and go unto the mountains, and seek that which goeth astray? And if so be that he find it, verily I say unto you, he rejoiceth over it more than over the ninety and nine which have not gone astray. Even so

**it is not the will of your Father who is in heaven, that one of these
little ones should perish.—Matt. 18:12-14.**

So religion grows with man's capacity to receive higher, finer
revelations of the divine. And in no age of the world has so great a
change passed over the intellectual framework of faith as in the
generation just gone. To live in protest against forms of belief a generation old is fighting men of straw; the vanguard of religious
thought and life has pushed ahead many a mile beyond the point of
such attack. Men who threw away the living water of the Gospel
because they disliked the water-buckets in which their boyhood
churches presented it, are living spiritually thirsty lives when there is
no reasonable need of their doing so. There is many an unbeliever
with a "God-shaped blank" in his heart, who could be a confident
and joyful believer if he only knew what religion means to men of
faith today.

*O God, who hast formed all hearts to love Thee, made all ways
to lead to Thy face, created all desire to be unsatisfied save in Thee;
with great compassion look upon us gathered here. Our presence is
our prayer, our need the only plea we dare to claim, Thy purposes
the one assurance we possess.*

*Some of us are very confused; we do not know why we were ever
born, for what end we should live, which way we should take. But
we are willing to be guided. Take our trembling hands in Thine,
and lead us on.*

*Some of us are sore within. We long for love and friendship, but
we care for no one and we feel that no one cares for us. We are
misunderstood, we are lonely, we have been disappointed, we have
lost our faith in man and our faith in life. Wilt Thou not let us love
Thee who first loved us?*

*Some of us are vexed with passions that affright us; to yield to
them would mean disaster, to restrain them is beyond our power,
and nothing earth contains exhausts their vehemence or satisfies their
fierce desire.*

*And so because there is no answer, no end or satisfaction in our-
selves; and because we are what we are, and yet long to be so different; we believe Thou art, and that Thou dost understand us. By
faith we feel after Thee, through love we find the way, in hope we
bring ourselves to Thee. Amen.—W. E. Orchard.*

Second Week, Fifth Day

Many minds are prejudiced against religion because, having gone so far as to feel the credulity of religious belief, they have never gone further and *seen the credulity of religious unbelief*. Irreligion implies a creed just as surely as religion does; and many a man's return to faith has begun when his faculties of doubt, which hitherto had been used only against belief in God, became active against belief in no-God. Mr. Gilbert Chesterton, with his characteristic vividness and exaggeration, narrates such an experience: "I never read a line of Christian apologetics. I read as little as I can of them now. It was Huxley and Herbert Spencer and Bradlaugh who brought me back to orthodox theology. They sowed in my mind my first wild doubts of doubt. Our grandmothers were quite right when they said that Tom Paine and the free-thinkers unsettled the mind. They do. They unsettled mine horribly. The rationalist made me question whether reason was of any use whatever; and when I had finished Herbert Spencer I had got as far as doubting (for the first time) whether evolution had occurred at all. As I laid down the last of Colonel Ingersoll's atheistic lectures the dreadful thought broke across my mind, 'Almost thou persuadest me to be a Christian.' I was in a desperate way." Lest Mr. Chesterton's whimsicality may hide the seriousness of such an experience, we may add that Robert Louis Stevenson's first break with his "youthful atheism" came when, under the influence of Professor Fleeming Jenkin, he too began to have his "first wild doubts of doubt." He began thinking, as he says, that "certainly the church was not right, but certainly not the anti-church either." Many a man has played unfairly with his doubts; he has used them against religion, but not against irreligion. When he is thorough with his doubts he may join the many who understand what the apostle meant when he wrote to Timothy:

O Timothy, guard that which is committed unto thee, turning away from the profane babblings and oppositions of the knowledge which is falsely so called; which some professing have erred concerning the faith.

Grace be with you.—I Tim. 6:20, 21.

O God, too near to be found, too simple to be conceived, too good to be believed; help us to trust, not in our knowledge of Thee, but

*in Thy knowledge of us; to be certain of Thee, not because we feel
our thoughts of Thee are true, but because we know how far Thou
dost transcend them. May we not be anxious to discern Thy will, but
content only with desire to do it; may we not strain our minds to
understand Thy nature, but yield ourselves and live our lives only to
express Thee.*

*Shew us how foolish it is to doubt Thee, since Thou Thyself dost
set the questions which disturb us; reveal our unbelief to be faith
fretting at its outworn form. Be gracious when we are tempted to
cease from moral strife: reveal what it is that struggles in us. Before
we tire of mental search enable us to see that it was not ourselves
but Thy call which stirred our souls.*

*Turn us back from our voyages of thought to that which sent us
forth. Teach us to trust not to cleverness or learning, but to that
inward faith which can never be denied. Lead us out of confusion
to simplicity. Call us back from wandering without to find Thee at
home within. Amen.*—W. E. Orchard.

Second Week, Sixth Day

Many men are biased in favor of their habitual doubt because they
do not see that *positive faith is the only normal estate of man.* We
live not by the things of which we are uncertain, but by the things
which we verily believe. Columbus doubted many of the old views
in geography, but these negations did not make him great; his greatness sprang from the positive beliefs which he confidently held and
on which he launched his splendid adventure. Goethe is right when
he makes Mephistopheles, his devil, say, "I am the spirit of negation," for negation, save as it paves the way for positive conviction,
always bedevils life. The psalmist reveals the ideal experience for
every doubter.

First, *uncertainty:*

But as for me, my feet were almost gone;
My steps had well nigh slipped.
For I was envious at the arrogant,
When I saw the prosperity of the wicked.

Psalm 73:2, 3.

Then *vision:*

When I thought how I might know this,
It was too painful for me;
Until I went into the sanctuary of God,
And considered their latter end.

—Psalm 73:16, 17.

Then, *positive assurance:*

Thou wilt guide me with thy counsel,
And afterward receive me to glory.
Whom have I in heaven but thee?
And there is none upon earth that I desire besides thee.
My flesh and my heart faileth;
But God is the strength of my heart and my portion for ever.

—Psalm 73: 24-26.

Doubt, therefore, does have real value in life; it clears away rubbish and stimulates search for truth; but it has no value unless it is
finally swallowed up in positive assurance. So Tennyson pictures the
experience of his friend, Arthur Hallam:

> "One indeed I knew
> In many a subtle question versed,
> Who touch'd a jarring lyre at first,
> But ever strove to make it true:
>
> Perplext in faith, but pure in deeds,
> At last he beat his music out.
> There lives more faith in honest doubt,
> Believe me, than in half the creeds.
>
> He fought his doubts and gather'd strength,
> He would not make his judgment blind,
> He faced the spectres of the mind
> And laid them: thus he came at length
>
> To find a stronger faith his own."

*O Most Merciful, whose love to us is mighty, long-suffering, and
infinitely tender; lead us beyond all idols and imaginations of our*

*minds to contact with Thee the real and abiding; past all barriers of
fear and beyond all paralysis of failure to that furnace of flaming
purity where falsehood, sin, and cowardice are all consumed away.
It may be that we know not what we ask; yet we dare not ask for
less.*

*Our aspirations are hindered because we do not know ourselves.
We have tried to slake our burning thirst at broken cisterns, to comfort the crying of our spirits with baubles and trinkets, to assuage the
pain of our deep unrest by drugging an accusing conscience, believing a lie, and veiling the naked flame that burns within. But now
we know Thou makest us never to be content with aught save Thyself, in earth, or heaven, or hell.*

*Sometimes we have sought Thee in agony and tears, scanned the
clouds and watched the ways of men, considered the stars and
studied the moral law; and returned from all our search no surer
and no nearer. Yet now we know that the impulse to seek Thee came
from Thyself alone, and what we sought for was the image Thou
hadst first planted in our hearts.*

*We may not yet hold Thee fast or feel Thee near, but we know
Thou holdest us. All is well. Amen.*—W. E. Orchard.

Second Week, Seventh Day

Men are often prejudiced against religion or any serious consideration of it, because they *never have felt any vital need of God.* To
study wireless telegraphy in the safe seclusion of a college laboratory
is one thing; to hear the wireless apparatus on a floundering ship
send out its call for help across a stormy sea is quite a different
matter. Many folk have never thought of faith in God save with a
mild, intellectual curiosity; they do not know those deep experiences
of serious souls with sin and sorrow and anxiety, with burden for
great causes and desire for triumphant righteousness in men and
nations—experiences that throw men back on God as their only
sufficient refuge and hope. *Men never really find God until they
need him;* and some men never feel the need of him until life
plunges them into a shattering experience. Even in scientific research
new discoveries are made because men *want* them, and Mayer,
lighting on a theory that proved to be of great value, says, "Engaged
during a sea voyage almost exclusively with the study of physiology,
I discovered the new theory, for the sufficient reason that I *vividly*

felt the need of it." How much more must the vital discovery of God
depend on life's conscious demand for him! And how certainly a
shallow, frivolous nature, unstirred by the deep concerns of life, is
biased against any serious interest in religious faith! Great believers
have first of all *thirsted* for God.

Ho, every one that thirsteth, come ye to the waters, and he that
hath no money; come ye, buy, and eat; yea, come, buy wine and
milk without money and without price. Wherefore do ye spend
money for that which is not bread? and your labor for that which
satisfieth not? hearken diligently unto me, and eat ye that which is
good, and let your soul delight itself in fatness. Incline your ear,
and come unto me; hear, and your soul shall live: and I will make
an everlasting covenant with you, even the sure mercies of David.
. . . Seek ye Jehovah while he may be found; call ye upon him
while he is near: let the wicked forsake his way, and the unrighteous
man his thoughts; and let him return unto Jehovah, and he will
have mercy upon him; and to our God, for he will abundantly
pardon.—Isa. 55:1-3, 6, 7.

Grant unto us, we pray Thee, the lost hunger and thirst after
righteousness—the longing for God. Grant unto us that drawing
power by which everything that is in us shall call out for Thee.
Become necessary unto us. With the morning and evening light, at
noon and at midnight, may we feel the need of Thy companionship.
. . . Though Thou dost not speak as man speaks, yet Thou canst
call out to us; and the soul shall know Thy presence, and shall
understand by its own self what Thou meanest. Grant unto us this
witness of the Spirit, this communion of the soul with Thee—and
not only once or twice: may we abide in the light.

Thou hast come unto Thine own; and even as of old, Thine own
know Thee not, and believe Thee not. How many are there that
have learned Thy name upon their mother's knee, but have forgotten
it! How many are there that grew up into the happiness of a child-
hood in which piety presided, but have gone away, and have not
come back again to their first love and to their early faith! How
many are there marching on now in the Sahara of indifference and
in the wilderness of unbelief! . . . Lord, look upon them; have
merciful thoughts toward them, and issue those gracious influences
of power by which what is best in them shall lift itself up and bear
witness against that which is worst. Amen.—Henry Ward Beecher.

COMMENT FOR THE WEEK

I

We are to deal in this chapter with one of the most common experiences of doubt and are to attempt the statement of a truth useful in meeting it. Many minds are undone at the first symptoms of religious uncertainty, because they suppose that their doubt is philosophical, and they feel a paralyzing inability to deal with philosophy at all. As men have been known to take to their beds at hearing the scientific names of illnesses which hitherto they had patiently endured, so minds are sometimes overwhelmed by an unsettlement of faith that takes the name of philosophic doubt. It is well, then, early in our study, to note the homely, familiar experience, which in most cases underlies and helps to explain the problem of theological unrest.

We all began, as children, with an unlimited ability to believe what we were told. We were credulous long before we became critical. God and Santa Claus, fairy stories and life after death—in what beautiful, unquestioning confusion we received them all! Our thinking was altogether imitative, as our talking was. From the existence of Kamchatka to the opinion that it was wrong to lie, we had no independent knowledge of our own. Reliance on authority was our only road to truth. One prescription was adequate for every need of information: ask our parents and be told.

This situation was the occasion of our first unsettlement of faith: we discovered the fallibility of our parents. They failed to tell us what we asked, or we found to be untrue what they had said, or they themselves confessed how much they did not know. To some this was a shock, the memory of which has never been forgotten. Edmund Gosse, the literary critic, tells us that up to his sixth year he thought that his father knew everything. Then came the fateful crisis when his father wrongly reported an incident which Edmund himself had witnessed. "Nothing could possibly have been more trifling to my parents," he writes, "but to me it meant an epoch. Here was the appalling discovery never suspected before that my father was not as God and did not know everything. The shock was not caused by any suspicion that he was not telling the truth, as it appeared to him, but by the awful proof that he was not, as I had supposed, omniscient." By most of us, however, the transfer of our faith from our parents' authority to some other basis of belief was easily accomplished. We found ourselves resting back on the priest or the church or the creed or the Bible. Still our convictions were not independently our own; we had never fought for them or thought them through; they were founded on the say-so of authority. What we wished to know we asked another, and what was told us we implicitly believed.

The time inevitably comes, however, to a normally developing mind, when such an attitude of unquestioning credulity becomes impossible. The curious "Why?" of the growing child, that began in early years to besiege all statements of fact, now ranges out to call in question the propositions of religious faith. For long-accepted truths, from the rotundity of the earth to the existence of God, the enlarging intellect wants reasons rather than dogmas. So normal is this period of interrogation that it is regularly slated on the timetables of psychological development. Starbuck fixes the average age of the doubt period at about eighteen years for boys and about fifteen for girls.

At whatever time and in whatever special form this period of doubt arises, the characteristic quality of its outcome is easily described. In the end the fully awakened mind is ill content to accept any authoritative statements that he dare not question or deny. He resents having a quotation from any source waved like a revolver in his face with the demand that he throw up his intellectual hands. No more in religion than in politics does he incline to stand before infallibility, like the French peasants before Louis XI, saying, "Sire, what are our opinions?" He claims his right to question everything, to make every truth advance and give the countersign of reasonableness, to weigh all propositions in the scales of his own thinking, and if he is to love the Lord his God at all, to do it, not with all his credulity, but, as Jesus said, with all his mind.

Biography reveals how many of the great believers have passed through this youthful period of rebellion against accepted tradition and have suffered serious religious unsettlement in the process. Robert Browning tells us that as a boy he was "passionately religious." When his period of questioning and revolt arrived, however, it carried him so far that he was publicly rebuked in church for intentional misbehavior, and in his sixteenth year, under the influence of Shelley's "Queen Mab," he declared himself an atheist. But in his

"Pauline," written when he was twenty-one, the direction in which
his quest was leading him was plain:

> "I have always had one lode-star; now
> As I look back, I see that I have halted
> Or hastened as I looked towards that star—
> A need, a trust, a yearning after God."

And when he grew to his maturity, had left his early credulousness
with the revolt that followed it far behind and had used his independent thinking to productive purpose, from what a height of
splendid faith did he look back upon that youthful period of storm
and stress which he called "the passionate, impatient struggles of a
boy toward truth and love"!

Henry Ward Beecher's intellectual revolution was postponed until
he had entered the theological seminary. "I was then twenty years
old," he writes, "and there came a great revulsion in me from all
this inchoate, unregulated, undirected experience. My mind took
one tremendous spring over into scepticism, and I said: 'I have been
a fool long enough—I will not stir one step further than I can see
my way, and I will not stand a moment where I cannot see the truth.
I will have something that is sure and steadfast.' Having taken that
ground, I was in that state of mind for the larger part of two years."
A wholesome restraint upon the wild perversions, the anarchic denials, the abysmal despairs of this period of life is the clear recognition that in some form it is one of the commonest experiences of
man.

II

The treatment accorded to a youth who is passing through this
difficult adjustment often determines, in a fine or lamentable way,
his subsequent attitude towards religion. *Negative repression of real
questions is of all methods the most fatal, whether it be practiced on
the youth by others or by the youth upon himself.* "I have not been
in church for twenty years," said a college graduate. "Why?" was
the inquiry. "Because in college I learned from geology through how
many ages this earth was slowly being built. Troubled by the conflict
between this new knowledge and my early training, I went to my
minister. He said that the Bible told us the earth was made in six

days and that I must accept that on faith. That's why." Thousands
of men are religious wrecks today because, when the issue was raised
in their thinking between their desire for a reason and their traditional beliefs, they were told that to ask a reason is sin. George
Eliot's experience unhappily is not unique. Just when in girlhood her
mind was waking to independent thought, a book now long unread,
Hennell's "Inquiry Concerning the Origin of Christianity," convinced her immature judgment that her early credulity had been
blind. No one was at hand to state the faith in a reasonable way or
to meet, not by denying but by using her right to think, the attacks
of Hennell, which now are forgotten in their futility. She never came
through her youthful unsettlement. Years after, F. W. H. Myers
wrote: "I remember how at Cambridge I walked with her once in
the Fellows' Garden of Trinity, on an evening of rainy May, and she,
stirred somewhat beyond her wont, and taking as her text the three
words which have been used so often as the inspiring trumpet calls
of men—the words God, Immortality, Duty—pronounced with terrible earnestness, how inconceivable was the first, how unbelievable
was the second, and how peremptory and absolute the third. Never,
perhaps, had sterner accents affirmed the sovereignty of impersonal
and unrecompensing law. I listened and night fell; her grave, majestic countenance turned toward me like a Sibyl's in the gloom; it
was as though she withdrew from my grasp one by one the two
scrolls of promise, and left me the third scroll only, awful with inevitable fate."

In this period of readjustment, whether one is the youth in the
midst of the struggle or the solicitous friend endeavoring to help,
one most needs a clear perception of the ideal outcome of such intellectual unrest. Let us attempt a picture of that ideal. The youth who
long has taken on his parents' say-so the most important convictions
that the soul can hold, or who, with no care to think or question for
himself, has looked to Book or Church for all that he believed about
God, now feels within him that intellectual awakening that cannot
be quieted by mere authority. He long has taken his truth preserved
by others' hands; now he desires to pick it for himself, fresh from the
living tree of knowledge. His declaration of independence from subjection to his parents or his Church is not at first irreverent desire
to disbelieve; it is rather desire to enter into the Samaritans' experience when they said to the woman who first had told them about
Jesus: "Now we believe, not because of *thy* speaking; for we have

heard for ourselves, and know that this is indeed the Saviour of the world" (John 4:41). The youth turns from second-hand rehearsal of the truth to seek a first-hand, original acquaintance with it. As he began in utter financial dependence on his father, then made a bit of spending money of his own, and at last moved out to make his living, ashamed to be a pensioner and parasite when he should be carrying himself, so from his old, intellectual dependence the youth passes to a fine responsibility for his own thinking and belief. He knows that such transitions, whether financial or intellectual, generally mean stress and perplexity, but if he is to be a man the youth must venture.

In this transition beliefs will certainly be modified. Not only do forms of religious thinking shift and change with the passing generations, but individuals differ in their powers to see and understand. Religious faith, like water, takes shape from the receptacles into whose unique nooks and crannies it is poured. If the truth which the youth possesses is to be indeed his own, it will surely differ from the truth which once he learned, by as much as his mind and his experience differ from his father's. Even in the New Testament one can easily distinguish James' thought from Paul's and John's from Peter's. But change of form need not mean loss of value. To pass by fine gradations from unquestioning credulity to thoughtful faith is not impossible. Thus a boy learns to swim with his father's hands beneath him and passes so gradually from reliance upon another to independent power to swim alone that he cannot tell when first the old support was quietly withdrawn.

Thus ideally pictured, this transition is nothing to be feared; it is one of life's steps to spiritual power. This period of questioning and venture we have called the passage from credulity to independence, but its significance is deeper than those words imply. *It is the passage from hearsay to reality.* Of all inward intimate experiences, religion reaches deepest and is least transferable. It is as incommunicable as friendship. A father may commend a comrade to his son and lay bare his own deep friendship with the man, but if the son himself does not see the value there nor for himself in loyalty and love make self surrender, the father can do nothing more. Friendship cannot be carried on by proxy. One can as easily breathe for another as in another's place be loyal to a friend or trust in God.

When, therefore, the youth moves out from mere dependence on his father, his Bible, or his Church to see and know God in his own right, he is fulfilling the end of all religion. *For this his father taught*

him, for this the Book was written and the Church was founded.
As George Macdonald put it, "Each generation must do its own
seeking and finding. The father's having found is only the warrant
for the children's search." Said Goethe: "What you have inherited
from your fathers you must earn for yourself before you can call it
yours." This individual experience makes religion real, and the
"awkward age" of the spirit when the old security of credulous
belief has gone and the new assurance of personal conviction has not
yet fully come, is a small price to pay for the sense of reality that
enters into religion when a man for himself knows God. Such is the
ideal transition from credulity to independence, from hearsay to
reality.

III

One fallacy which disastrously affects many endeavors after this
ideal transition is the prejudice that, since faith has hitherto in the
youth's experience meant credulous acceptance of another's say-so,
faith always must mean that. Faith and credulity appear to him
identical. In "Alice through the Looking Glass" the Queen asserts
that she is a hundred and one years, five months, and one day old.
"I can't believe that," said Alice. "Can't you?" said the Queen. "Try
again, draw a long breath and shut your eyes." So blind, irrational,
and wilful does faith seem to many! So far from being an essential
part of all real knowledge, therefore, faith seems to stand in direct
contrast with knowledge, and this impression is deepened by our
common phraseology. Tennyson, for example, sings:

> "We have but faith: we cannot know;
> For knowledge is of things we see."

Before there can be any profitable discussion of religious belief,
therefore, we need to see that faith is one of the chief ways in which
continually we deal with reality; it is a road to truth, without which
some truth never can be reached at all. The reason for its inevitableness in life is not our lack of knowledge, but rather that faith is as
indispensable as logical demonstration in any real knowing of the
world. Behind all other words to be said about our subject lies this
fundamental matter: *faith is not a substitute for truth, but a path-*

way to truth; there are realities which without it never can be known.

For one thing, no one can know *persons* without faith. The world of people, without whom if a man could live, he would be, as Aristotle said, either a brute or a god, is closed in its inner meaning to a faithless mind. Entrance into another life with insight and understanding is always a venture of trust. We cry vainly like Cassim before the magic cave, "Open, Barley," if we try to penetrate the secrets of a human personality without sympathy, loyalty, faith. These alone cry "Open, Sesame."

Surely this knowledge of persons, impossible without faith, is as important as any which we possess. While the physical universe furnishes the general background of our existence, the immediate world in which we really live is personal, made up of people whom we fear or love, by whom we are cheered, admonished, hurt, and comforted. "The world is so waste and empty," cried Goethe, "when we figure but towns and hills and rivers in it, but to know that someone is living on it with us, even in silence—this makes our earthly ball a peopled garden." A solitary Robinson Crusoe would give up any other knowledge, if in return he could know even a benighted savage like Friday. But even a savage cannot be known by logical demonstration. Crusoe could so have learned some things, but when he wanted to know Friday, he came by way of adventures in confidence, personal trust and self-commitment, growing reliance and appreciative insight, assured loyalty and faith. He *knew* whom he had *believed*.

Moreover, such knowledge of persons is as solid as it is important. That two plus two make four cannot be gain-said, and doubtless no other kinds of information can be quite so absolute as mathematical theorems. But when one thinks of a comrade, long loved and trusted until he is known through and through, for practical purposes one can think of nothing more stable than his knowledge of his friend. The plain fact is that we *do* know people, know them well, and that this knowledge never has been or can be a matter of logical demonstration. By taking Arthur Hallam to pieces and analyzing him, the inductive mind might work out all the laws that are involved in Arthur Hallam's constitution; but that mind with all its knowledge would not know Arthur Hallam. Tennyson's "In Memoriam," however, makes clear that knowledge of a friend is not interdicted because scientific demonstration cannot supply it. Tennyson knew

Hallam well, and this knowledge, far more solid and significant than most other information he possessed, was not achieved by grinding laws out of facts; it came, as all such knowledge comes, by faith.

As one considers what this understanding of the personal world, seen with the open eyes of trust and loyalty, means to us, how assured it is, how it enriches and deepens life, he perceives that here at least faith is something far more than a stop-gap for ignorance, a dream, a fantasy. It is positively a pathway to truth.

There is another realm where faith is our only way of dealing with reality; by it alone can we know *the possibilities of individuals and of society*. We are well assured now in the United States that the nation can be economically prosperous without slavery. But sixty years ago plenty of people were assured of the contrary, were convinced that if the abolitionists succeeded we could not economically endure. How did we come by this significant knowledge that the immoral system was dispensable? Not by logical demonstration. The economists of most of our universities logically demonstrated that slavery was essential. *Faith was the pathway to the truth.* Faith that a new order minus slavery was possible gained adherents, grew in certainty with access of new believers, fed its followers on hopes unrealized but passionately believed in, until *faith became experiment, and experiment became experience, and experience brought forth knowledge*. The nation trusted and tried. This is the only way to truth in the realm of moral possibilities. If the world were finished, its *i*'s all dotted and its *t*'s all crossed, we might exist on that sort of descriptive science that finds the facts and plots their laws. But the world is in the making; what is *actual* is not quite so important to us as what is *possible;* we live, as Wordsworth sings, in

> "Hope that can never die,
> Effort and expectation and desire,
> And something evermore about to be."

To endeavor to satisfy man, therefore, with descriptions of the actual is preposterous. The innermost meaning of personal and social life lies in the contrast between what we are and what we may become. Beyond the achieved present and the demonstrable future, stands the ideal, whose possibility we can never know as a truth without faith enough to try.

When, therefore, one hears disparagement of faith as a poor

makeshift for knowledge, he may be pardoned a sharp rejoinder.
When has man ever found solid knowledge in this most important
realm of human possibilities, without faith as the pioneer? We do
not know first and then supply by belief what knowledge lacks. *We
believe first, as Columbus did, and then find new continents because
what faith first suggested a great venture has confirmed.* When
Stephenson proposed to run a steam car forty miles an hour, a host
of wise-acres proved the feat impossible on the ground that no one
could move through the air so rapidly and still survive. If now we
know that one easily survives a speed of over a hundred miles an
hour in an aeroplane, it is because a faith that *saw* and *dared* introduced us to the information. We know now that democracy is not a
futile dream, nor the conquest of the air by wireless and of the land
by electricity a madman's frenzy; we know truths of highest import
and certainty from the usefulness of radium to the wisdom of religious liberty, and all this knowledge existed as belief in possibility
before it became truth in fact. Faith was "assurance of things hoped
for, a conviction of things not seen" (Hebrews 11:1). Faith is no
makeshift. Its power is nowhere felt more effectively than in the
achievement of knowledge.

IV

So far is faith, then, from being blind credulity, that it alone deserves to be called the Great Discoverer. Everywhere faith goes before
as a pioneer and the more prosaic faculties of the mind come after
to civilize the newly opened territory. In the evolution of the senses
touch developed first. All the knowledge that any creature had, concerned the tangible. But in time other senses came. Dimly and un-
certainly creatures discerned by hearing and seeing the existence of
distant objects. They became aware of presences which as yet they
could not touch; they were furnished with clues, in following which
they found as real what at first had been intangible. Such a relation
faith bears to knowledge. Faith, said Clement of Alexandria, is the
"ear of the soul." Said Ruskin, faith is "veracity of insight." By it we
hear what as yet we cannot touch and see what the arms of our
logic are not long enough to reach.

All the elemental, primary facts of life are faith's discoveries; we
have no other means of finding them. By faith we discover our
selves. We do not hold back from living until we can prove that we

exist. We never can strictly prove that we exist. The very self that we
are trying to demonstrate would have to be used in the demonstration. We have no other way of getting at ourselves except to take
ourselves for granted—accepting

> "This main miracle that you are you,
> With power on your own act and on the world."

As Mr. Chesterton remarked, "You cannot call up any wilder vision
than a city in which men ask themselves if they have any selves." By
faith all men go out to live as though their selves were real.

By faith we accept the existence of the *outer world*. We do not
restrain ourselves from acting as though the physical world were
really there, until we can prove it. We never can strictly prove it;
perhaps it is not there at all. When through a microscope an Indian
was shown germs in the Ganges' water, to convince him of the peril
of its use, he broke the instrument with his cane, as though when the
microscope was gone, the facts had vanished too. In his philosophy
all that we see is illusion. Perhaps this is true—the world a phantasm
and our minds fooling us. But none of us believes it. And we do not
believe it because we live by faith—the elemental faith on which all
common sense and science rest and without which man's thought
and work would halt—that our senses and our minds tell us the
truth. "It is idle to talk always of the alternative of reason and faith.
Reason itself is a matter of faith. It is an act of faith to assert that
one's thoughts have any relation to reality at all."

By faith we even discover the *universe*. We cannot think of the
world as a multiverse; we always think of it as having unity, and we
do so whether as scientists we talk about the uniformity of nature,
or as Christians we speak of one Creator. Not only, however, can no
one demonstrate that this is a universe; *it positively does not look as
though it were*. Opposing powers snarl at each other and clash in a
disorder that gives to the casual observer not the slightest intimation
that any unity is there. Thunder storms and little babies, volcanoes
and Easter lilies, immeasurable nebulæ in the heavens and people
getting married on the earth—what indescribable contrasts and con-
fusions! Still we insist on thinking unity into this seeming anomaly,
and out of it we wrest scientific doctrines about the uniformity of
law. As Professor James, of Harvard, put it, "The principle of uniformity in nature has to be *sought* under and in spite of the most

rebellious appearances; and our conviction of its truth is far more like religious faith than like assent to a demonstration."

One might suppose that beliefs so assumed and so incapable of adequate demonstration would make the knowledge based upon them insecure. *But the fact is that all our surest knowledge is thus based on assumptions that we cannot prove.* "As for the strong conviction," Huxley says, "that the cosmic order is rational, and the faith that throughout all duration, unbroken order has reigned in the universe, I not only accept it, but I am disposed to think it the most important of all truth." Faith then, in Huxley's thought, is not a makeshift when knowledge fails. Rather by faith we continually are getting at the most important realities with which we deal. As Prof. Ladd, of Yale, impatiently exclaims: "The rankest agnostic is shot through and through with all the same fundamental intellectual beliefs, all the same unescapable rational faiths, about the reality of the self and about the validity of its knowledge. You cannot save science and destroy all faith. You cannot sit on the limb of the tree while you tear it up by the roots."

V

If faith is thus the pioneer that leads us to knowledge of persons and of moral possibilities; if by faith we discover ourselves, the outer world's existence and its unity, why should we be surprised that faith is our road to God? Superficial deniers of religion not infrequently seek the discredit of a Christian's trust by saying that God is only a matter of faith. To which the Christian confidently may answer: Of course God is a matter of faith. Faith is always the Great Discoverer.

A man finds God as he finds an earthly friend. He does not go apart in academic solitude to consider the logical rationality of friendship, until, intellectually convinced, he coolly arms himself with a Q. E. D. and goes out to hunt a comrade. Friendship is never an adventure of logic; it is an adventure of life. It is arrived at by what Emerson called the "untaught sallies of the spirit." We fall in love, it may be with precipitant emotion; our instincts and our wills are first engaged; the whole personality rises up in hunger to claim the affection that it needs and without which life seems unsupportable; faith, hope, and love engage in a glorious venture, where logic plays a minor part. But to make friendship rational, to give it poise, to trace its origins and laws, to clarify, chasten, and direct—this is the necessary work of thought. Faith discovers and reveals; reason furnishes criticism, confirmation, and discipline.

So men find God. They are hungry for him not in intellect alone, but with all their powers. They feel with Tolstoi: "I remembered that I only *lived* at those times when I believed in God." They need him to put sense and worth and hope into life. As with the reality of persons, the validity of knowledge, the unity of the world, so in religion the whole man rises up to claim the truth without which life is barren, meaningless. His best convictions at the first are all of them insights of the spirit, affirmations of the *man*. But behind, around and through them all play clarifying thoughts, and reasons come to discipline and to confirm. But the reasons by themselves could not have found God. Faith is the Great Discoverer.

> "Oh! world, thou choosest not the better part,
> It is not wisdom to be only wise,
> And on the inward vision close the eyes;
> But it is wisdom to believe the heart.
> Columbus found a world and had no chart
> Save one that Faith deciphered in the skies;
> To trust the soul's invincible surmise
> Was all his science and his only art.
> Our knowledge is a torch of smoky pine
> That lights the pathway but one step ahead
> Across the void of mystery and dread.
> Bid then the tender light of Faith to shine
> By which alone the mortal heart is led
> Into the thinking of the thought Divine."[1]

---

[1] Professor Santayana, of Harvard.

CHAPTER III

Faith in the Personal God

DAILY READINGS

We are to consider this week the Christian faith that God is personal. Before, however, we deal with the arguments which may confirm our confidence in such a faith, or even with the explanations that may clarify our conception of its meaning, let us, in the daily readings, consider *some of the familiar attitudes in every normal human life, that require God's personality for their fulfilment.* Men have believed in a personal God because their own nature demanded it.

Third Week, First Day

Men have believed in a personal God because of a *deep desire to think of creation as friendly.* F. W. Myers, when asked what question he would put to the Sphinx, if he were given only one chance, replied that he would ask, "Is the universe friendly?" Some have tried to think of creation as an enemy which we must fight, as though in Greenland we strove to make verdure grow, although the soil and climate were antagonistic. Some have tried to think creation neutral, an impersonal system of laws and forces, which we must impose our will upon as best we can, although in the end the system is sure to outlast all our efforts and to bring our gains to naught. But at the heart of man is an irresistible desire to think creation a friend, with whose good purposes our wills can be aligned, and whose power can carry our efforts to victorious ends. Says Gilbert Murray, of Oxford University, "As I see philosophy after philosophy falling into this unproven belief in the Friend behind phenomena, as I find that I myself cannot, except for a moment and by an effort, refrain from making the same assumption, it seems to me that perhaps here too we are under the spell of a very old ineradicable instinct." *But friends are always persons, and if creation is friendly then God is in some sense personal.* This faith is the radiant center of the Gospel.

But thou, when thou prayest, enter into thine inner chamber, and having shut thy door, pray to thy Father who is in secret, and thy Father who seeth in secret shall recompense thee. And in praying use not vain repetitions, as the Gentiles do: for they think that they shall be heard for their much speaking. Be not therefore like unto them: for your Father knoweth what things ye have need of, before ye ask him. After this manner therefore pray ye: Our Father who art in heaven, Hallowed be thy name. Thy kingdom come. Thy will be done, as in heaven, so on earth. Give us this day our daily bread. And forgive us our debts, as we also have forgiven our debtors. And bring us not into temptation, but deliver us from the evil one. For if ye forgive men their trespasses, your heavenly Father will also forgive you.—Matt. 6:6-14.

O Lord, we would rest in Thee, for in Thee alone is true rest to be found. We would forget our disappointed hopes, our fruitless efforts, our trivial aims, and lean on Thee, our Comfort and our Strength. When the order of this world bears cruelly upon us; when Nature seems to us an awful machine, grinding out life and death, without a reason or a purpose; when our hopes perish in the grave where we lay to rest our loved dead: O what can we do but turn to Thee, whose law underlieth all, and whose love, we trust, is the end of all? Thou fillest all things with Thy presence, and dost press close to our souls. Still every passion, rebuke every doubt, strengthen every element of good within us, that nothing may hinder the outflow of Thy life and power. In Thee, let the weak be full of might, and let the strong renew their strength. In Thee, let the tempted find succor, the sorrowing consolation, and the lonely and the neglected their Supreme Friend, their faithful Companion.

O Lord, we are weary of our old, barren selves. Separate us from our spiritual past, and quicken within us the seeds of a new future. Transform us by the breath of Thy regenerating power, that life may seem supremely beautiful and duty our highest privilege, and the only real evil a guilty conscience. Let us be no longer sad, or downcast, or miserable, or despairing, vexed by remorse, or de-

pressed by our failures. Take from us the old self. Give us a new self, beautiful, vigorous, and joyous. Let old things pass away and let all things become new. Kindle within us a flame of heavenly devotion, so that to us work for Thee shall become a happiness, and rest in Thee shall become an energy, unchecked by fears within and foes without. Give us love, and then we shall have more than all we need, for Thou art Love, Thyself the Giver and the Gift. Amen.—
Samuel McComb.

Third Week, Second Day

Bless Jehovah, O my soul;
And all that is within me, bless his holy name.
Bless Jehovah, O my soul,
And forget not all his benefits:
Who forgiveth all thine iniquities;
Who healeth all thy diseases;
Who redeemeth thy life from destruction;
Who crowneth thee with lovingkindness and tender mercies;
Who satisfieth thy desire with good things,
So that thy youth is renewed like the eagle.

—Psalm 103:1-5.

Such an attitude of thankfulness as this psalm represents is native to man's heart. When he is glad he feels grateful; he has an irrepressible impulse to thank somebody. As between a boastful Nebuchadnezzar—"This great Babylon which I have built . . . by the might of my power and for the glory of my majesty" (Dan. 4:30)—and the Master, grateful for the dawning success of his cause—"I thank Thee, O Father, Lord of heaven and earth" (Matt. 11:25)—we can have no doubt which is the nobler attitude. Man at his best always looks upon his blessings as gifts, his powers as entrustments, his service as a debt which he owes, and his success as an occasion of gratitude rather than pride. *But we cannot be really thankful to impersonal power.* Little children blame chairs for their falls and thank apple trees for their apples, but maturity outgrows the folly of accusing or blessing impersonal things. Thankfulness, in any worthy interpretation of the term, can never be felt except toward friendly persons who *intended the blessing* for which we are glad. A thoughtful man, therefore, cannot be grateful to a godless world-machine, even

though it has treated him well, for the world-machine never purposed to treat him well and his happiness is a lucky accident, with
no good will to thank for it. Haeckel says that there is no God—only
"mobile, cosmic ether." Imagine a congregation of people, under
Haeckel's leadership, rising to pray, "O Mobile Cosmic Ether,
blessed be thy name!" It is absurd. *Unless God is personal, the deepest meanings of gratitude in human hearts for life and its benedictions have no proper place in the universe.*

*O God above all, yet in all; holy beyond all imagination, yet
friend of sinners; who inhabitest the realms of unfading light, yet
leadest us through the shadows of mortal life; how solemn and uplifting it is even to think upon Thee! Like sight of sea to wearied
eyes, like a walled-in garden to the troubled mind, like home to
wanderer, like a strong tower to a soul pursued; so to us is the sound
of Thy name.*

*But greater still to feel Thee in our heart; like a river glorious,
cleansing, healing, bringing life; like a song victorious, comforting
our sadness, banishing our care; like a voice calling us to battle,
urging us beyond ourselves.*

*But greater far to know Thee as our Father, as dear as Thou art
near; and ourselves begotten of Thy love, made in Thy image, cared
for through all our days, never beyond Thy sight, never out of Thy
thought.*

*To think of Thee is rest; to know Thee is eternal life; to see Thee
is the end of all desire; to serve Thee is perfect freedom and everlasting joy. Amen.*—W. E. Orchard.

Third Week, Third Day

Have mercy upon me, O God, according to thy lovingkindness:
According to the multitude of thy tender mercies blot out my trans-
   gressions.
Wash me thoroughly from mine iniquity,
And cleanse me from my sin.
For I know my transgressions;
And my sin is ever before me.
Against thee, thee only, have I sinned,
And done that which is evil in thy sight.

—Psalm 51:1-4.

Penitence is one of the profoundest impulses in man's heart. And man at his deepest always feels about his sin as the Psalmist did: he has wronged not only this individual or that, but he has sinned against the whole structure of life, against whatever Power and Purpose may be behind life, and his penitence is not complete until he cries to the Highest, "Against Thee, Thee only, have I sinned." While men, therefore, have always asked each other for forgiveness, they have as well asked God for it. *But such an attitude is utterly irrational if God is not personal.* Persons alone care what we do, have purposes that our sins thwart, have love that our evil grieves, have compassion to forgive the penitent; and to confess sin to a world-machine—careless, purposeless, loveless, and without compassion—is folly. Yesterday we saw how impossible it was really to feel grateful to a materialist's god; today imagine congregations of people addressing to the Cosmic Ether any such penitent confessions as Christians by multitudes continually address to their Father: "We have erred and strayed from Thy ways like lost sheep." *Plainly in a world where creative power is impersonal the deepest meanings of penitence have no place.* Read over the prayer that follows, considering the futility of addressing such a penitent aspiration to anything impersonal; and then really pray it to the God whom Christ revealed:

We beseech Thee, Lord, to behold us with favor, folk of many families and nations gathered together in the peace of this roof, weak men and women subsisting under the covert of Thy patience. Be patient still; suffer us yet awhile longer—with our broken purposes of good, with our idle endeavors against evil, suffer us awhile longer to endure and (if it may be) help us to do better. Bless to us our extraordinary mercies; if the day come when these must be taken, brace us to play the man under affliction. Be with our friends, be with ourselves. Go with each of us to rest; if any awake, temper to them the dark hours of watching; and when the day returns, return to us, our sun and comforter, and call us up with morning hearts—eager to labor—eager to be happy, if happiness shall be our portion—and if the day be marked for sorrow, strong to endure it.

We thank Thee and praise Thee; and in the words of him to whom this day is sacred, close our oblation. Amen.—Robert Louis Stevenson.[1]

Third Week, Fourth Day

Now the God of hope fill you with all joy and peace in believing, that ye may abound in hope, in the power of the Holy Spirit.— Rom. 15:13.

For in hope were we saved: but hope that is seen is not hope: for who hopeth for that which he seeth? But if we hope for that which we see not, then do we with patience wait for it.—Rom. 8:24, 25.

Hope is no fringe on the garment of human life; it is part of the solid texture of our experience; without it men may exist, but they cannot live. Now some minds live by hope about tomorrow, or at the most, the day after tomorrow, and do not take long looks ahead. But as men grow mature in thoughtfulness, such small horizons no longer can content their minds; they seek a basis for hope about the far issue of man's struggle and aspiration. They cannot bear to think that creation lacks a "far-off divine event"; they cannot tolerate a universe that in the end turns out to be

> "An eddy of purposeless dust,
> Effort unmeaning and vain."

But it is obvious that if God is not in control of creation, with personal purpose of good will, directing its course, there is no solid basis for hope. If the universe is in the hands of physical forces, then a long look ahead reveals a world collapsing about a cold sun, and humanity annihilated in the wreck. Some such finale is the inevitable end of a godless world. As another pictures it, mankind, like a polar bear on an ice floe that is drifting into warmer zones, will watch in growling impotence the steady dwindling of his home, until he sinks in the abyss. All optimistic philosophies of life have been founded on faith in a personal God, who purposes good to his children, and without such faith no hope, with large horizons, is reasonable. Paul is fair to the facts when he says, "Having no hope and without God in the world" (Eph. 2:12). When one asks why men have believed in a personal God, this clearly is part of the answer: only a personal God can be "the God of hope."

O God of heaven above and earth beneath! Thou art the constant hope of every age—the reliance of them that seek Thee with thoughtfulness and love. We own Thee as the guardian of our pilgrimage; and when our steps are weary we turn to Thee, the mystic companion of our way, whose mercy will uphold us lest we fall. Thou layest on us the burden of labor throughout our days; but in this sacred hour Thou dost lift off our load, and make us partakers of Thy rest. Thou ever faithful God, our guide by cloud and fire! without this blest repose our life were but a desert path; here we abide by the refreshing spring, and pitch our tents with joy around Thy holy hill. Yet when we seek to draw nigh to Thee, Thou art still above us, like the heavens. O Thou that remainest in the height, and coverest Thyself with the cloud thereof! behold, we stand around the mountain where Thou art; and if Thou wilt commune with us, the thunder from Thy voice of love shall not make us afraid. Call up a spirit from our midst to serve Thy will; and take away the veil from all our hearts, that with the eye of purity we may look on the bright and holy countenance of life. And when we go hence to resume our way, may it be with nobler spirits, with more faithful courage, and more generous will. For life and death we trust ourselves to Thee as disciples of Jesus Christ. Amen.—James Martineau.

Third Week, Fifth Day

Jehovah is the portion of mine inheritance and of my cup:
Thou maintainest my lot.
The lines are fallen unto me in pleasant places;
Yea, I have a goodly heritage.
I will bless Jehovah, who hath given me counsel;
Yea, my heart instructeth me in the night seasons.
I have set Jehovah always before me:
Because he is at my right hand, I shall not be moved.
Therefore my heart is glad, and my glory rejoiceth:
My flesh also shall dwell in safety.
For thou wilt not leave my soul to Sheol,
Neither wilt thou suffer thy holy one to see corruption.
Thou wilt show me the path of life:
In thy presence is fulness of joy;
In thy right hand there are pleasures for evermore.

                            —Psalm 16:5-11.

Many things in human life bring joy. From the sense of a healthy body and the exhilaration of a sunshiny day to the deep satisfactions of home and friends—there are numberless sources of happiness. But man has always been athirst to find joy in thinking about the total meaning of life. Lacking that, the details of life lose radiance, for, in spite of himself, man

> "Hath among least things
> An undersense of greatest; sees the parts
> As parts, but with a feeling of the whole."

If when he thinks about God, he can, like this psalmist, rejoice in the love behind life, the good purpose through it, the glorious future ahead of it, then all his other blessings are illumined. Not only are there happy things *in life,* but *life itself* is fundamentally blessed. But if when he raises his thought to the Eternal, he has no joyful thoughts about it, sees no love or purpose there, then a pall falls on even his ordinary happiness. Alas for that man who does not like to think about life's origin and destiny and meaning, because he has no joyful faith about God! Some men have what Epictetus called "paralysis of the soul" every time they think of creation, for to them it is a huge physical machine crashing on without reason or good will. But some men have such a joyful faith in the divine that their gladness about the whole of life redeems their sorrow about its details. So Samuel Rutherford in prison said, "Jesus Christ came into my room last night and every stone flashed like a ruby." For the thought of God in terms of friendly personality is the most joyful idea of him that man has ever had. Man's thirst for joy is one of the sources of his faith in a personal God. He has wanted what Paul called "joy and peace in believing" (Rom. 15:13).

We rejoice, O Lord our God, not in ourselves nor in the firm earth on which we tread, nor in the household, nor in the church, nor in all the procession of things where mankind moves with power and glory. We rejoice in the Lord. We rejoice in Thy strength. A strange joy it is. Day by day we find ourselves breaking out into gladness through the ministration of the senses, and by the play of inward thought; but Thou art never beheld by us. . . . Thou never speakest to us, nor do we feel Thy hand, nor do we discern Thy face of love and glory and power. We break away from all other experiences, and look up into the emptiness, as it seems to us, which yet is full of life; into that which seems cold and void, but wherein moves

*eternal power; into the voiceless and inscrutable realm where Thou
dwellest, God over all, blessed forever. . . . O Lord our God, how
near Thou art to us! and we do not know it. How near is the other
life! and we do not feel it. It clothes us as with a garment. It feeds
us. It shines down upon us. It rejoices over us. . . . Thither, out of
narrow and anguishful ways, out of sorrows, out of regrets, out of
bereavements, we look; and already we are rested before we reach it.*

Grant unto us, today, we beseech Thee, this beatific vision. Amen.
—Henry Ward Beecher.

Third Week, Sixth Day

**For when one saith, I am of Paul; and another, I am of Apollos;
are ye not men? What then is Apollos? and what is Paul? Ministers
through whom ye believed; and each as the Lord gave to him. I
planted, Apollos watered; but God gave the increase. So then
neither is he that planteth anything, neither he that watereth; but
God that giveth the increase. Now he that planteth and he that
watereth are one: but each shall receive his own reward according
to his own labor. For we are God's fellow-workers: ye are God's
husbandry, God's building.—I Cor. 3:4-9.**

One of the profoundest motives that can grip man's heart is the
conviction that he is a fellow-worker with the Divine. To feel that
there is a great Cause, on behalf of which God himself is concerned,
and in the furtherance of which we can be God's instruments and
confederates, is the most exhilarating outlook on life conceivable.
Even people who deny God try to get this motive for themselves.
One such man hopes for the success of his favorite causes in "the
tendency of the universe"; another talks about "the nature of things
taking sides." *But nothing save personality has moral tendencies,
and only persons take sides in moral issues.* If the guidance of the
world is personal, then, and then only, can we rejoice with confidence in a great Ally, who has moral purposes and who has committed to us part of his work. This was the Master's motive when he
said, "My Father worketh even until now, and I work" (John
5:17). But one clearly sees that such an inspiring consciousness of
cooperation with the Eternal depended on the certainty with which
the Master called the Eternal by a personal name—Father. When
men like Livingstone have gone out in sacrificial adventure for the

saving of men they have not banked on the "tendency of the universe," nor trusted in any abstract "nature of things taking sides"; they have been servants of a personal God, under orders from him, and they have counted on personal guidance in the service of a cause whose issue was safe in God's hands.

O God, we pray Thee for those who come after us, for our children, and the children of our friends, and for all the young lives that are marching up from the gates of birth, pure and eager, with the morning sunshine on their faces. We remember with a pang that these will live in the world we are making for them. We are wasting the resources of the earth in our headlong greed, and they will suffer want. We are building sunless houses and joyless cities for our profit, and they must dwell therein. We are making the burden heavy and the pace of work pitiless, and they will fall wan and sobbing by the wayside. We are poisoning the air of our land by our lies and our uncleanness, and they will breathe it.

O God, Thou knowest how we have cried out in agony when the sins of our fathers have been visited upon us, and how we have struggled vainly against the inexorable fate that coursed in our blood or bound us in a prison-house of life. Save us from maiming the innocent ones who come after us by the added cruelty of our sins. Help us to break the ancient force of evil by a holy and steadfast will and to endow our children with purer blood and nobler thoughts. Grant us grace to leave the earth fairer than we found it; to build upon it cities of God in which the cry of needless pain shall cease; and to put the yoke of Christ upon our business life that it may serve and not destroy. Lift the veil of the future and show us the generation to come as it will be if blighted by our guilt, that our lust may be cooled and we may walk in the fear of the Eternal. Grant us a vision of the far-off years as they may be if redeemed by the sons of God, that we may take heart and do battle for Thy children and ours. Amen.—Walter Rauschenbusch.

Third Week, Seventh Day

I will extol thee, my God, O King;
And I will bless thy name for ever and ever.
Every day will I bless thee;
And I will praise thy name for ever and ever.

Great is Jehovah, and greatly to be praised;
And his greatness is unsearchable.
One generation shall laud thy works to another,
And shall declare thy mighty acts.
Of the glorious majesty of thine honor,
And of thy wondrous works, will I meditate.
And men shall speak of the might of thy terrible acts;
And I will declare thy greatness.
They shall utter the memory of thy great goodness,
And shall sing of thy righteousness.
Jehovah is gracious, and merciful;
Slow to anger, and of great lovingkindness.
Jehovah is good to all;
And his tender mercies are over all his works.
All thy works shall give thanks unto thee, O Jehovah;
And thy saints shall bless thee.

—Psalm 145:1-10.

Adoration springs from the deeps of man's spirit. We never can be content with looking down on things beneath us, nor with looking out on things that find our level. We always must look up to things above us. As a mediæval saint said, *"The soul can never rest in things that are beneath itself."* Worship, therefore, is an undeniable impulse in man's heart. Poets worship Beauty; scientists worship Truth; every man of honor worships Right. That is, the good, true, and beautiful stand above us calling out our adoration, and all the best in us springs from our worshipful response to their appeal. But this impulse to adore is never fulfilled until we gather up all life into spiritual unity and bow down in awe and joy before God. That is adoration glorified, worship crowned and consummated. And the only God whom man can adore with awe and joy is personal. No impersonal thing is worshipful; however great a *thing* may be it still lies beneath our soul. No abstract Idea is worshipful; we still are greater than any *idea* that we can hold. Only God, thought of in personal terms but known to be greater than any terms which human life can use, is adorable. *Men have believed in Him because worship is man's holiest impulse.*

Such are the experiences of man, with which faith in a personal God is inseparably interwoven. Our demand for a friendly creation, our deepest impulses to thanksgiving, penitence, hope, joy, cooperation with the Eternal, and adoration of the highest—all require personality in God. As Professor William James said, "The universe is no longer a mere *It* to us, but a *Thou* if we are religious."

O Lord our God, Thy greatness is unsearchable, and the glory of Thy presence has overwhelmed us. Thou art hidden in excess of light; and if we were to behold Thee in the great sphere in which Thou art living, none of us would dare to draw near to Thee. Our imperfections, our transgressions, our secret thoughts, our wild impulses, that at times come surging in upon us, are such that we should be ashamed to stand before the All-searching Eye. Our lives are before Thee, open as a book, and Thou readest every word and every letter thereof. Blessed be Thy name, Thou hast taught us to come to Thee through the Lord Jesus Christ as through a friend, and thou hast taught us to draw near to Thee in person through the familiar way of Fatherhood; from our childhood we have said, Our Father, and in this way we are not afraid; in this way we come familiarly and boldly: not irreverently, but with the familiarity which love gives. Thou hast poured the light of Thy love upon the path which we tread, and Thou hast taught us to come rejoicing before Thee. . . . Open Thy hand and Thy heart, and say to every one of us, Peace be unto you! Amen.—Henry Ward Beecher.

COMMENT FOR THE WEEK

I

We have been using freely the most momentous word in human speech as though we clearly understood its meaning. We have been speaking of God as though the import of the term were plain. But most of us, asked to state precisely what we mean by "God," would welcome such a refuge from our confusion as Joubert sought. "It is not hard to know God," said he, "provided one will not force oneself to define him." Many people who stoutly claim to believe in God live in perpetual vacillation as to what they mean by him. Writes one: "God to my mind is an impersonal being, but whether for convenience or through sheer impotence I pray to him as a personal being . . . I know I talk on both sides of the fence, but that is just where I am."

At times, indeed, some question whether there is any need to

think or say what "God" may signify. They call him by vague names
—the All, the Infinite. In moods of exalted feeling, impatient of
definition, they wish to be left alone with their experience of the
Eternal; they resent the intrusion of theology, as a poet, lost in wonder at a landscape, might resent the coming of surveyors with their
clanking chains. So Walt Whitman wanted to see the stars rather
than hear the astronomer, and after listening to the learned lecture,
with its charts and diagrams, he says,

> "I became tired and sick,
>   Till rising and gliding out I wandered off by myself,
>   In the mystical moist night air, and from time to time
>   Looked up in perfect silence at the stars."

But, for all that, we well may be thankful for astronomers. At times
the "mystical, moist night air" is absent; we do not wish to "look up
in perfect silence at the stars"; and, even though we know in advance that they are bound to be inadequate, we do want as clear and
worthy ideas as possible about the universe. Moreover, when such
ideas are ours, looking up in perfect silence at the stars is more impressive than it ever was before. No more can men content themselves with a vague consciousness of God. Spirits like Wordsworth
have raptures of which they sing,

> "In such access of mind, in such high hour
>   Of visitation from the living God,
>   Thought was not—in enjoyment it expired."

In communion with nature, in love for family, in fellowship with
God, such hours may come, but nature, family, and God must also
be the objects of understanding thought. Days of vital need, if not
of mental doubt, inevitably come when it is impossible any longer to
use a term like "God" without knowing what we mean.

The special urgency of this is felt by most of us because as children
we were taught to picture the Divine in terms of personality. The
God of the Bible is personal. Little that persons do, save sinning, is
omitted from the catalogue of God's activities as he is pictured for
us in the Scripture. He knows, loves, purposes, warns, rebukes, allures, rewards, and punishes, as only persons can. And all our relationships with him are clearly personal. When we pray we say "Our
Father"; when we seek our duty we ask, "What wilt thou have me

to do?" God is *He* and *Thou,* not *It,* and friendship is the ideal relation of all souls with him.

Moreover, in our maturity we are not likely to be interested in a
God who is not personal. Whoever curiously asks why he believes
in God, will find not simply *reasons* but *causes* for his faith, and will
perceive that the causes of faith lie back of the reasons for it. Vital
need always precedes the arguments by which we justify its satisfaction. A man eats one thing and shuns another on principles of die-
tetics that can be defended before his intelligence; but behind all
such sophisticated reasons stands the vital cause of eating—hunger.
So back of intellectual arguments for belief in God lies the initial
cause of faith: *men are hungry.* Men believe in God because they
hunger for a world that is not chance and chaos, but that is guided
by a Purpose. They believe in God, because in their struggles after
righteousness they hunger for a Divine Ally in whom righteousness
has its origin, its ground and destiny. They believe in God because
they hunger for confidence that Someone cares about our race in its
conflicts and defeats and because in their individual experience they
want a friend. Without such faith man feels himself to be, in
Goethe's phrase, "a troubled wanderer upon a darkened earth."
Plainly this elemental human hunger for purpose, righteousness, and
friendship calls for something akin to personality in God. *Only persons have purpose, character, and friendliness.* The vital motives
which lead men to seek God's comfort, forgiveness, guidance, and
cooperation plainly imply his personality. Things do not forgive us,
love us, nor purpose good concerning us, nor can any thing be imagined so subtle and so powerful as to satisfy the needs on account of
which men come to God. If God is not personal, he can feel no concern for human life and a God of no concern is of no consequence.

The philosophers of India, with a well-reasoned pantheistic system and centuries to make their philosophy effective, have failed to
quell this deathless thirst for a God who counts. Every wayside
shrine of Hinduism incarnates the old faith in gods conceived as
friends, not things; and Buddha, who taught impersonal deity, is
now himself adored as the Personal Lord of Love and Blessedness.
Wherever one finds vital religion one finds that God is no dry impersonal abstraction, but man's friend. Boscamen, speaking of the
Egyptian Book of the Dead and of the Chaldean Tablets, says: "Six
thousand years ago in Egypt and Chaldea—it is not dread, but the
grateful love of a child to his father, of friend to friend, that meets

us in the oldest books of the world." And when one turns from the oldest to the newest books this inner demand of man's religious life has not ceased; it has been refined and confirmed. "The All would not be the All unless it contained a Personality," said Victor Hugo. "That Personality is God."

Biography is lavish in illustrations of this need in man's religious life. The biographer of Theodore Parker, the free-lance preacher of Boston, remarks: "In his *theology* God was neither personal nor impersonal, but a reality transcending these distinctions. In his *devotions* God was as personal as his own father or mother, and he prayed to him as such, daringly indifferent to the anthropomorphisms of his unfettered speech." When one passes from speculation to religion, he always comes into a realm where only a personal God will do. On this point even confessed unbelievers furnish confirmation. One who calls himself an agnostic writes: "At times in the silence of the night and in rare lonely moments, I experience a sort of communion of myself with Something Great that is not myself. Then the Universal Scheme of things has on me the effect of a sympathetic Person, and my communion therewith takes on a quality of fearless worship. These moments happen, and they are to me the supreme fact in my religious life." Always for the purposes of vital religion, God must have on us the "effect of a sympathetic Person."

II

When one, however, subjects this need of his religious life to searching thought, what difficulty he encounters! Multitudes, if they were candid, would confess what a college senior wrote: "When I am just thinking about God in a speculative or philosophical way, I generally think of him as impersonal, but for practical purposes I think of him as personal." Many folks feel thus distraught; at the heart of their religious life is the paralyzing doubt, that in a universe like this to think of God as personal is absurd. If a train moving a mile a minute should leave the earth, it must travel 40,000,000 years before it would reach the nearest star. The Creator of such a world is not readily reduced to the similitude of human life. Once men lived on a flat earth, small in compass and cosily tucked beneath the sky's coverlet, but now the world's vastness beggars imagination. As an astronomer remarked, coming from a session with his telescope, "This does away with a six-foot god; you cannot shake hands with the Creator of *this*." Men used to suppose that Arcturus was a single star, but now new telescopes reveal Arcturus as a galaxy of stars, thousands in number, with interstellar spaces so immense that thought breaks down in spanning them and imagination even cannot make the leap. Is the God of such a universe to be conceived in terms of a magnified man?

So to picture deity seems at first sight a survival of mere childishness. Professor John Fiske, of Harvard, has told us that when he was a boy God always conjured up in his imagination the figure of a venerable bookkeeper, with white flowing beard, standing behind a high desk and writing down the bad deeds of John Fiske. How many of us can recall such early crude and childish thoughts of God! A mother asked her young daughter what she was drawing. "A picture of God," was the answer. "But no one knows what God looks like," the mother said. "They will," came the rejoinder, "when I get through." We all began with some such primitive idea of deity. Indeed, these early conceptions long persist in many minds, as the following statements, written by college students, indicate: "I think of God as real, actual skin and blood and bones, something we shall see with our eyes some day, no matter what lives we lead on earth." "It may be a remnant of youth, but anyhow, every time I think of God there appears a vague image of a man, with all members of the body, just enormously large." "I have always pictured him according to a description in *Paradise Lost* as seated upon a throne, while around are angels playing on harps and singing hymns." "I think of God as having bodily form and being much larger than the average man. He has a radiant countenance beaming with love and compassion. He is erect and upright, fearless and brave."[2]

No one of us may be contemptuous of such crude ideas; we all possessed them once. Indeed the loss of them, with their picture of deity, clear in feature and distinct in outline, has been to some a shock from which faith has not recovered. When increasing knowledge discredited our immature theology, and our world immeasurably widened, the very human God of our first imaginations was lost among the stars. We learned that this is a universe where the light that falls upon our eyes tonight left the far heavens when Abraham was shepherding on Syrian hills. The Christian Gospel of the personal Father which once was good news became a serious problem.

---

[2]From a questionnaire, "Belief in God and Immortality," by Prof. James H. Leuba.

We still may cling to the old meanings of our religious faith; still we may pray in hours of need as though our childhood's God were really there; but at times we suspect that we are clinging to the beauty of an early memory while reluctantly we lose conviction of its truth. Many modern men and women can understand the plight of the famous Dr. Jowett of Oxford, who, so runs the tradition, inserted "used to" in a muffled voice, when he recited the creed: "I *used to* believe in God the Father Almighty."

With such misgivings, whether as habitual disturbers of our faith or as occasional moods of unbelief that come and go, most of us must be familiar. What Charles Darwin is reported to have said about himself, many if they spoke frankly would say too: "Sometimes I feel a warm sense of a personal God, and then"—with a shake of his head—"it goes away."

III

Whatever may be our theology, the fact is plain that the denial of a personal God solves no problem. For if we may not think of God in terms of personality, the query still remains, which was there before —*in what terms shall we conceive of the Eternal?* In a discussion on the nature of the sky, one boy, denying the idea of a solid canopy, exclaimed, "There ain't any sky." Said the other, seeing how little this negation solved the problem, "Well, what *is* it that ain't?" Some such inquiry one must put to his doubts about God's personality. Though we may deny a personal God, nevertheless in the place where he once stood, creator and sustainer of all existence, is Something that we do think of somehow. We may have but little of Carlyle's sublime imagination; may not easily transport ourselves to stand with him on the far northern cliff, "behind him all Europe and Africa fast asleep, except the watchmen, and before him the silent Immensity and Palace of the Eternal, whereof our sun is but the porch-lamp." Yet who of us, regarding the illimitable universe, on the far outskirts of which our little earth is whirling, so minute that through the strongest telescope from the nearest star its conflagration would be quite invisible, has escaped the sense of a Universal Power? And the human mind cannot so keep itself at home in little tasks and pleasures as to evade the question: How shall we think of the Power that made the universe? In what terms? By what analogies? Hours of revelation come in every serious life when no desire compares in urgency with the desire to know the character of the Eternal. It does make a prodigious difference what hands hold the leash of the universe.

This second fact is also clear, that if we are to think of the Eternal at all, we must think in terms of something drawn from our experience. When we sing of Paradise we speak of golden streets and gates of pearl, and Thoreau remarks that, arriving in heaven, he expects to find pine trees there. Such words we do not take literally, but such words we cannot utterly avoid, for if we are to speak at all of the unknown glory, we must use pictures from the known. So we think of God in human symbols. We cannot catch him in an abstract definition as though a boy with a butterfly net should capture the sun at noon. Our minds are not fitted for such enterprise. Of necessity we take something homely, familiar, close at hand, and lifting it up as far as we can reach, say *God is most like that*. No one who thinks at all of the Eternal escapes this necessity.

By this method the *materialist* reaches his philosophy. Haeckel laughs to scorn the opening clause of the "Apostles' Creed." "I believe in God the Father Almighty, maker of heaven and earth"—for such faith no words are contemptuous enough. This denial does not mean however that Haeckel has no faith; he deliberately offers a creedal substitute which runs in part: I believe in a "chemical substance of a viscous character, having albuminous matter and water as its chief constituents." In such terms does Haeckel think of the Eternal. A professor of medicine has remarked that such a theory reduces all reality to "phosphorus and glue." When some Psalmist cries, "Bless the Lord, O my soul," nothing substantial is speaking or is being spoken to save phosphorus and glue! When an Italian patriot cries, "The time for dying comes to all, but the time for dishonoring oneself ought never to come," nothing is real and causal save phosphorus and glue! And every gracious and redeeming deed in history from the love of mothers to the cross of Christ has been a complicated working out of phosphorus and glue! In whatever labored phrases he may state his case, the materialist's method there is obvious; he has taken physical energy, of whose presence in his own body he is first assured, and whose reality he has then read out into the world, and this homely and familiar experience he has lifted up as far as he can reach to say, the Eternal is most like that.

So far as method is concerned, the *theist* of necessity travels the same road; only he insists on a nobler symbol than physical energy in terms of which to think of God. He takes *mind*. He says in effect: There may be wide stretches of the universe where our intellects meet no answer and find no meaning. But in much of the universe we do see meaning; and how can intelligence find sense where intelligence has not put sense? A few scratches on a cliff's face in Assyria, after centuries of neglect, rendered up their meaning to the mind of Rawlinson. They were themselves the work of intelligence, and intelligence could read them. So, the theist continues, the universe is in part at least intelligible. Our minds fit into it and are answered by it. We can trace its laws and predict its movements. Man first worked out the nature of the ellipse in theoretical geometry, and then telescopes later showed the gigantic ellipses of planetary orbits in the heavens. Can it be that this intelligible world, readable by mind, is itself essentially mindless? As easily believe that the notes of Wagner's operas were accidentally blown together by a whirlwind and yet are playable by man! Therefore the theist believes the universe to be rational; he takes mind as he has known it in himself, and lifting it as high as he can reach, cries, God is most like that.

So far as the general method of approach is concerned, the Christian travels the same road to his idea of God. Only he cannot believe that the best he knows is too good or too great to be a symbol in terms of which to think of the Eternal. Therefore he will not take a byproduct of experience such as physical energy, nor a section of personality such as mind; he takes the full orb of personality, *self-conscious being that knows and purposes and loves,* and he affirms that God is most like this. Such in its simplest form is the Christian assertion of God's personality.

In one of his noblest passages Martineau has put into classic form this necessity, which we have been discussing, of thinking about God in terms of human experience: "God, being infinite, can never be fully comprehended by our minds; whatever thought of him be there, his real nature must still transcend: there will yet be deep after deep beyond, within that light ineffable; and what we see, compared with what we do not see, will be as the raindrop to the firmament. Our conception of him can never *correspond with the reality,* so as to be without omission, disproportion, or aberration; but can only *represent the reality,* and *stand for God* within our souls, till nobler thoughts arise and reveal themselves as his interpreters. And this is precisely what we mean by a symbolical idea. The devotee who prostrates himself before a black stone—the Egyptian who in his prayers was haunted by the ideal form of the graceful ibis or the monstrous sphinx—the theist who bends beneath the starry porch that midnight opens to the temple of the universe—the Christian who sees in heaven a spirit akin to that which divinely lived in Galilee, and with glorious pity died on Calvary—all alike assume a representation of him whose immeasurable nature they can neither compass nor escape. And the only question is, whether the conception they portray upon the wall of their ideal temple is an abominable idol, or a true and sanctifying mediatorial thought."

IV

In their endeavor thus to think of God in terms of personality, some are perplexed because in their imagination a person is inseparable from flesh. "I think of God as a personal being," writes a college student. "A personal being would have a form that you could see or touch." But this would be true only if the grossest materialism were accepted, and the spiritual life declared to be the product of brain as digestive fluids are of salivary glands. On any other basis, personality is not indissolubly bound to body nor by it necessarily delimited. A man cannot hear without his ear, but he is not his ear; he cannot hear without the auditory nerve, but he is not the auditory nerve; he cannot hear without the temporal lobe of the brain, but he is not the brain nor any portion of it. These may be the instruments which he uses; he is free when they are well, hampered when they are broken, and at last he is separable from them all. John Quincy Adams at the age of eighty met a friend upon a Boston street. "Good morning," said the friend, "and how is John Quincy Adams today?" "Thank you," was the ex-president's reply, "John Quincy Adams himself is well, quite well, I thank you. But the house in which he lives at present is becoming dilapidated. It is tottering upon its foundations. Time and the seasons have nearly destroyed it. Its roof is pretty well worn out. Its walls are much shattered and it trembles with every wind. The old tenement is becoming almost uninhabitable and I think John Quincy Adams will have to move out of it soon. But he himself is quite well, quite well." Such a conception of man as *being* a permanent personality and *having* a temporary body is essential to any worthy meaning when we use personal terms about God.

With such an elevated thought, however, of what personality does mean, it soon is evident that no other reality with which we deal is so worthy to be the symbol of an Eternal Spirit. Is one perplexed that God, who is invisible, should be pictured in the similitude of human persons? But *we* are invisible. The outward husks and fleshy garment of our friends we indeed have seen, but upon the friend himself—consciousness, love, purpose, ideal, and character—no eye has looked. No mirror ever has been strong enough to show us to ourselves. In every homely conversation this ineffable miracle is wrought: out of the unseen where I dwell, I signal by word and gesture to you back in the unseen where you dwell. We are inhabitants now of the intangible and unseen world; we are as invisible as God.

Indeed, personality is essentially the most unlimited reality with which we deal; in comparison a solar system is a little thing. Consider *memory,* by which we can retrace our youthful days, build our shanties once again at brooksides, replay our games, and recapitulate the struggles and the joys of the first days at school. Nothing in all the universe can remember except persons. Were we not so familiar with this element in human greatness, we would more often pause to exclaim, as did Augustine, fifteen centuries ago, "Great is the power of memory. Amazement overcomes me when I think of it. And yet men go abroad to gaze upon the mountains, the broad rivers, the wide ocean, the courses of the stars, and pass themselves, the crowning wonder, by!" Consider *imagination,* by which, sitting still in body we can project ourselves around the world, can walk down Princes Street in Edinburgh, or stand in mingled awe and condemnation before the tomb of Napoleon in Paris, or rise uncovered before the majesty of the Matterhorn. Nothing in all the universe can do that except persons. Were full power to act wherever we can *think* added to our gifts, we should come so near to incipient omnipresence as to be in dread of our responsibility. Consider *love,* by which we live not so much where our bodies are as where our friends and family may be. Love expands the individual until his real life is independent of geography. Says one lover to another:

> "The widest land
> Doom takes to part us, leaves thy heart in mine
> With pulses that beat double."

Many a mother in America has *lived* in the trenches of France; *many* a man has found that what might happen to him where his body was could not be compared with what might happen to him where his friendships were; and as we grow in love and loyalty we find ourselves scattered all over creation. How far such an expansion of life may go our Lord revealed when he said, "Inasmuch as ye did it unto one of these, my brethren, even these least, ye did it unto me" (Matt. 25:40). Nothing in heaven above or on the earth beneath can so extend itself in love save persons.

Finally, consider *creative power* by which human beings project themselves into the future, and, with masterful ideals in mind, lay hold on circumstance and bend it to their will. As if he shared creative power with the Eternal, an engineer summons nature's forces to his bidding and lays his will upon them, until where nothing was a structure stands that mankind may use for centuries. Nothing in all the universe can so create except persons. In that essentially creative act where deathless ideas and harmonies are given being by poets and musicians, so that something out of nothing is brought to pass by personality, man faces a mystery as abysmal as God's making of the world. "Paradise Lost" is wonderful; but not half as wonderful as the creative personality itself who years before projected it. "An inward prompting," Milton says, "which now grew daily upon me, that by labor and intense study, joined with the strong propensity of nature, I might perhaps leave something so written to after times as they should not willingly let it die." Nothing can so create save personality.

Personality is not so limited that we should be ashamed to think of God in terms of it. Rather, of all realities with which we deal, personality alone, invisible, reaching back in memory, reaching out in imagination, expanding itself in love, and laying hold upon the future with creative power, is a worthy symbol of the Eternal Spirit.

Even when the meaning of personality has been so enlarged and elevated, we should not leave our statement of belief in God as though our experience of personality were a mould into which our thought of him is poured and so delimited. We are not presumptuous Lilliputians, running out with verbal stakes and threads, to pin down the tall, majestic Gulliver of the Eternal and dance in theological exultation round our capture. We know better than that. We understand how insufficient is every human name for God. We know that when we have said our best—"How unsearchable are his judgments and his ways past tracing out!" (Rom. 11:33).

Nothing more has marred the Christian message and discredited the Christian faith than the unwise presumption that has forced its definitions into the secrets of the Infinite. "It is enough to say," exclaims Leslie Stephen, "that they defined the nature of God Almighty with an accuracy from which modest naturalists would shrink in describing the genesis of a black beetle." The antidote to such vain pride of theology is found in the wholesome modesty of the Bible. There man enquires, "Canst thou by searching find out God? Canst thou find out the Almighty unto perfection? It is high as heaven; what canst thou do? Deeper than Sheol; what canst thou know?" (Job 11:7). There God replies: "As the heavens are higher than the earth, so are my ways higher than your ways and my thoughts than your thoughts" (Isa. 55:9). Scripture bears abundant testimony to the symbolic nature of our human terms for God. "Like as a father pitieth his children, so Jehovah pitieth them that fear him" (Psalm 103:13). "As one whom his mother comforteth, so will I comfort you" (Isa. 66:13). "I will betroth thee unto me" (Hos. 2:20). "Return, . . . saith Jehovah, for I am a husband unto you" (Jer. 3:14). "The Lord spake unto Moses . . . as a man speaketh unto his friend" (Ex. 33:11). Father, Mother, Bridegroom, Husband, Friend—these are symbols of God. Men, endeavoring to frame some worthy thought of the Eternal, lift up their best in phrases such as these, and in them enshrine their noblest concepts of the divine. They have no better, truer thing to say of God, no wiser way in which to say it. But when they think of the Eternal as he must be, and of their human words, infinitesimal in comparison, they know that all their best names for God are like small measures of water dipped from an immeasurable sea. For all that, so much of God as they can grasp and understand is the most important truth that mankind knows. Let even a tea-cup of water be taken to a laboratory and it will tell the truth about the sea; *that one tea-cup will reveal the quality of the whole ocean.* Yet it will not reveal all the truth about the ocean. When one considers the reach of the sea over the rim of the world; thinks of the depths that no eye can pierce, the distances that no mind can imagine; remembers the currents that sweep through the sea, the tides that rise there, and the storms that beat it to its nether wells, he dare not try to put *these* into a tea-cup. So God sweeps out beyond the reach of human symbols. At once so true and so inadequate are all our words for him.

So we might speak to one who incredulously looks upon our faith, but for one who whole-heartedly approaches God as Christianity suggests, no negative and cautionary word is adequate. The Christian method of conceiving God brings the most exhilarating thought of him that man has ever had. It says in brief: Take your *best* and think of God as most truly symbolized in that. As to what our best is, not even the agnostics doubt. The physical universe belittles us on one side only; it makes a pigmy of the body. In our spirits we still tower above the physical; we are greater than the world we know. Our supreme good, the divinest reality with which we deal, is personality. Then lift that up, says Christianity; it is your best, and you dare not think of God in terms of less; you have Christ's example in arguing from the human best to the divine: "If ye, being evil, know how to give good gifts unto your children, *how much more* . . . your Father" (Matt. 7:11).

The Christian faith asserts that when a man thus thinks of God in terms of the best he knows he is on the road toward truth. How many billion spiritual miles he may have to travel to the end, no man can tell. Only he will never need to stop, retrace his steps, and start upon a lower path than personality, a road that lies beneath righteousness and love. The road leads on and up beyond our imagination, but it is the same road and not another. *God is personality plus, or else he alone is completely personal and we are but in embryo.*

If God so is personal, then all the deep meanings of religious life and faith that the saints, our spiritual sires, have known are open to us modern men and women. Forms of thought indeed have changed, but if God is thus our Father and our Friend, the essentials of Christian experience are waiting for us all. Life then is not purposeless; all creation is bound into spiritual unity by personal Will; and in sacrificial labor we are serving one who is able to guard that which we "have committed unto him against that day" (II Tim. 1:12). Old hymns of confidence in time of trial, we too can sing:

> "Still will we trust, though earth seem dark and dreary,
> And the heart faint beneath His chastening rod;
> Though steep and hard our pathway, worn and weary,
> Still will we trust in God."

And we can pray, not indeed with clamorous beggary as though the grace of God were a wayside stall where every greedy hand can pluck what passing whim may wish, but we can commune with God as the real saints have always prayed with humility and gratitude and confident desire for good. Most of all, that priceless privilege is open to us which is the center and sun of Christian thought and life. For if among all realities in our experience, we have dared take the best, personality, as a symbol in terms of which to think of God, how should we not, among all personalities, take the best we know as the highroad of approach to him. Therefore our real symbol of God shall be no man among us, frail and sinful, but our Lord himself "fairest among ten thousand"—"the one altogether beautiful." We shall think of God in terms of him. We shall see "the light of the knowledge of the glory of God in the face of Jesus Christ" (II Cor. 4:6).

CHAPTER IV

Belief and Trust

DAILY READINGS

We have tried to explain our faith in the personal God, and to
see the transfiguring influence of that faith on life. But is belief in
God always such a blessing as we have pictured? Rather faith, like
every other experience of man, has its caricatures and burlesques.
Many men are prevented from appreciation of faith in God, with
its inestimable blessings, because they have so continually seen
faith's perversions. The fact is that belief in God may be an utterly
negligible matter in a man's experience or may even become a positively pernicious influence. Let us, in the daily readings, consider
some of the *familiar travesties on faith.*

Fourth Week, First Day

Praise ye Jehovah.
Praise Jehovah, O my soul.
While I live will I praise Jehovah:
I will sing praises unto my God while I have any being.
Put not your trust in princes,
Nor in the son of man, in whom there is no help.
His breath goeth forth, he returneth to his earth;
In that very day his thoughts perish.
Happy is he that hath the God of Jacob for his help,
Whose hope is in Jehovah his God.

—Psalm 146:1-5.

No one can mistake the note of reality in this psalmist's experience of God. But every one of us knows people who, if asked whether

they believed in God, would readily assent, yet to whom faith makes
no such difference in life as this psalm expresses. Their faith is
nothing but an opinion about God, lightly held, a formal consent
that what church or family tradition says must be correct. They
have what Luther used to call "the charcoal burner's faith." A man
of that occupation, when asked what he believed, said, "What Holy
Church believes"; but, questioned further, he could not tell what it
was that Holy Church did believe. So formal, vitally unpossessed,
and practically unreal is much of our religious opinion that passes
for faith. Dean Swift was a churchman of high rank, and yet his
biographer is compelled to say of him: "He clung to the doctrines
of his church, not because he could give abstract reasons for his
belief, but simply because the church happened to be his." Vital
religious faith is a very different thing from such dry conventionality. A man may assent to the contents of a college catalogue and
yet never have experience of college life; he may agree that a menu
is dietetically correct and yet never grow strong from the food; and
he may believe in every creed in Christendom and not know what
faith in God really means. Opinions about God are a roadway to
God, but the end of the journey is a personal fellowship that trans-
figures life; and to seize opinions as though they were the object
of faith is, to use Tagore's figure, "like a man who tries to reach
his destination by firmly clutching the dust of the road."

*O Thou great Father of us all, we rejoice that at last we know
Thee. All our soul within us is glad because we need no longer
cringe before Thee as slaves of holy fear, seeking to appease Thine
anger by sacrifice and self-inflicted pain, but may come like little
children, trustful and happy, to the God of love. Thou art the only
true Father, and all the tender beauty of our human loves is the
reflected radiance of Thy lovingkindness, like the moonlight from
the sunlight, and testifies to the eternal passion that kindled it.*

*Grant us growth of spiritual vision, that with the passing years
we may enter into the fulness of this our faith. Since Thou art our
Father, may we not hide our sins from Thee, but overcome them
by the stern comfort of Thy presence. By this knowledge uphold us
in our sorrows and make us patient even amid the unsolved mysteries of the years. Reveal to us the larger goodness and love that
speak through the unbending laws of Thy world. Through this faith
make us the willing equals of all Thy other children.*

As Thou art ever pouring out Thy life in sacrificial father-love,
may we accept the eternal law of the cross and give ourselves to
Thee and to all men. We praise Thee for Jesus Christ, whose life
has revealed to us this faith and law, and we rejoice that he has
become the first-born among many brethren. Grant that in us, too,
the faith in Thy fatherhood may shine through all our life with such
persuasive beauty that some who still creep in the dusk of fear may
stand erect as free sons of God, and that others who now through
unbelief are living as orphans in an empty world may stretch out
their hands to the great Father of their spirits and find Thee near.
Amen.—Walter Rauschenbusch.

Fourth Week, Second Day

Faith is travestied in many lives not so much by the substitution
of opinion for experience, as by making religion consist in certain
devout practices, such as church-going. Ceremonialism, instead of
being an aid in making God real, takes the place of fellowship with
God. How scathing were the attacks of the prophets on this distor-
tion of religion!

**Hear the word of Jehovah, ye rulers of Sodom; give ear unto the
law of our God, ye people of Gomorrah. What unto me is the multitude of your sacrifices? saith Jehovah: I have had enough of the
burnt-offerings of rams, and the fat of fed beasts; and I delight not
in the blood of bullocks, or of lambs, or of he-goats. When ye come
to appear before me, who hath required this at your hand, to
trample my courts? Bring no more vain oblations; incense is an
abomination unto me; new moon and sabbath, the calling of assemblies—I cannot away with iniquity and the solemn meeting.
Your new moons and your appointed feasts my soul hateth; they
are a trouble unto me; I am weary of bearing them. And when ye
spread forth your hands, I will hide mine eyes from you; yea, when
ye make many prayers, I will not hear: your hands are full of blood.
Wash you, make you clean; put away the evil of your doings from
before mine eyes; cease to do evil; learn to do well; seek justice,
relieve the oppressed, judge the fatherless, plead for the widow.—
Isa. 1:10-17.**

Many young people, watching conventional observances in religious worship and perceiving no real life active there, come to the

conclusion that religious faith is a decent and negligible formality. So William Scott Palmer, tracing his progress from agnosticism to Christianity, describes the religion of his boyhood: "Religion as a personal matter, religion as a life, did not exist for me or for my family. The borderland of my native village went to church at eleven o'clock on fine Sundays, and I went in and with it. There were unlucky Sundays when the Litany was said, and the service prolonged by its unmeaning length; the lucky Sundays were wet ones that cleared up later. . . . I did not know that there was any vital meaning in religion." And even Sir Wilfred Grenfell, whose work in Labrador is one of this generation's outstanding triumphs of Christian faith, says of his young manhood: "The ordinary exponents of the Christian faith had never succeeded in interesting me in any way, or even in making me believe that they were more than professionally concerned themselves. Religion appeared to be a profession, exceedingly conventional, and most unattractive in my estimation—the very last I should have thought of selecting." No travesty on faith is more deadly in its effects than this substitution of conventional observance for life.

O Jesus, we thy ministers bow before Thee to confess the common sins of our calling. Thou knowest all things; Thou knowest that we love Thee and that our hearts' desire is to serve Thee in faithfulness; and yet, like Peter, we have so often failed Thee in the hour of Thy need. If ever we have loved our own leadership and power when we sought to lead our people to Thee, we pray Thee to forgive. If we have been engrossed in narrow duties and little questions, when the vast needs of humanity called aloud for prophetic vision and apostolic sympathy, we pray Thee to forgive. If in our loyalty to the Church of the past we have distrusted Thy living voice and have suffered Thee to pass from our door unheard, we pray Thee to forgive. If ever we have been more concerned for the strong and the rich than for the shepherdless throngs of the people for whom Thy soul grieved, we pray Thee to forgive.

O Master, amidst our failures we cast ourselves upon Thee in humility and contrition. We need new light and a new message. We need the ancient spirit of prophecy and the leaping fire and joy of a new conviction, and Thou alone canst give it. Inspire the ministry of Thy Church with dauntless courage to face the vast needs of the future. Free us from all entanglements that have hushed

*our voice and bound our action. Grant us grace to look upon the
veiled sins of the rich and the coarse vices of the poor through Thine
eyes. Give us Thine inflexible sternness against sin, and Thine inexhaustible compassion for the frailty and tragedy of those who do the
sin. Make us faithful shepherds of Thy flock, true seers of God, and
true followers of Jesus. Amen.*—Walter Rauschenbusch.

Fourth Week, Third Day

And he spake also this parable unto certain who trusted in themselves that they were righteous, and set all others at nought: Two
men went up into the temple to pray; the one a Pharisee, and the
other a publican. The Pharisee stood and prayed thus with himself,
God, I thank thee, that I am not as the rest of men, extortioners,
unjust, adulterers, or even as this publican. I fast twice in the week;
I give tithes of all that I get. But the publican, standing afar off,
would not lift up so much as his eyes unto heaven, but smote his
breast, saying, God, be thou merciful to me a sinner. I say unto you,
This man went down to his house justified rather than the other:
for every one that exalteth himself shall be humbled; but he that
humbleth himself shall be exalted.—Luke 18:9-14.

The men against whom the Master directed this parable were
bigots. Self-opinionated, self-conceited, dogmatic, and contemptuous—they wore all the attributes of bigotry. *And bigotry is a very
familiar perversion of faith.* Vital fellowship with God ought to
make men gracious, magnanimous, generous; it ought to make life
with God seem so incomparably important that when anyone has
that, his opinions about God will be tolerantly regarded, however
mistaken they may appear to be. Dr. Pritchett, when President of
the Massachusetts Institute of Technology, passed through a classroom where a young instructor was conducting a chemical experiment. "The reaction itself," says Dr. Pritchett, "was going on in a
retort on the table, while on a blackboard was written the conventional formula, which in the science of chemistry is used to describe
the reaction. It so happened that the instructor had made a mistake
in writing the formula; instead of CO^2 he had written CO_3. But
this made not the slightest difference in the reaction which was
going on in the flask." So, a man may live his life with an admirably
Christian spirit, although he describes it with a mistaken formula.

His error is theoretical, not vital. But a bigot is so sure that he alone knows the true formula, that a man without that formula is altogether wrong, and that he must either set him right or condemn him utterly, that he grows bitter, hard, unlovely. His opinions may be right, but his spirit is wrong. The faith that should make his life radiant is perverted to make it narrow, harsh, contemptuous. He renders hateful the very faith he seeks to commend and ruins the reputation of the God whom he is zealous to exalt. So the Pharisee of the parable missed all the beauty of the publican's life because he thought the publican's formula was wrong. No one can estimate the irreparable damage which zealous bigots have done to true faith.

O Thou who art of purer eyes than to behold iniquity, canst Thou bear to look on us conscious of our great transgression? Yet hide not Thy face from us, for in Thy light alone shall we see light.

Forgive us for the sins which crowd into the mind as we realize Thy presence; our ungovernable tempers, our shuffling insincerities, the craven fear of our hearts, the pettiness of our spirits, the foul lusts and fatal leanings of our souls. Not for pardon only, but for cleansing, Lord, we pray.

Forgive us, we beseech Thee, our unconscious sins; things which must be awful to Thy sight, of which we yet know nothing. Forgive by giving us in fuller measure the awakening of Thy presence, that we may know ourselves, and lose all love of sin in the knowledge of what Thou art.

Forgive us for the things for which we can never forgive ourselves; those sad turned pages of our life which some chance wind of memory blows back again with shame; for the moment of cruel passion, the hour beyond recall, the word that went forth to poison and defame, the carelessness that lost our opportunity, the unheeded fading of bright ideals.

Forgive us for the things that others can never forgive; the idle tale, the cruel wrong, the uncharitable condemnation, the unfair judgment, the careless criticism, the irresponsible conduct.

Forgive us for the sins of our holy things; that we have turned the sacred page without a sigh, read the confessions of holy men and women and never joined therein, lived in Thy light and never prayed to be forgiven or rendered Thee thanksgiving; professed to believe in Thee and love Thee, yet dared to injure and hate.

Naught save being born again, nothing but a miracle of grace, can ever be to us forgiveness. Cleanse our hearts, renew our minds, and take not Thy Holy Spirit from us. Amen.—W. E. Orchard.

Fourth Week, Fourth Day

Of all perversions of faith none is more fatal than the substitution of opinions about God for integrity of character and usefulness of life. With what scathing vehemence does James, as Dr. Moffatt renders him, attack this travesty on faith.

"My brothers, what is the use of anyone declaring he has faith, if he has no deeds to show? Can his faith save him? Suppose some brother or sister is ill-clad and short of daily food; if any of you says to them, 'Depart in peace! Get warm, get food,' without supplying their bodily needs, what use is that? So faith, unless it has deeds, is dead in itself. Someone will object, 'And you claim to have faith!' Yes, and I claim to have deeds as well; you show me your faith without any deeds, and I will show you by my deeds what faith is! You believe in one God? Well and good. So do the devils, and they shudder. But will you understand, you senseless fellow, that faith without deeds is dead? When our father Abraham offered his son Isaac on the altar, was he not justified by what he did?"—James 2: 14-21.

An American business man not long dead, who hated any word from the pulpit about social righteousness, used to complain: "Preachers are talking so everlastingly about this earth. I've done my best to get them to stick to the Gospel, and not allow 'worldliness' to get into the teachings of the Church; but the good old preachers have gone to glory." Yet this pious zealot helped wreck the finances of a great railroad system, and with part of the proceeds built a theological seminary. *There was no vital, intelligent connection between his faith in God and his ideals of character and service.* One verse should be made to flame in Christian pulpits: "If any provideth not for his own, and specially his own household, he hath denied the faith and is worse than an unbeliever" (I Tim. 5:8). Domestic fidelity is here only typical of all basic moral obligations. What this verse says in principle is clear: theoretical unbelief is not the worst sin in God's sight; any man who fails in the fundamental

duties of rectitude and service has thereby denied the faith and is
worse than an atheist.

O thou holy One and just! if alone the pure in heart can see thee,
truly we must stand afar off, and not so much as lift up our eyes
unto heaven. Were it not that thou hast help and pity for the con-
trite spirit, we could only cry, "Depart from us, we are sinful men,
O Lord!" For idle words, for proud thoughts and unloving deeds;
for wasted moments and reluctant duties, and too eager rest; for the
wandering desire, the vain fancy, the scornful doubt, the untrustful
care; for impatient murmurs, and unruly passions, and the hardness
of a worldly heart; thou, Lord, canst call us unto judgment, and we
have naught to answer thee. But, O thou Judge of men, thou art
witness that we do not love our guilty ways; make our conscience
true and tender that we may duly hate them, and refuse them any
peace as enemies to thee. Stir up within us a great and effectual
repentance that we may redeem the time which we have lost, and
in the hours that remain may do the work of many days. Thou
knowest all our secret snares; drive from us every root of bitterness:
with thy severity pluck out, O Lord, the thorns of sin from our
entangled souls, and bind them as a crown of contrition around our
bleeding brows; and having made our peace with thee may we hence-
forth watch and pray that we enter not again into temptation, but
bear our cross with patience to the close. Amen.—James Martineau.

Fourth Week, Fifth Day

Some of the most lamentable perversions of religious faith arise
from inadequate ideas of God. Consider, for example, the way
Manasseh thought that the Divine ought to be worshiped.

For he built again the high places which Hezekiah his father had
destroyed; and he reared up altars for Baal, and made an Asherah,
as did Ahab king of Israel, and worshipped all the host of heaven,
and served them. And he built altars in the house of Jehovah,
whereof Jehovah said, In Jerusalem will I put my name. And he
built altars for all the host of heaven in the two courts of the house
of Jehovah. And he made his son to pass through the fire, and
practised augury, and used enchantments, and dealt with them that
had familiar spirits, and with wizards: he wrought much evil in the
sight of Jehovah, to provoke him to anger.—II Kings 21:3-6.

Then compare the thought of the Master on the same subject.

But the hour cometh, and now is, when the true worshippers shall worship the Father in spirit and truth: for such doth the Father seek to be his worshippers. God is a Spirit: and they that worship him must worship in spirit and truth.—John 4:23, 24.

There is no reason to suppose that Manasseh was insincere; he is one of an innumerable company in whom the religious motive has been harnessed to warped and ignorant ideas of God. Religious faith, like any other tremendous power, is terrific in evil consequences when it goes wrong. Men, under its subtle and prevailing influence, have waged bloody wars, worshiped with licentious rituals, carried on pitiless persecutions, and in bigotry, cruelty, and deceit have grown worse than they would have been with no religion whatsoever. And men, in its inspiring light, have launched missionary movements, founded great philanthropies, built schools, hospitals, orphanages, and in sacrifice, courageous service, and hope of human brotherhood have made man's history glorious. Religion needs intelligence to save it from becoming a ruinous curse; like all power of the first magnitude it is a disaster if ignorantly used. Since religious faith will always be a major human motive, under what obligations are we to save it from perversion and to keep it clean and right!

Almighty God, our heavenly Father, we are most unworthy to be called Thy children; for when light and darkness have been set before us, we have often chosen darkness rather than light. Conscious that within us are the elements of a nobler and a meaner life, we have yet given way to the meaner appetites, and have not obeyed the inspiration Thou hast kindled within us. We entreat Thee now of Thy grace to call us back from the ways of temptation and sin into that higher life which Thou dost breathe upon us, and which is manifested in Jesus Christ our Lord. Give us the self-knowledge, the humility, the repentance, the aspiration which draw us to the Cross of Christ, that worshiping there in lowliness, we may see the weakness of falsehood and the strength of truth, the exceeding sinfulness of selfishness, and the beauty of love and sacrifice.

O Thou whose secret is with them that fear Thee, inspire us with that loyalty of soul, that willingness to do Thy will to which all things are clear. Darkness, we know, cometh upon the proud and disobedient; confusion is ever attendant upon self-will; while to the humble, the earnest, and the pure-minded, the way of duty and spiritual health is made clear. O Spirit of the Eternal, subdue within us all pride, all vain-glory, all self-seeking, and bring every thought and every desire into obedience to the law of Christ our Lord.

Almighty Father, to Thee would we consecrate these earthly days from infancy to age. Thee would we remember in childhood and youth. Thee would we serve in all the relations and activities of middle age. Thee would we teach our children to love and serve. Be Thou our stay and hope when health and strength shall fail. And when we are summoned hence, do Thou, O Life of our life, illumine the mystery of the invisible world with Thy presence and love. We ask these blessings in the spirit of Jesus Christ our Lord. Amen.— John Hunter.

Fourth Week, Sixth Day

The perversions of religious faith, working pitiable instead of benevolent consequences, are often seen on mission fields. Consider Paul's address in Athens:

And Paul stood in the midst of the Areopagus, and said,

Ye men of Athens, in all things I perceive that ye are very religious. For as I passed along, and observed the objects of your worship, I found also an altar with this inscription, TO AN UNKNOWN GOD. What therefore ye worship in ignorance, this I set forth unto you. The God that made the world and all things therein, he, being Lord of heaven and earth, dwelleth not in temples made with hands; neither is he served by men's hands, as though he needed anything, seeing he himself giveth to all life, and breath, and all things; and he made of one every nation of men to dwell on all the face of the earth, having determined their appointed seasons, and the bounds of their habitation; that they should seek God, if haply they might feel after him and find him, though he is not far from each one of us: for in him we live, and move, and have our being; as certain even of your own poets have said,

For we are also his offspring.

—Acts 17:22-28.

Paul did not need to plead for religion with the Athenians; they were already "very religious." Only religion was not doing for them what it ought; it was a power used "in ignorance"; and Paul, valu-

ing all that was good there, quoting their own poets with appreciation, nevertheless longed to take their strong religious motives and
so clarify and direct them that faith might mean unqualified benediction. Is not this always the right missionary method? The people
of India are intensely religious; no tribe in Africa lacks its gods;
and everywhere the faith-motive is immensely powerful. But often
it makes mothers drown their babies in sacred rivers, it conse-
crates caste systems as holy things, it centers man's adoration around
unworthy objects, its powers, gone wrong, are a curse and not a blessing. If in Jesus Christ religious faith has come to us, through no
merit of our own, as an unspeakable benediction, ought we not,
humbly, without dogmatism or intolerance, and yet with passionate
earnestness, to share our best with all the world? Religious faith may
either depress or lift a people's life; it is forever doing one or the
other in every nation under heaven; and *there is no hope for the
world until this master-motive is lifting everywhere.*

*Almighty God, our Father in heaven, who hast so greatly loved
the world that Thou hast given Thine only-begotten Son, the Redeemer, communicate Thy love to the hearts of all believers, and
revive Thy Church to preach the Gospel to every creature.*

*O Thou who rulest by Thy providence over land and sea, defend
and guide and bless the messengers of Christ; in danger be their
shield, in darkness be their hope; enrich their word and work with
wisdom, joy, and power, and let them gather souls for Thee in far
fields white unto the harvest.*

*O Thou who by Thy Holy Spirit workest wonders in secret, open
the eyes that dimly look for light to see the day-star in Christ; open
the minds that seek the unknown God to know their Heavenly Father
in Christ; open the hearts that hunger for righteousness to find
eternal peace in Christ. Deliver the poor prisoners of ignorance and
captives of idolatry, break down the bars of error, and dispel the
shadows of the ancient night; lift up the gates, and let the King
of glory and the Prince of Peace come in.*

*Thy kingdom, O Christ, is an everlasting kingdom! Strengthen
Thy servants to pray and labor and wait for its appearing; forgive
our little faith and the weakness of our endeavor; hasten the day
when all nations shall be at peace in Thee, and every land and every
heart throughout the world shall bless the name of the Lord Jesus,
to the glory of God the Father. Amen.*—Henry van Dyke.

Fourth Week, Seventh Day

The sad perversions of religious faith are not a matter for foreign missions only. At home, too, we find people who seem to be rather worse than better because they are religious. Just as power in any other form may be abused, so may religious faith. Some in the name of religion become censorious and intolerant, some superstitious, some slaves to morbid fears; and ignorance, self-conceit, pride, and worldly ambition when driven and enforced by a religious motive are infinitely worse than they would have been without it. Toward this fact two attitudes are possible. One is to throw over religion on account of its abuses; which is as reasonable as to deny all the blessings of electricity because in ignorant hands it is a dangerous power. The other is to take religious faith more seriously than ever, to see how great a force for weal or woe it always is in human life, and to strive in ourselves and in others for a high, intelligent, and worthy understanding and use of it. For religion can mean what Amiel said of it: "There is but one thing needful—to possess God. Religion is not a method: it is a life—a higher and supernatural life, mystical in its root and practical in its fruits; a communion with God, a calm and deep enthusiasm, a love which radiates, a force which acts, a happiness which overflows." From our study of the perversions and travesties of faith, we turn therefore in the weekly comment to consider faith's vital meanings. So Paul, writing to the Galatians, rejoices in religion as a gloriously transforming power in life.

But I say, Walk by the Spirit, and ye shall not fulfil the lust of the flesh. For the flesh lusteth against the Spirit, and the Spirit against the flesh; for these are contrary the one to the other; that ye may not do the things that ye would. But if ye are led by the Spirit, ye are not under the law. Now the works of the flesh are manifest, which are these: fornication, uncleanness, lasciviousness, idolatry, sorcery, enmities, strife, jealousies, wraths, factions, divisions, parties, envyings, drunkenness, revelings, and such like; of which I forewarn you even as I did forewarn you, that they who practise such things shall not inherit the kingdom of God. But the fruit of the Spirit is love, joy, peace, long-suffering, kindness, goodness, faithfulness, meekness, self-control; against such there is no law.

And they that are of Christ Jesus have crucified the flesh with the passions and the lusts thereof.—Gal. 5:16-23.

Thou, O God, hast exalted us so that no longer we walk with prone head among the animals that perish. Thou hast ordained us as Thine own children, and hast planted within us that spiritual life which ever seeks, as the flame, to rise upward and mingle with Thee. Every exaltation, every pure sentiment, all urgency of true affection, and all yearning after things higher and nobler, are testimonies of the divinity that is in us. These are the threads by which Thou art drawing us away from sense, away from the earth, away from things coarse and unspiritual, and toward the ineffable. We rejoice that we have in us the witness of the Spirit, the indwelling of God. For, although we are temples defiled, though we are unworthy of such a Guest, and though we perpetually grieve Thee, and drive Thee from us, so that Thou canst not do the mighty work that Thou wouldst within us, yet we rejoice to believe that Thou dost linger near us. Even upon the outside, Thou standest knocking at the door until Thy locks are wet with the night dews, and dost persuade us with the everlasting importunity of love, and draw us upward, whether with or without our own knowledge. Thou art evermore striving to imbue us with Thyself, and to give us that divine nature which shall triumph over time and sense and matter; and we pray that we may have an enlightened understanding of this Thy work in us and upon us, and work together with Thee. Amen.—Henry Ward Beecher.

COMMENT FOR THE WEEK

I

One might be tempted by the last chapter to suppose that, if he could accept the proposition that God is personal, he would be well upon his way toward Christianity. But in theory at least Plato accepted this proposition four hundred years before Christ, when he said: "God is never in any way unrighteous—He is perfect righteousness; and he of us who is most righteous is most like Him." He, too, used personality as a symbol of God. When, however, one compares Plato with Jesus, how incalculably greater is the religious meaning of our Lord! There is something more in the Master's experience and thought than the belief that God is personal. Evidently our quest must be followed further than the last chapter carried us.

In Scripture two kinds of faith in the personal God are clearly indicated. On the one side stand verses such as this: "Thou believest that God is one; thou doest well; the demons also believe and shudder" (James 2:19). On the other, one finds through both the Testaments witness and appeal for a kind of faith that plainly differs from the first: "O my God, in thee have I trusted" (Psalm 25:2). It is not difficult to guess the terms in which many would describe this difference. In the first, so the familiar explanation runs, we are dealing with the *mind's* faith in God; the man's intellect assents to the belief that God is and that He is one. In the second we are dealing with the *heart's* faith in God; the whole man is here involved in an adoring trust that finds in reliance upon God life's stimulus and joy.

This distinction between the faith of the intellect and of the heart is valid, but it does not go to the pith of the truth. When a professor in the classroom, discussing conflicting theories of life's origin, concludes that theism is the reasonable interpretation of the universe, the listener understands that the lecturer believes in God's existence. But if the professor could be followed home and overheard in a private prayer, like Fénelon's: "Lord, I know not what I ought to ask of Thee; Thou only knowest what I need; Thou lovest me better than I know how to love myself. O Father! give to Thy child that which he himself knows not how to ask," something incalculably more than the classroom talk disclosed would be revealed about the meaning of the teacher's faith. And as the classroom lecture and the private prayer stand so contrasted, the gist of the difference is plain. In the one, faith was directed toward a *theory;* in the other faith laid hold upon a *Person.* That the intellect was more involved in the first and the emotions in the second is incidental to the main matter, that *two differing objects were in view.* Toward these two objects we continually are exercising faith—*ideas and people, propositions and persons.*

Now faith in a proposition we conveniently may call belief; and faith in a person, trust. We believe that gravitation and the conservation of energy universally apply, that democracy will prove better than absolutism, and that prison systems can be radically reformed; these and innumerable other propositions that cannot be demonstrated we confidently believe. But in quite another way we daily are exercising faith; *we have faith in our friends.* How profound a change comes over the quality and value of faith when it thus finds its objective in a person! Our beliefs in propositions are of basic import and without them we could not well exist, but it is by trust in persons that we live indeed. Belief in monogamy, for all its importance, is a cold abstraction, and few could be found to die for it. Men do not lay down their lives for abstract theories, any more than they would suffer martyrdom, as Chesterton remarked, for the Meridian of Greenwich. But when monogamy is translated from theory into personal experience, when belief in the idea becomes trust in a lifelong comrade of whom one may sing:

"What I do
And what I dream include thee, as the wine
Must taste of its own grapes,"

faith has taken a form for which men do live and die in glad surrender. Although the same word, faith, be applied to both, trust in persons reaches deeper than belief in propositions and supplies a warmth and power that belief cannot attain.

In religion these two aspects of faith continually are found and both are indispensable. Trust in a person, for example, presupposes belief in his existence and fidelity. "He that cometh to God must believe that he is, and that he is a rewarder of them that seek after him" (Heb. 11:6). Trust cannot exist without belief, but when one seeks the inner glory of the religious life that has overflowed in prayer and hymn, supplied motive for service and power for character, he finds it not in belief, but in the vital relationships involved in trusting a Person. Men often have discussed their particular beliefs with cool deliberation, have stated them in formal creeds, have changed them with access of new knowledge and experience. But *trust,* the inner reliance of the soul on God and glad self-surrender to his will, has persisted through many changes, clothing itself with beliefs like garments and casting them aside when old. Trust has made rituals and churches and unmade them when they were ineffectual, it has been the life behind the theory, the experience behind the explanation; and its proper voice has been not creed and controversy, but psalm and song and sacrifice. Men have felt in describing this inward friendship that their best words were but the "vocal gestures of the dumb," able to indicate but unable to express their thoughts. *For while belief is theology, trust is religion.*

II

This central position of trust in the Christian life is evident when one considers that in its presence or absence lies the chief point of difference between a religious and an irreligious man. The peculiarity of religion is not that it has beliefs; everybody has them. As we have seen, Huxley, who called himself an agnostic, said that he thoroughly believed the universe to be rational, than which only a few greater ventures of faith can be imagined. A man may not want to have beliefs. He may say that knowledge is wool, warm to clothe oneself withal, that belief is cotton, and that he will not mingle them. But for all that he still does have beliefs and he cannot help it.

When, therefore, a Christian and an atheist converse they can match belief with belief. "I believe," says one, "in God the Father"; and "I believe," says the other, "in the eternal physical universe, without spiritual origin or moral purpose." Says the Christian, "I believe in the immortality of persons," and the atheist replies, "I believe that the spirit dies with the body as sound ceases when the bell's swinging iron grows still." Says the Christian, "I believe in the ultimate triumph of righteousness"; and the atheist replies, "I believe that all man's aspiration after good is but the endless sailing of a ship that never shall arrive." So the two may play battledore and shuttlecock, but if, so having paired beliefs, they part with no more said, they have missed the real point of their difference. The irreligious man can match the Christian's belief with his own, but one thing he cannot match—the Christian's trust. *He has nothing that remotely corresponds with that.*

The Christian always has this case to plead with an unbelieving man: Do not suppose that the difference between us is exhausted in a conflict of contrasting propositions. Great indeed is the divergence there! But the issue of all such difference lies in another realm. When you face life's abysmal mysteries that your eyes can no more pierce than mine, you have no one to trust. When misfortunes fall that send men to their graves, as Sydney Smith said, with souls scarred like a soldier's body, you have no one to trust. When you face the last mystery of all and whether going say farewell to those who stay, or staying bid farewell to those who go, you have no one to trust. You can match my belief with your belief, but for one thing you have no counterpart. "Jehovah is my shepherd, I shall

not want" (Psalm 23:1). You cannot match that! "My heart hath
trusted in him, and I am helped" (Psalm 28:7). You cannot match
that! "Shall not the Judge of all the earth do right?" (Gen. 18:25);
"We have our hope set on the living God" (I Tim. 4:10); "Father,
into thy hands I commend my spirit" (Luke 23:46). That trust you
cannot match!

III

In the light of this distinction between belief and trust some mistaken types of faith can be easily described. There, for example, is the
faith of formal creedalism. We cannot have trust without some belief,
but we may unhappily have belief without any trust. Now a man
who believes the doctrines that underly the Christian life but who
does not vitally trust the Person whom those doctrines present, has
missed the heart out of faith's meaning. He is like one who cherishes
a letter of introduction to a great personality, but has never used it;
he has the formal credentials, but not the transforming experience.
It follows that we cannot estimate a man merely by knowing his
beliefs. I believe in all the Christian truths, says one; and the curious question rises, how did these beliefs of his come into his possession? They may have been handed to him by his forbears like
a set of family jewels, a static and external heritage, which now
he keeps in some ecclesiastical safe-deposit vault and on state days,
at Christmas or at Easter, goes to see. Still he may claim that they
are his beliefs; he may even quarrel about their genuineness, not
because he ever uses them but because they are his. He may repeat
the creed with the same unquestioning assent that he gives to the
conventional cut of his clothes. His beliefs are not the natural utterance and explanation of his inner life with God and man, but are
put on as they were handed to him, like the fashions of his coats.
So easy is it to be formally orthodox!

Over against such conventional believers one thinks of other folk
whom he has known. They have no such stereotyped, clear-cut beliefs. They are very puzzled about life. It seems to them abysmally
mysterious. And when they speak they talk with a modesty the formal
creedalist has never felt: My beliefs are most uncertain. Confused
by many voices shouting conflicting opinions about truths which I
once accepted without thinking, I cannot easily define my thoughts.
But I do trust God. That assent of the mind which I cannot give to

propositions, I can give to him. Life is full of mystery, but I do not really think that the mystery is darkness at its heart. My faith has yet its standing ground in this, that the world's activities are not like the convulsions of an epileptic, unconscious and purposeless. There is a Mind behind the universe, and a good purpose in it.

> "Yet in the maddening maze of things,
>   And tossed by storm and flood,
>   To one fixed trust my spirit clings;
>   I know that God is good."

Say as one may that such an attitude is far from adequate, yet as compared with the merely formal acceptance of inherited opinions how incomparably superior its religious value is!

The people of placid, stiff beliefs are not the successors of the real saints. When one reads George Matheson's books of devotion, for example, or sings his hymn "O Love, that wilt not let me go," or learns of his great work in his church in Edinburgh, one might suppose that he never had a doubt. Yet listen to his own confession: "At one time with a great thrill of horror, I found myself an absolute atheist. After being ordained at Innellan, I believed nothing; neither God nor immortality. I tendered my resignation to the Presbytery, but to their honor they would not accept it, even though a Highland Presbytery. They said I was a young man and would change. I have changed." One need only read such books of his as "Can the Old Faith Live with the New?" to see through what a searching discipline of strenuous thought he passed in the regaining of his faith. But if one would know what held his religious life secure while he was working out his beliefs from confusion to clarity, one must turn to Matheson's poem:

> "Couldst thou love *Me*
>   When creeds are breaking—
>   Old landmarks shaking
>   With wind and sea?
>   Couldst thou refrain the earth from quaking
>   And rest thy heart on *Me*?"

Many a man has been held fast by his trust in God while in perplexity he thought out his beliefs about God.

Indeed, within the Scripture, whatever word is used to describe the attitude of faith, this vital personal alliance with God is everywhere intended. For convenience we have called faith in propositions belief, but that does not mean that when the Scriptures use "believe" they are urging the acceptance of propositions. Not often in the Bible are we invited merely to agree with an opinion; we are everywhere called to trust a Person. "Trust in the Lord" in the Old Testament, "Believe in the Lord Jesus Christ" in the New, are neither of them the proclamation of a theory, but the exaltation of a personality. Wherever in Scripture doctrines are insisted on—the unity of God, the deathlessness of the spirit, the divinity of Christ— they are never doctrines for their own sakes; *they are either commendatory truths about a Friend, that we may not fail to trust him, or they are ideas about life that have come to men because they did trust him. Trust in a Person is either the source or the goal of every Christian doctrine.* The Gospel at its center is not a series of propositions, but a concrete, personal relationship opened between the soul and the Divine, out of which new powers, joys, possibilities flow gloriously into human life. When out of this experience of divine fellowship Paul, for example, speaks of faith he means by it the alliance that binds him to his friend. He fairly sings of the peace that comes from such believing (Rom. 15:13), of the love that is its motive power and chief expression (Gal. 5:6), and of "the sacrifice and service" which are its issue (Phil. 2:17). He enthusiastically commends to everyone this divine alliance through which moral defeat is changed to victory in the "righteousness which is of God by faith" (Phil. 3:9); and his prose slips over into poetry when he describes his new transfigured life as "access by faith into that grace wherein we stand" (Rom. 5:2). Plainly he is not talking here about a set of propositions; he is rejoicing in a transforming personal relationship. Some faith is nothing but an inherited set of opinions and it gives a cold light like an incandescent bulb; some faith, like sunshine, is brighter for seeing than any incandescence can ever be, but warm too, so that under its persuasive touch new worlds of life spring into being. The faith of the New Testament and of the real saints is not the cold brilliance of a creed in whose presence one can freeze even while he sees; it is the warm, life-giving sunshine of a trust in God that makes all gracious things grow, and puts peace and joy, hope and love into life. Belief in propositions is there, but the crown and glory of it are trust in a Person.

IV

In the light of this distinction between belief and trust, the inadequacy of another type of faith can easily be understood. Many would protest that they have not accepted their beliefs as an external heritage from the past, but rather have thought them through, and hold them now as *reasonable theories to explain the facts of the spiritual life*. They would say that as a geologist observes the rocks and constructs an hypothesis to account for their origin and nature, so the mind, observing man's contacts with invisible powers, constructs religious beliefs as explanations of experience. They would insist that their theology is not merely traditional, but in large degree is independently appropriated and original. They hold it as an hypothesis to make intelligible man's experiences of the spiritual world.

There is significant truth in this view of faith. Man's ideals, his loves, hopes, aspirations, his unescapable sense of moral obligation, his consciousness of Someone other than himself, are facts, as solidly present in experience as stars and mountains. To explain these facts by theology is as rational as to explain the stars by astronomy. Every believer in religious truth should welcome this confirming word from Dr. Pritchett, written when he was President of the Massachusetts Institute of Technology: "Science is grounded in faith just as is religion, and scientific truth, like religious truth, consists of hypotheses, never wholly verified, that fit the facts more or less closely."

But when one turns from such a statement to inquire what faith has actually meant to religious men, he does not find that their experience could easily be defined as belief in an hypothesis. The prophets, standing their ground through national disaster, undiscourageable in their conviction of God's good purpose for His people, would have been surprised to hear their faith so described. When the Sons of Thunder were swept out into a new life by the influence of Jesus, or the seer of Patmos was ravished with visions of eternal victory, or Paul was made conqueror in a fight for character that had been his despair, they would hardly have spoken of their experiences as belief in an hypothesis. Real religion has always meant something more vital than holding a theory about life. When Robert Louis Stevenson says of his transformation of character, "I came about like a well-handled ship. There stood at the wheel that unknown steersman whom we call God"; when Tolstoi cries: "To know God and to live are one and the same thing"; when Professor William James, of Harvard, writes of his consciousness of God, "It is most indefinite to be sure and rather faint, and yet I know that if it should cease, there would be a great hush, a great void in my life"; one sees what conversion of character, what increase of life's value, what spiritual reenforcement religion has meant even to such unconventional believers. When they speak of it, they are evidently thinking of a vital power and not a theory.

The most obscure Christian to whom religion has become a necessity in living, knows how far short the plummet of hypothetical belief comes from reaching bottom. In sin, burdened by a sense of guilt that he could not shake off and unable to forgive himself, he has cried to be forgiven, and the Gospel that has been his hope was no injunction to hold hard by his hypothesis! In sorrow, when the blows have fallen that either hallow or embitter life, he has sought for necessary fortitude, and the Gospel which established him certainly was not, Cast thy care on thine hypothesis! And when, more than conqueror, he faces death, his confidence and hope will rest on no such prayer as this, O Hypothesis, guide me! The word of religion is of another sort, "Though I walk through the valley of the shadow of death, I will fear no evil, for *Thou* art with me." Not belief in propositions, but trust in a Person has been the heart of the Gospel, and to make any hypothesis, however true, do duty as religion is to give the soul a stone when it asks for bread.

The futility of seeking contentment in faith as an hypothesis alone is especially manifest in our time. This is an age of swiftly changing ideas in every realm. As in science, so in religion, today one theory holds the field to be displaced tomorrow by another. A man in theology, as much as in politics or psychology, goes to bed supposing he has settled his opinions, and wakes up to find a new array of evidence that disturbs his confidence. When, therefore, religious faith has meant no more to its possessor than theory, there is no security or rest. Each day the winds of opinion shift and veer, and minds at the beginning obstinate in their beliefs, at last, dismayed by the reiterated uncertainties of thought, give up their faith.

Where, then, have the men of faith found the immovable center of their confidence? Paul revealed the secret. On the side of his particular opinions he frankly confessed his limited and uncertain knowledge. "Now we know in fragments," he wrote, "now we see through a glass darkly." "How unsearchable are his judgments and

his ways past tracing out!" But on the side of his trust he is ada-
mant: "I know *him* whom I have believed." The certainty of his life
was his relationship with a person, and his beliefs were the best he
yet had thought in the explication and establishment of that trust.

The great believers of the Church continually have exhibited this
dual aspect of their faith. Even St. Augustine, facing the profound
mysteries involved in his trinitarian belief, complains that human
speech is pitiably futile in trying to explain what "Three persons"
means, and that if he uses the familiar phrase, he does so not because
he likes it, but because he may not be silent and knows no better
thing to say. But when Augustine prays to the God whose nature is
so unfathomable that no man can see it fully or express it adequately,
he reveals no such uncertain thought: "Grant me, even me, my
dearest Lord, to know Thee and love Thee and rejoice in Thee.
. . . Let the love of Thee grow every day more and more here, that
it may be perfect hereafter; that my joy may be great in itself and
full in Thee. I know, O God, that thou art a God of truth; O make
good Thy gracious promises to me!" So children do not fully understand an earthly father and often hold conceptions grotesquely insufficient to do justice to his life and work. But they may have for
him well-founded trust. Even in the years of infancy an ennobling
personal relationship begins, despite the inadequacy of their beliefs,
and that trust yearly deepens while mental concepts shift and change
with access of new knowledge. *The abiding core of a child's life
with his father is not belief but trust.*

Such has always been the secret of faith's stability in men who
have entered into personal fellowship with God. Even of the first
disciples it has been said—"They would have had difficulty sometimes to tell you *what* they believed, but they could always have told
you in *whom* they believed."

v

The truth of which we have been speaking has pertinent bearing
on the main object of our studies. We shall be considering the difficulties which Christians have with their beliefs, and the arguments
which may clarify and establish our minds' confidence in God. But
many problems in the realm of intellectual belief cannot be solved
by any arguments which the mind devises. The trouble often lies not
in our theories about the religious life, but in our religious life itself.

The deeper difficulty is not that our thinking is unreasonable, but that our experience is unreal.

To a man who never had seen the stars or felt the wonder of their distances, astronomy would be a lifeless topic and his endeavors to think about it a blundering and futile operation. Our theories about anything depend for their interest and worth upon the vividness with which we experience the thing itself and care to understand its meaning. This is true about matters like the stars; how much more true about the intimate affairs of man's own life! Democracy vs. autocracy is a crucial problem. But plenty of men are so careless about human weal, think so little of their country and the world as objects of solicitude and devotion, that to discuss in their presence democratic and autocratic theories of state is a waste of time. The trouble is not with their minds; they may be very clever and acute. The trouble is with their lives. They need to experience patriotism as a vital motive; they need to care immensely what happens to mankind. Only then will the problems of government grow vivid, and the need of a solution become so critical that thinking will be urgent and productive. We never think well about anything for which we do not care.

Plenty of people today discuss theology as an academic pastime. It is a speculative game at which they play, as they do at golf, for its fun and lure. They do not really care about God; they feel no crucial need of him. Of little use is all their ingenuity in argument, clever and astute though it may be. Blind men might so discuss the color scheme of an Italian landscape and deaf men debate the harmonies of Handel's oratorios. What is lacking is experience. For our theories are only the explanations of experience, and an emptier game cannot be played than debating explanations of experiences which we have not had.

Everyone in difficulty with his faith should give due weight to this important truth. Our intellectual troubles are not all caused by the bankruptcy of our spiritual lives, but many of them are. Men live with drained and unreplenished spirits, from which communion with God and service of high causes have been crowded out. God grows unreal. The self-evidencing experiences that maintain vital confidence in the spiritual life grow dim and unimperative. Men pass years without habitually thinking as though God really were, without making any great decisions as though God's will were King, without engaging in any sacrificial work that makes the thought of

God a need and a delight, without the companionship of great ideas or the sustenance of prayer. Then, when experience is denuded of any sense of God's reality, some intellectual doubt is suggested by books or friends, or fearful trouble shatters happiness. What recourse is there in such a case? The arguments of faith have no experience to get their grip upon; they can appeal to no solid and sustained fact of living. Religious confidence goes to pieces and men tell their friends that modern philosophy has been too much for faith. But the underlying difficulty was not philosophical; it was vital. The insolvency of "belief" was due to the bankruptcy of "trust." Personal fellowship with God failed first; the theory about him lapsed afterward.

Throughout our endeavor to deal with intellectual perplexity, this fundamental truth should not be forgotten. *The peril of religion is that vital experience shall be resolved into a formula of explanation, and that men, grasping the formula, shall suppose themselves thereby to possess the experience.* If one inquires what air is, the answer will probably be a formula stating that oxygen and nitrogen mixed in proportions of twenty-one to seventy-nine make air. But air in experience is not a formula. Air is the elixir we breathe and live thereby. Air is the magician who takes the words that our lips frame and bears them from friend to friend in daily converse. Air is the messenger who carries music to our ears and fragrance to our nostrils; it is the whisperer among the trees in June, and in March the wild dancer who shakes the bare branches for his castanets. Air is the giant who piles the surf against the rocky shore, and the nurse who fans the faces of the sick. One cannot put that into a formula. No more can God be put into a theology, however true. They who define him best may understand him least. God is the Unseen Friend, the Spiritual Presence, who calls us in ideals, warns us in remorse, renews us with his pardon, and comforts us with power. God is the Spirit of Righteousness in human life, whose victories we see in every moral gain, and allied with whom we have solid hopes of moral victory. God is the One who holds indeed the far stars in his hand, and yet in fellowship with whom each humblest son of man may find strength to do and to endure with constancy and fortitude and deathless hope. And when one lives close to him, so that the inner doors swing easily on quiet hinges to let him in, he is the One who illumines life with a radiance that human wills alone cannot attain. That is God—"Blessed is the man that taketh refuge in him" (Psalm 34:8).

CHAPTER V

Faith's Intellectual Difficulties

DAILY READINGS

Most people will readily grant that such a sense of personal fellowship with God as the last week's study presented is obviously desirable. Every one who has experienced such filial life with God will bear witness to its incomparable blessing. Said Tennyson, "I should be sorely afraid to live my life without God's presence, but to feel he is by my side just now as much as you are, that is the very joy of my heart." But many who would admit the desirability of the experience are troubled about the reasonableness of the beliefs that underly it. They want intellectual assurance about their faith. Let us in the daily readings present certain considerations which a mind so perplexed should take into account.

Fifth Week, First Day

We should let no one deny our right to bring religious belief to the test of reasonableness. Glanvill was right when in the seventeenth century he said, "There is not anything I know which hath done more mischief to Religion than the disparaging of Reason." In the New Testament Paul says:

Prove all things; hold fast that which is good.—I Thess. 5:21.

Peter says:

Yea, and for this very cause adding on your part all diligence, in your faith supply virtue; and in your virtue knowledge.—II Pet. 1:5.

This might be paraphrased to read, Faith should be *worked out* into character and *thought through* into knowledge. As for Jesus:

One of the scribes came, and heard them questioning together, and knowing that he had answered them well, asked him, What commandment is the first of all? Jesus answered, The first is, Hear, O Israel; The Lord our God, the Lord is one: and thou shalt love the Lord thy God with all thy heart, and with all thy soul, and with all thy mind, and with all thy strength.—Mark 12:28-30.

In many a life which has neglected these admonitions Lowell's words have proved true: "Nothing that keeps thought out is safe from thought." In our resolute endeavor to think through the mystery of life, however, and to find a reasonable basis for faith, we need to remember that *the very desire to know is an indication of the reality which we seek.* The dim intuition that the world with all its diverse powers was in some sense a unity, preceded by ages the statement of nature's uniformity which modern science knows; and man's tireless desire to reach a reasonable statement of the unity was an intimation in advance that unity was there. So men do not believe in God because they have proved him; they rather strive endlessly to prove him because they cannot help being sure that he must be there. This in itself is an intimation about reality which no thoughtful man will lightly set aside. Tennyson rightly describes the reason for man's quest after proof about God:

> "If e'er when faith had fall'n asleep,
> I heard a voice 'believe no more'
> And heard an ever-breaking shore
> That tumbled in the Godless deep;
>
> A warmth within the breast would melt
> The freezing reason's colder part,
> And like a man in wrath the heart
> Stood up and answer'd 'I have felt.' "

Eternal Father, Quest of ages, long sought, oft doubted or forsook; can it be that Thou art known to us, the Law within our minds, the Life of every breath we draw, the Love that yearneth in our hearts? Art Thou the Spirit who oft hast striven with us, and whom we greatly feared, lest yielding to His strong embrace we should become more than we dared to be?

An impulse toward forgiveness has sometimes stirred within us, we have felt moved to show mercy, the sacrificial life has touched our aspiration; but we were unprepared to pay the price. Was this Thyself, and have we turned from Thee? Something like this we must have done, so barren, joyless and so dead has life become. Canst Thou not visit us again?

We hush our thoughts to silence, we school our spirits in sincerity, and here we wait. O may we not feel once more the light upon our straining eyes, the tides of life rise again within our waiting hearts?

We never looked to meet Thee in the stress of thought, the toil of life, or in the call of duty; we only knew that somehow life had lost for us all meaning, dignity, and beauty. How then shall we turn back again and see with eyes that fear has filmed? How can we be born again, now grown so old in fatal habit?

If we could see this life of ours lived out in Thee, its common days exalted, its circumstances made a throne, its bitterness, disappointment, and failure all redeemed, then our hearts might stir again, and these trembling hands lay hold on life for evermore. Amen.—W. E. Orchard.

Fifth Week, Second Day

Not only is man's tireless quest for assurance about God an intimation that God must be here to be sought after; but *the spiritual nature of man which insists on the quest is itself a revelation that God actually is here.* Some men say that our spiritual life is the result of evolution, and they suppose that by this magic word they have explained it. But what comes out of a process of growth was somehow latent in the Original Beginning from which the growth started. Palm-trees do not grow from acorns; only oaks evolve from acorns and for the sufficient reason that oaks are somehow *involved in acorns* to start with. So a universe with spiritual life in it naturally presupposes an Original with spiritual life in It. Whatever evolves must first of all have been involved. The very fact that the seeker after God has a spiritual life, which is restless and unsatisfied without faith in the Eternal Spirit, is one of the clearest indications that, whatever else may be said about the source of life, it must be spiritual. The Nile for ages was a mystery; it flowed through Egypt—a blessed necessity to the land, enriching the soil, and sustaining the people—but nobody knew its source. Long before Victoria Nyanza was discovered, however, thinkers were sure that a great lake must be the explanation of the stream; and when at last they found the sources of the Nile, the lake was even greater than anyone had dreamed. So is man's spirit a revelation of a spiritual origin even before that origin is clearly known. As the Bible puts it:

Now he that wrought us for this very thing is God, who gave unto us the earnest of the Spirit.—II Cor. 5:5.

O God! mysterious and Infinite, Thou art the first and Thou the last: as our weeks pass away and our age rises or declines, we still return to Thee who ever art the same. We seek Thee as the sole abiding light amid the shadows of perishable things. O Thou most ancient God! to whom the heavens are but of yesterday, and the life of worlds but as the shooting star, there is no number of Thy days and mercies; and what can we do, O Lord, but throw ourselves on Thee who failest not, and from whom our pathway is not hid? With solemn and open heart we would meet Thee here. Cover not Thyself with a cloud, most High, but may our prayer pass through.

O Thou our constant Witness and our awful Judge! When we remember our thoughtless lives, our low desires, our impatient temper, our ungoverned wills, we know that Thou hast left us without excuse. For Thou hast not made us blind, O Lord, as the creatures that have no sin; nor hast Thou spared the light of holy guidance. Thy still small voice of warning whispers through our deepest conscience; and Thine open Word hath dwelt among us, full of grace and truth, and called us to the feet of Christ to choose the better part. We are not our own, and are ashamed to have lived unto ourselves. Thou hast formed us for Thy service, and we must hide our face that we have shrunk from the glorious hardships of our task, and slumbered on our holy watch. Our daily work has not been wrought as in Thy sight; and we have not made the outgoings of the morning and the evening to praise Thee. The trials of our patience we have received as earthly pains of nature, not as the heavenly discipline of faith; and the fulness of Thy bounties has come to us as dead comfort, not as the quickening touch of Thy everlasting love. O our true and only God! we have lived in a bondage of the world that bringeth no content; and the passions we serve are as strange idols that cannot deliver. Awake, awake, O Arm of the Lord! and burst our bonds in sunder; and help the spirit that struggles within

*us to turn unto Thee with a pure heart, and serve Thee in newness
of spirit. Amen.*—James Martineau.

Fifth Week, Third Day

Many stumble at the very beginning of their quest for God, because they are sure that finite mind can never know the Infinite. The Bible itself asserts that God is in one sense unknowable.

Touching the Almighty, we cannot find him out.—Job 37:23.

Man cannot find out the work that God hath done from the beginning even to the end.—Eccl. 3:11.

O the depth of the riches both of the wisdom and the knowledge of God! how unsearchable are his judgments, and his ways past tracing out! For who hath known the mind of the Lord? or who hath been his counsellor?—Rom. 11:33, 34.

But in the same sense in which God is unknowable, all the most important realities with which we deal are also beyond our comprehension. We do not know what electricity is, what matter is, what life is. Ether is utterly beyond the reach of our definitions, and an English scientist calls it "unknown, impalpable, the necessary condition of scientific thought." As for the constituent elements of the material world, we are told that atoms are so infinitesimally minute as to be indivisible, and yet that an "electron ranges about in the atom as a mouse might in a cathedral." The plain fact is that in any realm, human knowledge soon runs off into an unknown region where it deals with invisible realities, which it cannot define, but on which life is based. While therefore we do not know what electricity, ether, electrons, and life itself *are,* we do know them well *in their relationship with our needs.* So we may know God. Deep beyond deep in him will be past our fathoming, but what God means in his relationships with our lives we may know gloriously.

*O Thou who transcendest all thought of Thee as the heavens are
higher than the earth; we acknowledge that we cannot search Thee
out to perfection, but we thank Thee that Thou, the Invisible,
comest to us in the things that are seen; that Thy exceeding glory is
shadowed in the flower that blooms for a day, in the light that fades;
that Thine infinite love has been incarnate in lowly human life; and*

*that Thy presence surrounds all our ignorance, Thy holiness our sin,
Thy peace our unrest.*

*Give us that lowly heart which is the only temple that can contain
the infinite. Save us from the presumption that prides itself on a
knowledge which is not ours, and from the hypocrisy and carelessness which professes an ignorance which Thy manifestation has
made for ever impossible. Save us from calling ourselves by a name
that Thou alone canst wear, and from despising the image of Thyself Thou hast formed us to bear, and grant that knowledge of Thee
revealed in Jesus Christ which is our eternal life. Amen.*—W. E.
Orchard.

Fifth Week, Fourth Day

The assurance of God may come in part from looking outward at
his creation. This universe seems superficially to be material, but
really it is *saturated with the presence of mind.* So a city's streets,
buildings, bridges, subways, and railroads might appear to careless
thought grossly material; but the fact is that in their origin they all
are *mental.* They are not simply iron and steel and stone; they are
thought, plan, purpose materialized and made visible. The basic fact
about them is that mind shaped them and permeates every use to
which they are put. The most important and decisive force in their
origination was not anything that can be seen, but the invisible
thought that dreamed them and moulded them. So when one looks
at creation he finds something more than matter; he finds order, law,
uniformity; his mind is at home in tracing regularities, discovering
laws, and perceiving purposes. Creation is not grossly material; it is
saturated with the evidence of mind. Lord Kelvin, the chemist,
walking in the country with Liebig, his fellow-scientist, asked his
companion if he believed that the grass and flowers grew by mere
chemical forces; and Liebig answered, "No, no more than I could
believe that the books of botany describing them could grow by
mere chemical forces."

**Lift up your eyes on high, and see who hath created these, that
bringeth out their host by number; he calleth them all by name; by
the greatness of his might, and for that he is strong in power, not
one is lacking.**

**Why sayest thou, O Jacob, and speakest, O Israel, My way is hid
from Jehovah, and the justice to me is passed away from my God?**

Hast thou not known? hast thou not heard? The everlasting God, Jehovah, the Creator of the ends of the earth, fainteth not, neither is weary; there is no searching of his understanding. He giveth power to the faint; and to him that hath no might he increaseth strength. Even the youths shall faint and be weary, and the young men shall utterly fall: but they that wait for Jehovah shall renew their strength; they shall mount up with wings as eagles; they shall run, and not be weary; they shall walk, and not faint.—Isa. 40: 26-31.

O Thou Infinite Perfection, who art the soul of all things that are . . . we thank Thee for the world of matter whereon we live, wherewith our hands are occupied, and whereby our bodies are builded up and filled with food and furnished with all things needful to enjoy. We thank Thee for the calmness of Night, which folds Thy children in her arms, and rockest them into peaceful sleep, and when we wake we thank Thee that we are still with Thee. We bless Thee for the heavens over our head, arched with loveliness, and starred with beauty, speaking in the poetry of nature the psalm of life which the spheres chant before Thee to every listening soul.

We thank Thee for this greater and nobler world of spirit wherein we live, whereof we are, whereby we are strengthened, upheld, and blessed. We thank Thee for the wondrous powers which Thou hast given to man, that Thou hast created him for so great an estate, that thou hast enriched him with such noble faculties of mind and conscience and heart and soul, capable of such continual increase of growth and income of inspiration from Thyself. We thank Thee for the wise mind, for the just conscience, for the loving heart, and the soul which knows Thee as Thou art, and enters into communion with Thy spirit, rejoicing in its blessing from day to day. Amen.— Theodore Parker.

Fifth Week, Fifth Day

The vital assurance of faith always comes, not so much from observing the outer world, as from appreciating the meaning of man's inner life. Man knows that he is something more than a physical machine. Theorists may say that our minds are only a series of molecular changes in the brain; but man turns to ask: *Who is it that is watching these molecular changes? The very fact that we can discuss*

*them, is proof that we are something more than they are and of
another order.* Leslie Stephen was an agnostic, but at the thought of
man as merely a physical machine he grew impatient. "I knock down
a man and an image," he said, "and both fall down because both
are material. But when the man gets up and knocks me down, the
result is not explicable by any merely mechanical action." Man
denies his own inward consciousness of self when he refuses to acknowledge the mental and spiritual part of him as the thing he really
is. Man may have a body, but he surely is a soul. And when man lets
this highest part of him speak its own characteristic word, he always
hears a message like this: I am spirit; to grow into great character
is the one worthy end of my existence; but how came I to be spirit
with spiritual purpose unless my Creator is of like quality? and how
can I believe that my existence and my purpose are not a cruel joke
unless I am begotten by a Spiritual Life that will sustain my strength
and crown my effort? To believe that man's soul is a foundling, laid
on the doorstep of a merely physical universe, crying in vain for any
father who begot him or any mother who conceived him, is to make
our highest life a liar. Therefore man at his best has always believed
in God.

**For as many as are led by the Spirit of God, these are the sons
of God. For ye received not the spirit of bondage again unto fear;
but ye received the spirit of adoption, whereby we cry, Abba,
Father. The Spirit himself beareth witness with our spirit, that we
are children of God.—Rom. 8:14-16.**

*O Thou whom no name can tell, whom all our thoughts cannot
fully comprehend, we rejoice in all Thy goodness. . . . We thank
Thee for our body, this handful of dust so curiously and wonderfully
framed together. We bless Thee for this sparkle of Thy fire that we
call our soul, which enchants the dust into thoughtful human life,
and blesses us with so rich a gift. We thank Thee for the varied
powers Thou hast given us here on earth. We bless Thee for the far-
reaching mind, which puts all things underneath our feet, rides on
the winds and the waters, and tames the lightning into useful service.
. . . We thank Thee for this conscience, whereby face to face we
commune with Thine everlasting justice. We thank Thee for the
strength of will which can overpower the weakness of mortal flesh,
face danger and endure hardship, and in all things acquit us like
men. . . .*

We thank Thee for this religious sense, whereby we know Thee, and, amid a world of things that perish, lay fast hold on Thyself, who alone art steadfast, without beginning of days or end of years, forever and forever still the same. We thank Thee that amid all the darkness of time, amid joys that deceive us and pleasures that cheat, amid the transgressions we commit, we can still lift up our hands to Thee, and draw near Thee with our heart, and Thou blessest us still with more than a father's or a mother's never-ending love. Amen.— Theodore Parker.

Fifth Week, Sixth Day

One ground of assurance concerning faith is the way a sincere fellowship with God affects life. In a delicious passage of his autobiography, Benjamin Franklin says, "I was scarce fifteen, when, after doubting by turns of several points, as I found them disputed in the different books I read, I began to doubt of Revelation itself. Some books against Deism fell into my hands; they were said to be the substance of sermons preached at Boyle's Lectures. It happened that they wrought an effect on me quite contrary to what was intended by them; for the arguments of the Deists which were quoted to be refuted, appeared to me much stronger than the refutations; in short I soon became a thorough Deist. My arguments perverted some others, particularly Collins and Ralph; but, each of them having afterwards wrong'd me greatly without the least compunction, and recollecting Keith's conduct towards me (who was another free thinker), and my own towards Vernon and Miss Read, which at times gave me great trouble, I began to suspect that this doctrine, tho' it might be true, was not very useful." Many men, not yet able to see clearly the issue of conflicting arguments, are practically convinced in favor of faith by the relative effects on life of faith and unbelief. When one carries this thought out until he imagines a world where no one any more believes in God, he feels even more emphatically the negative results of unbelief. As Sir James Stephen said, "We cannot judge of the effects of Atheism from the conduct of persons who have been educated as believers in God, and in the midst of a nation which believes in God. If we should ever see a generation of men to whom the word God has no meaning at all, we should get a light on the subject which might be lurid enough." A practical working conviction is often gained in religion, as in every other realm, not by argument, but by acting on a principle until it verifies itself by its results, or, as in Benjamin Franklin's case, by trying a negation until one is driven from it by its consequences.

Beware of false prophets, who come to you in sheep's clothing, but inwardly are ravening wolves. By their fruits ye shall know them. Do men gather grapes of thorns, or figs of thistles? Even so every good tree bringeth forth good fruit; but the corrupt tree bringeth forth evil fruit. A good tree cannot bring forth evil fruit, neither can a corrupt tree bring forth good fruit. Every tree that bringeth not forth good fruit is hewn down, and cast into the fire. Therefore by their fruits ye shall know them.—Matt. 7:15-20.

O God, who remainest the same though all else fades, who changest not with our changing moods, who leavest us not when we leave Thee; we thank Thee that when we lose faith in Thee, soon or late we come to faith in something that leads us back again with firmer trust and more sincerity. Even if we wander into the far country we take ourselves with us; ourselves who are set towards Thee as rivers to the sea. If we turn to foolishness, our hearts grow faint and weary, our path is set with thorns, the night overtakes us, and we find we have strayed from light and life.

Grant to us clearer vision of the light which knows no shade of turning, that we stray not in folly away; incline our hearts to love the truth alone, so that we miss Thee not at last; give us to realize of what spirit we are, so that we cleave ever to Thee, who alone can give us rest and joy. Amen.— W. E. Orchard.

Fifth Week, Seventh Day

When all is said and done in the matter of intellectual assurance, many are confused by the seeming lack of finality in the result. After all these ages of debate, they say, see all the innumerable opinions of jarring sects about religious truth! Evidently there is no satisfying conclusion obtainable at all! But look at the innumerable schools of medicine—shall one on their account decide that health is a fruitless study? Consider the infinite variety of taste in food—shall we say that therefore hunger and its satisfaction is a futile question to discuss? Rather, the very variety of the answers in man's quest reveals the importance of the quest itself. Of course proof of God lacks the finality of a scientific demonstration, and this is true *because it moves in a realm so much more important than anything that science touches.* Exactness and finality are possible only in the least important realms. One can measure and analyze and describe to a minute nicety a table which a carpenter has made, but when one turns to the carpenter himself and endeavors to analyze his motives, weigh his thoughts, estimate his quality, and prove his purposes, one drops minute nicety at once. The carpenter is not to be put into a column of figures and added with mathematical precision as his table is. The farther up one moves in the scale the less precise and undeniable do his conclusions become. So science is exact just because it deals with measurable things; but religion, by as much as its realm is more important, can less easily pack its conclusions into neat parcels finally tied up and sealed. A man who will not believe anything which is not precisely demonstrable must eliminate from his life everything except what yardsticks can measure and scales can weigh. Let no man ever give up the fight for faith because he does not seem at once to be reaching an answer which he can neatly formulate. Let him remember Tolstoi, writing on his birthday: "I am twenty-four, and I have not done a thing yet. But I feel that not in vain have I been struggling for nearly eight years against doubt and temptation. For what am I destined? This only the future will disclose."

Hear, O Jehovah, when I cry with my voice:
Have mercy also upon me, and answer me.
When thou saidst, Seek ye my face; my heart said unto thee,
Thy face, Jehovah, will I seek.
Hide not thy face from me;
Put not thy servant away in anger:
Thou hast been my help;
Cast me not off, neither forsake me, O God of mv salvation.
When my father and my mother forsake me,
Then Jehovah will take me up.
Teach me thy way, O Jehovah;
And lead me in a plain path,
Because of mine enemies.
Deliver me not over unto the will of mine adversaries:
For false witnesses are risen up against me,
And such as breathe out cruelty.
I had fainted, unless I had believed to see the goodness of Jehovah
In the land of the living.

Wait for Jehovah:
Be strong, and let thy heart take courage;
Yea, wait thou for Jehovah.

—Psalm 27:7-14.

Deliver us, our Father, from all those mists which do arise from the low places where we dwell, which rise up and hide the sun, and the stars even, and Thee. Deliver us from the narrowness and the poverty of our conceptions. Deliver us from the despotism of our senses. And grant unto us this morning, the effusion of Thy Spirit, which shall bring us into the realm of spiritual things, so that we may, by the use of all that which is divine in us, rise into the sphere of Thy thought, into the realm where Thou dwellest, and whither have trooped from the ages the spirits of just men now made perfect. Grant, we pray Thee, that we may not look with time-eyes upon eternal things, measuring and dwarfing with our imperfectness the fitness and beauty of things heavenly. So teach us to come into Thy presence and to rise by sympathy into Thy way of thinking and feeling, that so much as we can discern of the invisible may come to us aright. Amen.—Henry Ward Beecher.

COMMENT FOR THE WEEK

I

While it is true that in many cases the apparent unreasonableness of Christian faith springs from the underlying unreality of Christian life, this is not always a sufficient diagnosis of doubt. Horace G. Hutchinson, the English golfer, who spent much of his life in agnosticism and has now come over into Christian faith, thus interprets the spirit of his long unbelief: "All the while I had the keenest consciousness of the comfort that one would gain could he but believe in the truth of the Christian promises. Surely that must always be the agnostic's mood. . . . It is not that they wilfully reject the appeal to the heart; their will is eager to respond to it. But man has his gift of reason; it cannot be that he is not intended to use it. Least of all can it be part of the great design that he should suspend its use in regard to the most important subject to which his thought can be directed."

Such sincere intellectual difficulties with faith must be met with intellectual arguments and not with moral accusations. Plenty of folk of elevated character and admirable lives grant, sometimes impatiently, that the Christian faith is beautiful—but is it *so?* Is not its solacing power a deceptive sleight of hand, by which our pleasing fancies and desires are made to look like truth? So a mirage is beautiful to weary travelers, but their temporary comfort rests on fallacy. McTaggart summed up one of the most wide-spread and masterful desires of this generation when he said, "What people want is a religion they can believe to be true."

As one sets himself to meet faith's intellectual difficulties, the attitude in which he is to approach the problem is all-important. Samuel M. Crothers tells us that a young man once left with him a manuscript for criticism, and remarked in passing, "It is only a little bit of my work, and it will not take you long to look it over. In fact it is only the first chapter in which I explain the Universe." When one outgrows this cocksure presumption of youth and gains a graver and more seasoned mind, he leaves behind the attempt to pierce to creation's last secret. He sees that we can no more neatly and finally demonstrate God than we can demonstrate any of life's important faiths.

Moreover proof of God, as a theorem in philosophy, is not a deep human need. Men often have supposed that they had such demonstration, but human experience was little affected by the fact. The exhaustless source of mankind's desire for assurance about God is not theoretical curiosity but vital need, and until a man feels the need, sees how urgently man's highest life reaches out toward God, he never will make much of any arguments. Browning's bishop asks his friend:

> "Like you this Christianity or not?
> It may be false, but will you wish it true?
> Has it your vote to be so if it can?"

Until a man gives an affirmative answer to that inquiry, until he possesses a life that itself suggests God and wants him, he is not likely to arrive anywhere by argument alone.

This is not the case with Christianity only. We cannot prove with theoretical finality that monogamy is the form of family life to which the universe is best adapted. But mankind, trying many experiments with family life, has found in the monogamous family values unique and indispensable. It is because men feel the value of such a love-bond, that they begin to argue for it. And their argument, when one sees deeply into it, is framed after this fashion: We know the *worth* of this family-life of faithful lovers. We want monogamy and we propose to have it. We do not pretend that our faith in monogamy, as the form of marriage best fitted to this universe, is capable of exact demonstration; but we do see arguments of great weight in favor of it and we do not see any convincing arguments against it. We are persuaded that our faith has reasonable right of way; and we propose to go on believing in monogamy and practicing it and combating its enemies, until we prove our case in the only way such cases ever can be finally proved, by the issue of the matter in the end.

So men come into the sort of personal and social life that Jesus represents. Apart from any theories, they value the life itself—its ideals of character, friendship, service, trust. If honesty allows, they propose to live that life. When a man has gone far enough in Christian experience, so that he comes up to his intellectual difficulties by such a road, he is likely to profit by a consideration of the reasons in favor of faith. He is in the attitude of saying: I have found great living in Christ. No argument for the Christian experience can be quite so convincing as the Christian experience itself. I am bound to have that life if I honestly can, and I will search to see whether there is any insuperable intellectual difficulty in the way of it.

II

One of the initial perplexities of faith concerns the sort of intellectual assurance which we have a right to expect. In a laboratory of physics, the investigator gathers facts, makes inductions as to their laws, and then verifies his findings. He uses a simplicity of procedure and gains a finality of result that makes all other knowledge seem relatively insecure. To be sure, the scientist may seek long for his truth and make many ineffectual guesses that prove false, but, in the end, he reaches a conclusion so demonstrable that every man of wit enough to investigate the subject must agree that it is so. How the Christian wishes for such certainty concerning God!

Before, however, any one surrenders confidence in God, because confessedly the affirmations of religious faith cannot be established by such methods as a physicist employs, there is ample reason for delay. We are certain that heat expands and cold contracts, and we can prove the fact and state its laws. But are we not also sure that it is wrong to lie and right to tell the truth? This conviction about truthfulness at least equals in theoretical certainty and in practical right to determine conduct, our confidence in heat's expanding power. This conviction about truthfulness does actually sway life more than does any single scientific truth that one can name. Let us then set ourselves to prove our moral confidence by such methods as the physical laboratory can supply—with yardsticks, and Troy weight scales, and test tubes, and meters! At once it is evident that if we are to hold only such truth as is amenable to the demonstration of a laboratory, we must bid farewell to every *moral conviction* that hitherto has influenced our lives. God, banished because the physicist cannot prove him, will have good company in exile!

Moreover, all our *esthetic convictions* will have to share that banishment. We know that some things are beautiful. The consensus of the race's judgment has not so much agreed to accept the new astronomy as it has agreed to think sunrise glorious and snow-capped mountains wonderful. Take from our lives our judgments on beauty, so that we may call no music marvelous, no poetry inspiring, no scenery sublime, and some of the most intimate and assured convictions we possess will have to go. A man who has seen the Matterhorn at dawn, when the first shaft of light reaches its rocky pinnacle and streams down in glory over the glaciers that cape its shoulders, will not disbelieve the splendor of the scene, though all the world beside unanimously should cry that it is not beautiful. But prove it by the methods of a laboratory? When the geologist has analyzed all the mountain's rocks, the chemist all its minerals; when the astronomer has traced the earth's orbit that brings on the dawn, and the physicist has counted and tabulated the rays of light that make the colors, our conviction of the scene's beauty will be as little explained or proved as is our confidence in God. It becomes clear that some convictions which we both do and must hold are not amenable to the sort of proof which a scientific laboratory furnishes.

Moreover, if we will have no truth beyond the reach of a physicist's demonstration, all our *convictions in the realm of personal relationship* will have to go. We *know* that friendship-love is the crown of every human fellowship. Father and son, mother and daughter, brother and sister, wife and husband—these relationships are in themselves bare branches wanting the foliage and fruit of friendship. Of no truth is man at his best more sure than he is that "Life is just our chance o' the price of learning love." But no laboratory ever can deal with such a truth, much less establish it. For this is the neglected insight, for the want of which our religious confidence is needlessly unstable: *Every realm of reality has its own appropriate kind of proof, and a method of proof available in one realm is seldom, if ever, usable in another.* That truthfulness is right is in a way provable, but methods proper to the moral realm must be allowed; that the Matterhorn is sublime is in a sense provable, but by methods which the esthetic realm permits; that love is the crown of life can be soundly established, but one must employ a method appropriate to personal relationships. If, obsessed by the procedure of a laboratory as the solitary path to knowledge, one will have no convictions which cannot meet its tests, then in good logic there must be a great emigration from his soul. All his convictions about morals and beauty, all his convictions about personal friendships and about God must leave together. He will have a depopulated spirit. No man could live on such terms for a single hour. The most essential and valuable equipment of our souls is in convictions which the demonstrations of a physicist can as little reach as an inch worm, clambering up the Himalayas, can measure the distance to the sun.

III

A man to whom the Christian life has come to be preeminently valuable, and who is asking whether it is intellectually justifiable, is set free, by such considerations as we just have noted, to seek assurance where religious assurance may properly be found. For one thing, he may find help by *trying out the creed of no-God.* Many a man is a wavering believer, makes little excursions into doubt and returns hesitant and unhappy, because he never has dared to see his doubts through to their logical conclusion and to face the world with God eliminated.

One may sense the general atmosphere of the world, under the no-God hypothesis, by saying, *In all this universe there is no mind essentially greater than mine.* The import of such a statement grows weightier the more one ponders it. All human minds are infinitesimal in knowledge; endless realities must lie beyond our reach; "our science is a drop, our ignorance a sea." Yet human knowledge is all that anywhere exists, if the no-God hypothesis is true. There is no knower who knows more, and the infinite reality beyond our grasp is not known by any mind at all. No one ever thought it or will think it through eternity. Then, let a man add, *In all this universe there is no goodness essentially greater than mine.* Human goodness is pitiably partial; it is but prophecy of what goodness ought to mean; "Man is a dwarf of himself," as Emerson said. But human goodness is all that anywhere exists, if the no-God hypothesis is true. There never will be any better goodness anywhere, and when the earth comes to its end in a solar catastrophe, there will be no goodness left at all. Certainly the hypothesis of no-God raises more questions than it easily can quell.

Indeed the Christian, long accused by unbelieving friends of gross credulity because he holds his creed, may well leave his defense and "go over the top" in an offensive charge. If it is a question of holding creeds, unbelief is a creed as certainly as belief is; it says, I believe that there is no God or that God cannot be known. If it is a question of credulity, the Christian suspects that of all the different kinds of credulousness which the world has seen, nothing ever has surpassed the capacity of modern sceptics to accept impossible beliefs. He who says, I believe that there is no God, nor anything which that name might reasonably connote, is saying, I believe that the fundamental reality everywhere is physical. Long ages ago atoms, electrons, "mobile cosmic ethers" began their mysterious organization, whose present issue is planetary orbits, rocks, organic life, and, highest point of all, the brain of man. Man's mind is but the moving shadow cast by the activity of brain. Man's character is the subtle fragrance of his nerves. Everywhere, if the no-God hypothesis be true, spirit is a *result,* physical energy the *cause.*

Some startling corollaries follow such a view. *No man can be blamed for anything.* Molecular action in the brain is responsible alike for saints and sinners, and we are as powerless to change our quality of character or action as a planet is to change its course. Judas and Jesus, Festus and Paul, the Belgian lads and the Prussian officers who mutilated them, the raper and the raped—why blame the one or praise the other when all characters alike are ground from a physical machine, whose action is predetermined by the push of universal energy behind? One man even says that to condemn an immoral deed is like Xerxes whipping the Hellespont—punishment visited on physical necessity which is not to blame.

The second corollary is not less startling: *every man thinks as he does because of molecular action in the brain.* A Christian believes in God because his molecules maneuver so, and his opponent is an atheist because his molecules maneuver otherwise, and all convictions of truth, however well debated and reasoned out, are fundamentally the work of atoms, not of mind. What we call intellect as little causes anything as steam from a kettle causes the boiling out of which it comes. Some brains boil Socialism, some do not; some brains boil Episcopalianism and some Christian Science. A determinist and a believer in freewill differ as do oaks and elm trees, for physical reasons only, and folk are Catholic in southern Europe—so we are informed—because their skulls are narrow, and in northern Europe Protestants because their skulls are broad. Truth is a nickname for a neurosis. The standing marvel is that on some matters like the multiplication table our brains boil so unanimously.

A third corollary still remains: *we have no creative power of mind and will.* All that is and is to be was wound up in primeval matter, and now in our thoughts and actions is ticking like a clock. "All of our philosophy," says Huxley, "all our poetry, all our science, and all our art—Plato, Shakespeare, Newton, and Raphael—are potential in the fires of the sun." That is to say, Plato had nothing to do with *creating* his philosophy, nor Shakespeare with writing plays—they were empty megaphones and the real voice is the physical machine from which all things come. Professor Bowne of Boston University, after the publication of his "Metaphysics," received from a physicist a protest against his emphasis on the reality of mind. The professor of physics insisted that the only fundamental reality was physical and that mind is always a result of brain's activity and never a cause of anything. To this Professor Bowne replied that according to the writer's own theory, as he understood it, the letter of protest was the result of certain physical forces issuing in nervous excitations that made scratches on paper, and that the writer's mind had nothing effectual to do with its composition. This, said Professor Bowne, might be a plausible explanation of the letter, but he was unwilling to apply it to the universe. What wonder that the physicist acknowledged to a friend that the retort nettled him, for he did not see just how to answer it?

IV

One's discontent with this reduction of our lives to physical causation is increased when he studies the *mental process* by which men *reach it.* It is as if a man should perceive in the works of Shake-

speare insight and beauty, pathos and laughter, despair and hope,
and should set himself to explain all these as the function of the
type. How plausibly he could do it! If one takes Shakespeare's sentences full of spiritual meaning he can readily resolve them into
twenty-six constituent letters of the alphabet, and these into certain
hooks and dashes, and these into arithmetical points diffused in
space. Starting with such abstract points, let one suppose that some
fortunate day they arranged themselves into hooks and dashes, and
these into letters of the alphabet, and these by fortuitous concourse
came together into sentences. Reading them we think we see deep
spiritual meaning, but they are all the work of type; the fundamental
reality is arithmetical points diffused in space. Such is the process by
which a man reduces the mental and moral life of man back to its
physical basis; then breaks up the physical basis into atoms; then,
starting with these abstractions, builds up again the whole world
which he just has analyzed, and thinks he has explained the infinitely
significant spiritual life of man. Not for a long time will we accept
such a method of explaining the works of Shakespeare! Nor can man
contentedly be made to follow so inconsequential a process of
thought as that by which the mind and character of Jesus are reduced to a maneuver of molecules.

The attractiveness of this explanation of the universe as a huge
physical machine is easily understood. It presents a simple picture,
readily grasped. It packs the whole explanation of the world into a
neat parcel, portable by any mind. In the days of monarchy the government of the universe was pictured in terms of an absolute sovereign; in feudal times the divine economy was pictured as a gigantic
feudalism; we always use a dominant factor in the life of man to
help us picture the eternal. So in the age whose builder and maker
is machinery we easily portray the universe as a huge machine. The
process is simple and natural, but to suppose that it is adequate is
preposterous. Lord Kelvin, the chemist, knew thoroughly the mechanistic idea of the world. He felt the fascination of it, for he said at
Johns Hopkins University, "I never satisfy myself until I make a
mechanical model of a thing. If I can make a mechanical model I
can understand it. As long as I cannot make a mechanical model all
the way through, I cannot understand." But Lord Kelvin knew
better than to suppose that this figure comprehended all of reality.
"The atheistic idea," said he, "is so nonsensical, that I do not know
how to put it into words."

The rejection of the no-God hypothesis does not necessarily imply that a man becomes fully Christian in his thought of deity. There are way-stations between no-God and Jesus' Father. *But it does mean that to him reality must be fundamentally spiritual, not physical.* What other hypothesis possibly can fit the facts? For consider the view of a growing universe which we see from the outlook that modern science furnishes. Out of a primeval chaos where physical forces snarled at each other in unrelieved antagonism, where no man had yet arisen to love truth and serve righteousness, something has brought us to a time, when for all our evil, there are mothers and music and the laughter of children at play, men who love honor and for service' sake lay down their lives, and homes in every obscure street where fortitude and sacrifice are splendidly exhibited. Out of a chaos, where a contemporary observer, could there have been one, would have seen no slightest promise of spirit, something has brought us to the Ten Commandments, and the Sermon on the Mount, to great character and growing achievements in social righteousness, to lofty thoughts of the Divine and hopes of life eternal. *Something has been at work here besides matter. No explanation of all this will do, without God.*

v

Another source of confirmation for the man who, valuing Christian experience, seeks assurance that it is intellectually justifiable, is to be found in the effect of Christian faith on life itself. The nautical tables can be proved by an astronomer in his observatory; but if they are given to a sailor and he beats about the seas with them in safety, finding that they make adventurous voyages practicable, that also would be important witness to their truth. So the Christian ideas of life have not been kept by studious recluses to ponder over and weave philosophies about; they have been down in the market place, men have been practically trying them for generations, and *they make great living.*

The ultimate ground of practical assurance about anything is that we have tried it and that it works. A man may have experience that other persons exist, may draw the inference that friendly relations with them are not impossible, but only when he launches out and verifies his thought in an adventure will he really be convinced of friendship's glory. In no other way has final assurance about God come home to man. They who have lived as though God *were* have been convinced that he *is;* they who have willed to do his will have known.

That religious faith does justify itself in life is a fact to which mankind's experience amply testifies. Men have come to God, not as chemists to bread curious to analyze it; they have come as hungry men, needing to eat if they would live. And they have found life glorified by faith in him. The difference between religion and ir-religion here is plain. *How seldom one finds enthusiastic unbeliev-ers!* When all that is fine spirited and resolute in agnostic literature is duly weighed and credited, the pessimistic undertone is always heard. Leslie Stephen thus summarizes life—"There is a deep sad-ness in the world. Turn and twist the thought as you may there is no escape. Optimism would be soothing if it were possible; in fact, it is impossible, and therefore a constant mockery." No gospel burns in the unbeliever's mind, urgent for utterance; he has no inspiring out-looks to offer, no glad tidings to declare. The more intelligent he is the more plainly he sees this. With Clifford he laments that "the spring sun shines out of an empty heaven to light up a soulless earth" and feels "with utter loneliness that the Great Companion is dead"; with Romanes he frankly states, "So far as the ruination of individ-ual happiness is concerned, no one can have a more lively concep-tion than myself of the possibly disastrous tendency of my work." An unbeliever whose admirable life raised the question as to the philos-ophy by which he guided it, gave this summary of his creed, "I am making the best of a bad mess." Unbelievers do not spontaneously utter in song the glory of a creed like this, and when they do write poetry, it is of a sort that music will not fit—

> "The world rolls round forever like a mill,
>   It grinds out death and life and good and ill,
>   It has no purpose, heart, or mind or will."

When from poetry one turns to philosophy, he can see good reasons why hymnals and unbelief should be uncongenial. There is little to make life worth while in a creed which holds as Haeckel does that morality in man, like the tail of a monkey or the shell of a tortoise, is purely a physiological effect, and that man himself is "an affair of chance; the froth and fume at the wave-top of a sterile ocean of matter." Shall the practical unserviceableness of such an idea for the purpose of life, awaken no suspicion as to its truth?

Upon the other hand, suppose that by some strange chance the principles of Jesus should over night take possession of mankind. Even as it is, when one starts his thought with the Stone Age, the progress of mankind has obviously been immense. From universal cannibalism after a battle, to massacre without cannibalism marked one great advance; from massacre of all prisoners taken in war to enslavement of them marked another; and when slavery ceased being a philanthropic improvement, as it was at first, and became a sin and shame, humanity took another long step forward. With all our present barbarity, a far look backwards shows a clear ascent. As for the influence of Jesus, Lecky, the historian, tells us that "The simple record of three short years of Christ's active life has done more to regenerate and soften mankind than all the disquisitions of philosophers and all the exhortations of moralists." What if this process were brought to its fulfilment between sunset and dawn, and the new day came with everyone sure of God's fatherhood and life eternal, of the law of love and the supremacy of character and with everyone living as though these were true? Whatever intellectual perplexities of belief a man may have, he knows that such a world would be divinely great. No war, no evil lust, no covetous selfishness, no drunkenness! Mankind, relieved of ancient burdens which have ruined character and crushed endeavor, confident of faiths that give life infinite horizons and deathless hopes, in cooperative international fraternity would be making the earth a decent home for God to rear his children in. One finds it hard to believe that ideas which, incarnate in life, would so redeem the world are false.

As to the effect of the Christian affirmations on individual character, we do not need to picture an imagined future. A Character has been here who has lived them out. A jury of philosophers might analyze the wood-work and the metals of an organ, and guess from form and material what it is, but we still should need for our assurance a musician. When he sweeps the keys in harmony we *know* that it is an organ. So when the philosophers have debated the pros and cons of argument concerning faith, Jesus *plays* the Gospel. His life *is* the Christian affirmations done into character. When religious faith, at its best, is incarnate in a Man, this is the consequence. And multitudes of folk, living out the implications of the faith, have found the likeness of the Master growing in them. Weighty confir-

mation of the Gospel's *truth* arrives when its meaning is translated
into life; the world will not soon reject the New Testament in this
edition—bound in a Man.

To one in perplexity about belief, this proper question therefore
rises: What do we think about the Christlike character? Is it not
life at its sublimest elevation? But to acknowledge that and yet to
deny the central faiths by which such life is lived is to say that those
ideas which, incarnate, make living great are false, and those ideas
which leave life meager of motive and bereft of hope are true. No
one lives on such a basis in any other realm. We always mistrust the
validity of any idea which works poorly or not at all. And so far from
being a practical makeshift, this "negative pragmatism" is a true
principle of knowledge. Says Professor Hocking, of Harvard, "If a
theory has no consequence, or bad ones; if it makes no difference to
men, or else undesirable differences; if it lowers the capacity of men
to meet the stress of existence, or diminishes the worth to them of
what existence they have; such a theory is somehow false, and we
have no peace until it is remedied." The last word against irreligion
is that it makes life unlivable; the last word for faith is that it makes
life glorious.

VI

One who is facing intellectual difficulties in the way of faith may
well consider that the very Christian life for whose possession he is
seeking justification is itself an argument of the first importance.
This life grew up in the universe; it is one expression of the universe;
and it is hard to think that it does not reveal a nature kindred to
itself in the source from which it came.

Mankind has always experienced a relationship with the Unseen
which has seemed like communion of soul with Soul. When a psy-
chologist like Professor James, of Harvard, reduces to its most general terms this religious Fact which has been practically universal in
the race, he puts it thus: "Man becomes conscious that this higher
part (his spiritual life) is coterminous and continuous with a MORE
of the same quality, which is operative in the universe outside of
him, and which he can keep in working touch with, and in a fashion
get on board of and save himself when all his lower being has gone
to pieces in the wreck." No experience of man is more common in
occurrence, more tremendous in result than this. From the mystics

whose vivid sense of God canceled their consciousness that anything else was real, to plain folk who in the strength of the divine alliance have lived ordinary lives with extraordinary spirit, mankind as a whole has known that the best in man is in contact with a MORE.

One does not need to be of a mystical temperament, given to raptures, to know what this means. Let him consider his own experience of love and duty, how he is bound by them to his ideals and woven into a community of personal life not only with his friends but with all humanity, until this spiritual life of his becomes the most august and commanding power he knows. When in our bodies we so discern a physical nature, whose laws and necessities we did not create, and whose power binds us into a community of need and labor with our fellows, our conclusion is confident. This experience is the basis of our assurance that a *physical universe is really here*. When, likewise in our inner selves we find a spiritual life, which man did not create, in obedience to which alone is safety, and peace, and power, what shall we conclude? That there is a *spiritual universe* as plainly evidenced in man's soul as the physical universe is in the body! And when we note the attributes of this Spiritual Order, how it demands righteousness, rebukes sin, welcomes obedience and holds out ideals of endless possibility, it is plain that we are talking about something close of kin to God. As in summer we beat out through some familiar bay, naming the headlands as we sail, until if we go far enough, we cannot prevent our eyes from looking out across the unbounded sea, so if a man moves out through his own familiar spiritual life far enough, he comes to the Spiritual Order which is God. Man has not drifted into his religion by accident or fallen on it merely as superstition; he has moved out from his inner life to affirm a Spiritual Order as inevitably as he has moved out from his bodily experiences to affirm a physical universe.

When from this general experience we turn to the specific experiences of religion, which prayer and worship represent, the testimony of the race is confident. Men have not all these ages been lifting up their souls to an unreality from which no response has come. The artesian well of transforming influence in human souls has not flowed from Nowhere. Some, indeed, hearing confidence in God founded on the individual experiences of man, derisively cry "Nonsense!" But if one were to prove that the Sistine Madonna is beautiful, he would have to offer his experience in evidence. "I went to Dresden," he might say, "up into the room where the Madonna

hangs . . . and it *is* beautiful. I saw it." Met with derision by a
doubter, as though his experience were no proof at all, how shall he
proceed? "I am not the only one," he might continue, "who has
perceived its beauty. All these centuries the folk best qualified to
judge have gone up into that room and have come down again, sure
that Raphael's work is beautiful." Is anyone in a position to deride
that? So through all ages men and women, from lowest savages to
the race's spiritual kings and queens, have gone up to the Divine,
and, at their best, from experiences of prayer, worship, forgiven sins,
transfigured lives, have come down sure that Reality is there. *One
may not call nonsense the most universal and influential experience
of the human race!*

The force of this fact is more clearly seen when one considers that
man has grown up in this universe, gradually developing his powers
and functions as responses to his environment. If he has eyes, so the
biologists assure us, it is because the light waves played upon the
skin and eyes came out in answer; if he has ears it is because the air
waves were there first and ears came out to hear. Man never yet,
according to the evolutionist, has developed any power save as a
reality called it into being. There would be no fins if there were no
water, no wings if there were no air, no legs if there were no land.
Always the developing organism has been trying to "catch up with
its environment." Yet some would tell us that man's noblest power of
all has developed in a vacuum. They would say that his capacity to
deal with a Spiritual World, to believe in God, and in prayer to
experience fellowship with him, has all grown up with no Reality to
call it into being. If so, it stands alone in man's experience, the only
function of his life that grew without an originating Fact to call it
forth. It does not seem reasonable to think that. The evidence of
man's experience is overwhelmingly in favor of a Reality to which
his spirit has been trying to answer. Said Max Müller, "To the
philosopher the existence of God may seem to rest on a syllogism; in
the eyes of the historian it rests on the whole evolution of human
thought."

CHAPTER VI

Faith's Greatest Obstacle

DAILY READINGS

The speculative doubts leave many minds untouched, but one universal human experience sooner or later faces every serious life with questions about God's goodness. We all meet trouble, in ourselves or others, and oftentimes the wonder why in God's world such calamities should fall, such wretchedness should continually exist, plunges faith into perplexity. Few folk of mature years can fail to understand Edwin Booth when he wrote to a friend, "Life is a great big spelling book, and on every page we turn the words grow harder to understand the meaning of." Now, the basis of any intelligent explanation of faith's problem must rest in a *right practical attitude toward trouble*. To the consideration of that we turn in the daily readings.

Sixth Week, First Day

Beloved, think it not strange concerning the fiery trial among you, which cometh upon you to prove you, as though a strange thing happened unto you: but insomuch as ye are partakers of Christ's sufferings, rejoice; that at the revelation of his glory also ye may rejoice with exceeding joy. If ye are reproached for the name of Christ, blessed are ye; because the Spirit of glory and the Spirit of God resteth upon you. For let none of you suffer as a murderer, or a thief, or an evil-doer, or as a meddler in other men's matters: but if a man suffer as a Christian, let him not be ashamed; but let him glorify God in this name. . . . Wherefore let them also that suffer according to the will of God commit their souls in well-doing unto a faithful Creator.—I Pet. 4:12-16, 19.

Such an attitude toward trouble as Peter here recommends is the most wholesome and hopeful possible to man. And it is reasonable too, if only on the ground that trouble *develops in men the essential qualities of strong character.* Our highest admiration is always reserved for men who master difficult crises. If the story of Joseph, begun beside Bedouin camp fires centuries ago, can easily be naturalized beside modern radiators; if Robinson Crusoe, translated into every tongue is understood by all, the reason lies in the depth of man's heart, where to make the most out of untoward situations is a daily problem. Not every one can grasp the argument or perceive the beauty of "Paradise Lost" and "Paradise Regained," but one thing about them every man appreciates—the blind Milton, sitting down to write them:

> "I argue not
> Against Heaven's hand or will, nor bate a jot
> Of heart or hope; but still bear up and steer
> Right onward."

The full understanding of Ole Bull's playing on the violin was necessarily restricted to the musical, but no restriction bounds the admiration of men, learned or simple, when in a Munich concert, his A string snaps and he finishes the composition on three strings. That is the human problem in epitome. Getting music out of life's remainders after the break has come; winning the battle with what is left from a defeat; going blind, like Milton, and writing sublimest poetry, or deaf, like Beethoven, and composing superb sonatas; being reared in an almshouse and buried from Westminster Abbey, like Henry M. Stanley; or, like Kavanagh, born without arms or legs and yet sitting at last in the British Parliament—all such hardihood and undiscourageable pluck reach back in a man's bosom beyond the strings that ease and luxury can touch, and strike there an iron, reverberating chord. Nothing in human life is so impressive as pluck, "fighting with the scabbard after the sword is gone." And no one who deeply considers life can fail to see that our best character comes when, as Peter says, we "suffer as a Christian."

O Lord our God, let our devout approach to Thee be that of the heart, not of the lips. Let it be in obedience to Thy spiritual law, not to any outward ritual. Thou desirest not temples nor offerings, but the sacrifice of a lowly and grateful heart Thou will not despise. Merciful Father, to all Thy dispensations we would submit ourselves, not grudgingly, not merely of necessity, but because we believe in Thy wisdom, Thy universal rule, and Thy goodness. In bereavement and in sorrow, in death as in life, in joys and in happiness, we would see Thy hand. Teach us to see it; increase our faith where we cannot see; teach us also to love justice, and to do mercy, and to walk humbly with Thee our God. Make us at peace with all mankind, gentle to those who offend us, faithful in all duties, and sincere in sorrow when we fail in duty. Make us loving to one another, patient in distress, and ever thankful to Thy divine power, which keeps, and guides, and blesses us every day. Lord, accept our humble prayer, accomplish in us Thy holy will. Let Thy peace reign in our hearts, and enable us to walk with Thee in love; through Jesus Christ our Lord. Amen.—Francis W. Newman, 1805.

Sixth Week, Second Day

Even unto this present hour we both hunger, and thirst, and are naked, and are buffeted, and have no certain dwelling-place; and we toil, working with our own hands: being reviled, we bless; being persecuted, we endure; being defamed, we entreat: we are made as the filth of the world, the offscouring of all things, even until now. —I Cor. 4:11-13.

If Paul could be questioned about the experience of trouble which these verses vividly express, would he not say that there had been qualities of character in him and resources in his relationship with God which he never would have known about had it not been for the test of adversity? Trouble not only develops but also *reveals* character; we do not know ourselves until we have been tried out in calamity. The simplest demand of adversity on every man is that he be "game." Henry Newbolt is not indulging in rhetoric when he tells of a Soudan battle where a British square made up of Clifton graduates is hard beset by a charge of fierce enemies, and, in that crisis, makes the cry of a Clifton football captain, "Play us, boys, play the game!" rally the men and save the day. At school or in the Soudan the problem is the same; the sling with which David plays in his youth is his chief reliance when Goliath comes; a "game" spirit is essential to character from birth to death. We turn from the story

of Nelson at Aboukir, nailing six flags to his mast so that if even five
were shot away no one would dream that he had surrendered, to
find that the spirit there exemplified is applicable to our most common day. The quality which made Nelson an Admiral of England,
in spite of his lost arm, his lost eye, his small stature, and his feeble
health is one of our elemental needs. And to a supreme degree this
quality was in great Christians like Paul. Read his letter to the Philippians and see! Adversity brought his spirit to light, and made it
an asset of the cause. In a real sense, trouble, however forbidding,
was one of Paul's best friends, and there was a good reason why he
should "rejoice in tribulations."

*O Father of spirits! Thou lovest whom Thou chastenest! Correct
us in our weakness as the children of men, that we may love Thee in
our strength as the sons of God. May the same mind be in us which
was also in Jesus Christ, that we may never shrink, when our hour
comes, from drinking of the cup that he drank of. Wake in us a soul
to obey Thee, not with the weariness of servile spirits, but with the
alacrity of the holy angels. Fill us with a contempt of evil pleasures
and unfaithful ease; sustain us in the strictness of a devout life. Daily
may we crucify every selfish affection, and delight to bear one another's burdens, to uphold each other's faith and charity, being
tender-hearted and forgiving as we hope to be forgiven. Hold us
to the true humility of the soul that has not yet attained; and may
we be modest in our desire, diligent in our trust, and content with
the disposals of Thy Providence. O Lord of life and death! Thy
counsels are secret; Thy wisdom is infinite: we know not what a day
may bring forth. When our hour arrives, and the veil between the
worlds begins to be lifted before us, may we freely trust ourselves
to Thee, and say, "Father, into Thy hands I commend my spirit."
Amen.*—James Martineau.

Sixth Week, Third Day

If adversity, rightly used, so develops and reveals character, we
may expect to find trouble as a background to the most admirable
men of the race. We read the luminous histories of Francis Park-
man and do not perceive, behind the printed page, the original
manuscript, covered with a screen of parallel wires, along which the
blind author ran his pencil that he might write legibly. We think of

James Watt as a genius at invention, and perhaps recall that Wordsworth said of him, "I look upon him, considering both the magnitude and the universality of his genius, as perhaps the most extraordinary man that this country ever produced." But Watt himself we forget—sickly of body, starving on eight shillings a week, and saying, "Of all things in life there is nothing more foolish than inventing." Kant's philosophy was a turning point in human thought, but lauding Kant, how few recall his struggle with a broken body! Said he, speaking of his incurable illness, "I have become master of its influence in my thoughts and actions by turning my attention away from this feeling altogether, just as if it did not at all concern me." Wilberforce, the liberator of British slaves, we know, and beside his grave in Westminster Abbey we recall the superb title that he earned, "the attorney general of the unprotected and of the friendless," but the Wilberforce who for twenty years was compelled to use opium to keep himself alive, and had the resolution never to increase the dose—who knows of him? One of the chief rewards of reading biography is this introduction that it gives to handicapped men; the knowledge it imparts of the world's great saints and scripture makers, conquerors and reformers, who, in the words of Thucydides, "dared beyond their strength, hazarded against their judgment, and in extremities were of excellent hope." And when one turns to the supreme Character, could the dark background be eliminated and still leave Him?

But now we see not yet all things subjected to him. But we behold him who hath been made a little lower than the angels, even Jesus, because of the suffering of death crowned with glory and honor, that by the grace of God he should taste of death for every man. For it became him, for whom are all things, and through whom are all things, in bringing many sons unto glory to make the author of their salvation perfect through sufferings.—Heb. 2:8-10.

O God, who art unsearchable in Thy judgments, and in Thy ways past finding out, we bow before the mystery of Thy Being, and confess that we know nothing, and can say nothing worthy of Thee. We cannot understand Thy dealings with us. We have faith, not sight; when we cannot see, we may only believe. Sometimes Thou seemest to have no mercy upon us. Thou dost pierce us through our most tender affections, quenching the light of our eyes in dreadful dark-

*ness. Death tears from us all that we love, and Thou art seemingly
deaf to all our cries. Our earthly circumstances are reversed and bitter poverty is appointed us, yet Thou takest no heed, and bringest
no comfort to the sorrow and the barrenness of our life. Still would
we trust in Thee and cling to that deepest of our instincts which tells
us that we come from Thee and return to Thee. Be with us, Father
of Mercies, in love and pity and tenderness unspeakable. Lift our
souls into Thy perfect calm, where all our wills are in harmony with
Thine. Amen.*—Samuel McComb.

Sixth Week, Fourth Day

To one perplexed and disheartened by adversity, a theoretical
explanation is generally not half as valuable as concrete instances
of courage and fortitude, founded on faith. Whether we be theologians or scientists or as ignorant of both as Caliban, there is an immediate, personal call to arms in the brave fight of George Matheson, one of Scotland's great preachers for all his blindness, or in
Louis Pasteur's indomitable will, making his discoveries despite the
paralytic stroke that in his forty-sixth year crippled his strength. The
qualities which we admire in them are a sort of apotheosis of the
qualities which we need in ourselves. For we all are handicapped,
some by ill-starred heredity, by unhappy environment, or by the consequences of our own neglect and sin; some by poverty, some by
broken bodies, or by dissevered family ties—and all of us by unfortunate dispositions. It does us good then to know that Phillips Brooks
failed as a teacher. His biographer tells us that so did his first ambition to be an educator cling to him, that in the prime of life, when
he was the prince of preachers, he came from President Eliot's office,
pale and trembling, because he had refused a professorship at Harvard. So Robertson, of Brighton, whose sermons began a new epoch
in British Christianity, was prevented from being a soldier only by
the feebleness of his body, and Sir Walter Scott, who wanted to be
a poet, turned to novel writing, anonymously and tentatively trying
a new role, because, as he frankly put it, "Because Byron beat me."
He is an excellent cook who knows how to make a good dinner out
of the left-overs, and hardly a more invigorating truth is taught by
history than that most of the finest banquets spread for the delecta-
tion of the race have been prepared by men who made them out of
the leavings of disappointed hopes.

Therefore let us also, seeing we are compassed about with so great a cloud of witnesses, lay aside every weight, and the sin which doth so easily beset us, and let us run with patience the race that is set before us, looking unto Jesus the author and perfecter of our faith, who for the joy that was set before him endured the cross, despising shame, and hath sat down at the right hand of the throne of God. For consider him that hath endured such gainsaying of sinners against himself, that ye wax not weary, fainting in your souls. —Heb. 12:1-3.

Our Father, we thank Thee that while we are sure of Thy protecting care, Thy casual providence, which foresees all things, we can bear the sorrows of this world, and do its duties, and endure its manifold and heavy cross. We thank Thee that when distress comes upon us, and our mortal schemes vanish into thin air, we know there is something solid which we can lay hold of, and not be frustrate in our hopes. Yea, we thank Thee that when death breaks asunder the slender thread of life whereon our family jewels are strung, and the precious stones of our affection fall from our arms or neck, we know Thou takest them and elsewhere givest them a heavenly setting, wherein they shine before the light of Thy presence as morning stars, brightening and brightening to more perfect glory, as they are transfigured by Thine own almighty power.

We thank Thee for all the truth which the stream of time has brought to us from many a land and every age. We thank Thee for the noble examples of human nature which Thou hast raised up, that in times of darkness there are wise men, in times of doubt there are firm men, and in every peril there stand up heroes of the soul to teach us feebler men our duty, and to lead all of Thy children to trust in Thee. Father, we thank Thee that the seed of righteousness is never lost, but through many a deluge is carried safe, to make the wilderness to bloom and blossom with beauty ever fragrant and ever new, and the desert bear corn for men and sustain the souls of the feeble when they faint. Amen.—Theodore Parker.

Sixth Week, Fifth Day

One distinguishing mark of the men who have won their victories with the remnants of their defeat is that they refuse to describe their unideal conditions in negative terms. If they cannot live in southern

California where they would choose to live, but must abide in New England instead, they do not describe New England in terms of its deficiencies—no orange groves, no acres of calla lilies, no palm trees. There are compensations even in New England, if one will carefully take account of stock and see what positively is there! Or if a man would choose to live in Boston and must live in Labrador, the case of Grenfell suggests that a positive attitude toward his necessity will discover worth, and material for splendid triumphs even on that inhospitable coast. The mark of the handicapped men who have made the race's history glorious has always been their patriotism for the country where they had to live. They do not stop long to pity themselves, or to envy another's opportunity, or to blame circumstances for their defeat, or to dream of what might have been, or to bewail their disappointed hopes. If the soil of their condition will not grow one crop, they discover what it will grow. They have insight, as did Moses, to see holy ground where an ordinary man would have seen only sand and sagebrush and sheep.

Now Moses was keeping the flock of Jethro his father-in-law, the priest of Midian: and he led the flock to the back of the wilderness, and came to the mountain of God, unto Horeb. And the angel of Jehovah appeared unto him in a flame of fire out of the midst of a bush: and he looked, and, behold, the bush burned with fire, and the bush was not consumed. And Moses said, I will turn aside now, and see this great sight, why the bush is not burnt. And when Jehovah saw that he turned aside to see, God called unto him out of the midst of the bush, and said, Moses, Moses. And he said, Here am I. And he said, Draw not nigh hither: put off thy shoes from off thy feet, for the place whereon thou standest is holy ground.— Exodus 3:1-5.

Father of life, and God of the living, Fountain of our being and Light of all our day; we thank Thee for that knowledge of Thyself which light our life with eternal splendor, for that giving of Thyself which has made us partakers of Thy divine nature. We bless Thee for everything around us which ministers Thee to our minds; for the greatness and glory of nature, for the history of our race, and the lives of noble men; for the thoughts of Thee expressed in human words, in the art of painters and musicians, in the work of builders and craftsmen. We bless Thee for the constant memories of what we are that rise within ourselves; for the pressure of duty, the hush

of solemn thoughts, for moments of insight when the veil on the face
of all things falls away, for hours of high resolve when life is quick-
ened within, for seasons of communion when, earth and sense for-
gotten, heaven holds our silent spirits raptured and aflame.

We have learned to praise Thee for the darker days when we had
to walk by faith, for weary hours that strengthened patience and
endeavor, for moments of gloom and times of depression which
taught us to trust, not to changing tides of feeling, but to Thee who
changest not. And now since Christ has won His throne by His cross
of shame, risen from His tomb to reign forever in the hearts of men,
we know that nothing can ever separate us from Thee; that in all
conflicts we may be more than conquerors; that all dark and hostile
things shall be transformed and work for good to those who know
the secret of Thy love.

Glory be to Thee, O Lord. Amen.—W, E. Orchard.

Sixth Week, Sixth Day

When folk have seen into human life deeply enough so that they
perceive how adversity can be used to high issues, faith in God becomes not so much a speculative problem as a practical need. They
want to deal with trouble nobly. They see that faith in God gives
the outlook on life which makes the hopeful facing of adverse situations reasonable and which supplies power to make it possible. The
result is that the *great sufferers have been the great believers*. The
idea that fortunate circumstances make vital faith in God probable
is utterly unsupported by history. Hardly an outstanding champion
of faith who has left an indelible impress on man's spiritual life can
anywhere be found, who has not won his faith and confirmed it in
the face of trouble. What is true of individuals is true of generations.
The days of Israel's triumphant faith did not come in Solomon's
reign, when wealth was plentiful and national ambitions ran high.
The great prophets and the great psalms stand out against the dark
background of the Exile and its consequences.

Awake, awake, put on strength, O arm of Jehovah; awake, as
in the days of old, the generations of ancient times. Is it not thou
that didst cut Rahab in pieces, that didst pierce the monster? Is
it not thou that driedst up the sea, the waters of the great deep;
that madest the depths of the sea a way for the redeemed to pass

over? And the ransomed of Jehovah shall return, and come with singing unto Zion; and everlasting joy shall be upon their heads: they shall obtain gladness and joy; and sorrow and sighing shall flee away.

I, even I, am he that comforteth you: who art thou, that thou art afraid of man that shall die, and of the son of man that shall be made as grass; and hast forgotten Jehovah thy Maker, that stretched forth the heavens, and laid the foundations of the earth; and fearest continually all the day because of the fury of the oppressor, when he maketh ready to destroy? and where is the fury of the oppressor? The captive exile shall speedily be loosed; and he shall not die and go down into the pit, neither shall his bread fail. For I am Jehovah thy God, who stirreth up the sea, so that the waves thereof roar: Jehovah of hosts is his name. And I have put my words in thy mouth, and have covered thee in the shadow of my hand, that I may plant the heavens, and lay the foundations of the earth, and say unto Zion, Thou art my people.—Isa. 51:9-16.

That is a voice out of the Exile. Such great believers, whose faith shone brightest when the night was darkest, have not pretended to know the explanation of suffering in God's world. But they have had insight to see a little and trust for the rest. Stevenson has expressed their faith: "If I from my spy-hole, looking with purblind eyes upon a least part of a fraction of the universe, yet perceive in my own destiny some broken evidences of a plan, and some signals of an overruling goodness; shall I then be so mad as to complain that all cannot be deciphered? Shall I not rather wonder, with infinite and grateful surprise, that in so vast a scheme I seem to have been able to read, however little, and that little was encouraging to faith?"

We thank Thee, O God, that Thou dost ride upon the cloud, and govern the storm. All that to us is dark is light to Thee. The night shineth as the day. All that which seems to us irregular and ungoverned, is held in Thine hand, even as the steed by the rein. From age to age Thou dost control the long procession of events, discerning the end from the beginning; and all the wild mixture, all the confusion, all the sorrow and the suffering, is discerned of Thee. As is the palette to the color, as is violence to development in strength, as is the crushing of the grape to the wine, so in Thy sight all things are beneficent that to us are most confusing and seemingly conflicting and threatening. Sorrow and pain and disaster are woven in the loom of God; and in the end we, too, shall be permitted to discern the fair pattern, and understand how that which brought tears here shall bring righteousness there.

O, how good it is to trust Thee, and to believe that Thou art wise, and that Thou art full of compassion, as Thou carriest on Thy great work of love and benevolence, sympathizing with all that suffer on the way, and gathering them at last with an exceeding great salvation! We trust Thee, not because we understand Thee, but because in many things Thou hast taught us where we should have been afraid to trust. We have crossed many a gulf and many a roaring stream upon the bridge of faith, and have exulted to find ourselves safe landed, and have learned to trust Thee, as a child a parent, as a passenger the master of a ship, not because we know, but because Thou knowest. Amen.—Henry Ward Beecher.

Sixth Week, Seventh Day

Every one therefore that heareth these words of mine, and doeth them, shall be likened unto a wise man, who built his house upon the rock: and the rain descended, and the floods came, and the winds blew, and beat upon that house; and it fell not: for it was founded upon the rock. And every one that heareth these words of mine, and doeth them not, shall be likened unto a foolish man, who built his house upon the sand: and the rain descended, and the floods came, and the winds blew, and smote upon that house; and it fell: and great was the fall thereof.—Matt. 7:24-27.

An important fact is here asserted by the Master, which is commonly obscured in the commentaries. He says that no matter whether a man's life be built on sand or on rock, he yet will experience the blasts of adversity; on both houses alike "the rain descended, and the floods came, and the winds blew." The Master repeatedly affirmed that trouble comes without necessary reference to character, that while we may always argue that sin causes suffering, we never can confidently argue that suffering comes from sin (Luke 13:4; John 9:1-3). Folks needlessly and unscripturally harass their souls when they suppose that some special trouble must have befallen them because of some special sin. The book of Job was written to disprove that, and as for the Master, he distinctly says that the man of faith with his house on a rock faces the same storm that wrecks the faithless man. *The difference is not in the adversity, but in the adversity's effect.* No more important question faces any soul than this: seeing that trouble is an unevadable portion of every life, good or bad, what am I to do with it? Says Oliver Wendell Holmes, "Did you ever happen to see that most soft-spoken and velvet-handed steam-engine at the Mint? The smooth piston slides backward and forward as a lady might slip her delicate finger in and out of a ring. The engine lays one of its fingers calmly, but firmly, upon a bit of metal; it is a coin now, and will remember that touch, and tell a new race about it, when the date upon it is crusted over with twenty centuries. So it is that a great silent-moving misery puts a new stamp on us in an hour or a moment—as sharp an impression as if it had taken half a lifetime to engrave it." The only flaw in that simile is that the coin cannot decide what impression shall be made. But we can. Rebellion, despair, bitterness, or triumphant faith—we can say which impression adversity shall leave upon us.

O God of our life, whom we dimly apprehend and never can comprehend, to whom nevertheless we justly ascribe all goodness as well as all greatness; as a father teaches his children, so teach us, Lord, truer thoughts of Thee. Teach us to aspire, so far as man may lawfully aspire, to a knowledge of Thee. Thou art not only a God to be honored in times of rest and ease, Thou art also the Refuge of the distressed, the Comforter of the afflicted, the Healer of the contrite, and the Support of the unstable. As we sympathize with those who are sore smitten by calamity, wounded by sudden accident, wrecked in the midst of security, so must we believe that Thy mighty all-embracing heart sympathizes. Pitier of the orphan, God of the widow, cause us to share Thy pity and become Thy messengers of tenderness in our small measure. Be Thou the Stay of all in life and death. Teach all to know and trust Thee, give us a portion here and everywhere with Thy saints; through Jesus Christ our Lord. Amen.—Francis W. Newman, 1805.

COMMENT FOR THE WEEK

I

Few who have sincerely tried to believe in God's goodness and who have lived long enough to face the harrowing facts of human wretchedness will doubt what obstacle most hampers faith. The major difficulty which perplexes many Christians, when they try to reconcile God's love with their experience, is not belief's irrationality but life's injustice. According to the Psalmist, "The fool hath said in his heart, 'There is no God' " (Psalm 14:1). But the fool is not the only one who has said that. He said it, jeering; he announced it in derision; he did not want God, and contemptuous denial was a joy. It was the temper of his negation that made him a fool. But many hearts, in tones far different from his, have said, "There is no God." Parents cry it brokenheartedly beside the graves of children; the diseased cry it, suffering from keener agony than they can bear; fathers cry it when their battle against poverty has failed and their children plead in vain for bread; and men who care about their kind say it as they watch the anguish with which war, drunkenness, lust, disease, and poverty afflict the race. No man of moral insight will call such folk fools. The wretchedness and squalor, the misery and sin which rest upon so much of humankind are a notorious difficulty in the way of faith.

In dealing with this problem two short cuts are often tried, and by them some minds endeavor to evade the issue which faith ought to meet. Some *minimize the suffering* which creation cost and which man and animals are now enduring. We must grant that when we read the experience of animals in terms of man's own life, we always exaggerate their pain. Animals never suffer as we do; their misery is not compounded by our mental agonies of regret and fear; and even their physical wretchedness is as much lower in intensity as their nerves are less exquisitely tuned. Darwin, who surely did not underestimate the struggle for existence, said in a letter, "According to my judgment, happiness decidedly prevails. All sentient beings have been formed so as to enjoy, as a general rule, happiness." We must grant also that man's practical attitude toward life gives the lie to pessimism. Only the suicides are the logical pessimists, and all the rest of men, most with good heart and multitudes with jubilant enthusiasm, do actually cling to life. Indeed, all normal men discover, that, within limits, their very hardships are a condition of their happiness and do not so much abate their love of life as they add zest and tang. We must grant further that suffering should be measured not by quantity, but by intensity. One sensitive man enduring bereavement, poverty, or disease represents *all* the suffering that ever has been or ever can be felt. To speak of limitless suffering, therefore, is false. There is no more wretchedness anywhere nor in all the world together, than each one can know in his own person.

When all this, however, has been granted, the facts of the world's misery are staggering. Modern science has given terrific sweep and harrowing detail to Paul's assertion, "The whole creation groaneth and travaileth in pain together until now" (Rom. 8:22). Let one whose insight into misery's meanings is quickened by even a little imagination, try to sum up the agony of drunkards' homes, of bereaved families, of hospitals, insane asylums, jails, and prisons, of war with its unmentionable horrors—its blinded, deafened, maddened, raped—and no small palliatives can solve his problem. Rather he understands the picture which James Russell Lowell said he saw years ago in Belgium: an angel holding back the Creator and saying, "If about to make such a world, stay thine hand."

Another short cut by which some endeavor to simplify the problem and content their thought is *to lift responsibility for life's wretchedness from God's shoulders and to put it upon man's*. Were man's sin no factor in the world, some say, life's miseries would cease; all the anguish of our earthly lot stands not to God's responsibility but to man's shame. But the sufferings of God's creatures did not begin with man's arrival, and the pain of creation before man sinned is a longer story than earth's misery since. Let Romanes picture the scene: "Some hundred of millions of years ago, some millions of millions of animals must be supposed to have become sentient. Since that time till the present, there must have been millions and millions of generations of millions and millions of individuals. And throughout all this period of incalculable duration, this inconceivable host of sentient organizations have been in a state of unceasing battle, dread, ravin, pain. Looking to the outcome, we find that more than one-half of the species which have survived the ceaseless struggle are parasitic in their habits, lower and insentient forms of life, feasting on higher and sentient forms, we find teeth and talons whetted for slaughter, hooks and suckers molded for torture—everywhere a reign of terror, hunger, sickness, with oozing blood and quivering limbs, with gasping breath and eyes of innocence that dimly close in deaths of cruel torture." Is man responsible for that? For cold that freezes God's living creatures, for lightning that kills them, for volcanoes that burn them, for typhoons that crush them—is man responsible? By no such easy evasion may we escape the problem which faith must meet. "In sober truth," as John Stuart Mill exclaimed, "nearly all the things which men are hanged or imprisoned for doing to one another, are Nature's everyday performances." Who can avoid seeing the patent contrast between the Father of Jesus and the Creator of such a world? "The power that launches earthquakes and arms cuttlefish," said one perplexed believer, "has but a meager relationship to the power that blesses infants and forgives enemies."

II

Could we hold this problem at arm's length, discussing it in speculative moods when we grow curious about the makeup of the universe, our case would be more simple. But of all life's problems, this most certainly—sometimes creeping, sometimes crashing—invades our private lives. Every man has a date with adversity which he must keep and which adversity does not forget. One notes the evidence of this in every normally maturing life. As children we wanted happiness and were impatient, lacking it. Our cups of pleasure easily brimmed and overflowed. A Christmas tree or a birthday party— and our hearts were like sun-parlors on cloudless days with all the windows open to the light! But the time comes to all when happiness like this is not our problem; we recognize that it is gone; our Edens are behind us with flaming angels at the gate. We have had friends and lost them and something has gone from our hearts that does not return; we have won successes which we do not estimate as highly in possession as we did in dreams, and it may be have lost what little we achieved; we have sinned, and though forgiven, the scars are still upon us; we have been weathered by the rains and floods and winds. Happiness in the old fashion we no longer seek. We want peace, the power to possess our souls in patience and to do our work. We want joy, which is a profound and spiritually begotten grace as happiness is not. This maturity which so has faced the tragic aspects of our human life is not less desirable than child-

hood; it may be richer, fuller, steadier. We may think of it as Wordsworth did about the English landscape—that not for all the sunny
skies of Italy would he give up the mists that spiritualize the English
hills. But when trouble comes, life faces a new set of problems that
childhood little knew. We have joined the human procession that
moves out into the inevitable need of comfort and fortitude.

The decisive crisis in many lives concerns the attitude which this
experience evokes. Some are led by it more deeply into the meanings
of religion. The Bible grows in their apprehension with the enlarging of their life; new passages become radiant as, in a great landscape, hills and valleys lately unillumined catch the rays of the rising
sun. At first the human friendliness of Jesus is most real, and the
Bible's stories of adventure for God's cause; then knightly calls to
character and service become luminous; but soon or late another
kind of passage grows meaningful: "Now our Lord Jesus Christ
himself, and God, our Father who loved us and gave us eternal comfort and good hope through grace, comfort your hearts and establish
them" (II Thess. 2:16). Others, so far from being led by adversity
into the deeper meanings of faith, renounce faith altogether, and
fling themselves into open rebellion against life and any God who
may be responsible for its tragedy. They may not dare to say what
James Thomson did, but they think it—

> "Who is most wretched in this dolorous place?
> I think myself; yet I would rather be
> My miserable self than He, than He
> Who formed such creatures to his own disgrace.
>
> The vilest thing must be less vile than Thou
> From whom it had its being, God and Lord!
> Creator of all woe and sin! abhorred,
> Malignant and implacable! I vow
>
> That not for all Thy power furled and unfurled,
> For all the temples to Thy glory built,
> Would I assume the ignominious guilt
> Of having made such men in such a world!"

Many, however, are not by adversity made more sure of God, nor
are they driven into rebellion against him. They are perplexed. It
had been so much easier, in the sheltered and innocent idealism of

their youth, to believe in God than it is now. As children they looked on life as they might have listened to Mozart's music, ravished with unqualified delight; but now they know that Mozart died in abject poverty, that the coffin which his wife could not buy was donated by charity, that as the hearse went to the grave the driver loudly damned the dead because no drink money had been given him, and that to this day no one knows where Mozart's body lies. Maturity has to deal with so much more tragic facts than youth can ever know. With all the philosophy that man's wit can supply, the wisest find themselves saying what Emerson did, two years after his son's death: "I have had no experience, no progress to put me into better intelligence with my calamity than when it was new." And in this inevitable wrestling with adversity, the cry of men is not simply for more courage. They might easily steady their hearts to endure and overcome, were only one question's answer clear—is there any *sense* in life's suffering? The one unsupportable thought is that all life's pain and hardship is meaningless and futile, that it has no worthy origin, serves no high purpose, that in misery we are the sport of forces that have no consciousness of what they do, no meaning in it and no care. Such folk want to believe in God, but—can they?

III

Two preliminary facts about Christianity's relationship with our problem may help to clarify our thought. The doubt sometimes obtrudes itself on minds perplexed about life's tragedies that the Christian's faith in a God of love is an idealistic dream. Such faiths as the Fatherhood of God have come to men, they think, in happy hours when calamity was absent or forgotten; they are the fruition of man's fortunate days. And born thus of a view of life from which the miseries of men had been shut out, this happy, ideal faith comes back to painful realities with a shock which it cannot sustain. But is Christian faith thus the child of man's happy days? Rather the very symbol of Christianity is the Cross. Our faith took its rise in one of history's most appalling tragedies, and the Gospel of a loving God, so far from being an ideal dream, conceived apart from life's forbidding facts, has all these centuries been intertwined with the public brutality of a crucifixion. Every emphasis of the Christian's faith has the mark of the Cross upon it. Jesus had said in words that God was love, but it was at Calvary that the words took fire: "God so loved the world that he gave his only begotton son" (John 3:16). Jesus had preached the divine forgiveness, but on Golgotha the message grew imperative: "God commendeth his own love toward us, in that, while we were yet sinners, Christ died for us" (Rom. 5:8). Jesus had put into parables the individual care of the Father for every child, but it was the Cross that drove the great faith home: Christ tasted "death for every man" (Heb. 2:9). Nothing in Christian faith has escaped the formative influence of the Tragedy. The last thing to be said about the Gospel is that it is a beautiful child-like dream which has not faced the facts of suffering. In the New Testament are all the miseries on which those who deny God's love count for support. We are at home there with suffering men: "they were stoned, they were sawn asunder, they were tempted, they were slain with the sword: they went about in sheepskins, in goatskins; being destitute, afflicted, ill-treated (of whom the world was not worthy), wandering in deserts and mountains and caves and the holes of the earth" (Heb. 11:37, 38). The men with whom Christianity began were not strangers to such trouble, so that some modern need remind their innocent and dreaming faith that life is filled with mysterious adversity. *Christianity was suckled on adversity; it was cradled in pain. At the heart of its Book and its Gospel is a Good Man crowned with thorns, nailed to a cross, with a spear wound in his side.*

Nor have the great affirmations of faith in God's fatherhood ever been associated with men of ease in fortunate circumstance. The voice that cried "Father, into thy hands I commend my spirit" spoke in agonizing pain. And through history one finds those words best spoken with a cross for a background. Thomas á Becket said them, martyred in his own cathedral; John Huss said them, going to the stake at Constance; George Wishart said them, roasted at the foot of the sea-tower of St. Andrews. Christian faith is not a dream that came in hours when human trouble had been forgotten; it has furnished from the beginning an interpretation of human trouble and an attitude in meeting it that has made men "more than conquerors."

The second preliminary fact is this: *Christianity has never pretended to supply a theoretical explanation of why suffering had to be.* This seeming lack has excellent reason, for such an explanation, if it be complete, is essentially beyond the reach of any finite mind. The most comprehensive question ever asked, some philosopher has said, was put by a child. "Why was there ever anything at all?" No finite mind can answer that. And next in comprehensiveness, and in penetration to the very pith of creation's meaning, is this query, "Why, if something had to be, was it made as it is?" One must be God himself fully to answer that, or to comprehend the answer, could it be written down. To expect therefore, from Christianity or from any other source a theoretical explanation that will plumb the depths of the mystery of suffering is to cry for the essentially impossible. So Carlyle says with typical vividness: "To the minnow every cranny and pebble, and quality and accident of its little native creek may have become familiar; but does the minnow understand the Ocean Tides and periodic Currents, the Trade-winds, and Monsoons, and Moon's Eclipses; by all which the condition of its little Creek is regulated, and may, from time to time (*un*miraculously enough), be quite overset and reversed? Such a minnow is Man; his Creek this Planet Earth; his Ocean the immeasurable All; his Monsoons and periodic Currents the mysterious Course of Providence through Aeons of Aeons."

So little is this inability of ours to know all that we wish about the world a cause for regret, that it ought to be an occasion of positive rejoicing. If *we* could understand the universe through and through, how small and meager the universe would have to be! The fact is that we cannot understand anything through and through. If one is disheartened because he cannot pierce to the heart of Providence and know all its secrets, let him try his hand upon a pebble and see how much better he will fare. What is a pebble? If one define it roughly as granite he must ask what granite is; if that be defined in terms of chemical properties, he must ask what they are; if they be defined as ultimate forms of matter, he must inquire what matter is; and then he will be told that matter is a "mode of motion," or will be assured by a more candid scientist, like Professor Tait, that "we do not know and are probably incapable of discovering what matter *is*." No one ever solves the innermost problems of a stone, but what can be done with stones our engineering feats are evidence.

If, therefore, we recognize at the beginning that the question why suffering had to be is an ultimate problem, essentially insoluble by finite minds, we need not be dismayed. Two opposing mysteries are in the world—goodness and evil. If we *deny* God, then *goodness* is a mystery, for no one has ever yet suggested how spiritual life could rise out of an unspiritual source, how souls could come from dust. If we *affirm* God, then *evil* is a mystery, for why, we ask, should love create a world with so much pain and sin? Our task is not to solve insoluble problems; it is to balance these alternatives—no God and the mystery of man's spiritual life, against God and the mystery of evil. Such a comparison is not altogether beyond our powers, nor are weighty considerations lacking to affect our choice.

IV

For one thing, we may well inquire, when we complain of this world's misery, what sort of world we are seeking in its place. Are we asking for a perfectly happy world? But happiness, at its deepest and its best, is not the portion of a cushioned life which never struggled, overpassed obstacles, bore hardships, or adventured in sacrifice for costly aims. A heart of joy is never found in luxuriously coddled lives, but in men and women who achieve and dare, who have tried their powers against antagonisms, who have met even sickness and bereavement and have tempered their souls in fire. Joy is begotten not chiefly from the impression of happy circumstance, but from the expression of overcoming power. Were we set upon making a happy world, therefore, we could not leave struggle out nor make adversity impossible. The unhappiest world conceivable by man would be a world with nothing hard to do, no conflicts to wage for ends worth while; a world where courage was not needed and sacrifice was a superfluity. Beside such an inane lotos-land of tranquil ease this present world with all its suffering is a paradise. Men in fact find joy where in philosophy we might not look for it. Said MacMillan, after a terrific twelve-month with Peary on the Arctic continent: "This has been the greatest year of my life."

The impossibility of imagining a worth-while world from which adversity had all been banished is even more evident when one grows ill-content to think of happiness as the goal of life. That we should be merely happy is not an adequate end of the creative purpose for us, or of our purpose for ourselves. In our best hours we acknowledge this in the way we handle trouble. *However much in doubt a man may be about the theory of suffering, he knows infallibly how suffering practically should be met.* To be rebellious, cursing fate and hating life; to pity oneself, nursing one's hurts in morbid self-commiseration—the ignobility of such dealing with calamity we indubitably know. Even where we fall feebly short of the ideal, we have no question what the ideal is. When in biography or among our friends we see folk face crushing trouble, not embittered by it, made cynical, or thrust into despair, but hallowed, sweetened, illumined, and empowered, we are aware that noble characters do not alone *bear* trouble; they *use* it. As men at first faced electricity in dread, conceiving toward it no attitude beyond building lightning-rods to ward away its stroke, but now with greater understanding harness it to do their will, so men, as they grow wise and strong, deal with their suffering. They make it the minister of character; they set it to build in them what nothing save adversity can ever build— patience, courage, sympathy, and power. They even choose it in vicarious sacrifice for the good of others, and by it save the world from evils that nothing save some one's suffering could cure. They act as though *character,* not happiness, were the end of life. And when they are at their best they do this not with stoic intrepidity, as though trouble's usefulness were but their fancy, but joyfully, as though a good purpose in the world included trouble, even though not intending it. So Robert Louis Stevenson, facing death, writes to a friend about an old woman whose ventriloquism had frightened the natives of Vailima, "All the old women in the world might talk with their mouths shut and not frighten you or me, but there are plenty of other things that frighten us badly. And if we only knew about them, perhaps we should find them no more worthy to be feared than an old woman talking with her mouth shut. And the names of some of these things are Death and Pain and Sorrow."

Whatever, then, may be our theoretical difficulty about suffering, this truth is clear: when we are at our best we practically deal with suffering as though moral quality were the goal of life. We *use* adversity, as though discipline were its purpose and good its end. It is worth noting that the only theory which fully fits this noblest attitude toward trouble is Christianity. Men may think God a devil, as James Thomson sang, and yet may be practically brave and cheer-ful, but their theory does not fit their life. Men may believe in no God and no purpose in the world, and yet may face adversity with courage and hope, but their spirit belies their philosophy. When men are at their best in hardship *they act as though the Christian faith in God were true, as though moral quality were the purpose of creation.*

If now, we really want a world in which character is the end and aim—and no other world is worth God's making—we obviously may not demand the abolition of adversity. If one imagines a life from its beginning lapped in ease and utterly ignorant what words like hardship, sorrow, and calamity imply, he must imagine a life lacking every virtue that makes human nature admirable. Character grows on struggle; without the overcoming of obstacles great quality in character is unthinkable. Whoever has handled well any calamitous event possesses resources, insights, wise attitudes, qualities of sympathy and power that by no other road could have come to him. For all our complaints against life's misery, therefore, and for all our inability to understand it in detail, who would not hesitate, foreseeing the consequence, to take adversity away from men? He who banishes hardship banishes hardihood; and out of the same door with Calamity walk Courage, Fortitude, Triumphant Faith, and Sacrificial Love. If we abolish the cross in the world, we make impossible the Christ in man. It becomes more clear the more one ponders it, that while this is often a hard world in which to be happy, to men of insight and faith it may be a great world in which to build character.

V

Before too confidently, however, we accept this conclusion, there is one objection to be heard. So far is the world from being absolved from cruelty, on the plea of moral purpose, one may say, that *its injustice is the very crux of its offense.* See how negligent of justice the process of creation is! Its volcanoes and typhoons slay good and bad alike, its plagues are utterly indifferent to character; and in the human world which it embosoms some drunken Caesar sits upon the throne while Christ hangs on the cross. Who for a single day can watch the gross inequities of life, where good men so often suffer and bad men go free, and still think that the world has moral purpose in it? The Bible itself is burdened with complaint against the seeming senselessness and injustice of God. Moses cries: "Lord, wherefore hast thou dealt ill with this people? Neither hast thou delivered thy people at all" (Exodus 5:22, 23); Elijah laments, "O Jehovah, my God, hast Thou also brought evil upon the widow, with whom I sojourn, by slaying her son?" (I Kings 17:20); Habakkuk complains, "Wherefore lookest thou upon them that deal treacherously, and holdest thy peace, when the wicked swalloweth up the

man that is more righteous than he?" (Hab. 1:13); and Job pro-
tests, "Although thou knowest that I am not wicked, . . . yet thou
dost destroy me" (Job 10:7, 8). Man's loss of faith springs often
from this utter disparity between desert and fortune. The time
comes to almost every man when he looks on, indignant, desperate,
at some gross horror uninterrupted, some innocent victim entreated
cruelly. He understands Carlyle's impatient cry, "God sits in heaven
and does nothing!"

Natural as is this attitude, and unjust as many of life's tragic
troubles are, we should at least see this: *man must not demand that
goodness straightway receive its pay and wrong its punishment.* He
may not ask that every virtuous deed be at once rewarded by proportionate happiness and every sin be immediately punished by proportionate pain. That, some might suppose, would put justice into
life. But whatever it might put into life, such an arrangement obviously would take out *character*. The men whose moral quality we
most highly honor were not paid for their goodness on Saturday
night and did not expect to be. They chose their course *for righteousness' sake alone,* although they knew what crowns of thorns,
what scornful crowds about their cross might end the journey. They
did not drive close bargains with their fate, demanding insurance
against trouble as the price of goodness. They chose the honorable
deed for honor's sake; they chose it the more scrupulously, the more
pleasure was offered for dishonor; their tone in the face of threatened suffering was like Milne's, Scotland's last martyr: "I will not
recant the truth, for I am corn and no chaff; and I will not be blown
away with the wind nor burst with the flail, but I will abide both."

Every man is instinctively aware and by his admiration makes it
known, that the kind of character which chooses right, willing to suffer for it, is man's noblest quality. The words in which such character has found utterance are man's spiritual battle cries. Esther, going
before the King, saying, "If I perish, I perish" (Esther 4:16); the
three Hebrews, facing the fiery furnace saying, "Our God whom we
serve is able to deliver us from the burning fiery furnace; and he will
deliver us out of thy hand, O king. But if *not,* be it known unto thee,
O king, that we will not serve thy gods" (Dan. 3:17, 18); Peter and
the apostles, facing the angry Council, saying, "We must obey God
rather than men" (Acts 5:29); Anaxarchus, the martyr, crying,
"Beat on at the case of Anaxarchus; Anaxarchus himself you cannot
touch"; Luther, defying the Emperor, "Here stand I; I can do no

other"—most words of men are easily dispensable, but no words like these can man afford to spare. They are his best. *And this sort of goodness has been possible, because God had not made the world as our complaints sometimes would have it.* For such character, a system where goodness costs is absolutely necessary. A world where goodness was paid cash in pleasant circumstance would have no such character to show. Right and wrong for their own sakes would be impossible; only prudence and imprudence for happiness' sake could there exist. Out of the same door with the seeming injustice of life goes the possibility of man's noblest quality—his goodness "in scorn of consequence." Many special calamities no one on earth can hope to understand. But when one has granted that fitness to grow character is the only worthy test of creation, it evidently is not so simple as at first it seemed to improve the fundamental structure of the world.

VI

Indeed, when one in imagination assumes the task of omnipotence and endeavors to construct a universe that shall be fitted for the growth of character, he cannot long hesitate concerning certain elements which must be there. *A system of regular law* would have to be the basis of that world, for only in a law-abiding universe could obedience be taught. If the stars and planets behaved "like swarms of flies" and nothing could be relied upon to act twice in the same way, character and intelligence alike would be impossible. In this new world, remolded, "nearer to our heart's desire," *progress* also would be a necessity. A stagnant world cannot grow character. There must be real work to do, aims to achieve; there must be imperfections to overpass and wrongs to right. Only in a system where the present situation is a point of departure and a better situation is a possibility, where ideal and hope, courage and sacrifice are indispensable can character grow. In this improved world of our dreams, *freewill* in some measure must be granted man. If character is to be real, man must not in his choice between right and wrong be as Spinoza pictured him, a stone hurled through the air, which thinks that it is flying; he must have some control of conduct, some genuine, though limited, power of choice. And in this universe which we are planning for character's sake, individuals could not stand separate and unrelated; *they must be woven into a community.* Love which is the crown of character, lacking this, would be impossible. What happens to one must happen to all; good and ill alike must be contagious in a society where we are "members one of another."

No one of these four elements could be omitted from a world whose test was its adaptability for character. Men with genuine power of choice, fused into a fellowship of social life, living in a law-abiding and progressive world—on no other terms imaginable to man could character be possible. *Yet these four things contain all the sources of our misery.* Physical law—what tragic issues its stern, unbending course brings with terrific incidence on man! Progress— how obviously it implies conditions imperfect, wrong, through which we have to struggle toward the best! Free-will—what a nightmare of horror man's misuse of it has caused since sin began! Social fellowship—how surely the innocent must suffer with the guilty, how impossible for any man to bear the consequence of his own sin alone! We may not see why these general conditions should involve the particular calamities which we bewail, but even our finite minds can see thus far into the mystery of suffering: *all our trouble springs from four basic factors in the universe, without any one of which, great character would be impossible.*

While, therefore, if one *deny* God, the mystery of goodness lacks both sense and solution; one may *affirm* God and find the mystery of evil, mysterious still but suffused with light. God is working out a spiritual purpose here by means without which no spiritual purpose is conceivable. Fundamentally creation is good. We misuse it, we fail to understand its meaning and to appropriate its discipline, and impatient because the eternal purpose is not timed by our small clocks, we have to confess with Theodore Parker, "The trouble seems to be that God is not in a hurry and I am." In hours of insight, however, we perceive how little our complaints will stand the test of dispassionate thought. Our miseries are not God's inflictions on us as individuals, so that we may judge his character and his thought of us by this special favor or by that particular calamity. The most careless thinker feels the poor philosophy of Lord Londonderry's petulant entry in his journal: "Here I learned that Almighty God, for reasons best known to himself, had been pleased to burn down my house in the county of Durham." One must escape such narrow egoism if he is to understand the purposes of God; one must rise to look on a creation, with character at all costs for its aim, and countless æons for its settling. In the making of this world God has *limited himself;*

he cannot lightly do what he will. He has limited himself in creating a law-abiding system where his children must learn obedience without special exemptions; in ordaining a progressive system where what *is* is the frontier from which men seek what *ought to be;* in giving men the power to choose right, with its inevitable corollary, the power to choose wrong; in weaving men into a communal fellowship where none can escape the contagious life of all. What Martineau said of the first of these is true in spirit of them all: "The universality of law is God's eternal act of self-limitation or abstinence from the movements of free affection, for the sake of a constancy that shall never falter or deceive."

When once a man has risen to the vision of so splendid a purpose in so great a world he rejoices in the outlook. Granted that now he sees in a mirror darkly, that many a cruel event in human life perplexes still—he has seen enough to give solid standing to his faith. What if an insect, someone has suggested, were born just after a thunderstorm began and died just before it stopped—how dark would be its picture of creation! But we who span a longer period of time, are not so obsessed by thunderstorms, although we may not like them. They have their place and serve their purpose; we see them in a broader perspective than an insect knows and on sultry days we even crave their coming. A broken doll is to a child a cruel tragedy, but to the father watching the child's struggle to accept the accident, to make the best of it and to come off conqueror, the event is not utterly undesirable. He is not glad at the child's suffering, but with his horizons he sees in it factors which she does not see. So God's horizons infinitely overpass our narrow outlooks. There is something more than whimsy in the theologian's saying, which President King reports, that an insect crawling up a column of the Parthenon, with difficulty and pain negotiating passage about a pore in the stone, is as well qualified to judge of the architecture of the Parthenon, as we of the infinitude of God's plans. Seeing as much as we have seen of sense and purpose in the structure of creation, we have seen all that our finite minds with small horizons could have hoped. We have gained ample justification for the attitude toward suffering which Dolly Winthrop in Silas Marner has immortalized: "Eh, there's trouble i' this world, and there's things as we can niver make out the rights on. And all as we've got to do is to trusten, Master Marner—to do the right thing as far as we know and to trusten. For if us, as knows so little, can see a bit o' good and rights, we may

be sure as there's a good and a rights bigger nor what we can know—
I feel it i' my own inside as it must be so."

VII

We may not truthfully leave our subject in such a case that faith's
concern with human misery will seem to lie merely in giving adversity
an explanation. Faith is concerned not alone to *explain* misery but
to *heal* it. For while it is impossible without hardship to develop
character, there are woeful calamities on earth that do not help
man's moral quality; they crush and mutilate it; they are barbarous
intruders on the plan of God and they have no business in his world.
Some ills are such that no theory can reconcile them with the love
of God and no man ought to desire such reconciliation; in the love
of God they ought to be abolished. Slavery must be a possibility in
a world where man is free; but God's goodness was not chiefly vindicated by such a theory of explanation. It was chiefly vindicated by
slavery's abolishment. The liquor traffic and war, needless poverty
in a world so rich, avoidable diseases that science can overcome—
how long a list of woes there is that faith should not so much explain
as banish! When some ills like drunkenness and war and economic
injustice are thrust against our faith, and men ask that the goodness
of God be reconciled with these, faith's first answer should be not
speculation but action. Such woes, so far from being capable of
reconciliation with God's goodness, are irreconcilable with a decent
world. God does not want to be reconciled with them; he hates them
"with a perfect hatred." We may not make ourselves patient with
them by any theory of their necessity. They are not necessary; they
are perversions of man's life; and *the best defense of faith is their
annihilation.*

Indeed, a man who, rebellious in complaint, has clamorously
asked an explanation of life's ills as the price of faith in God, may
well in shame consider God's real saints. When things were at their
worst, when wrong was conqueror and evils that seemed blatantly
to deny the love of God were in the saddle, these spiritual soldiers
went out to fight. The winds of ill that blow out our flickering faith
made their religion blaze—a pillar of fire in the night. The more
evil they faced, the more religion they produced to answer it. They
were the real believers, who "through faith subdued kingdoms,
wrought righteousness, obtained promises." In comparison with

such, it is obviously paltry business to drive a bargain with God that if all goes well we will believe in him, but if things look dark, then faith must go.

Many a man, therefore, who is no philosopher can be a great defender of the faith. He may not weave arguments to prove that such a world as this in its fundamental structure is fitted to a moral purpose. But he can join the battle to banish from the world those ills that have no business here and that God hates. He can help produce that final defense of the Christian faith—a world where it is easier to believe in God.

CHAPTER VII

Faith and Science

DAILY READINGS

The intellectual difficulties which trouble many folk involve the relations of faith with science, but often they do not so much concern the abstract theories of science as they do the particular attitudes of scientists. We are continually faced with quotations from scientific specialists, in which religion is denied or doubted or treated contemptuously, and even while the merits of the case may be beyond the ordinary man's power of argument, he nevertheless is shaken by the general opinion that what ministers say in the pulpit on Sunday is denied by what scientists say all the rest of the week. In the daily readings, therefore, we shall deal with the scientists themselves, as a problem which faith must meet.

Seventh Week, First Day

No one can hope to deal fairly with the scientists, in their relationship with faith, unless he begins with a warm appreciation of the splendid integrity and self-denial which the scientific search for truth has revealed.

Canst thou bind the cluster of the Pleiades,
Or loose the bands of Orion?
Canst thou lead forth the Mazzaroth in their season?
Or canst thou guide the Bear with her train?
Knowest thou the ordinances of the heavens?
Canst thou establish the dominion thereof in the earth?
Canst thou lift up thy voice to the clouds,
That abundance of waters may cover thee?

Canst thou send forth lightnings, that they may go,
And say unto thee, Here we are?
Who hath put wisdom in the inward parts?
Or who hath given understanding to the mind?
Who can number the clouds by wisdom?
Or who can pour out the bottles of heaven,
When the dust runneth into a mass,
And the clods cleave fast together?

—Job 38: 31-38.

Such is man's ancient wonder before the physical universe; and in the endeavor to discover the truth about it science has developed saints and martyrs whose selfless and sacrificial spirit is unsurpassed even in the annals of the Church. Men have spent lives of obscure and unrewarded toil to get at a few new facts; they have suffered persecution, and, even after torture, have reaffirmed the truth of their discoveries, as did Galileo, when he insisted, "The earth does move." They have surrendered place and wealth, friends and life itself in their passion for the sheer truth, and when human service was at stake have inoculated themselves with deadly diseases that they might be the means of discovering the cure, or have sacrificed everything that men hold most dear to destroy an ancient, popular, and hurtful fallacy. The phrase "pride of science" is often used in depreciation of the scientists. There is some excuse for the phrase, but in general, when one finds pride, dogmatism, intolerance, they are the work of ignorance and not of science. The scientific spirit has been characteristically humble. Says Huxley: "Science seems to me to teach in the highest and strongest manner the great truth which is embodied in the Christian conception of entire surrender to the will of God. Sit down before the fact as a little child, be prepared to give up every preconceived notion, follow humbly wherever and to whatever end nature leads, or you shall learn nothing. . . . I have only begun to learn content and peace of mind since I have resolved at all risks to do this." The Christian, above all others, is bound to approach the study of the controversy between science and theology with a high estimate of the integrity and disinterested unselfishness of the scientists.

O God, we thank Thee for the world in which Thou hast placed us, for the universe whose vastness is revealed in the blue depths of

*the sky, whose immensities are lit by shining stars beyond the strength
of mind to follow. We thank Thee for every sacrament of beauty;
for the sweetness of flowers, the solemnity of the stars, the sound of
streams and swelling seas; for far-stretching lands and mighty mountains which rest and satisfy the soul, the purity of dawn which calls
to holy dedication, the peace of evening which speaks of everlasting
rest. May we not fear to make this world for a little while our home,
since it is Thy creation and we ourselves are part of it. Help us
humbly to learn its laws and trust its mighty powers.*

*We thank Thee for the world within, deeper than we dare to look,
higher than we care to climb; for the great kingdom of the mind
and the silent spaces of the soul. Help us not to be afraid of ourselves, since we were made in Thy image, loved by Thee before the
worlds began, and fashioned for Thy eternal habitation. May we be
brave enough to bear the truth, strong enough to live in the light,
glad to yield ourselves to Thee.*

*We thank Thee for that world brighter and better than all, opened
for us in the broken heart of the Saviour; for the universe of love
and purity in Him, for the golden sunshine of His smile, the tender
grace of His forgiveness, the red renewing rain and crimson flood
of His great sacrifice. May we not shrink from its searching and
surpassing glory, nor, when this world fades away, fear to commit
ourselves to that world which shall be our everlasting home. Amen.—*
W. E. Orchard.

Seventh Week, Second Day

The Christian's appreciation of scientists should not stop short
of profound gratitude for their service to religion. If one reads
Burns's "Tam o' Shanter," with its "ghaists," "warlocks and witches,"
and "auld Nick," and remembers that these demonic powers were
veritable facts of terror once, he will see in what a world of superstitious fear mankind has lived. Bells were first put into church
steeples, not to call folk to worship, but to scare the devils out of
thunder-clouds, and the old cathedral bells of Europe are inscribed
with declarations of that purpose. The ancients hardly believed in
God so vividly as they believed in malicious demons everywhere.
Now the Gospel removed the *fear* of these from the first Christians;
it made men aware of a conquering alliance with God, so that believers no longer shared the popular dread of unknown demons. But

so long as thunderstorms, pestilences, droughts, and every sort of evil were supposed to be the work of devils, even the Gospel could not dispel the general dread. Only new knowledge could do that. While Christianity therefore at its best has removed the *fear* of evil spirits, science has removed the *fact* of them as an oppressive weight on life. Today we not only do not dread them, but we do not think of them at all, and we have science to thank for our freedom. By its clear facing of facts and tracing of laws, science has lifted from man's soul an intolerable burden of misbeliefs and has cleansed religion of an oppressive mass of credulity. *True religion never had a deadlier foe than superstition and superstition has no deadlier foe than science.* Little children, brought up in our homes to trust the love of the Father, with no dark background of malignant devils to harass and frighten them, owe their liberty to the Gospel of Jesus indeed, but as well to the illumination of science that has banished the ancient dreads.

These things have I spoken unto you, while yet abiding with you. But the Comforter, even the Holy Spirit, whom the Father will send in my name, he shall teach you all things, and bring to your remembrance all that I said unto you. Peace I leave with you; my peace I give unto you: not as the world giveth, give I unto you. Let not your heart be troubled, neither let it be fearful.—John 14:25-27.

To God the Father, God the Son, God the Spirit, we pour forth most humble and hearty supplications, that He, remembering the calamities of mankind, and the pilgrimage of this our life in which we spend our days, would please to open to us new consolations out of the fountain of His goodness for the alleviating of our miseries. We humbly and earnestly ask that human things may not prejudice such as are Divine, so that from the opening of the gates of sense, and the kindling of a greater natural light, nothing of incredulity . . . may arise in our minds towards Divine mysteries; but rather, O Lord, that our minds being thoroughly cleansed and purged from fancy, and yet subject to the Divine will, there may be given unto faith the things that are faith's, so that we may continually attain to a deeper knowledge and love of Thee, Who art the Fountain of Light, and dwellest in the Light which no man can approach unto; through Jesus Christ our Lord. Amen.—Francis Bacon, 1561.

Seventh Week, Third Day

If one approach the scientists, as we have suggested, with appreciation of their devoted spirit and of their beneficent service, he is likely to be fair and Christian in his judgment. For one thing, he will readily understand why some of them are not religious men. The laws of psychology are not suspended when religion is concerned; there as elsewhere persistent attention is the price of a vivid sense of reality. When, therefore, a man habitually thinks intensely of nothing but biological tissue, or chemical reactions, or the diseases of a special organ, the results are not difficult to forecast. Darwin's famous confession that in his exacting concentration on biology he utterly lost his power to appreciate music or poetry is a case in point. Said Darwin, "My mind seems to have become a kind of machine for grinding general laws out of a large collection of facts." It is needless to say that such a mind is not likely to be more vividly aware of God than it is to feel music's beauty or poetry's truth. The plain fact is that if any man should persistently restrict himself to a physical science, should never hear a symphony or an oratorio, should shut out from his experience any dealing with music or enjoyment of it, he would in the end lose all musical capacity, and would become a man whose appreciation of music was nil and whose opinion on music was worthless. *Just such an atrophy of life is characteristic of intense specialists.* When one understands this he becomes capable of intelligent sympathy with scientists, even when he does not at all agree with their religious opinions. Jude gives us a remarkable injunction, plainly applicable here. "On some have mercy who are in doubt."

But ye, beloved, building up yourselves on your most holy faith, praying in the Holy Spirit, keep yourselves in the love of God, looking for the mercy of our Lord Jesus Christ unto eternal life. And on some have mercy, who are in doubt; and some save, snatching them out of the fire; and on some have mercy with fear; hating even the garment spotted by the flesh.

Now unto him that is able to guard you from stumbling, and to set you before the presence of his glory without blemish in exceeding joy, to the only God our Saviour, through Jesus Christ our Lord, be glory, majesty, dominion and power, before all time, and now, and for evermore. Amen.—Jude 20-25.

*O God, who so fillest all things that they only thinly veil Thy
presence; we adore Thee in the beauty of the world, in the goodness
of human hearts and in Thy thought within the mind. We praise
Thee for the channels through which Thy grace can come to us;
sickness and health, joy and pain, freedom and necessity, sunshine
and rain, life and death.*

*We thank Thee for all the gentle and healing ministries of life;
the gladness of the morning, the freedom of the wind, the music of
the rain, the joy of the sunshine, and the deep calm of the night;
for trees, and flowers, the clouds, and skies; for the tender ministries
of human love, the unselfishness of parents, the love that binds man
and woman, the confidence of little children; for the patience of
teachers and the encouragement of friends.*

*We bless Thee for the stirring ministry of the past, for the story
of noble deeds, the memory of holy men, the printed book, the
painter's art, the poet's craft; most of all for the ministry of the
Son of Man, who taught us the eternal beauty of earthly things,
who by His life set us free from fear, and by His death won us from
our sins to Thee; for His cradle, His cross, and His crown.*

*May His Spirit live within us, conquer all the selfishness of man,
and take away the sin of the world. Amen.*—W. E. Orchard.

Seventh Week, Fourth Day

The tendency of scientific specialization to shut out the appreciation of life's other values has one notable result: the opinions of
scientific specialists in the physical realm on matters of religion are
generally not of major importance. There is a popular fallacy that
an expert in one realm must be listened to with reverence on all
subjects. But the fact is that a great physicist is not by his scientific
eminence thereby qualified to talk wisely on politics or literature
or religion; rather, so far as *a priori* considerations are concerned,
he is thereby disqualified. Mr. Edison cannot say anything on electricity that is insignificant; but when he gave an interview on immortality he revealed to everyone who knew the history of thought on
that subject and the issues involved in it, that on matters outside
his specialty he could say things very insignificant. The more one
personally knows great specialists, the more he sees how human they
are, how interest in one thing shuts out interest in others, how the
subject on which the mind centers grows real and all else unreal,

how very valuable their judgment is on their specialties, and how much less valuable even than ordinary men's is their judgment on anything beside. This truth does not concern religion only; it concerns any subject which calls into play appreciative faculties that their science does not use. For a man, therefore, to surrender religious faith because a specialist in another realm disowns it is absurd. If one wishes, outside of those whose vital interest in religion makes them specialists there, to get confirmation from another class of men, let him look not to physicists but to judges. They are accustomed to weigh evidence covering the general field of human life; and among the great judicial minds of this generation, as of all others, one finds an overwhelming preponderance of religious men.

But unto us God revealed them through the Spirit: for the Spirit searcheth all things, yea, the deep things of God. For who among men knoweth the things of a man, save the spirit of the man, which is in him? even so the things of God none knoweth, save the Spirit of God. But we received, not the spirit of the world, but the spirit which is from God; that we might know the things that were freely given to us of God. Which things also we speak, not in words which man's wisdom teacheth, but which the Spirit teacheth; combining spiritual things with spiritual words. Now the natural man receiveth not the things of the Spirit of God: for they are foolishness unto him; and he cannot know them, because they are spiritually judged. —I Cor. 2:10-14.

O Eternal and glorious Lord God, since Thy glory and honor is the great end of all Thy works, we desire that it may be the beginning and end of all our prayers and services. Let Thy great Name be glorious, and glorified, and sanctified throughout the world. Let the knowledge of Thee fill all the earth as the waters cover the sea. Let that be done in the world that may most advance Thy glory. Let all Thy works praise Thee. Let Thy wisdom, power, justice, goodness, mercy, and truth be evident unto all mankind, that they may observe, acknowledge, and admire it, and magnify the Name of Thee, the Eternal God. In all the dispensation of Thy Providence, enable us to see Thee, and to sanctify Thy Name in our hearts with thankfulness, in our lips with thanksgiving, in our lives with dutifulness and obedience. Enable us to live to the honor of that great Name of Thine by which we are called, and that, as we profess ourselves to be Thy children, so we may study and sincerely endeavor

*to be like Thee in all goodness and righteousness, that we may
thereby bring glory to Thee our Father which art in heaven; that
we and all mankind may have high and honorable thoughts concerning Thee, in some measure suitable to Thy glory, majesty, goodness, wisdom, bounty, and purity, and may in all our words and
actions manifest these inward thoughts touching Thee with suitable
and becoming words and actions; through Jesus Christ our Lord.
Amen.*—Lord Chief Justice Sir Matthew Hale, 1609.

Seventh Week, Fifth Day

So far in our thought we have tacitly consented to the popular
supposition, that the scientists are at odds with religion. Many of
them unquestionably are. But in view of the obsessing nature of
scientific specialties, the wonder is not that some scientists are non-
religious; the wonder is that so many are profoundly men of faith
in God. The idea that scientists as a whole are irreligious is untrue.
Lists of testimonials from eminent specialists in favor of religion are
not particularly useful, for, as we have said, the judgment of specialists outside their chosen realm is, at the most, no more valuable than
that of ordinary men. But if anyone tries to rest his case against
religion on the adverse opinions of great scientists, he easily can be
driven from his position. Sir William Crookes, one of the world's
greatest chemists, writes: "I cannot imagine the possibility of anyone with ordinary intelligence entertaining the least doubt as to the
existence of a God—a Law-Giver and a Life-Giver." Lord Kelvin,
called the "Napoleon of Science," said that he could think of nothing so absurd as atheism; Sir Oliver Lodge, perhaps the greatest
living physicist and certainly an earnest believer, writes, "The tendency of science, whatever it is, is not in an irreligious direction at
the present time"; Sir George Stokes, the great physicist (died 1903),
affirmed his belief that disbelievers among men of science "form a
very small minority"; and Sir James Geikie, Dean of the Faculty of
Science at Edinburgh University, impatiently writes, "It is simply
an impertinence to say that 'the leading scientists are irreligious or
anti-Christian.' Such a statement could only be made by some scat-
ter-brained chatterbox or zealous fanatic." The fact is that, in spite
of the tendency of high specialization to crowd out religious interest
and insight, our great scientists have never thrown the mass of their
influence against religion, and today, in the opinion of one of their

chief leaders, are growing to be increasingly men of religious spirit. Whatever argument is to be based on the testimony of the scientists is rather for religion than against it.

For this cause I also, having heard of the faith in the Lord Jesus which is among you, and the love which ye show toward all the saints, cease not to give thanks for you, making mention of you in my prayers; that the God of our Lord Jesus Christ, the Father of glory, may give unto you a spirit of wisdom and revelation in the knowledge of him; having the eyes of your heart enlightened, that ye may know what is the hope of his calling, what the riches of the glory of his inheritance in the saints, and what the exceeding greatness of his power to us-ward who believe.—Eph. 1:15-19.

O Lord, who by Thy holy Apostle hast taught us to do all things in the Name of the Lord Jesus and to Thy glory; give Thy blessing, we pray Thee, to this our work, that we may do it in faith, and heartily, as to the Lord, and not unto men. All our powers of body and mind are Thine, and we would fain devote them to Thy service. Sanctify them and the work in which we are engaged; let us not be slothful, but fervent in spirit, and do Thou, O Lord, so bless our efforts that they may bring forth in us the fruit of true wisdom. Strengthen the faculties of our minds, and dispose us to exert them for Thy glory and for the furtherance of Thy Kingdom. Save us from all pride and vanity and reliance upon our own power or wisdom. Teach us to seek after truth, and enable us to gain it; while we know earthly things, may we know Thee, and be known by Thee through and in Thy Son Jesus Christ, that we may be Thine in body and spirit, in all our work and undertakings; through Jesus Christ. Amen.—Thomas Arnold, 1795.

Seventh Week, Sixth Day

Far more important than the opinions of individual scientists for religion or against it, is the fact that scientists are coming increasingly to recognize the limitations of their field. The field of science *is* limited; its domain is the system of facts and their laws, which make the immediate environment of man's life; but with the Origin of all life, with the character of the Power that sustains us and with the Destiny that lies ahead of us science does not, cannot deal. The most superficial observance shows how little any great soul lives within the confines of science's discoveries. Carlyle, after his great bereavement, writes to his friend Erskine:

" 'Our Father which art in heaven, hallowed be Thy name, Thy will be done'—what else can we say? The other night in my sleepless tossings about, which were growing more and more miserable, these words, that brief and grand Prayer, came strangely to my mind, with an altogether new emphasis; as if written and shining for me in mild pure splendor, on the black bosom of the Night there; when I, as it were, read them word by word—with a sudden check to my imperfect wanderings, with a sudden softness of composure which was much unexpected. Not for perhaps thirty or forty years had I once formally repeated that prayer—nay, I never felt before how intensely the voice of man's soul it is; the inmost aspiration of all that is high and pious in poor human nature." But supposing that the facts of science were all of reality and the laws of science all of truth, what sort of prayer could Carlyle have offered? Another has suggested the form which the Lord's Prayer would take in a world that lacked religious faith: "Our brethren who are upon the earth, hallowed be our name; our Kingdom come; our will be done on earth; for there is no heaven. We must get us this day our daily bread; we know we cannot be forgiven, for Law knows no forgiveness; we fear not temptation, for we deliver ourselves from evil; for ours is the Kingdom and ours is the power, and there is no glory and no forever. Amen." In such a barren prayer *the whole of man's life is not represented.*

Let no man deceive himself. If any man thinketh that he is wise among you in this world, let him become a fool, that he may become wise. For the wisdom of this world is foolishness with God. For it is written, He that taketh the wise in their craftiness: and again, The Lord knoweth the reasonings of the wise, that they are vain. Wherefore let no one glory in men. For all things are yours; whether Paul, or Apollos, or Cephas, or the world, or life, or death, or things present, or things to come; all are yours; and ye are Christ's; and Christ is God's.—I Cor. 3:18-23.

O Thou Infinite Spirit, who occupiest all space, who guidest all motion, thyself unchanged, and art the life of all that lives, we flee unto thee, in whom we also live and move and have our being, and would reverence Thee with what is highest and holiest in our soul.

We know that Thou art not to be worshiped as though Thou needest aught, or askedst the psalm of praise from our lips; or our hearts poor prayer. O Lord, the ground under our feet, and the seas which whelm it round, the air which holds them both, and the heavens sparkling with many a fire—these are a whisper of the psalm of praise which creation sends forth to Thee, and we know that Thou askest no homage of bended knee, nor heart bowed down, nor heart uplifted unto Thee. But in our feebleness and our darkness, dependent on Thee for all things, we lift up our eyes unto Thee; as a little child to the father and mother who guide him by their hands, so do our eyes look up to Thy countenance, O Thou who art our Father and our Mother too, and bless Thee for all Thy gifts. We look to the infinity of Thy perfection with awe-touched heart, and we adore the sublimity which we cannot comprehend. We bow down before Thee, and would renew our sense of gratitude and quicken still more our certainty of trust, till we feel Thee a presence close to our heart, and are so strong in the heavenly confidence that nothing earthly can disturb us or make us fear. Amen.—Theodore Parker.

Seventh Week, Seventh Day

The difficulty which many Christians feel concerning science centers around their loyalty to the Bible. They still are under the domination of the thought that the Christian idea of the Bible is the same as the Mohammedan idea of the Koran or the Mormon idea of Joseph Smith's sacred plates. The Koran was all written in heaven, word for word, say orthodox Mohammedans, before ever it came to earth. As for the Mormon Bible, God buried the plates on which he wrote, said Smith, and then disclosed their hiding place, and his prophet translated them verbatim, so that the Mormon book is literally inerrant. But this is not the Christian idea of the Bible. Inspiration is never represented in Scripture as verbal dictation where human powers and limitations are suspended, so that like a phonographic plate the result is a mechanical reproduction of the words of God. Rather God spoke to men through their experience as they were able to understand him, and as a result the great Christian Book, like a true Christian man, represents alike the inbreathing of the Divine and the limitation of the human. So the Epistle to the Hebrews clearly states that God did what he could in revealing partially to partial men what they could understand:

God, having of old time spoken unto the fathers in the prophets by divers portions and in divers manners, hath at the end of these days spoken unto us in his Son, whom he appointed heir of all things, through whom also he made the worlds.—Heb. 1:1, 2.

Of all limitations that are entirely obvious in the ancient Hebrew-Christian world, the current view of the physical universe is the most unescapable. To suppose that God never can reveal to men anything about the world, transcending what the ancient Hebrews could understand, is to deny the principle which Jesus applied even to the more important realm of spiritual truth: "I have yet many things to say unto you, but ye cannot bear them now" (John 16:12).

O Thou who hast visited us with the Dayspring from on high, who hast made light to shine in the darkness, we praise Thy holy name and proclaim Thy wonderful goodness.

We bless Thee for the dawning of the light in far-off ages as soon as human eyes could bear its rays. We remember those who bore aloft the torch of truth when all was false and full of shame; those far-sighted souls who from the mountain tops of vision heralded the coming day; those who labored in the darkened valleys to lift men's eyes to the hills.

We thank Thee that in the fulness of the times Thou didst gather Thy light into life, so that even simple folk could see; for Jesus the Star of the morning and the Light of the world.

We commemorate His holy nativity, His lowly toil, His lonely way; the gracious words of His lips, the deep compassion of His heart, His friendship for the fallen, His love for the outcast; the crown of thorns, the cruel cross, the open shame. And we rejoice to know as He was here on earth, so Thou art eternally. Thou dost not abhor our flesh, nor shrink from our earthly toil. Thou rememberest our frailty, bearest with our sin, and tastest even our bitter cup of death.

And now we rejoice for the light that shines about our daily path from the cradle to the grave, and for the light that illumines its circuit beyond these spheres from our conception in Thy mind to the day when we wake in Thy image; for the breathing of Thy spirit into ours till we see Thee face to face: in God, from God; to God at last. Hallelujah. Amen.—W. E. Orchard.

COMMENT FOR THE WEEK

I

The innermost questions which some minds raise about religion cannot be answered without candid discussion of the obvious contrasts between faith and science. The conflict between science and theology is one of the saddest stories ever written. It is a record of mutual misunderstanding, of bitterness, bigotry, and persecution, and to this day one is likely to find the devotees of religion suspicious of science and scientists impatient with the Church.

If we are to understand the reason for this controversy between science and theology, we must take a far look back into man's history. Stephen Leacock remarks that whenever a professor discusses anything, he has to retreat at least 2,000 years to get a running start. Our retreat must be farther than that; it carries us to the earliest stage in which we are able to describe the thoughts of men. *At the beginning men attributed to superhuman spirits all activities in the world which they themselves did not perform.* If the wind blew, a spirit did it; if the sun rose, a spirit moved it; if a storm came, a spirit drove it. Natural law was non-existent to the primitive man; every movement in nature was the direct result of somebody's active will. From the mysterious whispering of a wind-swept field to the crashing thunder, what man did not cause the gods did.

If, therefore, a primitive man were asked the cause of rain, he had but one answer: a god made it rain. That was his *scientific* answer, for no other explanation of rain could he conceive. That was his *religious* answer, for he worshiped the spirit on whom he must depend for showers. This significant fact, therefore, stands clear: *To primitive man a religious answer and a scientific answer were identical.* Sunrise was explained, not by planetary movements which were unknown, but by the direct activity of a god, and the Dawn then was worshiped in the same terms in which it was explained. The historic reason for the confusion between science and religion at once grows evident. *At the beginning they were fused and braided into one; the story of their relationship is the record of their gradual and difficult disentangling.*

Wherever peace has come between science and religion, one finds a realm where the boundaries between the two are acknowledged

and respected. Ask *now* the question, What makes it rain? There is
a scientific answer in terms of natural laws concerning atmospheric
pressure and condensation. There is also a religious answer, since
behind all laws and through them runs the will of God. These two
replies are distinct, they move in different realms, and are held together without inconsistency. As Sabatier put it, "Since God is the
final cause of all things, he is not the scientific explanation of any
one thing." In how many realms where once confusion reigned between the believers in the gods and the seekers after natural laws, is
peace now established! Rain and sunrise, the tides and the eclipses,
the coming of the seasons and the growing of the crops—for all such
events we have our scientific explanations, and at the same time
through them all the man of religion feels the creative power of
God. Peace reigns in these realms because here *no longer do we force
religious answers on scientific questions or scientific answers on religious questions.* Evidently the old Deuteronomic law is the solution
of the conflict between science and religion: "Cursed be he that
removeth his neighbor's landmark" (Deut. 27:17).

II

Left thus in the negative, however, this might seem to mean that
we are to divide our minds into air-tight compartments, and allow
no influences from one to penetrate another. But science and religion
do tremendously affect each other, and no honest dealing ever can
endeavor to prevent their mutual reaction. Our position is not thus
negative; it affirms a positive and most important truth. Life has
many aspects; science, art, religion, approach it from different
angles, with different interests and purposes; and while they do *influence* each other, they are not *identical* and each has solid standing
in its own right. When science has grown domineering, as though
her approach to reality were the only one and her conclusions all
of truth, the poets have had as much distaste for her as have the
theologians. Shelley, who called himself an atheist, had no interest
in religion's conflict with the extreme claims of science; yet listen
to his aroused and flaming language as he pleads the case for poetry
against her: "Poetry is something divine. . . . It is the perfect and
consummate surface and bloom of all things; it is as the odor and
color of the rose to the texture of the elements which compose it, and
the form and splendor of unfaded beauty to the secrets of anatomy

and corruption. What were virtue, love, patriotism, friendship—
what were the scenery of this beautiful universe which we inhabit;
what were our consolations on this side of the grave—and what were
our aspirations beyond it, if poetry did not ascend to bring light and
fire from those eternal regions where the owl-winged faculty of calculation dare not even soar?" This involves no denial of science's
absolute right to her own field—the "texture of the elements which
compose" the rose, and the "secrets of anatomy." But it is a justified
assertion that this field of science is not all of reality, and that what
the "owl-winged faculty of calculation" can reach is not all of truth.

What is a sunset? Science sets forth the answer in tables where
the light waves that compose the colors are counted and the planetary movements that bring on the dusk are all explained. Poetry
answers in a way how different!

> "I've dreamed of sunsets when the sun, supine,
> Lay rocking on the ocean like a god,
> And threw his weary arms far up the sky,
> And with vermilion-tinted fingers,
> Toyed with the long tresses of the evening star."[1]

Is one of these answers more true than the other? Rather it is
absurd to compare their truth; they are not contradictory; they
approach the same fact with diverse interests, and seek in it different aspects of reality. Each has its rights in its own field. And so far
is it from being true that science has a clear case in favor of its own
superior importance, that Höffding, the philosopher, remarks, "It
well may be that poetry gives more perfect expression to the highest
Reality than any scientific concept can ever do."

Any great fact is too manifold in its meanings to be exhausted by
a single method of approach. If one would know the Bible thoroughly, he must understand the rules of grammar. Were one to make
grammar his exclusive specialty, the Bible to him, so far as he held
strictly to his science, would be nouns and verbs, adverbs, adjectives,
and prepositions, and the law-abiding relationships between them.
This mere grammarian would know by such a method one aspect
of the Bible, but how little of the Book would that aspect be! No
rules of grammar can interpret the thirteenth chapter of the First
Corinthians or explain the story of the Cross. The facts and laws of
the Book's language a grammarian could know, but the beauty and

[1] J. G. Holland.

the soul of it, the innermost transforming truth of it, would be unperceived.

So life is too rich and various to be exhausted by any one approach. Science seeks facts and arranges them in systems of cause and effect. Poetry sees these bare facts adorned with beauty, she suffuses them with her preferences and her appreciations. Religion sees the whole gathered up into spiritual unity, filled with moral purpose and good will, and in this faith finds peace and power. There need be no conflict between these various approaches; they are complementary, not antagonistic; and no man sees all the truth by any one of them alone. So a chemist might come to a spring to analyze it; a painter to rejoice in its beauties and reproduce them on his canvas; and a man athirst might come to drink and live. Shall they quarrel because they do not all come alike? Let them rather see how partial is the experience of each without the others!

III

In the mutual trespassing which has caused our problem, religion has had her guilty share, and the reason is not difficult to find. God did not have to give a modern scientific education to his ancient Hebrew saints before he could begin to reveal to them something of his will and character. And they, writing their experience and thought of him, could not avoid—as no generation's writers can avoid—indicating the view of the physical world which they and their contemporaries held. It is easy, therefore, from scores of Scripture passages to reconstruct the early Hebrew world. Their earth was flat and was founded on an underlying sea. (Psalm 136:6; Psalm 24:1, 2; Gen. 7:11); it was stationary (Psalm 93:1; Psalm 104:5); the heavens, like an upturned bowl, "strong as a molten mirror" (Job 37:18; Gen. 1:6-8; Isa. 40:22; Psalm 104:2), rested on the earth beneath (Amos 9:6; Job 26:11); the sun, moon, and stars moved within this firmament, of special purpose to illumine man (Gen. 1:14-19); there was a sea above the sky, "the waters which were above the firmament" (Gen. 1:7; Psalm 148:4), and through the "windows of heaven" the rain came down (Gen. 7:11; Psalm 78:23); beneath the earth was mysterious Sheol where dwelt the shadowy dead (Isa. 14:9-11); and all this had been made in six days, a short and measurable time before (Gen. I). This was the world of the Hebrews.

Because when the Hebrews wrote the Bible their thoughts of God, their deep experience of him, were interwoven with their early science, Christians, through the centuries, have thought that faith in God stood or fell with early Hebrew science and that the Hebrew view of the physical universe must last forever. In the seventeenth century, Dr. John Lightfoot, Vice-Chancellor of the University of Cambridge, said: "Heaven and earth, center and circumference, were created all together, in the same instant, and clouds full of water. . . . This work took place and man was created by the Trinity on October 23, 4004 B. C., at nine o'clock in the morning." Of what tragedy has this identification of science with religion been the cause!

When *astronomy* began to revolutionize man's idea of the solar universe, when for the first time in man's imagination the flat earth grew round and the stable earth began moving through space seventy-five times faster than a cannon-ball, Pope Paul V solemnly rendered a decree, that "the doctrine of the double motion of the earth about its axis and about the sun is false and entirely contrary to Holy Scripture." When *geology* began to show from the rocks' unimpeachable testimony the long leisureliness of God, laying the foundations of the world, a Christian leader declared geology "not a subject of lawful inquiry," "a dark art," "dangerous and disreputable," "a forbidden province," "an awful evasion of the testimony of revelation." This tragic record of theology's vain conflict with science is the most pitiable part of the Church's story. How needless it was! For now when we face our universe of magnificent distances and regal laws has religion really suffered? Has a flat and stationary earth proved essential to Christianity, as Protestants and Catholics alike declared? Rather the Psalmist could not guess the sweep of our meaning when now we say, "The heavens declare the glory of God and the firmament showeth his handiwork" (Psalm 19:1).

In the last generation the idea of *evolution* was the occasion of a struggle like that which attended the introduction of the new astronomy. How was the world made? asked the ancient Hebrew, and he answered, By the word of God at a stroke. That was his scientific answer, and his religious answer too. When, therefore, the evolving universe was disclosed by modern science, when men read in fossil and in living biological structure the undeniable evidence of a long history of gradually changing forms of life, until the world was seen *not made like a box but growing like a tree,* many men of

religion thought the faith destroyed. They identified the Christian
Gospel with early Hebrew science! Today, however, when the general idea of evolution is taken for granted as gravitation is, how
false this identification obviously appears! Says Professor Bowne,
"An Eastern king was seated in a garden, and one of his counselors
was speaking of the wonderful works of God. 'Show me a sign,' said
the king, 'and I will believe.' 'Here are four acorns,' said the counselor; 'will your Majesty plant them in the ground, and then stoop
down and look into this clear pool of water?' The king did so. 'Now,'
said the other, 'look up.' The king looked up and saw four oak
trees where he had planted the acorns. 'Wonderful!' he exclaimed;
'this is indeed the work of God.' 'How long were you looking into
the water?' asked the counselor. 'Only a second,' said the king.
'Eighty years have passed as a second,' said the other. The king
looked at his garments; they were threadbare. He looked at his
reflection in the water; he had become an old man. 'There is no
miracle here, then,' he said angrily. 'Yes,' said the other; 'it is God's
work whether he do it in one second or in eighty years.' "

Such an attitude as this is now a commonplace with Christian
folk. A vast and growing universe through which sweep the purposes of God is by far the most magnificent outlook for faith that
man has ever had. The Gospel and Hebrew science are *not* identical;
the Gospel is not indissolubly bound to any science ancient or modern; for science and religion have separable domains.

> "A fire-mist and a planet,
>   A crystal and a cell,
> A jelly-fish and a saurian,
>   And caves where cave men dwell.
> Then a sense of Love and Duty
>   And a face turned from the clod,
> Some call it Evolution
>   And others—call it God."

The same story of needless antagonism is now being written about
religion and *natural law*. When science began plotting nature's
laws, the control of the world seemed to be snatched from the
hands of deity and given over to a system of impersonal rules. God,
whose action had been defined in terms of miracle, was forced from
one realm after another by the discovery of laws, until at last even
comets were found to be not whimsical but as regular in their law-

abiding courses as the planets, and God seemed to be escorted to the edge of the universe and bowed out. When Newton first formulated the law of gravitation, the artillery of many an earnest pulpit was let loose against him. One said that Newton took "from God that direct action on his works so constantly ascribed to him in Scripture and transferred it to material mechanism" and that he "substituted gravitation for Providence." But now, when science has so plainly won her case, in her own proper field; when we know to our glory and profit so many laws by which the world is governed, and use our knowledge as the most splendid engine of personal purpose and freedom which man ever had, we see how great our gain has been. *Nor is it more a practical than a religious gain.* God once was thought of chiefly in terms of miraculous action; he came into his world now and again, like the *deus-ex-machina* of a Greek tragedy, to solve a critical dilemma in the plot. Now all the laws we know and many more are his regular ways of action, and through them all continuously his purpose is being wrought. As Henry Drummond exclaimed, "If God appears periodically, he disappears periodically. If he comes upon the scene at special crises, he is absent from the scene in the intervals. Whether is all-God or occasional God the nobler theory?"

Nothing, therefore, can be more pathetic than the self-styled "defenders of the faith" who withstand the purpose of reverent students to give scientific answers to scientific questions. Such men are not really defending the faith. They are doing exactly what Father Inchofer did when he said, "The opinion that the earth moves is of all heresies the most abominable"; what Mr. Gosse did when he maintained, in explanation of geology's discoveries, that God by the use of stratified rock and fossils deliberately gave the earth the *appearance* of development through long ages, while really he made it in six days; what Mr. Southall did when, in the face of established anthropology, he claimed that the "Egyptians had no Stone Age and were born civilized"; what the Dean of Chichester did when he preached that "those who refuse to accept the history of the creation of our first parents according to its obvious literal intention, and are for substituting the modern dream of evolution in its place, cause the entire scheme of man's salvation to collapse." These were not defending the faith; they were making it ridiculous in the eyes of intelligent men and were embroiling religion in controversies where she did not belong and where, out of her proper realm, she was foredoomed to defeat. *For scientific problems are not a matter for faith; they are a matter for investigation.* No one can settle by faith the movements of the planets, the method of the earth's formation, the age of mankind, the explanation of comets. These lie in science's realm, not in religion's, and religious faith demeans herself when she tries to settle them. Let science be the grammarian of the world to observe its parts of speech and their relations! Religion deals with the soul of the world, its deepest source, its spiritual meaning, its divine purpose.

IV

Science, however, has not always been content with the grammarian's task. When we have frankly confessed religion's sins in trespassing on scientific territory, we must note that *science has her guilty share in the needless conflict.* Today one suspects that the Church's vain endeavor by ecclesiastical authority to force religious solutions on scientific problems is almost over. But the attempt of many scientists to claim the whole field of reality as theirs and to force their solutions on every sort of problem is not yet finished. This, too, is a vain endeavor. To suppose that the process of scientific observation and inference can exhaust the truth of life is like supposing that there is no more meaning in Westminster Abbey than is expressed in Baedeker.

Scientists, for example, sometimes claim domains which are not theirs by *spelling abstract nouns with capitals, by positing Law or Evolution as the makers and builders of the world.* But law never did anything; law is only man's statement of the way, according to his observation, in which things are done. To explain the universe as the creation of Law is on a par with explaining homes as the creation of Matrimony. Abstract nouns do not create anything and the capitalizing of a process never can explain it. So, too, Evolution does nothing to the world; it is the way in which whoever makes the world is making it. As well explain the difference between an acorn and an oak by saying that Growth did it, as to explain the progress of creation from stardust to civilization by changing e to E. Science may describe the process as evolutionary, but its source, its moving power, and its destiny are utterly beyond her ken.

For another thing, scientists often invade realms which are not theirs, by *stretching the working theories of some special science to the proportions of a complete philosophy of life.* A generation ago, when geology and biology were in their "green and salad days," the enthusiasm inspired by the splendid results of their hypotheses went to strange lengths. One professor of geology seriously explained the pyramids of Egypt to be the remains of volcanic eruption which had forced its way upwards by slow and stately motion. The hieroglyphs were crystalline formations and the shaft of the great pyramid was the airhole of a volcano. Scientists are human like all men; their specialties loom large; the ideas that work in their limited areas seem omnipotent. So a student of the influence of sunlight on life thinks reactions to the sun explain everything. "Heliotropism," he says, "doubtless wrote Hamlet." A specialist on the influence of geography on human nature interprets everything as the reaction of man to seas, mountains, plains, and deserts, and Lombroso even thinks the revolutionary temperament especially native to men who live on limestone formations! Specialists in economic history are sure that man is little more than an animated nucleus of hunger and that all life is explicable as a search for food. And psychologists, charmed by the neatness of description which casual connections introduce into our inner life, leap to the conclusion, which lies outside their realm, that personality is an illusion, freedom a myth and our mental life the rattling of a casual chain forged and set in motion when the universe began. *All this is not science; it is making hypotheses from a limited field of facts masquerade as a total philosophy of life.*

The underlying reason why science, when she regards her province as covering everything, inevitably clashes with the interests of religion, is that *she starts her view of the world from the sub-human side.* The typical sciences are physics, chemistry, astronomy, geology, biology, and the view of the universe which they present is the basis on which all other sciences proceed. But this foundation is subhuman; the master ideas involved in it are all obtained with the life of man left out of account. Such an approach presents a world-machine, immense and regular, and when, later, psychology and sociology arise, how easy it is to call the human life which they study a by-product of the sub-human world, an exudation arising from the activities of matter.

Religion, on the contrary, *starts with human life.* Fall down in awe, Science cries, before this vast sub-human world! And the religious man answers: What world is this I am to bow before? Is it not the universe which my mind knows and whose laws my intellect has grasped? This universe, so far as it exists at all for me, is apprehended by my vision, penetrated by my thought, encompassed by my interpretations. *What is really great and wonderful here, is not the world which I understand, but the mind that understands it—not the sub-human but the human.* Man himself is the supreme Fact, and all the world that man could bow before, man's mind must first of all contain. The master truth is not that my mind exists within a physical universe, but that the physical universe is encompassed by my mind. Therefore, when I interpret life, I will start with man, and not with what lies below him.

Romanes, the English scientist, illustrates in his experience the difference which these two approaches make. When, returning from agnosticism to Christianity, he explained his lapse, he said, "I did not sufficiently appreciate the immense importance of *human* nature, as distinguished from physical nature, in any inquiry touching theism. . . . Human nature is the most important part of nature as a whole whereby to investigate the theory of theism. This I ought to have anticipated on merely *a priori* grounds, had I not been too much immersed in merely physical research." Of how many now does this same explanation hold! They segregate man from the rest of the universe, and endeavor an interpretation of the unhuman remainder. They forget that man is part and parcel of the universe, bone of its bone, as imperative an expression of its substantial nature as are rocks and stars, and that *any philosophy which interprets the world minus man has not interpreted the world.*

Here is the difference between a Haeckel and a Phillips Brooks. All the dominant ideas of the one are drawn from existence minus man; all the controlling convictions of the other are drawn from the heights and depths of man's own life. The first approach inevitably leads to irreligion, for Spirit cannot reveal itself except in spirit and until one has found God in man he will not find him in nature. The second as certainly leads to religion, for, as Augustine said, "If you dig deep enough in every man you find divinity." Over against the testimony of the sub-human that there is a mechanistic aspect to the world, stands the unalterable testimony of the human that there is as well an ideal, purposive, and spiritual aspect of the world. Surely the latter brings us nearer to the heart of truth. *We never understand anything except in terms of its highest expression and man is the summit of nature.*

Could religion find a voice, therefore, she would wish to speak not in terms of apology but of challenge, when science, assuming all of reality for its field, grows arrogant. Describe the aspect of the world that belongs to you, she would say. I have learned my lesson; your field is yours, and no interference at my hands shall trouble you again. But remember the limitations of your domain—to observe and describe phenomena and to plot their laws. That is an immense task and inexpressibly useful. But when you have completed it, the total result will be as unlike the real world as a medical manikin with his wire nerves and painted muscles is unlike a real man. The manikin is sufficiently correct; everything is truly pictured there— *except life.* So things are as science sees them, but things are more than science sees. Plot then the mechanistic aspect of the world, but do not suppose that you have caught all of truth in that wide-meshed net! When you have said your last word on facts observed and laws induced, man rises up to ask imperious questions with which you cannot deal, to present urgent problems for which no solution ever has been found save Augustine's, "I seek for God in order that my soul may *live.*"

v

Our thought so ended, however, would leave science and religion jealously guarding their boundaries, not cooperating as allies. *Such suspicious recognition of each other's realms does not exhaust the possibilities.* When once the separate functions each by the other have been granted, we are free to turn our thought to the inestimable service which each is rendering. Consider the usefulness of science to the ideal causes of which religion is the chief! Science has given us the *new universe,* not more marvelous in its vastness than in its unity. For the spectroscope has shown that everywhere through immeasurable space the same chemical properties and laws obtain; the telescope has revealed with what mathematical precision the orbits in the heavens are traced and how unwaveringly here or among the stars gravitation maintains its hold. Man never had so immense and various and yet so single and unified a world before. Polytheism once was possible, but science has banished it forever. Whatever may be the source of the universe, it is *one* Source, and whoever the creator, he is more glorious in man's imagination than he could ever have been before. Science also has put at the disposal of the ideal causes *such instruments as by themselves they would never have possessed.* We are hoping for a new world-brotherhood, and we pray for it in Christian churches as the Father's will. But the instruments by which the inter-racial fellowship must be maintained and without which it would be unthinkable are science's gift. Railroads, steamships, telegraphs, telephones, wireless—these are the shuttles by which the ideal faiths in man's fraternity may be woven into fact. When Christian physicians heal the sick or stamp out plagues that for ages have been man's curse and his despair, when social maladjustments are corrected by Christian philanthropy, and saner, happier ways of living are made possible; when comforts that once were luxuries are brought within the reach of all, and man's life is relieved of crushing handicaps; when old superstitions that had filled man's life with dread for ages are driven like fogs before science's illumination, and religious faith is freed of their incumbrance; when great causes of relief have at their disposal the unimaginable wealth which our modern economic system has created —can anyone do sufficient justice to man's debt to science? And once more science has done religion an inestimable service in establishing as a point of honor the ambition *to see straight and to report exactly.* The tireless patience, the inexorable honesty, the sacrificial heroism of scientists, pursuing truth, is a gift of incalculable magnitude. Huxley is typical of science at its best when he writes in his journal his ideal—"To smite all humbugs however big; to give a nobler tone to science; to set an example of abstinence from petty personal controversies and of toleration for everything but lying; to be indifferent as to whether the work is recognized as mine or not, so long as it is done." Countless obscurantisms and bigotries, shams and sophistries have been driven from the churches by this scientific spirit and more are yet to go. Science has shown intellectual dishonesty to be a sin of the first rank. Christianity never can be thankful enough for science; on our knees we should be grateful for her as one of God's most indispensable gifts. Nor should the fact that many a scientist whose contributions we rejoice in was not certain about God defer our gratitude. Cyrus, the Persian, is not the only one to whom the Eternal has said, "I will gird thee, though thou hast not known me" (Isa. 45:5).

When, however, science has done her necessary work, she needs her great ally, religion. Without the insight and hope which faith alone can bring, we learn a little about the world, our minds enclosed in boundaries beyond which is dark, unfathomable mystery. We rejoice in nature's beauty and in friendship, suffer much with broken bodies and more with broken family ties, until we die as we were born—the spawn of mindless, soulless powers that never purposed us and never cared. And the whole universe is purposeless, engaged with blind hands, that have no mind behind them, on tasks that mean nothing and are never done. Science and religion should not be antagonists; they are mutually indispensable allies in the understanding and mastery of life.

CHAPTER VIII

Faith and Moods

The relationship of faith to feeling, rather than faith's relationship to mind, is with many people the more vital interest. The emotional results of faith are rightfully of intense concern to everyone, for our feelings put the sense of value into life. To see a sunset without being stirred by its beauty is to miss seeing the sunset; to have friends without feeling love for them is not to have friends; and to possess life without feeling it to be gloriously worth while is to miss living. Now, in this regard, the attitude of faith stands sharply opposed to its direct contrary—the attitude of fear. Faith and fear are the two emotional climates, in one or the other of which everyone tends habitually to live. To the comparison of these we set ourselves in the daily readings.

Eighth Week, First Day

Give ear to my prayer, O God;
And hide not thyself from my supplication.
Attend unto me, and answer me:
I am restless in my complaint, and moan,
Because of the voice of the enemy,
Because of the oppression of the wicked;
For they cast iniquity upon me,
And in anger they persecute me.
My heart is sore pained within me:
And the terrors of death are fallen upon me.
Fearfulness and trembling are come upon me,
And horror hath overwhelmed me.

And I said, Oh that I had wings like a dove!
Then would I fly away, and be at rest.
Lo, then would I wander far off,
I would lodge in the wilderness.

—Psalm 55:1-7.

How many people are slaves to the mood from which this psalmist suffered! "Fearfulness and trembling" are their habitual attitude toward life. They fear to die and just as much they fear to live; before every vexatious problem, before every opposing obstacle, even before the common tasks and responsibilities of daily living, they stand in dread; and every piece of work is done by them at least three times—in previous worry, in anxious performance, and in regretful retrospect. Such fear *imprisons* the soul. No two men really live in the same world; for while the outward geography may be identical, the real environment of each soul is created by our moods, tempers, and habits of thought. Fear builds a prison about the man, and bars him in with dreads, anxieties, and timid doubts. And the man will live forever in that prison unless faith sets him free. *Faith is the great liberator.* The psalmist who found himself a prisoner of "fearfulness and trembling" obtained his liberty and became a "soul in peace" (v. 18); and the secret of his freedom he revealed in the closing words of his psalm—"But I will trust in Thee." Faith of some sort is the only power that ever sets men free from the bondage of their timidities and dreads. If a man is the slave of fearfulness, there is no substance in his claim to be a man of faith; a man who has vital faith is not habitually fearful. And as Emerson said, "He has not learned the lesson of life who does not every day surmount a fear."

O God, we remember with sadness our want of faith in Thee. What might have been a garden we have turned into a desert by our sin and wilfulness. This beautiful life which Thou hast given us we have wasted in futile worries and vain regrets and empty fears. Instead of opening our eyes to the joy of life, the joy that shines in the leaf, the flower, the face of an innocent child, and rejoicing in it as in a sacrament, we have sunk back into the complainings of our narrow and blinded souls. O deliver us from the bondage of unchastened desires and unwholesome thoughts. Help us to conquer hopeless brooding and faithless reflection, and the impatience of irritable weakness. To this end, increase our faith, O Lord. Fill us

with a completer trust in Thee, and the desire for a more whole-
hearted surrender to Thy will. Then every sorrow will become a joy.
Then shall we say to the mountains that lie heavy on our souls,
"Remove and be cast hence," and they shall remove, and nothing
shall be impossible unto us. Then shall we renew our strength, and
mount up with wings as eagles; we shall run and not be weary; we
shall walk and not faint. We offer this prayer in the name of Jesus
Christ our Lord. Amen.—Samuel McComb.

Eighth Week, Second Day

Not only is it true that fear imprisons while faith liberates; fear *paralyzes* and faith *empowers.* The only attitude in which a man has command of his faculties and is at his best, is the attitude of faith; while fear bewilders the mind and paralyzes the will. The physical effects of fear are deadly; it positively inhibits any useful thinking; and in the spiritual life its results are utterly demoralizing. Fear is the panic of a soul. Consider such an estate as the author of Deuteronomy presents:

And among these nations shalt thou find no ease, and there shall be no rest for the sole of thy foot: but Jehovah will give thee there a trembling heart, and failing of eyes, and pining of soul; and thy life shall hang in doubt before thee; and thou shalt fear night and day, and shalt have no assurance of thy life. In the morning thou shalt say, Would it were even! and at even thou shalt say, Would it were morning! for the fear of thy heart which thou shalt fear, and for the sight of thine eyes which thou shalt see.—Deut. 28: 65-67.

Such a situation oppresses every vital power, and the conquest of such a situation must always be inward before it can be outward; *the man must pass from fear to faith.* Let even a little faith arise in him, and power begins to return. Men fear that they cannot overcome evil habits, that they cannot successfully meet difficult situations, that they cannot hold out in the Christian life, and that great causes cannot be fought through to victory—and the weakness which appalls them is the creation of their own misgiving.

> "Our doubts are traitors,
> And make us lose the good we oft might win,
> By fearing to attempt."

But faith is tonic; the results which follow a change of heart from fear to faith are miraculous; spiritual dwarfs grow to giants and achieve successes that before would have been unbelievable. No verse in Scripture has behind it a greater mass of verifiable experience than: "This is the victory that hath overcome the world, even our faith" (I John 5:4).

Gracious Father, Thou hast invited us, unworthy as we are, to pray for all sorts and conditions of men. . . . We pray for all who are in bondage to fear, unable to face the tasks of life or bear the thought of death with peace and dignity. Free them from the tyranny of these dark dreads. Let the inspiration of a great faith or hope seize their souls, and lift them above their fruitless worry and idle torments, into a region of joy and peace and blessedness. We pray for the victims of evil habits, the slaves of alcohol or morphine, or any other pretended redeemer of the soul from weariness and pain. Great is the power of these degrading temptations; but greater still is the saving energy of Thy Spirit. So let Thy Spirit enter the hearts of these unhappy children of Thine, that their will may be made strong to resist, and that the burning heat of high thoughts may consume the grosser desires of the flesh. We pray for souls bound beneath self-imposed burdens, vexed by miseries of their own making; for the children of melancholy, who have lost their way and grope without a light; for those who do their work with no enthusiasm, and, when night falls, can find no sleep though they search for it as for hidden treasure. Let Thy light pierce through their gloom and shine upon their path. . . .

Unite us to Jesus Christ, Thy perfect Son, in the bonds of a living trust, so that sustained by His example, and sanctified by His Spirit, we may grow more and more into the image of His likeness. These, and all other blessings, we ask in His name and for His sake. Amen.
—Samuel McComb.

Eighth Week, Third Day

There are many situations in life which naturally throw the pall of dread over man's soul. Life is seldom easy, it is often overwhelmingly difficult, and if a man has worry in his temperament, circumstances supply plenty of occasions on which to exercise it. The difference between men lies here: those in whom the fear-attitude is master hold the oppressive trouble so close to the eye that it hides everything else; those whom the faith-attitude dominates hold trouble off and see it in wide perspectives. A copper cent can hide the sun if we hold it close enough to the eye, and a transient difficulty can shut out from a fearful soul all life's large blessings and all the horizons of divine good will. Fear *disheartens* men by concentrating their attention on the unhappy aspects of life; *but faith is the great encourager*. Whittier lived in a generation full of turmoil and trouble, and his own life is a story of prolonged struggle against illness, disappointments, and poverty. But, listen:

> "Yet sometimes glimpses on my sight
> Through present wrong, the eternal right;
> And, step by step, since time began
> I see the steady gain of man."

That is the attitude of faith; it does not deny the evil, but it sees around it, refuses to be obsessed or scared by it, and takes heart from a large view when a small view would be appalling. And history always confirms the large view. Fear may be right for the moment, but in the long run it is a liar; only faith tells the truth.

Be merciful unto me, O God; for man would swallow me up:
All the day long he fighting oppresseth me.
Mine enemies would swallow me up all the day long;
For they are many that fight proudly against me.
What time I am afraid,
I will put my trust in thee.

—Psalm 56:1-3.

Almighty and ever-living God, we draw near unto Thee, believing that Thou art, and that Thou wilt reward all those who diligently seek Thee. We are weak, mortal men, immersed in this world's affairs, buffeted by its sorrows, flung to and fro by its conflicts of right and wrong. We cry for some abiding stay, for some sure and steadfast anchorage. Reveal Thyself to us as the eternal God, as the unfathomable Love that encompasses every spirit Thou hast made, and bears it on, through the light and the darkness alike, to the goal of Thine own perfection. And yet, when Thou speakest to us, we are covered with confusion, for now we remember all the sadness and evil disorder of our lives. Thou hast visited our hearts with ideals fair and beautiful, but alas! we have grown weary in aspiration, and have declined into the sordid aims of our baser selves. Thou hast given us the love of parent and of friend, that we might thereby learn something of Thine own love; yet too often have we despised Thy gift and shut our hearts to all the wonder and the glory. We make confession before Thee of our sin and folly and ignorance. Again and again we have vowed ourselves to Thy service; again and again our languid wills have failed to do Thy Will. We have been seduced by the sweet poison of sin, and even against light and knowledge we have done that which Thou dost abhor, and which in our secret hearts we loathe. And now we almost fear to repent, lest Thou shouldst call us into judgment for a repentance that must needs be repented of. O mighty Saviour of men! be patient with us a little longer. Take us back to Thyself. Without Thee, we are undone; with Thee, we will take fresh heart of hope, and bind ourselves with a more effectual vow, and laying aside every weight and the sin which doth so easily beset us, we will follow Thee whithersoever Thou leadest. Amen.—Samuel McComb.

Eighth Week, Fourth Day

Fear depresses vitality and is a fruitful cause of nervous disorders, with all their disastrous reactions on man's health. Modern investigation has shown beyond any reasonable doubt that while illness comes often by way of the body, it comes also by way of the mind; our moods and tempers have a physical echo, and of all fatal mental states none is so ruinous as fear. It is not strange, therefore, that some people never are well. As Dr. McComb puts it, "Many play at living—they do not really live. They fear the responsibilities, the struggles, the adventures, not without risk, which life offers them. They fear illness. They fear poverty. They fear unhappiness. They fear danger. They fear the passion of sacrifice. They fear even the exaltation of a pure and noble love, until the settlements in money and social prestige have been duly certified. They fear to take a plunge into life's depths. They fear this world, and they fear still more the world beyond the grave." In such a mood no man can possibly be well. Faith, therefore, which drives out fear, has always been a minister of health. The Master's healings, which to the rationalism of a previous generation seemed incredible, in the light of the present knowledge seem inevitable. He had faith and he demanded faith, and wherever the faith-attitude can be set in motion against the fear-attitude and all its morbid brood, the consequences will be physical as well as moral. An outgrown custom of the early Church does not now seem so strange as it did a generation ago:

Is any among you suffering? let him pray. Is any cheerful? let him sing praise. Is any among you sick? let him call for the elders of the church; and let them pray over him, anointing him with oil in the name of the Lord: and the prayer of faith shall save him that is sick, and the Lord shall raise him up; and if he have committed sins, it shall be forgiven him. Confess therefore your sins one to another, and pray one for another, that ye may be healed. The supplication of a righteous man availeth much in its working.—James 5:13-16.

Eternal God, who art above all change and darkness, whose will begat us, and whose all present love doth enfold and continually redeem us, Holy Guest who indwellest, and dost comfort us; we have gathered to worship Thee, and in communion with Thee to find ourselves raised to the light of our life, and the Heaven of our desires.

Pour upon our consciousness the sense of Thy wonderful nearness to us. Reveal to our weakness and distress the power and the grace that are more than sufficient for us. May we see what we are, Thy Spirit-born children linked by nature, love, and choice to Thy mighty being; and may the vision make all fears to fade, and a Divine strength to pulse within.

Enable us to carry out from this place the peace and strength that here we gain, to take into our homes a kinder spirit, a new thoughtfulness; that we may brighten sadness, heal the sick, and make happiness to abound. May we take into our daily tasks and life of labor, a sense of righteousness that shall be as salt to every evil and corrupting influence.

Because we have walked here awhile with Thee, may we be able to walk more patiently with man. Send us forth with love to the fallen, hope for the despairing, strength to impart to the weak and wayward; and carry on through us the work Thou didst commence in Thy Son our Brother Man and Saviour God. Amen.—W. E. Orchard.

Eighth Week, Fifth Day

Fear makes impossible any satisfying joy in life. A man of faith may be deeply joyful even in disastrous circumstances, but a man of fear would be unhappy in heaven. Stevenson sings in "the saddest and the bravest song he ever wrote":

"God, if this were faith? . . .
To go on for ever and fail and go on again,
And be mauled to the earth and arise,
And contend for the shade of a word and a thing not seen with the
      eyes:
With half of a broken hope for a pillow at night
That somehow the right is the right,
And the smooth shall bloom from the rough:
Lord, if that were enough?"

Sad this song may be, but at the heart of it is yet a fierce joy because faith is there. But put a man of fear in luxury and remove from him every visible cause of disquiet and he will still be miserable. The more a man considers these two determinant moods in life, the more he sees that somehow the faith-attitude must be his, if life is to be worth living. Without it life dries up into a Sahara; with it, he comes into a company of the world's glad spirits, who one way or another have felt what the Psalmist sings:

Jehovah is my light and my salvation;
Whom shall I fear?
Jehovah is the strength of my life;
Of whom shall I be afraid?
When evil-doers came upon me to eat up my flesh,
Even mine adversaries and my foes, they stumbled and fell.
Though a host should encamp against me,
My heart shall not fear:
Though war should rise against me,
Even then will I be confident.
One thing have I asked of Jehovah, that will I seek after:
That I may dwell in the house of Jehovah all the days of my life,
To behold the beauty of Jehovah,

And to inquire in his temple.
For in the day of trouble he will keep me secretly in his pavilion:
In the covert of his tabernacle will he hide me;
He will lift me up upon a rock.
And now shall my head be lifted up above mine enemies round
    about me;
And I will offer in his tabernacle sacrifices of joy;
I will sing, yea, I will sing praises unto Jehovah.

                    —Psalm 27:1-6.

Gracious Father! We confess the painful riddle of our being, that, while claiming kinship with Thee, we feel far from Thee. O, what means this strange bewilderment, this never-ending war between our worse and better thoughts? We are Thine by right, yet we have not given ourselves wholly to Thy care. Our hearts know no rest, save in Thee, yet they have sought it in this world's vainglory, which passeth away. We seek to quench our thirst at the cisterns of this earth, but they are broken cisterns, that can hold no water. Lead us to Thy well of life that springeth up eternally. Give us to drink of that spiritual water, of which, if any man drink, he shall never thirst again. We lament our want and poverty before Thee. Open Thou our eyes to behold the unsearchable riches of Thy grace, and increase our faith that we may make them ours. Unite us to Thee in the bonds of will and love and purpose. Out of Thy fulness, which is in Christ, give to each one of us according to his need. Make us wise with His Wisdom; pure with His purity; strong with His strength; that we may rise into the power and glory of the life that is life indeed. Hear our hearts' weak and wandering cries, and when Thou hearest, forgive and bless, for His sake. Amen.—Samuel McComb.

Eighth Week, Sixth Day

No man can serve two masters: for either he will hate the one, and love the other; or else he will hold to one, and despise the other. Ye cannot serve God and mammon. Therefore I say unto you, Be not anxious for your life, what ye shall eat, or what ye shall drink; nor yet for your body, what ye shall put on. Is not the life more than the food, and the body than the raiment? Behold the birds of the heaven, that they sow not, neither do they reap, nor gather into barns; and your heavenly Father feedeth them. Are not ye of much more value than they? And which of you by being anxious can add one cubit unto the measure of his life? And why are ye anxious concerning raiment? Consider the lilies of the field, how they grow; they toil not, neither do they spin: yet I say unto you, that even Solomon in all his glory was not arrayed like one of these.

But if God doth so clothe the grass of the field, which to-day is, and to-morrow is cast into the oven, shall he not much more clothe you, O ye of little faith? Be not therefore anxious, saying, What shall we eat? or, What shall we drink? or, Wherewithal shall we be clothed? For after all these things do the Gentiles seek; for your heavenly Father knoweth that ye have need of all these things. But seek ye first his kingdom, and his righteousness; and all these things shall be added unto you.—Matt. 6:24-33.

The meaning of this passage hinges on the first "therefore." You cannot serve God and selfish gain at the same time, says Jesus; you should choose decisively to serve God; and *therefore* you must not be anxious about yourself. For *anxious fear so concentrates a man's thought on himself that he can serve no one else*. That this is the meaning of this familiar passage is clear also from its conclusion. The real reason for conquering anxious fear is that a man may give himself wholeheartedly to the service of the Kingdom. That fear does spoil usefulness is obvious; a man cannot be fearful for himself and considerate of his fellows. As Stevenson puts it in "Aes Triplex," "The man who has least fear for his own carcass has most time to consider others. That eminent chemist who took his walks abroad in tin shoes and subsisted wholly upon tepid milk had all his work cut out for him in considerate dealings with his own digestion. So soon as prudence has begun to grow up in the brain, like a dismal fungus, it finds its first expression in a paralysis of generous acts." The shame of our fearful living is that it circles about self, is narrowed down to mean solicitudes about our own comfort, and is utterly incapable of serving God or seeking first his Kingdom. Only faith puts folk at leisure from their small anxieties so that they can be servants of a worthy cause. Jesus, therefore, in this passage, is not giving us the impossible injunction not to think about tomorrow; he is stating a truth of experience, that anxious fear for oneself which so draws in the thought that God's great causes are forgotten is a deadly peril in man's life. By faith thrust out the mean and timid solicitudes, is his injunction, that life may be free to put first things first.

*We come to Thee, our Father, that we may more deeply enter
into Thy joy. Thou turnest darkness into day, and mourning into
praise. Thou art our Fortress in temptation, our Shield in remorse,
our Covert in calamity, our Star of Hope in every sorrow. O Lord,
we would know Thy peace, deep, abiding, inexhaustible. When we
seek Thy peace, our weariness is gone, the sense of our imperfection
ceases to discourage us, and our tired souls forget their pain. When,
strengthened and refreshed by Thy goodness, we return to the task
of life, send us forth as servants of Jesus Christ in the service and
redemption of the world. Send us to the hearts without love, to men
and women burdened with heavy cares, to the miserable, the sad,
the broken-hearted. Send us to the children whose heritage has been
a curse, to the poor who doubt Thy Providence, to the sick who
crave for healing and cannot find it, to the fallen for whom no man
cares. May we be ministers of Thy mercy, messengers of Thy helpful
pity, to all who need Thee. By our sympathy, our prayers, our kindness, our gifts, may we make a way for the inflow of Thy love into
needy and loveless lives. And so may we have that love which alone
is the fulfilling of Thy law. Hasten the time when all men shall love
Thee and one another in Thee, when all the barriers that divide us
shall be broken down, and every heart shall be filled with joy and
every tongue with melody. These gracious gifts we ask, in Jesus'
name. Amen.*—Samuel McComb.

Eighth Week, Seventh Day

Fear does not reveal its disastrous consequences to the full until
it colors one's thoughts about the source and destiny of life. Folk
work joyfully at a picture-puzzle so long as they believe that the
puzzle can be put together, that it was meant, completed, to compose a picture, and that their labor is an effort made in reasonable
hope. But if they begin to fear that they are being fooled, that the
puzzle is a hoax and never can be pieced together anywhere by anyone, how swiftly that suspicion will benumb their work! So joyful
living depends on man's conviction that this life is not a hapless
accident, that a good purpose binds it all together, and that our
labor for righteousness is not expended on a futile task without a
worthy outcome. But fear blights all such hope; it whispers what
one pessimist said aloud: "Life is not a tragedy but a farcical melo-
drama, which is the worst kind of play." That fear benumbs worthy

living, kills hope, makes cynical disgust with life a reasonable attitude, and with its frost withers all man's finest aspirations. *Only
faith in God can save men from such fear.* Fear or faith—there is no
dilemma so full of consequence. Fear imprisons, faith liberates; fear
paralyzes, faith empowers; fear disheartens, faith encourages; fear
sickens, faith heals; fear makes useless, faith makes serviceable—and,
most of all, fear puts hopelessness at the heart of life, while faith
rejoices in its God.

Oh give thanks unto Jehovah; for he is good;
For his lovingkindness endureth for ever.
Let Israel now say,
That his lovingkindness endureth for ever.
Let the house of Aaron now say,
That his lovingkindness endureth for ever.
Let them now that fear Jehovah say,
That his lovingkindness endureth for ever.
Out of my distress I called upon Jehovah:
Jehovah answered me and set me in a large place.
Jehovah is on my side; I will not fear:
What can man do unto me?

—Psalm 118:1-6.

*O God, we invoke Thy blessing upon all who need Thee, and who
are groping after Thee, if haply they may find Thee. Be gracious to
those who bear the sins of others, who are vexed by the wrongdoing and selfishness of those near and dear to them, and reveal to
them the glory of their fellowship with the sufferings of Christ.
Brood in tenderness over the hearts of the anxious, the miserable, the
victims of phantasmal fear and morbid imaginings. Redeem from
slavery the men and women who have yielded to degrading habits.
Put Thy Spirit within them, that they may rise up in shame and
sorrow and make confession to Thee, "So brutish was I, and ignorant: I was as a beast before Thee." And then let them have the
glad assurance that Thou art with them, the secret of all good, the
promise and potency of better things. Console with Thy large consolation those who mourn for their loved dead, who count the
empty places and long for the sound of a voice that is still. Inspire
them with the firm conviction that the dead are safe in Thy keeping,
nay, that they are not dead, but live unto Thee. Give to all sorrowing ones a garland for ashes, the oil of joy for mourning, and the*

*garment of praise for the spirit of heaviness. Remember for good all
who are perplexed with the mysteries of existence, and who grieve
because the world is so sad and unintelligible. Teach them that Thy
hand is on the helm of affairs, that Thou dost guide Thine own
world, and canst change every dark cloud into bright sunshine. In
this faith let them rest, and by this faith let them live. These blessings we ask in the name of our Lord and Saviour Jesus Christ.
Amen.*—Samuel McComb.

COMMENT FOR THE WEEK

I

Many people do not find their most perplexing difficulty either in
the realm of trust or of belief, but in a problem which includes both.
They are confused because neither their experience of God nor their
intellectual conviction of the reasonableness of faith is dependable
and steady. Faith comes and goes in them with fluctuating moods
that bring an appalling sense of insecurity. Their religious life is not
stable and consistent; it runs through variant degrees of confidence
and doubt, and its whimsical ups and downs continually baffle them.
To classify some folk as men of faith and some as men of doubt does
not, in the light of this experience, quite tally with the facts. There
are moods of faith and moods of doubt in all of us and rarely does
either kind secure unanimous consent. Were we to decide for irreligion, a minority protest would be vigorously urged in the interests of
faith, and when most assuredly we choose religion, the prayer,
"Lord, I believe, help thou mine unbelief" (Mark 9:24) is still
appropriate. We often seem to be exchanging, as Browning's bishop
says:

> "A life of doubt diversified by faith,
> For one of faith diversified by doubt."

Some hope arises when we observe that this experience which so
perplexes us is fully acknowledged in the Bible. The popular supposition is that when one opens the Scripture he finds himself in a world
of constant and triumphant faith. No low moods and doubts can
here obscure the trust of men; here God is always real, saints sing in
prison or dying see their Lord enthroned in heaven. When one, how-

ever, really knows the Bible, it obviously is no serene record of untroubled faith. It is turbulent with moods and doubt.

Here, to be sure, is the fifteenth chapter of First Corinthians, on
Immortality, but here too is another cry, burdened with all the doubt
man ever felt about eternal life, "That which befalleth the sons of
men befalleth beasts; even one thing befalleth them: as the one
dieth, so dieth the other; yea, they have all one breath; and man
hath no preeminence above the beasts" (Eccl. 3:19). The Scripture
has many exultant passages on divine faithfulness, but Jeremiah's
bitter prayer is not excluded: "Why is my pain perpetual, and my
wound incurable, which refuseth to be healed? Wilt thou indeed be
unto me as a deceitful brook, as waters that fail?" (Jer. 15:18). The
confident texts on prayer are often quoted, but there are cries of
another sort: Job's complaint, "Behold, I go forward, but he is not
there; and backward, but I cannot perceive him" (Job 23:8); Habakkuk's bitterness, "O Jehovah, how long shall I cry, and thou wilt
not hear? I cry unto thee of violence and thou wilt not save" (Hab.
1:2). The Bible is no book of tranquil faith. From the time when
Gideon, in a mood like that of multitudes today, cried, "Oh, my
Lord, if Jehovah is with us, why then is all this befallen us?" (Judges
6:13) to the complaint of the slain saints in the Apocalypse, "How
long, O Master, the holy and true, dost thou not judge and avenge
our blood" (Rev. 6:10), the Bible is acquainted with doubt. It
knows the searching, perplexing, terrifying questions that in all ages
vex men's souls. If the Psalmist, in an exultant mood, sang, "Jehovah
is my shepherd," he also cried, "Jehovah, why casteth thou off my
soul? Why hidest thou thy face from me?" (Psalm 88:14).

No aspect of the Scripture could bring it more warmly into touch
with man's experience than this confession of fluctuating moods. At
least in this the Bible is our book. Great heights are there, that we
know something of. Psalmists sing in adoration, prophets are sure of
God and of his coming victory; apostles pledge in sacrifice the certainty of their belief, and the Master on Transfiguration Mountain
prays until his countenance is radiant. And depths are there, that
modern men know well. Saints cry out against unanswered prayer
and cannot understand how such an evil, wretched world is ruled by
a good God; in their bitter griefs they complain that God has cast
them off, and utterly forgotten and, dismayed, doubt even that a
man's death differs from a dog's. This is our book. For the faith of
many of us, however we insist that we are Christians, is not tranquil,

steady, and serene. It is moody, occasional, spasmodic, with hours of great assurance, and other hours when confidence sags and trust is insecure.

II

Faith so generally is discussed as though it were a creed, accepted once for all and thereafter statically held, that the influence of our moods on faith is not often reckoned with. But the moods of faith are the very pith and marrow of our actual experience. When a Christian congregation recite together their creedal affirmation, "I believe in God," it *sounds* as though they all maintained a solid, constant faith. But when in imagination, one breaks up the congregation and interprets from his knowledge of men's lives what the faith of the individuals actually means, he sees that they believe in God not evenly and constantly, but more or less, sometimes very much, sometimes not confidently at all. Our faith in God is not a static matter such as the recitation of a creed suggests. Some things we do believe in steadily. That two plus two make four, that the summed angles of a triangle make two right angles—of such things we are unwaveringly sure. No moods can shake our confidence; no griefs confuse us, no moral failures quench our certainty. Though the heavens fall, two and two make four! But our faith in God belongs in another realm. It is a vital experience. It involves the whole man, with his chameleon moods, his glowing insights, his exalted hours, and his dejected days when life flows sluggishly and no great thing seems real.

This experience of variable moods in faith does not belong especially to feeble folk, whose ups and downs in their life with God would illustrate their whole irresolute and flimsy living. The great believers sometimes know best this tidal rise and fall of confidence. Elijah one day, with absolute belief in God, defied the hosts of Baal and the next, in desolate reaction, wanted to die. Luther put it with his rugged candor, "Sometimes I believe and sometimes I doubt." John Knox, at liberty to preach, "dings the pulpit into blads" in his confident utterance; but the same Knox recalled that, in the galleys, his soul knew "anger, wrath, and indignation which it conceived against God, calling all his promises in doubt." The Master himself was not a stranger to this experience. He believed in God with unwavering assurance, as one believes in the shining of the sun. But the fact that the sun perpetually shines did not imply that every day was a sunshiny day for him. The clouds came pouring up out of his dark horizons and hid the sun. "Now is my soul troubled; and what shall I say?" (John 12:27). And once the fog drove in, so dense and dark that one would think there never had been any sun at all. "My God, my God, why hast thou forsaken me?" (Matt. 27:46).

This experience of fluctuating moods is too familiar to be denied, too influential to be neglected. There can be no use in hiding it from candid thought behind the recitation of a creedal formula. There may be great use in searching out its meaning. For there are ways in which this common experience, at first vexatious and disquieting, may supply solid ground for Christian confidence.

III

In dealing with these variant moods of faith we are not left without an instrument. We have *the sense of value*. We discern not only the *existence* of things, but their *worth* as well. When, therefore, a man has recognized his moods as facts, he has not said all that he can say about them. Upon no objects of experience can the sense of value be used with so much certainty as upon our moods. *We know our best hours when they come.* The lapidary, with unerring skill, learns to distinguish a real diamond from a false, but his knowledge is external and contingent, compared with the inward and authoritative certainty with which we know our best hours from our worst. Our great moods carry with them the authentic marks of their superiority.

Experience readily confirms this truth. We all have, for example, *cynical and sordid moods.* At such times, only the appetites of physical life seem much to matter; only the things that minister to common comfort greatly count. When Sydney Smith, the English cleric, writes, "I feel an ungovernable interest in my horses, my pigs, and my plants. But I am forced and always was forced to task myself up to an interest in any higher objects," most of us can understand his mood. We grow obtuse at times to all that in our better moods had thrilled us most. Nature suffers in our eyes; great books seem dull; causes that once we served with zest lose interest, and personal relationships grow pale and tame. From such mere dullness we easily drift down to cynicism. Music once had stirred the depths, but now our spirits tally with the scoffer's jest, "What are you crying about with your Wagner and your Brahms? It is only horsehair scraping on catgut." Man's most holy things may lose their grandeur and become a butt of ridicule. When the mood of Aristophanes is on, we too may hoist serious Socrates among the clouds, and set him talking moonshine while the cynical look on and laugh. The spirit that "sits in the seat of the scornful" is an ancient malady.

But every man is thoroughly aware that these are not his best moods. From such depleted attitudes we come to worthier hours; *real life* arrives again. Nature and art become imperatively beautiful; moral causes seem worth sacrifice, and before man's highest life, revealed in character, ideal, and faith, we stand in reverence. These are our great hours, when spiritual values take the throne, when all else dons livery to serve them, and we find it easy to believe in God.

Again, we have *crushed and rebellious moods*. We may have been Christians for many years; yet when disaster, long delayed, at last descends, and our dreams are wrecked, we *do* rebel. Complaint rises hot within us. Joseph Parker, preacher at the City Temple, London, at the age of sixty-eight could write that he had never had a doubt. Neither the goodness of God nor the divinity of Christ, nor anything essential to his Christian faith had he ever questioned. But within a year an experience had fallen of which he wrote: "In that dark hour I became almost an atheist. For God had set his foot upon my prayers and treated my petitions with contempt. If I had seen a dog in such agony as mine, I would have pitied and helped the dumb beast; yet God spat upon me and cast me out as an offense—out into the waste wilderness and the night black and starless." No new philosophy had so shaken the faith of this long unquestioning believer. But his wife had died and he was in a heartbroken mood that all his arguments, so often used on others, could not penetrate. He believed in God as one believes in the sun when he has lived six months in the polar night and has not seen it.

These heartbroken moods, however, are not our best. Out of rebellious grief we lift our eyes in time to see how other men have borne their sorrows off and built them into character. We see great lives shine out from suffering, like Rembrandt's radiant faces from dark backgrounds. We see that all the virtues which we most admire —constancy, patience, fortitude—are impossible without stern settings, and that in time of trouble they find their aptest opportunity, their noblest chance. We rise into a new mood, grow resolute not to be crushed, but, as though there were moral purpose in man's trials,

to be hallowed, deepened, purified. The meaning of Samuel Rutherford's old saying dawns upon us, "When I am in the cellar of affliction, I reach out my hand for the king's wine." And folk, seeing us,
it may be, take heart and are assured that God is real, since he can
make a man bear off his trial like that and grow the finer for it.
These are our great hours too, when the rains descend, and the
winds blow, and the floods come, and beat upon our house, and it is
founded on a rock!

Once more, we have hours of *discouragement about the world.*
The more we have cared for moral causes and invested life in their
advancement, the more we are desolate when they seem to fail. Some
rising tide in which we trusted turns to ebb again, injustice wins its
victories, the people listen to demagogues and not to statesmen,
social causes essential to human weal are balked, wars come and
undo the hopes of centuries. Who does not sometimes fall into the
Slough of Despond? Cavour, disheartened about Italy, went to his
room to kill himself. John Knox, dismayed about Scotland, in a
pathetic prayer entitled, "John Knox with deliberate mind to his
God," wrote, "Now, Lord put an end to my misery." We generally
think of Luther in that intrepid hour when he faced Charles V at
Worms; but he had times as well when he was sick with disappointment. "Old, decrepit, lazy, worn out, cold, and now one-eyed," so
runs a letter, "I write, my Jacob, I who hoped there might at length
be granted to me, already dead, a well-earned rest." During the
Great War, this mood of discouragement has grown familiar. Many
can understand what Robert Louis Stevenson meant when he wrote,
of the Franco-Prussian war, "In that year, cannon were roaring for
days together on French battlefields, and I would sit in my isle (I
call it mine after the use of lovers) and think upon the war, and the
pain of men's wounds, and the weariness of their marching . . . It
was something so distressing, so instant, that I lay in the heather on
the top of the island, with my face hid, kicking my heels for agony."

But these dismayed hours are not our best. As Bunyan put it, even
Giant Despair has fainting fits on sunshiny days. In moods of clearer
insight we perceive out of how many Egypts, through how many
round-about wilderness journeys, God has led his people to how
many Promised Lands. The Exodus was not a failure, although the
Hebrews, disheartened, thought it was and even Moses had his dubious hours; the mission of Israel did not come to an ignoble end in
the Exile, although multitudes gave up their faith because of it and

only prophets dared believe the hopeful truth. The crucifixion did not mean the Gospel's end, as the disciples thought, nor did Paul, imprisoned, lose his ministry. *Nothing in history is more assured than this, that only men of faith have known the truth.* And in hours of vision when this fact shines clear we rise to be our better selves again. What a clear ascent the race has made when wide horizons are taken into view! What endless possibilities must lie ahead! What ample reasons we possess to thrust despair aside, and to go out to play our part in the forward movement of the plan of God!

> "Dreamer of dreams? we take the taunt with gladness,
>   Knowing that God beyond the years you see,
> Has wrought the dreams that count with you for madness
>   Into the texture of the world to be."

These are our better hours.

IV

Such sordid, cynical, crushed, rebellious, and discouraged moods we suffer, but we have hours of insight, too, when we are at our best. And as we face this ebb and flow of confidence, which at the first vexatiously perplexed our faith, an arresting truth is clear. The creed of irreligion, to which men are tempted to resign their minds, is simply the *intellectual formulation of what is implied in our less noble hours.* Take what man's cynical, sordid, crushed, rebellious, and discouraged moods imply, and set it in a formal statement of life's meaning, and the result is the creed of irreligion. But take man's best hours, when the highest seems the realest, when even sorrows cannot crush his soul, and when the world is still the battle-field of God for men, and formulate what these hours imply, and the result is the central affirmations of religious faith. Even Renan is sure that "man is most religious in his best moments." Of this high interpretation our variant moods are susceptible, that *we know our best hours when they come, and the faith implied in them is essential Christianity.* As Browning sings it:

> "Faith is my waking life:
> One sleeps, indeed, and dreams at intervals,
> We know, but waking's the main point with us."

This fact which we so have come upon is a powerful consideration in favor of religion's truth. *Are we to trust for our guidance the testimony of our worse or better hours?* We have low moods; so, too, we have cellars in our houses. But we do not *live* there; we live upstairs! It is not unnatural to have irreligious moods. There may be hours when the eternal Energy from which this universe has come seems to be playing solitaire for fun. It shuffles the stars and planets to see what may chance from their combinations, and careless of the consequence, from everlasting to everlasting it shuffles and plays, and shuffles and plays again. But these are not our best hours. We may have moods when the universe seems to us, as Carlyle's figure pictures it, "as if the heavens and the earth were but boundless jaws of a devouring monster, wherein, I, palpitating, lay waiting to be devoured," but we are inwardly ashamed of times like that. Man comes to this brutal universe of irreligion by way of his ignoble moods. When he lifts up his soul in his great hours of love, of insight, and of devotion, life never looks to him as irreligion pictures it; it never has so looked to him and it never will!

In his best hours man always suspects that the Eternal must be akin to what is best in us, that our ideals are born from above, have there their source and destiny, that the Eternal Purpose reigns and yet shall justify the struggle of the ages, and that in anyone who is the best we know, we see most clearly what the Eternal is and means. That goodness is deeper than evil, that spirit is more than flesh, that life is lord of death, that love is the source of all—such convictions come naturally to us when we are at our best. When one examines such affirmations, he perceives that Christianity in its essential faiths is the expression of our finest hours. This is the source whence Christianity has come; it is man's best become articulate. Some used to say that Christian faith had been foisted on mankind by priests. Christian faith has no more artificially been foisted upon human life than the full blown rose is foisted on the bud. Christianity springs up out of man's best life; it is the utterance of his transcendent moods; *it is man believing in the validity of his own noblest days.*

Christianity, therefore, at its heart can never fail. Its theologies may come and go, its institutions rise and fall, its rituals have their dawn, their zenith, and their decline, but one persistent force goes on and will go on. *The Gospel is saying to man what man at his best is saying to himself.* Christ has a tremendous ally in human life— our noblest hours. They are all upon his side. What *he* says, *they* rise to cry "Amen" to. When we are most truly ourselves we are nearest to him. Antagonistic philosophies, therefore, may spring up to assail the Gospel's influence, and seem to triumph, and fall at last and be forgotten. Still Christ will go on speaking. Nothing can tear him from his spiritual influence over men. *In every generation he has man's noblest hours for his ally.*

v

In the fact to which our study of man's variant moods has brought us we have not only a confirming consideration in favor of religion's truth, but an *explanation of some people's unbelief.* They live habitually in their low moods; they inhabit spiritual cellars. We are accustomed to say that some friend would be saved from his ignoble attitudes by a vital religious faith; but it is also true that his persistent clinging to ignoble attitudes may be the factor that makes religious faith impossible. According to Dickens's "Tale of Two Cities" a prisoner in the Bastille, who had lived in a cell and cobbled shoes for many years, became so enamored of the narrow walls, the darkness, the task's monotony, that, when liberated, he built a cell at the center of his English home, and on days when the skies were clear and birds were singing, the tap of his cobbler's hammer in the dark could still be heard. So men, by an habitual residence in imprisoning moods, render themselves incapable of loving the wide horizons, the great faiths and hopes of religion. They do not merely make excursions of transient emotion into morose hours and, like men that find that the road is running into malarial swamps, turn swiftly to the hills. They dwell in their moroseness; they *choose* it, and often obstinately resist deliverance.

The common moods that thus incapacitate the soul for faith are easily seen in any man's experience. There are *sullen* tempers when we are churlish and want so to be. There are *stupid* tempers, when our soul is too negligent to care, too dull to ask for what only aspiring minds can crave or find. There are *bored* moods when we feel about all life what Malachi's people felt about worship, "Behold, what a weariness is it!" (Mal. 1:13); *rebellious* moods when, like Jonah, deprived of a comfort he desired, we cry, "I do well to be angry, even unto death" (Jonah 4:9); *suspicious* moods, when we mistrust everyone, and even of some righteous Job hear Satan's insinuating sneer, "Does Job fear God for nought?" (Job 1:9). No man is altogether strange to *frivolous* hours, when those thoughts are lost which must be handled seriously if at all, and *wilful* hours, when some private desire assumes the center of the stage and angrily resents another voice than his. To say that one who habitually harbors such moods cannot know God is only a portion of the truth; such a man cannot know anything worth knowing. He can know neither fine friends nor great books; he cannot appreciate beautiful music or sublime scenery; he is lost to the deepest loves of family and to every noble enthusiasm for human help. Athwart the knowledge of these most gracious and necessary things stand our obtuse, ignoble moods. The sullen, stupid, bored, rebellious, suspicious, frivolous, or wilful tempers, made into a spiritual residence, are the most deadly prison of the soul. Of course one who dwells there has no confidence in God. Lord Shaftesbury, the English philanthropist, made too sweeping a statement about this, but one can see the basis for his judgment: "Nothing beside ill-humor, either natural or forced, can bring a man to think seriously that the world is governed by any devilish or malicious power. I very much question whether anything beside ill-humor can be the cause of atheism." At least one may be sure that where ill-humor habitually reigns, vital faith in God is made impossible.

After full acknowledgment, therefore, of the momentous intellectual problems of belief, we must add that there is a *moral qualification for faith in God.* So great a matter is not achieved by any sort of person, with any kind of habitual moods and tempers. There are views which cellar windows do not afford; one must have balconies to see them. When Jesus said that the pure in heart are blessed because they see God, he was not thinking merely, perhaps not chiefly, of sexual impurity as hindering vision. He was pleading for a heart cleansed of all such perverse, morose, and wayward moods as shut the blinds on the soul's windows. He knew that men could not easily escape the sense of God's reality if they kept their vision clear. On elevated days we naturally think of Spirit as real, and see ourselves as expressions of spiritual purpose, our lives as servants of a spiritual cause. When one habitually dwells in these finer moods, he cannot tolerate a world where his Best is a transient accident. *He must have God, for faith in God is the supreme assertion of the reality and eternity of man's Best.* Any man who habitually lives in his finest moods will not easily escape the penetrating sense of God's reality.

VI

The certainty with which we tend to be most deeply religious in our best hours is clear when we consider that a man does practically believe in the things which he counts of highest worth. Lotze, the philosopher, even says that "Faith *is* the feeling that is appreciative of value." It is conceivable that one might be so constituted that without any sense of value he could study facts, as a deaf man might observe a symphony. The sound-waves such a man could mechanically measure; he could analyze the motions of the players and note the reactions of the crowd, but he would hear no music. He would not suffuse the whole performance with his musical appreciations; he would neither like it nor condemn. Man might be so constituted as to face facts without feeling, but he is not. Facts never stand in our experience thus barren and unappreciated—mere neutral *things* that mean nothing and have no value. The botanist in us may analyze the flowers, but the poet in us estimates them. The penologist in us may take the Bertillon measurements of a boy, but the father in us best can tell how much, in spite of all his sin, that boy is worth. This power to estimate life's *values* is the fountain from which spring our music, painting, and literature, our ideals and loves and purposes, our morals and religion. Without it no man can live in the real world at all.

If we would know, therefore, in what, at our highest altitudes, we tend to believe, we should ask *what it is that we value most, when we rise toward our best.* In our lowest hours what sordid, mercenary, beastly things men may prize each heart knows well. But ever as we approach our best the things that are worth most to us become elevated and refined. Our better moods open our eyes to a world where character is of more worth than all the rest beside, and through which moral purpose runs, to be served with sacrifice. We become aware of spiritual values in behalf of which at need physical existence must be willingly laid down; and words like honor, love, fidelity, and service in our hours of insight have halos over them that poorer moods cannot discern. Man at his best, that is to say, *believes in* an invisible world of spiritual values, and he furnishes the final proof of his faith's reality by sacrificing to it all lesser things. The good, the true, the beautiful command him in his finer hours, and at their beck and call he lays down wealth and ease and earthly hopes to be their servant. Men really *do believe in* the things for which they sacrifice and die.

In no more searching way can a man's faith be described than *in terms of the objects which thus he values most.* Wherever men find some consuming aim that is for them so supreme in worth that they sacrifice all else to win it, we speak of their attitude as a religion. The "religion of science" describes the absolute devotion of investigators to scientific research as the highest good; the "religion of art" describes the consuming passion with which some value beauty. When we say of one that "money is his God" we mean that he estimates it as life's highest treasure, and when with Paul we speak of others, "whose god is the belly" (Phil. 3:19), we mean men whose sensual life is to them the thing worth most. *What men believe in, therefore, is most deeply seen not by any opinions which they profess, but by the things they prize.* Faith, as Ruskin said, is "that by which men act while they live; not that which they talk of when they die." Many a man uses pious affirmations of Christian faith, but it is easy to observe from his life that what he really believes in is money. Where a man's treasure is, as Jesus said, his heart is, and there his faith is, too.

Is there any doubt, then, what we most believe in when we are at our best? While in our lower altitudes it may be easy to believe that the physical is the ultimately real, in our upper altitudes we so value the spiritual world, that we tend with undeniable conviction to feel sure that it must be causal and eternal. Materialism is man's "night-view" of his life; but the "day-view" is religion. Tyndall the scientist was regarded by the Christians of his generation as the enemy of almost everything that they held dear. Let him, then, be witness for the truth which we have stated. "I have noticed," he said, speaking of materialism, "during years of self-observation, that it is not in hours of clearness and vigor that this doctrine commends itself to my mind."

The challenge, therefore, presented to every one of us by Christian faith is ultimately this: *Shall I believe the testimony of my better hours or of my worse?* Many who deny the central affirmations of the Gospel put the object of their denial far away from them as though it were an external thing; they say that they deny the creed or the Bible or the doctrine about God. Such a description of a man's rejection of religious faith is utterly inadequate—the real object of his denial is inward. One may, indeed, discredit forms of doctrine and either be unsure about or altogether disbelieve many things that Christians hold, but when one makes a clean sweep of religion and banishes the central faiths of Christianity *he is denying the testimony of his own finest days.* From such rejection of faith one need not appeal to creed nor Bible, nor to anything that anybody ever said. Let the challenge strike inward to the man's own heart. From his denial of religious faith we may appeal to the hours that he has known and yet will know again, when the road rose under his feet and from a height he looked on wide horizons and knew that he was at his best. To those hours of clear insight, of keen thought, of love and great devotion, when he knew that the spiritual is the real and the eternal, we may appeal. They were his best. He *knows* that they were his best. And as long as humanity lives upon the earth this conviction must underlie great living—that *we will not deny the validity of our own best hours.*

CHAPTER IX

Faith in the Earnest God

DAILY READINGS

Throughout our studies we have been thinking of the effect of faith on the one who exercises it. As an introduction to this week's thought on the earnestness of God, let us approach the effect of faith from another angle. Faith has enormous influence on the one in whom it is reposed; not only the believer but the one in whom he believes is affected by his faith.

Ninth Week, First Day

I commend unto you Phœbe our sister, who is a servant of the church that is at Cenchreæ: that ye receive her in the Lord, worthily of the saints, and that ye assist her in whatsoever matter she may have need of you: for she herself also hath been a helper of many, and of mine own self.

Salute Prisca and Aquila my fellow-workers in Christ Jesus, who for my life laid down their own necks; unto whom not only I give thanks, but also all the churches of the Gentiles: and salute the church that is in their house. Salute Epænetus my beloved, who is the first-fruits of Asia unto Christ. Salute Mary, who bestowed much labor on you. Salute Andronicus and Junias, my kinsmen, and my fellow-prisoners, who are of note among the apostles, who also have been in Christ before me. Salute Ampliatus my beloved in the Lord.—Rom. 16:1-8.

This series of personal commendations is only the beginning of the last chapter of Paul's letter to the Romans. All the way through one hears the individual names of Paul's friends and fellow-laborers, with his discriminating and hearty praise of each. It is clear that he has faith in these men and women; he believes in them and relies on them. Consider the effect on them that Paul's confidence in their Christian fidelity would naturally have. There is no motive much more stirring than the consciousness that somebody believes in us, is trusting and counting on us. Whatever is fine and noble in human life responds to that appeal. Soldiers who feel that their country is relying upon their fidelity, children who are conscious that their parents believe in them, friends who are heartened by the assurance that some folk completely trust them—how much of the best in all of us has come because we have been the objects of somebody's faith! A Connecticut volunteer in the American Revolution has written that George Washington once paused for a moment in front of his company and said simply, "I am counting on you men from Connecticut." And the recruit clasped his musket in his arms and wept with the devotion which Washington's confidence evoked. Would not the sixteenth chapter of Romans have a similar effect on those who read it?

O Thou loving and tender Father in heaven, we confess before Thee, in sorrow, how hard and unsympathetic are our hearts; how often we have sinned against our neighbors by want of compassion and tenderness; how often we have felt no true pity for their trials and sorrows, and have neglected to comfort, help, and visit them. O Father, forgive this our sin, and lay it not to our charge. Give us grace ever to alleviate the crosses and difficulties of those around us, and never to add to them; teach us to be consolers in sorrow, to take thought for the stranger, the widow, and the orphan; let our charity show itself not in words only, but in deed and truth. Teach us to judge as Thou dost, with forbearance, with much pity and indulgence; and help us to avoid all unloving judgment of others; for the sake of Jesus Christ Thy Son, who loved us and gave Himself for us. Amen.—Johann Arndt, 1555.

Ninth Week, Second Day

And it came to pass in these days, that he went out into the mountain to pray; and he continued all night in prayer to God. And when it was day, he called his disciples; and he chose from them twelve, whom also he named apostles: Simon, whom he also

named Peter, and Andrew his brother, and James and John, and
Philip and Bartholomew, and Matthew and Thomas, and James
the son of Alphæus, and Simon who was called the Zealot, and
Judas the son of James, and Judas Iscariot, who became a traitor.
—Luke 6:12-16.

The power that comes to men when someone believes in them
must have come to these disciples whom Jesus trusted with his work.
We often note the power that was theirs through their faith in
Christ; consider today the inspiration that came from Christ's faith
in them. He picked them out, commissioned them, relied on them,
and believed in their ability with God's help to carry his work to a
successful issue. All that is most distinctive and memorable in their
character came from their response to that divine trust. How they
must have encouraged themselves in times of failure and disheartenment by saying: He believes in us; even though we are ignorant and
sinful, he believes in us; he has trusted his work to us, and for all our
inability he has faith that we can carry it to triumph! Their faith in
themselves and what they could do with God's help must have been
almost altogether a reflex of his faith in them. Our contention,
therefore, that faith is the dynamic of life has now a new confirmation: *the faith that lifts and motives life is not simply our faith in
the Divine, but the faith of the Divine in us.* One of the most glorious results of believing in God is that a man can press on to the
further confidence that God believes in us. If he did not, he would
never have made us. The very fact that we are here means that he
does believe in us, in our possibilities of growth, in our capacities of
service, in what he can do in and for and through us before he is
done. Man's faith in God and God's faith in man together make an
unequalled motive for great living. Yet there is always a sad appen-
dix to every list of trusted men, with somebody's blighted name:
"Judas Iscariot, who became a traitor."

*Loving Father, our hearts are moved to gratitude and trust when
we look up to Thee. We rejoice that through our fleeting days there
runs Thy gracious purpose. We praise Thee that we are not the
creatures of chance, nor the victims of iron fate, but that out from
Thee we have come and into Thy bosom we shall return. We would
not, even if we could, escape Thee. Thou alone art good, and to
escape from Thee is to fall into infinite evil. Thy hand is upon us*

*moving us on to some far-off spiritual event, where the meaning and
the mystery of life shall be made plain and Thy glory shall be revealed. Look in pity upon our ignorance and childishness. Forgive
us our small understanding of Thy purpose of good concerning us.
Be not angry with us, but draw us from the things of this world
which cannot satisfy our foolish hearts. Fill us with Thyself, that we
may no longer be a burden to ourselves. So glorify the face of goodness that evil shall have no more dominion over us. Amen.*—Samuel
McComb.

Ninth Week, Third Day

The fact that God has faith in us is not alone a source of comfort;
it presents a stirring challenge. It means that he is in earnest about
achieving his great purposes in human life and that he is counting
upon us to help. He has set his heart on aims, about which he cares,
and to whose achievement he is calling us; he is confident that with
him we can work out, if we will, loftier character and a better world.
Let us consider some of the purposes which God is counting on us,
in fellowship with him, to achieve. The prophet Micah, in a brief
but perfect drama, gives one clue. First the Lord summons his people
to a trial, with the eternal mountains for judges:

**Hear ye now what Jehovah saith: Arise, contend thou before the
mountains, and let the hills hear thy voice. Hear, O ye mountains,
Jehovah's controversy, and ye enduring foundations of the earth;
for Jehovah hath a controversy with his people, and he will contend
with Israel.—Micah 6:1, 2.**

Then, the Lord presents his case:

**O my people, what have I done unto thee? and wherein have I
wearied thee? testify against me. For I brought thee up out of the
land of Egypt, and redeemed thee out of the house of bondage; and
I sent before thee Moses, Aaron, and Miriam. O my people, remember now what Balak king of Moab devised, and what Balaam the
son of Beor answered him; remember from Shittim unto Gilgal,
that ye may know the righteous acts of Jehovah.—Micah 6:3-5.**

Then the people put in their hesitant, questioning plea.

**Wherewith shall I come before Jehovah, and bow myself before
the high God? shall I come before him with burnt-offerings, with**

calves a year old? will Jehovah be pleased with thousands of rams, or with ten thousands of rivers of oil? shall I give my first-born for my transgression, the fruit of my body for the sin of my soul?—Micah 6:6, 7.

Then the mountains pronounce judgment:

He hath showed thee, O man, what is good; and what doth Jehovah require of thee, but to do justly, and to love kindness, and to walk humbly with thy God?—Micah 6:8.

God, then, is in earnest about *just, kind, and humble character.* He believes in it as a possibility; he sees the making of it now in human hearts; he is pledged to further and establish it with all his power; and he is counting on us for loyal cooperation with all our powers of choice. Vital faith means a transforming partnership with a God who is in earnest about character.

O Thou who art the Father of that Son which hast awakened us and yet urgeth us out of the sleep of our sins, and exhorteth us that we become Thine, to Thee, Lord, we pray, who art the supreme Truth, for all truth that is, is from Thee. Thee we implore, O Lord, who art the highest Wisdom, through Thee are wise, all those that are so. Thou art the supreme Joy, and from Thee all have become happy that are so. Thou art the highest Good and from Thee all beauty springs. Thou art the intellectual Light, and from Thee man derives his understanding. To Thee, O God, we call and speak. Hear us, O Lord for Thou art our God and our Lord, our Father and our Creator, our Ruler and our Hope, our Wealth and our Honor, our Home, our Country, our Salvation, and our Life; hear, hear us, O Lord. Few of Thy servants comprehend Thee, but at least we love Thee—yea, love Thee above all other things. We seek Thee, we follow Thee, we are ready to serve Thee; under Thy power we desire to abide, for Thou art the Sovereign of all. We pray Thee to command us as Thou wilt; through Jesus Christ Thy Son our Lord. Amen.—King Alfred, 849.

Ninth Week, Fourth Day

God also is in earnest about *social righteousness.*

I hate, I despise your feasts, and I will take no delight in your solemn assemblies. Yea, though ye offer me your burnt-offerings and meal-offerings, I will not accept them; neither will I regard the peace-offerings of your fat beasts. Take thou away from me the noise of thy songs; for I will not hear the melody of thy viols. But let justice roll down as waters, and righteousness as a mighty stream.—Amos 5:21-24.

Anyone who cares about character must care about social conditions, for every unfair economic situation, every social evil left to run its course means ruin to character. And the God of the Bible, because he cares supremely for personal life at its best, is zealously in earnest about social justice; his prophets blazed with indignation at all inequity, and his Son made the coming Kingdom, when God's will would be done on earth, the center of his message. To fellowship with this earnest purpose of God we all are summoned; God believes in the glorious possibilities of life on earth; he is counting on us to put away the sins that hold the Kingdom back and to fight the abuses that crush character in men. To believe in God, therefore— the God who is fighting his way with his children up through ignorance, brutality, and selfishness to "new heavens and a new earth wherein dwelleth righteousness"—is no weakly comfortable blessing. It means joining a moral war; it means devotion, sacrifice; its spirit is the Cross and its motive an undiscourageable faith. And our underlying assurance that this war for a better world can be won is not simply our belief that it can be done, but *our faith that God is, and that he believes that it can be done.* When we pray we say, "Thy Kingdom come," and we are full of hope about the long, sacrificial struggle, for the purpose behind and through it all is first of all God's. Our earnestness is but an echo of his.

O Thou Eternal One, we adore Thee who in all ages hast been the great companion and teacher of mankind; for Thou hast lifted our race from the depths, and hast made us to share in Thy conscious intelligence and Thy will that makes for righteousness and love. Thou alone art our Redeemer, for Thy lifting arms were about us and Thy persistent voice was in our hearts as we slowly climbed up from savage darkness and cruelty. Thou knowest how often we have resisted Thee and loved the easy ways of sin rather than the toilsome gain of self-control and the divine irritation of Thy truth. . . .

We pray Thee for those who amid all the knowledge of our day

*are still without knowledge; for those who hear not the sighs of the
children that toil, nor the sobs of such as are wounded because
others have made haste to be rich; for those who have never felt the
hot tears of the mothers of the poor that struggle vainly against
poverty and vice. Arouse them, we beseech Thee, from their selfish
comfort and grant them the grace of social repentance. Smite us all
with the conviction that for us ignorance is sin, and that we are
indeed our brother's keeper if our own hand has helped to lay him
low. Though increase of knowledge bring increase of sorrow, may
we turn without flinching to the light and offer ourselves as instruments of Thy spirit in bringing order and beauty out of disorder and
darkness. Amen.*—Walter Rauschenbusch.

Ninth Week, Fifth Day

The thought which we have been pursuing leads us to a truth of
major importance: if God is thus in earnest, believing in man's possibilities and laboring for them, then he cannot be known by anyone
who does not share his purpose and his labor. *Action is a road to
knowledge and some things never can be known without it.* If one
would know the business world, he must be an active business man;
no amount of abstract study and speculation can take the place of
vital participation in business struggle. The way to understand any
movement or enterprise is to go into it, share its enthusiasms and
hopes, labor sacrificially for its success, bear its defeats as though
they were our own, and rejoice in its achievements as though nothing so much mattered to our happiness. Such knowledge is thorough
and vital; when one who so has learned what war is, or the missionary enterprise, or the fight against the liquor traffic, stands up to
speak, a merely theoretical student of these movements sounds unreal and tame. If therefore God is earnest Purpose, with aims in
which he calls us to share, no one can thoroughly know him merely
by *thinking;* he must know him by *acting.*

**But he that doeth the truth cometh to the light, that his works
may be made manifest, that they have been wrought in God.—
John 3:21.**

**Jesus therefore answered them, and said, My teaching is not
mine, but his that sent me. If any man willeth to do his will he
shall know of the teaching, whether it is of God, or whether I speak
from myself.—John 7:16, 17.**

Many people endeavor to reach a satisfactory knowledge of God by clarifying their thought and working out a rational philosophy. But, by such intellectual means alone, they could not gain satisfactory knowledge of so familiar a thing as home life. To know home life one elemental act is essential: get into a home and share its problems, its satisfactions, and its hopes. So the most adequate philosophy by itself can bring no satisfactory knowledge of God; only by working with God, sharing his purposes for the world, sacrificially laboring for the aims he has at heart can men know him.

Eternal God, who hast formed us, and designed us for companionship with Thee; who hast called us to walk with Thee and be not afraid; forgive us, we pray Thee, if craven fear, unworthy thought, or hidden sin has prompted us to hide from Thee. Remove the suspicion which regards Thy service as an intrusion on our time and an interference with our daily task. Shew to us the life that serves Thee in the quiet discharge of each day's duty, that ennobles all our toil by doing it as unto Thee. We ask for no far-off vision which shall set us dreaming while opportunities around slip by; for no enchantment which shall make our hands to slack and our spirits to sleep, but for the vision of Thyself in common things for every day; that we may find a Divine calling in the claims of life, and see a heavenly reward in work well done. We ask Thee not to lift us out of life, but to prove Thy power within it; not for tasks more suited to our strength, but for strength more suited to our tasks. Give to us the vision that moves, the strength that endures, the grace of Jesus Christ, who wore our flesh like a monarch's robe and walked our earthly life like a conqueror in triumph. Amen.—W. E. Orchard.

Ninth Week, Sixth Day

Because action with God is essential to any satisfying knowledge of him, action is one of the great resolvers of doubt. Many minds, endeavoring to think through the mystifying problems of God's providence, find themselves in a clueless labyrinth. The more they think the more entangled and confused their minds become. Their thoughts strike a fatal circle, like wanderers lost in the woods, and return upon their course, baffled and disheartened. To such perplexed minds the best advice often is: Cease your futile thinking and go to work. Let action take the place of speculation. Break the fatal round of circular thought that never will arrive, and go out to act on the basis of what little you do believe. Your mind like a dammed stream is growing stagnant; set it running to some useful purpose, if only to turn mill-wheels, and trust that activity will bring it cleansing in due time. Horace Bushnell, the great preacher, while a skeptical tutor at Yale, was disturbed because so many students were unsettled by his disbelief. In the midst of a revival he said that like a great snag he caught and stopped the newly launched boats as fast as they came down. Unable to think his way out of his intellectual perplexity, he faced one night this arresting question: "What is the use of my trying to get further knowledge, so long as I do not cheerfully yield to what I already know?" And kneeling he prayed after this fashion: "O God, I believe there is an eternal difference between right and wrong, and I hereby give myself up to do the right and to refrain from the wrong. I believe that Thou dost exist, and if Thou canst hear my cry and wilt reveal Thyself to me, I pledge myself to do Thy will, and I make this pledge fully, freely, and forever." What wonder that in time the light broke and that Bushnell became a great prophet of the faith!

Even Paul, finishing his laborious discussion of God's providence toward Israel, acknowledges his baffled thought:

O the depth of the riches both of the wisdom and the knowledge of God! how unsearchable are his judgments, and his ways past tracing out! For who hath known the mind of the Lord? or who hath been his counsellor? or who hath first given to him, and it shall be recompensed unto him again? For of him, and through him, and unto him, are all things. To him be the glory for ever. Amen.—Rom. 11:33-36.

And then, as if he turned from philosophy to action with gratitude, he begins the twelfth chapter:

I beseech you therefore, brethren, by the mercies of God, to present your bodies a living sacrifice, holy, acceptable to God, which is your spiritual service. And be not fashioned according to this world: but be ye transformed by the renewing of your mind, that ye may prove what is the good and acceptable and perfect will of God.—Rom. 12:1, 2.

O God, we thank Thee for the sweet refreshment of sleep and for the glory and vigor of the new day. As we set our faces once more

*toward our daily work, we pray Thee for the strength sufficient for
our tasks. May Christ's spirit of duty and service ennoble all we do.
Uphold us by the consciousness that our work is useful work and a
blessing to all. If there has been anything in our work harmful to
others and dishonorable to ourselves, reveal it to our inner eye with
such clearness that we shall hate it and put it away, though it be at
a loss to ourselves. When we work with others, help us to regard
them, not as servants to our will, but as brothers equal to us in
human dignity, and equally worthy of their full reward. May there
be nothing in this day's work of which we shall be ashamed when
the sun has set, nor in the eventide of our life when our task is done
and we go to our long home to meet Thy face. Amen.*—Walter
Rauschenbusch.

Ninth Week, Seventh Day

Then shall the King say unto them on his right hand, Come, ye
blessed of my Father, inherit the kingdom prepared for you from
the foundation of the world: for I was hungry, and ye gave me to
eat; I was thirsty, and ye gave me drink; I was a stranger, and ye
took me in; naked, and ye clothed me; I was sick, and ye visited
me; I was in prison, and ye came unto me. Then shall the righteous
answer him, saying, Lord, when saw we thee hungry, and fed thee?
or athirst, and gave thee drink? And when saw we thee a stranger,
and took thee in? or naked, and clothed thee? And when saw we
thee sick, or in prison, and came unto thee? And the King shall
answer and say unto them, Verily I say unto you, Inasmuch as ye
did it unto one of these my brethren, even these least, ye did it unto
me.—Matt. 25:34-40.

The earnestness of God is not about any diffuse generality; it is
about persons. His purposes concern them, and he believes in them
and in their capacities for fellowship with him, for growing character and for glorious destiny. If, therefore, one wishes the sense of
God's reality which comes from active co-partnership, let him serve
persons, believe in them, and be in earnest about them. A woman,
troubled by invincible doubts, was given by a wise minister the Gospel of John and a calling-list of needy families, and was told to use
them both. She came through into a luminous faith, and which
helped her more, her reading or her service, she could never tell.
When the Master said that the good we did to the least of his breth-

ren, we did to him, he indicated a road to vital knowledge of him; he said in effect that we can always find him in the lives of people to whom we give love and help. Many will never find him at all unless they find him there. The great believers have been the great servants; and the reason for this is not simply that faith produced service, but also that *service produced faith.* The life of Sir Wilfred Grenfell, for example, makes convincingly plain that his faith sent him to Labrador for service, and that then he drew out of service a compound interest on his original investment of faith.

O God, the Father of the forsaken, the Help of the weak, the Supplier of the needy, who hast diffused and proportioned Thy gifts to body and soul, in such sort that all may acknowledge and perform the joyous duty of mutual service; Who teachest us that love towards the race of men is the bond of perfectness, and the imitation of Thy blessed Self; open our eyes and touch our hearts, that we may see and do, both for this world and for that which is to come, the things which belong to our peace. Strengthen us in the work we have undertaken; give us counsel and wisdom, perseverance, faith, and zeal, and in Thine own good time, and according to Thy pleasure, prosper the issue. Pour into us a spirit of humility; let nothing be done but in devout obedience to Thy will, thankfulness for Thine unspeakable mercies, and love to Thine adorable Son Christ Jesus. . . . Amen.—Earl of Shaftesbury, 1801.

COMMENT FOR THE WEEK

I

Throughout our studies we have been asserting that faith in God involves confidence that creation has a purpose. But we shall not see the breadth and depth of the affirmation, or its significant meaning for our lives, unless more carefully we face a question, which, as keenly as any other, pierces to the marrow of religion: *Is God in earnest?*

That the God of the Bible is in earnest is plain. If we open the Book at the Exodus, we hear him saying, "I have surely seen the affliction of my people, . . . and have heard their cry, . . . and I am come down to deliver them" (Exodus 3:7, 8). If we turn to the prophets, we find Hosea, interpreting the beating of God's heart:

"How am I to give thee up, O Ephraim? How am I to let thee go, O Israel? How am I to give thee up? My heart is turned upon me, my compassions begin to boil"[1] (Hos. 11:8). Everywhere in the Old Testament, God is in earnest: about personal character—"What doth Jehovah require of thee, but to do justly, and to love kindness, and to walk humbly with thy God?" (Micah 6:8); about social righteousness—"Let justice roll down as waters, and righteousness as a mighty stream" (Amos 5:24); about the salvation of the world— "It is too light a thing that thou shouldest be my servant to raise up the tribes of Jacob and to restore the preserved of Israel: I will also give thee for a light to the Gentiles, that thou mayest be my salvation unto the end of the earth" (Isa. 49:6). When from the Old Testament one turns to the New, he faces an assertion of God's earnestness that cannot be surpassed: "God so loved the world that he gave his only begotten Son." God in the New Testament is as much in earnest as that, and all the major affirmations of the Book cluster about the magnetism of this central faith. God is even like a shepherd with a hundred sheep, who having lost one, leaves the ninety and nine and goes after that which is lost, until he finds it (Luke 15:4). From the earliest Hebrew seer dimly perceiving him, to the last apostle of the New Covenant, the God of the Bible is tremendously in earnest.

How profoundly the acceptance of this faith deepens the meaning and value of life is evident. For a moment some might think that the major question is not whether *God* is in earnest but whether *we* are; but when a man considers the hidden fountains from which the streams of his human earnestness must flow, he sees how necessary is at least the hope that at the heart of it creation is in earnest too. Von Hartmann, the pessimist, makes one of his characters say, "The activities of the busy world are only the shudderings of a fever." How shall a man be seriously in earnest about great causes in a world like that? The men whose devoted lives have made history great have seen in creation's busyness more than aimless shuddering. Moses was in earnest, but behind his consecration was his vision of the Eternal, saying to Pharaoh, "Let my people go!" The Master was in earnest, but with a motive that took into its account the purposefulness of God, "My Father worketh hitherto, and I work" (John 5:17).

Indeed, no satisfying meaning, no real unity are conceivable in a

---

[1]George Adam Smith's Translation.

purposeless universe. The plain fact is that *within* the universe nobody explains anything without the statement of its purpose. A chair is something to sit down on; a watch is something to tell time by; a lamp is something to give illumination in the dark—and lacking this purposive description, the story of the precedent history of none of these things, from their original materials to their present shape, would in the least tell what they really are. One who knows all else about a telephone, practically knows nothing, unless he is aware of what it is *for*. Nor is the necessity of such explanation lessened when scientists endeavor descriptions in their special realms. Huxley, narrating the growth of a salamander's egg, writes, "Let a moderate supply of warmth reach its watery cradle, and the plastic matter undergoes changes so rapid, and yet so steady and so purposelike in their succession, that one can only compare them to those operated by a skilled modeler upon a formless lump of clay. As with an invisible trowel, the mass is divided and subdivided into smaller and smaller portions, until it is reduced to an aggregation of granules not too large to build withal the finest fabrics of the nascent organism. And, then, it is as if a delicate finger traced out the line to be occupied by the spinal column and moulded the contour of the body; pinching up the head at one end, the tail at the other, and fashioning flank and limb into the due salamandrine proportions, in so artistic a way, that, after watching the process hour by hour, one is almost involuntarily possessed by the notion that some more subtle aid to vision than an achromatic, would show the hidden artist, with his plan before him, striving with skilful manipulation to perfect his work." The obvious fact is that salamanders' eggs act as though they were seriously intent on making salamanders; and lions' cells as though they were tremendously in earnest about making lions. As Herbert Spencer said of a begonia leaf, "We have therefore no alternative but to say, that the living particles composing one of these fragments, have an innate tendency to arrange themselves into the shape of the organism to which they belong." *But if this is so, purpose is essential in the description of every living thing.* All about us is a world of life with something strikingly like purposeful action rampant everywhere, so that in describing an elm tree it will not do to say only that forces from behind pushed it into being; one must say, too, that from our first observation of its cells they acted as though they were intent on making nothing else but elm. They went about their business as though they had a purpose. The tree's cause is not alone the forces from behind; it is as well the aim that in the cells' action lay ahead.

Men can describe nothing in heaven above or on the earth beneath without the use of purposive terminology. How shall they try otherwise to describe the universe? *A world in which the minutest particles and cells all act as though they were eagerly intent on achieving aims, can only with difficulty be thought of as an aimless whole.* Man's conviction is insistent and imperious that creation, so surcharged with purposes, must have Purpose. The greatest scientists themselves are often our best witnesses here. Charles Darwin and Alfred Russel Wallace are the twin discoverers of evolution. Said the former: "If we consider the whole universe the mind refuses to look at it as the outcome of chance." Said the latter: the world is "a manifestation of creative power, directive mind, and ultimate purpose."

What such men have coldly said, the men of devout religion have set on fire with passionate faith. They have been sure that this world is not

> "A tale
> Told by an idiot, full of sound and fury,
> Signifying nothing."

In every cause that makes for man's salvation they have seen the manifest unveiling of divine intent. *God is in earnest*—this conviction has possessed them utterly, and to live and die for those things on behalf of which the Eternal is tremendously concerned has been the aim, the motive, and the glory of their lives.

II

One need only watch with casual observance the multitudes who say that they believe in God, to see how few of them believe in this God who is in earnest. When they confess their faith in deity they have something else in mind beside the God of the Bible, compassionately purposeful about his world and calling men to be his fellow-workers. Let us therefore consider some of the fallacies that enable men to believe in a God who is *not* in earnest.

For one thing, some *put God far away.* Missionaries in Africa's interior find tribes worshiping stocks, stones, demons, ghosts, but this does not mean that no idea of a great original god is theirs.

Often they are not strangers to that thought, but, as an old Afrikander woman said, "He never concerned himself with me; why should I concern myself with him?" To such folk a great god exists, but he does not care; he dwells apart, an indifferent deity, who has left this world in the hands of lesser gods that really count. The task of the missionary, therefore, is not to prove the existence of a creator—"No rain, no mushrooms," said an African chief; "no God, no world"— but it is to persuade men that the God who seems so far away is near at hand, that he really cares, and over each soul and all his world is sacrificially in earnest.

Such missionary work is not yet needless among Christian people. Said a Copenhagen preacher in a funeral discourse, "God cannot help us in our great sorrow, because he is so infinitely far away; we must therefore look to Jesus." One feels this Siberian exile of God from all vital meaning for our humanity, when he is called the "Absolute," the "Great First Cause," the "Energy from which all things proceed." Like the man, examined by the Civil Service, who, asked the distance from sun to earth, answered, "I do not know how far the sun is from the earth; but it is far enough so that it will not interfere with the proper performance of my duties at the Customs Office," so men with phrases like the "Great First Cause" put God an immeasurable distance off. No man has dealings with a "Great First Cause," no "Great First Cause" ever had vital, personal, constraining meanings for a man. Rather across infinite distance and time unthinkable, we vaguely picture a dim Figure, who gave this toboggan of a universe its primal shove and has not thought seriously of it since. So a wanderer down the street might put a child upon her sled and giving her a start down-hill, go on his way. She may have a pleasant slide, but he will not know; she may fall off, but he will not care; there may be a tragic accident, but that will not be his concern—he has gone away off down the street. Multitudes of nominal believers have a god like that.

In comparison with such, one thinks of men like Livingstone. His God was compassionately concerned for Africa, spoke about black folk as Hosea heard him speak concerning Israel, "How can I give thee up? How can I let thee go?" until the fire of the divine earnestness lit a corresponding ardor in Livingstone's heart and he went out to be God's man in the dark continent. Such men have smitten the listless world as winds fill flapping sails, crying "Move!" And the God of such has been tremendously in earnest.

III

Some gain a God lacking serious purpose, not by putting him afar off, but by endeavoring to bring him so near that they *diffuse him everywhere*. Writers tell us that God is in every rustling leaf and in every wave that breaks upon the beach; we are assured that God is in every gorgeous flower and in every flaming sunset. And the poetry of this is so alluring that we cannot bear to have God specially anywhere, because we are so anxious to keep him everywhere. Preachers delight to illustrate their thought of God with figures drawn from nature's invisible energies—

> "Who has seen the wind?
>   Neither I nor you:
> But when the leaves hang trembling
>   The wind is passing through.
>
> Who has seen the wind?
>   Neither you nor I:
> But when the trees bow down their heads
>   The wind is passing by."

By such comparisons are we taught to see that God invisibly is everywhere.

For all the valuable truth that such speech contains, its practical issue, in many minds today, is to strip God of the last shred of personality, and with that loss to end the possibility of his being in earnest about anything. He has become refined Vapor thinly diffused through space. Folk say they love to meditate on him, and well they may! For such a god asks nothing of anybody except meditation; he has no purposes that call for earnestness in them. When little children are ruined in a city's tenements, when the liquor traffic brutalizes men, when economic inequity makes many poor that a few may be made rich, when war clothes the world with unutterable sorrow, such a god does not care. He is not in earnest about anything. For the only thing in the universe that can be consciously in earnest is personality, and when one depersonalizes God, the remainder is a deity who has no love, no care, no purpose. Thousands do obeisance to such a gaseous idol.

From this fallacy spring such familiar confessions of faith as this,

"God is not a person; he is spirit." If by this negation one intends to say that God is not a limited individual, that is obviously true; but *the contrast between personality and spirit is impossible.* One may as well speak of dry water as of impersonal spirit. Rays of radium are unimaginably minute and swift, but they are not spirit. Nothing in the impersonal realm can be conceived so subtle and refined that it is spirit. Spirit begins only where love and intelligence and purpose are, and these all are activities of personality. No one can *really* believe what Jesus said, "God is a Spirit," without being ready to pray as Jesus prayed, "Our Father."

Between an impersonal, diffused, and gaseous god, and the God of the Bible, how great the difference! God's pervading omnipresence is indeed affirmed in Scripture. There, as much as in any modern thought, the heavens declare his glory, the flowers of the field are illustrations of his care, and the influences of his spirit are like the breeze across the hills. To the ancient Hebrew, heaven and Sheol were the highest and the lowest, but of each the Psalmist says to God, "Thou art there," and as for the uttermost parts of the sea, "even there shall thy hand lead me" (Psalm 139:7-10). Cries Jeremiah from the Old Testament, "Am I a God at hand, saith Jehovah, and not a God afar off? Can any hide himself in secret places so that I shall not see him? saith Jehovah. Do not I fill heaven and earth?" (Jer. 23:23, 24). And Paul answers from the New Testament, "Not far from every one of us: for in him we live, and move, and have our being" (Acts 17:27, 28). But the God of the Bible who so pervades and sustains all existence never degenerates into a Vapor. When Egyptian taskmasters crack their whips over Hebrew slaves, he cares. When exiles try in vain to sing the songs of Zion in a strange land, he cares. When evil men build Jerusalem with blood, and rapacious men pant after the dust on the head of the poor, he cares. He is prodigiously in earnest, and those who best represent him, from the great prophets to the sacrificial Son, are like him in this, that they are mastered by consuming purpose. The God of the Bible is sadly needed by his people. For lack of him religion grows often listless and churches become social clubs.

IV

By another road men travel to believe in a God who is not in earnest: *they think of him as an historic being.* It was said of Car-

lyle, shrewdly if unjustly, that his God lived until the death of Oliver
Cromwell. Whatever may be the truth about Carlyle, it is easy to
find folk whose God to all intents and purposes is dead. Long since
he closed his work, spoke his last word, and settled down to inactiv-
ity and silence. He made the world, created man, thundered from
Sinai, established David's kingdom, brought back the exiles, inspired
the prophets and sent his Son. He *once* was earnest; the record of
his ancient acts is long and glorious, and men find comfort in reading what he used to do. They would not explicitly confess it, but in
fact they habitually think of God in the past tense. They cannot conceive the universe as happening by chance, and they posit God as
making it; they cannot believe that the transcendent characters of
olden times were uninspired, so God becomes the explanation of their
power. When such believers wish to assure themselves of God they
go to the stern of humanity's ship and watch the wake far to the
rear; but they never stand on the ship's bridge, and feel it sway and
turn at the touch of a present Captain in control. They have not
risen to the meaning of the Bible's reiterated phrase, *"the living
God."*

Höffding tells us that in a Danish Protestant church, well on into
the nineteenth century, worshipers maintained the custom of bowing, when they passed a certain spot upon the wall. The reason,
which no one knew, was discovered when removal of the whitewash
revealed a Roman Catholic Madonna. Folk had bowed for three
centuries before the place where the Madonna *used to be*. So some
folk worship deity; he is not a present reality but a tradition; their
faith is directed not toward the living God himself, but toward what
some one else has written about a God who used to be alive. They do
not feel now God's plans afoot, his purposes as certainly in progress
now as ever in man's history. They stand rather like unconverted
Gideon, facing backwards and lamenting, "Where are all his wondrous works which our fathers told us of?" (Judges 6:13).

Not by what we say, but by our practical attitudes we most reveal
how little we believe in an earnest, living God whose voice calls *us,*
whose plans need *us,* as much as ever Moses or David or Paul was
summoned and required. If we say that we do believe in this living
God we are belied by our discouragements, deserving as we often
do the rebuke which Luther's wife administered to the Reformer.
"From what you have said," she remarked, standing before him
clothed in deep, mourning black, "and from the way you feel and

act I supposed that God was dead." If we say that we believe in a living, earnest God, we are belied by our reluctance to expect and welcome new revelations of God's truth and enlarging visions of his plan. Willing to believe what the astronomers say, that light from a new star reaches the earth each year, we act as though God's spiritual universe were smaller than his physical, and do not eagerly await the new light perpetually breaking from his heavens. But most of all the little influence which our faith in God has upon our practical service is a scathing indictment of its vitality and power. No one who really believes in an earnest, living God can have an undedicated life. He may not think of the Divine in the past tense chiefly; the present and the future even more belong to God; and through each generation runs the earnest purpose of the Eternal, who has never said his last word on any subject, nor put the final hammer blow on any task. A faith like this, deeply received and apprehended, is a masterful experience. It changes the inner quality of life; it makes the place whereon we stand holy ground; it urgently impresses us into the service of those causes that we plainly see have in them the purpose of God. No outlook upon life compares with this in grandeur; no motive for life is at once so weighty and so fine.

v

One of the subtlest fallacies by which we miss believing in an earnest God is not describable as an opinion. Men fall into it, who neither reduce God to a Great First Cause, nor diffuse him into a vapor, nor regard him as an historic being. *They rather allow their superstitious sentiments to take the place of worthy faith.* Plenty of people who warmly would insist on their religion, reveal in their practical attitudes how utterly bereft of serious moral purpose their God is. They think their fortune will be better if they do not sit thirteen at a table or occupy room thirteen at a hotel; on occasion they throw salt or look at the moon over their right shoulders and rap on wood to assure their safety or their luck; and to be quite certain of divine favor they hang fetishes, like rabbits' feet, about their necks. Their attitude toward such surviving pagan superstitions is like Fontenelli's toward ghosts. "I do not believe in them," he said, "but I am afraid of them." That this is a law-abiding universe with moral purpose in it, such folk obviously do not believe. Their God is not in earnest. He spends his time watching for dinner parties of thirteen or listening for folk who forget to rap on wood when they boast that they have not been ill all winter. The utter poverty to which great words may be reduced by meager minds is evident when such folk say that they believe in God.

Even when these grosser forms of superstition are not present, others hardly more respectable may take their place. God is pictured as a King, surrounded with court ritual, in the complete and proper observance of which he takes delight, and any rupture in whose regularity awakes his anger. To go to church, to say our prayers, to read our Bibles, to be circumspect on Sunday, to help pay the preacher's salary and to contribute to the missionary cause—such things as these comprise the court ritual of God. These Christian acts are not presented as gracious privileges, opportunities, like fresh air and sunshine and friendship, to make life rich and serviceable; they are presented as works of merit, by which we gain standing in God's favor and assure ourselves of his benignity. For with those who so conform to his ordinances and respect his taboos, he is represented as well-pleased, and he blesses them with special favors. But any infraction of these rituals is sure to bring terrific punishment. God watches those who do not sing his praises or who fail in praying, and he marks them for his vengeance! Dr. Jowett tells us that in the Sunday school room of the English chapel where as a child he worshiped, a picture hung that to his fascinated and frightened imagination represented the character of God: a huge eye filled the center of the heavens, and from it rays of vision fell on every sort of minute happening and small misdeed on earth. As such a monstrous Detective, jealous of his rights and perquisites, God is how often pictured to the children! So H. G. Wells indignantly interprets his experience: "I, who write, was so set against God, thus rendered. He and his Hell were the nightmare of my childhood; I hated him while I still believed in him, and who could help but hate? I thought of him as a fantastic monster, perpetually spying, perpetually listening, perpetually waiting to condemn and to strike me dead; his flames as ready as a grill-room fire. He was over me and about my feebleness and silliness and forgetfulness as the sky and sea would be about a child drowning in mid-Atlantic. When I was still only a child of thirteen, by the grace of the true God in me, I flung this lie out of my mind, and for many years, until I came to see that God himself had done this thing for me, the name of God meant nothing to me but the hideous sear in my heart where a fearful demon had been."

This "bogey God" is in earnest about nothing except the observance of his little rituals; he is unworthy of a good man's worship, he has no purpose that can capture the consent and inspire the loyalty of serious folk. How many so-called unbelievers are in revolt against this perversion of the idea of God, taught them in childhood! The deity whom they refuse to credit is not the Father, with "the eternal purpose which he purposed in Christ" (Eph. 3:11); often they have not heard of him. Their denial is directed against another sort of God. "I wish I could recall clearly," writes one, "the conception of God which I gained as a boy in Sunday school. He was as old as grandfather, I know, but not so kind. We were told to fear him." Surely the real God must sympathize with those who hate his caricature. A vindictive Bogey, querulous about the mint, anise, and cummin of his ritual, in earnest about nothing save to reward obsequious servants and to have his vengeance out on the careless and disobedient, is poles asunder from the God and Father of our Lord Jesus Christ with his majestic purpose for the world's salvation.

VI

Of all the sentiments, however, by which a worthy faith is made impossible, none is so common, in these recent years, *as the ascription to God of a weak and flaccid affectionateness.* God's love is interpreted by love's meaning in hours when we are gentle with our children or tender with our friends. The soft and cosy aspects of love, its comforts, its pities, its affections, are made central in our thought of God. We are taught, as children, that he loves us as our mothers do; and as from them we look for coddling when we cry for it, so are our expectations about God. Our religion becomes a selfish seeking for divine protection from life's ills, a recipe for ease, an expectant trust, that as we believe in God he in return will nurse us, unharmed and happy, through our lives. No one intimately acquainted with the religious life of men and women can be unaware of this widespread, ingrained belief in a soft, affectionate, grandmotherly God. What wonder that life brings fearful disillusionment! What wonder that in a world where all that is valuable has been

> "Battered with the shocks of doom
> To shape and use,"

the God of coddling love seems utterly impossible!

The lack in this fallacious faith is central; there is no place in it for the movement of God's moral purpose. *To ascribe love to God without making it a quality of his unalterable purpose, which must sweep on through costs in suffering however great, is to misread the Gospel.* Many kinds of love are known in our experience, from a nursing mother with her babe to a military leader with his men. In Donald Hankey's picture of "the Beloved Captain" we see affection and tenderness, as beautiful as they are strong: "It was a wonderful thing, that smile of his. It was something worth living for, and worth working for. . . . It seemed to make one look at things from a different point of view, a finer point of view, his point of view. There was nothing feeble or weak about it. . . . It meant something. It meant that we were his men and that he was proud of us. . . . When we failed him, when he was disappointed in us, he did not smile. He did not rage or curse. He just looked disappointed, and that made us feel far more savage with ourselves than any amount of swearing would have done. . . . The fact was that he had won his way into our affections. We loved him. And there isn't anything stronger than love, when all's said and done."

Yet, this Captain, loving and beloved, will lead his men in desperate charges, where death falls in showers, but where the purpose which their hearts have chosen forces them to go. The love of God must be like that; it surely is if Jesus' love is its embodiment. His affection for his followers, his solicitude and tenderness have been in Christian eyes, how beautiful! They shine in words like John's seventeenth chapter where love finds transcendent utterance. Yet this same Master said: "Behold, I send you forth as sheep in the midst of wolves" (Matt. 10:16); "Blessed are ye when men shall reproach you, and persecute you, and say all manner of evil against you falsely for my sake" (Matt. 5:11); "Then shall they deliver you up unto tribulation, and shall kill you; and ye shall be hated of all the nations for my name's sake" (Matt. 24:9); "They shall put you out of the synagogues; yea, the hour cometh, that whosoever killeth you shall think that he offereth service unto God" (John 16:2); "If any man cometh unto me, and hateth not his own father, and mother, and wife, and children, and brethren, and sisters, yea, and his own life also, he cannot be my disciple" (Luke 14:26). The love of Jesus was no coddling affection; it had for its center a moral purpose that balked at no sacrifice. He took crucifixion for himself, and to his beloved he cried, "If any man would come after me, let him deny him-

self, and take up his cross, and follow me" (Matt. 16:24). Such love
is God's; and *preachers who advertise his Fatherhood as a gentle
nurse that shelters us from suffering have sapped the Gospel of its
moral power.* God's love is austere as well as bountiful; he is, as
Emerson said, the "terrific benefactor."

Indeed, faith in a God of coddling love may be one of the most
pernicious influences in human life. Our trust, so misinterpreted,
becomes a cushion on which to lie, a sedative by which to sleep.
When ills afflict the world that men could cure, such misbelievers
merely trust in God; when tasks await man's strength, they quietly
retreat upon their faith that God is good and will solve all, until
religion becomes a by-word and a hissing on the lips of earnest men.
Such misbelievers have not dimly seen the Scripture's meaning,
where faith is not a pillow but a shield, from behind which plays a
sword (Eph. 6:16) and where men do not sleep by faith, but "fight
the good fight of faith" instead (I Tim. 6:12). Or if such misbelievers do rouse themselves to lay hold on their Divinity, it is to demand
God's love for them and not to offer their lives to God. As Sydney
Smith exclaimed about some people's patriotism, "God save the
King! in these times too often means, God save my pension and my
place, God give my sisters an allowance out of the Privy Purse, let
me live upon the fruits of other men's industry and fatten upon the
plunder of the public."

Faith in God never is elevated and ennobling until we overpass
"God for our lives!" to cry *"Our lives for God!"* Then at the luminous center of our faith shines the divine purpose, costly but wonderful, that binds the ages together in spiritual unity. To that we dedicate our lives; in that we exceedingly rejoice. No longer do we test
God's goodness by our happiness or our ill-fortune; we are *his*
through fair weather and through foul. No longer do we merely hold
beliefs, we are held by them, captured now and not simply consoled
by faith. Only so are we learning discipleship to Christ and are beginning really to believe in the Christian God.

VII

From all these common fallacies of thought and sentiment one
turns to the New Testament to find the God of the Gospel. The very
crux of the Good Tidings is that God is so much in earnest that he
is the eternal Sufferer. The ancient Greeks had a god of perfect bliss;

he floated on from age to age in undisturbed tranquillity; no cry of man ever reached his empyrean calm; his life was an endless stream of liquid happiness. How different this Greek deity is from ours may be perceived if one tries to say of him those things which the Scripture habitually says of God. "In all their affliction he was afflicted" (Isa. 63:9); "Can a woman forget her sucking child, that she should not have compassion on the son of her womb? yea, these may forget, yet will not I forget thee" (Isa. 49:15); "God, being rich in mercy, for his great love wherewith he loved us even when we were dead through our trespasses" (Eph. 2:4, 5); "God so loved the world that he gave his only begotten Son" (John 3:16). None of these things that Christians say about their God can be said of a deity who dwells in tranquil bliss.

Indeed let one stand over against a war-torn, unhappy world and try to think that God does not suffer in man's agony, and he will see how useless and incredible such a God would be. God looks on Belgium and he does not care; he looks on Armenia desolate and Poland devastated, and he does not care; he sits in heaven and sees his children wounded and alone in No-man's land, watches the deaths, the heart-breaks, the poverty of war, its ruined childhood and its shattered families, and he does not care—how impossible it is to believe in such a God! A God who does not care does not count.

Christians, therefore, have the God who really meets the needs of men. He cares indeed, and, with all the modesty that words of human emotion must put on when they are applied to him, he suffers in the suffering of men and is crucified in his children's agonies. God limited himself in making such a world as this; in it he cannot lightly do what he will; he has a struggle on his heart; he makes his way upward against obstacles that man's imagination cannot measure. There is a cross forever at the heart of God. He climbs his everlasting Calvary toward the triumph that must come, and he is tremendously in earnest.

One important consequence follows such faith as this. Confidence in such an earnest, sacrificial God makes inevitable the Christian faith in immortality. Our solar system is no permanent theater for God's eternal purposes; it is doomed to dissolution as certainly as any human body is doomed to die. In the Lick observatory one reads this notice under a picture of the sun: "The blue stars are considered to be in early life, the yellow stars in middle life, the red stars in old age. . . . From the quality of its spectrum the sun is classified as a star in middle age." Those, therefore, who, denying their own immortality, comfort themselves with prophesying endless progress for the race upon the earth, have no basis for their hopes. "We must therefore renounce those brilliant fancies," says Faye the scientist, "by which we try to deceive ourselves in order to endow man with unlimited posterity, and to regard the universe as the immense theater on which is to be developed a spontaneous progress without end. On the contrary, life must disappear, and the grandest material works of the human race will have to be effaced by degrees under the action of a few physical forces which will survive man for a time. Nothing will remain—'Even the ruins will perish.' "

If one believes, therefore, in the God who is in earnest, he cannot content himself with such a universe—lacking any permanent element, any abiding reality in which the moral gains of man's long struggle are conserved. God's purpose cannot be so narrow in horizon that it is satisfied with a few million years of painful experiment, costly beyond imagination, yet with no issue to crown its sacrifice. In such a universe as Faye pictures, lacking immortality, generation after generation of men suffer, aspire, labor, and die, and this shall be the history of all creation, until at last Shakespeare's prophecy shall be fulfilled,

> "The cloud-capp'd towers, the gorgeous palaces,
> The solemn temples, the great globe itself,
> Yea, all which it inherit, shall dissolve
> And, like this insubstantial pageant faded,
> Leave not a rack behind."

If such is to be the story of creation, there is no purpose in it and the Christian faith in an earnest God is vain.

Only one truth is adequate to crown our confidence in a purposeful universe and to make it reasonable: *personality must persist*. We believe in immortality, not because we meanly want rewards ahead, but because in no other way can life, viewed as a whole, find sense and reason. If personality persists, this transient theater of action and discipline may serve its purpose in God's time, and disappear. He is in earnest, but not for rocks and suns and stars, he is in earnest about persons—the sheep of his pasture are men. They are not mortal; they carry over into the eternal world the spiritual gains of earth; and all life's struggle—its vicarious sacrifice, its fearful punishments, its labor for better circumstance and worthier life—is justified in its everlasting influence on personality. When we say that God cares, we mean no vague, diffusive attitude toward a system that lasts for limited millenniums and then comes to an uneventful end in a cold sun and a ruined earth. We mean that he cares for personality which is his child, that he suffers in the travail of his children's character, and that this divine solicitude has everlasting issues when the heavens "wax old like a garment." Still Paul's statement stands, one of the most worthy summaries of God's earnestness that ever has been written: "The creation waits with eager longing for the sons of God to be revealed" (Rom. 8:19).[2]

_____

[2]Moffatt's Translation.

CHAPTER X

Faith in Christ the Savior: Forgiveness

DAILY READINGS

During the next two weeks we are to consider some of the distinctive meanings which faith in Christ has had for his disciples. They have found in that faith unspeakable blessing and have uttered their gratitude in radiant language. But, just because of this, many folk find themselves in difficulty. Their expectations concerning the Christian life have been lifted very high, and in their experience of it they have been disappointed. Their problem is not theoretical doubt, but practical disillusionment. Their difficulty lies in their experience that the Christian life, while it may be theoretically true, is not practically what it is advertised to be. At this common problem let us look in the daily readings.

Tenth Week, First Day

Many expect in the Christian experience an emotional life of joy and quietude which they have not found. They are led to expect this by many passages of Scripture about "peace in believing," by many hymns of exultation where a mood of unqualified spiritual triumph finds voice, and by testimonies of men who speak of living years without any depressed hours or flagging spirits. Such a wonderful life of elevated emotion many crave for themselves; they came into the Christian fellowship expecting it; and they neither have it, nor are likely to achieve it. Now the beauty of a clear, high emotional life no one can doubt, but *we must not demand it as a condition of our keeping faith.* We ought not to seek God simply for the sake of sensational experiences, no matter how desirable they may be. In all the ages before Christ, the outstanding example of deep personal religion, expressing itself in over forty years of splendidly courageous prophetic ministry, is Jeremiah, and his temperament was never marked by quietude and joy. His emotional life was profoundly affected by his faith: *courage was substituted for fear.* But if he had demanded the mood of the 103rd Psalm as a price for continued faith, he would have lost his faith. He was not temperamentally constructed like the psalmist—and he was a far greater personality. We must not be too much concerned about our spiritual sensations. Consider the Master's parable about the two sons: one had amiable feelings, but his will was wrong, the other lacked satisfactory emotions, but he did the work.

But what think ye? A man had two sons; and he came to the first, and said, Son, go work to-day in the vineyard. And he answered and said, I will not: but afterward he repented himself, and went. And he came to the second, and said likewise. And he answered and said, I go, sir: and went not. Which of the two did the will of his father? They say, The first.—Matt. 21:28-31.

Ah, Lord, unto whom all hearts are open; Thou canst govern the vessel of our souls far better than we can. Arise, O Lord, and command the stormy wind and the troubled sea of our hearts to be still, and at peace in Thee, that we may look up to Thee undisturbed, and abide in union with Thee, our Lord. Let us not be carried hither and thither by wandering thoughts, but, forgetting all else, let us see and hear Thee. Renew our spirits; kindle in us Thy light, that it may shine within us, and our hearts may burn in love and adoration towards Thee. Let Thy Holy Spirit dwell in us continually, and make us Thy temples and sanctuary, and fill us with Divine love and light and life, with devout and heavenly thoughts, with comfort and strength, with joy and peace. Amen.—Johann Arndt, 1555.

Tenth Week, Second Day

Many came into the Christian life because they needed conquering power in their struggle against sin. They were told that absolute victory could be theirs through Christ, and they set their hearts on that in ardent hope and expectation. But they are disappointed. That they have been helped they would not deny, but they find that the battle with besetting sin is a running fight; it has not been concluded by a final and resounding victory. This seems to them a denial of what Christian preachers and Christian hymns have promised, and perhaps it is. Hymns and preachers are not infallible. Christian experience, however, is plainly aligned against their disappointment. Some men under the power of Christ are immediately transformed so that an old sin becomes thenceforth utterly disasteful; even the desire for it is banished altogether. But a great preacher, only recently deceased, no less really under the power of Christ, had all his life to fight a taste for drink which once had mastered him. His battle never ceased. His victory consisted not in the elimination of his appetite, but in abiding power to keep up the struggle, to refuse subjugation to it, and at last gloriously to fall on sleep, admired and loved by his people who had seen in him steadfast, unconquerable will, sustained by faith. To have done with a sinful appetite in one conclusive victory is glorious; but we must not demand it as a price of keeping faith. Perhaps our victory must come through the kind of patient persistence which James the Apostle evidently knew.

Count it all joy, my brethren, when ye fall into manifold temptations; knowing that the proving of your faith worketh patience. And let patience have its perfect work, that ye may be perfect and entire, lacking in nothing.

But if any of you lacketh wisdom, let him ask of God, who giveth to all liberally and upbraideth not; and it shall be given him. But let him ask in faith, nothing doubting: for he that doubteth is like the surge of the sea driven by the wind and tossed. For let not that man think that he shall receive anything of the Lord; a double-minded man, unstable in all his ways.—James 1:2-8.

O Lord God Almighty, who givest power to the faint, and increasest strength to them that have no might; without Thee we can do nothing, but by Thy gracious assistance we are enable for the performance of every duty laid upon us. Lord of power and love, we come, trusting in Thine almighty strength, and Thine infinite goodness, to ask from Thee what is wanting in ourselves; even that grace which shall help us such to be, and such to do, as Thou wouldst have us. O our God, let Thy grace be sufficient for us, and ever present with us, that we may do all things as we ought. We will trust in Thee, in whom is everlasting strength. Be Thou our Helper, to carry us on beyond our own strength, and to make all that we think,

*and speak, and do, acceptable in Thy sight; through Jesus Christ.
Amen.*—Benjamin Jenks, 1646.

Tenth Week, Third Day

Jehovah is my shepherd; I shall not want.
He maketh me to lie down in green pastures;
He leadeth me beside still waters.
He restoreth my soul:
He guideth me in the paths of righteousness for his name's sake.
Yea, though I walk through the valley of the shadow of death,
I will fear no evil; for thou art with me;
Thy rod and thy staff, they comfort me.

—Psalm 23:1-4.

What expectations are awakened by such a passage! Many have
come into the Christian life because in experience they have found
that "it is not in man that walketh to direct his steps." They wanted
a Guide in the mysterious pilgrimage of life, and in the words of
hymns like, "He leadeth me, O blessed thought!" they saw the promise of a God-conducted experience. But they are disappointed. They
have the same old puzzles to face about what they ought to do; they
have no divine illumination that clears up in advance their uncertainty as to the wisdom of their choices; they are not vividly aware
of any guidance from above to save them from the perplexities which
their companions face about conduct and career. Of course part of
their difficulty is due to false expectation. Not even Paul or John
was given mechanical guidance, infallible and unmistakable; they
never had a syllabus of all possible emergencies with clear directions
as to what should be done in every case; they were guided through
their normal faculties made sensitive to divine suggestion, and doubtless they never could clearly distinguish between their thought and
their inspirations. Divine guidance did not save them from puzzling
perplexities and unsure decisions. But it did give them certainty that
they were in God's hands; that he had hold of the reins behind their
human grasp; that when they did wisely and prayerfully the best they
knew, he would use it somehow to his service. And so far as the vivid
consciousness of being guided is concerned, that probably came *in
retrospect;* when they saw how the road came out, they agreed that
God's hand must have been in the journey. Such an experience it is
reasonable to expect and possible to have.

O God our Lord, the stay of all them that put their trust in Thee, wherever Thou leadest we would go, for Thy ways are perfect wisdom and love. Even when we walk through the dark valley, Thy light can shine into our hearts and guide us safely through the night of sorrow. Be Thou our Friend, and we need ask no more in heaven or earth, for Thou art the Comfort of all who trust in Thee, the Help and Defence of all who hope in Thee. O Lord, we would be Thine; let us never fall away from Thee. We would accept all things without murmuring from Thy hand, for whatever Thou dost is right. Blend our wills with Thine, and then we need fear no evil nor death itself, for all things must work together for our good. Lord, keep us in Thy love and truth, comfort us with Thy light, and guide us by Thy Holy Spirit; through Jesus Christ our Lord. Amen.— S. Weiss, 1738.

Tenth Week, Fourth Day

Many folk grow up into the Christian life, and so interpret the love of God that they expect from him affectionate mothering; they look to him to keep them from trouble. In childhood, sheltered from life's tragic incidents, this expectation was more or less realized; but now in maturity they are disappointed. God has not saved them from trouble; he has not dealt with them in maternal tenderness. Rather Job's complaint to God is on their lips:

I cry unto thee, and thou dost not answer me:
I stand up, and thou gazest at me.
Thou art turned to be cruel to me;
With the might of thy hand thou persecutest me.

.   .   .   .

Did not I weep for him that was in trouble?
Was not my soul grieved for the needy?
When I looked for good, then evil came;
And when I waited for light, there came darkness.
My heart is troubled, and resteth not;
Days of affliction are come upon me.

—Job 30:20, 21; 25-27.

One such disappointed spirit says that in youth, even if she hurt her finger, she was told to pray to God and he would take away the

bruise; but now life does not seem to be directed by that kind of a
God at all. It isn't! A pregnant source of lost faith is to be found
in this unscriptural presentation of God's love. In Scripture God's
love for his people and their tragic suffering are put side by side,
and the Cross where the well-beloved Son is crucified is typical of
the whole Book's assertion that God does not keep his children from
trouble. Sometimes he leads them into it; and always he lets the
operation of his essential laws sweep on, so that disease and accident
and death are no respecters of character. When Ananias was sent
with God's message to the newly converted Paul, that greeting into
the Christian life concerned "how many things he must suffer"
(Acts 9:16). Whatever else our faith must take into account, this is
an unescapable fact: we are seeking the impossible when we ask that
our lives be arranged on the basis that we shall not face trouble.
Faith means a conquering confidence that good will, a purpose of
eternal love, runs through the whole process. It says, not apart from
suffering, but in the face of it:

> "I'm apt to think the man
> That could surround the sum of things, and spy
> The heart of God and secrets of his empire,
> Would speak but love—with him the bright result
> Would change the hue of intermediate scenes,
> And make one thing of all Theology."

*Almighty God to whom all things belong, whose is light and dark-
ness, whose is good and evil, Master of all things, Lord of all; who
hast so ordered it, that life from the beginning shall be a struggle
throughout the course, and even to the end; so guide and order that
struggle within us, that at last what is good in us may conquer, and
all evil be overcome, that all things may be brought into harmony,
and God may be all in all. So do Thou guide and govern us, that
every day whatsoever betide us, some gain to better things, some
more blessed joy in higher things may be ours, that so we, though
but weaklings, may yet, God-guided, go from strength to strength,
until at last, delivered from that burden of the flesh, through which
comes so much struggling, we may enter into the land of harmony
and of eternal peace. Hear us, of Thy mercy; through Jesus Christ
our Lord. Amen.—George Dawson, 1877.*

Tenth Week, Fifth Day

Till we all attain unto the unity of the faith, and of the knowledge of the Son of God, unto a fullgrown man, unto the measure of the stature of the fulness of Christ: that we may be no longer children, tossed to and fro and carried about with every wind of doctrine, by the sleight of men, in craftiness, after the wiles of error; but speaking truth in love, may grow up in all things into him, who is the head, even Christ.—Eph. 4:13-15.

Many came into the Christian life familiar with such an idea of growth. They expected the new life to be an enlarging experience, with new vistas, deepening satisfactions, increasing certitude. If at the beginning the Christian way did not content them, they blamed their immaturity for the unsatisfactory experience; they appealed to the days ahead for fuller light. But they are disappointed. They have not grown. The most they can claim is that they are stationary; the haunting suspicion cannot altogether be avoided that their faith is dwindling and their fervor burning down. This difficulty is not strange—with many folk it is inevitable; for they have never grasped the fact that the Christian life, like all life whatsoever, is law-abiding, and that to expect effects without cause is vain. That a Christian experience has begun with promise does not mean that it will magically continue; that the spirit will naturally drift into an enlarging life. An emotional conversion, like a flaming meteor, may plunge into a man's heart, and soon cool off, leaving a dead, encysted stone. But to have a real life in God, that begins like a small but vital acorn and grows like an aspiring oak, one must obey the laws that make such increasing experience possible. To keep fellowship with God unimpeded by sin, uninterrupted by neglect; to think habitually as though God were, instead of casually believing that he is; to practice love continually until love grows real; and to arrange life's program conscientiously as though the doing of God's will were life's first business—such things alone make spiritual growth a possibility.

We desire to confess, O Lord, that we have not lived according to our promises, nor according to the thoughts and intents of our hearts. We have felt the gravitation of things that drew us downward from things high and holy. We have followed right things how feebly! Weak are we to resist the attraction of evils that lurk about the way of goodness; and we are conscious that we walk in a vain show. We behold and approve Thy law, but find it hard to obey; and our obedience is of the outside, and not of the soul and of the spirit, with heartiness and full of certainty. We rejoice that Thou art a Teacher patient with Thy scholars, and that Thou art a Father patient with Thy children. Thou art a God of long-suffering goodness, and of tender mercies, and therefore we are not consumed.

And now we beseech of Thee, O Thou unwearied One, that Thou wilt inspire us with a heavenly virtue. Lift before us the picture of what we should be and what we should do, and maintain it in the light, that we may not rub it out in forgetfulness; that we may be able to keep before ourselves our high calling in Christ Jesus. And may we press forward, not as they that have attained or apprehended; may we press toward the mark, for the prize of our high calling in Christ Jesus, with new alacrity, with growing confidence, and with more and more blessedness of joy and peace in the soul. Amen.—Henry Ward Beecher.

Tenth Week, Sixth Day

The Christian experience which disappoints its possessor by lack of growth is common, because so many leave the idea of growth vague and undefined. They expect in general to grow, but in what direction, to what describable results, they never stop to think. If we ran our other business as thoughtlessly, with as little determinate planning and discipline, as we manage our Christian living, any progress would be impossible. What wonder that as Christians we often resemble the child who fell from bed at night, and explained the accident by saying, "I must have gone to sleep too near the place where I got in"!

Growth is always in definite directions, and folk will do well at times, without morbid self-examination, to forecast their desired courses. Becoming Christians from motives of fear, as many do, we should press on to a fellowship with God in which fear vanishes in divine friendship and cooperation. Choosing the Christian life for self-centered reasons, because it can do great things for us, we should press on to glory in it as a Cause on which the welfare of the race depends and for which we willingly make sacrifice. Beginning with narrow ideas of service to our friends and neighborhood, we should press on to genuine interest in the world-field, in international fraternity, and in Christ's victory over all mankind. Such definite lines of progress we well may set before us. And a life that does grow, so that each new stage of maturing experience finds deeper levels and greater heights, is never disappointing; it is life become endlessly interesting and worth while.

Not that I have already obtained, or am already made perfect: but I press on, if so be that I may lay hold on that for which also I was laid hold on by Christ Jesus. Brethren, I count not myself yet to have laid hold: but one thing I do, forgetting the things which are behind, and stretching forward to the things which are before, I press on toward the goal unto the prize of the high calling of God in Christ Jesus. Let us therefore, as many as are perfect, be thus minded: and if in anything ye are otherwise minded, this also shall God reveal unto you: only, whereunto we have attained, by that same rule let us walk.—Phil. 3:12-16.

Our Father, we pray Thee that we may use the blessings Thou hast given us, and never once abuse them. We would keep our bodies enchanted still with handsome life, wisely would we cultivate the intellect which Thou hast throned therein, and we would so live with conscience active and will so strong that we shall fix our eye on the right, and, amid all the distress and trouble, the good report and the evil, of our mortal life, steer straightway there, and bate no jot of human heart or hope. We pray Thee that we may cultivate still more these kindly hearts of ours, and faithfully perform our duty to friend and acquaintance, to lover and beloved, to wife and child, to neighbor and nation, and to all mankind. May we feel our brotherhood to the whole human race, remembering that nought human is strange to our flesh but is kindred to our soul. Our Father, we pray that we may grow continually in true piety, bringing down everything which would unduly exalt itself, and lifting up what is lowly within us, till, though our outward man perish, yet our inward man shall be renewed day by day, and within us all shall be fair and beautiful to Thee, and without us our daily lives useful, our whole consciousness blameless in Thy sight. Amen.—Theodore Parker.

Tenth Week, Seventh Day

While some, for reasons such as we have suggested, have made at least a partial failure of the Christian life, and are tempted to feel that their experience is an argument against it, we may turn with confidence to the multitude who have found life with Christ an ineffable blessing.

There is therefore now no condemnation to them that are in Christ Jesus. For the law of the Spirit of life in Christ Jesus made me free from the law of sin and of death. For what the law could not do, in that it was weak through the flesh, God, sending his own Son in the likeness of sinful flesh and for sin, condemned sin in the flesh: that the ordinance of the law might be fulfilled in us, who walk not after the flesh, but after the Spirit. For they that are after the flesh mind the things of the flesh; but they that are after the Spirit the things of the Spirit. For the mind of the flesh is death; but the mind of the Spirit is life and peace.—Rom. 8:1-6.

Innumerable disciples of Jesus can subscribe to this Pauline testimony, and the center of their gratitude, as of his, is the victory over sin which faith in Christ has given them. The farther they go with him the more wonderful becomes the meaning of his Gospel. What Thomas Fuller, in the seventeenth century, wrote about the Bible, they feel about their whole relationship with Christ: "Lord, this morning I read a chapter in the Bible, and therein observed a memorable passage, whereof I never took notice before. Why now, and no sooner, did I see it? Formerly my eyes were as open, and the letters as legible. Is there not a thin veil laid over Thy Word, which is more rarified by reading, and at last wholly worn away? I see the oil of Thy Word will never leave increasing whilst any bring an empty barrel." As for the consciousness of filial alliance with the God and Father of Jesus, that has been a deepening benediction. How many can take over the dual inscription on an ancient Egyptian temple, as an expression of their own experience! A priest had written, in the name of the Deity, "I am He who was and is and ever shall be, and my veil hath no man lifted." But near at hand, some man of growing life and deepening faith has added: "Veil after veil have we lifted, and ever the Face is more wonderful."

Eternal and Gracious Father, whose presence comforteth like sunshine after rain; we thank Thee for Thyself and for all Thy revelation to us. Our hearts are burdened with thanksgiving at the thought of all Thy mercies; for all the blessings of this mortal life, for health, for reason, for learning, and for love; but far beyond all thought

*and thankfulness, for Thy great redemption. It was no painless tra-
vail that brought us to the birth, it has been no common patience that
has borne with us all this while; long-suffering love, and the breaking of the eternal heart alone could reconcile us to the life to which
Thou hast ordained us. We have seen the Son of Man sharing our
sickness and shrinking not from our shame, we have beheld the
Lamb of God bearing the sins of the world, we have mourned at
the mysterious passion and stood astonished at the cross of Jesus
Christ; and behind all we have had the vision of an altar-throne
and one thereon slain from the foundation of the world; heard a
voice calling us that was full of tears; seen beyond the veil that was
rent, the agony of God.*

*O for a thousand tongues to sing the love that has redeemed us.
O for a thousand lives that we might yield them all to Thee. Amen.*
—W. E. Orchard.

COMMENT FOR THE WEEK

I

Hitherto in our studies we have thought of God as the object of
our faith. From the beginning, to be sure, we have been using the
Master as the Way. The God who is in earnest about immortal personalities is supremely revealed in Jesus Christ. But through Christ's
mediation we have been trying to pierce to the Eternal character
and purpose; we have been taking Jesus at his word, "He that believeth on me, believeth not on me but on him that sent me" (John
12:44).

The meaning of faith for the Christian, however, cannot be left
as though Christ were an instrument which God used for his revealing and then thrust aside, a symbol in terms of whom we may poeti-
cally picture God. Christ has been for his people more than a transparent pane, itself almost forgettable, through which the divine light
shone. His personality has been central and dominant, and when
his disciples have most vividly expressed the meaning of their faith
they have said that they believed in him. The first Christians whose
experience is enshrined in the New Testament did not deal with
faith in God alone. They adored Jesus; they were illimitably thankful to him; they rejoiced to call themselves his bondservants and to
suffer for him; they claimed him as a brother, but they acknowledged

him their Lord as well; and they bowed before him with inexpressible devotion. "They all set him in the same incomparable place. They all acknowledged to him the same immeasurable debt."

One need not read far in the New Testament to see why these first disciples so adored their Lord. He was their Savior. They called him by many other names—Messiah, *Logos,* Son of Man, and Son of God—in their endeavor to do justice to his work and character, but one name shines among all the rest and swings them about it like planets round a sun. He is the Savior. From the annunciation to Joseph, "Thou shalt call his name Jesus; for it is he that shall save his people from their sins" (Matt. 1:21), to the New Song of the Apocalypse (Rev. 5: 5-13), the New Testament is written around the central theme of saviorhood. These first disciples were vividly aware of an abysmal need, which had been met in Christ, a great peril from which through him they had escaped; and throughout the New Testament one never loses the accent of astonished gratitude, from folk who were once slaves and now are free, who from victims have been turned to victors. When Wilberforce's long campaign for the freeing of British slaves was at its climax, the population of Jamaica lined the shore for days awaiting the ship that should bring news of Parliament's decision. And when from a boat's prow the messenger cried "Freedom," the island rang with the thanksgiving of the liberated. Such rejoicing one hears in the New Testament. The disciples speak of the freedom wherewith Christ has set them free (Gal. 5:1); they say that they were dead and now are made alive (Rom. 6:11-13); once overwhelmed by sin, they now cry, "More than conquerors" (Rom. 8:37). Nor have they any doubt who is the agent or what is the agency of their salvation: Christ is the Savior and faith the means. "This is the victory that hath overcome the world," they cry, "even our faith" (I John 5:4).

If we are to understand this attitude of the first disciples toward Christ the Savior, *we must appreciate as they did the peril from which he rescued them.* One cannot understand the meaning of any character who, like Moses, delivered a people from their bondage, unless he deeply feels the importance of the problem to whose solution the man contributed. Moses shines out against the background of a nation's trouble like a star against the midnight sky. When the blackness of the night is gone, the star has vanished, too. The race's deliverers never can retain their brightness in our gratitude unless we keep alive in our remembrance the evil against which they fought.

If we would know Moses, we must know Pharaoh; if we would know Wellington, we must know Napoleon. If we are to value truly the great educators, we must estimate aright the blight that ignorance lays on human life. John Howard will be nothing to us, if we do not know the ancient prison system in comparison with which even our modern jails are paradise; and Florence Nightingale will be an empty name, if we cannot imagine the terrors of war without a nurse. Always we must see the stars against the night.

Nor is there any other way in which a Christian can keep alive a vital understanding of his Lord. Many modern Christians seem to have lost vision of the problem that Jesus came to solve, of the human peril to whose conquest he made the supreme contribution. They think that the Church has adored Jesus because of a metaphysical theory about him, but all theories concerning Christ have arisen from a previous devotion to him. Or they think that Jesus is adored because he was so uniquely beautiful in character. But while without this his people never would have called him Lord, not on this account chiefly have they looked on him with inexpressible devotion. No one can understand the Christian attitude toward Jesus except in terms of the bondage from which he came to rescue us. There is a human cry that makes his advent meaningful; it is like the night behind the star of Bethlehem. Long ago a Psalmist heard that cry and every age and land and soul has echoed it, "My sins are mightier than I" (Psalm 65:3).[1]

II

The peril of sin as the innermost problem of human life is in these days obscure to many minds. For one thing, sin has been so continuously preached about, that it seems to some an ecclesiastical question, fit for discussion, it may be, in a church on Sunday, but otherwise not often emerging in ordinary thought. But sin is no specialty of preaching. If a man, forgetting churches and sermons, seriously ponders human life as he knows it actually to be, if he gathers up in his imagination the deepest heartaches of the race, its worst diseases, its most hopeless miseries, its ruined childhood, its dissevered families, its fallen states, its devastated continents, he soon will see that the major cause of all this can be spelled with three letters—sin. To make vivid this peril as the very crux of humanity's

---

[1]"Iniquities prevail against me."

problem on the earth, one needs at times to leave behind the customary thoughts and phrases of religion and to seek testimony from
sources that the Church frequently forgets. When governments try
to build social states where equity and happiness shall reign, their
prison systems, their criminal codes, their courts of law loudly advertise that their problem lies in sin. When jurists plan leagues of nations
and sign covenants to make the world a more fraternal place, only
to find greed, hate, and cruelty demolishing their well-laid schemes,
their failure uncovers the crucial problem of man's sin. When phi-
lanthropists try to lift from man's bent back the burdens that oppress
him, it becomes plain how infinitely their task would be lightened,
if it were not for sin. As for literature—where the seers, regardless
of religious prejudice, have tried to see into the human heart and
truly to report their insights—its witness is overwhelming as to what
man's problem is. No great book of creative literature was ever written without sin at the center. Macbeth, Hamlet, Othello, Faust, Les
Misérables, Romola, The Scarlet Letter—let the list be extended in
any direction and to any length! Always the insight of the creative
seers reports one inner peril of the race. Sin is no bogey erected by
the theologians, no ghost imagined by minds grown morbid with the
fear of God. Sin to every seeing eye is the one most real and practical
problem of mankind.

For another reason this crucial problem is dimly seen by many
minds: we do not often use the word about ourselves. The hardest
thing that any man can ever say is "I have sinned." We make mistakes, we have foibles of character and conduct, we even fall into
error—but we do not often sin. By such devices we avoid the painful consciousness of our inward malady and even the name of our
disease is banished from decorous speech. But sin does not go into
exile with its name. Sin has many aliases and can swiftly shift its
guise to gain a welcome into any company.

Sin in the slums is gross and terrible. It staggers down the streets,
blasphemes with oaths that can be heard, wallows in vice unmentionable by modest lips. Then some day prosperity may visit it. It
moves to a finer residence, seeks the suburbs, or finds domicile on
a college campus. It changes all its clothes. No longer is it indecent
and obscene. Its speech is mild, its civility is irreproachable. It
gathers a company of friends who minister to pleasure and respectability, and the cry of the world's need dies unheard at its peaceful
door. It presses its face continually through the pickets of social

allowance, like a bad boy who wishes to trespass on forbidden ground but fears the consequence. Its goodness is superficial seeming; at heart it is as bad as it dares to be. It has completely changed its garments, but it is the same sin—indulgent, selfish, and unclean. Sin, as anyone can easily observe, takes a very high polish.

Neither by calling sin an ecclesiastical concern nor by covering its presence in ourselves with pleasant euphemisms can we hide its deadly bane in human life. The truth and import of this negative statement become clear and convincing when its positive counterpart is faced. The world needs *goodness*. The one thing in which mankind is poor and for the lack of which great causes lag and noble hopes go unfulfilled is character. With each access of that humanity leaps forward; with the sag of that all else is failure. And the one name for every loss and lack and ruin of character is sin. That is our enemy. Upon the defeat of that all our dearest hopes depend, and in its victory every dream of good that the race has cherished comes to an end.

III

The urgency of this truth is manifest when we note the consequence of sin in our own lives. No statement from antiquity has accumulated more confirming evidence in the course of the centuries than the Psalmist's cry, "My sins are mightier than I." Let us consider its truth in the light of our experience.

Our sins are stronger than we are *in their power to fasten on us a sense of guilt that we cannot shake off*. Sinful pleasures lure us only in *anticipation,* dancing before us like Salome before her uncle, quite irresistible in fascination. Happiness seems altogether to depend upon an evil deed. But on the day that deed, long held in alluring expectation, is actually done—how swift and terrible the alteration in its aspect! It passes from anticipation, through committal, into memory, and it never will be beautiful again. We lock it in remembrance, as in the bloody room of Bluebeard's palace, where the dead things hung; at the thought of it we shrink and yet to it our reminiscence continually is drawn. Something happens in us as automatic as the dropping of a loosened apple from a tree; all the laws of the moral universe conspire to further it and we have no power to prevent: sin becomes guilt. When on a lonely ocean the floating bell buoys toll, no human hands cause them to ring; the waste of an unpeopled ocean surrounds them everyway. The sea by its own restlessness is ringing its own bells. So tolls remorse in a man's heart and no man can stop it.

Our sins are stronger than we are *in their power to become habitual*. If one who steps from an upper window had only the single act to consider, his problem would be simple. He could step or not as he chose. But when one steps from an upper window he finds himself dealing with a power over which his will has no control. Master of his single act, he is not master of the *gravitation* that succeeds it. Many a youth blithely plays with sin, supposing that separate deeds —which he may do or refrain from as he will—make up the problem. Soon or late he finds that he is dealing with moral laws, built into the structure of the universe as gravitation is—laws which he did not create and whose operation he cannot control. By them with terrific certainty thoughts grow to deeds, deeds to habits, habits to character, character to destiny.

At the beginning sin always comes disguised as liberty. Its lure is the seductive freedom which it promises from the trammels of conscience and the authority of law. But every man who ever yet accepted sin's offer of a free, unfettered life, discovered the cheat. Free to do the evil thing, to indulge the baser moods—so men begin, but they end *not free to stop*, bound as slaves to the thing that they were free to do. They have been at liberty to play with a cuttle-fish, and now that the first long arm with its suckers grasps them, and the second arm is waving near, they are not at liberty to get away.

Our sins are mightier than we are *in their power to make us tempt our fellows*. When we picture our sinfulness, even to ourselves, we naturally represent our lives assailed by the allurements of evil and passively surrendering. We are the tempted; we pity ourselves because the outward pressure was too strong for the inward braces. We forget that in sin we are not simply the passive subjects of temptation; sin always makes us active tempters of our fellows. No drug fiend ever is content until he wins a comrade in his vice; a thief would have his friends steal, too; a gossip is not satisfied until other lips are tearing reputations into shreds; and vindictiveness is happiest when other hearts as well are lighted with lurid tempers. Sin always is contagious as disease is; the tempted becomes the tempter on the instant that he falls. Peter weak, lures Jesus to his weakness, and the Master recognizes the active quality of his disciple's sin; "Get thee behind me, Satan!" (Matt. 16:23). Sin satanizes men and sends them out to seduce their fellows. When, therefore, a sensitive man repents of his evil, he abhors himself—not mildly as a victim, but profoundly as a victimizer. He repents of the way he has played Satan to others, sometimes deliberately, sometimes by the unconscious influence of an unworthy spirit. He remembers the times when his words have poisoned the atmosphere which others breathed, when his tempers have conjured up evil spirits in other hearts, when his attitude has made wrongdoing easy for his friends and family, and well-doing hard. And his desperate helplessness in the face of sin is made most evident when he recalls the irrecoverable injury which lives have suffered and are suffering, hurt, perhaps ruined, by his evil.

Our sins are mightier than we are in their power to bring their natural consequences upon other lives. The landlord, of whom President Hyde has told, who without disinfection rented to a new family an apartment where a perilous disease had been, is typical of every evil-doer. When the only child of the incoming family fell sick of the disease and died, and the landlord was faced with his guilt, he pleaded his unwillingness to spend the money which the disinfection would have cost. He denied his Lord for ten dollars. Let the law punish him as it can, the crux of his moral problem lies in the fact that however much he may be sorry now, he never can bear all the consequences of his sin. Somewhere there is a childless home bearing part of the result of his iniquity. One who had done a deed like that might well crave death and oblivion. But everyone who ever sinned is in that estate. No man ever succeeded in building around his evil a wall high and thick enough to contain all evil's consequences. They always flow over and seep through; they fall in cruel disaster on those who love us best. One never estimates his sin aright until he sees that no man ever bears all the results of his own evil. Always our sins nail somebody else to a cross; they even "crucify . . . the Son of God afresh" (Heb. 6:6).

Such is the meaning of the peril against whose background the New Testament believers saw the luminous figure of the Savior. Sin brings men into the debt of a great guilt which they cannot pay and into the bondage of tyrannous habits which they cannot break; it makes men tempting satans to their fellows, and it hurls its results like vitriol across the faces of their family and friends. And when one looks on the lamentable evils of the world at large, its sad inequities, its furious wars, he sees no need to deal delicately with sin or to speak of it in apologetic tones. Sin is, as the New Testament saw it, the central problem of mankind. If anyone has ever come with the supreme contribution to its conquest, the face of the world may well be turned toward him today. In the Christian's faith, such a Savior has come. For if the visitor from Mars who so often has been imagined coming to earth, should come again, and amazed at the churches built, the anthems sung, the service wrought in Jesus' name, should curiously inquire what this character had done to awaken such response, we should have to answer: Jesus of Nazareth made no direct contribution to science or art or government or law—with none of these important realms did he concern himself. Only one thing he did: *he made the indispensable contribution to man's fight for great character against sin.* And because that is man's crucial problem, all science, art, government, and law are under an unpayable indebtedness to him. Because that is man's innermost need, his birthday has become the hinge of history, until one cannot write a letter to his friend without dating his familiar act from the advent of him who came to save us in our struggle for godliness against evil.

IV

Faith in Christ has a double relationship with the problem of man's sin; it concerns the *basis on which we are to be judged* and *the strength by which we are to conquer.* Christ has brought to men a gospel of forgiveness and power. With regard to the first—and with the first alone this chapter is concerned—the opinion of many modern men is swift and summary: folk are to be judged by what they do; the output of a man, as of a machine, is the test of him. Until this popular method of judgment is convicted of inadequacy, there is no hope of understanding what Christians have meant by being "saved through faith" (Eph. 2:8). We must see that men are worth more than they *do*.

A man's deeds alone are an insufficient basis for judgment, because *motives for the same act may be low or high.* No one can be unaware of the Master's meaning when he speaks of those who do their alms before men to be seen of them (Matt. 6:1ff), or of Paul's when he says, "If I bestow all my goods to feed the poor . . . but have not love" (I Cor. 13:3). Some men habitually shine to good advantage by such means; they have the facile gift of putting their best foot forward. Like a store at Christmas time, its finest goods in the

window and inferior stock for sale upon the counters, they are infinitely skilful in gaining more credit than their worth deserves. One
who has dealt with such folk becomes aware that to estimate an
isolated deed is superficial; one must know the motive. A cup of cold
water or a widow's penny may awake the Master's spirited approval,
and millions rung into the temple treasury by showy Pharisees meet
only scorn.

Deeds alone are an insufficient basis for judgment because, while
we are more than body, *our bodies are the instruments of all that
visibly we do.* Many a man in spirit is like a swift mill race, eager
for service, but the flesh, a battered mill wheel, ill sustains the spirit's
vehemence; it breaks before the shock. One must shut the gates and
patch up the wheel, before the spirit, impatient for utterance, may
have its way again; and some mill-wheels never can be mended.
Says one of Robert Louis Stevenson's biographers: "When a temporary illness lays him on his back, he writes in bed one of his most
careful and thoughtful papers, the discourse on 'The Technical Elements in Style.' When ophthalmia confines him to a darkened room,
he writes by the diminished light. When after hemorrhage, his right
hand has to be held in a sling, he writes some of his 'Child's Garden'
with his left hand. When the hemorrhage has been so bad that he
dare not speak, he dictates a novel in the deaf and dumb alphabet."
When one has lived with handicapped folk, discerning behind the
small amount of work the infinite willingness for more, and in the
work done a quality that makes quantity seem negligible, he perceives that deeds are no sufficient measure of spiritual value. Only
an eye that pierces behind the unwrought work to the *man,* willing
while the flesh was weak, can ever estimate how much some spirits
are worth.

Deeds alone are an insufficient basis for judgment because *men
face unequal opportunities.* Some start with one talent, some with
ten. The cherished son of a Christian family ought to live a decent
life; how favorable his chance! But if a vagrant wharf-rat by some
mysterious vision of decency and determination of character makes
a man of himself, how much more his credit! The worth of goodness
cannot be estimated without knowledge of the struggle which it cost.
When one considers the smug, conventional respectability of some,
possessing every favorable help to goodness, and the rough but genuine integrity of others who have fought a great fight against crippling
handicaps to character, he sees why, in any righteous judgment, the

last will be first, as Jesus said, and the first last. Only God, with
power to understand what heredity and circumstance some men
have faced, what enticements they have met, what a fight they have
really waged even when they may have seemed to fail, can tell how
much they are worth.

> "What's done we partly may compute,
> But know not what's resisted."

Judgment based on deeds alone can never truly estimate a man,
because in every important decision of our lives an *"unpublished
self" finds no expression in our outward act.* Duty is not always
clear; at times it seems a labyrinth without a clue. Perplexed, we
balance in long deliberation the opposing reasons for this act or that,
until, forced to choose, we obtain only a majority vote for the decision. Yet that uncertain majority alone is published in our deed;
man's eyes never see the unexpressed protestant minority behind.
And when the choice proves wrong, and friends are grieved and
enemies condemn and what we did is hateful to ourselves, only one
who knows how much we wanted to do right, and who accounts not
only the published but the unpublished self can truly estimate our
worth. Peter, who denied his Lord, it may be because he wanted the
privilege of being near him at the trial, is not the only one who has
appealed from the outward aspect of his deed to the inner intention
of his heart: "Lord, thou knowest all things; thou knowest that I
love thee" (John 21:17).

Moreover, even when we choose aright, *no deed can ever gather
into utterance all that is best and deepest in us.* A mother's love is
as much greater than any word she speaks or act she does, as the
sunshine is greater than the focused point where in a burning glass
we gather a ray of it. We are infinitely more than words can utter
or deeds express. No adequate judgment, therefore, can rest on deeds
alone. A machine may be estimated by its output, but a man is too
subtle and profound, his motives and purposes too inexpressible, his
temptations and inward struggles too intimate and unrevealed, his
possibilities too great to be roughly estimated by his acts alone.

> "Not on the vulgar mass
> Called 'work' must sentence pass,
> Things done, that took the eye and had the price;

O'er which, from level stand,
The low world laid its hand,
Found straightway to its mind, could value in a trice:

But all, the world's coarse thumb
And finger failed to plumb,
So passed in making up the main account;
All instincts immature,
All purposes unsure,
That weighed not as his work, yet swelled the man's amount:

Thoughts hardly to be packed
Into a narrow act,
Fancies that broke through language and escaped;
All I could never be,
All, men ignored in me,
This, I was worth to God, whose wheel the pitcher shaped."

v

If, however, we are to understand the Christian's meaning when he speaks of being saved by faith (Rom. 3:28; 5:1; Gal. 3:24), we need to see not only that men are worth more than they *do*, but as well that they are worth more than they *are*. Some things always start large and grow small; some things always start small and grow large; but a man may do either, and his value is determined not so much by the position he is in, as it is by the direction in which he is moving. Even of stocks upon the market in their rise and fall this truth is clear. The figure at which a stock is quoted is important, but the meaning of that figure cannot be understood unless one knows whether it was reached on the way up or the way down. How much more is any static judgment of a man impossible! One starts at the summit, with endowments and opportunities that elevate him far above his fellows, and frittering away his chance, drifts down. Another, beginning at the bottom, by dint of resolute endeavor climbs upward, achieving character in the face of odds before which ordinary men succumb. Somewhere these two men will pass, and, statically judged, will be of equal worth. But one is drifting down; one climbing up. The innermost secret of their spiritual value lies in that hidden fact. *When, therefore, one would judge a man, he must pierce*

*behind the deeds that he can see, behind the present quality that he
can estimate, back to the thing the man has set his heart upon, to the
direction of his life, to the ideal which masters him—that is, to his
faith.* There lies the potential future of the man, his ultimate worth,
the seed of his coming fruit. If one has eyes to see what that faith is,
he knows the man and what the man is bound to be.

When, therefore, men set their hearts on Christ, lay hold on him
by faith as life's Master and its goal, that faith opens the door to
God's forgiveness. In Augustine's luminous phrase, "The Christian
already has in Christ what he hopes for in himself." He is Christ's
brother in the filial life with God, young, immature, undeveloped—
but the issue of that life is the measure of the stature of Christ's fulness. God does not demand the end when only the beginning is possible, does not scorn the dawn because it is not noon. He welcomes
the first movement of man's spirit toward him, not for the fruit
which yet is unmatured, but for the seed which still is in the germ;
he takes the will for the deed, because the will is earnest; he sees
the journey's end in Christlike character, when at the road's beginning the pilgrim takes the first step by faith. There is no fiction here;
God ought to forgive and welcome such a man. All good parents act
so toward their children. This divine grace corresponds with truth,
for a man is *worth* the central, dominant faith, that determines life's
direction and decides its goal. And the Gospel that God so deals
with man, announced in the words of Jesus, illustrated in his life,
sealed in his death, has been a boon to the race that puts all men
under an immeasurable debt to Christ.

VI

This method of judgment which all good men use with their
friends and families has been often disbelieved, in its Christian
formulations, because it has been misrepresented and misunderstood. But human life, far outside religious boundaries, continually
illustrates the wisdom and righteousness of so judging men by faith.
Roswell McIntyre deserted during the Civil War; he was caught,
court-martialed, and condemned to death. He stood with no defense
for his deed, no just complaint against the penalty, and with nothing to plead save shame for his act, and faith that, with another
chance, he could play the man. On that, the last recourse of the
condemned, President Lincoln pardoned him.

"EXECUTIVE MANSION,
Oct. 4, 1864.

Upon condition that Roswell McIntyre of Co. E, 6th Reg't of
New York Cavalry, returns to his Regiment and faithfully serves out
his term, making up for lost time, or until otherwise discharged, he
is fully pardoned for any supposed desertion heretofore committed,
and this paper is his pass to go to his regiment.

ABRAHAM LINCOLN."

Was such clemency an occasion for lax character? The answer is
written across the face of Mr. Lincoln's letter in the archives:
"Taken from the body of R. McIntyre at the Battle of Five Forks,
Va., 1865." Five Forks was the last cavalry action of the war; Mc-
Intyre went through to the finish.

Any one who knows the experience of being forgiven understands
the motives that so remake a pardoned deserter. The relief from the
old crushing condemnation, the joy of being trusted again beyond
desert, the gratitude that makes men rather die than be untrue
a second time, the unpayable indebtedness from which ambition
springs, "whether at home or absent, to be well-pleasing unto him"
(II Cor. 5:9)—this is the moral consequence of being pardoned.
Goodness so begotten reaches deep and high, has in it conscious
joy and hope, feels vividly the value of its moral victories, possesses
great motives for sacrificial service in the world. The Apocalypse is
right. There is a song in heaven that angels cannot sing. Only men
like McIntyre will know how to sing it.

The vital and transforming faith that saves is always better presented in a story than in an argument, and in the Scripture the best
description of it is Jesus' parable of the Prodigal. As the Master drew
that portrait of life in the far country, all the watching Pharisees
thought that such a boy was lost. The Prodigal himself must have
guessed that his case was hopeless. His friends, his character, his
reputation, his will were gone, and in the inner court-room of his
soul with maddening iteration he heard sentence passed, Guilty.
Only one hope remained. If he was unspoiled enough by the far
country's pitiless brutality to think that at home they might bear
no grudge, might find forgiveness possible, might offer him another
chance as a hired servant, if he could think that perhaps his father
even *wanted* him to come home, then there was hope. With such
slender faith the boy turned back from the far country. He had the

same lack of character, the same weakened will, the same evil habits. Only one difference had as yet been wrought. Before, he had been facing toward swine, now he was facing toward home. The *direction* of his life was changed by faith. And when the father saw him, homeward bound, *"while he was yet afar off,"* forgiveness welcomed him. No pardon could unload from the lad's life all the fearful consequences of his sin. As long as he lived, the scars on health, repute, and usefulness were there. But forgiveness could take the sin away *as a barrier to personal friendship with the father;* the old relationships of mutual confidence, helpfulness, and love could be restored; the glorious chance could be bestowed of fighting through the battle for character, not hopelessly in the far country, but victoriously at home.

One of the chief glories of the Gospel is that it has so reclaimed the waste of humanity, made sons of Prodigals and patriots of McIntyres. Its Pauls were persecutors, its Augustines the slaves of lust, and its rank and file men and women to whom Christ's message has meant forgiveness, reinstatement, a new chance, and boundless hope. Scientific business conserves its waste and makes invaluable by-products from what once was slag; but Christ has been the conserver of mankind. The lost and sick have been returned to sanity and wholesomeness and service; humanity has been enriched beyond computation, with Bunyans and Goughs and Jerry McAuleys. Tolstoi's simple confession in "My Religion" is typical of multitudes: "Five years ago I came to believe in Christ's teaching, and my life suddenly became changed: I ceased desiring what I had wished before, and began to desire what I had not wished before. What formerly had seemed good to me appeared bad, and what had seemed bad appeared good. . . . The direction of my life, my desires became different: what was good and bad changed places." Tolstoi had indulged, as he acknowledges, in every form of unmentionable vice practiced in Russia; and yet forgiven, reinstated, transformed, he was carried to his burial by innumerable Russian peasants with banners flying. Where Christ's influence has vitally come, the loss and wreck and flotsam of the moral world have been so reclaimed to character and power.

At the beginning of the Christian era, a few desolate sand lagoons lay off the Paduan coast of Italy. There the wild fowl made their nests; the lonely skiffs of fishermen threaded the reedy channels; the storms washed the shifting and uncertain sands. And possibly to this day the lagoons would have been thus barren and deserted, had not the Huns swept down on Italy. The Huns made the building of Venice necessary. They did not intend so fair a consequence of their terrific onslaughts. Their thoughts were on death and pillage. But because they came, the Italians fled to the lagoons, built there, behind the barricade of restless waters, their gleaming city, developed there the commerce that combed the world, built the Doge's palace as the abode of justice, and raised St. Mark's in praise of God. Venice was the city of Salvation; it rose resplendent because the Huns had come. So Christ turns the ruin of sin to victory, and builds in human life character, recovered and triumphant. If his Gospel can have its way, a spiritual Venice will arise to make the onslaught of the moral Huns an evil with a glorious issue. What wonder that inexpressible devotion has been felt for him by all his people?

CHAPTER XI

Faith in Christ the Savior: Power

DAILY READINGS

As we saw in the last week's study, Christian faith has always centered around the person of Jesus himself. This week let us consider some testimonies from the New Testament as to the meaning and effect of this definitely Christian faith.

Eleventh Week, First Day

It must be clear to any observing mind that the world does not suffer from lack of faith. There is faith in plenty; everybody is exercising it on some object. In the Bible we read of folk who "trust in vanity" (Isa. 59:4), who "trust in lying words" (Jer. 7:4), or "in the abundance of riches" (Psalm 52:7); and the Master exclaims over the difficulty which those who "trust in riches" have when they try to enter the Kingdom of God (Mark 10:24). Faith, then, is a necessary faculty of the soul: the power by which we commit ourselves to any object that wins our devotion and commands our allegiance. No man avoids its use, and men differ only in the objects toward which their faith is directed. Of all the tragedies caused by the misuse of human powers, none is more frequent and disastrous than the ruin that follows the misuse of faith. With this necessary and powerful faculty in our possession, capable of use on things high or low, to what determination can a man more reasonably set himself than this?—*since I must and do use faith on something, I will choose the highest.* It is with such a rational and worthy choice that the Christian turns to Jesus. He is the best we know; we will direct our faith toward him. This does not mean that in the end our faith does not rest on God; it does, for Jesus is the Way, the Door, as he said, and faith in him moves up through him to the One who sent him. As Paul put it, "Such confidence have we through Christ to God-ward" (II Cor. 3:4). But faith in Jesus is the most vivid, true, and compelling way we have of committing ourselves to the highest and best we know. In the light of this truth, we can understand why John calls such faith the supreme "work" which God demands of us.

Work not for the food which perisheth, but for the food which abideth unto eternal life, which the Son of Man shall give unto you: for him the Father, even God, hath sealed. They said therefore unto him, What must we do, that we may work the works of God? Jesus answered and said unto them, This is the work of God, that ye believe on him whom he hath sent.—John 6:27-29.

Gracious Father! Thou hast revealed Thyself gloriously in Jesus Christ, the Son of Thy love. In Him we have found Thee, or rather, are found of Thee. By His life, by His words and deeds, by His trials and sufferings, we are cleansed from sin and rise into holiness. For in Him Thou hast made disclosure of Thine inmost being and art drawing us into fellowship with Thy life. As we stand beneath His Cross, or pass with Him into the Garden of His Agony, it is Thy heart that we see unveiled, it is the passion of Thy love yearning over the sinful, the wandering, seeking that it may save them. No man hath seen Thee at any time, but out from the unknown has come the Son of Man to declare Thee. And now we know Thy name. When we call Thee Father, the mysteries of existence are not so terrible, our burdens weigh less heavily upon us, our sorrows are touched with joy. Thy Son has brought the comfort that we need, the comfort of knowing that in all our afflictions Thou art afflicted, that in Thy grief our lesser griefs are all contained. Let the light which shines in His face, shine into our hearts, to give us the knowledge of Thy glory, to scatter the darkness of fear, of wrong, of remorse, of foreboding, and to constrain our lives to finer issues of peace and power and spiritual service. And this prayer we offer in Christ's name. Amen.—Samuel McComb.

Eleventh Week, Second Day

The New Testament clearly reveals the experience that *forgiveness* comes in answer to such self-committing faith in Christ as we spoke of yesterday.

And he said unto her, Thy sins are forgiven. And they that sat at meat with him began to say within themselves, Who is this that even forgiveth sins? And he said unto the woman, Thy faith hath saved thee; go in peace.—Luke 7:48-50.

In popular thought forgiveness is often shallowly conceived. It is thought to be an easy agreement to forget offense, a good-natured waving aside of injuries committed as though the evil done were of no consequence. But forgiveness is really a most profound and searching experience; and it takes two persons, each sacrificially desirous of achieving it, before it can be perfected. In the pardoner, the passion for saviorhood must submerge all disgust at the sin in love for the sinner; and in the pardoned, desire for a new life must create sacrificial willingness to hate and forsake the evil and humbly accept a new chance. It follows, therefore, that no one can forgive another, no matter how willing he may be to do so, unless the recipient fulfils the conditions that make pardon possible. Forgiveness is a mutual operation; no forgetting or good will on the part of one person is forgiveness at all; and the attitude in the forgiven man that makes the reception of pardon possible is negatively penitence and positively faith. Any experience of human forgiveness reveals that the offender must detest his sin and turn from it in trust and self-commitment to claim the mercy and choose the ideals of the one whom he has wronged. That God in Christ is willing to forgive is the Christian Gospel; and if we go unforgiven it is for lack of faith. That is the hand which grasps the proffered pardon.

Almighty God, whose salvation is ever nigh to them that seek Thee, we think of our little lives, of their wayward ways, and we remember Thee and are troubled. Our days pass from us and we are heated with strifes, and troubles and restless, with mean temptations and fugitive desires. We spend our years in much carelessness, and too seldom do we think of the greatness of our trust and the wonder and mystery of our being. We are vexed with vain dreams and trivial desires. We live our days immersed in petty passions. We strain after poor uncertainties. We pursue the shadows of this passing life and continually are we visited by our own self-contempt and bitterness. We have known the better and have chosen the worse. We have felt the glory and power of a higher life and yet have surrendered to ignoble temptations and to satisfactions that end with the hour.

Almighty Father, of Thy goodness do Thou save our lives, so smitten with passion, from the failure and misery that else must come to us. Be with us in our hours of self-communion, and inspire us with good purpose and service to Thee. Be with us when heart and flesh faint, and there seems no help or safety near us. Be with us when we are carried into the dry and lonely places, seeking a rest that is not in them. Sustain us, we beseech Thee, under the burden of our many errors and failures. From the confused aims and purposes of our lives may there be brought forth, by the aid of Thy Spirit, and the teaching and discipline of life, lives constant and assured in service and obedience to Thee. Amen.—John Hunter.

Eleventh Week, Third Day

It is clear in the New Testament that all the *free movements of divine help* depend on the presence of man's faith. Words like these are continually on the lips of Jesus: "Be of good cheer; thy faith hath made thee whole" (Matt. 9:22); "According to your faith be it done unto you" (Matt. 9:29); "Great is thy faith: be it done unto thee even as thou wilt" (Matt. 15:28). Human life as a whole confirms the truth which such words suggest: *Man's faith is always the limit of his blessing; he never obtains more than he believes in.* Men live in a world of unappropriated truth and unused power; and the blessings of truth and power can be reached only by ventures of faith. Even electricity withholds its service from a man who, like Abdul Hamid, has not faith enough to try. In personal relationships this fact becomes even more clear. Whatever gifts of good will may be waiting in the heart of any man, we are shut out from them forever, unless we have the grace of faith in the man and open-hearted self-commitment to him. As the Christian Gospel sees man's case, the central tragedy lies here: that God in Christ is willing to do so much more in and for and through us than we have faith enough to let him do. Our unbelief is not a matter of theoretical concern alone; it practically disables God, it handicaps his operation in the world, it is

an "evil heart of unbelief, in falling away from the living God"
(Heb. 3:12). The divine will is forced to wait upon the lagging
faith of man. How often the Master exclaimed, "O ye of little faith!"
(Matt. 6:30; 8:26). And the reason for his lament was eminently
practical.

And coming into his own country he taught them in their synagogue, insomuch that they were astonished, and said, Whence hath
this man this wisdom, and these mighty works? Is not this the carpenter's son? is not his mother called Mary? and his brethren,
James, and Joseph, and Simon, and Judas? And his sisters, are they
not all with us? Whence then hath this man all these things? And
they were offended in him. But Jesus said unto them, A prophet is
not without honor, save in his own country, and in his own house.
And he did not many mighty works there because of their unbelief.
—Matt. 13:54-58.

*Almighty God, our Heavenly Father, we desire to come to Thee
in all humility and sincerity. We are sinful; pardon Thou us. We are
ignorant; enlighten Thou our darkness. We are weak; inspire us
with strength. In these times of doubt, uncertainty, and trial, may
we ever feel conscious of Thine everlasting light. Soul of our soul!
Inmost Light of truth! Manifest Thyself unto us amid all shadows.
Guide us in faith, hope, and love, until the perfect day shall dawn,
and we shall know as we are known.*

*Almighty God, teach us, we pray Thee, by blessed experience, to
apprehend what was meant of old when Jesus Christ was called the
power of God unto salvation, for we stand in need of salvation from
sin, from doubt, from weakness, from craven fear; we cannot save
ourselves; we are creatures of a day, short-sighted, and too often
driven about by every wind of passion and opinion. We need to be
stayed upon a higher strength. We need to lay hold of Thee. Manifest Thyself unto us, our Father, as the Saviour of our souls, and
deliver us from the bondage of corruption into the glorious liberty of
the children of God. Amen.*—John Hunter.

Eleventh Week, Fourth Day

Not only is man's power to appropriate the divine blessing dependent on faith; in the experience of the New Testament man's
power of achievement has the same source.

Then came the disciples to Jesus apart, and said, Why could not we cast it out? And he saith unto them, Because of your little faith: for verily I say unto you, If ye have faith as a grain of mustard seed, ye shall say unto this mountain, Remove hence to yonder place; and it shall remove; and nothing shall be impossible unto you.—Matt. 17:19, 20.

Mountains are symbols of difficulty, and the Master's affirmation here that faith alone can remove them is clearly confirmed in human experience. It may seem at times as though faith, compared with the obstacles, were like a minute mustard seed before the ranges of Lebanon, but faith can overcome even that disproportion in size. Great leaders always must have such confidence. Listen to Mazzini: "The people lack faith . . . the faith that arouses the multitudes, faith in their own destiny, in their own mission, and in the mission of the epoch; the faith that combats and prays; the faith that enlightens and bids men advance fearlessly in the ways of God and humanity, with the sword of the people in their hand, the religion of the people in their heart, and the future of the people in their soul." In any great movement for human good, the ultimate and deciding question always is: How many people can be found who have faith enough to believe in the cause and its triumph? When enough folk have faith, any campaign for human welfare can be won. Without faith men "collapse into a yielding mass of plaintiveness and fear"; with faith they move mountains. And when men have faith in Christ as God's Revealor—faith, not formal and abstract, but real and vital—they begin to feel about the word "impossible" as Mirabeau did, "Never mention to me again that blockhead of a word!"

O God, our Father, our souls are made sick by the sight of hunger and want and nakedness; of little children bearing on their bent backs the burden of the world's work; of motherhood drawn under the grinding wheels of modern industry; and of overburdened manhood, with empty hands, stumbling and falling.

Help us to understand that it is not Thy purpose to do away with life's struggle, but that Thou desirest us to make the conditions of that struggle just and its results fair.

Enable us to know that we may bring this to pass only through love and sympathy and understanding; only as we realize that all are alike Thy children—the rich and the poor, the strong and the weak, the fortunate and the unfortunate. And so, our Father, give us an ever-truer sense of human sisterhood; that with patience and stead- fastness we may do our part in ending the injustice that is in the land, so that all may rejoice in the fruits of their toil and be glad in Thy sunshine.

Keep us in hope and courage even amid the vastness of the un- dertaking and the slowness of the progress, and sustain us with the knowledge that our times are in Thy hand. Amen.—Helen Ring Robinson.

Eleventh Week, Fifth Day

Faith in Christ has always been consummated, in the experience to which the New Testament introduces us, in an inward transfor- mation of life.

I have been crucified with Christ; and it is no longer I that live, but Christ liveth in me: and that life which I now live in the flesh I live in faith, the faith which is in the Son of God, who loved me, and gave himself up for me.—Gal. 2: 20.

Such conversion of life is the normal result of a vital fellowship whose bond is faith. For one thing, a man at once begins to care a great deal more about his own quality when he believes in Christ and in Christ's love. "What a King stoops to pick up from the mire cannot be a brass farthing, but must be a pearl of great price." To be loved by anyone is to enter into a new estimate of one's possible value; to be loved by God in Christ is to come into an experience where our possible value makes us alike ashamed of what we are and jubilant over what we may become. We begin saying with Irenæus, "Jesus Christ became what we are that he might make us what he is." And then, faith, ripening into fellowship, opening the life sensi- tively to the influence of the friend, issues in a character infused by the friend's character. He lives in us. Such transformation of life does not happen in a moment; it requires more than instantaneous expo- sure to take the Lord's picture on a human heart; but time-exposure will do it, and "Christ in us" be alike our hope of glory and our secret of influence.

O Father Eternal, we thank Thee for the new and living way into Thy presence made for us in Christ; the way of trust, sincerity, and sacrifice. Beneath His cross we would take our stand, in communion with His Spirit would we pray, in fellowship with the whole Church of Christ we would seek to know Thy mind and will.

We desire to know all the fulness of Christ, to appropriate His unsearchable riches, to feed on His humanity whereby Thou hast become to us the bread of our inmost souls and the wine of life, to become partakers of Thy nature, share Thy glory, and become one with Thee through Him.

Give unto us fellowship with His sufferings and insight into the mystery of His cross, so that we may be indeed crucified with Him, be raised to newness of life, and be hidden with Christ in Thee.

We desire to make thankful offering of ourselves as members of the body of Christ; in union with all the members may we obey our unseen Head, so that the Body may be undivided, and Thy love, and healing power, and very Self may be incarnate on the earth in one Holy Universal Church. Amen.—W. E. Orchard.

Eleventh Week, Sixth Day

With faith in Christ so seen as the secret of divine forgiveness and assistance, of achieving power and inward transformation, there can be little surprise at the solicitude which the New Testament shows concerning the disciples' faith. We find this urgent interest in Paul:

Wherefore when we could no longer forbear, we thought it good to be left behind at Athens alone; and sent Timothy, our brother and God's minister in the gospel of Christ, to establish you, and to comfort you concerning your faith; . . . night and day praying exceedingly that we may see your face, and may perfect that which is lacking in your faith.—I Thess. 3:1, 2, 10.

We are bound to give thanks to God always for you, brethren, even as it is meet, for that your faith groweth exceedingly, and the love of each one of you all toward one another aboundeth.—II Thess. 1: 3.

And one of the most appealing revelations of Jesus' habit in prayer concerns his supplication for Peter's faith.

Simon, Simon, behold, Satan asked to have you, that he might sift you as wheat: but I made supplication for thee, that thy faith fail not; and do thou, when once thou hast turned again, establish thy brethren.—Luke 22: 31, 32.

In all such passages one feels at once that faith is used as Paul uses it in the thirteenth chapter of First Corinthians—a comrade and ally of hope and love. It is not a matter of dogma and does not move in the realm of opinion, although ideas of the first magnitude may be involved in it. It is primarily a bond of divine fellowship, which at once keeps the life receptive to all that God would do for the man and moves the man to do all that he should for God. If that fails, even Peter would fall in ruins, and the expression is none too strong, when in I Timothy the failure of such vital faith is described as a "shipwreck" (I Tim. 1:19). But when by faith the consciousness of God has grown clear, and alliance with him is so real that we stop arguing about it and begin counting on it in daily living, the increment of power and confidence and stability which a man may win is quite incalculable.

O Thou plenteous Source of every good and perfect gift, shed abroad the cheering light of Thy seven-fold grace over our hearts. Yea, Spirit of love and gentleness, we most humbly implore Thy assistance. Thou knowest our faults, our failings, our necessities, the dulness of our understanding, the waywardness of our affections, the perverseness of our will. When, therefore, we neglect to practice what we know, visit us, we beseech Thee, with Thy grace, enlighten our minds, rectify our desires, correct our wanderings, and pardon our omissions, so that by Thy guidance we may be preserved from making shipwreck of faith, and keep a good conscience, and may at length be landed safe in the haven of eternal rest; through Jesus Christ our Lord. Amen.—Anselm, 1033.

Eleventh Week, Seventh Day

Some who gladly acknowledge the surprising results which faith can work in life, do not see any great importance in the object to which faith attaches itself. They say that faith is merely a psychological attitude, and that faith in one thing does as well as faith in another. Folk are healed, they point out, by all kinds of faith, whether directed toward fetishes, or saints' relics, or metaphysical theories, or God himself. It is the faith, they say, and not the object, which does the work. There is a modicum of truth in this. Faith, by its very power to organize man's faculties and give them definite set and drive, is itself a master force, and if a man has no interest beyond the achievement of some immediate end, like conquering nervous qualms or getting strength for a special task, he may achieve that end by believing in almost anything, provided he believes hard enough. *But to believe in some things may debauch the intelligence and lower the moral standards, even while it achieves a practical end.* To win power for a business task by believing in a palm-reader's predictions is entirely possible, but it is a poor bargain; a man sells out his intelligence for cash. The object in which a man believes does make an immense difference in the effect of his faith on his *mind* and *character.* An African savage may gain courage for an ordeal by believing in his fetish—but how immeasurable is the abyss between the meaning of that faith for the whole of life and the meaning of a Christian's faith in God! We have no business, for the sake of immediate gain, to allow our faith to rest in anything lower than the highest.

Blessed be the God and Father of our Lord Jesus Christ, who according to his great mercy begat us again unto a living hope by the resurrection of Jesus Christ from the dead, unto an inheritance incorruptible, and undefiled, and that fadeth not away, reserved in heaven for you, who by the power of God are guarded through faith unto a salvation ready to be revealed in the last time. Wherein ye greatly rejoice, though now for a little while, if need be, ye have been put to grief in manifold trials, that the proof of your faith, being more precious than gold that perisheth though it is proved by fire, may be found unto praise and glory and honor at the revelation of Jesus Christ: whom not having seen ye love; on whom, though now ye see him not, yet believing, ye rejoice greatly with joy unspeakable and full of glory: receiving the end of your faith, even the salvation of your souls.—I Peter 1:3-9.

Gracious Father of our spirits, in the stillness of this worship may we grow more sure of Thee, who art often closest to us when we feel Thou hast forsaken us. The toil and thought of daily life leave us little time to think of Thee; but may the silence of this holy place make us aware that though we may forget Thee, Thou dost never forget us. Perhaps we have grown careless in contact with common things, duty has lost its high solemnities, the altar fires have gone untended, Thy light within our minds has been distrusted or ignored. As we withdraw awhile from all without, may we find Thee anew within, until thought grows reverent again, all work is hallowed, and faith reconsecrates all common things as sacraments of love.

If pride of thought and careless speculation have made us doubtful of Thee, recover for us the simplicity that understands Thou art never surer than when we doubt Thee, that through all failures of faith Thou becomest clearer, and so makest the light that once we walked by seem but darkness. Help us then to rest our faith on the knowledge of our imperfection, our consciousness of ignorance, our sense of sin, and see in them shadows cast by the light of Thy drawing near.

If Thy purposes have crossed our own and Thy will has broken ours, enable us to trust the wisdom of Thy perfect love and find Thy will to be our peace.

So lead us back to meet Thee where we may have missed Thee. Amen.—W. E. Orchard.

COMMENT FOR THE WEEK

I

The forgiveness which the Gospel offers—reinstating a man in the personal relationships against which he sinned, and giving him another chance—opens opportunity, but by itself it does not furnish power. The saviorhood of Christ, however, so far from failing at this crucial point, makes here its chief claim to preeminence. However one may explain it, the normal quality of a genuine Christian life is moral energy. The Gospel not alone to Paul, but to all generations of Christ's disciples, had been "God's saving power for everyone who has faith" (Rom. 1:16).[1]

Faith always supplies moral dynamic. Emerson's challenge "They can conquer who believe they can," is easily verified in daily life. In practical business, in social reform, in personal character, no more common or fatal barrier to success exists than disbelief in possibilities. While some who think they can when they cannot, prove the rule by its exception, we are sure in advance that one who believes he cannot, has lost his battle before it has begun. Granted a task worth doing, sufficient strength for its accomplishment, and motives in plenty to make success desirable, and one insinuating enemy can

---

[1] Moffatt's translation.

spoil the enterprise. Let the subtle fear that the task is impossible obsess the thought, paralyze the nerve, and no hope is left. Like chlorine gas, such fear defeats us before we have begun to fight and fills our trenches with asphyxiated powers.

Anyone who is to be a savior to mankind, therefore, must be able to make men say, "I can." That Christ has had that influence on men is the commonplace of Christian biography from the beginning until now. "In him who strengthens me I am able for anything" (Phil. 4:13)[2] is a word of Paul's which the best Christian experience confirms. It does not mean that men can do what they will, overriding all obstacles to chosen goals; it means that they are aware of resources in reserve, of power around them and in them, so that they are not afraid of anything which they may face. If a duty ought to be done, they are confident that they can do it; if a trouble must be borne, they are assured that they can bear it.

This buoyant faith is more than a grace of temperament. In Paul's case, for example, it was not due to rugged health, for that he lacked; it was not the easy optimism of some happiness cult, for he was a persecuted man, bearing in his body "the marks of the Lord Jesus"; and such a note of assured resource as we just have quoted did not come from the hopefulness of fortunate circumstance, but from a prison where he wore a chain. Paul himself is certain that his sense of power springs from discipleship to Jesus. And when one turns to the gospels, he sees that whenever the Master had opportunity to exert to the full his influence on men, some such result as here appears in Paul is evident. A contagious personality always enlarges the sense of possibilities and powers in other men. A man, leaving Trinity Church, where he had heard Phillips Brooks, exclaimed, "He always makes me feel so strong." It was said that one could not stand for a moment with Edmund Burke under an archway, to let a shower pass by, without emerging a greater man. Each one of us knows folk who so impress him. We go into their presence, weak, self-pitiful; when we come out, the horizons are broader, the possibilities have enlarged, there is more in us than we had suspected, we are convinced that we *can*.

To a degree that escapes our estimation Jesus exerted that influence on men. Napoleon said that he made his generals out of mud. Out of what, then, did the Master make his apostles? At the beginning, Peter, for example, is protesting, "Depart from me, for I am a

---

[2]Moffatt's translation.

sinful man, O Lord," and Jesus is bending over him, saying: Come after me, and I will make you a fisher of men; if you will, you can. After months of influence, Peter, still shamed and weak, is pleading his love against his deed, and Jesus is saying: Feed my sheep; feed my lambs; if you will, you can. In Jesus' relationship with his disciple, a great personality stands over a lesser one, by life and word insistently saying, *You can,* until power is vitally transmitted, and in the vacillating, vehement Simon there emerges rock-like, stable Peter.

Throughout the Christian centuries nothing has been more typical than this of the Master's influence on men. He has come to innumerable sodden lives, held slaves to tyrannous sin, saying in the hopelessness of bondage, "I cannot," and he has touched them with his contagious confidence, until they rose into freedom, saying, "By the help of God, I can!" He has come into social situations where ancient evils, long entrenched and seemingly invincible, withstood the assault of reformation, and he has put inexhaustible resource into his people, until they said with an old reformer, "Impossible? If that is all that is the matter, let us go ahead!" He has come to his Church, reluctant to undertake a world-wide mission, staggered by the task's magnitude, and he has made men pray with *life* and not alone with lip, "Thy Kingdom come, Thy will be done on earth as it is in heaven." Wherever the influence of Christ vitally has come, the horizons of possibility have widened and the sense of power grown inexhaustible.

Such influence is of the very essence of saviorhood and the attitude that appropriates it is saving faith. When John B. Gough, desperately enmeshed in habit, faces the Christian Gospel of release one easily may trace his changing response. Dubious at first, he wants to believe it but he does not dare. He wishes it were true, but the whole logic of his situation, his long habit, his spoiled reputation, his weakened will, argue against the possibility. As Augustine said about his lust, "The worse that I knew so well had more power over me than the better that I knew not." Still, a note of authority in the Gospel, as though spoken by one whose power to perform is equal to the thing he promises, arrests Gough's mind, captures his imagination, awakens his spirit's deep desire, until at last the Master's call, "You can," is answered by the human cry, "I will," and the man moves out into new possibilities, new powers, and increasing liberty. That *is* salvation. It is no formal status decreed by legal enactment, as though a judge technically acquitted a-prisoner. It is new life, inward liberation from old habits, apprehensions, anxieties, and fears. It lifts horizons, consumes impossibilities, and at the center of life sets the stirring conviction that what ought to be done can be done.

Christians who are accustomed lightly to assert that they are saved need specially to take this truth to heart. Some speak as though salvation were a technicality and they sing about it,

> " 'Tis done, the great transaction's done."

To many such, were candor courteous, one would wish to say: Saved? Saved from what? You are habitually anxious. Your life is continually vexed with little fears and apprehensions. When trouble comes, you are sure that you cannot stand it; when tasks present themselves, you are certain that you cannot perform them. You have pet self-indulgences, from major sins to little meannesses; you know that they are wrong; but when suggestion comes that you surrender them, you are sure that you have not the strength. When causes, plainly Christian, on whose successful issue man's weal depends, appeal to you for help, you weaken every enterprise by your disheartenment. Saved from *what?* Not from fear, timidity, selfishness, and stagnation! And if you say, Saved from Hell—what is Hell but the final subjugation of the soul to such sins as you now are cherishing? The words of Jesus are promises of saviorhood from real and present evils: "Be not *anxious*" (Matt. 6:34); "Go, *sin* no more" (John 8:11); "*Fear* not, little flock" (Luke 12:32). When one, by faith, turns his face homeward from such destroyers of life, he begins to be saved; but only as he lives by faith in fellowship with the Divine and so achieves progressive victory, does he keep on being saved. *The heart of salvation is victorious power.*

II

Not all men feel the need of the power which comes from discipleship to Christ. They live content without such increment of strength as Christians find in faith. Their power is equal to their tasks because their tasks are levelled to their power. One cannot understand, therefore, what the Saviorhood of Christ has meant to men, unless he sees how Christ has created the need of the very power he furnishes. He has done this, in part, *by awakening the desire for an ascending life.* Men do not naturally want to believe in possibilities too great and taxing; it always is easier to leave undisturbed the *status quo.* Even changing one's residence is difficult. Though one may move to a better house, yet to decide to move, to break old relationships, to tear up and refit the furnishings, and to adjust oneself to new associations mean stress and strain. So men come to be at home with habits; they are comfortably accustomed to timidity and self-indulgence. Release into a new life does not lure as privilege; it repels as hardship. Some sins, indeed, are followed by remorse, but others, grown habitual, bring a sense of well-being and content. We like ourselves; we do not want a better life; we are unwilling to pay its cost. Our sins are no bed of nettles, but a lotus land of decent ease. Were we candidly to speak to them, we should say, O Sin, you are a comfortable friend! When most we want forbidden fruit you suggest excuses. You side happily with our inclinations and save us from the struggle that high duty costs and the sacrifice of striving for the best. Among the blessings of our lives, we count you not the least, O decent, comfortable, self-indulgent Sin!

Idlers thus drift listlessly and refuse a voyage with a purpose and a goal; youths living by low standards, look on Christlike character as beyond their interest and possibility; undedicated men find excuse for holding back devotion to great causes in the world—we shelter ourselves from aspiration and enterprise behind our faithlessness. Into such a situation Christ repeatedly has come, bringing a vision of what life ought to be, too imperative to be neglected, too challenging to be denied. Men have been shaken out of their content; the true color of their lives has been revealed against his white background, the meanness of their plans against the wide ranges of his purpose. From seeing him they have gone back to be content in their old habits, but in vain. Can one who has seen a home be happy in a hovel? Ranke, the historian, says, "More guiltless and more powerful, more exalted and more holy, has naught ever been on earth than his conduct, his life, and his death. The human race knows nothing that could be brought even afar off into comparison with it." So he has been the disturber of man's ignoble self-content, and to say that we believe in him means that, no longer able to endure the thing we are, we go on pilgrimage toward the thing he is. Faith means that we decide to *move.* This first essential work of saviorhood Christ has wrought, and when men start to follow him, they feel the need of power.

For another thing, Christ has created a thirst for the power he furnishes by *revealing the quality of character in the possession of which salvation ultimately consists.* At the beginning of the ethical development whether of the individual or of the race, goodness is defined in terms of prohibitions. There are many things which men ought *not* to do; they walk embarrassed in the presence of their duty like courtiers before an exacting prince. How negative and repelling such goodness is! As another exclaims: "They do not break the Sabbath themselves, but no one who has to spend it with them likes to see the dreadful day come round. They do not swear themselves, but they make all who know them want to. They are just as good as trying not to be bad can make them."

Discerning spirits, therefore, turn to goodness positively conceived. "Thou shalt not" becomes "Thou shalt"; duty consists of rules to be kept, precepts to be observed, principles to be applied, and we go out to do good deeds to men. But whoever seriously tries to do deeds really good, faces a need of moral elevation, as much beyond the outward act of good as that surpasses the observance of prohibitions. *Good deeds are not a matter of will alone, but of spiritual quality.* Let the wind blow to fan the faces of the sick, but if it discover that it is laden with disease, what shall it do? To blow this way or that may be within volition's power, but not to *cleanse* oneself. The task of character reaches inward, beyond the things we do or refrain from doing to the man we are. Goodness is something more than girding up the loins, blowing upon the hands, and setting to the work of being dutiful. It springs from the spirit's depths; it is tinctured with the spirit's quality; and deeds are never really better than the soul whose utterances they are. From "Thou shalt not do" to "Thou shalt do" and from "Thou shalt do" to "Thou shalt be," man's flying goal of goodness moves. And this ideal in Christ has been incarnate, visible, imperative. He *was* right in the inner quality and flavor of his life; and to be like him involves a pure and powerful personality. Whoever sets that task ahead knows that he cannot strut proudly into it. Like Alice entering Wonderland he must grow very small before he can grow large. The Christ who has power to give has revealed the need of it.

Not only by the intensifying of the ideal, but by its extension, has Christ created thirst for divine help. In youth the problem of character concerns personal habits. Our untamed strength must be broken to the harness, and the snaffle bit be used upon our wayward powers. We justly fear our sins and in their triumph we see the wreck of individual prospects and the ruin of our families' hopes. Our concern centers about ourselves, and its crux is self-mastery. But when in maturity, somewhat "at leisure from ourselves" in settled habits, we no longer fear our own ruin nor think it probable, goodness extends its meaning. To play our part in man's advancement, to live, work, sacrifice, and if need be die for causes on which our children's hopes depend, becomes our ideal. As boys in spring-time when the ice is melting see from a hill-top the swirling flood that overflows the plain, and know that somewhere underneath the unfamiliar and tumultuous rapids the main channel runs, from which the floods have broken, to which in time they must return, so in a generation when man's life has broken its banks in fury we still believe that the main course of the divine purpose is not forever lost. To believe that, and in the strength of it to toil for the ends God seeks, becomes to awakened spirits the essential soul of goodness.

When such meanings enter into his ideal, a man runs straight upon the need of God. For we may make our contribution to the cause of man's good upon the earth and our children may make theirs, but if this world is a spiritual Sahara, never meant for character and social weal, and against the dead set of the desert's power we are building oases here with our unaided fingers, then the issue of our work stands in no doubt. The Sahara will pile its burning sands about us and hurl its blistering winds across us, and we and our works together come to naught. By as much, then, as a man really cares about democracy and liberty and social equity, about human brotherhood and Christian civilization, by so much he needs God, who gathers up the scattered contributions of his children and builds them into victory. A man alone may keep the decalogue, but alone he cannot save the world. Who dreams of that wants power. And Christ has made men dream of that, believe in that with passionate certainty, until "Thy Kingdom come" is the daily prayer of multitudes. To no human strength can such prayer be offered; we are not adequate to an eternal, universal task. Again Christ has brought us to the need of power, and his people call him Savior, because the need which he creates he also satisfies.

In one of the tidal rivers near New York, the building of a bridge was interrupted by a derelict sunk in the river's bottom. Divers put chains about the obstacle and all day long the engineer directed the maneuvering of tugs as they puffed and pulled in vain endeavor to dislodge the hulk. Then a young student, fresh from the technical school, asked for the privilege of trying, and from the vexed, impatient chief obtained his wish. "What will *you* do it with?" the engineer enquired. "The flat-boats in which we brought the granite from Vermont," the young man answered. So when the tide was out, the flat boats were fastened to the derelict. The Atlantic began to come in; its mighty shoulders underneath the boats lifted—lifted until the derelict had to come. The youth had harnessed infinite energy to his task. To the consciousness of such resource in the spiritual world Christ has introduced his people. They have meant not formula but fact, not technicality but experience, when they have called him Savior.

III

This consciousness of power has come in part from Christ's revelation of God the Father. Whoever has sinned against his friend or unkindly wronged a child knows what sin does to personal relationships. How swift a change comes over a son's thought of his father when the son has sinned! The wrong may have been done secretly so that his sire does not know, and the boy alone on earth is conscious of it. But for all that the filial relationship has lost its glory. Before the sin, the son was happy with his father near; they were companions, confidants, and to the boy fatherhood was very beautiful. Now, he is most unhappy with his father near; the father's eyes like a detective's pierce him through, the face like a judge's waits sternly to condemn. He is looking at his father through the dark glasses of his sin, and they distort his vision. When one considers the gods whom men have worshiped, approaching them by bloody altarstairs, offering their first-born to assuage wrath or win from apathy to favor, he sees, extended to a racial scale, our boyhood's tragedy. *Mankind has been looking at the Father through its ignorance and sin and it has seen him beclouded and awry.* Christ changed all that. By what he taught, by what he was, by what he suffered he has said to man, so that man increasingly has believed it—You are wrong about God. He does not stand aloof—careless or vindictive; he is not as he looks to you through the twisted lenses of your evil. He loves you. He *cares* beyond your power to understand, and all my compassion but reveals in time what is eternally in him. He is pledged to the victory of goodness in you and in the world, and you have not used all your power until you have used his, for that, too, is yours.

From that day the fight against sin has been a new thing, and men have gone into it with battle-cries they never used before— "*God* was in Christ, reconciling the world unto himself" (II Cor. 5:19); "*God* commendeth his own love toward us, in that, while we were yet sinners, Christ died for us" (Rom. 5:8); "If *God* is for us, who is against us?" (Rom. 8:31).

This access of power has come in part from Christ's revelation of *man*. When a jewel is taken from darkness into sunlight, there is a two-fold revealing. The sunlight is disclosed in new glory, for it never seemed so beautiful before as it appears breaking in splendor through the jewel's heart. And there is a revelation of the jewel. Dull and unillumined in the dark, it is lustrous when the sun enlightens it. So Christ brought us an unveiling of the Father; the Divine never had seemed so wonderful as when it poured in glory through his purity and love. And he brought as well a new revelation of man. Our human nature, bedimmed by sin and lusterless, he in his own person took up into the light, and lifting it where all mankind could see he cried—This *is* human nature—man as God intended him to be—no slave of fate and dupe of sin, but a free man and a victor. And from that day the war on sin has had new spirit in it, and battle cries that presage triumph have grown familiar on the fighters' lips: "Now are we children of God, and it is not yet made manifest what we shall be" (I John 3:2); "Till we all attain unto the unity of the faith, and of the knowledge of the Son of God, unto a full-grown man, unto the measure of the stature of the fulness of Christ" (Eph. 4:13); "His precious and exceeding great promises; that through these ye may become partakers of the divine nature" (II Pet. 1:4).

IV

Christ's double revelation of God and man, however, has had its vital impact of power on life in what Christians have always called *the experience of the Spirit*. When the New Testament speaks its characteristic word about the Spirit, it means the conscious presence of the living God in the hearts of men, and that is the very essence of religion. The first Christians did not know God in one way only; they knew him in three ways. So one man might know Beethoven the composer and be an authority upon his works; another might know Beethoven the performer and delight in his playing; and another might know Beethoven the man and rejoice in his friendship—but no one could know the whole of Beethoven until he knew him all three ways. The New Testament Christians came thus to God. He was the Father, Creator of all; he was the Character, revealed in Jesus; but as well he was the Spiritual Presence in their lives, their sustenance and power. "The grace of the Lord Jesus Christ, and the love of God, and the communion of the Holy Spirit" (II Cor. 13:14) —such was their experience of the Divine. It was not dogma; it was *life*. God was Creator, Character, and Comforter.

Christian experience is in continual danger of drifting from this vital center. In our age especially, we are prone to find God at the end of an argument and to leave him there. We have been compelled by militant agnosticism to put our apologetic armies on the defensive. Finding it impossible to hold the respect of men's intelligence without reasonable arguments in the faith's behalf we have had to draw such inferences from the nature of the material universe, from the necessities of human thought, the demands of human conscience, and the progress of moral evolution in history, that materialism should be made, what indeed it is, a discredited affair. But God so arrived at, by way of reason, is an external matter. He is an hypothesis to explain the universe. "He sitteth upon the circle of the earth and the inhabitants thereof are as grasshoppers before him." Granted the incalculable value in such faith, putting unity into history and purpose into life—it is not religion and it never can be. *Religion begins when the God outwardly argued is inwardly experienced.* Religion begins when we cease using the tricky and unstable aeroplane of speculation to seek Him among the clouds, and retreat into the fertile places of our own spirits where the living water rises, as Jesus said. God outside of us is a theory; God inside of us becomes a fact. God outside of us is an hypothesis; God inside of us is an experience. God the Father is the possibility of salvation; God the Spirit is actuality of life, joy, peace, and saving power. God the transcendent may do for philosophy, but he is not enough for religion.

Without this completion of the Gospel, Christ's saviorhood does not reach inward to our need. For lacking it, we stand before the Master with the same admiration that a man who is no painter feels when he sees a Raphael. He knows the work is sublime, but he is not proposing to reproduce it. He is conquered by its beauty, but he knows no possibility of its imitation. If, however, there were a spirit of Raphael that could lay hold upon a man's life and transform him to the master's skill and power, then his admiration would become inwardly effective. *It takes the spirit of Raphael to do Raphael's work.* If this gospel of an indwelling dynamic is not coupled with our admiration for Jesus, we are like a student practicing the fingering of the Hallelujah Chorus on an organ from which the power has been shut off. With what accuracy his fingers travel the keys, who can tell? Once Handel's soul, on fire with the passion of harmony, burned itself into that composition. He wrote it upon his knees. But with whatever agility the student's fingers follow the notes, no Hallelujah Chorus comes from his organ to praise God and move men. So the record of this matchless character handed to us in the gospels, like notes of music meant to be played again, is but our despair, if we must attempt its reproduction on a powerless organ. Our admiration for it is external and ineffectual. We fall thereby into a static religion of creed; we have no dynamic religion of progress and hope. This then is the glorious message, where the Christian Gospel reaches its climax, and which alone puts fullest meaning into Jesus' perfect life: *the Spirit of God in Jesus made his quality; that same Spirit is underground in our lives, striving to well up in characters like his, until we live, yet not we, but Christ lives in us.*

Any spring day may serve to illustrate this faith. Where does the restlessness in nature have its source? Every tree, in discontent, hastens to make buds into leaves, and every blade of grass is tremulous with impatient life. No tree, however, is a sufficient explanation of its own haste and dissatisfaction; no flower has in itself the secrets of its eager growth. The spirit of life is abroad, and crowding itself everywhere on old, dead forms, is making them bloom again. Explain then, the moral restlessness of our hearts in other wise! We do ill, and are distraught with remorse until we repent and make reparation. We attain money or talents, and are chased day and night by the urgent call to their spiritual dedication. We conform ourselves to decency and still hear a call for goodness beyond all earthly need. We succeed as the world calls it, and we know that it is failure; we fail as the world sees it, and our hearts sing for joy because we know that we have succeeded. Everywhere we are confronted with a pulsing life that longs to get itself expressed in us. We cannot get away from God. He is not far, he is here. This Spirit, for whom there is no better name than the Spirit of Jesus, is our continual com-

panion. We are locked in an enforced fellowship with him. There is
no friend with whom we deal more directly and continually than
with him. Every time we open an inspiring book and devoutly study
it, this Spirit is pleading for entrance. Every time we pray he stands
at the door and knocks. Every time some child in need, or some great
cause demanding sacrifice, lays claim on us, this Spirit is crying to be
let in. Men's hunger for food, their love for family and friends, are
not more direct, concrete, immediate experiences than our dealings
with this Spirit of the Lord. He is not only God the Father; he is
God the Spirit, striving to dwell in us and work through us.

Into a vital use of this relationship with the Divine, Christ opened
the way and multitudes have followed. He has taught men to find
that same resourcefulness in the spiritual world which science finds
in the physical. Every successful invention of a man like Edison involves a twofold faith: that there is inexhaustible power in the universe and that, with persistent patience and cooperation, there is no
telling what marvels yet may come from the employment of it. Faith
is science's flying column. It runs out into engineering, agriculture,
medicine, and refuses to limit the possibilities. Science is a tremendous believer; it lives by faith that almost anything may yet be done.
Such a relationship Paul sustained with the Spirit. He was confident
of resources there, "exceeding abundantly above all that we ask or
think" (Eph. 3:20). He was a spiritual Edison, a believer in the
divine reality and power and their availability by faith in human life.

Only such a Gospel is adequate to man's deepest need. Sin,
whether its forms be decent or obscene, cripples men's wills with the
appalling certainty that they are slaves. As a hypnotist draws imaginary circles around his victims, across which they cannot step, so Sin,
that Svengali of the soul, whether in personal or social life, paralyzes
its dupes with disbelief in possibilities. To innumerable folk, empris-
oned by their fears and sins, Christ has been the Savior. He has
awakened that faith which, as he said, is the greatest mountain-
mover known to men. They have been "strengthened with power
through his Spirit in the inward man" (Eph. 3:16).

v

When one considers, as we have in these two chapters, what Christ
has meant in the experience of his people, little wonder can remain
that they have called him by such high names as have aroused man's

incredulity. For this Gospel of power has never been separable from
him, as though he were its historic fountain and could easily be forgotten by those who far down-stream enjoyed the water. His personality itself has been the inspiration of his people. At Marston Moor,
when the Puritans and Cavaliers were aligned for battle and all was
in readiness for conflict to begin, Oliver Cromwell came riding across
the plain. And the chronicler says that at the sight of him the Puritans sent up a great victorious shout, as though their battle already
had been won. Some such effect our Lord has had on his disciples.
To explain that effect one would have to speak not so much of his
teaching as of himself—his character and purpose; nor so much of
them as of the Cross where all he taught and was came to a point of
flame that has set the world on fire. Christ was the

> "nerve o'er which do creep
> The else unfelt oppressions of the earth."

He suffered with man and for man, he uniquely embodied in his
own experience the universal law that the consequences of sin fall
in part on the one who loves the sinner and tries to save him; and in
that sacrifice his work for man was consummated, and his influence
over man confirmed. When his people have bowed before him in
unutterable devotion they have been thinking not only of what he
has done for them, but of what it cost him to do it.

Why, therefore, should we wonder that his disciples at their best
have called Jesus divine? His first followers began with no abstract
ideas of deity; they began with "the man, Christ Jesus" (I Tim.
2:5). They had no idea at the first that he was more. His bodily and
mental life had obeyed the laws of normal human development, advancing "in wisdom and stature, and in favor with God and men"
(Luke 2:52). He hungered after his temptation, thirsted on the
Cross, slept from weariness while the boat tossed in a storm, and
exhausted, sat beside the well. Like other men he had elevated hours
of great rejoicing; times when compassion moved him to tears, as
when he saw a multitude unshepherded or, swinging round the brow
of Olivet, beheld Jerusalem; and hours of hot indignation, too, as
when he found his Father's house a den of thieves or spoke out his
heart against the Pharisees. He asked questions, and was astonished,
now at the people's lack of faith, again at the centurion's excess of
it. His fellowship with God was nourished by secret prayer, his

power replenished by retreat to quiet places for communion, and all his life was lived, his temptations faced, his troubles borne, and his work done in a spirit of humble, filial dependence on his Father.

Thus real and human, a sharer in their limitations, their sorrows, and their moral trials, the first disciples saw the Master. But ever as they lived with him, whether in physical presence or in spiritual fellowship, he wrought in them a Savior's work. He became to them manhood indeed, but manhood plus. He grew in their apprehension, as though a boy had thought an ocean's inlet were a lake enclosed, and now discovers that it is the sea itself, and all its tides the pulse of the great deep. How should they name this greatness in their Lord? They were not utterly without a clue, for he himself had introduced them to the life divine. They had learned through him to say about themselves that they were temples in which God dwelt (II Cor. 6:16), that God abode in them (I John 4:12), that he stood ever waiting to come in (Rev. 3:20), and that the possession of the divine nature was the Gospel's promise (II Pet. 1:4). By what other element in their experience could they interpret the greatness of their Lord? It might be inadequate, but it was the best they had. They rose to understand the divine life in him from the experience of the divine life in themselves. "God was in Christ," they said. They never dreamed of claiming equality with him. Like pools beside the sea, they understood the ocean's quality from their own. There are not two kinds of sea-water; nor, with one God, can there be two kinds of divine life. But so understanding the sea, shall the pool claim equality with it? Rather, the sea has deeps, tides, currents, and relationships with the world's life that no pool can ever know. So Christ was at once their brother and their Lord. He was real, because they interpreted his life divine from the foregleams of God's presence in themselves. He was adorable, because he was an ocean to their landlocked pools, and they waited for his tides.

Only by some such road as these first disciples trod can men come to a vital understanding of the Lord. Nothing but *experience* can give us a living estimate of anything; without that theory is vain. Let a man live with the Master's manhood until it grows luminous and through it he sees the character of God; let a man avail himself of the Master's saviorhood until forgiven and empowered he finds the "life that is life indeed"; let a man grow in the experience of God's presence until he knows not only the God without but the God within; and then if he rises to estimate his Lord, he will not hesitate to see in Jesus the incarnate presence of the living God. After that, theology may help or hinder him, according as it is wise and vital or cold and formal; but with theology or not, he knows the heart of the New Testament's attitude toward Jesus. He understands why the first Christians summed up their faith as "believing in the Lord Jesus Christ."

CHAPTER XII

The Fellowship of Faith

DAILY READINGS

Our thought turns, in our closing week of study, from believers taken one by one, to believers gathered in fellowship. This community of faith has wider boundaries than the organized churches; in a real sense it includes all servants of man's ideal aims; yet in the Church we naturally seek the chief meanings of fellowship for faith. Why men do not go to church, is often asked. But why men do go, so that in spite of countless failures in the churches, attendance on public worship and loyalty to organized religion are among mankind's most usual habits, is an inquiry far more important. To that inquiry let us in the daily readings turn our thought.

Twelfth Week, First Day

But woe unto you, scribes and Pharisees, hypocrites! because ye shut the kingdom of heaven against men: for ye enter not in yourselves, neither suffer ye them that are entering in to enter.

Woe unto you, scribes and Pharisees, hypocrites! for ye compass sea and land to make one proselyte; and when he is become so, ye make him twofold more a son of hell than yourself. . . .

Woe unto you, scribes and Pharisees, hypocrites! for ye tithe mint and anise and cummin, and have left undone the weightier matters of the law, justice, and mercy, and faith: but these ye ought to have done, and not to have left the other undone. Ye blind guides, that strain out the gnat, and swallow the camel!—Matt. 23:13-15; 23, 24.

Jesus' indictment of the Jewish Church is terrific, and yet no one who knows the story of the Christian churches can doubt that they often have deserved the same condemnation. They have at times committed all the sins that can be laid at any institution's door; they have been selfish, formal, worldly, cruel. A wonder-story from the Arctic says that once the candle-flames froze and the explorers broke them off and wore them for watch charms; the flames of the great fire congealed and were wound like golden ornaments around men's necks. So repeatedly the burning words of Scripture, the blazing affirmations of old creeds, on fire at first with the passion of souls possessed by God, have been frozen in the churches' Arctic climate, and handed to men like talismans and amulets, with no saving warmth or light. Creeds, rituals, organizations—how often these frozen forms of life have taken the place of inward spiritual power! Dr. Washington Gladden would not be alone in saying: "While therefore I had as large an experience of church-going in my boyhood as most boys can recall, I cannot lay my hand on my heart and say that the church-going helped me to solve my religious problems. In fact, it made those problems more and more tangled and troublesome." And yet the Church goes on. Voltaire prophesied its collapse in fifty years, and in fifty years the house where he made the prophecy was a depot for the circulation of the Scriptures. The Church's persistence, continual adaptation to new conditions, and apparently endless power of revival must have some deep reason. It may be because prayer like this which follows has never utterly died out in the sanctuary.

O Thou that dwellest not in temples made with hands! We ever stand within the courts of Thy glorious presence, only we open now the gates of our poor praise. Thou hast enriched this day of rest, O Lord, with Thy choicest gifts of peace; and lo! Thou unforgetting God, its record is before Thee, for ages past, moistened with penitential tears, and illumined with glad hopes, and hallowed by the innumerable prayers of faithful and saintly men. In this our day may the churches of Thy Holy One seek Thee still in spirit and truth; may we also enter in and find our rest, being of one heart and mind, and serving Thee with a wakeful and humble joy. Teach us now how we may converse with Thee, for we cannot order our speech by reason of darkness. We are naked and without disguise before Thee; oh! hide not Thyself from us behind our ignorance and sin. May we at least in this Thine hour shake off the sluggish clouds of sense and self that cling around our souls; and strenuously open our whole nature to the breath of Thy free spirit, and the healthful sunshine of Thy grace. Let the divine image of the Son of God visit us with power; driving out, with the chastisement of penitence, all obtruding passions that profane the temple of our hearts, and turn into a place of traffic that native house of prayer. O God of glory, God of grace! let not the things which are spiritually discerned be foolishness unto us through the blindness of our conscience: Thou knowest the thoughts of our wisdom that they are vain; take them from us, and bid them vanish away, lost in that wisdom from above which is revealed only to the pure in heart. Not unto us, O Lord, not unto us, but unto Thee be every thought of praise! Amen.—James Martineau.

Twelfth Week, Second Day

Some men doubtless go to church from traditional habit only, but such a motive obviously is not adequate to explain why the recurrent tides of humanity, even after an ebb in interest, sweep back to the Church again. In the eighteenth century, for example, Butler reports the common opinion that all that remained for Christianity was decent obsequies. But in a few years the Wesleys began a movement that changed the spiritual complexion of the English-speaking world, and swept multitudes into Christian fellowship. One reason for this repeated fact is clear. Mankind cannot and will not consent to live without faith in God, and faith in God in its genesis and its sustenance is largely a matter of contagion. We are not so much taught it; we catch it. It is vitally imparted in the family circle, and wherever kindred and believing spirits gather. No man is so independent as to escape the vital fact that his noblest emotions, attitudes, ideals, and faiths are socially engendered and socially sustained; he never would have had them in a solitary life and a solitary life would soon spoil those which he has now. A man may believe in his country and love her; but let him join in a patriotic movement or even attend a high-spirited patriotic meeting, and he will believe in her and love her more ardently. Man's religious life is not lawless; it is regulated by the same necessities of fellowship. The Church has made many mistakes, but on her altar the fire has never utterly gone out, and in her fellowship the faith of multitudes has been kindled.

Let us hold fast the confession of our hope that it waver not; for he is faithful that promised: and let us consider one another to pro-

voke unto love and good works; not forsaking our own assembling together, as the custom of some is, but exhorting one another; and so much the more, as ye see the day drawing nigh.—Heb. 10:23-25.

Great is Thy name, O God, and greatly to be praised. In Thee all our discordant notes rise into perfect harmony. It is good for us to think of the wonder of Thy being. Thou art silent, yet most strong; unchangeable, yet ever changing; ever working, yet ever at rest, supporting, nourishing, maturing all things. O Thou Eternal Spirit, who hast set our noisy years in the heart of Thy eternity, lift us above the power and evils of the passing time, that under the shadow of Thy wings we may take courage and be glad. So great art Thou, beyond our utmost imagining, that we could not speak to Thee didst Thou not first draw near to us and say, "Seek ye my face." Unto Thee our hearts would make reply, "Thy face, Lord, will we seek." . . . We thank Thee for our birth into a Christian community, for the Church and the Sacraments of Thy grace, for the healing day of rest, when we enter with Thy people into Thy House and there make holyday; for the refreshment of soul, the joys of communion, the spiritual discipline, the inspiration of prayer and hymn and sermon. . . . We praise Thee for the myriad influences of good, conscious and unconscious, that have been about us, deeply penetrating our inner life, shaping and fitting us for Thy Kingdom. Thou hast indeed forgiven all our iniquities, and healed all our diseases, and redeemed our life from destruction, and crowned us with lovingkindness. Therefore would we call upon our souls, and all that is within us, to bless Thy holy Name. Amen.—Samuel McComb.

Twelfth Week, Third Day

For ye, brethren, were called for freedom; only use not your freedom for an occasion to the flesh, but through love be servants one to another. For the whole law is fulfilled in one word, even in this: Thou shalt love thy neighbor as thyself. But if ye bite and devour one another, take heed that ye be not consumed one of another.—Gal. 5:13-15.

One fundamental reason for the endless revival of the Church is that faith never is satisfied until it issues in work. It insists on our being "servants one to another." We have spoken of God's merciful acceptance of a man when out of sin he turns his life by faith toward

Christ; but to interpret this as meaning the adequacy of faith without effective service is to misread Scripture and to demoralize life. Faith that does not lead to service is no real faith at all. But whenever men endeavor to express in work any faith which they may hold they must come together. Service involves cooperation. A hermit may have faith, but his faith does not concern any ideal hopes on earth; it has no outlooks save upon his own soul's condition in the world to come; it is a narrow, selfish, inoperative thing. As soon as men are grasped by some moving faith about what ought to be done for God's service and man's welfare here and now, a hermit's solitude or any sort of unaffiliated life becomes impossible. They must combine in a fellowship of faith and of labor to seek common ends. They begin to say with Edward Rowland Sill, "For my part I long to 'fall in' with somebody. This picket duty is monotonous. I hanker after a shoulder on this side and the other." And to fall in with others to serve Christian ends means some kind of church. Let us pray today for a church more fit to express this passion to serve.

God, we pray for Thy Church, which is set today amid the perplexities of a changing order, and face to face with a great new task. We remember with love the nurture she gave to our spiritual life in its infancy, the tasks she set for our growing strength, the influence of the devoted hearts she gathers, the steadfast power for good she has exerted. When we compare her with all other human institutions, we rejoice, for there is none like her. But when we judge her by the mind of her Master, we bow in pity and contrition. Oh, baptize her afresh in the life-giving spirit of Jesus! Grant her a new birth, though it be with the travail of repentance and humiliation. Bestow upon her a more imperious responsiveness to duty, a swifter compassion with suffering, and an utter loyalty to the will of God. Put upon her lips the ancient Gospel of her Lord. Help her to proclaim boldly the coming of the Kingdom of God and the doom of all that resist it. Fill her with the prophet's scorn of tyranny, and with a Christ-like tenderness for the heavy-laden and down-trodden. Give her faith to espouse the cause of the people, and in their hands that grope after freedom and light to recognize the bleeding hands of the Christ. Bid her cease from seeking her own life, lest she lose it. Make her valiant to give up her life to humanity, that like her crucified Lord she may mount by the path of the cross to a higher glory. Amen.—Walter Rauschenbusch.

Twelfth Week, Fourth Day

For the scripture saith, Whosoever believeth on him shall not be put to shame. For there is no distinction between Jew and Greek: for the same Lord is Lord of all, and is rich unto all that call upon him: for, Whosoever shall call upon the name of the Lord shall be saved. How then shall they call on him in whom they have not believed? and how shall they believe in him whom they have not heard? and how shall they hear without a preacher? and how shall they preach, except they be sent? even as it is written, How beautiful are the feet of them that bring glad tidings of good things!— Rom. 10:11-15.

The necessity of affiliation for effective faith is clear when one considers the missionary enterprise. One of the noblest qualities in human life is our natural desire to share our blessings. Every normal child is happier when some other child is joining in the play; every lover of music is gladdened by sharing with a friend enjoyment of a favorite symphony; save in singularly churlish folk the love of having others partake our joys is spontaneous and hearty. To those whom Christian faith has blessed with hope and power, the undeniable impulse comes to share these finest benedictions with all other men. The missionary enterprise does not rest upon a text; it wells up from one of the worthiest impulses in man's life. One may be fairly sure, that save as some perverted theology inhibits a spirit of love, a man's missionary interest will be proportionate to the reality and value of his own experience. If he himself has something well worth sharing, he will want to share it. But the missionary enterprise is more than any individual can compass; it demands organization, cooperation, and massed resources; it cannot be prosecuted without a church. The further our thought proceeds the more clear it becomes that the question is not, shall we have churches? but rather, since churches are inevitable, of what sort shall they be?

O Thou who hast made all nations of men to seek Thee and to find Thee; bless, we beseech Thee, Thy sons and daughters who have gone forth, into distant lands, bearing in their hands Thy Word of Life. We rejoice that, touched with the enthusiasm of Christ, so many have consecrated their lives to proclaiming the mes-

sage of Thy love to those other sheep of Thine who are not of our fold, that they may be united with us and that there may be one flock and one Shepherd. Help Thy ministering servants to recognize the fragments of truth and goodness that are ever found where men are sincere and to claim these glimpses of Thyself as the prophecies of a fuller revelation. When discouraged by the hardness of their task, and the meager fruit of all their labor, give them faith to see the far-off whitening harvest. Inspire them with Thy gracious promise that though the sower may go forth weeping, bearing precious seed, he will come again with joy, bringing his sheaves with him. Comfort them in their exile and loneliness with a sense of Thy companionship and with the prayers and sympathy of their brethren at home. Through them let Thy Word have free course and be glorified. And so let Thy Kingdom come, and Thy Will be done on earth as in Heaven, for Jesus Christ's sake. Amen.—Samuel McComb.

Twelfth Week, Fifth Day

After this manner therefore pray ye: Our Father who art in heaven, Hallowed be thy name. Thy kingdom come. Thy will be done, as in heaven, so on earth. Give us this day our daily bread. And forgive us our debts, as we also have forgiven our debtors. And bring us not into temptation, but deliver us from the evil one. For if ye forgive men their trespasses, your heavenly Father will also forgive you. But if ye forgive not men their trespasses, neither will your Father forgive your trespasses.—Matt. 6:9-15.

The central ideal of Christian effort is set for us in the first petition of the Master's prayer. But a Kingdom on earth, with God's will done here in heavenly fashion, is a social idea. It means not only right personal quality; it means right family life, and economic, political, and international relationships Christianized. No amount of fine individual character, necessary as it is, will of itself rectify the social maladjustments and inequities. Were everyone as good as possible, we still should need organized action. All parts of an engine may be correct, and yet they may be wrongly fitted together. As it is, social relations obviously demand concerted action; we must join together to combat immoral industrial conditions, to throttle the liquor traffic, to make human fraternity a fact and not a dream. The opposition to all such reforms is organized, and no haphazard attack will succeed. Now, many organizations may arise to serve special ends and may do excellent service to the cause, but what has proved true in the conflict with the liquor traffic, is true also of enterprises for industrial justice and international cooperation—*only when the churches see the moral issue and put their power in, is there any hope of victory.* A Christian whose faith involves the Kingdom sees plainly that he cannot go on without the Church.

O Lord, we praise Thy holy name, for Thou hast made bare Thine arm in the sight of all nations and done wonders. But still we cry to Thee in the weary struggle of our people against the power of drink. Remember, Lord, the strong men who were led astray and blighted in the flower of their youth. Remember the aged who have brought their gray hairs to a dishonored grave. Remember the homes that have been made desolate of joy, the wifely love that has been outraged in its sanctuary, the little children who have learned to despise where once they loved. Remember, O Thou great avenger of sin, and make this nation to remember.

May those who now entrap the feet of the weak and make their living by the degradation of men, thrust away their shameful gains and stand clear. But if their conscience is silenced by profit, do Thou grant Thy people the indomitable strength of faith to make an end of it. May all the great churches of our land shake off those who seek the shelter of religion for that which damns, and stand with level front against their common foe. May all who still soothe their souls with half-truths, saying "Peace, peace," where there can be no peace, learn to see through Thy stern eyes and come to the help of Jehovah against the mighty. Help us to cast down the men in high places who use the people's powers to beat back the people's hands from the wrong they fain would crush.

O God, bring nigh the day when all our men shall face their daily task with minds undrugged and with tempered passions; when the unseemly mirth of drink shall seem a shame to all who hear and see; when the trade that debauches men shall be loathed like the trade that debauches women; and when all this black remnant of savagery shall haunt the memory of a new generation but as an evil dream of the night. For this accept our vows, O Lord, and grant Thine aid. Amen.—Walter Rauschenbusch.

Twelfth Week, Sixth Day

Neither for these only do I pray, but for them also that believe on me through their word; that they may all be one; even as thou, Father, art in me, and I in thee, that they also may be in us: that the world may believe that thou didst send me. And the glory which thou hast given me I have given unto them; that they may be one, even as we are one; I in them, and thou in me, that they may be perfected into one; that the world may know that thou didst send me, and lovedst them, even as thou lovedst me.—John 17:20-23.

To the Christian the Church is a problem, just because she is a necessity. He caught his faith from the contagion of her fellowship and he sees that if he is to serve effectively the ideals of Christ and the coming of the Kingdom he must work through some church. But because the Church is necessary, he is not thereby made content with her. She is at once helping and hindering the spread of the faith; she is the source of immeasurable good and yet she is not "one, that the world may believe." A traveler across the American plains in springtime sees fences, tiresomely prominent, staring at him from the landscape; but in summer when he returns the fences are invisible. The wheat and corn are growing, the earth is bearing fruit, and while the old divisions may be there, they all are hidden. One suspects that if Christians everywhere set themselves with hearty zeal to bear the fruit of service for the common weal, if they gave themselves to achieve the aims of Christ for men with ardor and thoroughness, the sectarian divisions would grow unimperative and disappear. We may not be able to think the disagreements through, but we may be able to work them out; even where we cannot recite a common creed, we can share a common purpose. The War, where Jewish rabbis have held crucifixes before the eyes of dying soldiers, and where Catholic priests have met death, as one did at Gallipoli, following a Wesleyan chaplain—"my Protestant comrade"—into danger, has revealed how deeply underneath our sharp divisions our spiritual loyalties seek unity when crisis comes. For all the unity that can come without compromise to conscience, surely the Christian people are bound to pray and work.

O God, the Father of our Lord Jesus Christ, our only Saviour, the Prince of Peace; give us grace seriously to lay to heart the great

*dangers we are in by our unhappy divisions. Take away all hatred
and prejudice, and whatsoever else may hinder us from godly union
and concord; that as there is but one body and one Spirit, and one
hope of our calling, one Lord, one faith, one baptism, one God and
Father of us all, so we may be all of one heart and of one soul, united
in one holy bond of truth and peace, of faith and charity, and may
with one mind and one mouth glorify Thee, through Jesus Christ
our Lord. Amen.*—"The Book of Common Prayer."

Twelfth Week, Seventh Day

**For I am already being offered, and the time of my departure is
come. I have fought the good fight, I have finished the course, I
have kept the faith: henceforth there is laid up for me the crown
of righteousness, which the Lord, the righteous judge, shall give to
me at that day; and not to me only, but also to all them that have
loved his appearing.—II Tim. 4:6-8.**

The fellowship of faith is not bounded by the earth. Paul's expectation took into its account a communion that far overreached the
confines of temporal experience. The New Testament believers not
only held but vividly apprehended that the "whole family" to which
they belonged in Christian communion was "in heaven and on
earth." Their outlook Wordsworth has expressed in modern words:

> "There is
> One great society alone on earth:
> The noble Living and the noble Dead."

To that society of the world's prophets and martyrs, seers and
servants, it may well be a man's ambition to belong. And that ideal
is not impossible to anyone, for the mark and seal of their fellowship
is that they have "kept the faith." When others despaired, lost heart,
and deserted causes on which man's welfare hung, they kept the
faith. When mysteries perplexed their minds and discouragement,
to human vision, was more rational than hope, they turned from
sight to insight and they kept the faith. When new knowledge, half-
understood, disturbed old forms of thought and multitudes were
confused in uncertainty and disbelief, they kept the faith. And they
often came to their end, like Paul, having "suffered the loss of all
things"—yet not *all,* for they had kept the faith.

"For all the saints, who from their labors rest,
Who Thee by faith before the world confessed,
Thy name, O Jesus, be forever blest,
        Alleluia!

O may Thy soldiers, faithful, true, and bold,
Fight as the saints who nobly fought of old,
And win with them the victor's crown of gold,
        Alleluia!

O blest communion, fellowship Divine!
We feebly struggle; they in glory shine;
Yet all are one in Thee, for all are Thine.
        Alleluia!"

O God, Thou only Refuge of Thy children! who remainest true though all else should fail, and livest though all things die; cover us now when we fly to Thee. Thy shelter was around our fathers. Thy voice called them away, and bids us seek Thee here till we depart to be with them. In Thy memory are the lives of all men from of old. Before Thy sight are the secret hearts of all the living. We stand in awe of Thy justice which, since the ages began, hath never changed: and we cling to Thy mercy that passeth not away.

Almighty Father, Thou art a God afar off as well as nigh at hand. Thou who in times past didst pity the prayers of our forerunners, and especially of that suffering servant of Thine whom Thou hast made our Leader unto Thee! be pleased to strengthen us now, O Lord, to bear our lighter cross and surrender ourselves for duty and for trial unto Thee. Show us something of the blessed peace with which they now look back on their days of strong crying and tears, and teach us that it is far better to die in Thy service than to live for our own. Rebuke within us all immoderate desires, all unquiet temper, all presumptuous expectations, all ignoble self-indulgence, and feeling on us the embrace of Thy Fatherly hand, may we meekly and with courage go into the darkest ways of our pilgrimage, anxious not to change Thy perfect will, but only to do and bear it worthily. May we spend all our days in Thy presence, and meet our death in the strength of Thy grace, and pass thence into the nearer light of Thy knowledge and love. Amen.—John Hunter.

COMMENT FOR THE WEEK

I

So far in our studies we have been dealing with the individual believer in his search for a reasonable faith. But we must face at last what from the beginning has been true, that there is no such thing as an individual believer. *All faiths are social.* However little we may be aware of each other's influence, however intangible the social forces which shape the convictions by which we live, no man builds or keeps his faiths alone. We may pride ourselves on our independent thought, but the fact remains as Prof. William James has stated it: "Our faith is faith in some one else's faith, and in the greatest matters this is most the case."

The realm of religious conviction is not the only place where we hold with a strong sense of personal possession what has been given us by others, and often forget to acknowledge our indebtedness. We believe in democracy and popular education, not because by some gift of individual genius we are wiser than our unbelieving sires, but because, in the advance of the race, that faith has been wrought out by many minds, and, with minute addition of our own thought, we share the general conviction. As a man considers how rich and varied are the faiths he holds, how few of them he ever has thought through or ever can, and how helpless he would be, if he were set from the beginning to create any one of them, he gains new insight into Paul's words, "What hast thou that thou didst not receive? but if thou didst receive it, why dost thou glory as if thou hadst not received it?" (I Cor. 4:7).

Indeed, this same truth holds in every relationship. Nothing is more impossible than a "self-made man." In no realm can that common phrase be intelligently applied to anyone. If in business one has risen from poverty to wealth, he has used railroads that he did not invent and telephones that he does not even understand; he has built his business on a credit system for which he did not labor and whose moral basis has been laid in the ethical struggles of unnumbered generations. For the clothes he wears, the food he eats, the education he receives, he is debtor to a social life that taps the ends of the earth and that has cost blood not his and money which he never can repay. If granting this, a man still say, "My power and the might of my hand hath gotten me this wealth" (Deut. 8:17), he may well consider whence his power has come. His distant ancestors stalked through primeval forests, their brows sloped back, their hairy hides barren of clothes, and in their hands stone hatchets, by the aid of which they sought their food. What has this Twentieth Century boaster done to change the habits of the Stone Age to the civilization on which his wealth is based or to elevate man's intellect to the grasp and foresight of the modern business world? All the power by which he wins his way is clearly a social gift, and any contribution which he may add is infinitesimal compared with his receipts.

By this truth all declarations of individual independence need to be chastened and controlled and all boasting cancelled utterly. Normal minds have their times of self-assertion in religion, when they grow impatient of believing anything simply because they have been told. As a college Junior put it: "I must clear the universe of God, and then start in at the beginning to see what I can find." But to assert a reasonable independence ought not to mean that one cut himself off from the support of history, the accumulated experience of the race, the insight of the seers, and in unassisted isolation walk, like Kipling's cat, "by his wild lone." No man can do that anywhere and still succeed. Imagine a man, in politics, dubious of his old affiliations and disturbed by the conflicting opinions of his day. If, so perplexed, he should throw over all that ever had been thought or done in civic life, and in an unaided individual adventure attempt out of his own mind to constitute a state, in what utter confusion would he land! No mind can begin work as though it were the first mind that ever acted, or were the only mind in action now. All effective thinking is social; contributions from innumerable heads pour in to make a wise man's knowledge. And to suppose that any man can climb the steep ascent of heaven all alone and lay his hands comprehensively on the Eternal is preposterous. No one ever apprehended a science so, much less God! Even Jesus fed his soul on the prophets of his race.

II

Indeed, Jesus' attitude toward the fellowship of faith is most revealing, seen against the background of his nation's history. In the beginning, there was in Israel no such thing as individual religion. In the earliest strata of the Bible's revelation, we find no indication of a faith that brought God and each of his people into intimate relationships. Jehovah was the God of the nation as a whole and not of the people one by one. When he spoke, he spoke to the community through a leader; "Speak thou with us and we will hear," the people cried to Moses, "but let not God speak with us lest we die" (Exodus 20:19). It was at the time of the Exile, when the nation fell in ruins, and the hearts of faithful Jews were thrown back one by one on God that individual trust, peace, joy, and confidence found utterance. It was Jeremiah (Chap. 31) and Ezekiel (Chap. 18) who saw men individually responsible to God, and who opened the way for loyal Jews to be his people even when the nation was no more. And what they began Jesus completed. He lifted up the individual and made each man the object of the Father's care. "It is not the will of your Father . . . that *one* of these little ones should perish" (Matt. 18:14). "What man of you, having a hundred sheep, and having lost *one* of them . . ." (Luke 15:4). "The very hairs of your head are all numbered" (Matt. 10:30). As for religion's inner meaning, it became in Jesus' Gospel not a national ritual but a private faith: "But thou, when thou prayest, enter into thine inner chamber, and having shut thy door, pray to thy Father who is in secret" (Matt. 6:6).

While Jesus, however, so emphasized the inward, individual aspects of religion, he did not leave it there, as though persons could ever be like jugs in the rain, separate receptacles that share neither their emptiness nor their abundance. He bound his disciples into a fellowship. He joined their channels until, like interflowing streams, one contributed to all and the spirit of all was expressed in each. He braided them into friendship with himself and with each other, so close that the community did what no isolated believer ever could have done—it survived the shock of the crucifixion, the agony of sustained persecution, the frailties of its members, and the discouragements of its campaign. On that *group* the Master counted for his work: "The gates of Hades shall not prevail against it" (Matt. 16:18). And when the New Testament Church emerged, the fellowship which Christ himself had breathed into it was clear and strong. Men who became Christians, in the New Testament, came into a new relationship with God indeed, but into a new human fraternity as well. They were "builded together for a habitation of God through the Spirit" (Eph. 2:22), and even when death came that fellowship was not destroyed. They were still "the whole family in heaven and on earth" (Eph. 3:15). John Wesley was right: "The Bible knows nothing of a solitary religion." In the Old Testament religion was predominantly national; in the New Testament, individuals rejoicing in the "Beloved Community" could not describe their life without the reiteraton of "one another." They were to "pray one for another" and "confess sins one to another" (James 5:16); they were to "love one another" (I Pet. 1:22), "exhort one another" (Heb. 3:13), "comfort one another" (I Thess. 4:18); they were to "bear one another's burdens" (Gal. 6:2) and in communal worship "admonish one another with psalms and hymns and spiritual songs" (Col. 3:16).

So when they thought of their faith, they never held it in solitary confidence; they were "strong to apprehend *with all the saints* what is the breadth and length and height and depth, and to know the love of Christ which passeth knowledge" (Eph. 3:18).

III

When a modern believer endeavors to interpret this spirit in the New Testament in terms of his own wants, he sees at once that he needs fellowship for the *enriching* of his faith. Cooperation for achievement is a modern commonplace, but when Paul prayed, as we have quoted him, that the Ephesians might be "strong to *apprehend* with all the saints," he was stating the more uncommon proposition that men must cooperate for knowledge. He saw the divine love in its length, breadth, depth, and height on one side, and on the other a solitary man endeavoring to understand it. Impossible! said Paul; the divine love in its fulness cannot be known in solitude, it must be apprehended in fellowship.

At first nothing seems more strictly individual than knowledge. To know is an intimate, personal affair; it cannot be carried on by proxy. But even casual thought at once makes clear that in solitude we cannot know even the physical universe. No man can go apart and through the narrow aperture of his own mind see the full round of truth. For astronomers study the stars, geologists the rocks, chemists know their special field and physicists know theirs; each scientist understands in part, and if one is to know the breadth and length and height and depth of the physical world he must be strong to apprehend with all the scientists.

In religion this necessity of cooperation in knowing God may not at first seem evident. In the secret session behind closed doors, as Jesus said, one finds his clearest thought of God, and in the individual heart the divine illumination comes. So some insist; and the answer does not deny, but surpasses the truth in the insistence. *Is yours the only heart where God is to be found? Does the sea of his grace exhaust itself in what it can reveal in your bay?* Rather, in how many different ways men come to God, how various their experiences of him, and how much each needs the rest for breadth and catholicity of view!

One man comes to God by way of intellectual perplexity and he knows chiefly faith's illumination of life's puzzling problems; another comes through the experience of sin and he responds to such a phrase as "God our Saviour" (I Tim. 1:1); another comes to God through trouble and has found in faith "eternal comfort and good hope through grace" (II Thess. 2:16); and another by way of a happy life has found in God the object of devoted gratitude. One, a mystic, finds God in solitary prayer; another, a worker, knows him chiefly as the Divine Ally. Some are very young and have a child's religion; some are at the summit of their years and have a strong man's achieving faith; and some are old and are familiar with the face of death and the thought of the eternal. How multiform is man's experience of God! Some compositions cannot be interpreted by a solo. Let the first violinist play with what skill he can, he alone is not adequate to the endeavor. There must be an orchestra; the oboes and viols, the drums and trumpets, the violins and cellos must all be there. So faith in God is too rich and manifold to be interpreted by individuals alone; a fellowship is necessary. Even Paul, in one of his most gloriously mixed-up and yet revealing sentences, prays for fellowship that his faith may be enriched: "I long to see you, that I may impart unto you some spiritual gift, to the end ye may be established; that is, that I with you may be comforted in you, each of us by the other's faith, both yours and mine" (Rom. 1:11, 12).

Poverty of faith, therefore, is not due only to individual lapses of character and perplexities of mind; *it is due to neglect of Christian fellowship.* One who with difficulty has clung to his slender experience of God, goes up to the church on Sunday. Even though it be a humble place of prayer, if the worship is genuine, the hymns, the prayers, the Scriptures gather up the testimony of centuries to the reality of God. Here David speaks again and Isaiah answers; here Paul reaffirms his faith and John is confident that God is love. Here the saints before Christ cry, "Jehovah is my rock, and my fortress, and my deliverer" (Psalm 18:2), and the sixteenth century answers, "A mighty fortress is our God"; and the nineteenth century replies, "How firm a foundation, ye saints of the Lord!" We go up to the church finding it hard to sing, *"My Jesus, I love thee, I know thou art mine";* we go down with a *Te Deum* in our hearts:

"The glorious company of the apostles praise thee;
The goodly fellowship of the prophets praise thee;
The noble army of martyrs praise thee;
The holy Church throughout all the world doth acknowledge thee."

In the rich and varied faiths of the Church we find a far more fruitful relationship with God than by ourselves we ever could have gained. Without such an enriching experience men can only with difficulty keep faith alive. Twigs that snap out of the camp-fire lose their flame and fall, charred sticks; but put them back and they will burn again, for fire springs from fellowship. Amiel, after an evening of solitude with a favorite book on philosophy, wrote what is many a Christian's prayer: "Still I miss something—common worship, a positive religion, shared with other people. Ah! when will the church to which I belong in heart rise into being? I cannot, like Scherer, content myself with being in the right all alone. I must have a less solitary Christianity."

IV

Men need fellowship, not only for the enrichment of their faith, but for its *stability.* No man can successfully believe anything all alone. Let an opinion in any realm be denied, despised, neglected by common consent of men, and not easily do we hold an unshaken conviction of its truth. But let it be agreed with, supported and endorsed by many, especially by men of insight, and with each additional testimony to its truth our faith grows confident. A fundamental experience of man is that his faiths are socially confirmed.

Authority of some sort, therefore, never is outgrown in any province of knowledge, and strugglers after faith have solid right to the sustenance which it can give. For one thing the authority of the *expert* is acknowledged everywhere. When a great astronomer speaks about the stars, most of us put our hands upon our mouths and humble ourselves to listen. If in science, expert knowledge has this authority—not artificial, infallible, and externally enforced, but vital, serviceable, and real—how much more in realms where insight and spiritual quality are indispensable! Such authority comes in the spirit of Paul: "Not that we have lordship over your faith, but are helpers of your joy" (II Cor. 1:24).

An amateur stands before a picture like Turner's "The Building of Carthage" and either does not notice the details, or noticing sees no special meaning there. But when Ruskin, Turner's seer, begins to speak—how wonderful the children in the foreground sailing toy boats in a pool, prophecy of Carthage's future greatness on the sea! —one by one the details take fire and glow with meaning as our eyes are opened. Such is the service of a real authority. It does not, as Weigel says, put out a person's eye and then try to persuade him to see with some one else's. It rather cures our blindness and enables us to see what by ourselves we were incapable of seeing. Christ supremely, when allowed to be himself, has helped men thus. He has not oppressed the mind with burdensome authority, denying us our right to think. He has come appealing to our little insight with his own clear vision, "Why even of yourselves judge ye not what is right?" (Luke 12:57). Things which we see dimly he has clarified; things which we did not see at all, he has made manifest. He has been what he called himself, the Light, and his people have said of him what the man in John's ninth chapter said, "He opened mine eyes" (John 9:30). A struggler after faith may well count among his assets the insight of the seers and of the Seer. As another states it: "Our weak faith may at times be permitted to look through the eyes of some strong soul, and may thereby gain a sense of the certainty of spiritual things which before we had not."

Beside the authority of the seers, there is *the authority of racial experience,* to which indeed no mind ought slavishly to subject itself, but from which all minds ought to gain insight and confidence. Tradition has done us much disservice. Oppressions that might long before have been outgrown have been counted holy because they were hoary. There must be something to commend an opinion or a custom beside its age, and all progress depends upon recognizing that

"Times makes ancient good uncouth."

But if out of the past have come evils to be overthrown, out of the past also have come the best possessions of the race. "Traditional" has grown to be an adjective of ill repute; it signifies in common parlance the inheritance of oppressive ideals and institutions that hold the "dead hand" over hopes of progress. But our best music also, our poetry, and our art are traditional; the discoveries of our scientists on the long road from alchemy to chemistry, from magic to physics are traditional; all that each new generation begins with, fitted out like the well-favored child of a provident father, is traditional. No one can describe the utter barrenness of life, if we could not build on the accumulations of our sires, using the result of their toil as the basis of our work, their hardly won wisdom as our guide. To discount anything because it is traditional is to discount everything, except that comparatively minute addition which each new generation makes to the slowly accumulating wisdom and wealth of the race. As Mr. Chesterton has put it: "Tradition may be defined as the extension of the franchise. Tradition means giving votes to the most obscure of all classes, our ancestors. It is the democracy of the dead. Tradition refuses to submit to the small and arrogant oligarchy of those who merely happen to be walking about. All democrats object to men being disqualified by the accident of birth; tradition objects to their being disqualified by the accident of death. Democracy tells us not to neglect a good man's opinion, even if he is our groom; tradition asks us not to neglect a good man's opinion, even if he is our father."

Now racial experience is dubious at many points and at very few does it approach finality. But on one matter it speaks with a unanimity that is nothing short of absolute. *Man cannot live without religion*—like the earth beneath the mountain peaks this universal experience of the race underlies the special insights of the seers. When during the mid-Victorian discomfiture of faith at the first disclosures of the new science, Tennyson's "In Memoriam" appeared, Prof. Sidgwick wrote of it, "What 'In Memoriam' did for us, for me at least in this struggle, was to impress on us the ineffable and irradicable conviction that *humanity* will not and cannot acquiesce in a godless world." That conviction is confirmed by the whole experience of the race. To be sure religion, like love, exists in all degrees. From degraded lust to the relationship of Robert Browning and Elizabeth Barrett, love is infinite in variety; it takes its quality from the character of those whom it affects; yet through all its

changes it is itself so built into the structure of mankind, that though
there be loveless individuals, life as a whole is unimaginable without
it. So religion runs the gamut of human quality. In a Hindu idolater
it performs disgusting rites to placate an angry god, and in Rabindranath Tagore it cries: "If thou speakest not I will fill my heart
with thy silence and endure it. I will keep still and wait like the
night with starry vigil and its head bent low with patience. The
morning will surely come, the darkness will vanish, and thy voice
pour down in golden streams, breaking through the sky." In Torque-
mada it is cruel; in Father Damien it becomes a passion for saviorhood. Religion helped Sennacherib to his campaigns and Isaiah to
his prophecies; it preached the Sermon on the Mount and it dragged
Jesus before Pilate. Can the same spring send forth sweet water and
bitter? But religion does it, for religion is life motived by visions of
God; it is tremendous in strength, but with man's unequal power to
understand the Divine, it is ambiguous in quality. Like electricity, it
is magnificent in blessing or terrible in curse. Yet through all its degrees man's relationship with the Invisible is so essentially a part of
his humanity that lacking it he has never yet been discovered, and
without it he cannot be conceived. It was this impressive witness of
racial experience that made John Fiske, of Harvard, say, "Of all the
implications of the doctrine of evolution with regard to man, I believe the very deepest and strongest to be that which asserts the
Everlasting Reality of Religion."

This testimony of the spiritual seers and this cumulative experience of the race have a right to play a weighty part in any consideration of religious faith. Even a rebellious youth might pause before
he scoffs at a mature and thoughtful mind, letting his Church, his
Scripture, and his Christ speak impressively to him about the reality
of God. What we all do in every other realm, when we are wise, this
mind is doing in religion. His individual grasp on truth he sets in the
perspective of history. He does not feel himself upon a lonely quest
when he seeks God; rather he feels behind him and around him the
race of which he is a part and which never yet has ceased to believe
in the Divine, and he sees his own insights illumined by those supreme spirits who have talked with God "as a man talketh with his
friend." He knows as well as any youth that authority has been
stereotyped in theories of artificial infallibility, to which no mature
mind for a moment can weakly surrender its right to think, but he
refuses to give up a real authority because some have held a false

one. The authority of the dictionary is one thing—literal and external. But the authority of a good mother moves on a different plane. It is not artificial and oppressive. It is vital and inspiring. She has lived longer, experienced more than her children; she is wiser, better, more discerning than they. A man who has had experience of great motherhood comes to feel that if his mother thinks something very strongly and very persistently, he would better consider that thing well, for the chances are overwhelming that there is truth in it. How much more shall he feel so about the age-long experience of the saints with God! In this respect at least there still is truth in Cyprian's words, "He that hath God for his Father, hath the Church for his Mother."

V

Faith needs fellowship not alone for enrichment and stability, but for *expression*. For faith, as from the beginning we have maintained, is not an effortless acceptance of ideas or personal relationships; it is an active appropriation of convictions that drive life, and Christian faith especially has always involved a campaign whose object is the saving of the world. Such an expression of religious life involves cooperation; men cannot effectively support the "work of faith" (I Thess. 1:3) apart from fellowship.

The necessity for this cooperative expression of religion is clear when we consider the *one in whom we believe*. How anyone can expect in solitude to believe in Christ is a mystery. For Christ, with overflowing love to those who shared his filial fellowship with God, said, "No longer do I call you servants . . . I have called you friends" (John 15:15); his care encompassed folk who never heard of him and whom he never saw, "Other sheep I have, which are not of this fold: them also I must bring . . . and they shall become one flock, one shepherd" (John 10:16); and beyond his generation's life his love reached out to followers yet unborn, "Them also that believe on me through their word" (John 17:20). Whatever other quality a movement sprung from such a source may possess, it must be social. Moreover, Jesus' faith was active; the meaning of it he himself disclosed, "All things are possible to him that believeth" (Mark 9:23). In such a spirit, both by himself and through his followers, he sought the lost, healed the sick, preached the Gospel, and expectantly proclaimed an earth transformed to heaven. Such a character cannot be known in contemplation under the trees in June or through the pages of an interesting book. If Garibaldi, leading his men to the liberation of Italy, had found a devotee who said, I believe in you; I love to read your deeds, and often in my solitary, meditative hours I am cheered by the thought of you—one can easily imagine the swift and penetrating answer! That you believe in me is false; no one believes in me who does not share my purpose; the army is afoot, great business is ahead, the cause is calling, he who believes follows. Such a spirit was Christ's. The hermits, whether of old time in their cells, or of modern time with their unaffiliated lives, are wrong. *The final test of faith in Christ is fellowship in work.*

The Church itself has been to blame for much undedicated faith. Correctness of opinion has been substituted, as a test, for fidelity of life. "Believe in the Lord Jesus Christ and thou shalt be saved," has been interpreted to mean: accept a theory about Christ's person and all is well. But one need only go back in imagination to the time when first that formula was used to see how vital was its import. To believe in Christ then meant to accept a despised religion, to break ties that men value more than life, to face the certainty of contempt and the risk of violence. To believe in Christ then meant coming out from old relationships and going to a sect where one was pilloried with derision, that one might work for the things which Christ represents. No one did that as a theory; it required a tremendous thrust of the will, a decision that reached to the roots of life. All this was involved in believing on Christ, and our decent holding of a theory about him, in a time when all lips praise him, is a poor substitute for such vital faith. John tells us that once a multitude of Jews professed belief in Jesus, but the Master, hearing their affirmations, saw the superficial meaning there. "Many believed on his name," says John —"but Jesus did not trust himself unto them" (John 2:23, 24). How many believe in Christ in such a way that he cannot believe in them! They forget that while the test of a man is his faith, the test of faith is faithfulness. An apostolic injunction needs modern enforcement, "that they who have believed God may be careful to maintain good works" (Titus 3:8).

The necessity for a cooperative expression of religion is evident again in the *truth which we believe*. Take in its simplest form the Gospel which Christianity presents, that God is in earnest about personality, and what urgency is there for associated work! For personality is being ruined in this world. False ideas of life, idolatry whether to fetishes in Africa or to money here, irreligion in all its manifold and blighting forms, are destroying personality from within, and from without sweatshops, tenements, war, the liquor traffic, industrial inequity, are engaged in the same task of ruin. The common contrast between individual and social Christianity is superficial. The one thing for which the Christian cares is personal life, and in its culture and salvation he sees the aim of God and God-like men. Whatever, therefore, affects *that* is his concern, and what is there that does not affect it? What men believe about life's meaning and its destiny strikes to the core of personal life, and the houses in which men live, the conditions under which they work, the wages that they are paid, and the environments which surround their plastic childhood—these, too, mould for good or ill the fortunes of personality.

The Christian, therefore, who intelligently holds the faith that he professes cannot be negligent either of evangelism, education, and missionary enterprise upon the one side, or of social reformation on the other. These are two ends of the tunnel by which the Gospel seeks to open out a way for personality to find its freedom. A man who says that he believes in Jesus Christ, and yet is complacent about child labor and commercialized vice, poor housing conditions and unjust wages, the trade in liquor and the butchery of men in war, stands in peril of hearing the twenty-third chapter of Matthew's gospel brought up to date for his especial benefit by the same lips that spoke it first. The indignation of the Master falls on priests and Levites who, speeding to the temple service, "pass by on the other side" the victims of social injury.

Isolated Christians, however, cannot further this campaign for personality redeemed from inward ills and outward handicaps. *Evil is organized, and goodness must be, too.* As wisely would a single patriot shoulder a rifle and set out for France as would an unaffiliated Christian set his solitary strength against the massed evil of the world. Men increase effectiveness by a large per cent through fellowship, as ancient Hebrews saw: "Five of you shall chase a hundred, and a hundred of you shall chase ten thousand" (Lev. 26:8).

VI

Many secondary fellowships offer to a Christian opportunity for associated service; no cooperative endeavor to make this a better

world for God to rear his children in should lack Christian sympathy
and support. But the primary fellowship of Christians is the Church.
Some indeed would have no church; they would have man's spiritual life a disembodied wraith, without "a local habitation and a
name." But no other one of all man's finer interests has survived
without organized expression. Justice is a great ideal; any endeavor
to incarnate it in human institutions sullies its purity. One who
dwelt only on the lofty nature of justice, who thought of it uncon-
taminated and ideal, might protest against its embodiment in the
tawdry ritual and demeaning squabbles of a law court. Between the
poetry of justice and the recriminations of lawyers, the perjury of
witnesses, the fumbling uncertainty of evidence, the miscarriages of
equity, how bitterly a scornful mind could point the contrast! But
a reverent mind, sorry as it may be at the misrepresentation of the
ideal in the human institution, is ill content with scorn. He who with
insight reads the history of jurisprudence, perceives how the courts
of law, with all their faults, have conserved the gains in social equity,
have propagated the ideal for which they stand, have made progress
sometimes slowly, sometimes with a rush like soldiers storming a re-
doubt, and in times of stress have been a bulwark against the invasion of the people's rights. The poetry of justice would have been an
idle dream without equity's laborious embodiment in codes and
courts.

Some minds dwell with joy upon the spiritual Church. Its names
are written on no earthly roster, but in the Book of Life; its worship
is offered in no earthly temple, but in the trysting places where soul
meets Over-soul in trustful fellowship; its baptism is not with water
but with spirit, its eucharist not with bread but with the shared life
of the Lord. Or, ranging out to think of the Church as an ideal
human brotherhood, men dream as Manson did in "The Servant
in the House":

"If you have eyes, you will presently see the church itself—a loom-
ing mystery of many shapes and shadows, leaping sheer from floor
to dome. The work of no ordinary builder! . . . The pillars of it go
up like the brawny trunks of heroes: the sweet human flesh of men
and women is moulded about its bulwarks, strong, impregnable: the
faces of little children laugh out from every corner-stone: the terrible spans and arches of it are the joined hands of comrades; and
up in the heights and spaces there are inscribed the numberless

musings of all the dreamers of the world. It is yet building—building
and built upon. Sometimes the work goes forward in deep darkness:
sometimes in blinding light: now beneath the burden of unutterable
anguish: now to the tune of a great laughter and heroic shoutings
like the cry of thunder. Sometimes, in the silence of the night-time,
one may hear the tiny hammerings of the comrades at work up in
the dome—the comrades that have climbed ahead."

All such ideals, like pillars of fire and cloud, lead the march toward a promised land. They are to the actual Church what the
poetry of justice is to the actual courts. But in one case as in the
other, such ideals are dreams if, with labor and struggle, through
many mistakes, against the disheartenment of man's frailty and sin,
we do not work out an institution that shall embody and express
man's spiritual life. Even now a discerning spirit whose own faith
has been nourished at the altar regards the Church with boundless
gratitude. She has indeed been to the Gospel what courts are to
justice, indispensable and yet burdensome, an institution that the
ideal cannot live without and yet often cannot easily live with. No
one feels her faults so acutely as one who devotedly values the Gospel and longs for its adequate expression on the earth. Yet the
Church conserves the race's spiritual gains, fits out our youth with
the treasure of man's accumulated faith, is a power house of endless
moral energy for good causes in the world, exalts the ideal aims of
life amid the crushing pressure of material pursuits, holds out a gospel of hope to men whom all others have forsaken, and to the ends
of the earth proclaims the good news of God and the Kingdom. No
other fellowship offers to men of faith so great an opportunity to
make distinctive contribution to the race's spiritual life. In the presence of the Church's service and the Church's need an unaffiliated
believer in Jesus Christ is an anomaly. For enrichment, stability, and
expression, faith must have fellowship.

*"Oh magnify Jehovah with me, and let us exalt His name to-
gether"* (Psalm 34:3).

SCRIPTURE PASSAGES
USED IN THE DAILY READINGS

Exodus 3:1-5 (VI-5); 4:24-26 (II-4).

Deuteronomy 28:65-67 (VIII-2).

II Kings 21:3-6 (IV-5).

Job 30:20, 21, 25-27 (X-4); 37:23 (V-3); 38:31-38 (VII-1).

Psalms 16:5-11 (III-5); 23:1-4 (X-3); 27:1-6 (VIII-5); 27:7-14
    (V-7); 51:1-4 (III-3); 55:1-7 (VIII-1); 56:1-3 (VIII-3);
    73:2, 3, 16, 17, 24-26 (II-6); 103:1-5 (III-2); 118:1-6 (VIII-
    7); 145:1-10 (III-7); 146:1-5 (IV-1).

Proverbs 2:1-5 (II-3); 4:1-9 (II-2).

Ecclesiastes 3:11 (V-3).

Isaiah 1:10-17 (IV-2); 40:26-31 (V-4); 51:9-16 (VI-6); 55:1-3
    (II-7).

Amos 5:21-24 (IX-4).

Micah 6:1-8 (IX-3).

Matthew 6:6-14 (III-1); 6:9-15 (XII-5); 6:24-33 (VI-6); 7:15-
    20 (V-6); 7:24-27 (VI-7); 13:54-58 (XI-3); 17:19-20 (XI-
    4); 18:12-14 (II-4); 21:28-31 (X-1); 23:13-15, 23, 24 (XII-
    1); 25:34-40 (IX-7).

Mark 12:28-30 (V-1).

Luke 6:12-16 (IX-2); 7:48-50 (XI-2); 18:9-14 (IV-3); 22:31,
    32 (XI-6).

John 3:21 (IX-5); 4:23, 24 (IV-5); 6:16, 17 (IX-5); 6:27-29
    (XI-1); 7:16, 17 (IX-5); 14:25-27 (VII-2); 17:20-23 (XII-
    6).

Acts 17:22-28 (IV-6).

Romans 8:1-6 (X-7); 8:14-16 (V-5); 8:24, 25 (III-4); 10:11-15
    (XII-4); 11:33, 34 (V-3); 11:33-12:2 (IX-6); 15:13 (III-4);
    16:1-8 (IX-1).

I Corinthians 2:10-14 (VII-4); 3:4-9 (III-6); 3:18-23 (VII-6);
    4:11-13 (VI-2).

II Corinthians 5:5 (V-2).

Galatians 2:20 (XI-5); 5:13-15 (XII-3); 5:16-23 (IV-7).

Ephesians 1:15-19 (VII-5); 4:13-15 (X-5).

Philippians 3:12-16 (X-6).

SOURCES OF PRAYERS
USED IN THE DAILY READINGS

ALFRED, KING—IX-3. "A Chain of Prayer Across the Ages," by S. F. Fox.

ANSELM, ST.—XI-6. "A Chain of Prayer Across the Ages," by S. F. Fox.

ARNDT, JOHANN—IX-1; X-1. "A Chain of Prayer Across the Ages," by S. F. Fox.

ARNOLD, THOMAS—VII-5. "A Chain of Prayer Across the Ages," by S. F. Fox.

BACON, FRANCIS—VII-2. "A Chain of Prayer Across the Ages," by S. F. Fox.

BEECHER, HENRY WARD—I-4; I-7; II-7; III-5; III-7; IV-7; V-7; VI-6; X-5. "A Book of Public Prayer."

BOOK OF COMMON PRAYER—XII-6.

DAWSON, GEORGE—X-4. "A Chain of Prayer Across the Ages," by S. F. Fox.

HALE, SIR MATTHEW—VII-4. "A Chain of Prayer Across the Ages," by S. F. Fox.

HUNTER, JOHN—I-1; IV-5; XI-2; XI-3; XII-7. "Devotional Services for Public Worship."

JENKS, BENJAMIN—X-2. "A Chain of Prayer Across the Ages," by S. F. Fox.

McCOMB, SAMUEL—I-6; II-1; III-1; VI-3; VIII-1; VIII-2; VIII-3; VIII-5; VIII-6; VIII-7; IX-2; XI-1; XII-2; XII-4. "A Book of Prayers for Public and Personal Use."

MARTINEAU, JAMES—III-4; IV-4; V-2; VI-2; XII-1. "Prayers in the Congregation and in College."

NEWMAN, FRANCIS W.—VI-1; VI-7. "A Chain of Prayer Across the Ages," by S. F. Fox.

ORCHARD, W. E.—I-2; I-3; II-2; II-3; II-4; II-5; II-6; III-2; IV-3; IV-6; V-1; V-3; V-6; VI-5; VII-1; VII-3; VII-7; VIII-4; IX-5; X-7; XI-5; XI-7. "The Temple."

PARKER, THEODORE—I-5; V-4; V-5; VI-4; VII-6; X-6. "Prayers."

RAUSCHENBUSCH, WALTER—III-6; IV-1; IV-2; IX-4; IX-6; XII-3; XII-5. "Prayers of the Social Awakening."

ROBINSON, HELEN RING—XI-4. "Thy Kingdom Come," by Ralph E. Diffendorfer.

SHAFTESBURY, EARL OF—IX-7. "A Chain of Prayer Across the Ages," by S. F. Fox.

STEVENSON, ROBERT LOUIS—III-3. "Prayers Written at Vailima."

VAN DYKE, HENRY—IV-6. "Thy Kingdom Come," by Ralph E. Diffendorfer.

WEISS, S.—X-3. "A Chain of Prayer Across the Ages," by S. F. Fox.

THE MEANING OF SERVICE

THE MEANING OF
SERVICE

HARRY EMERSON FOSDICK

Author of "The Manhood of the Master," "The Meaning of Prayer,"
"The Meaning of Faith," etc.

Garden City Books

GARDEN CITY, NEW YORK

PRINTED IN THE UNITED STATES OF AMERICA

The Bible Text used in this volume is taken from the American Standard Edition of the Revised Bible, copyright, 1901, by Thomas Nelson & Sons, and is used by permission.

To

Frank Sheldon Fosdick

MY FATHER

WHO FOR NEARLY HALF A CENTURY, AS AN
EDUCATOR OF YOUTH, HAS ILLUSTRATED
IN HIS LIFE THE MEANING OF SERVICE.

Preface

Thirty years ago this book was written—the last of a trilogy, the first two volumes of which were *The Meaning of Prayer* and *The Meaning of Faith*. I am amazed at the continuous demand which has kept them in lively circulation ever since and which now calls for a new edition.

To be sure, the subject with which this book deals is of vital importance now. No decent person can live in a generation such as this with its cruel suffering, its widespread devastation, its millions of dispossessed, starving, and enslaved people, and not feel the imperious demand to do his best to help. If this little volume can kindle afresh in anyone the sense of worth and significance in the individual's contribution to the world's vast need, I shall be grateful that I wrote it.

I hoped, when it first was published, that it might be a challenge to our churches, as well as to individuals. Too many churches talk endlessly about Christianity, but do all too little to express it in public service. Sermons can be important—but only when they issue in deeds. How can we endure so many underprivileged areas, with poverty and delinquency, so close to our sanctuaries where we pray and preach?

Such were the motives behind this little volume and for all the friends who have welcomed it and who now ask for a new edition, I am very grateful.

HARRY EMERSON FOSDICK

January 9, 1950.

Acknowledgments

Special acknowledgment is gladly made to the following: to E. P. Dutton & Company for permission to use prayers from "A Chain of Prayer Across the Ages"; to the Rev. Samuel McComb and the publishers for permission to quote from "Prayers for Today," Copyright, 1918, Harper & Brothers; to the Pilgrim Press for permission to make selections from "Prayers of the Social Awakening" by Walter Rauschenbusch and "The Original Plymouth Pulpit" by Henry Ward Beecher; to Little, Brown & Company for permission to quote one prayer from "Prayers, Ancient and Modern" by Mary W. Tileston; to George H. Doran Company for permission to use one prayer from "Pulpit Prayers" by Alexander Maclaren; to Jarrolds (London) Ltd. for permission to make quotations from "The Communion of Prayer" by William Boyd Carpenter, Bishop of Ripon; and to Longmans, Green & Company for permission to quote from "Prayers for the City of God," by Gilbert Clive Binyon.

None of the above material should be reprinted without securing permission.

CONTENTS

CONTENTS

THE MEANING OF SERVICE

CHAPTER I

Service and Christianity

DAILY READINGS

One of the most inveterate and ruinous ideas in the history of human thought is that neither service to man nor any moral rightness whatsoever is essential to religion. In wide areas of religious life, to satisfy God has been one thing, to live in righteous and helpful human relations has been another. As Professor Rauschenbusch put it: "Religion in the past has always spent a large proportion of its force on doings that were apart from the real business of life, on sacrificing, on endless prayers, on traveling to Mecca, Jerusalem, or Rome, on kissing sacred stones, bathing in sacred rivers, climbing sacred stairs, and a thousand things that had at best only an indirect bearing on the practical social relations between men and their fellows."

The conviction that a man who is not living in just and helpful relations with his fellows by no means whatever can be on right terms with God, is one of man's greatest spiritual illuminations, the understanding of which cost long centuries of slow and painful progress out of darkness into light. Note in the daily readings some old, pre-Christian attitudes toward this matter. They are still in evidence, for even yet we have on the one side appalling human need, and on the other an immense amount of religious motive power and zeal, which are not harnessed to the problems of human welfare. *Even yet one of mankind's most insistent needs is the interpretation of religion in terms of service and the attachment of religion's enormous driving power to the tasks of service.*

First Week, First Day

How much of the latent moral energy of religious faith is wasted *because many people, even yet, have only a partially righteous God!* We still need to go back for instruction to a Hebrew prophet like Micah.

Wherewith shall I come before Jehovah, and bow myself before the high God? shall I come before him with burnt-offerings, with calves a year old? will Jehovah be pleased with thousands of rams, or with ten thousands of rivers of oil? shall I give my first-born for my transgression, the fruit of my body for the sin of my soul? He hath showed thee, O man, what is good; and what doth Jehovah require of thee, but to do justly, and to love kindness, and to walk humbly with thy God?—Micah 6:6-8.

Translate that into modern terms: Wherewith shall I come before the Father of Jesus, and bow myself before the God who is love? Shall I come before him with gorgeous ceremonies, with elaborate rituals? Will the Father of all mercies be pleased with thousands of repeated credos or with ten thousands of eloquent sermons? Shall I give the bending of the knee for my transgression, the offering of my purse for the sin of my soul? He hath shewed thee, O man, what is good; and what doth the Father require of thee, but to do justly, and to love kindness, and to walk humbly with thy God? How many of us need such instruction yet in the utterly righteous character of God, and his demands on men! Raymond Lull, who, after a life of splendid usefulness, was stoned to death by Muhammadans in North Africa in 1315, urging his "sweet and reasonable appeal" for Christ, put a primary truth into worthy words: "He who would find Thee, O Lord, let him go forth to seek Thee in love, loyalty, devotion, faith, hope, justice, mercy, and truth; for in every place where these are, there art Thou."

O Father of Light and God of all Truth, purge the world from all errors, abuses, corruptions, and sins. Beat down the standard of Satan, and set up everywhere the standard of Christ. Abolish the reign of sin, and establish the kingdom of grace in all hearts; let humility triumph over pride and ambition; charity over hatred, envy, and malice; purity and temperance over lust and excess; meek-

ness over passion; disinterestedness and poverty of spirit over covet-
ousness and the love of this perishable world. Let the Gospel of
Christ in faith and practice prevail throughout the world.—French
Coronation Order.

First Week, Second Day

Another reason why so much of religion's driving power is unhar-
nessed to the tasks of service is *man's curious ability to keep divine*
relationships in one compartment of life and human relationships
in another. Are we yet beyond the reach of Isaiah's swift and terrible
indictment?

What unto me is the multitude of your sacrifices? saith Jehovah:
I have had enough of the burnt-offerings of rams, and the fat of fed
beasts; and I delight not in the blood of bullocks, or of lambs, or of
he-goats. When ye come to appear before me, who hath required
this at your hand, to trample my courts? Bring no more vain oblations; incense is an abomination unto me; new moon and sabbath,
the calling of assemblies,—I cannot away with iniquity and the
solemn meeting. Your new moons and your appointed feasts my
soul hateth; they are a trouble unto me; I am weary of bearing
them. And when ye spread forth your hands, I will hide mine eyes
from you; yea, when ye make many prayers, I will not hear: your
hands are full of blood. Wash you, make you clean; put away the
evil of your doings from before mine eyes; cease to do evil; learn
to do well; seek justice, relieve the oppressed, judge the fatherless,
plead for the widow.—Isa. 1:11-17.

Here are people who are religious, but their piety does not involve
goodness, nor their faith justice, nor their worship humaneness.
Their life with God has no connection with their daily relationships; it does not make them better home-folk, friends, neighbors,
or citizens. Are not plenty of such cases in the Christian churches?
How many folk believe in God's good purpose for mankind with
the religious side of their minds, but never order their practical ambitions as though there were such a purpose in the world! Or with
the religious part of their nature they believe that God loves all men,
while with the practical side they themselves neglect, mistreat, and
condemn men. We still need the advice which was given to David

Livingstone by an aged Scotchman: "Now, lad, make religion the everyday business of your life, and not a thing of fits and starts."

Lord! Our Light and our Salvation, help us, we beesech Thee, to enter into, and abide in, the secret place of the Most High; and may the shadow of the Almighty be our covering defense. Help each of us to set his love upon Thee, to bring thoughts and affections and purposes to Thyself, to think as Thou dost teach us, to love as Thou hast loved us, to do and will as Thou dost command us. So may we live in union with Thyself, and our word-worship in this place be in harmony with our consecration of life in our daily work.—Alexander Maclaren.

First Week, Third Day

Unmoral religion such as we are considering is often caused by *a preoccupying interest in the subordinate and trivial corollaries of religion*, its external expressions, its accidental accompaniments. Still the thunder of Amos is needed to clear our air!

I hate, I despise your feasts, and I will take no delight in your solemn assemblies. Yea, though ye offer me your burnt-offerings and meal-offerings, I will not accept them; neither will I regard the peace-offerings of your fat beasts. Take thou away from me the noise of thy songs; for I will not hear the melody of thy viols. But let justice roll down as waters, and righteousness as a mighty stream.—Amos 5:21-24.

How impatiently the prophet contrasts the etiquette of religious ritual with the importance of human justice! Many a man needs so to take his religion out of doors from the suffocating narrowness of small rubrics and petty rules, and to see it in terms not of "mint and anise and cummin," but of "justice and mercy and faith." Quintin Hogg poured out his life in Christian service for the poor boys of London. In a letter to one of the reclaimed lads, he wrote: "I do not care a rush what denomination you belong to, I do not very much care what special creed you profess, but I do care beyond all expression that the result of that creed in your daily life should be to make you a power for good amongst your fellowmen. . . . We hear much talk about creeds, professions of faith and the like; but I want you to remember that when God started to write a creed for us, He did it, not in words that might change their meaning, but He set before us a life, as though to teach us that whereas theology was a science which could be argued about, religion was a life and could only be lived."

Guide me, teach me, strengthen me, till I become such a person as Thou wouldst have me be; pure and gentle, truthful and high-minded, brave and able, courteous and generous, dutiful and useful.—Charles Kingsley.

First Week, Fourth Day

Still another familiar source of a religious life divorced from practical goodness and daily usefulness is the *segregation of the Church,* setting it apart from life, as though God dwelt in a temple instead of living in the struggles of humanity. So, of old time, Hosea cried:

O Ephraim, what shall I do unto thee? O Judah, what shall I do unto thee? for your goodness is as a morning cloud, and as the dew that goeth early away. Therefore have I hewed them by the prophets; I have slain them by the words of my mouth: and thy judgments are as the light that goeth forth. For I desire goodness, and not sacrifice; and the knowledge of God more than burnt-offerings.—Hos. 6:4-6.

When the Master, for service's sake, ate with the ceremonially unclean (Matt. 9:13) and again when for human helpfulness he transgressed the Sabbath rules (Matt. 12:7), and in both cases was denounced as an enemy of God, he fell back upon this passage from Hosea: "Go ye and learn what this meaneth, I desire mercy and not sacrifice." He felt as General Booth did, of whom it was said that, in comparison with the importance of helping men, "Every canon of society appeared in his eyes as the trivial and pitiful etiquette of a child's doll's house." The Master could not patiently see his Father treated as old fire-worshipers might have treated their sacred fire, keeping it aloof in their shrine and refusing it to the people to warm their houses, cook their food, and illumine their darkness. For, in Jesus' eyes, God was not primarily in church; God was in the midst of needy, sinning, aspiring, failing humanity. And religion was not professional piety. As Henry Ward Beecher said: "Religion means work. Religion means work in a dirty world. Religion means peril; blows given, but blows taken as well. Religion means transformation. The world is to be cleaned by somebody and you are not called of God if you are ashamed to scour and scrub."

Almighty God, Fountain of Life and Light, who didst raise up prophets in ancient times to warn and instruct, and whose Son Jesus Christ did send abroad into the world apostles, evangelists, pastors, and teachers, we beseech Thee to raise up in these days an increasing number of wise and faithful men, filled with the old prophetic fire and apostolic zeal, by whose labours Thy Church may be greatly blessed, and Thy Kingdom come and Thy Will be done on earth as it is in heaven.—John Hunter.

First Week, Fifth Day

Still another reason for the great quantity of religious motive power not yet belted into human service is *defective ideas of what is morally right.* Religious zeal does not necessarily argue ethical enlightenment. We are shocked to read of an ancient temple in Mexico, surrounded by 136,000 human skulls symmetrically piled; we wince at the thought of serving God, as some cults do, by murder and prostitution. But one need only read the prophets to see what a struggle it cost to be rid of such abominations in our own religious heritage. Are we yet rid of the heavy incubus of ethical blindness on religious life? Is "zeal without knowledge" a past problem? Rather Jeremiah might still hurl his invective at Christendom:

Thus saith Jehovah of hosts, the God of Israel, Amend your ways and your doings, and I will cause you to dwell in this place. Trust ye not in lying words, saying, The temple of Jehovah, the temple of Jehovah, the temple of Jehovah, are these. For if ye thoroughly amend your ways and your doings; if ye thoroughly execute justice between a man and his neighbor; if ye oppress not the sojourner, the fatherless, and the widow, and shed not innocent blood in this place, neither walk after other gods to your own hurt: then will I cause you to dwell in this place, in the land that I gave to your fathers, from of old even for evermore.

Behold, ye trust in lying words, that cannot profit. Will ye steal,

murder, and commit adultery, and swear falsely, and burn incense
unto Baal, and walk after other gods that ye have not known, and
come and stand before me in this house, which is called by my
name, and say, We are delivered; that ye may do all these abominations? Is this house, which is called by my name, become a den of
robbers in your eyes? Behold, I, even I, have seen it, saith Jehovah.
—Jer. 7:3-11.

Here were people who were zealous in their religious life. Feel the
ardent intensity with which they cry up "the Temple." But they had
not learned that simple lesson which Dr. Wilfred Grenfell, from his
practical service on the Labrador Coast, has put into wholesome
words: "Whether we, our neighbor, or God is the judge, absolutely
the only value of our 'religious' life to ourselves or to anyone is what
it fits us for and enables us to do."

*My Father and My God . . . let the fire of Thy love consume the
false shows wherewith my weaker self has deceived me. Make me
real as Thou art real. Inspire me with a passion for righteousness
and likeness to the Man of Nazareth, that I may love as He loved,
and find my joy as He found His joy in being and doing good. Dwell
Thou within me to give me His courage, His tenderness, His simplicity, to transform my own poor shadow-self into the likeness of
His truth and strength. Amen.*—Samuel McComb.

First Week, Sixth Day

And as for thee, son of man, the children of thy people talk of
thee by the walls and in the doors of the houses, and speak one to
another, every one to his brother, saying, Come, I pray you, and
hear what is the word that cometh forth from Jehovah. And they
come unto thee as the people cometh, and they sit before thee as
my people, and they hear thy words, but do them not; for with
their mouth they show much love, but their heart goeth after their
gain. And, lo, thou art unto them as a very lovely song of one that
hath a pleasant voice, and can play well on an instrument; for they
hear thy words, but they do them not.—Ezek. 33:30-32.

Ezekiel here has run upon unmoral religion in a common form.
See how amiable the spirit of these people was, how ingratiating
their manners, how ready their responsiveness! They loved to *hear*

about God's will, but they did not *do* it. So aspen leaves, tremulous, sensitive, quivering, sway with agitated responsiveness in every breath of wind. Endlessly stirring, the night finds them just where they were in the morning. They move continuously but they move nowhere. Many a man's religion is *emotional responsiveness without practical issue.* He substitutes delight in hearing the Gospel for diligence in living it. He does not see that religion is "action, not diction."

From infirmity of purpose, from want of earnest care and interest, from the sluggishness of indolence, and the slackness of indifference, and from all spiritual deadness of heart, save us and help us, we humbly beseech Thee, O Lord.

From dullness of conscience, from feeble sense of duty, from thoughtless disregard of others, from a low ideal of the obligations of our position, and from all half-heartedness in our work, save us and help us, we humbly beseech Thee, O Lord.—Bishop Ridding

First Week, Seventh Day

Woe unto you, scribes and Pharisees, hypocrites! for ye compass sea and land to make one proselyte; and when he is become so, ye make him twofold more a son of hell than yourselves.

Woe unto you, ye blind guides, that say, Whosoever shall swear by the temple, it is nothing; but whosoever shall swear by the gold of the temple, he is a debtor. Ye fools and blind: for which is greater, the gold, or the temple that hath sanctified the gold? And, Whosoever shall swear by the altar, it is nothing; but whosoever shall swear by the gift that is upon it, he is a debtor. Ye blind: for which is greater, the gift, or the altar that sanctifieth the gift? . . .

Woe unto you, scribes and Pharisees, hypocrites! for ye tithe mint and anise and cummin, and have left undone the weightier matters of the law, justice, and mercy, and faith: but these ye ought to have done, and not to have left the other undone. Ye blind guides, that strain out the gnat, and swallow the camel!—Matt. 23:15-19, 23, 24.

The greatest single contribution of the Hebrew prophets to human thought was their vision of the righteous nature of God and of his demands on men. Their supreme abhorrence was unmoral religion. In all our study we shall see the Master sharing their conviction, ele-

vating it to heights they never dreamed, stating it in terms that flash
and pierce and burn as theirs could not. The Master, too, hated unmoral religion. He pilloried the Pharisees in everlasting scorn. Their
pettiness, their quibbling, their false emphases, their bigotry, their
uncharitableness, their lack of forthright honesty, aroused his indignation. Their religion made them worse, not better; one feels that
they would have been improved without it; their religion was the
most unlovely thing about them. What should have made them large
had made them little; what should have made them generous had
made them mean. But to the Master religion meant graciousness
and magnanimity, self-forgetfulness and self-denial, high purpose
and deep joy in ministry, boundless brotherhood and a love balked
by no ingratitude or sin. The heights of his faith in God conspired
to send service pouring down to men in inexhaustible good will. He
was sure that the good God can be content with nothing less than
goodness in his children, and that the crown of goodness is a positive
life of outgoing service to all mankind.

*O Lord, grant to me so to love Thee, with all my heart, with all
my mind, and with all my soul, and my neighbor for Thy sake, that
the grace of charity and brotherly love may dwell in me, and all
envy, harshness, and ill will may die in me; and fill my heart with
feelings of love, kindness, and compassion, so that, by constantly rejoicing in the happiness and good success of others, by sympathizing
with them in their sorrows, and putting away all harsh judgments
and envious thoughts, I may follow Thee, who art Thyself the true
and perfect Love. Amen.*

COMMENT FOR THE WEEK

I

No one can doubt the central place which service held in the life
and teaching of the Master. Consider the parable of the good Samaritan (Luke 10:30-37), or that other more solemn utterance, where
the standing of the dead before the throne of God depended on
whether they had fed the hungry, clothed the naked, given drink
to the thirsty, and visited the imprisoned and sick (Matt. 25:31-46).
Consider his sayings, sparks from the anvil where he hammered out
the purpose of his life: "The Son of man came not to be ministered

unto, but to minister, and to give his life a ransom for many" (Matt.
20:28) ; "He that is greatest among you shall be your servant" (Matt.
23:11) ; "I am in the midst of you as he that serveth" (Luke 22:27).
Consider even more his life itself. In devoted love to individuals, so
that, with the whole Kingdom of God upon his heart, he yet poured
out his care on a blind Bartimeus, or a discouraged prodigal, or an
evilly entreated widow crying for her rights; in the revealing of great
truths that bless and redeem human life; in the starting of a movement that with all its faults has flowed like a river down from
Nazareth to revive man's character; in the possession of a radiant
spirit that throws out light on every side as naturally as the sun
shines, so that his very personality has been man's greatest benediction; in that ultimate test of service, vicarious sacrifice, that gives
up life itself for the sake of others; everywhere one sees that the
characteristic expression of the Master's spirit was ministry. Nor
was this ministry expended first upon the amiable and the great.
Who can read Rabindranath Tagore's lines and not think of Jesus?

"Here is thy footstool and there rest thy feet where live the poorest
    and lowliest and lost.
When I try to bow to thee, my obeisance cannot reach down to
    the depth where thy feet rest among the poorest and lowliest
    and lost.
Pride can never approach to where thou walkest in the clothes of
    the humble among the poorest and lowliest and lost.
My heart can never find its way to where thou keepest company
    with the companionless among the poorest, the lowliest, and
    the lost."

Surely there is little use in any man's calling himself the disciple
of such a Master if he does not possess the spirit and know the meaning of service.

It is evident, however, that plenty of professed Christians have
not interpreted their religion in such terms as these. Consider those
social evils—war, poverty, disease, ignorance, vice—the endless tragedy of which is the commonplace of the modern world! One sees
that, with one third of the population of the globe nominally Christian, there must have been some misunderstanding as to what Christianity is all about to allow so many professed disciples of Jesus to
live side by side for so long a time with such dire need. Christianity

has been content, in wide areas of its life, with some other interpretation of its own meaning than that which at first kindled the passion for service in the hearts of its disciples and sent them out from the shadow of the Cross, the spirit of the Cross within them. "I promise you," cried Hugh Latimer, preaching in Cambridge in 1529, "if you build one hundred churches, give as much as you can make to gilding of saints and honouring of the Church; and if thou go on as many pilgrimages as thy body can well suffer and offer as great candles as oaks; if thou leave the works of mercy and the commandments undone, these works shall nothing avail thee. . . . If you list to gild and paint Christ in your churches and honour Him in vestments, see that before your eyes the poor people die not for lack of meat, drink, and clothing." One catches there the authentic accent of the Christian spirit. Surely our world would be a far more decent and fraternal place if such an interpretation of the will of Christ in terms of practical service had been deeply apprehended and faithfully obeyed by the great body of his professed disciples.

At the beginning of our study, therefore, we well may examine some of the partial and perverted ways in which we Christians are tempted to misconceive our faith and so to mistake the message of the Master.

II

For one thing, Christianity to many people who profess it is no more than a formality. It is one of life's decent conventions. They were taught it in youth; they have never doubted its theoretical validity; they perceive that its profession is a mark of respectability; and they would no more be thought atheists than anarchists. But Christ's love for all sorts and conditions of men has never become the daily motive of their lives, and Christ's sacrificial faith in the possibility of a redeemed earth has never captured their imagination and their purpose.

The story of the religious experience of too many folk runs like this: they take the heavy lumber of their lives and build the secular dwelling in which habitually they abide; there they live and move and have their being in family and social life, in business and politics and sports; but because religion is a part of every conventionally well-furnished life they build as well, with what lumber may remain, an appended shrine, and there at times they slip away and pay their respects to the Almighty. Their religion is an isolated and uninfluential afterthought. Especially on Sundays when the banks are shut, the shops are closed, the rush of life is still, and finer forces stir within them, they go in company with their fellows to the church for formal worship. And when it is over they close the door on that experience and go back to their ordinary life again. So Bliss Carman sings:

> "They're praising God on Sunday.
> They'll be all right on Monday.
> It's just a little habit they've acquired."

When, in the midst of their customary lives, this isolated religious experience rises in their memory, it seems vague, unreal, like a sonata of Beethoven heard long ago or a poem once listened to and half remembered. They recall it as one thinks of his summer home beside the sea, when in the galloping turmoil of the city a chance recollection strays to it. It is a long way off in another kind of world.

So flying fish live in the sea; that is their native and habitual realm, but once in a while they make a brief excursion into the upper air and glisten for an instant in the sun—only to fall back into the sea again. To how many people is religion such a brief, occasional experience! And yet they call themselves disciples of him whose heart beat with an unintermittent passion to help people, whose God was love, whose worship was daily service, whose hope was the Kingdom, whose instrument was the Cross. They are not really Christians. They are flying fish. For true discipleship to Jesus is the opposite of spasmodic conventionality. We are even wrong when we call our public worship on Sunday "church service." Church service really begins on Monday morning at seven o'clock and lasts all the week. Church service is helpfulness to people; public worship is preparation for it. For the church service which the Master illustrated and approved is a life of ministry amid the dust and din of daily business in a sacrificial conflict for a Christian world.

III

The obscuring of practical service as the indispensable expression of the Christian Gospel is effected in many folk, not by thus making religion a listless and spasmodic formality but by *stressing, often with heated earnestness, all sorts of trivial accompaniments of religion that do not really matter.* So an English lord complained that the severest blow religion ever had received was the loss of the bishops' wigs!

Historic Christianity is like a river that carries with it not only its own pure water but all manner of debris as well, silt from its own bottom, logs from its banks, flotsam from its tributaries. At last these accumulations that came from the river block the river; the rising water frets against the impediments that once expressed its life; and the river has to burst a new course through them and toss them impatiently aside. Such was the work of the Hebrew prophets amid the religious trivialities of their day and such the conflict of the Master with quibbling minds that tithed "mint and anise and cummin," and neglected "the weightier matters of the law."

Even yet when men say "Christianity" they often mean not so much the pure spirit at the heart of it as all the clutter collected on its way. But the World War through which we have lived has made multitudes discriminate. It is clear that some things in so-called Christianity matter very much and some things do not count at all. Too often Christianity becomes like a city's streets where all forms of traffic, big and little, jostle each other upon equal terms. The gutter-snipe and the merchant, the pushcart and the limousine, all have their rights, and in the fusion of them discrimination lapses and the streets are cluttered and confused. Then fire breaks out, and the whole street from end to end is cleared to let the engines by. When disaster comes the main business must be given gangway.

Such an effect the Great War has had on men's thoughts of Christianity. They see that some things once deemed important are of small account. Denominational distinctions in Protestantism, for the most part, do not matter. A man who becomes excited about them in such a day as this is an anachronism. Old questions of biblical criticism that were once discussed as though men's very lives depended upon them, do not crucially matter. A man who becomes vexed and quarrelsome about such questions today is hopelessly belated. He has an ante-bellum mind. Many questions in theology that have vexed human hearts and have furnished basis for heresy trials do not matter. They may have a place upon the side streets of Christian thinking, but they ought to be kept from littering up the avenues. *For there is one thing that does matter.* There is nothing on earth that begins to matter so much. Can Jesus Christ, his faith and

principles, be made regnant on this earth? Can we get men to believe vitally in him and in the truths he represents and to join the
great crusade to make over this shattered world upon the basis of
his ideals? Can lives now battered and broken by misfortune and by
sin be reclaimed, and can our social life, its business, its statecraft,
its international relationships be transformed by the renewing of
men's minds until they shall be truly Christian? In comparison with
that, nothing else matters.

In the presence of such a cause, for a man to have a sectarian
mind, to ride theological hobbies, to be obsessed with favorite
fashions in religious phylacteries, is to miss the main issue of the
Gospel. One who, like General Booth, founder of the Salvation
Army, knows thoroughly and feels deeply the physical, moral, and
spiritual desolation of millions who live under the very shadow of
our church spires, feels also with impatience the frivolous futility of
much popular religion. "It is no better than a ghastly mockery," he
says, "to call by the name of One, who came to seek and to save that
which was lost, those churches which, in the midst of lost multitudes,
either sleep in apathy or display a fitful interest in a chasuble. Why
all this apparatus of temples, of meeting houses, to save men from
perdition in a world which is to come, while never a helping hand
is stretched out to save them from the inferno of their present life?
Is it not time that, forgetting for a moment their wrangling about
the infinitely little and the infinitely obscure, they should concentrate
all their energies on a united effort to break this terrible perpetuity
of perdition and to rescue some at least of those for whom they profess to believe their Founder came to die?"

IV

Of all the reasons why Christian people miss the indispensable
fruit of real Christianity in service none is commoner than this:
religion can itself become one of the most selfish influences in life.
Men can accept religion, love it, cleave to it, not from any unselfish
motives whatsoever but solely because of the inward peace, the
quieted conscience, and the radiant hope which they themselves get
from it. Religion becomes not a stimulus but a sedative; it is used
not as an inspiration to service but as a substitute for it. Mystical
experiences of spiritual delight; a peaceful sense of being pardoned
by God and reconciled with him; an emotional share, sometimes

soothing, sometimes ecstatic, in the fellowship of public praise; hope of a future heaven—these blessings and others like them men get from religion. And sometimes these are all that they get. Religion reaches them only on their receptive side. It is life's supreme appeal to their selfishness.

Indeed the very nature of the Christian message lays us open to this special form of failure. For Christianity has two sides. On one side Christianity is the best news to which human ears ever listened. The fatherhood of God, the saviourhood of Christ, the friendship of the Spirit, the victory of righteousness, the life eternal— no other message half so exhilarating and comfortable has ever stirred the hearts of men. It is good to hear and the New Testament bears abundant witness that from the beginning of the Gospel's proclamation a peril arose from this very fact. The Good News was so good to hear that even in the first century folk began the pleasant but hopeless endeavor to absorb it by hearing only, and the New Testament keeps ringing out a warning. Says Jesus: "Everyone that heareth these words of mine, and doeth them not, shall be likened unto a foolish man, who built his house upon the sand" (Matt. 7:26). Says Paul: "Not the hearers of the law are just before God but the doers of the law" (Rom. 2:13). Says James: "Be ye doers of the word, and not hearers only, deluding your own selves" (James 1:22).

This insistence of the New Testament on the peril of a facile and passive response to the Gospel is no accident. It springs warm and urgent from the New Testament's thought of what the Gospel is. It is good news to be heard, but it is something more; it presents a task to be achieved. It calls for devoted, sacrificial service. It has launched a movement which for breadth and depth of present influence and for latent power cannot be matched in history. It has meant a crusade to turn the world upside down. Christianity is not simply a message to be heard; it is a deed to be done.

All the profoundest experiences in human life are thus two-sided, and are complete only as reception and action are balanced. The love which makes a home has two aspects. On one side it is romance. The poets sing about it endlessly—the

> "tender and extravagant delight,
> The first and secret kiss by twilight hedge,
> The insane farewell repeated o'er and o'er."

But on the other side a complete love involves unselfishness, willing sacrifice, mutual forbearance, absolute fidelity, boundless devotion. In one aspect love is all lure and witchery and enchantment; in the other it is loyalty and self-denial and fidelity "till death us do part." On one side it is responsiveness; on the other it is responsibility. Miserable bargain hunters in the realm of spirit are those who try to get one side without the other!

Christian history bears painful testimony to the absorbing preference of multitudes of so-called Christians for the comfortable aspects of the Gospel. There never has been any lack of folk to listen with ready receptiveness to the consolations of the faith. Religion made impressive in architecture, beautiful in music, glorious in art, vocal in preaching, vivid in sacrament, has brought hope, cheer, and comfort to multitudes. But too often this elemental fact has been forgotten, that every Christian truth, gracious and comfortable, has a corresponding obligation, searching and sacrificial. Every doctrine has its associated duty, every truth its task. On a Sunday morning, for example, a congregation listens to a sermon on the central message of the Christian faith, God's love for every son of man. None is so small and so obscure, so lost to general observation and to private care, the preacher cries, that God does not think on him. He loves us every one as though he had no other sons to love. It is a glorious Gospel. And if the preacher be a master of gripping phrase and luscious paragraph, how surely with such a theme he will cast a witching spell over any audience! But such a spell, however delectable, may be an unwholesome experience. That Gospel, when the Master first proclaimed it, was not intended primarily for preaching; it was intended for action. Do we not see, as he did, the appalling sin, the haggard want, the infuriating oppression, which are befalling these folk, every one of whom God loves? If personality is as sacred as that teaching says, then there is urgent business afoot upon this earth to challenge the service of all who believe the teaching. For on every side ruin is befalling these countless men and women for whom Christ died because he thought that they were worth dying for.

One of the most remarkable sights in the high Rockies is "timber line." One mounts from the valleys where the forests are immense and bountiful and ever as he rises the trees grow dwarfed. At last he comes to "timber line." It is the final frontier of the trees, the last stand where they have been able to maintain themselves against the furious tempests of the upper heights. Far above stretch the snow-clad summits, and here are such twisted, stunted, whipped, and beaten trees as one could not imagine without seeing them. Twenty-eight rings were counted in one courageous struggler there, two inches high. Twenty-eight years of bitterest fighting against impossible odds had brought two inches of misshapen growth!

What is this, however, in comparison with the human timber line? Consider the terribly handicapped and beaten masses of mankind, whipped by poverty, sickness, ignorance, sin. The most beautiful religious poem of recent years, "The Hound of Heaven," was written by Francis Thompson. But Thompson, a few years before he wrote it, was a tatterdemalion figure on the streets of London, holding the heads of strangers' horses to make a few pence for opium to drug himself. The tragedy there was pitiful: Francis Thompson so outwardly circumscribed and inwardly cowed that he could not *be* Francis Thompson at all. In ways dramatic or obscure how common that story is! Personality with rich possibilities in it is everywhere nipped and stunted, its flowers unopened, its fruit unborne.

Only recently a young man sailed from New York City for Liberia. See what amazing contrasts that young man's experience presents! When first he comes upon our view, he is a naked savage nine years old, discovered by a missionary in the jungle of Africa. His father is a worshiper of demons, obsessed by witchcraft; his mother is a native of the forest; his tribe is sunk in the depths of barbarism. He borrows a bit of calico from his mother for a loin cloth and leaves his home for a Wesleyan school. Yet only yesterday that young man, now in his twenty-ninth year, a graduate of Harvard University with high honors, a Christian of beautiful spirit, whose presentation of the cause of Liberia in Washington, so competent authorities report, was worthy of the finest traditions of British and American statesmanship, sailed back to Liberia to help his people. One rejoices in that single experience of personality released from crippling handicaps. But what a woeful waste in multitudes of other lives, also capable of fine expansion, who still are dwarfs of their real selves!

A sheer question of sincerity is raised, therefore, if one professes to believe that all these folk, battered and undone, are infinitely valuable in the sight of God. That is not chiefly a message to be enjoyed. That is chiefly a challenge to be answered with self-denying toil. The sacredness of personality is the most disturbing faith a man can hold. We are wretched bargain hunters in religion if we try to keep the comforts of the Gospel and to avoid its sacrifices.

> "No mystic voices from the heavens above
> Now satisfy the souls which Christ confess;
> Their heavenly vision is in works of love,
> A new age summons to new saintliness.
> Before th' uncloistered shrine of human needs
> And all unconscious of the worth or price,
> They lay their fragrant gifts of gracious deeds
> Upon the altar of self-sacrifice."[1]

V

This, then, is the conclusion of the matter: *the inevitable expression of real Christianity is a life of sacrificial service.* If by making religion a spasmodic formality, or by centering our thought upon its trivial corollaries, or by choosing its comfortable aspects and avoiding its self-denials, we refuse this characteristic expression of the Master's spirit, we cannot really have the Master's spirit at all. One law of the spiritual life from the operation of which no man can escape is that nothing can come into us unless it can get out of us. We commonly suppose that study is the road to learning. Upon the contrary, long-continued acquisitive study, absorbing information without expressing it, is the surest way to paralyze the mind. He who would be a scholar must not only study but teach, write, lecture, apply his knowledge to practical uses. Somehow he must give what he gets or soon he will get no more. As with a swamp, so with a mind, an inlet is useless without an outlet, since he who gets to keep can in the end get nothing good.

So a man who tries to assimilate Christianity by impression without expression can receive no real Christianity at all. If one stands perfectly insulated on a glass foundation he may handle live wires with impunity. Electricity may not come in where it cannot flow through. So the Christian Gospel demands outlet before it can find inlet. The failure of many Christians lies at the point of intake; they are estopped from real faith and prayer; they have no vital contact with divine realities. But the disaster of multitudes comes from a cluttered outlet. They do not know the meaning of service.

---

[1] Professor Francis G. Peabody.

CHAPTER II

The Peril of Uselessness

DAILY READINGS

Lord Melbourne is reported to have said: "If we are to have a religion, let us have one that is cool and indifferent; and such a one as we have got." Here is a candid desire for a faith which does not involve devoted service, but which makes possible a life insipidly neutral. Such a man is not outrageously cruel and inhuman, but he frankly accepts the ideal of negative harmlessness. Let us consider this week certain familiar attitudes which cause plenty of decent, not unamiable people, even though they may be religious, to accept for themselves such a colorless, useless life.

Second Week, First Day

And he came to Nazareth, where he had been brought up: and he entered, as his custom was, into the synagogue on the sabbath day, and stood up to read. And there was delivered unto him the book of the prophet Isaiah. And he opened the book, and found the place where it was written,
The Spirit of the Lord is upon me,
Because he anointed me to preach good tidings to the poor:
He hath sent me to proclaim release to the captives,
And recovering of sight to the blind,
To set at liberty them that are bruised,
To proclaim the acceptable year of the Lord.
And he closed the book, and gave it back to the attendant, and sat down: and the eyes of all in the synagogue were fastened on him. And he began to say unto them, To-day hath this scripture been fulfilled in your ears.—Luke 4:16-21.

When Jesus went to church he thought about service. Service was the crux of his whole spiritual experience; it was the great matter with which, in his eyes, public worship and all that it represents were concerned. When he worshiped his Father, he worshiped One, who was not willing "that one of these little ones should perish" (Matt. 18:14); when he prayed in solitude, he remembered friends like Peter, sorely tempted and needing help (Luke 22:31, 32); when he thought of immortality, he rejoiced that some, cruelly handicapped in this life, would have another chance (Luke 16:19-31); when he was transfigured he straightway harnessed his refreshed power to practical ministry (Matt. 17:9-18). *His public worship, his faith in God, his private prayer, his eternal hope, and his transfigured hours all centered round and issued in a devoted life of helpfulness to people.* The first reason why many folk are content with a "cool and indifferent religion" is that they have missed utterly the meaning of the Master's life. Whatever their religion may mean to them—correctness of formal belief, historic continuity of church establishments, exactness of ritual, respectable conventionality—it is not of that quality which causes them in the church to be thinking, as Jesus did, about the poor, the captive, the blind, and the bruised.

O Thou, who art the Light of the minds that know Thee, the Life of the souls that love Thee, and the Strength of the thoughts that seek Thee; help us so to know Thee, that we may truly love Thee, so to love Thee that we may fully serve Thee, whose service is perfect freedom; through Jesus Christ our Lord. Amen.—Gelasian Sacramentary (A. D. 494).

Second Week, Second Day

Another reason for that type of decent religion, which nevertheless is "cool and indifferent" to human service, is *the strange idea that God, like some vain earthly potentate, enjoys being praised,* and that, therefore, a due amount of adoration is highly gratifying to him and quite sufficient for us. But consider the clear teaching of the Master:

If therefore thou art offering thy gift at the altar, and there rememberest that thy brother hath aught against thee, leave there thy gift before the altar, and go thy way, first be reconciled to thy brother, and then come and offer thy gift.—Matt. 5:23, 24.

Religion is like patriotism in this respect: both of them at the beginning are emotions which we enjoy. We praise our country in patriotic oratory and resounding song, and we like it. But the days come when a man's country expects of him something more than praise. Patriotism lays its hands on all the active, outgoing, courageous elements in his life; it means sacrificial self-denial; it may even lead a man to vicarious death. So, says Jesus, does God ask something far more than worship. He asks self-sacrificing, brotherly relations between men. God is no fool to be pleased by flattery. What does he care for our songs, except as our lives are serving his other children? "Not every one that saith unto me, Lord, Lord," cried Jesus, "but he that doeth the will of my Father" (Matt. 7:21).

Almighty and most merciful Father, who hast given us a new commandment that we should love one another; give us also grace that we may fulfil it. Make us gentle, courteous, and forbearing. Direct our lives, so that we may look each to the good of the other in word and deed. And hallow all our friendships by the blessing of Thy Spirit; for His sake who loved us, and gave Himself for us, Jesus Christ our Lord. Amen.—Bishop Westcott (1825-1901).

Second Week, Third Day

Another reason for a neutral, useless life among amiable and decent people is *sheer lack of information about the needs of folk beyond the borders of our social circles.*

And they came to the other side of the sea, into the country of the Gerasenes. And when he was come out of the boat, straightway there met him out of the tombs a man with an unclean spirit, who had his dwelling in the tombs: and no man could any more bind him, no, not with a chain; because that he had been often bound with fetters and chains, and the chains had been rent asunder by him, and the fetters broken in pieces: and no man had strength to tame him. And always, night and day, in the tombs and in the mountains, he was crying out, and cutting himself with stones.— Mark 5:1-5.

How many of the people in the neighboring village of Gadara knew of this man, or had tried to help him? But Jesus, by an instinctive sympathy, never went into any neighborhood without finding at once the sick, the poor, the bedeviled. We live in our secluded social circles; we do not know even the maids in our kitchens, the workmen in our factories, the bootblacks and the newsboys who serve us. We deal with our fellows on a cash basis, not on a basis of human interest. And as for the conditions of life in the slums of our own communities, in the jails and asylums, among the sick, the vicious, the homeless, the unemployed, the mentally defective, how little do many of us know—or care! But imagine Jesus in one of our communities! He would not live in a social cocoon. He would soon know all the worst need of the town.

O Lord God, arise, for the spoiling of the poor, for the sighing of the needy; for Thou respectest not the persons of princes nor regardest the rich more than the poor. Give justice to the afflicted and destitute, rescue the weak, and may Thy Kingdom come on earth, through Jesus Christ our Lord.—Bishop Vernon Herford.

Second Week, Fourth Day

Jesus made answer and said, A certain man was going down from Jerusalem to Jericho; and he fell among robbers, who both stripped him and beat him, and departed, leaving him half dead. And by chance a certain priest was going down that way: and when he saw him, he passed by on the other side. And in like manner a Levite also, when he came to the place, and saw him, passed by on the other side. But a certain Samaritan, as he journeyed, came where he was: and when he saw him, he was moved with compassion, and came to him, and bound up his wounds, pouring on them oil and wine; and he set him on his own beast, and brought him to an inn, and took care of him. And on the morrow he took out two shillings, and gave them to the host, and said, Take care of him: and whatsoever thou spendest more, I, when I come back again, will repay thee. Which of these three, thinkest thou, proved neighbor unto him that fell among the robbers? And he said, He that showed mercy on him. And Jesus said unto him, Go, and do thou likewise. —Luke 10:30-37.

The Master presents clearly here three familiar types. The robbers are aggressively destructive, cruel, inhuman. The Good Samaritan is aggressively unselfish. The priest and the Levite are neither one nor the other. They did not hurt the man; they did not help him. They refused to mix in the unpleasant affair at all. They stood aloof alike from robbery and service. Preoccupied about their own affairs, they did not wish to distract their thought, disarrange their schedule, or soil their hands with this sorry business of a wounded man. How like they are to many among us, who, *from mere dislike of having our ordinary, comfortable course of life disturbed, miss countless opportunities for usefulness!* Consider the intense indignation of the Master, which this parable reveals, against such a listless, apathetic attitude toward human need!

They that are ensnared and entangled in the extreme penury of things needful for the body, cannot set their mind upon Thee, O Lord, as they ought to do; but when they be disappointed of the things which they so mightily desire, their hearts are cast down and quail from excess of grief. Have pity upon them, therefore, O merciful Father, and relieve their misery from Thine incredible riches, that by Thy removing of their urgent necessity, they may rise up to Thee in mind. Thou, O Lord, providest enough for all men with Thy most liberal and bountiful hand; but whereas Thy gifts are, in respect of Thy goodness and free favour, made free unto all men, we (through our haughtiness and niggardship and distrust) do make them private and peculiar. Correct Thou the things which our iniquity hath put out of order; let Thy goodness supply that which our niggardliness hath plucked away. Give Thou meat to the hungry and drink to the thirsty; comfort Thou the sorrowful; cheer Thou the dismayed; strengthen Thou the weak; deliver Thou them that are prisoners; and give Thou hope and courage to them that are out of heart.—Queen Elizabeth's Prayer Book.

Second Week, Fifth Day

Still another reason for a listlessly useless life is that *folk content themselves with meditating on the fact that they are not doing any harm.*

Ye are the salt of the earth: but if the salt have lost its savor, wherewith shall it be salted? it is thenceforth good for nothing, but to be cast out and trodden under foot of man.—Matt. 5:13.

Salt is good: but if the salt have lost its saltness, wherewith will ye season it?—Mark 9:50.

In view of this familiar condemnation, consider what evil in denatured salt can so deserve the Master's disapproval. What harm
does it do? It is not poison that one should dread it. It is a neutral,
harmless thing, by which no ruin is brought on anyone. Yet to this
homely example of savorless salt the Master turned for the picture of
a kind of life which seemed to him intolerable. Poor Richard's Almanac contains this sentiment: "The noblest question in the world
is, What good can I do in it?" That is a test on which the Master
insisted. When, therefore, any man contents himself with asking of
his empty life, What harm do I do? he may expect the scathing
rebuke of Jesus. Such self-satisfied negativeness, in his eyes, reduced
the glorious possibilities of useful manhood to insipidity. He could
no more endure denatured personality than denatured salt.

*Eternal God, who committest to us the swift and solemn trust of
life; since we know not what a day may bring forth, but only that
the hour for serving Thee is always present, may we wake to the
instant claims of Thy Holy Will; not waiting for tomorrow, but
yielding today. Lay to rest, by the persuasion of ·Thy Spirit, the resistance of our passion, indolence, or fear. Consecrate with Thy
presence the way our feet may go; and the humblest work will shine,
and the roughest places be made plain. Lift us above unrighteous
anger and mistrust into faith and hope and charity by a simple and
steadfast reliance on Thy sure will. In all things draw us to the mind
of Christ, that Thy lost image may be traced again, and Thou
mayest own us as at one with Him and Thee. Amen.*—James
Martineau.

Second Week, Sixth Day

**But the unclean spirit, when he is gone out of the man, passeth
through waterless places, seeking rest, and findeth it not. Then he
saith, I will return into my house whence I came out; and when he
is come, he findeth it empty, swept, and garnished. Then goeth he,
and taketh with himself seven other spirits more evil than himself,
and they enter in and dwell there: and the last state of that man
becometh worse than the first.—Matt. 12:43-45.**

The Master, illustrating a familiar experience, uses the popular
ideas of his time with regard to the activity of demons. A man succeeds in expelling from his life some cruel temper, selfish passion,

mean animosity; he rejoices in a heart "empty, swept, and garnished." What he rejoices in, however, the Master heartily condemns. *He cannot tolerate an empty life.* Many people suppose that to be a Christian is thus a suppression of their instincts, a banishment of their impulses, a prohibition of their natural powers. Their whole ideal is negative. Consider, however, Henry Ward Beecher's description of Paul: "He was a man of immense conscience, immense pride, and immense combativeness. He was converted. His conscience did not diminish, his pride did not shrink, his combativeness did not flow out. All those great elements remained in him. Before he was converted, his conscience worked with malign feelings. Afterwards, his conscience worked with benevolent feelings. Before he was converted, his pride worked for selfishness. After he was converted, his pride worked for benevolence. Before he was converted, his combativeness worked for cruelty. After he was converted, it worked for zeal." A merely empty life always ends, as Jesus said, by being seven times more bedeviled than it was at first. But a thorough Christian is a man with all his active powers awake, well harnessed, and at work.

O Lord God of hosts, who maketh the frail children of men to be Thy glad soldiers in the conquest of sin and misery, breathe Thy Spirit, we pray Thee, into the students of this country and of all lands, that they may come together in faith and fellowship, and stand up an exceeding great army for the deliverance of the oppressed and for the triumph of Thy Kingdom; through Jesus Christ our Lord. Amen.—"A Book of Prayers for Students."

Second Week, Seventh Day

A life of negative uselessness is also caused by *mere frivolity.*

Now the parable is this: The seed is the word of God. And those by the way side are they that have heard; then cometh the devil, and taketh away the word from their heart, that they may not believe and be saved. And those on the rock are they who, when they have heard, receive the word with joy; and these have no root, who for a while believe, and in time of temptation fall away. And that which fell among the thorns, these are they that have heard, and as they go on their way they are choked with cares and riches and pleasures of this life, and bring no fruit to perfection. And that in the good ground, these are such as in an honest and good heart, having heard the word, hold it fast, and bring forth fruit with patience.—Luke 8:11-15.

Consider the third kind of soil, where worldly cares, and love of gain, and delight of life's good times destroyed the fruit. Such a description does not involve conduct notoriously evil, but it does picture a style of living which lacks seriousness. Some of these folk were evidently light-headed, frivolous; they were preoccupied with pleasure, instead of being served by it. They may have been very gay and winsome, and not by any means unamiable, but, for all their engaging qualities, the fact remains that they flitted through life; frivoled their time and energy away; were tickled by many transient pleasures, tiring of which they sought for new; and their selfish and frittered lives "ended like a broom, in a multitude of small straws."

How familiar are these causes of useless living among decent folk! Some do not associate their churchgoing, as Jesus did, with service; some praise God indeed, but have never had their active powers captured by him; some do not know human life outside their little circles; some do not want their comfortable schedule of life disturbed; some are content with harmlessness; some define duty in terms of repression rather than expression; and some are absorbed in frivolity. Is there any one of us who is altogether free from such unserviceable faults?

Lord, let me not live to be useless!—John Wesley.

COMMENT FOR THE WEEK

I

Over against the virtues of a serviceable life stand in sharp contrast destructive qualities like cruelty, rapacity, and hatred. Against these and all their kin the Master loosed his wrath. *But he knew well that the majority of folk are not so much tempted to fall away from positive service into positive destructiveness, as they are tempted to fall between the two into negative uselessness.* It is worth our while, therefore, to note the intensity and persistency with which the Master bore down upon this deadly sin.

No outbreaking evil is reported of the pious travelers, the priest and the Levite, who in the parable of the good Samaritan left the robbed and wounded man untended in his trouble. One asks in vain what positive wrong they did. The Master's condemnation falls on them because they did nothing. They "went by on the other side." No oppressive wrongs are mentioned in the story of Dives who feasted sumptuously while Lazarus lay uncared for at his gate (Luke 16:19-31). The indictment concerns only what Dives did not do. He was useless. No destructive vices are reported of those who stand condemned in the great parable of the judgment (Matt. 25:31-46). The indictment against them is a comprehensive charge of uselessness: "I was hungry, and ye did not give me to eat; I was thirsty, and ye gave me no drink; I was a stranger, and ye took me not in; naked, and ye clothed me not; sick, and in prison, and ye visited me not."

Everywhere in the teaching of our Lord this central emphasis is found. Sometimes he illustrates his thought in terms of *business*. No positive dishonor is charged against the man of one talent who hid his entrustment in a napkin while his fellows profitably traded with their capital and multiplied it (Matt. 25:14-30). He is accused by the Master of doing nothing. But in the Master's eyes no charge is more terrific. He was "a good-for-nothing servant"; he must be cast into "outer darkness." Sometimes the Master illustrates his thought in terms of *agriculture*. Three kinds of ground stand heartily condemned in the parable of the sower (Mark 4:1-20). One was hard and would not take the seed; one was stony and gave the seed thin rootage; one was rich and grew choking weeds. But the gist of the final fault in every case lay here: the ground was useless. Sometimes the Master illustrates his thought in terms of *domestic life*. A most amiable boy is pictured in the parable where the father asks his two sons for service in the vineyard (Matt. 21:28-31). "I go, sir," said one, a winsome, well-intentioned, gracious lad. *"But he went not,"* said Jesus. That negative is one of the most damning charges that can be brought against a human life. However, well-intentioned, the boy was useless. The Master's praise goes rather to the other son, whose words were not gracious but who did the work.

When the Master speaks of the future life, it is with useless people that his most fearful apprehensions are concerned. The useless chaff will be consumed, he says (Matt. 3:12); the useless weeds must necessarily be burned (Matt. 13:30). The very word Gehenna, which

we translate Hell, means Valley of Hinnom, the place of incineration
outside Jerusalem where the rubbish of the city was consumed. Such
a picturesque and flaming figure may be uncertain in its doctrinal
implications, but it makes convincingly clear the principle on which
the Master estimated men. Above all other things he hated uselessness. Recall his condemnation of savorless salt, harmless but insipidly
good for nothing. Recall his rebuke of lives that like candles under
the bed or covered by a vessel burn, but burn uselessly (Luke 8:16).
And consider his incisive words in the parable of the fig tree: "A
certain man had a fig tree planted in his vineyard; and he came
seeking fruit thereon, and found none. And he said unto the vine-
dresser, Behold, these three years I come seeking fruit on this fig tree,
and find none: cut it down; why doth it also cumber the ground?"
(Luke 13:6-9).

II

This same standard of judgment the Master used concerning institutions as well as persons. *In his eyes the only solid claim on perpetuity for any organization must rest on usefulness,* and he did not
hesitate to force this issue home with ruthless severity on the most
venerable religious institutions of his day. Nothing, for example, was
more sacred in his people's thought than the Sabbath. They said that
God himself had rested on the Sabbath; that the deliverance from
Egypt took place on the Sabbath; that God with his own fingers had
written the Sabbath law on Sinai. The rabbis said that God had
created the human race that he might have some one to keep the
Sabbath. Then Jesus came, and even that sacred day he subjected
to the ruthless test of usefulness. The rabbis had said that men were
created to keep the Sabbath; he answered that "the sabbath was
made for man and not man for the sabbath" (Mark 2:27). He said
that with all its venerable history and sacred associations, that holiest
of days would stand or fall by one test: usefulness to people. If by it
human life grew richer, well! If not, no theory of divine institution
could sustain it. And because the Sabbath became a burden and not
a blessing, it is gone in Christendom and the Lord's Day takes its
place.

As the Master tested the Sabbath, so he tested the temple. The
House of God on Zion was the most sacred spot the Jews had ever
known. During long centuries of passionate devotion they had loved

it when possessed, longed for it in exile, rebuilt it when regained, and in spirit from the ends of the earth had revisited it continually with ardent prayer. The Master shared this loyalty. From the time when twelve years old he stood within his Father's house and questioned the doctors of the law, to the day when, ready to face the Cross, he swung around the brow of Olivet and, seeing the gleaming dome on Zion, burst into tears, he was a lover of the temple. But he saw also the inviolable law which even the temple could not escape. Priests using the sacred courts to squeeze ill-gotten gains from the people's piety; rabbis loving to be called rabbi, seeking the chief places at the feasts; Levites hurrying up the Jerusalem-Jericho road to be on time at the temple sacrifice, but careless of victims who had fallen among thieves; Pharisees wearing their broad phylacteries and loading on the people's conscience burdens grievous to be borne; the temple, a place of special privilege and not of service—all that he saw, and though it broke his heart to say it, he cried out that not one stone should be left upon another.

Many dubious problems concerning the Master's life and teaching baffle our inquiry, but one central fact stands clear: in his eyes uselessness was a deadly sin, and no permanence or greatness could belong to any person however eminent or to any institution however sacred unless it served the people.

III

All history is a running commentary on the truth of this principle of Jesus. Even in the sub-human world, before ethical meanings are evident, we can perceive that there is some relationship between permanence and usefulness. We cannot answer our children's simple questions about the animals they love without recourse to it. Why do squirrels have bushy tails? Because they are useful for balancing in the branches of trees. Why do cats and dogs have eyes in the front of their heads? Because they are hunters, and eyes in front are useful to spy the game they seek. Why do rabbits have eyes on the sides of their heads? Because they are not hunters but are hunted, and eyes at the side are useful to watch in every direction for approaching foes. From such homely facts to the most learned explanation of the evolution of species, this truth is evident: that a useful function is the best guaranty of permanence, and that outgrowing that useful function any living thing falls into peril of extinction. If it survives at all, it is crowded as a derelict into the shallows and back eddies, out of the main stream of life. So the sense of smell, the most useful safeguard of the animals, become less necessary among men, grows immeasurably less acute. As Huxley says, *"The sense of uselessness is the severest shock that any organism can sustain."*

When one turns from sub-human nature to human society, this principle becomes even more evident. The history of man is strewn with the wrecks of social customs and political institutions that seemed great and permanent. Men thought them inextricably wrought into the fabric of life. A world without them was unimaginable. But they were not useful to the progress and enrichment of mankind, and they have vanished.

Consider so contemporary a matter as the prohibition of the liquor traffic in the United States! Convivial drinking goes back to the dawn of history. It is one of the immemorial traditions of the race. It has been enshrined in story, exalted in art, made fascinating in song, and countless customs of private friendship and public ceremonial have been entwined with it. Moreover, in our modern time billions of dollars have been invested in the traffic. It seemed absurd to propose its abolition. But one unescapable fact was more than a match for this enormous weight of power: the liquor traffic was not useful. All men who knew the facts saw that from the cavernous maw of the liquor traffic came an endless stream of wrecked homes and blasted lives, of unspeakable personal filth and public degradation, of economic inefficiency and unproductiveness. Whatever else the liquor traffic involved, it always involved this. Tradition, wealth, the ingrained habit of millions of men—not all these together could withstand that fact. The liquor traffic must go, for usefulness is the only assured basis of survival for any institution in society.

Countless social customs and organizations now fallen on ruin bear witness to this ruthless impatience of life with unserviceable things. Though they may long survive, they are at infinite disadvantage. Absolute monarchy, slavery, the duel, the ordeal, judicial torture, great empires built on conquest and by brute force maintained —how long is the list of proud, inveterate institutions, once boastfully sure of their reasonableness and perpetuity, that now are gone because they were not useful! Serviceableness is not a pleasant ideal, superimposed on life by ethical dreamers. Serviceableness is one of the most formidable demands of life, by the satisfaction of which alone can any institution hope finally to survive. For though men scoff at it, rebel and chafe against it, seek escape by subterfuge, or try to brush back the sea with a broom, the truth remains that no international policy, no economic system, no social custom, no ecclesiastical establishment, no personal eminence, has any sure tenure of permanence and power unless it serves the people.

IV

The importance of this principle to Christian folk is evident. The institutions and the people that call themselves by the name of Jesus are not exempt from the laws of Jesus. Only usefulness can assure their continued influence. Without that all successfully defended doctrines, all possession of regal station, of social prestige and wealth, all theories of divine ordination, all venerable associations accumulated through long centuries, are powerless to sustain their strength. With nothing more than such things to plead, our churches will disappear like a thousand other organizations, whose

> "pomp of yesterday
> Is one with Nineveh and Tyre."

To pour out into the world a multitude of people who have caught the sacrificial spirit of the Master, and who, in his faith and purpose, give themselves to the service of mankind—that alone is the sustaining glory and hope of the Christian Gospel.

Indeed, this principle of Jesus, severe as it is and ruthless as its operation often seems, is full of hopeful prophecy. In the life of our churches today are many belated elements, from outgrown ideas to needless sectarian divisions, which are no longer useful. They serve no purpose in enriching the spiritual life of men and in spreading the Kingdom of God. If the Master in person were here, he would visit on them the same treatment which he visited on the Sabbath and on the temple. And for all men of forward-looking spirit it means courage to perceive that the universe itself conspires against these unserviceable things. When any custom once useful loses its function, the very stars in heaven fight with us against that Sisera.

Alike the spirit of the Master, therefore, and the special call of our times urge on Christians the aspect of the Gospel which we have set ourselves to study. The passing generations have their various needs, and under the urgency of changing circumstances, the manifold aspects of the Christian faith, one by one, are lifted to the front. Now this truth is specially demanded, now that duty must be specially enforced. In our day, for the sake of the integrity of Christian character, the progress of the Christian Church, and the salvation of the world, we need a new hatred of uselessness in institutions and persons, and a new baptism of the spirit of sacrificial and effective service.

V

In particular, as Christians and churchmen we well may give thought to the necessary extension of the idea of Christian service with which our times manifestly face us. *We are here not simply to save people out of the world but to save the world.* A lamentable feud exists between the partisans of personal and social Christianity. I believe in personal Christianity, says one. I believe in preaching the Gospel of Jesus to individuals. The sole business of the Church is to proclaim the evangel of divine forgiveness and regeneration until those who accept it are soundly saved and inwardly transformed. On the other side another cries: I believe in social Christianity. I seek the application of the principles of Jesus to our economic and international order. I am a patriot for the Kingdom of God upon the earth, and only as our social wrongs are righted does that Kingdom come. So do the devotees of personal and social Christianity confront each other.

The dilemma, however, on which they impale themselves is false. The full truth, as so often happens, flies like a bird with two wings, and maimed in either by our partial thinking it flutters a crippled creature on the ground. The partisans of individual Christianity are right in this: the Christian Gospel seeks the redemption of personality. Men and women are the infinitely valuable children of God. Christianity ardently desires to save them from every enemy that cripples and enslaves them, to unfold their possibilities, to lead them into spiritual triumph and abundant life. And the partisans of social Christianity are right in this: that you cannot really be in earnest about saving personality and still neglect the social life from which personality springs and by which it is tremendously affected. Those who plead for the personal evangel against social reformation contradict themselves.

To say that we have Christian love for children, while we are careless of the conditions of child labor that deaden and damn the souls of children before they are old enough to know their hapless plight; to say that we long to save men from the power of lust, when we placidly allow city officials to grow rich on the gains of lust, commercially organized and publicly flaunted; to say that we desire personality redeemed, while we passively let disease and poverty beat men in body and in soul, and unstirred see families live in hovels where all reticence and modesty are made impossible and vice grows rank; to say that we long to lead men into abundant life, while we hear unmoved of tens of thousands of men in one American corporation who work twelve hours a day, seven days a week; to say that we want Christ to triumph in the spirits of all men, while we let international relationships remain un-Christianized, with their inevitable issue in bitterness and hatred and all the ugly tempers that are the spawn of war—what is all this but sheer hypocrisy?

To be sure, some of the most thrilling stories of Christian victory concern folk touched to fine issues by Christ's Gospel, who came up out of the lowest conditions to spiritual triumph. So, though a plank thrown on the sward have but a single nail hole in it, some aspiring blade of grass will find it and come up from the obscurity and darkness underneath to rejoice in the splendor of the sun. But one who sees, with understanding eyes, that miracle of individual triumph, cannot be content. Consider all the dead and withered grass for which no way of escape was found! So blighting conditions lie across the lives of millions of folk today alike in heathendom and Christendom. Here and there some few break through to liberty. But the crushed multitudes—how can a disciple of Jesus think of them with equanimity? Men are not disembodied spirits. They are tremendously moved and molded by the environment in which they live. No one can hope to save the world without saving men; but neither can one hope to save men without saving the world. The two involve each other; they are one. The Church's best gift to mankind is redeemed personality; but redeemed personality's best gift to mankind is a better world, more fit to be a home for the family of God. He who is a partisan for either of these avenues of service against the other is a fair target for that newly discovered saying of our Lord: "Thou hearest with one ear, but the other thou hast closed."

Too long have many Christians been content with the ideal of negative unworldliness. The true antidote for worldliness is not unworldliness alone, but better-worldliness. Worldliness says, Indulge as you will in drink; unworldliness says, Be a teetotaler! better-worldliness says, The whole accursed liquor traffic can be stopped. Worldliness says, Salacious drama is a permissible delight; unworldliness says, The theater is utterly taboo; better-worldliness says, The recreation of the people must be redeemed to decency and worth. Worldliness says, Play politics according to the current rules of the game; unworldliness says, Eschew politics altogether; better-worldliness says, The State can be as Christian as a man and Christian men must make it so. Worldliness says, Business is a selfish conflict for revenue only; unworldliness says, Seek not to be rich; better-worldliness says, Business is an indispensable service to mankind, and if it be organized and fairly run for man's sake and not for money only, it can be made as Christian as a church. Worldliness says, When war comes, fight; unworldliness says, No Christian must ever fight at all; better-worldliness says, International anarchy is a relic of barbarism and if Christian folk will seriously set themselves to organize the good will of the world, it can be stopped. In a word, worldliness says, Let the world be; unworldliness says, Come out from the world; better-worldliness says, In God's name, save the world!

The great days of the Church come when that full scope of service is accepted as the Christian task. When Carey gives the Bible in translation to millions of people; when Livingstone throws wide the doorways of a new continent to civilization; when Paton lays the foundation of a new social order in the Hebrides; when Hamlin drives the opening wedge of Christian civilization into Constantinople—then come the great days of the Church. When of William Wilberforce's fight against the slave traffic it can be said: "The clergy to a man are favorable to the cause" and "the people have taken up the matter in view of duty and religion, and do not inquire what any man or set of men think of it," then come great days to the Church. For great days never can come to the Church, except as she shares the spirit of her Lord, and her Lord's demand was not simply new men in an old world but a new world to house new men.

CHAPTER III

The Strong and the Weak

DAILY READINGS

We are to consider this week the problem created by human inequality. Where some are by nature and privilege more highly endowed than others, Christianity at once insists on the use of the superior strength in service. In our daily readings we shall endeavor to see the dangers associated with the possession of superior strength, if this Christian principle is not observed.

Third Week, First Day

Paul from his prison writes to his friends at Philippi as follows:

But I rejoice in the Lord greatly, that now at length ye have revived your thought for me; wherein ye did indeed take thought, but ye lacked opportunity. Not that I speak in respect of want: for I have learned, in whatsoever state I am, therein to be content. I know how to be abased, and I know also how to abound: in everything and in all things have I learned the secret both to be filled and to be hungry, both to abound and to be in want. I can do all things in him that strengtheneth me.—Phil. 4:10-13.

One half of that passage is not at all surprising. I know how to be abased; I know how to be hungry; I know how to be in want—how familiar that testimony is, from those who have learned from Christ faith, steadiness, and overcoming power in times of hardship! But the other half of the passage is decidedly unusual. "I know how to abound"; Paul writes as though *that* were a difficult affair. "I know how to be filled," he says, "I can do all things in him that strengtheneth me." Paul evidently feels that dealing with abundance is quite as difficult as dealing with abasement. It is as though he said: I am now an old man. In my experience I have swept the gamut of human life. I have experienced proud eminence and contemptuous ostracism. I have had culture, education, money; and I have been tossed about the earth, a poor tentmaker, apostle of a persecuted faith. At the end I bear witness that Jesus Christ enables a man to stand anything that can happen to him. I could even stand success. I know how to abound.

How often have we so considered our privileges as a difficult problem to be spiritually mastered?

O most liberal Distributer of Thy gifts, who givest us all kinds of good things to use, grant to us Thy grace, that we misuse not these Thy gracious gifts given to our use and profit. Grant us to be conversant amongst Thy gifts, soberly, purely, temperately, holily, because Thou art such a one; so shall not we turn that to the poison of our souls, which Thou hast given for the medicine of our bodies, but using Thy benefits thankfully, we shall find them profitable both to soul and body. Amen.—"Christian Prayers," 1566.

Third Week, Second Day

Now there was a certain rich man, and he was clothed in purple and fine linen, faring sumptuously every day: and a certain beggar named Lazarus was laid at his gate, full of sores, and desiring to be fed with the crumbs that fell from the rich man's table; yea, even the dogs came and licked his sores. And it came to pass, that the beggar died, and that he was carried away by the angels into Abraham's bosom: and the rich man also died, and was buried. And in Hades he lifted up his eyes, being in torments, and seeth Abraham afar off, and Lazarus in his bosom. And he cried and said, Father Abraham, have mercy on me, and send Lazarus, that he may dip the tip of his finger in water, and cool my tongue; for I am in anguish in this flame. But Abraham said, Son, remember that thou in thy lifetime receivedst thy good things, and Lazarus in like manner evil things: but now here he is comforted, and thou art in anguish. And besides all this, between us and you there is a great gulf fixed, that they that would pass from hence to you may not be able, and that none may cross over from thence to us.—Luke 16:19-26.

The minds of the Pharisees who heard Jesus were already furnished with the popular, lurid picture of future punishment which Jesus uses here. What is new to them is not the background of flaming condemnation, but the character of the person who is condemned. Jesus takes a familiar setting and puts into it an unfamiliar personnel. For what the Master says is this: *The condemned character is a man who having superior privileges proves himself unfit to have them.* How much we need that lesson! In our eyes, success is in itself an estate most to be desired; we forget that success is a fine art, of all arts most difficult to handle. We clamor for power—fortune, wealth, prestige. How can I succeed? is our question. We do not ask, Am I *fit* to succeed? Yet the second question is the more important. It is one thing to be in a happy and fortunate estate; it is another to be fit to be there. It is one thing to be well fed; it is another to be worth feeding. It is one thing, like Dives, to have money and influence and social position, and it is another to be the kind of man who is fit to have them. And the Master insists that fitness to possess any privilege can be proved only by service to the unprivileged. There is no hope for Dives until he learns to pray like this:

Blessed Lord, who for our sakes wast content to bear sorrow and want and death; Grant unto us such a measure of Thy Spirit that we may follow Thee in all self-denial and tenderness of soul. Help us by Thy great love, to succour the afflicted, to relieve the needy and destitute, to share the burdens of the heavy-laden, and ever to see Thee in all that are poor and desolate. Amen.—Bishop Westcott (1825-1901).

Third Week, Third Day

And he spake a parable unto them, saying, The ground of a certain rich man brought forth plentifully: and he reasoned within himself, saying, What shall I do, because I have not where to bestow my fruits? And he said, This will I do: I will pull down my barns, and build greater; and there will I bestow all my grain and my goods. And I will say to my soul, Soul, thou hast much goods laid up for many years; take thine ease, eat, drink, be merry. But God said unto him, Thou foolish one, this night is thy soul required of thee; and the things which thou hast prepared, whose shall they be? So is he that layeth up treasure for himself, and is not rich toward God.—Luke 12:16-21.

Let us imagine this colossal failure in his youth. He may have been able, steady, energetic, ambitious. He wished to succeed and he was willing to pay the price. He gave himself efficiently to his labor; he lived a clean, hard-working life; he made no fool of himself with debauchery. So long as he had success to gain he was a good man. But when he had gained it—there the Master's record of his utter ruin begins! For it is often easier to gain success than to use it well. Some men are ruined by adversity. But alas! for the many who do not fail, who climb high and higher yet before the applauding eyes of their fellows, until they fall over the precipice of their own prosperity! It is not easy to abound. With what appreciation do we read Erasmus's description of his powerful friend, Sir Thomas More: "Elevation has not elated him or made him forgetful of his humble friends. He is always kind, always generous. Some he helps with money, some with influence. When he can give nothing else he gives advice. He is Patron-General to all poor devils."

For those who in their plenty live delicately, contemn the poor, and forget God; for all people whose hearts are so perished within them that pity has departed; Shew them Thy ways. Amen.—"A Book of Prayers for Students."

Third Week, Fourth Day

Charge them that are rich in this present world, that they be not highminded, nor have their hope set on the uncertainty of riches, but on God, who giveth us richly all things to enjoy; that they do good, that they be rich in good works, that they be ready to distribute, willing to communicate; laying up in store for themselves a good foundation against the time to come, that they may lay hold on the life which is life indeed.—I Tim. 6:17-19.

Why is such an injunction so apt in every generation? Is it not in part because the possession of power in any form, whether political prestige, social station, popularity, or wealth, always begets the thirst for more? Success for its own sake becomes an absorbing passion. If a man have none of it, he may solace himself without it. But if a man gain even a little of it, like strong drink it may soon become indispensable to him. He must have more and more of it. At last he joins the multitude whose portrait the New Testament so exactly sketches: "They that are minded to be rich fall into a temptation and a snare" (I Tim. 6:9). Paul does not say, "They that *are* rich"; he says, "They that *are minded to be rich.*" The thirst is on them. At all costs they propose for themselves to be rich. Whether with one kind of wealth and power or another, in some degree we are all endowed; and the only attitude that can make possible a Christian character is revealed in such a prayer as this:

O my God, make me a good man! O my Father, come what may, make me a simple-minded, honest, humble, and brave Christian! Let me seek no favour but Thine, and give my heart to no labour but in Thee and for Thee! With God my Saviour as my help and guide may I, ere I die, be a blessing to the city in which I dwell, especially to the poor and miserable in it, for whom my heart bleeds. Amen.—Norman Macleod.

Third Week, Fifth Day

Consider the Master's description of the scribes and Pharisees:

But all their works they do to be seen of men: for they make broad their phylacterics, and enlarge the borders of their garments, and love the chief place at feasts, and the chief seats in the synagogues, and the salutations in the marketplaces, and to be called of men, Rabbi. But be not ye called Rabbi: for one is your teacher, and all ye are brethren. And call no man your father on the earth: for one is your Father, even he who is in heaven. Neither be ye called masters: for one is your master, even the Christ. And he that is greatest among you shall be your servant. And whosoever shall exalt himself shall be humbled; and whosoever shall humble himself shall be exalted.—Matt. 23:5-12.

The scribes and Pharisees were the privileged classes of their day. They had social rank, education, culture, public influence. And the issue of such possessions the Master saw there, as he can see it in any generation: pride, exclusiveness, unbrotherliness. For one peril that is always associated with any kind of success or power is that it will kill humility, beget pride, and break brotherhood. Wrote the Duchess of Buckingham to Lady Huntingdon about the early Methodists: "Their doctrines are most repulsive, and strongly tinctured with impertinence and disrespect to their superiors. It is monstrous to be told that you have a heart as sinful as the common wretches that crawl the earth. This is highly insulting, and I wonder that your Ladyship should relish any sentiment so much at variance with high rank and good breeding."

Let us pray!

Thou, O God, who givest Grace to the Humble, do something also for the Proud Man: Make me Humble and Obedient; take from me the Spirit of Pride and Haughtiness, Ambition and Self-Flattery, Confidence and Gayety; Teach me to think well, and to expound all things fairly of my Brother, to love his worthiness, to delight in his Praises, to excuse his Errors, to give Thee thanks for his Graces, to rejoice in all the good that he receives, and ever to believe and speak better things of him than of myself.

O teach me to love to be concealed and little esteem'd, let me be truly humbled and heartily ashamed of my Sin and Folly. Teach me to bear Reproaches evenly, for I have deserv'd them; to refuse all Honours done unto me, because I have not deserv'd them; to return all to Thee, for it is Thine alone; to suffer Reproach thankfully; to amend my faults speedily, and when I have humbly, patiently, charitably, and diligently served Thee, change this Habit into the shining Garment of Immortality, my Confusion into Glory, my Folly into perfect Knowledge, my Weakness and Dishonours into the Strength and Beauties of the Sons of God. Amen.—Thomas à Kempis (1379-1471).

Third Week, Sixth Day

And Jesus looked round about, and saith unto his disciples, How hardly shall they that have riches enter into the kingdom of God! And the disciples were amazed at his words. But Jesus answereth again, and saith unto them, Children, how hard is it for them that trust in riches to enter into the kingdom of God! It is easier for a camel to go through a needle's eye, than for a rich man to enter into the kingdom of God. And they were astonished exceedingly, saying unto him, Then who can be saved? Jesus looking upon them saith, With men it is impossible, but not with God: for all things are possible with God.—Mark 10:23-27.

We marvel at men who, heavily handicapped by *adversity*, succeed in achieving victorious lives. The Master marveled at men who, heavily handicapped by *prosperity*, were able to rise above it. It seemed to him a superhuman task to get the spiritual mastery of success. Abraham Lincoln and William Ewart Gladstone were born in the same year. One was born in a cabin, and the other in a castle. One was so poor that he says the first day he earned a dollar was the proudest day of his life; and the other was so rich that from his birth to his death he never had to give an anxious thought to his ample fortune. One was so bereft of opportunity that all his books he borrowed and read by a pine knot on the hearth; the other had everything the schools of England could afford and Christ Church College, Oxford, could furnish. The one was so homely that a member of his Cabinet called him a gorilla, and the other was one of the handsomest men in Europe. One started with nothing; the other started with everything. Put yourself in the place of each, and consider: if a humble, brotherly, serviceable Christian life were your ideal, under which set of circumstances do you think that you would meet the greater obstacles?

Take from us, O God, all pride and vanity, boasting and forward-
ness; and give us the true courage that shows itself by gentleness;
the true wisdom that shows itself by simplicity; and the true power
that shows itself by modesty.—Charles Kingsley.

Third Week, Seventh Day

And he spake also this parable unto certain who trusted in themselves that they were righteous, and set all others at nought: Two men went up into the temple to pray; the one a Pharisee, and the other a publican. The Pharisee stood and prayed thus with himself, God, I thank thee, that I am not as the rest of men, extortioners, unjust, adulterers, or even as this publican. I fast twice in the week; I give tithes of all that I get. But the publican, standing afar off, would not lift up so much as his eyes unto heaven, but smote his breast, saying, God, be thou merciful to me a sinner. I say unto you, This man went down to his house justified rather than the other: for every one that exalteth himself shall be humbled; but he that humbleth himself shall be exalted.—Luke 18:9-14.

Here is the final consequence of a successful, prosperous life: this Pharisee in his pride and self-content loses any genuine sense of the

need of God. How often indeed do we ourselves secretly feel that
religion is for the wicked and the weak! It comforts people when
they are sad; it steadies them when they are sick; it offers forgiveness
when they are condemned; it gives them hope when they come to
die. Religion is medicine for feebleness. If one has health, fortune,
and reputation, he needs it little. As one calls in a nurse when he is
ill, so folk when fortune fails them turn to religious faith. It is
narcotic; it soothes them.

Over against this familiar idea, set what we have been saying this
week. Not adversity but prosperity is for many men the greater strain
upon their characters. Multitudes of folk in each generation collapse
into uselessness, not because they were weak, but because they could
not master the strength entrusted to them. The fact is that we never
need a deep, convincing, and powerful spiritual life more than when
all things are going well with us. Let us hold this in mind as we turn
to study the obligation which the strong, if they are to be Christian,
must discharge to the weak.

*O God, who knowest us to be set in the midst of so many and
great dangers, that, by reason of the frailty of our nature, we cannot
always stand upright; grant to us such strength and protection as
may support us in all dangers and carry us through all temptations;
through Jesus Christ our Lord. Amen.*—Book of Common Prayer,
1662.

COMMENT FOR THE WEEK

I

One fact which plunges us at once into the heart of the problem
of service is inequality. Popular interpretations of the Declaration of
Independence to the contrary notwithstanding, men are not born
equal. All men by right of birth should have an equal chance to
become all that they are capable of being, but this principle is yet a
long way from producing actual equality. *On some terms the strong
and the weak must live together.*

Men are not equal in *practical ability.* Under any easily predict-
able economic system, if riches were to fall like snow upon a wind-
less day, making dead level everywhere, upon that scene of financial
equality the wind of unequal ability would blow and some fields

would be drifted high and some fields blown quite bare. Men are not
equal in *intellectual capacity*. How shall we explain a family where
eight children come, none destined to any eminence, but where the
ninth, Daniel Webster, grows to a personal impressiveness that used
to make the houses on Beacon Street look smaller when he walked
by, and to a mental power that in debate was irresistible? We get no
answer to our curious inquiry. Only we know that some men put the
pressure on their brains and find them there, alert and eager; and
others turn on the current of their intellectual ambition with no
better consequence than burning out the fuse. Men are not equal in
spiritual capacity. All men have in them the power to open up their
lives to the influence of the Divine Spirit, and by him to be transformed, but some are thimbles in comparative capacity, and others
are oceans with tides and gulf streams and commerce-bearing depths.
Whatever may be the possibilities in the far reaches of eternal life,
we see upon the earth small souls in all degrees growing alongside
the capacious spirits through whom supremely God reveals himself.

What is true of individuals is true of groups of men. Races are not
equal. We know why no more than we can tell why one son in a
family may be a genius and his twin a dunce. Only the fact is clear
that some races, put anywhere on earth, will at once construct a
stable government and live by law. But others, after unimpeded
tenure of a continent for ages, cannot unaided establish a settled
government at all. Whatever the solution of this puzzling problem,
the fact is clear. The strong and the weak, in individuals and races,
must somehow live together on the earth. Moreover, we all are involved in this complication. None is so weak as not to bear, in some
aspect of his life, the relationship of strength to some one weaker
still. Consider the children, the tendrils of whose slender vines reach
up for the sustenance of our maturer lives. Recall our friends, who
in giving us their trust give us enormous power over their welfare
and their happiness.

This relationship of the strong to the weak claims our special attention because it has been the fruitful mother of the cruelest tragedies of human life. How has God stood it through the ages, watching
the strong squeeze the weak like grape clusters into their chalices
that they might drink blood like wine! One cannot easily open his
Bible without running upon some outburst of indignation over this
tragic sin. Moses rips his dignities and titles off that he may not even
indirectly share in Pharaoh's oppression of his helpless countrymen.

Nathan falls like lightning upon David because, being very rich in sheep, he has robbed his neighbor of his one ewe lamb. Isaiah cries: "What mean ye that ye crush my people and grind the face of the poor?" (Isa. 3:15). Amos cries: "Ye kine of Bashan . . . that oppress the poor, that crush the needy" (Amos 4:1). And when the Master comes, with what overflowing wrath does he denounce strong men who rob widows' houses and cover their crime with the pretense of prayer!

II

If one asks, then, what Christianity proposes as the solution of this difficult relationship, Paul tersely sums up the spirit of the whole New Testament: "We that are strong ought to bear the infirmities of the weak and not to please ourselves" (Rom. 15:1). *The strong bearing the burdens of the weak*—was ever a more revolutionary principle announced? The weak, the undefended, the immature, have always been the prey of the strong. They have been ruthlessly cut up, strewn in, and plowed under to make a richer soil for the strong to grow in. The saddest chapters in history recount the story of the strong, wringing the weak dry of their toil and flinging them heedlessly aside, or displaying their power in shameless cruelties, as when a Roman patron crucified two thousand slaves beside a highway to satisfy his whim.

Indeed, this right of the strong over the weak has been in our day asserted as the true teaching of science and philosophy. "The struggle for existence" and "the survival of the fittest" have been interpreted to suit the strong and have been erected into a theory of conduct for all life. So far from seeing any law of usefulness running through creation, men have seen only a law of grasping selfishness and bitter war. The tall tree in the forest does not solicitously serve the sapling at its base. It stamps the sapling out, steals its sustenance, blots out its sun, rots it back into the forest mold, that the strong tree may be stronger yet. The horticulturist when he finds a few blooms upon his rosebush and many stunted ones, does not pinch back the finer flowers that the nipped and feeble ones may have a chance. He amputates the weak. He is no democrat seeking the welfare of all the people. He is an aristocrat sacrificing the common run to the finest specimens. He does not plead for humanity; he seeks the superman. Such a philosophy of life, alike in the theory and practice, has in recent years been tragically influential, and its consequences are written in lines of fire across the world. So Nietzsche reviles the Gospel for the very reason that makes us praise it: "Christianity is the one great curse, the one great spiritual corruption." And Nietzsche can truly claim that large areas of human life, personal, economic, and political, are founded upon principles the very opposite of Christian. Empires for conquest, industrial systems for exploitation, individual ambition rising on steppingstones of fallen folk—how much of life is based upon the pagan principle that the weak must bear the burdens of the strong and must not please themselves!

The scientific answer to this heathen doctrine is being written by the experts. In Kropotkin's "Mutual Aid," in the works of Novikov, we see Greek meet Greek in the scientific field. The fact is that even a forest represents cooperation quite as much as it represents conflict, and the story of animal life shows clearly that capacity for mutual aid, far more than brute strength, has made species fit to survive. The bees have lasted; the ichthyosaurus is gone. Conflict and carnage are in nature, but the development of altruism is an integral part of the story from the beginning and the higher the scale of existence rises, the less does brute force count and the more life's progress depends upon cooperation. A few facts in the origin of life may seem to favor the exploitation of the weak by the strong. The whole course of evolving life, which has lifted spiritual powers into preeminence and has made life's continuance and worth depend upon good will and mutual aid, is overwhelmingly against it.

The Christian Gospel, however, did not wait for the battledore and shuttlecock of scientific argument. It leaped at once by the insight of love to the heart of the matter. Many things in so-called Christianity can be dispensed with—dogmas, institutions, rituals, of which when they are gone the world will cry, "Good riddance!" But the principle that the highest strength should be put at the service of the lowliest weakness is a central pillar of the Gospel, around which if any blind Samson ever winds antagonistic arms and breaks it down, all the Gospel will come clattering into ruin. "Though he was rich, yet for your sakes he became poor that ye through his poverty might become rich"—no truer summary of the Master's spirit does the New Testament contain. And wherever that spirit has come to its proper utterance in his followers, this ministry of strength to weakness is its characteristic expression. To be sure, the *prevention* of weakness, perpetuating itself through evil heredity and circumstance, is primary, but the weak who are already here are not, in the Christian program, to be left to hopelessness. Father Damien going out to serve the lepers; John Howard visiting the vilest prisons in Christendom, passionate for the redemption of the criminals; Mackay laying his life upon Uganda and breathing a new spirit into depraved and barbarous folk; William Booth plunging into "Darkest England" and seeking a way out for squalid millions—these are the proper fruits of the Christian Gospel. And so far has this principle at last ceased to be a paradox and become a principle of sane government that, as Lord Asquith has said: "The test of every civilization is the point below which the weakest and most unfortunate are allowed to fall."

III

We may well consider, therefore, some of the facts which make this central principle of Christian conduct seem convincing. For one thing, if we regard human history in the large it is clear that, *strong and weak alike, we all are coming up together from the same primitive conditions, and that we who in any sense are strong are simply those who are a little way ahead.* Our strength does not belong to us in fee simple to possess and to use as we will. We are the custodians of the gains of the whole race for the sake of all mankind.

An English-speaking Christian may be tempted to look down upon a cannibal as a hopeless specimen of a degenerate race. Why spend strength upon such a wretch? Our condescension might be chastened by these words of Jerome, the Christian scholar of the fourth century: "When I was a boy living in Gaul, I saw the Scottish people in Britain eating human flesh and though they had plenty of cattle and sheep at their disposal, yet they would prefer a ham of the herdsman or a slice of the female breast as a luxury." Is it any special merit of ours that we, whose ancestors were also cannibals, have now a little ahead of our brethren climbed out of that horrible morass?

Or a modern man, heir to the scientific labors of these last few generations, reads with horror a missionary's story like "Mary Slessor of Calabar." The blasting superstitions of witchcraft and demon worship fall with such tragic incidence upon the African tribes where Miss Slessor toiled, that one wonders whether such expenditure of consecrated strength on such degraded feebleness can be

worth while. But a pause is given to our doubt when as late as the
sixteenth century in our own racial history, we read the words of
Montaigne: "The day will never come when the common ruck of
men will cease to believe in witchcraft. If the lawyers and judges of
our modern sixteenth century France, men trained to sift evidence
and learned in science, can be so far deceived as to send thousands
of victims to their death for impossible crimes, how can we ever
hope that the common man will avoid these errors?" Is supercilious
pride particularly befitting us, who so recently have escaped slavery
to a superstition which still shackles thousands of God's children
upon the earth?

There is no end to such comparisons. All races, however superior
they now may seem, are but the advance guard of an emerging
humanity. If we are tempted to think meanly of ignorance because
we are educated, let us read again a couplet from our own literature
only a few centuries behind us:

> "There was a wight who such a scholar was
>   That he the letters in a book could read."

If we shudder at the sacrifice of children by their parents in heathen
cults, let us recall that our fathers in Britain used to put young girls
in wicker baskets and run swords through them, that they might
tell from the way the blood flowed what the will of the gods was.
One principle is given us in Scripture so simple and so human that
no fair-minded man can escape its grip: we are bound to show
mercy to folk who still struggle in difficulties where we ourselves
have been: "Love ye therefore the sojourner; for ye were sojourners
in the land of Egypt" (Deut. 10:19).

If in a family two children grew up together, could their relations
be regulated on any other principle than that which Christianity
suggests? One of the children comes first to the age of poise, self-
mastery, and power. The other still is infantile. If the older should
use his superiority to mistreat the younger, with what indignant admonition would the father speak! "You two are growing together
in the same home," so he would say, "and *you* are a little way ahead.
That is not greatly to your credit; you had the first start. This maturity of growth was not given you for self-inflation, but for service.
You hold it in trust for the whole family's sake."

No good home could be run on any other principle. Nor can God

run his world otherwise. Strength ought to be put at the service of
weakness, for in all possession of privilege and power we are trustees
of the advance gains of the race for the sake of the whole human
family.

IV

A second reason has always undergirded this Christian principle
of putting the best strength at the service of the lowliest weakness.
The weak are worth serving. The Master's life is based upon this
faith and is aglow with its meaning. If at an auction of musical instruments a battered violin with dusty body and sagging strings had
been bid for in cents as a worthless article; if some one should pick
up the instrument, dust it, look at the maker's name, bid it up into
the hundreds of dollars, and when pressed bid higher still; if word
went round that the man was Kreisler, that Fritz Kreisler wanted
the violin, no matter what it cost; how the estimate of the instrument's worth would rise! So Jesus put new value into despised men.
Boys in a far country, rotten with harlotry and sunk to low estate
among the swine—all the world called them lost and good for nothing. But the Master bid his life for them. Let the cost be the crown
of thorns, the spear, the Cross; the Master counted personality, however ruined, worth it all. Wherever the Gospel has gone, its characteristic fruitage has been service for all sorts of men in the faith that
all sorts of men are worth serving.

This Christian confidence in the worth and latent possibility of all
mankind is not a faith neatly to be proved in theory, but in practice
it has been justified upon a scale that only the most optimistic could
have dreamed. *The spread of civilization* justifies it. The Greeks despised the barbarians as an inferior breed, until Alexander the Great
conquered the barbarians and brought Greek and non-Greek culture
into vital contact. Then it was discovered that the barbarians could
learn anything that the Greeks had to teach, and within a few centuries the center of the world's culture had shifted from Athens to
Alexandria. So within our own time great nations and races long
despised have awakened out of sleep and have displayed an aptitude
for progress, a capacity for learning all that the most advanced races
know and for pushing farther still the boundaries of enterprise, that
ought to humble any racial pride. *The spread of democracy* justifies
it. Democracy means not only political copartnership; it means the

right of all men everywhere to all the privileges the race has won. It means popular access to education, leisure, economic self-control. It means copartnership rather than autocracy in industry as well as in government. But all this has underneath it an amazing venture of faith in human nature and in the power of whole classes of the population long despised to achieve intelligence, self-mastery, and the cooperative spirit. Wherever democracy succeeds in any realm, the triumph of Christian faith in the capacities of lowly folk is seen.

Perhaps most of all *the missionary movement* has justified the Christian faith in the worth of the weak. When Charles Darwin sent his subscription to the Christian orphanage on Tierra del Fuego, he wrote: "The success of the Tierra del Fuego Mission is most wonderful and shames me, as I always prophesied utter failure. . . . I certainly should not have predicted that all the missionaries in the world could have done what has been done." As glass is made of sand, so repeatedly out of the dull, opaque material of low castes and degraded races the Christian Gospel has made the most transparent sainthood. Into the office of the dean of one of the greatest American universities walked recently a man from one of the South Sea Islands, whose cheeks were scarred with the mutilations of primitive savage rites. He was eight years old before he had seen a white man. He was asking now for a course in advanced Semitics that he might translate the Old Testament from its original sources into his own tongue. He had passed in a single lifetime from the lowest pit of barbarism to the highest intellectual privileges of the modern world. When the Master announced the direction of his ministry "unto the least of these my brethren," who could have foreseen the wide areas of human life in which that revolutionary principle would be justified? For this is the Christian conviction which underlies the greatest practical venture of social faith in the race's history: that the outcast, downtrodden, and despised are worth saving, that every son of man, however ignorant and bestial, is not beyond redemption to sanity and virtue; that there is no personal or social inferiority that need be final; and that, therefore, the weak by their potential capacity to become strong have a right to the service of strength.

v

Another fact underlies this Christian principle. *Any strength that does not serve weakness is itself doomed.* Why should Midas in his

palace care for Tom-all-alone in his cellar? asks Dickens; and he
answers: "There is not an atom of Tom's slime, not a cubic inch of
any pestilential gas in which he lives, not one obscenity or degradation about him but shall work its retribution." We read the story of
strength's oppression of weakness with pity for the weak. But no
cruelty of the mighty toward the feeble ever worked agony for the
feeble any more certainly than it worked ruin for the strong. "For
the oppression of the poor, for the sighing of the needy, now will I
arise, saith the Lord"—such is the habitual accent of the Scripture.
That judgment of Scripture is everywhere carried out in history. No
retributions surpass the penalties for misused strength. "Who reckless rules right soon may hope to rue." After Louis XVI comes Ro-
bespierre; after the Czar comes Lenin; after industrial despotism
comes revolution. The slave trade, from its sources in Africa to its
consummation in Christendom, was as cruel and apparently as safe
an exploitation of the weak by the strong as history knows. But all the
agony of the enslaved was matched by the punishment of the en-
slavers, and Lincoln's words have application far beyond the immediate circumstances that gave them birth: "Yet, if God wills that
. . . every drop of blood drawn with the lash shall be paid by another drawn with the sword, as was said three thousand years ago,
so still it must be said, 'The judgments of the Lord are true and
righteous altogether.' "

Nor is this inevitable incidence of penalty upon the strong for any
wrong they do the weak an arbitrary matter. The reason for it is
wrought deeply into the texture of human life. We are all bound up
together, rich and poor, learned and ignorant, sick and well, good
and bad, in one bundle of life. No harm can fall on any which does
not in the end affect all. No isolating walls can keep the ills of the
weak from reaching the strong. Carlyle tells us of an Irish widow
who in Edinburgh with three helpless children sought help in vain,
fell ill of typhus, and, infecting seventeen others, died. "The forlorn
Irish widow," cries Carlyle grimly, "applies to her fellow creatures,
'Behold I am sinking bare of help. I am your sister; one God made
us. You must help me.' They answer, 'No, impossible: thou art no
sister of ours!' But she proves her sisterhood; her typhus kills *them;*
they actually were her brothers though denying it."

This inevitable sharing of the strong in the ills of the weakest and
most helpless people with whom they deal has now been stretched to
take in all mankind, and every day the intermeshing relationships

grow more intimate and unescapable. The laying of the first Atlantic cable was heralded everywhere as opening a new era in man's life; it was one of the most stirring bits of news that Stanley told Livingstone in the heart of Africa; it woke Whittier to rhapsody:

"For lo, the fall of Ocean's wall,
Space mocked and time outrun;
And round the world the thought of all
Is as the thought of one."

But the relationship of all races, advanced and backward, Christian and non-Christian, high and low, which the laying of the cable thus foretokened is more than a welcome gain. It is a portentous fact. All ignorance everywhere, all sin, superstition, ill will, disease, and blasting poverty are now a peril everywhere. No one is safe till all are safe. No privilege is secure till all possess it. No blessing is really owned until it universally is shared. That service to "one of the least of these my brethren," so far from being a superfluous ideal, is an ineradicable law of life, is indicated by this basic fact: in the last analysis self-preservation depends upon it. For whenever the strong neglect or oppress the weak, they must face that same principle at the heart of the Eternal which found impressive utterance on the lips of Caliph Omar: "By God! he that is weakest among you shall be in my sight the strongest until I have vindicated for him his rights; but him that is strongest will I treat as the weakest until he complies with the laws."

VI

Because strong and weak emerge together toward the light and the strong for the sake of all have been trusted with the lead; because the weak are potentially strong and the release of their life from weakness into strength is their right; because no ill can rest upon the weak that does not also smite the strong; for such reasons the strong should bear the burdens of the weak. But not all these reasons together plumb the depth of the Christian motive. *The strong should bear the burdens of the weak, because they, too, are weak.* At first we said that none is so weak as not to bear the relationship of strength to some one weaker still; it is equally true that none is so strong as not to bear the relationship of weakness to some one stronger yet.

We have called Paul's principle paradoxical; but in one institution it always has been the fundamental law. Who is king of the home? Not the father, however strong, nor the mother, however important. The baby is king of the home. He is feebleness incarnate, yet if he cries all are attent; if he is ill no science is too skilled to serve him, no sacrifice of comfort too prolonged to meet his needs. At home the mother's thoughts, in business the father's ambitions center in the cradle. In this basic institution of human life we that are strong *do* bear the burdens of the weak and do not please ourselves. Each of us had that done for him. It were a shame if we could not live for others on a principle without which we ourselves never could live at all.

Nor have we escaped dependence upon superior strength because we now are grown to adult years. Strong in some respects, how weak we are in others! A thousand human ministries from family and friends support us in our frailties. Without such constant sustenance of superior strength we could not live for a day in worthiness, happiness, and peace. Moreover, when we think of standing in the presence of the Living God all conceit of independent strength vanishes utterly. The world looks up to a man and cries, "Strong!" But when he looks at himself he knows that he is dependent upon a mercy for which he cannot pay and on a power that he must receive with thankfulness, not earn with pride. He goes out to serve the immature, the handicapped, the backward, the oppressed, with no condescending superiority. He feels himself in a fellowship of mutual dependence upon a strength greater than his own. He is too heavily indebted to One who lavished the highest gifts upon the lowliest needs to find condescension possible. He signs all his service as our fathers signed their letters, "I am, sir, your most obliged and humble servant."

CHAPTER IV

The Abundant Life

DAILY READINGS

That the love of pleasure is one of the chief enemies of an unselfish life is a commonplace of experience. We all wish to be happy, and we are not wrong in wishing it. "A happy man or woman," says Robert Louis Stevenson, "is a better thing to find than a five pound note. He or she is a radiating focus of good will; and their entrance into a room is as though another candle had been lighted." But what makes life really happy? Let us consider a few of the elements, distinctly *not* selfish, which we at once recognize as necessary to abiding happiness.

Fourth Week, First Day

This is my commandment, that ye love one another, even as I have loved you. Greater love hath no man than this, that a man lay down his life for his friends. Ye are my friends, if ye do the things which I command you. No longer do I call you servants; for the servant knoweth not what his lord doeth: but I have called you friends; for all things that I heard from my Father I have made known unto you.—John 15:12-15.

Friends are necessary to a happy life. When friendship deserts us we are as lonely and helpless as a ship, left by the tide high upon the shore; when friendship returns to us, it is as though the tide came back, gave us buoyancy and freedom, and opened to us the wide places of the world. Proteus in "Two Gentlemen of Verona" says: "I to myself am dearer than a friend." How clearly such a man has blocked from his life one of the great avenues of happiness! But

friendship is essentially unselfish; its proper voice is heard in such
words as Jesus spoke to his disciples that last night at the Table. To
be sure, friendship can be perverted and caricatured, but even in its
low forms some self-forgetfulness creeps in, and in its high ranges,
where it brings the richest joy, it is nearest to pure unselfishness. Evidently a happy life cannot be all self-seeking.

*O Lord of Love, in whom alone I live, kindle in my soul Thy fire
of love; give me to lay myself aside, and to think of others as I kneel
to Thee. For those whom Thou hast given me, dear to me as my
own soul, Thy best gift on earth, I ask Thy blessing. If they are now
far away, so that I cannot say loving words to them today, yet be
Thou near them, give them of Thy joy, order their ways, keep them
from sickness, from sorrow, and from sin, and let all things bring
them closer to Thee. If they are near me, give us wisdom and grace
to be true helpers of one another, serving in love's service all day
long. Let nothing come between us to cloud our perfect trust, but
help each to love more truly, more steadfastly, more unselfishly.
Amen.*—Samuel McComb.

Fourth Week, Second Day

For yourselves know how ye ought to imitate us: for we behaved
not ourselves disorderly among you; neither did we eat bread for
nought at any man's hand, but in labor and travail, working night
and day, that we might not burden any of you: not because we have
not the right, but to make ourselves an ensample unto you, that ye
should imitate us. For even when we were with you, this we commanded you, If any will not work, neither let him eat. For we hear
of some that walk among you disorderly, that work not at all, but
are busybodies. Now them that are such we command and exhort
in the Lord Jesus Christ, that with quietness they work, and eat
their own bread. But ye, brethren, be not weary in well-doing.—
I Thess. 3:7-13.

One of Paul's most engaging qualities was his sturdy self-respect,
his love of economic independence, his pride in his handicraft. *Honest and useful work* in self-support, with something left over with
which to help others, was necessary to his happiness. "Let him that
stole steal no more," he wrote to the Ephesians, "but rather let him
labor, working with his hands the thing which is good, that he may

have to give to him that needeth." Any normal man understands
Paul's feeling in this respect. Idleness is the most deadly boredom
that life can know, and hard work, honestly done, with just pride in
efficiency and skill, is life's fundamental blessing. Deprive us of it for
many months and we are as restless, unsatisfied, and unhappy as a
homesick boy away from his own household. But good work is self-
expenditure; it is the forthputting of personality in creative labor.
Manifestly, happiness has in it requirements of self-investment as
well as of self-regard.

*Accept the work of this day, O Lord, as we lay it at Thy feet.
Thou knowest its imperfections, and we know. Of the brave purposes of the morning only a few have found their fulfilment. We
bless Thee that Thou art no hard taskmaster, watching grimly the
stint of work we bring, but the Father and Teacher of men who
rejoices with us as we learn to work. We have naught to boast before
Thee, but we do not fear Thy face. Thou knowest all things and
Thou art love. Accept every right intention, however brokenly fulfilled, but grant that ere our life is done we may under Thy tuition
become true master workmen, who know the art of a just and valiant
life. Amen.*—Walter Rauschenbusch.

Fourth Week, Third Day

First, I thank my God through Jesus Christ for you all, that your
faith is proclaimed throughout the whole world. For God is my
witness, whom I serve in my spirit in the gospel of his Son, how
unceasingly I make mention of you, always in my prayers making
request, if by any means now at length I may be prospered by the
will of God to come unto you. For I long to see you, that I may
impart unto you some spiritual gift, to the end ye may be established; that is, that I with you may be comforted in you, each of
us by the other's faith, both yours and mine.—Rom. 1:8-12.

Of course Paul wished to see Rome. Paul was an imperial man
and Rome was the imperial city. Paul's happiness consisted in part
in this very fact, that he had *large interests,* and was not shut up to
provincial enthusiasms. Wherever good and evil met in combat,
wherever great business was afoot, wherever Christ was building up
his Church, Paul's heart was engaged. How much of happiness
depends upon such breadth of interest! Joy is the tingling sense of

being fully alive, and that cannot come to narrow minds, absorbed by selfish concerns. They are pent, cooped up, suffocated; they lack the expansion of life which comes with large interests and generous enthusiasms. But an expanded life is of the very essence of unselfishness. How much of the throbbing joy which runs through the whole New Testament is due to the fact that Christ had taken many narrow, provincial spirits and had widened them to great hopes, liberal interests, and large devotions!

I am weary of my island life, O Spirit; it is absence from Thee. I am weary of the pleasures spent upon myself, weary of that dividing sea which makes me alone.

I look out upon the monotonous waves that roll between me and my brother, and I begin to be in want; I long for the time when there shall be no more sea.

Lift me on to the mainland, Thou Spirit of humanity, unite my heart to the brotherhood of human souls. Set my feet "in a large room"—in a space where many congregate. Place me on the continent of human sympathy where I can find my brother by night and by day—where storms divide not, where waves intervene not, where depths of downward distance drown not love.

Then shall the food of the far country be swine husks; then shall the riot and the revel be eclipsed by a new joy—the music and dancing of the city of God. Amen.—George Matheson.

Fourth Week, Fourth Day

These things have I spoken unto you, while yet abiding with you. But the Comforter, even the Holy Spirit, whom the Father will send in my name, he shall teach you all things, and bring to your remembrance all that I said unto you. Peace I leave with you; my peace I give unto you: not as the world giveth, give I unto you. Let not your heart be troubled, neither let it be fearful.—John 14:25-27.

Even as the Father hath loved me, I also have loved you; abide ye in my love. If ye keep my commandments, ye shall abide in my love; even as I have kept my Father's commandments, and abide in his love. These things have I spoken unto you, that my joy may be in you, and that your joy may be made full.—John 15:9-11.

Read these verses to observe one thing: the Master's earnest desire to share with his disciples the best blessings he had. His peace, his love, his joy—he did not wish to keep them to himself. And undoubtedly the more he shared, the more he possessed, for spiritual goods always multiply by division. Are we not facing here a basic truth in our lives? *Before we can fully enjoy anything we must share it.* Even a good book, good music, beautiful scenery—anything is enjoyed the more when we divide with others the experience. But this prerequisite for full happiness is distinctly unselfish. No man can achieve this special brand of abiding satisfaction by any manipulating of self-regard alone.

> "All who joy would win
> Must share it. Happiness was born a twin."

Everlasting Father, I beseech Thee to enable me to love Thee with all my heart and soul and strength and mind, and my neighbor as myself.

Help me to be meek and lowly in heart. Sweeten my temper and dispose me to be kind and helpful to all men. Make me kind in thought, gentle in speech, generous in action. Teach me that it is more blessed to give than to receive; that it is better to minister than to be ministered unto; better to forget myself than to put myself forward.

Deliver me from anger and from envy; from all harsh thoughts and unlovely manners. Make me of some use in this world; may I more and more forget myself and work the work of Him who sent me here; through Jesus Christ our Lord. Amen.—W. Angus Knight.

Fourth Week, Fifth Day

For this cause I bow my knees unto the Father, from whom every family in heaven and on earth is named, that he would grant you, according to the riches of his glory, that ye may be strengthened with power through his Spirit in the inward man; that Christ may dwell in your hearts through faith; to the end that ye, being rooted and grounded in love, may be strong to apprehend with all the saints what is the breadth and length and height and depth, and to know the love of Christ which passeth knowledge, that ye may be filled unto all the fulness of God.—Eph. 3:14-19.

Here surely was a source of happiness in Paul's life, without which he would have been utterly bereft: he had *spiritual resources* within

him on which even in his Roman prison he could fall back for recreation and refreshment. Sooner or later all men come to the need
of such inner wells of living water. Trouble falls upon us and by it
we are driven in upon ourselves. The days arrive when happiness
cannot spring from outward circumstance; we must discover it
within, and carry it with us amid forbidding conditions. But a selfish
man never can find such sources of joy within himself. Pascal was
right: "The man who lives only for himself hates nothing so much
as being alone with himself." A life inwardly rich and resourceful
must be, as Paul prayed, "rooted and grounded in love." Alas! for
a man, thrown back by fickle fortune on himself, who discovers in
his own narrow cupboard nothing to live on except the resentments,
the irritabilities, the peevish tempers, the jealousies, the exaggerated
self-regard, the disappointed ambitions of a selfish heart!

*O God of patience and consolation, give us such good will, we
beseech Thee, that with free hearts we may love and serve Thee and
our brethren; and, having thus the mind of Christ, may begin
heaven on earth, and exercise ourselves therein till that day when
heaven where love abideth shall seem no strange habitation to us.
For Jesus Christ's sake. Amen.*—Christina G. Rossetti.

Fourth Week, Sixth Day

**For I am already being offered, and the time of my departure is
come. I have fought the good fight, I have finished the course, I
have kept the faith: henceforth there is laid up for me the crown
of righteousness, which the Lord, the righteous judge, shall give to
me at that day; and not to me only, but also to all them that have
loved his appearing.—II Tim. 4:6-8.**

In these farewell words of Paul there is the unmistakable accent
of a victorious and joyful spirit. And this is the secret of his joy: *he
has lived his life for a cause that is worth living and dying for.* The
deep satisfactions of a purposeful existence, dedicated to a worthy
end, remain with him to the death. His final note is that of a happy
warrior: "I have fought the good fight." Compare with this the retrospect of a self-centered, frittered life! The selfish man may have
been carnal, deserving Carlyle's terrific comment on the eighteenth
century, "Soul extinct; stomach well alive!" He may have been
cruel, like Milton's "sons of Belial, flown with insolence and wine."

Or he may have been only a languid, pulseless, self-centered man. But in any case he has missed the supreme satisfaction of life. "This is now to be said," wrote Alfred the Great, "that whilst I live I wish to live nobly, and after life to leave to the men who come after me a memory of good works."

Help us, O Lord, to live out on the open sea of Thine all-reaching love, and to move with the currents of Thy power; to fill life's sails with the fresh winds of spiritual truth and freedom; to sail up and down time's glorious coast, carrying a heaven-scented cargo of better life to men; to be conscious less of effort and more of power; to see the needy men on the shore and bring them the bread of life; trusting always that when the sails grow gray and the spars and planks begin to groan in the gale, Heaven's safe harbor may welcome in peace the Captain of the Abundant Life. Amen.—George A. Miller.

Fourth Week, Seventh Day

Is it not plain from this week's study that he who seeks for happiness without unselfishness has missed his road? Friends, useful work, expanded interests, the delights of shared experience, inward spiritual resources, and a worthy purpose at life's center—such unselfish things as these are of the very substance of a joyful and abundant life.

All wise men in all ages have perceived that love and life thus belong together, and all of us do indulge in more or less unselfishness. But our service is fluctuating and unsteady. When the Master takes possession of us, straightway the principle of service begins to flower out. It widens its horizons to take in all the world; it deepens its vision to take in the most unlovely and the lost; it enlarges its scope to include even our enemies; it surrounds itself with majestic motives in the love of God, and at last a real Christian stands unfolded, with the spirit of service grown to a "lordly great compass" within. Such a development is not unhappy; it is the very blossom and fruitage of joy. So the Master said:

I am the door; by me if any man enter in, he shall be saved, and shall go in and go out, and shall find pasture. The thief cometh not, but that he may steal, and kill, and destroy: I came that they may have life, and may have it abundantly.—John 10:9, 10.

O God, Author of the world's joy, Bearer of the world's pain, make us glad that we are men and that we have inherited the world's burden; deliver us from the luxury of cheap melancholy; and, at the heart of all our trouble and sorrow, let unconquerable gladness dwell; through our Lord and Saviour Jesus Christ. Amen.
—Henry S. Nash.

COMMENT FOR THE WEEK

I

Such a dedicated use of strength in service as we have been considering plainly involves self-sacrifice. George Eliot in "Romola" says of Tito: "He was to be depended on to make any sacrifice that was not unpleasant." Such a costless amiability is common, but seriously to put service for all sorts of folk at the center of one's purpose involves readiness for self-renunciation which hurts. We run at once, therefore, upon that stumbling block which more than any other trips people up who start to be of use. We want *happiness* for ourselves; we want for ourselves a full, rich, vibrant life; and this clamorous self-regard seems desperately at war with self-sacrifice.

Of all arresting words of Jesus, none is stranger than his declaration on this seeming conflict between self-regard and self-renunciation. So significant is it that oftener than any other single thing he said it is referred to in the gospels: "Whosoever would save his life shall lose it: and whosoever shall lose his life for my sake shall find it." (Matt. 16:25. cf. Matt. 10:39; Mark 8:34, 35; Luke 9:23, 24; Luke 17:33; John 12:25.) He too, then, is in love with happiness; he too is seeking for his followers a tingling, copious, satisfying life. The fourth gospel expressly states his purpose: "I have come that they may have life and have it to the full." And the New Testament is radiant with the consciousness of having found the secret of abundant living. But whether in the Master himself or in those who closely followed him, one everywhere finds a strange prescription for their overflowing joy. If you wish blessedness, head for service; if you wish the crown of joy, take up the cross of sacrifice; if life is to be yours, lose your life in other lives and in causes that have won your love. *So far from seeing abundant living and sacrificial service as mutually exclusive, they see one as the road to the other.*

However reluctant we may be to base our daily conduct upon

this principle, however the subtle suspicion may intrude that the paradox is not quite true, there are times when its truth is evident. Crises come, sudden, unforeseen, that shake men down into the deeper levels of experience, where there is no keeping life except through life's surrender. "If I save my life, I lose it," is the motto engraved upon a statue of Sir Galahad in Ottawa. These are the last words of a youth, in whose memory the statue stands, who, seeing two skaters fall through the ice, plunged in and was drowned in rescuing them. Any such crisis makes evident to a courageous spirit, as it did to this youth, the truth of the Master's words. During the Great War who has not wonderingly watched men and women finding their joy and glory in self-renouncing devotion to a cause? Multitudes of folk faced selfish ease and terrific sacrifice, and chose sacrifice. Not for all the world in such an hour of need would they have chosen anything besides.

> "Though love repine and reason chafe,
> There came a voice without reply,
> 'Tis man's perdition to be safe
> If for the truth he ought to die."

Nevertheless, while this principle of Jesus is thus written in sympathetic ink upon the hearts of men so that the acid of a world catastrophe does bring it out where all can read, it pales again in common days. Men find it easier to die for a cause in a crisis than to live for it in ordinary hours. They do not really believe that self-realization through self-surrender is a universal law of life. But the Master saw this principle not as an occasional motive in a tragic hour, but as the common property of all hours. He saw that as surely as a seed must give itself up or else fail of increase, so only in sacrificial service can men find the secret of abundant life (John 12:24).

II

When we seek thus to understand, as the Master did, the relationship between self-realization and self-sacrifice, we need first of all to consider what the *self* is of which we speak. Children in the nursery play with a fascinating toy, which superficially seen appears to be a single box, but which on investigation reveals box within box, and ever more boxes still, each drawn from the interior of another until the floor is littered with them. So multiple and complicated a thing is the human self. When, therefore, one cries, I must care for myself, the answer comes, Which self? This smallest, meanest self, that last of all comes up from the interior of your life? This infinitesimal creature of narrow, clamorous, egoistic needs? To live for that self is to lose real life utterly. For all the while there is the larger possible self, that may inclose and glorify the smaller, compounded of family love, of friendship, of devotion to neighborhood and country, of loyalty to human kind, and to good causes on which man's weal depends. To live for that larger self is to live the abundant life.

Consider how true it is that our personalities are thus *a telescoping series of larger and smaller selves!* A young girl begins her life petted, pampered, spoiled. Her innermost and narrowest self is the only one she knows. Then love draws her out. She lives not quite so much within that narrow self as in the larger area of another's life, which to her has become dearer than her own. Then children come to increase the acreage of her spirit. Some day in that home toddling feet go down to the edge of the valley of the shadow. Her own life is in the balance then. Not something outside her stands hesitating there upon the valley's brink; it is part of her very being; and when her child's feet come clambering up the slippery slope again it is her own life that has come back to her. Expanded thus by experience she looks with increasing sympathy and understanding eyes upon humanity. She sees, as Chaucer sang:

> "Infinite been the sorwes and the teres
> Of oldé folk and folk of tendre yeres."

In her awakened womanhood she spends herself in unselfish service that this earth may be a more decent place for the family of God. Philanthropy, good government, the Christian cause—these things become part of herself. When she prays, "Thy Kingdom come" she means it. She can understand now what Milton felt: "I conceive myself to be not as mine own person, but as a member incorporate into that truth whereof I am persuaded." If now some friend who knew her coddled youth should say, "See! you have lost your old self!" would she not answer? "Thank God, I have lost it! I have lost my life and found it."

The paradoxical principle of Jesus, therefore, that self-surrender is necessary to self-realization is true in everyday experience. We all have this series of possible selves, from the meanest egoism that like a fledgling bird yammers with open mouth for the world to feed it, to that great self that can embrace within its sympathy and incorporate into its life the welfare of the world. The fundamental question is, Which self shall be subjugated to the other? Washington could have saved his self, his Virginia planter self, in ease and comfort, but so he would have lost his real self, Father of the Nation. The Master could have saved his self, his carpenter of Nazareth self, redeeming words unspoken, compassionate love unexpressed, the Cross unborne, but so he would have lost his real self, Savior of the World. We can save ourselves, our infinitesimal and futile selves, in unsacrificial ease. But what we have really done is to throw away the greatness of our lives.

Self-sacrifice is not, therefore, a bitter amputation of our personalities. *It is the enlargement of our personalities to comprehend the interests of others.* It is finding life, disguised as losing it. We overpass the boundary that separates *I* from *You;* we learn to think and live in terms of *We* and *Our,* and lo! we have found our greater selves. Sometimes the preacher pleads for self-regard. Care for yourselves, he says. Your personality is the most sacred entrustment God has given you. "What shall it profit a man if he gain the whole world and lose his own self?" And sometimes the preacher pleads for self-denial. You must sacrifice yourselves, he says. What is self that it should stand athwart the progress of God's good causes in the world? No one has learned the rudiments of Christian living who has not learned to deny, abnegate, crucify self. So do self-regard and self-denial appear in conflict. Nor is there any solution of this dilemma, except as we learn to incorporate our life by love into the life of others, until we live in them and they in us. Then self-sacrifice and self-realization flow together. What has become of the conflict between self-regard and self-denial in a great friendship, where two persons blend? When I care for myself, I am caring for my friend, and when I think of my friend, I am thinking of myself. We live in each other's lives. So Mrs. Browning sings of her husband:

> "The widest land
> Doom takes to part us, leaves thy heart in mine
> With pulses that beat double. What I do
> And what I dream include thee, as the wine
> Must taste of its own grapes."

Indeed, let any generous man ask himself where his *self* is, and how surprising is the answer! It is not alone where his body is. It is where his children dwell. What strikes them strikes him. It is where his friends are. What befalls them befalls him. It is where with difficulty causes forge ahead, on which his heart is set. Every large-hearted man is scattered over all creation. Where was David when, safe in the watchtower, he cried, "O my son, Absalom! would God I had died for thee, O Absalom, my son"? Where was Livingstone, when he cried of Africa, "All I can add in my loneliness is, may Heaven's rich blessing come down on every one—American, English, Turk— who will help to heal the open sore of the world"? Personality is marvelously extensible. Like an alarm system with a central register- ing bell and many sensitive wires stretching everywhither, so is a human person. We are not narrowly delimited things; we are spirit- ual beings, capable of infinite expansion, able to live ourselves out in other people and in causes that have claimed our love. No man is complete in himself; all that he cares for is part of him. The glory of the Master is that he so lived out his life in the lives of all man- kind that he could say and mean it, "Inasmuch as ye did it unto one of these my brethren, even these least, ye did it unto me." This is self- sacrifice; but it is also self-realization. It is the effulgence of life into its full size and glory, even though it be true that

"He who lives more lives than one
More deaths than one must die."

III

In spite of the acknowledged truth just presented, one may be tempted still to plead the case in favor of self-regard. The necessity and duty of caring for our individual selves, however narrow one may call them, are imperative. A solid and important truth lies in Shakespeare's words in "Henry V," "Self-love, my liege, is not so vile a sin as self-neglecting." To till a field for wheat that one self- ishly may eat it all, while starving neighbors look on unhelped, is bad enough. But to let a good field run to weeds untilled for any purpose, is still worse. A man's first responsibility is his own individ- ual life, to till it, enlarge it, to enrich it, to make it bear all that it will yield. The summary of the law and the prophets tells us to love ourselves well and then to love others just as much (Luke 10:27).

Because this is a Christian's primary responsibility, as it is any other man's, a charge of insincerity is sometimes lodged against the preacher and his congregation when self-sacrifice is exalted in the church. "See!" cries the scoffer, "all your words about self-renouncing service are hypocrisy. You and all your parishioners, like everybody else, want good things for yourselves. Homes, food, clothes, books, music, leisure, the elemental creature comforts and the luxuries that minister to fullness of life—you want all these, and you propose to have them if you can. In what, then, do you differ from any other men?"

To such an objection this parable may be an answer: The Sea of Galilee and the Dead Sea are made of the same water. It flows down, clear and cool, from the heights of Hermon and the roots of the cedars of Lebanon. The Sea of Galilee makes beauty of it, for the Sea of Galilee has an outlet. *It gets to give.* It gathers in its riches that it may pour them out again to fertilize the Jordan plain. But the Dead Sea with the same water makes horror. For the Dead Sea has no outlet. *It gets to keep.* That is the radical difference between selfish and unselfish men. We all do want life's enriching blessings; we ought to; they are divine benedictions. But some men get to give, and they are like Galilee; while some men get to keep and they are like the brackish water that covers Sodom and Gomorrah. "We Florentines," says one of George Eliot's characters, "live scrupulously that we may spend splendidly."

The Master's principle, then, that only by self-surrender can we win through to self-fulfilment, does not mean that the individual self is unimportant. It means that the individual self is but a fragment of the whole personality, and if it is to come to its fullness, must expand to take in its brethren. "Love to one's neighbor," says Professor Todd, "does not mean the annihilation of one's self, but simply the recognition that self and neighbor are fundamentally one."

One corollary of this truth is clear. *The selfish man is not a complete man; he is not whole, normal, healthy.* He is a truncated section of himself. He may think himself a natural, sensible, hardheaded, practical person. The truth is that he is sick.

Indeed, our insistence that unselfishness and abundant life involve each other and to be meanly selfish is to renounce the glory of living, is illustrated by the fact that the symptoms of invalidism and the symptoms of selfishness are the same. No one suffers long with a debilitating, nagging illness without being tempted to think wholly of his narrowest self. His mind tends to wind inward with circular, moody thoughts about himself. He is absorbed in his own needs. Querulous, touchy, waspish, wanting attention, impatient when he does not receive it, discontented when he does—unless it be spiritually conquered, such is the mood of illness.

Consider then the road by which a man moves out from this lamentable state toward health again! He begins to worry less and less about himself. He gains some surplus energy of thought to spend on some one besides himself. He feels in time a dawning capacity to be happy in the happiness of others. At length he eats and sleeps again with relish and delight, and sheds his returning radiance on all around. Rising within him like a tossing mill race, he feels returning vigor, fretting to be let loose upon some mill wheel. He wants to do something for somebody. At last, his sickness gone, happily objective, not moodily subjective, thinking of others, not worrying about himself, spending abroad his surplus vigor, not hoarding it greedily for his depleted strength, he goes out into life, a dynamic man come back to health again. By as much as he expends himself, giving more than he gets, making his contributions offered greater than his contributions levied, he shows the marks of a well man. For selfishness is sickness, and overflowing usefulness is spiritual health and abounding life.

IV

The necessary relationship between self-surrender and self-fulfilment is seen clearly in one more basic fact. Existence is given to us all to start with; our problem is somehow out of existence to make life. Existence is an entrustment; life is an achievement. Now all human experience is unanimous that real life can come only when *a worthy purpose runs down through the center of existence, to give it meaning.* This is plain when one tests its truth by the lives of the greatest men. As on raised letters, so on the outstanding characters of history even blind folk can read the truth that a worthy purpose is essential to abundant life. Amid infinite variety in details one attribute is always present when a great man comes: he has centered his existence around some aim concerning which he feels like Paul, "This one thing I do." The one intolerable life from which

all high-minded men must shrink, as Matthew Arnold says his father
shrank from it, is a frittered existence:

> "Not without aim to go round
> In an eddy of purposeless dust,
> Effort unmeaning and vain."

Nor is this attitude the peculiarity of the most capacious souls
alone. We all may have it. The Mississippi River makes the central
plains of the United States a rich and fruitful place. From the
Rockies to the Gulf, calling in tributaries from every side, it has
organized the life of a continent. What, then, has made the beauty
and productiveness of some small valley, whose woods and farms,
though quite unheralded, are a benediction to the few who know
them? There, too, a stream with tributary rivulets has organized and
fructified the valley's life. So a central, serviceable purpose is the
secret of abundant living, whether in continental men or in obscure
and lowly folk. No man lives at all until he lives for something great.

To many, such a purposeful and dedicated life seems stern, forbidding. We want pleasure: "the loose beads with no straight string
running through." We cannot wake and sleep and spend the hours
between, we say, concentrated on a serious aim. But a serviceable
purpose does not thus somberly becloud life and exclude its free-
hearted happiness. It rather is the one element in life that can put
foundation under happiness. When one goes from New York to San
Francisco he does not tensely sit through a week, saying with deliberate insistence, I must go to San Francisco. His purpose to reach
his destination does not exhaust his thought. He thinks of a thousand
other things; his delight in friendship and scenery upon the way is
unaffected and spontaneous; no single happy or interesting experience need he miss. But all the same his major purpose controls his
action; nothing is allowed to keep him from going on to San Francisco; and when he reaches his destination all that has happened on
the way—the pleasant fellowships, the gorgeous scenery—has been
but incidental to his dominant desire which brought him to his
journey's end.

So whatever may be his special calling, through a real Christian's
life runs a controlling purpose to be of use. It does not substitute
itself for other things; it permeates everything. Its subtle secret influence flows through all the rest. It shuts out no wholesome, happy

experience of good report. Rather it includes them all, and irradiates them with significance and worth. Such a man alone is truly happy, for pleasure never lasts when it is made the main business of life. It has abiding quality only when it is founded upon a worthy purpose. As a life that is all vacation knows no vacation, since the very essence of a holiday lies in having hard work upon all sides of it, so a life that is all pleasure-seeking knows no pleasure. For the essence of all abiding pleasure is to be mainly busy about some serviceable task.

Too long have the pallid and tubercular figures of saints in medieval cathedrals symbolized the meaning of Christian life! Consider rather a man like Henry Drummond. Few men have been more mastered by a central purpose. He lived to bring men into fellowship with Jesus Christ. The influence of his preaching and his personal interviews upon the student life of Scotland abides long after he has gone. His biographer says that writing the story of his life is "like writing the record of a fragrance." Yet as to the glow and buoyancy of his daily life, let a friend testify:

"He fished, he shot, he skated as few can, he played cricket; he would go any distance to see a fire or a football match. He had a new story, a new puzzle, or a new joke every time he met you. Was it on the street? He drew you to watch two message boys meet, grin, knock each other's hats off, lay down their baskets and enjoy a friendly chaffer of marbles. Was it on the train? He had dredged from the bookstall every paper and magazine that was new to him. . . . If it was a rainy afternoon in a country house, he described a new game, and in five minutes everybody was playing it. If it was a children's party, they clamored for his sleight of hand. . . . The name he went by among younger men was The Prince."

As a brook flows down from the high hills, sparkling in the sunlight, gathering itself in friendly pools, playing among the shallows near the shore, or running out into deep places where all is cool and still, so spirits like Drummond's flow among men. But whether they seem serious or happy they are mastered by one thing: the gravitation from the high hills whence they came. Their flow is all one way: a testimony to the fullness and beauty of Christian life and to the sufficiency of the Master from whom it comes.

Once more, therefore, losing the smaller self in a larger self, organized around a serious desire to serve mankind, is self-renunciation indeed, but it is self-fulfilment, too. The man who achieves it possesses an expansive personality which is the secret of abiding joy. Even when disasters fall, he is not undone as selfish men must be, for his smallest self is not the whole of himself, and what happens to his smallest self leaves still the larger areas of his life untouched. Like soldiers who fall wounded upon the battlefield, he himself may suffer, but still rejoice exceedingly to see his cause advanced.

Paradoxical as it may seem, therefore, the Master was speaking from a rich and real experience of fact when he said, "Whosoever will be great among you, let him be your minister, and whosoever will be chief among you let him be your servant." To be sure, the natural grain of the human wood runs another way altogether. Whosoever would be great among you, let him conquer or rule or gain wealth; let him *be served* by multitudes of slaves, by millions of subjects, by the labor of the poor—such is the idea which underlies the larger part of human history. The Master turned topsy-turvy this inveterate conviction that a man's glory consists in service received. He substituted in its place the amazing proposition that man's glory consists in the extent and quality and unselfishness of service rendered. And none who ever dared to live upon the Master's principle has denied its truth. The way of the Cross is the way of overflowing life. "He that will take that crabbit tree, and will carry it cannily," said Samuel Rutherford, "will yet find it to be such a burden as wings are to a bird and sails to a boat."

CHAPTER V

Self-Denial

DAILY READINGS

Our study during the last week centered about the Master's principle that in the expenditure of life lies the saving of it. There are times, however, when this truth is anything but obvious. A mountain's summit may glisten in the sunlight, while its lower altitudes are all beclouded. So this ideal of finding life through losing it may shine in its loftiest exhibitions, as in the character of Christ, while, on our common levels, it is obscure and difficult of access. Self-denial at times seems not to be glorious and life-giving at all. We shall try, this week, to deal with the meaning of such self-denial. Let us in our daily readings deal with the fact of it.

Fifth Week, First Day

And if thy right eye causeth thee to stumble, pluck it out, and cast it from thee: for it is profitable for thee that one of thy members should perish, and not thy whole body be cast into hell. And if thy right hand causeth thee to stumble, cut it off, and cast it from thee: for it is profitable for thee that one of thy members should perish, and not thy whole body go into hell.—Matt. 5:29, 30.

One elemental form of self-denial, demanded by a life of Christian service, is the *resolute rejection of positive evils* that mar character and therefore hurt usefulness. "There never was a bad man," said Edmund Burke, "that had ability for good service." How much this kind of self-denial costs, anyone who has ever seriously tried it knows. We must continually resist the down-drag of popular habits, to the practice of which the majority of folk consent. For the majority, however we must commit to it the arbitrament of political affairs, is almost sure to be wrong about any matter that requires fine discrimination. Put to popular vote the preference between ragtime and Chopin's nocturnes, the cinema and Shakespeare, cheap love-stories and the English classics, and is there any question what the majority would decide? So to be a good Christian is an achievement, won only by resistance to the pull of popular tastes and common practices. It costs to be among those whose characters lift up against the gravitation of commonly accepted evil. "The world is upheld," said Emerson, "by the veracity of good men: they make the earth wholesome."

My Father, may the world not mould me today, but may I be so strong as to help to mould the world! Amen.—John Henry Jowett.

Fifth Week, Second Day

The kingdom of heaven is like unto a treasure hidden in the field; which a man found, and hid; and in his joy he goeth and selleth all that he hath, and buyeth that field.

Again, the kingdom of heaven is like unto a man that is a merchant seeking goodly pearls: and having found one pearl of great price, he went and sold all that he had, and bought it.—Matt. 13:44-46.

Christian service plainly demands this second form of self-denial: *the abandonment of scattered loyalty for a life of dominant interest in the Kingdom of God on earth.* To be a Christian is not negative absence of outbreaking sin, as some seem to suppose. "I have known men," said Henry Ward Beecher, "who thought the object of conversion was to clean them, as a garment is cleaned, and that when they were converted they were to be hung up in the Lord's wardrobe, the door of which was to be shut so that no dust could get at them. A coat that is not used the moths eat; and a Christian who is hung up so that he shall not be tempted—the moths eat him; and they have poor food at that." Rather, a Christian life is one of positive, single-hearted devotion to the welfare of man, to the service of the lowliest and lost, to the support of all good causes, to the hope of the Kingdom. But a life so centrally dedicated costs its price. Sometimes a man, as Jesus said, must give up for it all that he has. Under any circumstances, a life that cares, suffers. So when the

Fugitive Slave Law was passed, a great New Englander wrote: "There is infamy in the air. I have a new experience. I wake in the morning with a painful sensation, which I carry about all day, and which, when traced home, is the odious remembrance of the ignominy which has fallen on Massachusetts, which robs the landscape of beauty and takes the sunshine out of every hour." Do you care for any good cause as much as that?

O Lord, fill us with the simplicity of a divine purpose, that we may be inwardly at one with Thy holy will, and lifted above vain wishes of our own. Set free from every detaining desire or reluctance, may we heartily surrender all our powers to the work which Thou hast given us to do; rejoicing in any toil, and fainting under no hardness that may befall us, as good soldiers of Jesus Christ, and counting it as our crown of blessing, if we may join the company of the faithful who have kept Thy Name, and witnessed to Thy kingdom in every age. Amen.—James Martineau.

Fifth Week, Third Day

And he looked up, and saw the rich men that were casting their gifts into the treasury. And he saw a certain poor widow casting in thither two mites. And he said, Of a truth I say unto you, This poor widow cast in more than they all: for all these did of their superfluity cast in unto the gifts; but she of her want did cast in all the living that she had.—Luke 21:1-4.

Christian service plainly demands *self-denial in money*. Extravagant expenditure while millions of people are in want, needless luxury, while good causes fail for funds—there is no use in claiming the Christian name if one indulges in such obviously unchristian conduct. Some have said that even luxurious expenditure is useful because it furnishes work for the laborer, but what it really does is to call both work and money away from necessary tasks to unproductive and needless investments. How justly does this satire fall on Dives!

> "Now Dives daily feasted
> And was gorgeously arrayed;
> Not at all because he liked it,
> But because 'twas good for trade.

> That the poor might have more calico,
> He clothed himself with silk;
> And surfeited himself on cream
> That they might have more milk.
> And e'en to show his sympathy
> For the deserving poor
> He did no useful work himself
> That they might do the more."

Compare such a character with the woman of the parable. She was taking her religion in earnest; and she gave good proof of it in her use of money. For the use of money can be made a touchstone of sincerity. If a man say that he loves his family, but, being able, makes no provision for their financial security, spending his income rather in his present pleasures, something is seriously the matter with his love. If a man say that he loves God and his fellows, but does not give till it hurts for their service, his professed love is not likely to be more than a theatrical gesture.

O Lord, who though Thou wast rich, yet for our sakes didst become poor, and hast promised in Thy Gospel that whatsoever is done unto the least of Thy brethren, Thou wilt receive as done unto Thee; give us grace, we humbly beseech Thee, to be ever willing and ready to minister, as Thou enablest us, to the necessities of our fellow-creatures, and to extend the blessings of Thy kingdom over all the world, to Thy praise and glory, who art God over all, blessed for ever. Amen.—St. Augustine (354-430).

Fifth Week, Fourth Day

And Zacchæus stood, and said unto the Lord, Behold, Lord, the half of my goods I give to the poor; and if I have wrongfully exacted aught of any man, I restore fourfold. And Jesus said unto him, To-day is salvation come to this house, forasmuch as he also is a son of Abraham. For the Son of man came to seek and to save that which was lost.—Luke 19:8-10.

Christian service demands not only self-denial in giving money, but *self-denial in making it.* Zacchæus had pressed the opportunities of his position to the limit; he had charged all that the traffic would bear; he had narrowly looked at all chances for gain—honest, half-honest, or dishonest—and had squeezed them as dry as he could. The invasion of his life by Jesus meant an economic revolution. He was forced to review the sources of his income and to plan a radical change. One of the acutest self-denials demanded by Christianity and too often disregarded, is such a renunciation of profits. Needlessly high prices, needlessly low wages, needlessly unwholesome conditions of labor make dividends poisonous. No true Christian can ever knowingly coin the suffering and degradation of his fellows into cash for his own pocket. The problem presented by this fact, under conditions of modern industry, is enormously difficult for the individual to handle. As Professor Rauschenbusch wrote: "Stockholders are scattered absentee owners. A corporation might be composed of retired missionaries, peace advocates, and dear old ladies, but their philanthropy would cause no vibrations in the business end of the concern." The solution of the problem can come only with general alterations in public ideals of business and with economic changes to give such better ideals expression; but this does not excuse any man from an earnest, sacrificial endeavor to purge the sources of his income from unchristian elements.

Deliver us, we beseech Thee, O Lord, from all kinds of stealing, extortion, fraud in trade and contracts; from all making haste to be rich, and from taking advantage of the ignorance or necessity of the persons we deal with.—Bishop Ken.

Fifth Week, Fifth Day

And Jesus said unto Simon, Fear not; from henceforth thou shalt catch men. And when they had brought their boats to land, they left all, and followed him. . . . And after these things he went forth, and beheld a publican, named Levi, sitting at the place of toll, and said unto him, Follow me. And he forsook all, and rose up and followed him.—Luke 5:10, 11, 27, 28.

Not everybody was thus called on to leave the ordinary business of life. Sometimes Jesus called men to stay where they were. So to the healed Gadarene demoniac, who wanted to join the traveling company of the apostles, the Master said, "Go to thy house and unto thy friend" (Mark 5:19). *But some men and women are called out for special work.* The comfort and security of home life and a set-

tled business are denied them. They are missionaries; they toil in
the slums of the cities; they undertake ventures in philanthropy;
they pioneer fresh fields of truth and bear the brunt of the attacks
that always fall on unaccustomed enterprises; they are the unusual
folk, the martyrs in whom the sacrifice of Jesus is fulfilled, "He
saved others, himself he cannot save" (Mark 15:31). Christian character involves the willingness to answer such a call as this. The self-
denial involved in it is sharply obvious. Only the loftiest motives can
sustain men in such self-sacrifice. So St. Bernard put it: "The faithful soldier does not feel his own wounds when he looks with love
on those of his King."

O God, the God of all goodness and of all grace, who art worthy
of a greater love than we can either give or understand; fill our
hearts, we beseech Thee, with such love toward Thee, that nothing
may seem too hard for us to do or to suffer in obedience to Thy
will; and grant that thus loving Thee, we may become daily more
like unto Thee, and finally obtain the crown of life which Thou hast
promised to those that love Thee; through Jesus Christ our Lord.
Amen.—"A Book of Prayers for Students."

Fifth Week, Sixth Day

Recall today the familiar scene where Naomi bids farewell to her
daughters-in-law, and turns her face from Moab toward her home
country:

And they lifted up their voice, and wept again: and Orpah kissed
her mother-in-law; but Ruth clave unto her.

And she said, Behold, thy sister-in-law is gone back unto her
people, and unto her god: return thou after thy sister-in-law. And
Ruth said, Entreat me not to leave thee, and to return from fol-
lowing after thee; for whither thou goest, I will go; and where thou
lodgest, I will lodge; thy people shall be my people, and thy God
my God; where thou diest, will I die, and there will I be buried;
Jehovah do so to me, and more also, if aught but death part thee
and me. And when she saw that she was steadfastly minded to go
with her, she left off speaking unto her.—Ruth 1:14-18.

Of how much self-denial in family relationships is this a type!
To be a real Christian in a home often means costly self-renunci-

ation. Controlled temper, decent demeanor no matter how you feel, a radiant spirit even under irritating circumstances—even such simple elements of Christian home life are not easy. Carlyle did not master that much self-denial in his relationships with his wife. "Ah! if I only had five minutes with her," he said after her death, "if only to assure her that I loved her through all that." And often the demands of self-renunciation in a home go deeper. When poverty must be faced together, when sickness falls, the tragedy of which all share, when children are sent to college by parents who cannot afford it, when sin wrecks lives which nevertheless love will not give up—how intimate, exacting, and continuous are the gracious self-bestowals of a true home! Here live the modest martyrs of service whose names are written in heaven. For Ruth is one of an innumerable company who have found their sphere of self-renouncing love in the home and whose reward, like Ruth's, lies here, that she bore Obed, and "he is the father of Jesse, the father of David."

O Heavenly Father, shed forth Thy blessed Spirit richly on all the members of this household. Make each one of us an instrument in Thy hands for good. Purify our hearts, strengthen our minds and bodies, fill us with mutual love. Let no pride, no self-conceit, no rivalry, no dispute ever spring up among us. Make us earnest and true, wise and prudent, giving no just cause for offense; and may Thy holy peace rest upon us this day and every day, sweetening our trials, cheering us in our work, and keeping us faithful to the end; through Jesus Christ our Lord. Amen.—Church Guild.

Fifth Week, Seventh Day

Such are the familiar self-denials which a Christian life involves: the withstanding of popular sins; the refusal of loose and scattered loyalty; the conquest of niggardliness; the renunciation of tainted income; the sacrifice of comfort, home, country, and life itself, if need be, to fulfil a special vocation; and, if that be not demanded, the daily self-renunciation without which home, neighborhood, and friendship are impossible. Such a program of self-denial the Master demanded without diminution or apology.

From that time began Jesus to show unto his disciples, that he must go unto Jerusalem, and suffer many things of the elders and

chief priests and scribes, and be killed, and the third day be raised up. And Peter took him, and began to rebuke him, saying, Be it far from thee, Lord: this shall never be unto thee. But he turned, and said unto Peter, Get thee behind me, Satan: thou art a stumbling-block unto me: for thou mindest not the things of God, but the things of men. Then said Jesus unto his disciples, If any man would come after me, let him deny himself, and take up his cross, and follow me. For whosoever would save his life shall lose it: and whosoever shall lose his life for my sake shall find it.—Matt. 16:21-25.

St. Francis Xavier, who knew from experience to what extremes Christian self-sacrifice could go, wrote once about this closing verse:

"It may be easy to understand the Latin, and the general meaning of this saying of the Lord, but when dangers arise, where the life about which you wish to decide will probably be lost, and when, in order to prepare yourself to decide to lose your life for God's sake that you may find it in Him, you get down to details, everything else, even this clear Latin, begins to get hazy. And in such a case, however learned you may be, you can understand nothing, unless God, in His infinite mercy, makes your particular case plain."

Surely we may take it for certain, that if we have no idea what Xavier means, if we never have been hard put to it to bring ourselves to the point of a decisive and costly self-denial, we have not been following very closely in the footsteps of the Master.

Yea, O my God, we lay hold of Thy Cross, as of a staff that can stand unshaken, when the floods run high. The tale told us is no fairy story of some far-away land: it is this world, and not another— this world with all its miseries and its slaughter and its ruin—that Thou hast entered to redeem, by Thine Agony and bloody Sweat.
—H. Scott Holland.

COMMENT FOR THE WEEK

I

All that we have said about self-sacrifice as the road to self-fulfil-ment may be true, but it will take a fairer and more gracious world than ours to make it constantly seem true. There are persons with whom it is easy for our lives to blend, until in losing self in them we find our selves returned to us, enlarged and glorified. So Paul said, "He that loveth his own wife loveth himself" (Eph. 5:28). There are causes in the service of which our interest runs high, so that, giving ourselves to them, we find an expanded and satisfying life. But the spending of self in service is not always so obviously associated with rich return. There are times when self-sacrifice and self-fulfilment do not beautifully blend. Tennyson put the truth of our last chapter into poetry:

"Love took up the harp of Life, and smote on all the chords with
     might;
 Smote the chord of Self, that, trembling, pass'd in music out of
     sight."

But often our individual selves, with all their clamorous rights and needs, are not so easily disposed of. They do not pass out of sight "in music," but in agony and rebellion. They chafe against the piercing self-denials that often are involved when we do our serviceable duty.

Some people it is a delight to serve. They are obviously worth it. Their response in gratitude, their alert capacity to avail themselves of proffered aid, their swift recovery from need to independence, visit any service rendered them with immediate reward. But one who sets himself, in the spirit of the Master, to lead a serviceable life, does not float day after day through such idyllic experiences. He sends boys through college and they turn out to be thankless rascals; he endeavors to advance an able girl to a more responsible position and she grows heady and hopeless; he conceives a fine plan to redeem an unsanitary neighborhood and with chagrin discovers that the hapless sufferers prefer it as it is; he ministers tirelessly through many years to the exacting demands of a querulous and selfish relative, only to wonder at the end whether such poignant self-denial was right.

Moreover, self-sacrificial service that ideally should expand the life, often in practice seems to narrow it. Helpfulness, alluring at first, lapses into drudgery. Living in a settlement, going as a missionary, championing a worthy cause, helping all sorts of folk, may appear romantic; in fact, it is extraordinarily hard work. So when Florence Nightingale and her first corps of nurses were sailing up the Bos-

porus to deal with the nameless horrors in the Crimea, the glow
of adventure still was exciting the young women's thoughts. They
uttered ecstatic exclamations over the coming days of service. But
Miss Nightingale silenced them. "Young women," she said, "the
strongest will be wanted at the washtub."

Not only does a serviceable spirit find itself dealing thus with
unresponsive folk and monotonous tasks, but, as well, the times come
when self-sacrifice means self-sacrifice with a vengeance. The claims
of others cut clean across the dearest interests of our own lives. Not
any expansion of the sacrificing self is obvious, but rather the utter
self-renunciation with which the sweetest, wholesomest, choicest joys
are given up for others' sake. Times come when saving others means
that we cannot save ourselves. So David Livingstone laid his wife
away, dead of the jungle fever, and broken-hearted and alone
turned his face toward his last terrific journey into the interior. In
his diary we find this outburst of agony: "Oh, my Mary, my Mary!
How often we have longed for a quiet home, since you and I were
cast adrift at Kolobeng!"

II

Granting, therefore, that only in unselfish service can any life find
true enlargement and satisfaction, we need still to consider in terms
of concrete experience the problem of costly self-denials. For one
thing, when the Master says, "If any man would come after me let
him deny himself and take up his cross and follow me," he is not
in the least unique. *Every art, science, feat of skill, and enterprise
on earth says the same thing.* So Paul at the Greek games saw men
who could not have guided so unerringly their swerving chariots, so
tirelessly have run their races and sustained their combats, if with
unwearying self-denial they had not disciplined themselves. And the
apostle in whose heart it well may be that a fight was on against
some resurgent wish for ease and comfort, went back to his own self-
denying life, with the figures of the athletes in his thought: "They
do it to obtain a corruptible crown; but we an incorruptible" (I
Cor. 9:25).

Consider, then, the self-denial of *acrobats*. To children they are
like automata, nimble in action, marvelous in skill. But older folk
must think of the discipline that lies behind the precision of their
feats. They have guarded their bodies by self-restraint and hardened

them by exercise; they have risked life to learn new exploits; they
have let neither boredom nor weariness nor illness prevent their continual appearances. And "they do it to obtain a corruptible crown."

Consider the *musicians*. When a master violinist plays a great passage from Beethoven, flawless in technique, gorgeous in coloring,
till eyes grow wet and nerves are taut with exquisite delight, like the
strings of the violin on which he plays, who can compute the cost
of such consummate skill? Self-denial is no special property of Christian service. It is an elemental law of life.

Consider the *explorers*. What rigor of the northern cold, what
exile from the comforts of home, what sustained and perilous self-
renunciation did Peary undergo that he might be the discoverer of
the North Pole! Or when, amid his freezing comrades, Scott lay
dying on the homeward march from the South Pole, what splendid
capacity for sustained self-sacrifice is revealed in what he wrote:
"We took risks; we knew we took them, and therefore we have no
cause for complaint, but bow to the will of Providence, determined
still to do our best to the last. Had we lived, I should have had a
tale to tell of the hardihood, endurance, and courage of my companions, which would have stirred the heart of every Englishman."

Consider *men of business*. One who deliberately risks life for a
philanthropic cause is widely heralded, but business men in multitudes break down their health each year or, seeking their fortunes
at the ends of the earth, put life in jeopardy. Missionaries leave
country, family, comfort, and cherished opportunities, to bury themselves in obscure and uninviting places, often among folk whom only
the grace of God can make one love at first. But is there any place
where men go for Christ's sake, where they do not go for money's
sake? Is there any outpost so remote where men carry the Gospel,
to which also men do not carry the products of our factories? So
Livingstone cried: "Can the love of Christ not carry the missionary
where the slave trade carries the slaver?"

Or if one would know the lengths to which self-denial commonly
goes in human life, let him consider the *patriot*. If the Master had
said to us, I have a cause that at all costs and hazards must be
pushed to a victorious issue; within five years it will cost twenty
million dead and such a lavish outpouring of treasure that all the
race in half a century cannot repay it, what would we have done?
But patriotism has said that and we have answered. How common
in history is the spirit of Ricasoli: "I would have killed my daugh-

ter, who was my great affection on earth, if she had been an obstacle to achieving the great end toward which so many Italians were straining."

One who shrinks from costly self-denial for service's sake may well consider, first of all, that self-denial is common coin, rung on every counter in the world where men buy anything which in serious earnest they desire.

"They do it to obtain a corruptible crown."

III

Such an approach to the problem of self-denial reveals its true nature. It is not the negative, forbidding thing that often we shake our heads about. In one sense there is no such thing as self-denial, for what we call such is the necessary price we pay for things on which our hearts are set.

This truth stands clear in all concerns of moral character. Many a young man is warned against the evils of illicit love, as though he were being asked chiefly to give up pleasure. The emphasis is all upon the repression of an appetite. Purity is made to seem merely a negative denial of deep desire. In the young man's thought, dissipation is the positively alluring life, full of charm and music, while purity is life stripped, straitened, and set in the forbidding grasp of prohibitory laws. What wonder that so many turn to the warmth and color of a wayward life!

The truth, however, about the self-denial which purity involves is based upon this positive fact: *the most beautiful possession on this earth which man has ever imagined or achieved is a Christian home*. Who has one is rich, and who may have one and meanly misses it, has played the fool. But so priceless a possession does not come by accident. Men do not drift into it. They must pay the price. If a man would have the full beauty of a Christian home, there are some kinds of life that he must not live.

The gripping appeal for self-denying purity, therefore, is not negative. Young man, so it might run, the girl whom you are going to marry is now alive. You may never have met her, but somewhere she is walking down a path which in the providence of God some day will cross yours. Wherever she may be, she keeps herself for you, and in her imagination you are even now a prince whom some day she will gladly marry. Not for the wealth of the world would she be grossly untrue to you. How, then, are you living? You have no right to take to such a girl a life smirched and rotted with unchastity. If you do, there is a secret shame you never will outgrow, a pang that you will feel whenever your children clamber to your arms. To have a home free from all that, with memories high and beautiful, is worth anything that it may cost. Those who have such homes do not call the price of them self-denial. It is all clear gain. They have surrendered dust for diamonds. For this is the deepest truth about self-denial: that men positively set their hearts upon some high possession which they greatly want, and, paying the price of it in self-restraint, they count themselves the happiest of men to possess their treasure. Self-denial is not negative repression, but the cost of positive achievement.

So inextricably indeed is the fact of self-denial wrought into life that by no devious dodging can one escape it. Let a man say, Not self-denial but self-indulgence is my choice; I set no high and costly aims ahead of me; I seek an unrestrained and uncostly life! Has he then escaped self-renunciation? *Rather he has plunged head foremost into the most terrific self-denial that human life can anyhow sustain.* For if we will not deny ourselves *for* a Christian home, we shall deny ourselves a *Christian home!* What more appalling self-renunciation can there be? If we will not deny ourselves a loose and unchaste life, then we shall deny ourselves self-respect and a conscience fit to live with. If we will not deny ourselves bad temper and a wagging tongue, then we shall deny ourselves friendship—God pity us! If we will not deny ourselves those habits of thought and life that keep divine fellowship away from human hearts, then we shall deny ourselves God. In short, if we will not give up evil for good, we shall surely give up good for evil. Where there is a will there is a won't. Self-denial is unescapable. It is not the negative, forbidding amputation of self from which men often shrink. It is the price men pay when they have positively set their hearts upon some chosen goal. At its highest it is the privilege life offers us of buying the best at the sacrifice of something less desired.

IV

The difference between men, therefore, does not lie in the presence of self-denial in their experience. That comes inevitably into every life. *The difference lies in the ends for which men deny themselves.* Some men place their individual selves at the center of their lives, and sacrifice everything beside in the service of that little god. George Eliot describes an ancient silver mirror, on which, if one brought a candle near, the multitudinous fine lines, wrought by much polishing, arranged themselves in concentric circles around the light of the candle flame. So to a mean man the large interests of human kind center about his self. *Self-centered* is the exact description of his life. The costly gains of civilization, the securities of government, the hard-won opportunities of trade, ties of family and friendship— all these in his eyes exist for his special benefit. They are to be dressed in livery, if he can manage it, and made to serve his interests. As in Joseph's dream, the sun, the moon, and the eleven stars all bow in obeisance before him. Does such a life escape self-denial? Rather to any man of spiritual vision such a man is practicing self-denial in its most extreme form.

He is denying himself that *generous outlook upon life* which alone can open human eyes to the worth and beauty of God's world. Moffatt gives the true translation of the Master's words: "If your Eye is generous, the whole of your body will be illumined, but if your Eye is selfish, the whole of your body will be darkened" (Matt. 6:23). Look on mankind with self-forgetful, benevolent, magnanimous eyes, and life is radiant; look on mankind with churlish, avaricious, greedy eyes, and life, as Hobbes the philosopher of selfishness called it, "is solitary, poor, nasty, brutish, and short." Wordsworth confesses that his first view of the Alps was spoiled for him by irritation over an unsatisfactory lunch. So does our clamorous self-regard, allowed to usurp the central place and to obsess our thought, blind our vision, though all life's splendor were unrolled before us. Whatever gracious, helpful, inspiring thing is to be seen on earth, only an eye unspoiled by self-centeredness can see it.

Moreover, the self-centered man denies himself *friendship*. The games of children are the playful replicas of manhood's serious pursuits. "Tag"—the heated chasing of things hard to catch; "I Spy"— the diligent searching for things hard to find; "Puss Wants a Corner" —the competitive struggle for positions too few in number to supply the demand—so do children's games represent adult life. But "Prisoner's Base," where, caught by the enemy, only the touch of a friend can set us free, goes deeper yet. Our friends are our deliverers. They call us out of our narrow selves; they believe in our possibilities which we cannot discern; they stand by us when else we would surrender hope; they shine upon us like the sun and rain in refreshing fellowship; and they bring to maturity within us all that is excellent and of good report. Cries Emerson: "I can do that by another which I cannot do alone. I can say to you what I cannot first say to myself." But friendship is reciprocal. Only the friendly spirit can keep friends. The self-centered man has denied himself the most inspiring relationship on earth.

He has also denied himself *the thrilling satisfaction of helping men.* "Are you not lonely out here?" asked a visitor of a lighthouse keeper on an isolated reef. "Not since I saved my first man," came the swift answer. To be of use to people, to see them redeemed from misery and sin, to know in one's own experience the truth which Clement of Alexandria spoke long centuries ago, "At all times God, the lover of men, clothes himself with man to the attainment of the salvation of men," is one of the most penetrating and abiding joys of life. General Booth in the slums of London, through long weeks of eager, unrelenting pursuit, sought the reclamation of one wayward man. At last the sustained, compassionate friendship of the General wore through the man's obstinate resistance. "Kindness and love!" the wretched fellow cried as he broke down, "kindness and love! Then there is a God!" Can ordinary plummets fathom the depth of satisfaction that lies in such an experience of saviorhood? But the self-centered man has denied himself all that.

He has denied himself as well the enlarging and enriching experience which belongs to the *cooperative fellowships of men.* The worth of life lies not where we self-centeredly cry *My* but where we loyally cry *Our.* Our family, our friends, our church, our college, our country—in such centers of self-effacing and self-expanding loyalty life finds its satisfaction. One man alone is no man at all. Robinson Crusoe is a poor segment of a man, segregated from his human fellowships, and only when braided back into the common loyalties and patriotisms that make life fruitful can he be himself again. But the self-centered man has denied himself all that. He lives in spiritual isolation, with walls about him more impassable than the seas that surrounded Crusoe's island. He is a human derelict. His soul has been marooned.

The self-centered man has denied himself also the exhilaration of believing in and working for *the consummation of all human hopes, the Kingdom of God upon earth.* In troubled hours the progress of mankind indeed seems dubious. We pass through a catastrophic war, with high expectations that out of it may come a redeemed earth. But the war over-passed, we fall into more baffling problems still, bewildering to our hopes. So in the seventeenth century the central part of London burned down. Terrific suffering was involved, but one thought buoyed up the spirits of the people. They saw that the disaster might contribute to a lasting benefit. They would rebuild a new and better London. Sir Christopher Wren drew up the plan. St. Paul's Cathedral was to be its center. The city officials sanctioned the enterprise; the citizens were eager to achieve it. When they faced the practical details, however, so many folk insisted that as for them their houses must be placed exactly where they were before, that in the end a new and better London was not built. They reared the city once again upon its old foundations. So after the war are we rebuilding the old world upon old bases, and disillusionment is rampant everywhere. Human life seems like a brook, that cascading down the mountain, grows weary of the rapids and waterfalls and eagerly anticipates the quiet pool at the cataract's bottom. But come now to the pool, so long anticipated, it stays there not an instant, but is straightway shot out again into new rapids and waterfalls more tumultuous by far, it may be, than those just left behind. So have we passed from war, through the days of armistice, into the problems of peace.

Now the self-centered man looks on all this with cynical eyes. It well accords with his philosophy. As one who in the midst of conflagration thinks first of loot which he may seize, so the self-centered man in this mad and scrambling world gets what he can for himself while getting is possible. He sees no vision of man's circuitous rise to possibilities of finer life. No hope of a better day emerging even from the chaos of a world in ferment stirs his heart. No voice cries in his ear the words of Jeremiah to his nephew centuries ago in another catastrophic time, "Seekest thou great things for thyself? Seek them not" (Jer. 45:5). No faith that by God's grace and man's endeavor this earth can be made the home of human society more fair and fruitful than we have yet dared to dream, allures his loyalty. He cares nothing for the world and has no hopes for it. He is a profiteer on other men's disasters. He is a slacker from man's most ennobling

war against the inner sins and outer circumstances that cripple
human life—

> "Unconcerned,
> Tranquil almost, and careless as a flower
> Glassed in a greenhouse, or a parlour shrub
> That spreads its leaves in unmolested peace,
> While every bush and tree the country through
> Is shaking to the roots."

Last of all, the self-centered man has denied himself all *fellowship
with God*. For selfishness is a *cul-de-sac*, and no man ever yet broke
through it into the Divine Presence. There is no thoroughfare to the
love of God except through the love of man. The stories of all true
saints are illustrations of this truth. The warm and vital religious life
of Whittier has voiced itself in poems which, read as meditations or
sung as hymns, are familiar expressions of Christian piety. Many
think of him as achieving his spirituality by the wise use of solitude
alone. He is to us a mystic, a quietist. But even Whittier's central
fight was against selfishness. "I am haunted," he said, "by an immedicable ambition—perhaps a very foolish desire of distinction, of
applause, of fame, of what the world calls immortality." Even Whittier's victory came when he unselfishly threw himself into the campaign for the abolition of slavery. That crusade was the most forlorn
of all unpopular causes when he espoused it. So far from living a
quiet life he was for years a busy agitator; he lost many of his
friends; he was bitterly maligned; once in Philadelphia he was forced
in disguise to flee the assaulting mob.

> "We may not climb the heav'nly steeps
> To bring the Lord Christ down;
> In vain we search the lowest deeps
> For Him no depths can drown. . . .
>
> "But warm, sweet, tender even yet
> A present help is he;
> And faith has still its Olivet
> And love its Galilee."

How winsome and profound his fellowship with God was! But one
of the deep secrets of it he himself revealed, when in his old age he

said to a young man: "My lad, if thou wouldst win success, join thyself to some unpopular but noble cause!"

So Moses began with indignant pity for the suffering Israelites in
Egypt and ended beside the burning bush in fellowship with the
Eternal. So Elijah began with righteous wrath against the tyranny
of Ahab and ended on the mountain's side alone, listening to a "still
small voice." So Dante began with a great passion for a united Italy
and ended with Beatrice standing before the Great White Throne.
So many a humble servant of his fellows has found that God is love,
and that where love is there God is also.

No self-denial in a self-centered life! A self-centered man surrenders the spiritual insight which can perceive life's worth and beauty
and the spirit of friendliness which alone can make friendship possible; he loses the thrill of saving men, the joys of cooperative fellowship, the ennobling influence of a conscious share in the coming
Kingdom of Righteousness upon the earth; he surrenders the possibility of fellowship with God. In a word, he denies himself everything that makes life significant.

> "The wretch concentered all in self
> Living shall forfeit fair renown,
> And, doubly dying, shall go down
> To the vile dust from whence he sprung,
> Unwept, unhonoured, and unsung."

v

From such a miserable life all men of depth and insight instinctively have shrunk. As one traces to its source the difference between
the self-centered men and these generous servants of mankind, he is
led back to the inner chambers of the heart where dwell our dominant desires. The secret of a selfish man is that all his masterful,
controlling wants concern himself. Nothing seems so desirable to
him as that he himself should be safe and fortunate. The secret of a
useful man is that his heart is set on the happiness of his family, the
welfare of his friends, the progress of good causes in the world, the
redemption of the victims of want and sin, the coming of the
brotherhood of man. His thoughts, affections, ambitions, and desires
are centered outside his narrow self. And because he so wants in
serious earnest to see these great ends gained, he willingly will pay

the price. Such men never count their wounds or call their labors self-denial. To give up their work—that would be the renunciation of their real selves. So Sir Wilfred Grenfell, loving the fisher folk of Labrador, remarks that he dislikes to speak of self-sacrifice, for he cannot recall that he ever has indulged in it. So Livingstone, passionately desiring the salvation of Africa, could write: "People talk of the sacrifice I have made in spending so much of my life in Africa. . . . It is emphatically no sacrifice. Say rather it is a privilege." So is it written of the Master: "Who for the joy that was set before him endured the cross, despising shame" (Heb. 12:2).

CHAPTER VI

Justice

DAILY READINGS

We are to accept this week the challenge of those who appeal from self-denying love to justice, as a more possible and practical ideal of conduct. They are suspicious of so lofty a standard as self-sacrificing service for all sorts of folk, but they are willing to be *just* to everybody. Let us see in our daily readings some very searching principles which are involved in justice, however much one may endeavor to reduce it to simple terms.

Sixth Week, First Day

And as ye would that men should do to you, do ye also to them likewise.—Luke 6:31.

But the Pharisees, when they heard that he had put the Sadducees to silence, gathered themselves together. And one of them, a lawyer, asked him a question, trying him: Teacher, which is the great commandment in the law? And he said unto him, Thou shalt love the Lord thy God with all thy heart, and with all thy soul, and with all thy mind. This is the great and first commandment. And a second like unto it is this, Thou shalt love thy neighbor as thyself. On these two commandments the whole law hangeth, and the prophets.—Matt. 22:34-40.

Here stand Jesus' two summaries of justice: to do as one would be done by, and to love others as one loves one's self. In a word, simple justice involves the treatment of another's personality as, equally with one's own, an object of respect and consideration. A just man, therefore, must *refuse to claim for himself what he is unwilling to grant to others.* That is no easy principle of conduct, on so much lower a plane than Christian love that with relief a man can fall back upon it. Picture children in a home being thus perfectly fair with one another; imagine men in business always treating others as though they themselves were in the others' places; conceive nations never claiming for themselves what they would be unwilling to grant to others; and how marvelously changed would be our home life, business life, and international relationships! If we mean by love affectionate good will, it is often far easier to feel that for individual people who come in contact with us closely enough to claim it, than it is to be scrupulously and impersonally just to people whom we do not know. "Because," says Professor George Herbert Palmer, "justice seeks to benefit all, but all alike. It knows no persons, or rather it knows everyone as a person and insures each his share in the common good. All the altruism of love is here, but without love's arbitrary selection and limited interest. . . . In this extended and superpersonal love altruism attains its fullest and steadiest expression."

O Almighty God, who hast entrusted this earth unto the children of men, and through Thy Son Jesus Christ callest us unto a heavenly citizenship; grant us, we humbly beseech Thee, such shame and repentance for the disorder and injustice and cruelty that is in our midst, that fleeing unto Thee for pardon and for grace we may henceforth set ourselves to establish that city which has justice for its foundation and love for its law, whereof Thou art the Architect and Maker; through the same Jesus Christ, Thy Son, our Saviour.— "Prayers for the City of God."

Sixth Week, Second Day

And the scribes and the Pharisees bring a woman taken in adultery; and having set her in the midst, they say unto him, Teacher, this woman hath been taken in adultery, in the very act. Now in the law Moses commanded us to stone such: what then sayest thou of her? And this they said, trying him, that they might have whereof to accuse him. But Jesus stooped down, and with his finger wrote on the ground. But when they continued asking him, he lifted up himself, and said unto them, He that is without sin among you, let him first cast a stone at her. And again he stooped down, and with his finger wrote on the ground. And they, when they heard it, went out one by one, beginning from the eldest, even unto the last: and Jesus was left alone, and the woman, where she was, in the midst. And Jesus lifted up himself, and said unto her, Woman, where are they? did no man condemn thee? And she said, No man, Lord. And Jesus said, Neither do I condemn thee: go thy way; from henceforth sin no more.—John 8:3-11.

This narrative is often used as an exhibition of the Master's superlative charity. But what is it in the woman's accusers that arouses his indignation? They are not *just*. They are visiting on another judgment which they are unwilling to have visited on themselves. They are neglecting the basic principle, not only of mercy but of law: "He who cometh into court must have clean hands." It is perfectly clear that if they had put themselves in the woman's place before they judged her case, they would have had some contribution to make beside flinging stones. *To be just in our judgments of others, weighing fairly the circumstances which explain their conduct, letting no gusty excess of resentment distort our estimate, and willing that with what measure we mete it should be measured to us again* —what a searching requirement is that! Yet that is simple fairness. "Judge not that ye be not judged. For with what judgment ye judge ye shall be judged" (Matt. 7:1, 2).

O God, we pray that Thou wilt bless the outcast, the poor, the ignorant, the wanderers—those that do not know better than to live in hatreds, in strifes, in every evil passion. Grant that we may not turn inhumanly away from them, as if they were not of us; as if they did not belong to our households; as if they were not men like ourselves; as if they were not parts of the great family to which we belong. Grant that those who go forth especially to seek them, to preach to them, to relieve them, and to succor them, may themselves be filled with the Spirit of the Master. May none turn back from well doing because they find among the poor and needy ingratitude, intractableness, indocility, and all manner of evil requitings. May they, too, bear men's sins and carry their sorrows, as Christ bore our sins and carried our sorrows. And so may they learn to follow Christ through good report, and through evil report, and exalt the concep-

tion of a Christian manhood in the eyes of men. Amen.—Henry Ward Beecher.

Sixth Week, Third Day

Ye have heard that it was said to them of old time, Thou shalt not kill; and whosoever shall kill shall be in danger of the judgment: but I say unto you, that every one who is angry with his brother shall be in danger of the judgment; and whosoever shall say to his brother, Raca, shall be in danger of the council; and whosoever shall say, Thou fool, shall be in danger of the hell of fire.—Matt. 5:21, 22.

Justice, in Jesus' eyes, involves abstinence not only from deliberately unfair judgment but from all *hasty, contemptuous treatment of our fellows.* Who can measure the harm done daily in the world by spoken scorn? How it withers the fine spirit of men, and rouses rancor and bitterness! It discourages hope, blights confidence, breaks friendship, and leaves everywhere a trail of disheartened, resentful lives. The Psalmist is right: to walk in the counsel of the ungodly is bad enough, to stand in the way of sinners is worse still, but to sit in the seat of the scornful is worst of all. No good thing is safe from an unjust tongue. Even King Arthur's Round Table goes to pieces before Vivien's contemptuous speech. She

> "let her tongue
> Rage like a fire among the noblest names,
> Polluting, and imputing her whole self,
> Defaming and defacing, till she left
> Not even Launcelot brave, nor Galahad clean."

To be just in speech, never saying of another what we would resent if said about ourselves, to love our neighbor's reputation with our tongue as much as we love our own—is that an easy standard to attain?

If from all Thy good gifts, O Lord, I may ask but one, let that one be the spirit of kindness!

Let others have fame and fortune and jewels and palaces, if I may but have the kindly spirit! Give greatness and power to those that want them, but give to me Brotherly Kindness! Make somebody else to be comely of visage, if only I may wear a kindly countenance.

May I never wound the heart of any faltering child of Thine! Make me to do the little unremembered acts that quietly help without intending it. Grant me to bear about the unconscious radiance of a life that knows no grudge, but loves all men because they are children of my Father Who loved them enough to send His Son to save them. Amen.—George A. Miller.

Sixth Week, Fourth Day

And Jesus entered into the temple of God, and cast out all them that sold and bought in the temple, and overthrew the tables of the money-changers, and the seats of them that sold the doves; and he saith unto them, It is written, My house shall be called a house of prayer: but ye make it a den of robbers.—Matt. 21:12, 13.

Jerusalem was ordinarily a city of about 50,000 inhabitants. But at the time of the great feasts, pilgrims to the number of 1,000,000 sometimes thronged the city. What an opportunity for loot! To victimize these pious pilgrims, to squeeze them dry of their money by ingenious profiteering schemes, became a lucrative means of livelihood. Here the Master faces this system of exploitation, overflowing into the temple courts. He resents it, as he always resented the victimizing of people for private gain. Now, in any case of such exploitation, the man who is making gain at another's expense is not doing what he would like to have done to himself. He is not just. For justice rules out *taking unfair advantage of another's position,* trading on another's weakness, ignorance, or necessity, making gain for oneself by making a victim of another man. Is that an easy principle to live by? Upon the contrary, many a man will find it far simpler to practice self-denying love in home and neighborhood for a year, than to practice such ordinary justice for a single day in business.

Dig out of us, O Lord, the venomous roots of covetousness; or else so repress them with Thy grace, that we may be contented with Thy provision of necessaries, and not to labour, as we do, with all toil, sleight, guile, wrong, and oppression, to pamper ourselves with vain superfluities. Give us grace continually to read, hear, and meditate Thy purposes, judgments, promises, and precepts, not to the end we may curiously argue thereof, or arrogantly presume thereupon, but

to frame our lives according to Thy will. Amen.—Archbishop E.
Grindal (1519-1583).

Sixth Week, Fifth Day

And he called to him a little child, and set him in the midst of
them, and said, Verily I say unto you, Except ye turn, and become
as little children, ye shall in no wise enter into the kingdom of
heaven. Whosoever therefore shall humble himself as this little
child, the same is the greatest in the kingdom of heaven. And whoso
shall receive one such little child in my name receiveth me: but
whoso shall cause one of these little ones that believe on me to
stumble, it is profitable for him that a great millstone should be
hanged about his neck, and that he should be sunk in the depth
of the sea.—Matt. 18:2-6.

The Master so often and so rightly is regarded as the exemplar of
sacrificial love, that it is well to remind ourselves, as we are doing
this week, how much of his teaching is an appeal for justice. To
wrong children, to refuse them a fair chance to become all that they
have it in them to be, to make them stumble, and above all to use
up their slender strength for our selfish benefit is not first of all lack
of charity; it is outrageous injustice, against which the Master's
spirit flames in anger. No one would wish his own childhood to have
been so treated. "Some think we shall be born again on this earth
under conditions such as we have deserved," writes Professor
Rauschenbusch. "It would certainly be a righteous judgment of God
if he placed us amid the conditions we have created and allowed us
to test in our own body the after-effects of our life. How would a
man feel if he knew that the little daughter that died in his arms
twelve years ago was born as the child of one of his mill hands and
is spinning his cotton at this moment?" Is not that a plain, straightforward application of the Golden Rule? Evidently the appeal from
love to justice is not an easy one to live up to.

*O Thou great Father of the weak, lay Thy hand tenderly on all
the little children on earth and bless them. Be good to all children
who long in vain for human love, or for flowers and water, and the
sweet breast of Nature. But bless with a sevenfold blessing the young
lives whose slender shoulders are already bowed beneath the yoke of
toil, and whose glad growth is being stunted forever. Suffer not their*

little bodies to be utterly sapped, and their minds to be given over to stupidity and the vices of an empty soul. We have all jointly deserved the millstone of Thy wrath for making these little ones to stumble and fall. Grant all employers of labor stout hearts to refuse enrichment at such a price. Grant to all the citizens and officers of states which now permit this wrong the grace of holy anger. Help us to realize that every child of our nation is in very truth our child, a member of our great family. By the Holy Child that nestled in Mary's bosom; by the memories of our own childhood joys and sorrows; by the sacred possibilities that slumber in every child, we beseech Thee to save us from killing the sweetness of young life by the greed of gain.—Walter Rauschenbusch.

Sixth Week, Sixth Day

See that ye despise not one of these little ones: for I say unto you, that in heaven their angels do always behold the face of my Father who is in heaven. How think ye? if any man have a hundred sheep, and one of them be gone astray, doth he not leave the ninety and nine, and go unto the mountains, and seek that which goeth astray? And if so be that he find it, verily I say unto you, he rejoiceth over it more than over the ninety and nine which have not gone astray. Even so it is not the will of your Father who is in heaven, that one of these little ones should perish.—Matt. 18:10-14.

Here is a characteristic expression of the Master's outreaching mercy toward the weak, the strayed, the lost. Surely such an attitude of positive saviorhood involves more than justice. Yet when one takes the Golden Rule seriously, and asks himself what he would wish done, were he in the place of the victim, will he not run straight into the necessity of outgoing love? A man lost in the Welsh mountains in a heavy fog gave himself up to the prospect of a miserable night; when suddenly, as though at his very elbow, he heard a voice: "I wonder if he could have come this way." He was being searched for! The consciousness that some one was looking for him and that therefore he could be found thrilled through him. In any such situation, would not we wish so to be cared about and sought? Then what does the Golden Rule mean, if not that *positive saviorhood is also the demand of justice?* After all, justice and love run very close together. "We can be just only to those we love."

We beseech of Thee, O Lord our God, that Thou wilt have com-
passion upon all those for whom we should pray; those that are
thralled; those that are ensnared; those that have fallen into the pit;
those that are in great darkness and trouble and gloom and despond-
ency; those who are sick; those whose prosperity has been overturned
as by the wind from the desert; those who are strangers in a strange
land; those who are filled with bitterness and self-condemnation;
those that taste remorse; those that are neglected and outcast; those
who are in prison, and who are appointed unto death; all that are
wandering in poverty and abandonment; all that are steeped in ig-
norance, in vice, and in crime.

O good Lord, what dost Thou do? Is this world dear to Thee?
Dost Thou love man? Our souls shake within us, and we are full of
anguish when we look upon the face of man, and see how men
betray; how men hate and devour; how full of wretchedness and sin
the world is, that goes on repeating itself from generation to genera-
tion; how the voice of time is a wail; how all things are most sad
to behold. And dost Thou sit looking forevermore upon these things?
O Lord, reveal the right hand of Thy power. Come; for this desolate
earth doth wait for Thy coming, more than for the coming of sum-
mer. Amen.—Henry Ward Beecher.

Sixth Week, Seventh Day

Ye have heard that it was said, Thou shalt love thy neighbor, and
hate thine enemy: but I say unto you, Love your enemies, and pray
for them that persecute you; that ye may be sons of your Father who
is in heaven: for he maketh his sun to rise on the evil and the good,
and sendeth rain on the just and the unjust.—Matt. 5:43-45.

One would suppose that loving one's enemies and doing them
good were practices which clearly overpassed justice. Yet the Master
here distinctly appeals for them on the basis of that fine impartiality
which we ourselves have profited by and which is of the very essence
of a just and equitable life. Consider the impartial service which a
lighthouse keeper renders to all the wayfarers of the sea! Good men
and bad men pass in the night-going ships, but he shines on all. If his
worst enemy were passing and he knew it, he would not dim his
light. He is magnanimous. He allows no personal petulance, no
selfish pique, to interfere with his steady beneficence. *Such an im-*

partial spirit, unswayed by individual resentment, is of the very sub-stance of justice.

Justice does not include all that love does. Love goes deeper, is more intense, will sacrifice more, and carries in its heart a personal self-bestowal which justice alone does not know. But if the Golden Rule is its summary, justice is something far beyond the infliction of appropriate penalties. When a man does as he would be done by, he judges fairly, speaks kindly, refuses to exploit personality for private gain, protects the weak, rescues the fallen, and treats even his enemies as though they might some day become his friends.

O God, who has taught us in Thy holy Word that we must always do to others as we would they should do to us: give me grace to cleanse my heart and hands from all falsehood and wrong, that I may hurt nobody by word or deed, but be true and just in all my dealings and do my duty in that state of life into which it shall please Thee to call me, that so keeping innocency and taking heed to the thing that is right, I may obtain peace at the last for the sake of Jesus Christ, Thy Son, our Lord. Amen.—"A Book of Prayers for Students."

COMMENT FOR THE WEEK

I

Self-denying service, such as we have been considering, so far from being difficult and unnatural, is in some of our relationships happily spontaneous. For there are people whom we love with eager, self-forgetful affection. To argue with us that we should serve them is absurd. A true mother does not need argument that she should care for her child, nor a true lover that he should give himself in loyal service to the girl whom he adores. Nature herself plays upon our instincts to secure such self-bestowals as we lavishly pour out in family love and intimate friendship. Without the privilege of giving vent to love in ministry, we should be utterly bereft; the acutest agony we can imagine would be the stoppage of our power to help those whose hearts are ours.

Outside this inner area of intimate friendships, however, there are wide stretches of human relations where such tenderness of affection does not apply. Whatever may be the ideal, the fact is evident: there

are vulgar people from whom we shrink, bestial people who are re-
pellent to us, unfriendly people whose unkindness we resent. There
are racial boundaries across which affectionate relationships do not
easily pass; cultural boundaries where, in spite of ourselves, our
theoretical brotherhood encounters practical difficulties. Moreover,
there are criminally minded people, cruel and conscienceless, whose
depredations on society must be hated and withstood. In a word,
there are multitudes of people whom we do not like. To be told to
love them seems a counsel of perfection, not to be taken seriously in
daily life.

One attitude toward them, however, we all agree is both possible
and right. We can be just. So at a football game one cannot easily
imagine the coaches urging the opposing players to love one another.
But one can easily imagine the coaches saying: Young men, you will
play this game fairly; you will take for yourselves no advantage that
you would deny to others; you will be just.

It is of the first importance, therefore, that we should see what is
involved in the idea of justice. As there are masterpieces of literature, like Milton's "Paradise Lost," which all agree to praise, but
which few read, so there are virtues which all applaud but few
examine. Justice is one of them. Men may differ about loving everyone, but they agree concerning the duty of being just to everyone.
Yet the unappreciated depth and height and breadth of this applauded virtue is at once suggested by the fact that its most succinct,
complete description is the Golden Rule. Consider what large matters are involved in that!

The keeping of the Golden Rule is quite impossible without the
use of *generous and sympathetic imagination*. No man can do to
another what he wishes another to do to him, unless he has the
gracious power to put himself in another's place. Two boys in the
depth of New York City were overheard in controversy: "I can
write"; "I can, too"; "You can't"; "I can"; "Prove it." And the
challenged lad took from his pocket a piece of chalk and scribbled
on a brick wall the words "Keep off the grass." Can you who were
brought up where grass was green and plentiful, and all the country-
side was open to your wandering feet, put yourself into that boy's
place? Yet if you *were* that boy, who could handle fairly the delicate
scales of judgment save one who could see your problem from
within?

A critic has said of Robert Browning that he was born with a

passion for living in other people's experiences—"Rabbi ben Ezra,"
"Fra Lippo Lippi," "Andrea del Sarto," "Bishop Blougram," the
characters in "The Ring and the Book," and a host of others. He saw
their points of view, he thought their thoughts, he said the things
they had to say. What the master of verse did for art's sake, the
Master of spiritual life did for the sake of service. He saw by sympathy the prodigal's problem from within, when all the Pharisees
around were condemning him as lost. He saw from within the meaning of the widow's slender gift and the passionate outpouring of
Mary's gratitude in costly oil. He saw from within the way life
looked to Zacchæus and from within he knew the secret sifting of
Peter's soul by Satan. The woman taken in adultery, with the crowd
of angry men around, their robes girt up, and stones in hand to slay
her—even her problem he saw from within, and perceived in her
what no one looking from without could possibly have guessed.
Whoever kept to the full the Golden Rule except the Master? It is
not easy to keep. No one is just who does not put himself in the place
of those with whom he deals. And to do that one must see men as he
does stained glass in a cathedral window, not from without in, but
from within out.

John Wesley tells us of a man against whom year after year his
choler rose. He thought of him contemptuously as covetous. One day
when he gave to one of Wesley's favorite philanthropies a gift that
seemed too small, Wesley's indignation burst all bounds, and he
raked him fore and aft with scathing condemnation. Wesley tells us
in his diary that the man quietly said: "I know a man who at the
week's beginning goes to the market and buys a penny's worth of
parsnips and takes them home to boil in water, and all that week he
has the parsnips for his meat and the water for his drink; and meat
and drink alike cost him a penny a week." "Who is the man?" said
Wesley. "I am," was the reply. And Wesley adds, "This he constantly
did, although he then had two hundred pounds a year, that he might
pay the debts he had contracted before he knew God. And this was
the man that I had thought to be covetous." We cannot be just to
anyone whom we do not understand. If, then, we agree that across
all boundaries of personal dislike and racial difference we should be
just, we set for ourselves a task that will take all the insight and
generosity we have.

II

Moreover, to do to others what we wish them to do to us involves not only sympathy, but *active good will*. Who of us has not been served with constant, sacrificial care, by family and friends; and lacking such attendant ministry would not have slipped and fallen on ruin, moral and practical, a hundred times? So Wendell Phillips might magnificently sway his hostile audiences, and seem the very incarnation of audacity, but those who know perceive behind him his wife, invalid in everything but spirit, who used to lay her hand upon his shoulder with a parting charge: "Wendell, don't you shilly-shally!" So George Matheson may claim the homage of the world for his brave victory over blindness, but those who know perceive the truth of his biographer's comment: "The chief factor, undoubtedly, in his harmonious, successful, and marvelously fruitful life, was his sister, Miss Matheson." To do for others what we desire to have done for us is not a negative ideal. Too often justice is pictured in terms of abstinence from rank injustice. Not to be cruel, not to oppress the poor or to crush the faces of the needy, that is to be just. But the Golden Rule cannot so negatively be kept. Justice is positive. It means the painstaking bestowal upon other lives of the same sort of constant, sacrificial ministry by which we ourselves have lived and without which we could not really live at all.

Consider so elemental a relationship as that between a father and his son. All that is best in the father's life came from the impact of friendly persons. Like a lake with two outlets far up in the Rockies, where a passing breeze sends the water to the east until it finds the Mississippi and the Gulf, or to the west until it flows to the Pacific, so was that father's life in boyhood. He might have flowed down either slope, and if he did flow aright, it was because some strong, radiant spirits blew persuasively upon him. The justice of a father to his son, therefore, is no negative refraining from ill treatment. It is a positive outpouring on the boy's life of that companionship, which, were he a boy again, the father would crave for himself. If, remembering what it costs a boy to grow up right amid the terrific lure of sin, the father had to live his youth again, he would wish *his* father to take time to know him very well; for all the pressure of busy days to lay his life close alongside in fraternal comradeship; to be, when one desires not talk but help, a constant and unfailing friend; above all, to lift up a Christian character so winsome, strong, convincing, that in the fiercest storms that beat on life, the thought of it would hold as an anchor holds a ship.

Now justice does not cease making this demand for active good will when one moves out from the inner realm of affectionate relationships into the wider areas where personal affection does not instinctively extend. When in imagination anyone puts himself in the place of the disinherited, the forsaken, the outcast, however unlovely and degraded they may be, he at once is crying for help. Father Damien goes out to the lepers because he knows that if he were a leper he would not wish to be left in hapless, unbefriended isolation, unrelieved by any touch of human kindliness. Florence Nightingale goes out to the Crimea because she knows that if she were a wounded soldier brought in from the battlefield, she would not want to toss in pain unnursed by a woman's gentleness. Pioneers blaze the trail of medical missions, because they know that if means of healing were anywhere available, they would not wish to lie in needless pain or see their loved ones die in agony amid the rattle of witch doctors' drums. If once the Golden Rule were seriously taken, if men in earnest put themselves in the place of all oppressed, benighted folk, unbefriended, and cheated of their share in civilization's gains, and if in earnest they set themselves to do for them what they themselves in similar case would need, there would come a world-wide transformation of social life.

The far-flung meanings of the Golden Rule are evident, when a man puts himself in the place of young men and women who have gone to the ends of the earth for Christian service. As during the War the most alert and venturesome spirits sought France, desiring the post of danger at the front, so many daring Christian spirits among our youth turn their faces toward the foreign field. If he were one of them, above all else a man would desire that the Christian people at home should support his work with instruments of service to make his toil effective. He offers up the most precious thing a man can give—his life. He passionately craves that his investment of life shall be effective. To do lamely what could be done well with decent instruments—that is desolating. To stand in a great city where the sick and dying gather about him, like the sick round Jesus in the streets of old Capernaum, to have for investment in that great need the best medical education that modern science can bestow, and yet to have no adequate hospital, few nurses, no associates, to be compelled to do feebly what could be done magnificently—that is crushing. When a man sees missions and philanthropy not in abstract terms but interpreted in concrete personalities, and imagines himself to be one of them, he sees how wide is the scope and how searching the requirement of justice in realms where affection does not apply.

Justice says: You are a white man. Then put yourself in the place of the Negro, whose father was freed when he was a youth, and whose great-great-great-grandfather was brought over against his will on a slave ship from Africa, and see from the inside, how the problem of that man's life must appear to him. You are an American. Put yourself in the place of Britain, and France, and Italy, and Japan, and China, and those who but lately were our enemies, to see how this tangled world's problem must appear to them! You are a laboring man. Put yourself in the place of the employer, and see from his angle the perplexing problem of our economic life. You are an employer. Then put yourself in the place of the laboring man, to see how his life must appear to him. Justice is not less exciting than emotional affection, but more. It applies in realms where affection does not move. It holds a man to understanding sympathy and generous good will toward people whom instinctively he may dislike. At last it leads him to attack the organized injustice of our social and economic order, not because he himself is hurt, but because others are oppressed, in whose place he has imagined himself to be.

III

This extension of the Golden Rule into areas of human relationship where our affections do not easily go meets its greatest difficulty when it deals with *positively unfriendly folk*. Sympathy and good will may justly be expended upon some people beyond the borders of our emotional tenderness, but can it be just to give one's self in generous ministry to enemies? Is not justice comprehended in the old law of Leviticus (24:20) "Breach for breach, eye for eye, tooth for tooth; as he hath caused a blemish in a man, so shall it be rendered unto him"? Such strict retribution appears just, but the Master's command to love our enemies and do them good seems far to overpass the limits of fair play.

Yet the fact is that the Sermon on the Mount is not the denial but the fulfilment of the Levitical law. In an age of barbarous morals, when none disputed the right of vengeance, this old law was set up

to restrain the extravagant wrath of angry men. Its message is not:
you may return to a man whatever harm he has done to you. Its
message is rather: you may not return to a man *more* harm than he
has done to you. Eye for an eye, tooth for a tooth—so much revenge
you may take, if you must; no more.

What youth has not known hours when he was goaded to ungovernable rage? He lost his hold upon the throttle of his temper.
He assailed his enemy with a mad desire to satisfy the anger he could
not control. All calculations of exact retribution were forgotten.
There was no nice estimate of proposed damage to the foe. Ability
was the limit of purpose. Consider in such a case the restraint imposed by the old law: exact retaliation, no more! The commandment in Leviticus was intended to set limits to the vindictiveness of
angry men. The river of vengeance might flow on; the time had not
yet come utterly to dry its springs; but the stream had banks. When
therefore the Master *annulled* what Leviticus had *limited,* he was
not destroying the law but was fulfilling it; he was carrying an ethical
reform to its logical conclusion.

That this logical conclusion to the old law of retaliation is indispensable ought to be evident to even ordinary moral insight. For one
thing, the principle of tit for tat *makes too small business for a real
life to be preoccupied about.* Even in legal procedure the rule of an
eye for an eye issues in absurdity. In the code of Henry I, one finds
this law: if a boy standing under a tree is killed by another boy who
falls upon him out of the tree, then the boy who fell and did the
killing must in his turn stand under a tree and let another boy fall
on him until he dies. The ridiculous pettiness of such a legal principle is obvious; yet to that pass is anyone led who takes seriously
the law of retaliation. To go through life slapping back each time
one is slapped, is the cheapest form of wasting life.

After Appomattox, when Robert E. Lee was President of Washington College, a professor derided Grant harshly in his presence. In
swift indignation Lee thundered: "Sir, if ever I hear you speak again
in my presence disrespectfully of General Grant, either you or I will
sever his connection with this institution." A man in earnest about
serious tasks has no time for vindictiveness. The Master, with the
salvation of the world upon his heart, praying "Thy Kingdom come"
with passionate desire, could not be expected to content himself with
the narrow vengefulness of the Levitical law. Retaliation is a rule
of little men; retaliation makes little men. Large spirits always are

magnanimous. They even "love their enemies and do them good."

Moreover, the law of an eye for an eye is inadequate because *it makes no provision for the betterment of evil men*. Even the stern business of criminal law is discovering this. As late as 1833, in England, we are informed that, "Sentence of death was passed on a child of nine who poked a stick through a pane of glass in a shop front and stole some pieces of paint worth two-pence. This was housebreaking and the penalty of housebreaking was death." Even though after delay that sentence was commuted, it illustrates the appalling course of legal cruelty in Christendom. And if little by little the torture chamber, the racks and thumbscrews, the public pillories and whipping posts, the barbarous executions on wayside gibbets, the loathsome dungeons, are vanishing like nightmares when the sun rises, and prisons increasingly are reformatory in their aim, it is not mawkish sentiment that motives the change, but the sound sense of the Master. Retaliation gets nowhere. It is not only barbarous but it is stupid. Think of going out to save manhood with this device upon our banners, "Tit for tat," and with this for our slogan, "When you are slapped, slap back!" The only aim worth seeking is better men in a more decent world and the law of an eye for an eye is a futile instrument for such an enterprise.

IV

Not only does retaliation turn out to be too petty for large-minded men and too feeble for serious purposes, but despite the first appearance, *it is not just*. No one of us dares to suggest that he himself be treated on the principle of tit for tat. The parable of Jesus, where a servant, pardoned a debt of twelve million dollars, goes out to choke a fellow-servant who owed him seventeen dollars, cuts deep into the truth about us all. Such churlishness was not fair play. The pardoned debtor was refusing to another the forgiveness which he had himself received. He was taking what he would not give. So are we all pensioners on mercy, human and divine, and long since would have been utterly undone if retaliation without mercy had been given us. With no more sustenance than the principle of tit for tat can furnish, all the most beautiful human relationships would starve and die. From mothers who love before love is appreciated and keep on loving when it is not appreciated, to the world's saints and martyrs, prophets and apostles, who love human weal and serve

it through the gainsaying and persecution of the very men they seek
to help, our lives are all upborne by mercies which we have not deserved and for which we can never pay. And when one lifts his
thought to God's judgment of him, he sees that he would have no
hope if the Great White Throne were marked all over with the
motto, "Tit for tat." Let a man face the mercies he already has
received from family and friends, the unearned benedictions he already has been given, bought by other blood than his and the toil of
other hands, the forgiveness he has needed and will need again from
sources human and divine, and then let him face the Golden Rule!
He will see that the Lord's Prayer is urging him to simple justice:
"Forgive us our trespasses as we forgive them who trespass against
us."

The justice of the Golden Rule involves understanding sympathy,
active good will, and far-flung service. Its kingdom is wider than
the narrow realm where our intimate affections dwell. It takes in
even enemies. Only by such justice does a man contribute to life
what to make living rich and worthy he must take from life. Only so
does he find in himself the answer to an old prayer of the sixteenth
century—a Christian's plea for a just spirit:

"Open our hearts, O Lord, that we may be no less moved at the
needs and griefs of our neighbors than if they were our own. O most
mild and merciful Christ, breathe upon us the spirit of Thy meekness and Thy goodness that, as Thy pitying of us made Thee endure
most bitter death and torment for our sake, so our pitying of our
neighbors may lead us to succor them."

CHAPTER VII

Small Enemies of Usefulness

DAILY READINGS

We have been speaking of the spirit and practice of service as the necessary and beautiful expression of a Christian life. But here as everywhere else, the perversion of the best is the worst. As Bunyan found a passage to hell from under the walls of the celestial city, so are there ways to unlovely uselessness that run out from the very desire and intention to be of use. Let us consider this week some of these perversions of service.

Seventh Week, First Day

For we hear of some that walk among you disorderly, that work not at all, but are busybodies. Now them that are such we command and exhort in the Lord Jesus Christ, that with quietness they work, and eat their own bread.—II Thess. 3:11, 12.

For let none of you suffer as a murderer, or a thief, or an evildoer, or as a meddler in other men's matters: but if a man suffer as a Christian, let him not be ashamed; but let him glorify God in this name.—I Peter 4:15, 16.

One of the commonest caricatures of usefulness is *meddlesomeness*. Intent on helping folk, we become busybodies; we assume responsibility where we are not wanted; we intrude ourselves where we would have helped more by minding our own business; our overweening ambition to do something for somebody makes our very presence a vexation. How many such folk there are! Desiring to be useful, they become presumptuous, officious, and obtrusive. They lack reticence, humility, tact. Their desire to help is commendable, but its effect is spoiled by their own loudness, awkwardness, impertinence. They have generosity, but they lack discrimination. After all, no amount of zeal can make up for the want of modesty and good sense in service. Those who help most are often not those who try hardest, but those who, like a full-laden apple tree, are so rich in their own spiritual fruitage that no one can brush against a branch without bringing down something good to eat. Many a hurried, fuming, pushing, presumptuous worker for the help of others might well pause to consider another type of spirit:

"An incidental greatness charactered
Her unconsidered ways."

Lord, let me be ever courteous and easie to be entreated; never let me fall into a peevish or contentious Spirit, but follow Peace with all Men, offering forgiveness, inviting them by Courtesies, ready to Confess my own Errors, apt to make amends and desirous to be reconcil'd. Let no Sickness or Cross Accident, no Imployment or Weariness make me angry or ungentle, and discontented or unthankful or uneasie. Give me the Spirit of a Christian, Charitable, Humble, Merciful, and Meek, Useful and Liberal, Complying with every Chance, Angry at nothing but my own Sins, and Grieving at the Sins of Others. That while my Passion obeys my Reason, and my Reason is Religious, and my Religion is pure and undefiled, managed with Humility, and adorn'd with Charity, I may dwell in Thy Love, and be Thy Son and Servant for ever, through Jesus Christ our Lord. Amen.—Thomas à Kempis (1379-1471).

Seventh Week, Second Day

If there is therefore any exhortation in Christ, if any consolation of love, if any fellowship of the Spirit, if any tender mercies and compassions, make full my joy, that ye be of the same mind, having the same love, being of one accord, of one mind; doing nothing through faction or through vainglory, but in lowliness of mind each counting other better than himself; not looking each of you to his own things, but each of you also to the things of others.—Phil. 2:1-4.

Paul takes for granted here that the Philippian Christians will practice mutual helpfulness, but he is concerned about the spirit in which their service for each other will be bathed. That they should be modest, whole-hearted, without vainglory or condescending pride, "humbly considering each other the better man," is, in his eyes, essential to Christian usefulness. *For service can be utterly spoiled by the opposite attitude of superciliousness, condescension, lordliness.* Service may be flung to people as coins are flung to beggars. So Moses, about to bestow a blessing, cried: "Hear now, ye rebels; shall we bring you forth water out of this rock?" He was doing a gracious deed, but he was not doing it graciously. A good deal of intended usefulness is spoiled by this "flunkeyism of benevolence." We condescend to people, we stoop when we help, we are secretly puffed up by the superiority which our ability to serve makes evident. We have not, as Paul points out in the succeeding verses, "the mind of Christ."

O my God, enable me to thwart and utterly mortify my cursed vanity and pride, by giving me strength to hide all my good in this sense: not to speak to my nearest of good deeds done, but to do them cheerfully before Thee only, and to have the delight in making others happier and better. Let me please Thee, my Father, for I know Thou art so good as to be pleased with Thy children who by Thy grace are in any degree imbued with Thy goodness! Amen.— Norman Macleod (1812-1872).

Seventh Week, Third Day

And why beholdest thou the mote that is in thy brother's eye, but considerest not the beam that is in thine own eye? Or how wilt thou say to thy brother, Let me cast out the mote out of thine eye; and lo, the beam is in thine own eye? Thou hypocrite, cast out first the beam out of thine own eye; and then shalt thou see clearly to cast out the mote out of thy brother's eye.—Matt. 7:3-5.

The notable fact in this passage is the enthusiasm for service on the part of the man with a beam in his eye. He was zealous to be of use; he was positively officious about it; but the Master did not commend him. Sometimes it is easier to work up zeal for helping another than it is to handle well the problem of one's own life. So Charles Dickens, with clever strokes, drew the portrait of Mrs. Jellyby. To be of use was her ambition. So far from being deliberately selfish, she was resolutely unselfish. But her kind intentions all centered about Borrioboola-Gha in Africa. Her home disordered, her children neglected, her most obvious duties slatternly performed, she lavished her sentimental, long range interest upon a need thousands of miles away. She wished well, but she was useless. The beam in her own eye made negligible her strenuous ministries to the Africans.

O Lord, our heavenly Father, by whose Providence the duties of men are variously ordered, grant to us all such a spirit that we may labour heartily to do our work in our several stations, as serving one Master and looking for one reward. Teach us to put to good account whatever talents Thou hast lent to us, and enable us to redeem our time by patience and zeal; through Jesus Christ Thy Son. Amen. —Bishop Westcott (1825-1901).

Seventh Week, Fourth Day

For I say, through the grace that was given me, to every man that is among you, not to think of himself more highly than he ought to think; but so to think as to think soberly, according as God hath dealt to each man a measure of faith. For even as we have many members in one body, and all the members have not the same office: so we, who are many, are one body in Christ, and severally members one of another.—Rom. 12:3-5.

Bear ye one another's burdens, and so fulfil the law of Christ. For if a man thinketh himself to be something when he is nothing, he deceiveth himself.—Gal. 6:2, 3.

This is a characteristic note in Paul's epistles. In both these passages the apostle is speaking about service, and in each he is anxious lest intended helpfulness should be spoiled by *self-conceit*. Many folk are earnestly desirous to be of use, but they are so self-confident about their own aims and methods, so intolerantly cocksure about social remedies, that they do their cause more harm than good. They lack the grace to see that at least occasionally they may be mistaken. One of the most familiar forms of such self-conceit among us is found in the man or woman, who having lighted upon some notion, likely to be of use to the world, at once erects it into the one panacea for which all the ages have been waiting. He becomes a crank. All other ideas save his seem negligible; all folk who do not appreciate

his notion or assist him in it he marks down for fools; he rides the
hobby of his special cure-all tirelessly. The pathos of the situation
often lies in the man's self-renouncing devotion. But the devotion is
so heavily cumbered with conceit, intolerance, dogmatism, and extravagant claims of unique importance, that a spectator finds it
easier to stomach the original sin of selfishness than such a highly
developed perversion of self-sacrifice.

*O God, who hast promised to hear the prayers of Thy people,
give me, I beseech Thee, the spirit of wisdom and understanding, of
counsel and knowledge: keep me from folly and rashness: when I
am right do Thou confirm me, when I am wrong do Thou correct
me, and so give me, O Thou wisdom of God, a right judgment in all
things, that I be not barren nor unfruitful in the knowledge of Thee
and in the service of my fellowmen. Amen.*—"A Book of Prayers for
Students."

Seventh Week, Fifth Day

**Now when Jesus saw great multitudes about him, he gave com-
mandment to depart unto the other side. And there came a scribe,
and said unto him, Teacher, I will follow thee whithersoever thou
goest. And Jesus saith unto him, The foxes have holes, and the birds
of the heaven have nests; but the Son of man hath not where to lay
his head.—Matt. 8:18-20.**

In spite of the brevity of the record the scene is not difficult to
imagine. The popularity of the Master is at its height, the multitudes
throng about him, association with him is fashionable, and a sentimental scribe is swept off his feet and proposes to join his company.
But Jesus pricks the bubble of his effervescent feeling. He pictures
the reality of hardship and self-denial. Today service has gained
remarkable vogue. It is good form to be engaged in philanthropic
work. People take up organized charity or settlement work or "slum-
ming" as they do golf or bridge. A few such interests are to be expected in a well-furnished life. Philanthropy has become a fad.
Many sentimental folk are emotionally ready, like the scribe, to
follow Jesus in service. But they do not go far. They are caricatures
of his real disciples, and often they bring into contempt the causes
with which they dally. When folk are cruelly in need they are not

thankful for the service of those who make a fashionable game of helping them. One cannot easily imagine any character more likely to receive the scathing rebuke of the Master than the one who tried to make a fad of service to "the least of these," his brethren.

Give us, O Lord, a mind after Thine own heart, that we may delight to do Thy will, O our God; and let Thy Law be written on our hearts. Give us courage and resolution to do our duty, and a heart to be spent in Thy service, and in doing all the good that possibly we can the few remaining days of our pilgrimage here on earth. Grant this, we humbly beseech Thee, for the sake of Jesus Christ Thy Son our Lord. Amen.—John Tillotson (1630-1694).

Seventh Week, Sixth Day

And as these went their way, Jesus began to say unto the multitudes concerning John, What went ye out into the wilderness to behold? a reed shaken with the wind? But what went ye out to see? a man clothed in soft raiment? Behold, they that wear soft raiment are in kings' houses. But wherefore went ye out? to see a prophet? Yea, I say unto you, and much more than a prophet. This is he, of whom it is written,
    Behold, I send my messenger before thy face,
    Who shall prepare thy way before thee.
Verily I say unto you, Among them that are born of women there hath not arisen a greater than John the Baptist: yet he that is but little in the kingdom of heaven is greater than he.—Matt. 11:7-11.

Of all the perversions of service none makes it more distasteful than *sentimental softness.* Some, endeavoring to live by love and to express love in usefulness, succeed only in achieving an oily, obsequious imitation of the splendidly rugged and vigorous ministry of Jesus. For Jesus approved folk like John the Baptist, where the stern, masculine qualities were prominent. He himself could serve by fearless words, audacious deeds, fierce denunciation, and unbending endurance as well as by tenderness. Scientists tell us that if there be health in the body when disease enters, the white corpuscles go out into the blood like warriors to attack the evil. A healthy body has capacity to resent the intrusion of destructive things; it had capacious power to repel invaders and to cast them out; and if any body lacks that protective force it dies. What is true of the body is true of the person. The power of repulsion against evil, of swift and eager indignation against cruelty and hypocrisy, is indispensable to any soul. General Booth said, "Go on hating, night and day, in every place, under all circumstances. Bring this side of your nature well into play." Nor is it easy to see how one can be in any worthy sense a disciple of Jesus, if he has not harnessed his combative faculties to the service of human weal. Of all misadventures in the imitation of Jesus, none can be farther from the mark than a pallid, pulseless, sentimental man.

Grant, O Lord, as Thou hast cast my lot in a fair ground, that I may show forth contentment by rejoicing in the privileges with which Thou hast strewn my path, and by using to the full my opportunities for service.

In hours of hardship, preserve me from self-pity and endow me with the warrior's mind, that even in the heat of battle I may be inspired with the sense of vocation and win the peace of the victor; through Jesus Christ our Lord. Amen.—Bishop Charles H. Brent.

Seventh Week, Seventh Day

Then came to him the mother of the sons of Zebedee with her sons, worshipping him, and asking a certain thing of him. And he said unto her, What wouldest thou? She saith unto him, Command that these my two sons may sit, one on thy right hand, and one on thy left hand, in thy kingdom. But Jesus answered and said, Ye know not what ye ask. Are ye able to drink the cup that I am about to drink? They say unto him, We are able. He saith unto them, My cup indeed ye shall drink: but to sit on my right hand, and on my left hand, is not mine to give; but it is for them for whom it hath been prepared of my Father. And when the ten heard it, they were moved with indignation concerning the two brethren. But Jesus called them unto him, and said, Ye know that the rulers of the Gentiles lord it over them, and their great ones exercise authority over them. Not so shall it be among you: but whosoever would become great among you shall be your minister; and whosoever would be first among you shall be your servant: even as the Son of man came not to be ministered unto, but to minister, and to give his life a ransom for many.—Matt. 20:20-28.

To seek notoriety and prominence even in the circle of Jesus' disciples, is a common perversion of service. We give ourselves to a sacrificial life, as James and John did, but we twist the meaning of our very sacrifice until we are thinking of the gains in fame and popularity and power which may accrue to us. How few St. Francis Xaviers there are, of whom it can be said that he "would like to reform the world without his own existence being known." Old John Donne put such self-effacement at the summit of spiritual achievement:

> "I have done one braver thing
> Than all the worthies did;
> And yet a braver thence doth spring,
> Which is, to keep that hid."

Such are a few of the familiar perversions of service: we become meddlesome, we condescend, we make officious care for others a substitute for the cleansing of ourselves, we become fanatics, faddists, sentimentalists, or seekers after notoriety. When we cannot be driven from the desire to be useful, we may yet be drawn into some caricature of usefulness.

I have been careless, cowardly, mutinous. Punishment I have deserved, I deny it not; yet have mercy on me for the sake of the truth I long to learn, and of the good which I long to do. Take the will for the deed, good Lord. Accept the partial self-sacrifice which Thou didst inspire, for the sake of the one perfect self-sacrifice which Thou didst fulfil upon the Cross. Pardon my faults, out of Thine own boundless pity for human weakness. Strike not my unworthy name off the roll call of the noble and victorious army, which is the blessed company of all faithful people; and let me, too, be found written in the Book of Life, even though I stand the lowest and last upon its list.—Charles Kingsley.

COMMENT FOR THE WEEK

I

Hitherto we have been thinking of a generously useful life against the background of thoroughgoing selfishness, ungracious and unjust.

While it is true, however, that the blatant enemy of serviceableness is selfishness, it is also true that not often do men deliberately set themselves to live self-centered lives. Selfishness, like any other sin, is not often seen dressed in full uniform and advertising candidly her true designs. Her ways are subtle; she disguises herself in winsome forms; her ample box of tricks supplies many such subterfuges as making proposed service unlovely by tactlessness or twisting an unselfish intention into a useless result.

Some characters, to be sure, have been and doubtless are avowedly and colossally selfish. To their ambition for aggrandizement they have deliberately handed the reins of their lives. They have concluded like Napoleon, "I am not an ordinary man, I am an extraordinary man, and ordinary rules do not apply to me," and in their unabashed self-seeking they have ridden roughshod across all considerations of justice and mercy. But probably such folk are few. Even Napoleon, doubtless deceiving himself as well as others, clothed his insatiable personal ambition in the plausible desire to spread the ideals of French liberty. One must turn to the imagined characters of literature to be sure that he has found utter selfishness, deliberate and unashamed. There, like Milton's Satan, some do indeed say, "Better to reign in hell than serve in heaven."

The uselessness of most of us, however, springs from meaner causes than such deliberate self-inflation. On the slope of Long's Peak in Colorado lies the ruin of a forest giant. The naturalist tells us that the tree had stood for four hundred years; that it was a seedling when Columbus landed on San Salvador; that it had been struck by lightning fourteen times; that the avalanches and storms of four centuries had thundered past it. In the end, however, beetles killed the tree. A giant that age had not withered nor lightnings blasted nor storms subdued fell at last before insects that a man could crush between his forefinger and his thumb. So human characters collapse into futile uselessness not only through "presumptuous sins" but more frequently through "secret faults." And nowhere is this subtle cause of ruined character more obvious than in the destructive work of the small enemies of usefulness.

II

The best intentions to live a serviceable life may evaporate for no other reason than the *habitual substitution of well-wishing for well-*

doing. Superficially to wish people well is a habit easily acquired. In church under the spell of worship, or alone stirred by meditation or by a book, a man can warmly wish well to all humanity. So in an old jingle a captain brought to his crew the map of a shoreless sea:

> "He brought them a map representing the sea,
>   Without the least vestige of land;
> And the crew were all glad when they found it to be
>   A map they could all understand.
> 'What's the use of Mercators, North Pole and equators,
>   Tropics, zones, and meridian lines?'
> So the captain would cry, and the men would reply,
>   'They are only conventional signs.' "

On such a zoneless, shoreless sea of well-wishing how many folk congenially are sailing! Their lives are not storm-tossed with hate nor wrecked by tempests of selfish ambition. Rather the breeze of a mild good will fills their sails, their skies are benignantly blue, and underneath is the gentle heave of kindly feeling. But they never *land*. The sea of their well-wishing has no shore. They arrive nowhere. They mean well but they mean well feebly. To no concrete deed of service, to no practical assumption of responsibility, to no costly and efficient expenditure of time, thought, energy, and money in useful work, do they ever come.

The peculiar peril of such well-wishing lies in the complacent opinion of oneself which it induces. Good intentions and kindly emotions are the most efficient opiates for an uneasy conscience. We hear an address on the need of China or the sufferings of the Armenians and we are deeply stirred. We wish well to all the yellow race, to all oppressed and stricken people everywhere, to Australian bushmen, the hill tribes of the Himalayas, the barbarians of Timbuctoo, to Asia, Africa, and the islands of the sea! In our swelling and inclusive sympathy—and that, too, without the need of stirring from the pew—we may gather up all the sick, afflicted, and despised on earth, feeling in secret that so compassionate a spirit must argue an admirable life. When a rapacious man revels in cruelty, or a truculent man seeks vengeance, or a miser worships mammon, one easily can see that they are wrong. But kindly wishing, such as rises in a man of humane and generous emotions, quiets the accusing conscience and, like a vampire, lulls the victim while it sucks his blood. For well-wishers, while often in appearance the most sensitive, kindly, sympathetic, responsive folk one meets, still deserve the scathing rebuke of James, the Lord's brother: "If a brother or sister be naked and in lack of daily food, and one of you say unto them, Go in peace, be ye warmed and filled; and yet ye give them not the things needful to the body; what doth it profit?" (James 2:15, 16).

There comes a time in certain experiments in chemistry when the fluid in solution awaits the decisive jar of the operator's finger to make it crystallize. So does many a well-intentioned spirit await the resolute act of will which will precipitate his kindly feelings into practical deeds. A large part of true religion is fulfilled when a man takes himself deliberately in hand and walks himself up to tasks undone, concerning which he long has been wishing well. Sign that check; write that letter; pay that call; seek that interview; bear that testimony; accept that office; assume that responsibility—such crisp imperatives are indispensable, if well-wishing is not to prove the ruin of a serviceable life.

III

Another enemy of usefulness whose alluring disguise makes the peril greater is *the substitution of pleasing people for serving them.* One who sets himself to the task can soon become an adept at making himself agreeable. Consider these smooth and plausible folk who like human chameleons crawl across life, taking a new color from every person whom they meet! What infinite adaptability! Vain people enjoy flattery; they purr like kittens when their favorite vanities are stroked; and the specialist in pleasing folk knows how to touch each vain man's favorite nerve, until it tingles with delight. Weak people want pity; they are in a minor mood and they wish all who meet them to wail, like dogs at a sad tune upon a violin; and the adept in agreeableness can wail to the satisfaction of the most self-pitying. Proud folk wish deference; when it shines upon them, they preen their feathers like peacocks in the sunlight; and your specialist in congeniality is positively radiant with deference when proud folk are near. Optimists enjoy the company of hopeful spirits who agree that the world is at the dawning of a great new day; and the adept in giving pleasure can affirm that hope with an enthusiastic assurance that puts new color into the roseate visions of the most optimistic. Pessimists love to see heads shaken over the world's lamentable state, and to hear sad affirmations that things will be much worse before they are better; and the specialist in adaptability can do both with an abandoned lugubriousness which makes the most pessimistic sure that conditions are even worse than he had hitherto supposed.

So Hamlet and Polonius in the drama talked together. Says Hamlet, "Do you see yonder cloud that's almost in shape of a camel?" "By the mass," says Polonius, "and 'tis like a camel, indeed." "Methinks," says Hamlet, "it is like a weasel." "It is backed like a weasel," agrees Polonius. "Or like a whale?" says Hamlet. And Polonius consents, "Very like a whale." After a day so spent in being agreeable, the congenial man comes home well satisfied. Has he not pleased people? Has he not made the world happier? Is he not a useful character?

It should be obvious that so far from being thus identical, pleasing folk and serving them are often opposite. Ex-President Eliot of Harvard University once was asked to name the fundamental quality essential to a successful college president. After thinking a moment he replied, "The capacity to inflict pain." No serious mind can miss his meaning. Without that stern capacity no great leadership, friendship, or parenthood is imaginable. For lack of it lives that might have been useful now are fallen into soft futility. Parents to please their children relax all discipline and allow perilous indulgences; preachers to please their congregations prophesy smooth things; legislators to please their constituencies deny their own most assured convictions; husbands and wives to please each other give up their own most cherished principles. How frequently agreeableness is the enemy of usefulness! A serviceable man is congenial when he can be, but for the sake of leaving folk temporarily pleased he will not leave them permanently worse. Service sometimes shines as pleasantly as the sun in June, and sometimes it bursts like a thunder storm and clears the air. Now it is as delicate and refreshing as dew; and again it is as brisk and hearty as a winter day. For service and softness are two different things, and deeply to help folk sometimes involves displeasing them.

IV

Another familiar enemy of usefulness is discouragement over *the humdrum and monotony of commonplace living* to which the large and glowing ideals of service seem so little applicable. The principles of the self-sacrificial life, finding its fullness in its outpouring, are alluring when set in fitting words, and those self-denying lives, the remembrance of which is the glory of history, are stimulating when we read of them. But when from the contemplation of the great ideals of service and their supreme embodiments we turn to the narrow horizons, the petty tasks, the tiresome drudgery, the limited opportunities of our ordinary days, the vision often fades and the examples seem inapplicable.

The fact is that, save in a small proportion of cases, service does not involve any dramatic surrender of life at all, but rather the faithful, painstaking use of life in ordinary tasks. One wonders which of the two is harder. It is said that thirty-seven flashes of lightning would be needed to keep one common incandescent lamp burning for a single hour. So the assumption of commonplace responsibilities, carried with constancy and fortitude through many years, may be far harder than one supreme adventurous deed of self-sacrifice that puts a name forever into manhood's memory. Thousands of soldiers in France would gladly have gone to the first line trenches that they might thereby escape the monotony of service in the camps.

One wonders also which of the two, the flaming deed of self-sacrifice or the obscure humdrum practice of it, is in the end more useful. There are two ways of saving folk at sea. Grace Darling's way is startling, unforgettable. All honor to her for that one wild night when with her father she risked her life to save the shipwrecked mariners on Longstone Ledge! There is, however, the blacksmith's way of saving mariners. A few old-fashioned smithies still are left where one may see the links of an anchor chain forged by hand with conscientious thoroughness. In the worker's imagination, for all the commonplaceness of his task, there well may be the picture of a mad night upon the ocean, when only that chain will stand between rocks and foundering ship. He will not be there to achieve a rescue that will make his name rememberable in the annals of the sea. But for all that, by conscientious work in the smoke of the smithy, he can save that ship. He who loses the ideal of a serviceable life because he cannot serve in Grace Darling's way lacks vision. Only a few are called to that. It is more fundamental to forge strong anchor chains than to rescue the victims of broken ones; it is more basic to build fireproof buildings than to save the occupants when buildings burn; the most important business in the world is the undergirding of home, and neighborhood, and nation with

"Plain devotedness to duty
Steadfast and still, nor paid with mortal praise,
But finding amplest recompense
For life's ungarlanded expense
In work done squarely and unwasted days."

An American soldier in France won the Croix de Guerre but refused to wear it, and this is his explanation: "I was no good back home. I let my sister and my widowed mother support me. I was a dead beat. And now they have given me the Croix de Guerre for something I did at the front. I am not going to put it on. I am going back home first. I am going to win out there. I am going to show my mother that I can make good at home. Then I will put on the Croix de Guerre." He is not the only one who has discovered that being heroic in a crisis is sometimes easier than being useful at home.

v

Kindred with what we just have said is this further fact: many people lose the ideal of usefulness because they are discouraged not about the commonplaceness of their tasks, but about their own *meanly endowed or severely handicapped lives*. Exhortation to usefulness so far from inspiring them, sickens them. They would count it their crown and joy to be useful, but what can they do?

By how many roads does Selfishness contrive to offer an escape from service! Some folk are *not* humbly dismayed about themselves. They are too conceited to be of use. They will not work on committees except as chairmen, nor in societies except as presidents. They are always seeking vainly for opportunities ample enough to be worthy of the exercise of their exalted powers. They are habitually aggrieved because, being eagles, folk expect them to hatch eggs on humming-birds' nests. Their professed desire to be of use is extraordinary, but the conditions which they insist on as indispensable are dictated by pride. They have not learned that effective service is the child of humility; they do not see that the real way to get things done is not to care who gets the credit for doing them.

When, however, Selfishness cannot so contrive to make pride a stumbling-block to usefulness, but finds instead a deeply humble soul, he is too experienced and wily a foe to be discouraged. Humility, if it be skillfully handled, will do quite as well as self-conceit to make life useless. Let a humble man's self-depreciation become exaggerated; let him meditate morbidly upon his poorly endowed life, his meagerness of mind, his crippled health, his slender store of strength, his little reputation; let him handle his one talent in disheartened comparison with the larger gifts of other men! He will soon be ready to lay what power he has away in a napkin; he will soon be as useless through false humility as Selfishness ever could have made him through false pride. It is a clever foe who knows how to persuade his victim to fall on his own sword. But so Selfishness uses a man's humility to his own undoing.

The fact is, however, that one thing in human life of which illfortune and crippling handicap never can deprive an earnest man is the privilege of being useful. One door which no man and no circumstance can shut is the opportunity to serve. Paul at liberty can give himself to splendid tasks. Paul in prison is deprived of many privileges which he had loved; but Paul in prison is not deprived of the privilege of being useful. Even the men to whom he is chained present a chance to preach the Gospel to an audience which cannot escape, and enforced leisure he can use for the writing of letters which thrill and burn in the Christian churches yet. When a man is earnestly set on being useful, he is in a country where he can dig anywhere and strike water.

Indeed, the indispensableness of all sorts of people, from the genius to the most meanly endowed, was clearly illustrated during the Great War. Everybody counted. In the saving of food, in the raising of crops, in the disposal of bonds, the fidelity of all the population was needed, and the children were mobilized in the schools for work as were the armies in the field. There was no one too small in ability to share in the campaign. Great handles to the burden there were which needed great hands to lift them, but all around the task were little handles also on which the smallest fingers could obtain a hold. Even the blind, whose hearing by nature's compensation is keener than ordinary men's, were set to the task of listening for the hostile airplanes on the English coast. Each person found some gift, however small, which could be contributed to the general fund.

It were a pity to forget in peace a truth which shone so clearly in the War. Life seldom gives to any man so barren a day that chances to help somebody are not plentiful. To be cheerful under difficulties, by fortitude and patience making even sick rooms holy lands; to appreciate some fine unadvertised endeavor of an unnoticed man; to display that rare virtue, magnanimity to an unfriendly person; to speak a stout word for a good cause; to be kind to the humiliated and gracious to the hurt; to touch some youth with new confidence in human goodness and with fresh resolve to live life for noble ends—such opportunities are as free as air to breathe. The chance to serve is the great democrat. He comes to all doors. He lodges in all houses. To any who will take he gives

> "That best portion of a good man's life,
> His little, nameless, unremembered acts
> Of kindness and of love."

It is not lack of opportunity or of endowment that makes us useless. It is lack of insight, thoughtfulness, sympathy, imagination, and love.

Moreover, no trouble need keep any man from the joys of service. Some forms of work strong folk must do, but for those deeper ministries to the souls of men—the inbreathing of new hope, the conquest of disillusionment and doubt, the inspiration of fresh faith in the reality of the spiritual world—the most useless man is one who has had no trouble. What can *he* do for us? In all the deeper needs of life, we turn not to the fortunate, the popular, the merry and unhurt, but to One "despised and rejected of men, a man of sorrows and acquainted with grief." His troubles did not prevent his usefulness; they are the chief instruments of his service. His incomparable influence on human hearts would have been impossible, if men had not known that he was "touched with the feeling of our infirmities." His Cross was not an interruption of his usefulness but the climax of it. For when anyone gives himself wholeheartedly to helping men, any experience of life, glad or sorrowful, transfiguration or crucifixion, can be used in ministry. When life digs pickaxes into us, this indeed is the deepest comfort—that new springs of understanding, sympathy, and service may be opened up.

Ask who most of all have influenced your life for good, and to what unlikely places does the trail of the answer lead! Folk whose outward eyes have been long blinded but whose inward eyes have

been opened wide to things invisible; shut-ins whose patient, unem-
bittered faith re-creates in the young and strong a new confidence
that spirit alone is real; men who live in unbreakable companionship with pain, but whose courage is not broken nor their spirits
crushed; martyrs of the home, whose failing health is the evidence of
unfailing preference of other's welfare to their own; the aged, grown
beautifully old, whose increasing frailty of flesh the better lets the
light of the eternal through—such people are not shut out from
service. They are often the most efficient ministers to some of man's
profoundest needs. Many an admired warrior for the common good
whose resounding blows are everywhere applauded draws his secret
inspiration from some upper room where, like the light in a lighthouse, a life is shut in but still is luminous.

To all folk discouraged about crippled lives, this then is the message: The world is in trouble and none can help more than hearts by
trouble touched to understanding. Where millions are in adversity,
serviceable men taught by hardship are deeply needed. So when
John Bright sat mourning in his widowed home, Cobden came to
comfort him: "Bright," he said, "there are thousands of homes in
England at this moment, where wives, mothers, and children are dying of hunger. When the first paroxysm of your grief is past, I would
advise you to come with me and we will never rest until the Corn
Laws are repealed." That is real comfort, to know that one's trouble
can be capitalized into usefulness. As "the Lady of the Decoration"
said, "The most miserable, pitiful, smashed-up life could blossom
again if it would only blossom for others."

The substitution of well-wishing for well-doing, of pleasing people
for serving them, disheartenment over small opportunities, self-conceit, and humility overdone—such beetles gnaw at the pith of our
usefulness. Our prayers against colossal selfishness are often wide of
the mark. We are not deliberately selfish. We are driven from a useful life, like travelers from the woods, not by lions but by midgets.
We need to pray not, "O God, save me from the brutal self-seeking
of Milton's Satan!" but rather, "Who can understand his errors?
Cleanse Thou me from secret faults!"

CHAPTER VIII

Cooperation

DAILY READINGS

We need to recognize, before we go further in our thought of service, how much of our helpfulness must be extended, not individually from one person to another, but through the medium of cooperative organizations. Unless one sees the necessity of this, understands its principles, and practically accepts it in his program of usefulness, he will inevitably be robbed of a large part of his possible service.

Eighth Week, First Day

And they were bringing unto him little children, that he should touch them: and the disciples rebuked them. But when Jesus saw it, he was moved with indignation, and said unto them, Suffer the little children to come unto me; forbid them not: for to such belongeth the kingdom of God. Verily I say unto you, Whosoever shall not receive the kingdom of God as a little child, he shall in no wise enter therein. And he took them in his arms, and blessed them, laying his hands upon them.—Mark 10:13-16.

Service for children, personally rendered, lies within reach of most of us. But consider in any community what numbers of children may be beyond the reach of casual individual good will. Christian people have no right to avoid such questions as these: Do we need a day nursery or a home for the care of orphaned and destitute children? Are our boys and girls being supplied with such organized help as the Christian Associations or the Boy Scouts or the Camp Fire Girls could supply? Does the community face the problem of children in industry, and is the problem being rightly and thoroughly handled? Are decent opportunities for play and recreation being provided for the young? Are the day schools what they ought to be? Are the Sunday schools effective? The time has gone by when personal service, individually rendered, can suffice in any form. "Nowadays the water main is my well, the trolley car my carriage, the banker's safe my old stocking, the policeman's billy my fist." *Service cannot refuse to face the necessities and to use the instruments which the new age has brought.*

*O Heavenly Father, whose unveiled face the angels of little children do always behold, look with love and pity, we beseech thee, upon the children of the streets. Where men, in their busy and careless lives, have made a highway, these children of thine have made a home and a school, and are learning the bad lessons of our selfishness and our folly. Save them, and save us, O Lord. Save them from ignorance and brutality, from the shamelessness of lust, the hardness of greed, and the besotting of drink; and save us from the greater guilt of those that offend thy little ones, and from the hypocrisy of those that say they see and see not, whose sin remaineth. Amen.—*Walter Rauschenbusch.

Eighth Week, Second Day

And when he was come down from the mountain, great multitudes followed him. And behold, there came to him a leper and worshipped him, saying, Lord, if thou wilt, thou canst make me clean. And he stretched forth his hand, and touched him, saying, I will; be thou made clean. And straightway his leprosy was cleansed. And Jesus saith unto him, See thou tell no man; but go, show thyself to the priest, and offer the gift that Moses commanded, for a testimony unto them.—Matt. 8:1-4.

All of us at times have the privilege of ministering directly to the comfort and recovery of the sick. *But no Christian who uses his imagination can be content with those opportunities which chance throws in his way.* The sick who most need care are often outside the range of individual ministry. Has your community a hospital properly equipped to minister to the whole community? Are there visiting nurses to be summoned in case of need? Is there a health department in your community which is cleaning up unsanitary districts, removing the cause of disease, and preventing its spread? Is there need of a convalescent home, a fresh air program, a special physician's superintendence of school children? No wordy profession of Christian care about the sick amounts to much in a modern community, save as such questions are answered. What multitudes of Christians need a baptism of public-mindedness!

Lord, have mercy on all miserable bodies; those that are ready to famish for want, feed them; those that are bound to beds of pain, loose them; those that are in prison and bonds, release them; those that are under the fury of persecution, and cry under the yoke of oppression, relieve them; those that lie smarting in their pains and wounds, cure them; those that are distracted in their thoughts and wits, settle them; those that are in perils of their estates and lives, preserve them. Wherever they are, and whosoever they be, what help I would pray for myself from Thee, or comfort from men, in their condition, I beseech Thee, the God of all help and comfort, to give it to them; take them to Thy care and tend them; supply them, and succour them; have compassion on them and heal them. Amen.
— Dr. Brough.

Eighth Week, Third Day

Then shall the King say unto them on his right hand, Come, ye blessed of my Father, inherit the kingdom prepared for you from the foundation of the world: for I was hungry, and ye gave me to eat; I was thirsty, and ye gave me drink; I was a stranger, and ye took me in; naked, and ye clothed me; I was sick, and ye visited me; I was in prison, and ye came unto me. Then shall the righteous answer him, saying, Lord, when saw we thee hungry, and fed thee? or athirst, and gave thee drink? And when saw we thee a stranger, and took thee in? or naked, and clothed thee? And when saw we thee sick, or in prison, and came unto thee? And the King shall answer and say unto them, Verily I say unto you, Inasmuch as ye did it unto one of these my brethren, even these least, ye did it unto me.—Matt. 25:34-40.

It is the commonplace of Christian teaching that we should care for the poor, afflicted, destitute. And most of us, touched by special instances of need, are ready to give help. *But how many fail either to see need or to feel obligation beyond those particular cases that come under their individual observance!* It stands to reason, however, that the most hopeless, abject want will be found in precisely those places where our casual observation does not fall. It stands to reason, also, that the most self-respecting poor, to whom beggary is agony and who would almost rather die than ask alms, are the very ones whose cries for help will never reach our ears. A modern community, therefore, of any size, which has not organized its philanthropy, mapped out the districts where poverty is frequent, studied scientifically its problem of destitution, examined the reasons for all cases of habitual want, and provided systematic measures for relief and constructive help, is not really caring for the poor at all. No words, no kindly feelings, no prayers, no individual beneficence, ever can make up for lack of cooperative organization in relief of want.

O Thou, who art Love, and who seest all the suffering, injustice, and misery which reign in this world, have pity, we implore Thee, on the work of Thy hands. Look mercifully upon the poor, the oppressed, and all who are heavy laden with error, labour, and sorrow. Fill our hearts with deep compassion for those who suffer, and hasten the coming of Thy kingdom of justice and truth; for the sake of Jesus Christ our Lord. Amen.—Eugène Bersier.

Eighth Week, Fourth Day

Now all the publicans and sinners were drawing near unto him to hear him. And both the Pharisees and the scribes murmured, saying, This man receiveth sinners, and eateth with them.

And he spake unto them this parable, saying, What man of you, having a hundred sheep, and having lost one of them, doth not leave the ninety and nine in the wilderness, and go after that which is lost, until he find it? And when he hath found it, he layeth it on his shoulders, rejoicing. And when he cometh home, he calleth together his friends and his neighbors, saying unto them, Rejoice with me, for I have found my sheep which was lost. I say unto you, that even so there shall be joy in heaven over one sinner that repenteth, more than over ninety and nine righteous persons, who need no repentance.—Luke 15:1-7.

No one would doubt the Christian's duty to work for reclamation of character. Many chances for personal service to tempted and beaten men come to any Christian who is looking for them. But even here no Christian ought to content himself with individual service alone. Have the Christians of your community ever faced together the moral conditions of your town? Do you know whether organized vice has invaded your city, whether the police are in cahoots with evil or are honestly about their business, whether vile plays that could be stopped are being given and vile resorts are debauching the town's youth? A few spoonfuls of reclaimed humanity are dipped up in churches; but often the full stream of moral filth pours into the community, unnoticed by any collective Christian attention, unopposed by any Christian public-mindedness. There is hardly a neighborhood in Christendom which the Christian people could not cleanse, putting the fear of God into corrupt officials, and driving out blatantly vicious influences, if they earnestly chose.

O Lord, who dost not willingly afflict the sons of men, behold from Thy holy habitation the multitude of miserable souls and lives among us, and have mercy upon them.

Have mercy upon all ignorant souls, and instruct them; upon all deluded minds, and enlighten them; on all seducing and seduced spirits, and convert them.

Have mercy upon all broken hearts, and heal them; on all struggling with temptation, and rescue them; on all languishing in spiritual desertion, and revive them.

Have mercy on all who stagger in faith, and establish them; that are fallen from Thee, and raise them; that stand with Thee, and confirm them.

Have mercy on all who groan under their sins, and ease them; that go on in their wickedness, and curb them.

O Blessed Jesus, who didst shed Thy Blood for our souls to save them; shed Thy Holy Spirit upon all and heal them, for Thy mercy's sake. Amen.—Dr. Brough.

Eighth Week, Fifth Day

We have been saying that Christians ought to take collective responsibility for such communal affairs as the care of children and of the sick, the relief of the poor and the cleaning up of moral conditions. This collective responsibility, however, ought to be extended far beyond the individual community. Our worst sins are no longer merely individual or communal; they are organized on a national scale. We have now "the man who picks pockets with a railway rebate, murders with an adulterant instead of a bludgeon, burglarizes with a 'rake-off' instead of a jimmy, cheats with a company prospectus instead of a deck of cards, or scuttles his town instead of his ship." Nothing can handle such forms of iniquity except public-mindedness. If a man hates sin, but hates it only in its individual forms, how far short has he fallen from his full share of service! To be a public-minded citizen, to make citizenship an agency of Christian usefulness, to understand public needs, public sins, public remedies—such coöperative ministry is indispensable to a full-sized Christian life. What would the world become if all Christians felt for their countries what the prophet felt for Zion?

For Zion's sake will I not hold my peace, and for Jerusalem's sake I will not rest, until her righteousness go forth as brightness, and her salvation as a lamp that burneth. And the nations shall see thy righteousness, and all kings thy glory; and thou shalt be called by a new name, which the mouth of Jehovah shall name. Thou shalt also be a crown of beauty in the hand of Jehovah, and a royal diadem in the hand of thy God. Thou shalt no more be termed Forsaken; neither shall thy land any more be termed Desolate: but thou shalt be called Hephzi-bah, and thy land Beulah; for Jehovah delighteth in thee, and thy land shall be married. For as a young man marrieth a virgin, so shall thy sons marry thee; and as the bridegroom rejoiceth over the bride, so shall thy God rejoice over thee.—Isa. 62:1-5.

O God, whose Kingdom is an everlasting kingdom and whose dominion endureth from generation to generation, abase our pride and shatter our complacency. Open our eyes to see the vanity of this world's riches and renown; make us to understand that there is no wealth but life, that living men are Thy glory and our life is the vision of Thee. Keep us from being terrorized by wealth and influence, or beguiled by pleas of custom and expediency, or distracted by the glamor of prosperity and aggrandizement; keep us securely in Thy way of righteousness and truth. Amen.—"Prayers for the City of God."

Eighth Week, Sixth Day

And it shall come to pass in the latter days, that the mountain of Jehovah's house shall be established on the top of the mountains,

and shall be exalted above the hills; and all nations shall flow unto it. And many peoples shall go and say, Come ye, and let us go up to the mountain of Jehovah, to the house of the God of Jacob; and he will teach us of his ways, and we will walk in his paths: for out of Zion shall go forth the law, and the word of Jehovah from Jerusalem. And he will judge between the nations, and will decide concerning many peoples; and they shall beat their swords into plowshares, and their spears into pruning-hooks; nations shall not lift up sword against nation, neither shall they learn war any more. —Isa. 2:2-4.

Cooperative responsibilty must overpass national lines, if this hope of the prophet is to be fulfilled. The old age still lifts up its voice to cry, War is inevitable; the new age cries, War is no more inevitable than slavery! The old age still insists, The State has no obligation but power; the new age answers, The State can be as Christian as a man. The old age urges, All nations must be armed against each other; the new age replies, All nations must cooperate for the world's peace. In this choice between Christ and Satan, Christians have an enormous stake. War in its origins, motives, methods, and issues is the most powerful anti-Christian influence on earth. But individual service alone cannot handle the problem. The cooperative organization of all the international good will there is, is indispensable. What an expanded, steady, wise, and ardent public-mindedness will be necessary to make such cooperation win the day!

Almighty God, who art the Father of all men upon the earth, most heartily we pray that Thou wilt keep Thy children from the cruelties of war, and lead the nations in the way of peace. Teach us to put away all bitterness and misunderstanding, both in Church and State; that we, with all the brethren of the Son of Man, may draw together as one comity of peoples, and dwell evermore in the fellowship of that Prince of Peace, who liveth and reigneth with Thee in the unity of the Holy Spirit, now and ever.—Percy Dearmer.

Eighth Week, Seventh Day

Consider this paragraph from the Edinburgh Conference Report:

"The evangelization of Africa means something more than the introduction of the Gospel into existing forms of social life. It means the introduction of education and letters, of agriculture and industries, of Christian marriage and due recognition of the sanctity of human life and property. The problem before the Church is the creation of an African civilization."

That is to say, Christianity cannot content itself with the cure of evil already done; it must seek, in the reconstruction of social life, the prevention of the evil at its source. Here lies the ultimate necessity of cooperation as contrasted with individual service. Our personal usefulness may occasionally *cure,* but only collective effort can finally *prevent* the ravages of sin, sickness, poverty, and social wrong. To relieve famine sufferers in India is good; to teach them collectively to practice irrigation and scientific agriculture, so that there will be no famines, is better. In how far are you, through influence and gift, supporting the great cooperative endeavors to reach the social roots of man's ills in community, nation, and the world?

And the word of Jehovah came unto me, saying, Son of man, prophesy against the shepherds of Israel, prophesy, and say unto them, even to the shepherds, Thus saith the Lord Jehovah: Woe unto the shepherds of Israel that do feed themselves! should not the shepherds feed the sheep? Ye eat the fat, and ye clothe you with the wool, ye kill the fatlings; but ye feed not the sheep. The diseased have ye not strengthened, neither have ye healed that which was sick, neither have ye bound up that which was broken, neither have ye brought back that which was driven away, neither have ye sought that which was lost; but with force and with rigor have ye ruled over them. And they were scattered, because there was no shepherd; and they became food to all the beasts of the field, and were scattered. My sheep wandered through all the mountains, and upon every high hill: yea, my sheep were scattered upon all the face of the earth; and there was none that did search or seek after them.

Therefore, ye shepherds, hear the word of Jehovah: As I live, saith the Lord Jehovah, surely forasmuch as my sheep became a prey, and my sheep became food to all the beasts of the field, because there was no shepherd, neither did my shepherds search for my sheep, but the shepherds fed themselves, and fed not my sheep; therefore, ye shepherds, hear the word of Jehovah: Thus saith the Lord Jehovah, Behold, I am against the shepherds; and I will require my sheep at their hand, and cause them to cease from feeding the sheep; neither shall the shepherds feed themselves any more; and I will deliver my sheep from their mouth, that they may not be food for them.—Ezek. 34:1-10.

O God, we praise Thee for the dream of the golden city of peace and righteousness which has ever haunted the prophets of humanity, and we rejoice with joy unspeakable that at last the people have conquered the freedom and knowledge and power which may avail to turn into reality the vision that so long has beckoned in vain. We pray Thee to revive in us the hardy spirit of our forefathers, that we may establish and complete their work, building on the basis of their democracy the firm edifice of a cooperative commonwealth, in which both government and industry shall be of the people, by the people, and for the people. May we, who now live, see the oncoming of the great day of God, when all men shall stand side by side in equal worth and real freedom, all toiling and all reaping, masters of nature, but brothers of men, exultant in the tide of the common life, and jubilant in the adoration of Thee, the source of their blessings and the Father of all. Amen.—Walter Rauschenbusch.

COMMENT FOR THE WEEK

I

Hitherto our thought of service has largely concerned itself with one individual's usefulness to another. But the finest forms of serviceable living are reached not when *I* give some helpful ministry to *you*, but when *we* in mutual fellowship work out our welfare together. The most gracious and the most useful ministries are found in co-operation. So a mother long blind complimented her son: "It is not so much that he does things for me, as that he so arranges matters that we can do things together."

In the mutual loyalties which such partnerships involve most of us find our richest satisfaction. To be sure, some men are made to work in solitude. Newton forbade the publication of his name in connection with his solution of the problem of the moon. "It would perhaps increase my acquaintance," he wrote, "the thing which I chiefly study to decline." Such solitary living, however, is reserved for geniuses. Most of us were made for comradeship, and we are bereft without it. Said a very young and lonely lad, "Mother, I wish that I were two little puppies, so that I could play together." Why, from the time our primitive forefathers communicated with one another by grunt and gesture because they had no other speech, has man so tirelessly worked out his elaborate languages, until now in the marvel and mystery of words we have so facile an instrument? The motive behind the development of language is men's irresistible desire to break over the isolating barriers that separate individuals and to achieve their proper destiny in thinking together and working together for common ends. Self-preservation may be the strongest instinct in men, but close alongside is the companion instinct for comradeship. "Only mankind together is the true man," said Goethe, "and the individual can be joyous and happy only when he feels himself in the whole."

So deeply is this need for cooperation wrought into all life that it reveals itself long before man arrives. The lowest orders of animals do indeed appear to talk like this: There is barely enough food to go around. What I gain you lose and what I lose you gain. We are natural enemies; there is between us an unavoidable hostility. But one rises only a little way in the scale of animal life before he hears a different tone: It may be that we were mistaken, they seem to say. It may be that our mutual antagonisms are superficial, our mutual interests profound. It may be that if you and I were blended into we, we could do more for both of us than either you or I could do for either of us. So the bees hive and the birds flock and the wolves hunt in packs.

"As the creeper that girdles the tree-trunk the law runneth forward and back—
For the strength of the Pack is the Wolf, and the strength of the Wolf is the Pack."

What begins thus among animals continues among men. The story of advancing civilization is mainly the record of mankind's enlarging capacity to cooperate. From the days when humanity began, not with a solitary individual, but with a unit of three—father, mother, and child—to the days when internationalism becomes a live issue and increasing numbers of people think in planetary terms, we can mark the major changes that have passed over human life in terms of cooperation, its enlargements and lapses, its victories and failures. In our time the whole structure of human life is so intricately interrelated, men, no matter how various their colors, customs, or habi-

tats, are so inextricably interdependent, that the problem of cooperation has become supremely the critical question of the world.

*No kind of help, therefore, that individuals can give each other
exhausts the meaning of service.* For all the fine spirit manifest, it is
vain for one man to lug water in a bucket from a spring to give
drink to the thirsty of a modern town. He must serve in another way.
He must call a town meeting and arouse the citizens to build a water
system in cooperative effort for the good of all. However admirable
in intention it may be, it is of negligible import for one man to
sweeten the bitterness of war by maintaining personal friendship
with one enemy citizen. The problem must be met in another way.
The people as a whole must be aroused to see the immedicable evils
of war, to hate it with a blazing hatred, to purpose its abolishment
with all their hearts, and mutually to seek those covenants that will
achieve their end. From the smallest enterprises to the greatest, the
direst human need is far beyond the reach of individual usefulness.

II

This basic problem in human relationships received its classic
Christian treatment in the twelfth and thirteenth chapters of Paul's
first letter to the Corinthians. The twelfth chapter pictures the cooperative unity of human life, ideally presented in the Church, as
one body with many members. Not like loose shot in a bag, isolate
and unrelated, does Paul see human kind, but like eyes, ears, hands,
feet, in one body, vitally joined and mutually interdependent. Having presented this unforgettable picture of a human society where
cooperation is indispensable, he swings out into the thirteenth chapter in praise of that most excellent and necessary of all gifts, love.
The thirteenth chapter did not by accident follow the twelfth. *It is
the fine flower that grows up out of the roots of the twelfth.* Paul
saw a basic fact about life, that we are cooperating members one
of another; then he declares that only one quality of relationship
can keep such members from catastrophe. Love in Paul's thirteenth
chapter is the necessary principle of conduct in life, based upon the
major fact about life which his twelfth chapter has presented.

Thoroughly to grasp the fact, therefore, that we are vitally related
members of one social body, to see it vividly, to feel it convincingly,
is the first step toward understanding the meaning of Christian love.
Two sets of forces continually play upon us like centrifugal and

centripetal forces among the planets. One set pulls us apart, disentangles us from each other, sets us over against each other, sharply individual and competitive. The other set of forces weaves us together, places the solitary in families, welds us into friendships, braids us into neighborhoods, nations, and mankind. Both these sets of forces are present in life and both are needful, but one of them is primary and the other is secondary. We are not first of all isolated individuals, says Paul; first of all we are members of the social body and have no true life apart from it. Therefore, the primary law of life is not selfishness; the primary law is love.

A man can assure himself that this is true by many tests. Let him look *back* to the source out of which his life has sprung. If from the day of birth he had been cast upon a desert island and like some Romulus had been suckled by a wolf, and then had grown, utterly cut off from the whole heritage of mankind's past, its national traditions, its social accumulations, its intellectual gains, its religious faiths, would he be himself? Rather he would not be anybody. He would be an animal, highly organized, it may be, but lacking all the characteristic qualities of human life. A person so abstracted from his social background is no person at all.

Let a man look *in* and, granting all the gains of past inheritance, let him consider the contributions of social relationships that immediately surround him! If he goes down into the thing he calls his self and rummages through its contents as one searches an old chest, how little he will find that is not social! His wife and children are there; they are a part of his self. His relatives and friends are there, his neighborhood and nation, the recreations he enjoys, the causes that he loves. So far from being isolatedly individual, he is like a tree in a forest, whose trunk indeed stands separate, but whose branches are twined and whose roots are woven into an inextricable network with all the other trees, and whose source is the seeds of forests that reach back into the past.

Or let a man look *out* into the world about him, and endeavor to picture a life independent of the society from which he came and to which he belongs! Such an isolated self is as difficult to imagine as the grin on the face of the cat in "Alice in Wonderland" that stayed after the cat had gone. Ex-President Harris of Amherst College has drawn for us the details of one small area of a man's unescapable membership in human kind: "When he rises, a sponge is placed in his hand by a Pacific Islander, a cake of soap by a French-

man, a rough towel by a Turk. His merino underwear he takes from
the hand of a Spaniard, his linen from a Belfast manufacturer, his
outer garments from a Birmingham weaver, his scarf from a French
silk-grower, his shoes from a Brazilian grazier. At breakfast his cup
of coffee is poured by natives of Java and Arabia, his rolls are passed
by a Kansas farmer, his beefsteak by a Texan ranchman, his orange
by a Florida Negro."

Let a man look *back,* or *in,* or *out,* he sees one primary fact. We
are members one of another. Out of society we came, to it we belong, from it we are not separable. God made us what we are, in
and through our fellows. "We are told that our body is a little con-
densed air living in the air," says Gabriel de Tarde. "Might we not
say that our soul is a little bit of society incarnate, living in society?
Born of society, it lives by means of it."

But if the principle of the twelfth chapter of First Corinthians is
true, the thirteenth chapter is inevitable. Nothing can solve the problems of human life, so constituted, except cooperative love. "Is it
true," some one asked, "that all the people in the world could get
into the state of Texas?" "Yes," was the answer, "if they were
friends." So always, increase of contacts demands access of friendliness. Love is not a luxury. It is the profoundest practical need of
mankind. On no other terms can human life sustain the mutual
relationships into which by its very nature it is increasingly com-
pressed.

III

It is a great day for a Christian when he sees that the gospel of
love is founded on the rock of *fact.* Many people think of love as
an ideal sentiment, a gracious iridescent quality, which gives a touch
of radiant color to life's solid structure, otherwise complete. "Upon
the top of the pillars was lily work": runs an Old Testament verse,
"so was the work of the pillars finished." Such floral decoration upon
the substantial column of man's life does love appear to be. Ask a
man what makes life strong and he thinks of self-seeking power; ask
him what makes life winsome and he thinks of love. He changes
gear from business to sentiment when he picks up the thirteenth
chapter of First Corinthians. But that chapter is not sentiment. It
is the plain statement of the way of living which alone corresponds
with the facts of life. On no other basis can humanity, constituted
as it is, live decently and fortunately upon the earth.

The solid grounding which the gospel of cooperative love has in the facts of life is clear when one considers history. Whatever real progress mankind has made has lain in the redemption of new areas of life from the regime of violence to the regime of good will. The *family* used to be founded upon force. Men did not woo their wives, they captured them by violence and held them by constraint. Parents were not bound to love their children. Infants were exposed at birth if the parents chose, and fathers held the absolute power of life and death over their growing offspring. Moreover, this regime of violence was counted on in theory as well as fact as necessary to sustain the home. Could anyone from a modern Christian family have entered such a household and explained the constitution of a home where marriage is an affair of mutual love and mutual consent, where the children from their earliest childhood are cooperating members of the family, not driven by violence but won by love, and where so far from having power to kill their children, parents administer the simplest corporal punishment only as a last resort, the visitor would have been met with utter incredulity. He would have seemed an arrant sentimentalist to suppose that a family could so be run by love instead of violence. The fact is, however, that family life over wide areas has actually been thus redeemed. Only when such redemption is wrought does a family come to its true nature, and no one who knows what a family can thus become, would propose relapse into the old barbarism.

So, too, the *school* used to be founded upon force. An unwhipped child was a lost opportunity. Of the Rev. James Boyer, an English schoolmaster, it was said that "it was lucky the cherubim who took him to heaven were nothing but wings and faces, or he infallibly would have flogged them by the way." The stories of cruel punishment pitilessly inflicted as a matter of principle upon unwary children are almost incredible to a modern mind. But they are not so incredible as would have been the description of a modern school to one of the old schoolmasters. To have a school the children deeply love, around which their thoughts of play center as well as their thoughts of work, in which they are cooperating members, and from which violence has been excluded as a needless intruder—that would have left an ancient pedagogue utterly incredulous. The man who proposed it would have seemed impossibly sentimental. But the taunted dreamers have turned out to be right. The facts were too much for the old educators, who, like the Sadducee, cried, "My right arm is my god." No one who knows the truth supposes that in a school cooperative good will will not work. It is the only thing that will work.

Religion also used to be under the domain of force. Let a man come into the Church willingly, if he would, but if he willfully refused, then violence was the swift and terrible resort. The Christian centuries are sick with cruelties born of the endeavor to make terror a motive for the Christian life, and violence an effective minister of the Christian Church. One does not wonder at accounts of black-haired priests going into torture chambers to force the recantation of disapproved beliefs and coming out white-haired with the horror of their own performances. It seemed incredible that the Church could be made a matter of voluntary cooperation. To tolerate in other men beliefs you did not hold yourself seemed as much as denying your convictions. Cried Thomas Edwards: "Could the devil effect a toleration, he would think he had gained well by the Reformation, and make a good exchange of the hierarchy to have a toleration for it." Said the saintly Baxter: "I abhor unlimited liberty and toleration of all, and think myself easily able to prove the wickedness of it." The Long Parliament in 1648 made death the penalty for eight errors in doctrine and indefinite imprisonment the penalty for sixteen others. But the facts were too much for these blind champions of forced religion. Human life is fundamentally built to be voluntarily cooperative, and the highest area of human life, religion, never came to its own until it was redeemed from the regime of force.

All progress moves thus to the rescuing of some new area of life from violence to the domain of cooperative good will. Already we have gone a long way on that road in *local government*. Once family feuds were matters of course. How else could one sustain the honor of his clan? But wherever that old barbarism still maintains its belated sway, it is the butt of general contempt and ridicule. Yet there was a time when the whole idea of settled local government, with ordered justice strong enough to make armed residences needless and family feuds a shame, seemed as Utopian as a warless world. From the city of Florence in the fourteenth century to the city of Florence in the twentieth century is as long a step as from the Europe of 1914 to the Europe of the internationalist's dream.

Moreover, what has been done in the government of neighborhoods has become indispensable in the larger *government of nations*.

Once all sovereignty was assumed to rest on power. The king could slay or keep alive and by that right he ruled. But one day mankind turned a corner and came face to face with a prodigious and revolutionary thought: all the people can be trusted in cooperative fellowship to establish laws which then all the people together will obey. That idea seemed incredible to multitudes. That the great mass of men could be trusted loyally to say *our* government—for that is the gist of democracy—was Utopian beyond belief. But the facts were all on the side of the new hope, for human life is essentially built to be cooperative and cooperation is the only way of life that in the end will work.

In family, school, church, neighborhood, state, all progress has consisted in this substitution of cooperative good will for violence. This is the essence of the redemption by which the social life of humanity is saved. And when in our generation the hopes of increasing multitudes begin to center around a cooperative industrial system instead of a continuance of disorder and violence, and around a cooperative internationalism instead of a continuance of worldwide chaos and anarchy, the facts of life are all on the side of the new hopes. Many experiments will have to be tried; blunders and excesses may mark the trail of the advance; obstacles at times may well appear to faint-hearted folk to be insuperable; and always there are some—the belated, the obstinate, the criminally-minded—who refuse to move up into the spirit of the new regime, upon whom force must still be used. But the general mass of human kind are capable of enlarging cooperation, and already mankind has gone too far on the road from force toward fellowship to turn back.

IV

Tolerance, patience, selflessness, faith, courage, fairness, tact, magnanimity—what fineness and strength of character are required by anyone who undertakes to be a cooperator! Many a man finds it far easier to be individually useful. He enjoys the flattering sense of his own munificence, when he as one individual gives service to another. Charles Lamb once said that the happiest sensation in the world is to do a good deed in secret and to have it found out by accident. So does a superior's helpfulness to an inferior prove one of the most personally gratifying experiences which the superior enjoys. It increases his consciousness of superiority. But to be a good cooperator means the abnegation of pride, the esteeming of others better than oneself, the willingness to take a lowly place in the fellowship of common enterprise, the loss of anxious self-seeking in collective enthusiasm. To be a good cooperator involves the possession of a love that suffers long and is kind, envies not, vaunts not itself, is not puffed up, does not behave itself unseemly, is not easily provoked, keeps no record of injuries, bears, hopes, believes, and endures all things.

Even in individual service this spirit of cooperation is indispensable to real effectiveness. A great industrial leader is said to have called to his office a young man in his employ who was going wrong with drink. The employee with shaking knees went up to his chief, expecting his discharge. The end of an hour's conversation ran like this: "My boy," said the chief, "we are not going to drink any more, are we?" "No, sir," said the youth, "we're not!" "And we are going to send each week so much money home to the wife and kiddies, aren't we?" "By heaven, sir!" said the youth, "we will!" To serve folk not only by doing service *for* them, but working *with* them, is the very essence of the finest helpfulness.

When one's thought moves out from such individual relationships to the problems of philanthropy, the same truth stands clear. Charles Kingsley once told Huxley the story of two mullahs who came to a heathen khan in Tartary to win his allegiance to their gods. The first mullah argued, "O Khan, worship my god, he is so wise that he made all things!" The second mullah argued, "O Khan, worship my god, he is so wise that he makes all things make themselves!" For an obvious and sufficient reason the second god won out. For, whether with God or man, to work *upon* another from without is not half so serviceable as to work *with* another from within. Parental dictatorship in a family is easier than comradeship, but it is correspondingly valueless. Welfare work in a factory, handed down from above, is easier than cooperative industrial democracy, but it is correspondingly ineffective. Munificent largess to a ne'er-do-well is easier than cooperative measures to encourage him in self-support, but only the latter amounts to much. No normal person wishes to be served by condescension; any normal person welcomes service by cooperation. "If I bestow all my goods to feed the poor," said Paul, "and have not love, it profiteth me nothing."

If the spirit of cooperation is so essential to the finest usefulness in individual relationships, and in family, factory, and philanthropy, how deep is the need of it and how searching its demands if one is to serve the coming of world-wide human brotherhood! No small, provincial soul can ever understand the hopes of international fraternity. The cooperative mind at its largest and its best is needed here. What holds back the coming of human brotherhood is not basic impossibility in achieving a world where reason and fraternity have taken the place of violence and exploitation; it is the provincial mind. All false pride of caste and class and rank, of race and nation, is provincialism, and provincialism is simply self-inflation in one of its most deadly forms. The Hottentots call themselves "the men of men"; the Eskimos call themselves "the complete people," but their neighbors the Indians are "louse-eggs"; the Haytian aborigines believed their island was the first of all created things, that the sun and moon issued from one of its caves and men from another; to the Japanese Nippon was the middle point of the world, and the Shah of Persia yet retains the title "The Center of the Universe." That is provincialism. When Americans or British or Frenchmen or Germans talk in the same spirit, it is provincialism still, a wretched survival of belated racial egoism—one of the deadliest forms of selfishness known to men.

This does not mean that a man should not love his own people best of all. A man should love his own people, as his own mother, with a unique devotion. Ties of nature are there which it is folly to deny. A man can mean to his own mother and she can mean to him what no other man's mother can mean to him or he can mean to any other man's mother. What is true of mothers is true of motherlands. We are bone of their bone, blood of their blood, bred in their traditions, and suckled at their breasts. We can do for our own people and they can do for us, what no other people can give to us or claim from us. Unique relationships are sacred because they offer the opportunity for unique service.

One primary effect, however, of such devotion to one's own mother should be the making of all motherhood everywhere infinitely sacred. He is a poor son whose sonship does not make him desire to serve all men's mothers. He is a poor patriot whose patriotism does not enable him to understand how all men everywhere feel about their altars and their hearthstones, their flags and their fatherland. Local patriotism should be the open door into universal sympathy. Nationalism should not hold back from but lead to internationalism. He who thinks that loyalty to his family means dislike of his village is a fool. A good family and a good village are fulfilled in each other; so are a good nationalism and a good internationalism the complement one of the other. But it requires a conquest of self-inflation by the cooperative spirit to perceive it. Such a victory over his own provincialism is one of the first necessities for the man who seeks to be useful to his generation's deepest need and greatest task. He must rise above inveterate racial prejudices and animosities, above the scorn that embitters the color line, above the petty pride that is contemptuous of strange customs, strange clothes, strange speech, above the jingoism of perverted patriots. He must learn to say *our* in friendship and family, in factory and philanthropy, in world-wide sympathy and good will, or else he ought forever to forgo the Lord's Prayer, "Our Father who art in heaven."

CHAPTER IX

New Forms of Service

"Truth is compar'd in Scripture to a streaming fountain," wrote Milton. "If her waters flow not in perpetual progression, they sick'n into a muddy pool of conformity and tradition." What is true of man's ideas is true also of their practical expressions. Methods of work change. To print from Gutenberg's movable wooden type after the Hoe multiple press and the linotype machine have arrived, is misdirected energy. Methods of service also change, or, refusing to progress, may harden into set forms which a new generation will find inadequate. In this week's study let us see the application of this general truth to our own generation's problems.

Ninth Week, First Day

Pure religion and undefiled before our God and Father is this, to visit the fatherless and widows in their affliction, and to keep oneself unspotted from the world.—James 1:27.

But whoso hath the world's goods, and beholdeth his brother in need, and shutteth up his compassion from him, how doth the love of God abide in him? My little children, let us not love in word, neither with the tongue; but in deed and truth.—I John 3:17, 18.

Some people still need to see with unmistakable clearness that Christian service is not simply a spiritual ministry to men's souls. A certain type of mind always is tempted to conceive this present life as a short, narrow-gauge railroad, whose one objective is the junction of death, where the through express of immortality is met. All questions of comfort, health, and wholesome circumstance upon

this present shuttle-train seem negligible. We shall not be here long.
To achieve a fortunate immortality is the one absorbing and exclusive aim of religion. But long since it has become evident that the
spiritual interests of men are powerfully affected by outward circumstance. "Here then is Africa's challenge to its missionaries," writes
Dan Crawford in "Thinking Black": "Will they allow a whole continent to live like beasts in hovels, millions of negroes cribbed, cabined,
and confined in dens of disease? No doubt it is our diurnal duty to
preach that the soul of all improvement is the improvement of the
soul. But God's equilateral triangle of body, soul, and spirit must
never be ignored. Is not the body wholly ensouled, and is not the
soul wholly embodied? . . . In other words, in Africa the only true
fulfilling of your heavenly calling is the doing of earthly things in a
heavenly manner." In view of the plain insistence of the New Testament, is there any other way of fulfilling our heavenly calling in
Britain or America?

*Pour into our hearts the spirit of unselfishness, so that, when our
cup overflows, we may seek to share our happiness with our brethren.
O Thou God of Love, who makest Thy sun to rise on the evil and
on the good, and sendest rain on the just and on the unjust, grant
that we may become more and more Thy true children, by receiving
into our souls more of Thine own spirit of ungrudging and unwearying kindness; which we ask in the name of Jesus Christ. Amen.*
—John Hunter.

Ninth Week, Second Day

I planted, Apollos watered; but God gave the increase. So then
neither is he that planteth anything, neither he that watereth; but
God that giveth the increase. Now he that planteth and he that
watereth are one: but each shall receive his own reward according
to his own labor. For we are God's fellow-workers: ye are God's
husbandry, God's building.—I Cor. 3:6-9.

Many folk need to achieve in a modern way *this happy blending
of dependence on God with energetic work.* For many are still
living in the pre-scientific age before the law-abiding forces of the
world were so largely delivered into man's hands, and they are
tempted to trust God to do *for* them what he is waiting to do

through them. Before medical science came, a plague was the occasion of public penitence in the churches. Men knew no other help for a pestilence than dependence on God. Now, however, we know that God has put into our hands the means by which, if we will, age-long plagues can be driven from the earth. He is waiting to do through man, by means of the wise and devoted use of law-abiding forces, more than our fathers ever dared ask him to do for man. A plague now ought indeed to drive us to our knees, but in penitence that we have used to so little purpose the powers intrusted to us. A pestilence ought indeed to make us cry to God, but for help to be more faithful in letting him use our dedicated knowledge for the saving of the race from its inveterate ills. A new and massive meaning has come into the old truth, "We are God's fellow-workers." Dependence on God does not mean sitting still: it means in part letting God use us to put at man's disposal all the potential service which is still folded in our new knowledge of natural law.

O God, we rejoice in the tireless daring with which some are now tracking the great slayers of mankind by the white light of science. Grant that under their teaching we may grapple with the sins which have ever dealt death to the race, and that we may so order the life of our communities that none may be doomed to an untimely death for lack of the simple gifts which Thou hast given in abundance. Make Thou our doctors the prophets and soldiers of Thy kingdom, which is the reign of cleanliness and self-restraint and the dominion of health and joyous life. Amen.—Walter Rauschenbusch.

Ninth Week, Third Day

When a man recognizes thus his Christian responsibility to minister to *all* the needs of men, and his further obligation to use in that ministry *all* the powers available, he finds himself faced in our modern world with four new conditions which must somehow be handled in the interests of service.

First, the modern Christian faces the *new powers conferred by science.* Whether man is going to wreck himself with these or with them rebuild a fairer world is one of the crucial questions of the coming centuries. Saloman Reinach, looking forward to the Peace Conference at Versailles, wrote:

"At the future Congress, among the seats reserved for the delegates of the great Powers, one seat should remain vacant, as reserved to the greatest, the most redoubtable, though youngest of Powers: science in scarlet robes. That is the new fact; that is what diplomacy should not ignore, if that imminent and execrable scandal is to be averted—the whole of civilization falling a victim to science, her dearest daughter, brought forth and nurtured by her, now ready to deal her the death-blow. The all-important question is the muzzling of the mad dog. Science, as subservient to the will to destroy, must be put in chains; science must be exclusively adapted to the works of peace."

How prodigious a problem is this which the servants of man must somehow succeed in solving, if we are not to be lost! For if we cannot harness science to service, all our vaunted knowledge will come to no better issue than that long ago reported by a disillusioned naturalist:

I the Preacher was king over Israel in Jerusalem. And I applied my heart to seek and to search out by wisdom concerning all that is done under heaven: it is a sore travail that God hath given to the sons of men to be exercised therewith. I have seen all the works that are done under the sun; and behold, all is vanity and a striving after wind. That which is crooked cannot be made straight; and that which is wanting cannot be numbered. I communed with mine own heart, saying, Lo, I have gotten me great wisdom above all that were before me in Jerusalem; yea, my heart hath had great experience of wisdom and knowledge. And I applied my heart to know wisdom, and to know madness and folly: I perceived that this also was a striving after wind. For in much wisdom is much grief; and he that increaseth knowledge increaseth sorrow.—Eccl. 1:12-18.

We praise Thee, O Lord, for that mysterious spark of thy light within us, the intellect of man, for Thou hast kindled it in the beginning and by the breath of Thy spirit it has grown to flaming power in our race.

We rejoice in the men of genius and intellectual vision who discern the undiscovered applications of Thy laws and dig the deeper springs through which the hidden forces of Thy world may well up to the light of day. We claim them as our own in Thee, as members with us in the common body of humanity, of which Thou art the all-pervading life and inspirer. Grant them, we pray Thee, the divine humility of Thine elect souls, to realize that they are sent of Thee as brothers and helpers of men and that the powers within them are but part of the vast equipment of humanity, entrusted to them for the common use. May they bow to the law of Christ and live, not to be served, but to give their abilities for the emancipation of the higher life of man. Amen.—Walter Rauschenbusch.

Ninth Week, Fourth Day

The second factor with which the modern Christian must deal is *new contacts between races and people.*

When the proposal to evangelize the heathen was brought before the Assembly of the Scotch Church in 1796, it was met by a resolution, that "to spread abroad the knowledge of the Gospel amongst barbarous and heathen nations seems to be highly preposterous, in so far as philosophy and learning must in the nature of things take the precedence, and that while there remains at home a single individual every year without the means of religious knowledge, to propagate it abroad would be improper and absurd." And then Dr. Erskine called to the Moderator, "Rax me that Bible," and he read the words of the great commission in a voice which burst upon them like a clap of thunder. Such a policy of aloofness as that proposed by the Scotch Assembly now would be impossible whether to churches or to states. The world is webbed into one fabric; we cannot longer live apart. In the new contacts lie possibilities of organized fraternity such as mankind never before possessed; in the same contacts lie terrific possibilities of friction, strife, and endless war. In what new and unexplored regions must the old spirit of service in our day become a pioneer!

So, in his smaller world, long centuries ago, Isaiah dreamed:

In that day shall there be a highway out of Egypt to Assyria, and the Assyrian shall come into Egypt, and the Egyptian into Assyria; and the Egyptians shall worship with the Assyrians.

In that day shall Israel be the third with Egypt and with Assyria, a blessing in the midst of the earth; for that Jehovah of hosts hath blessed them, saying, Blessed be Egypt my people, and Assyria the work of my hands, and Israel mine inheritance.—Isa. 19:23-25.

Almighty God, Ruler of the nations . . . quicken our consciences that we may feel the sin and shame of war. Inspire us with courage and faith that we may lift up our voices against private greed, social injustice, the aggression of the strong on the weak, and whatsoever else works enmity between man and man, class and class, nation and nation. Create within us a passion for the reign of righteousness, the spread of brotherhood and good will among the nations, so that we may hasten the fulfilment of Thine ancient word, "Nation shall not lift up sword against nation, neither shall they learn war any more." Amen.—Samuel McComb.

Ninth Week, Fifth Day

The third factor with which the modern Christian must deal is *new wealth*. There never has been so much wealth in the world. We are right in our indignation against injustice in its making and in its distribution, but the fact remains that history offers no parallel to the increase of wealth which the last few generations have created. Nor has the comparative centralization of that wealth in a few hands prevented widespread increase in the general comfort of living for the majority of the people. An average laboring man takes for granted luxuries of which a medieval princeling never dreamed. Now wealth is a potential servant or destroyer of manhood, with almost magical powers. To harness money for usefulness, to create the sense of stewardship in those who possess it, to educate all the people in the ministries to which it can be put, to redeem money from sordidness and to baptize it into the service of God and his children, this is one of the great tasks of the modern age.

Moreover, brethren, we make known to you the grace of God which hath been given in the churches of Macedonia; how that in much proof of affliction the abundance of their joy and their deep poverty abounded unto the riches of their liberality. For according to their power, I bear witness, yea and beyond their power, they gave of their own accord, beseeching us with much entreaty in regard of this grace and the fellowship in the ministering to the saints: and this, not as we had hoped, but first they gave their own selves to the Lord, and to us through the will of God.—II. Cor. 8:1-5.

Lord of all things in heaven and earth, the land and the sea and all that therein is; take from us, we humbly implore Thee, the spirit of gain and covetousness; give us the spirit of service, so that none may want, but each according to his need may share in Thy bounti-

ful liberality; for the love of Thine only Son Jesus Christ our Lord. Amen.

Ninth Week, Sixth Day

The fourth factor with which modern Christian service must deal is the *new personal equipment of educated folk*. Widespread popular education is a comparatively new thing in Christendom. Not until 1832 did England recognize any national responsibility for popular education or impose on parents any legal constraint to see that their children were taught. Sixty-five years ago in the United States it was still an open question whether state-supported education was wise. We are dealing now with a problem which no previous ages ever faced: a large majority of the people possessed of the privileges and powers of education. And we face in consequence the peril which Froude described, "Where all are selfish, the sage is no better than the fool, and only rather more dangerous." We face the tragedy of unguided and undedicated personal ability. We face the opportunity of harnessing to the cause of service a mass and force of trained skill such as the world never before had at its disposal.

Let not sin therefore reign in your mortal body, that ye should obey the lusts thereof: neither present your members unto sin as instruments of unrighteousness; but present yourselves unto God, as alive from the dead, and your members as instruments of righteousness unto God.—Rom. 6:12, 13.

Thou knowest, O heavenly Father, the duties that lie before me this day, the dangers that may confront me, the sins that most beset me. Guide me, strengthen me, protect me.

Give me Thy life in such abundance that I may this day hold my soul in Thy pure light. Give me Thy power, that I may become a power for righteousness among my fellows. Give me Thy love, that all lesser things may have no attraction for me; that selfishness, impurity, and falseness may drop away as dead desires, holding no meaning for me. Let me find Thy power, Thy love, Thy life, in all mankind, and in the secret places of my own soul. Amen.—"A Book of Prayers for Students."

Ninth Week, Seventh Day

Such, then, is a modern Christian servant. He knows that the Master would serve *all* the needs of men, with *all* the resources available. He is challenged to new forms of ministry by the new powers conferred by science, the new contacts which make all people one in interest, the new wealth at the world's disposal, and the new equipment of trained personal ability. Finally, into all these he tries to pour the old spirit of self-renouncing love.

Brethren, I count not myself yet to have laid hold: but one thing I do, forgetting the things which are behind, and stretching forward to the things which are before, I press on toward the goal unto the prize of the high calling of God in Christ Jesus. Let us therefore, as many as are perfect, be thus minded: and if in anything ye are otherwise minded, this also shall God reveal unto you: only, whereunto we have attained, by that same rule let us walk. Brethren, be ye imitators together of me, and mark them that so walk even as ye have us for an ensample. For many walk, of whom I told you often, and now tell you even weeping, that they are the enemies of the cross of Christ: whose end is perdition, whose god is the belly, and whose glory is in their shame, who mind earthly things.—Phil. 3:13-19.

So Paul presses forward in service, and at the same time harks back to the Cross of Christ, to the love which it reveals and to the self-sacrifice which it demands. Laurence Oliphant has said that our great need is a "spiritually minded man of the world." Have we not this week been pleading for such a character? Alive to the needs of his time and the movements of his generation, as keen as the Athenians not to miss any new thing worth knowing, seeking ever for more efficient methods, as canny and alert in service as a merchant keeping pace with the requirements of business, and through it all shedding the radiance of that eternal spirit of love, most ancient yet ever new, which shone in the Master's ministry—may we all be such spiritually minded men of the world!

O God, the Enlightener of men, who of all graces givest the most abundant blessing upon heavenly love; we beseech Thee to cleanse us from selfishness, and grant us, for Thy love, so to love our brethren

*that we may be Thy children upon earth; and thereby, walking in
Thy Truth, attain to Thy unspeakable joy, who art the Giver of life
to all who truly love Thee. Grant this prayer, O Lord, for Jesus
Christ's sake. Amen.*—Rowland Williams.

COMMENT FOR THE WEEK

I

While the spirit of unselfishness remains constant through passing
generations, the forms of its expression continually change. *One of
the most fatal enemies of effective service, therefore, is the belated
mind,* which while it feels unselfishly has not caught up with new
ways in which efficient usefulness must work. Many people of sincere
good will are spoiled in their service because they are behind the
times; they lack intelligent grasp on present human needs and on
present means available for meeting them. To pole a neighbor's
stranded rowboat off a shoal is useful service; but to try to pole an
ocean liner off a reef, while the effort may reveal the same good
intention, is distinctly not useful. A modern ocean liner cannot be
gotten off a reef that way, and no amount of willingness to help can
make up for lack of knowledge as to how it should be done.

This peril of a belated mind to efficiency of service is grounded in
the deeper truth, that much of man's most ruinous sin consists in
being behind the times. It is a most disturbing fact that God is not
dead but alive. We love to settle down in customary ways; we put
our minds to bed and tuck them in. But the forward moving purposes of the living God are forever disturbing our repose and forcing
us to move. Humanity settled down on a flat and stationary earth,
with the vault of heaven a few miles above, and to that cosmology
scaled all its thinking, but of a sudden the flat earth rounded out into
a sphere and went spinning through space. God tipped the minds of
all the world out of bed that day and cried "Move on!" Humanity
settled down in a universe large in space but limited in time, created
by fiat a few thousand years before Christ, but of a sudden the years
gave way to aeons and men saw the long leisureliness of the Eternal
unfolding a growing world. God tumbled the minds of men out of
their beds that day and forced a forward march.

What the living God does with our minds he does with our *morals.*
Polygamy once was practiced by the Hebrew patriarchs whose names

still are precious in our memory. Paul's phrase about idolatry is true of polygamy as well: "The times of this ignorance God winked at" (Acts 17:30). But neither God nor man winks at polygamy now, and those who live as the Hebrew patriarchs did are put in jail. Slavery was taken for granted in the ancient world; without a word against it as an institution, the Bible in law, precept, and parable, assumes its presence. But the day came when God commanded all men everywhere to repent of it. Under old aristocracy, commercial monopolies given by royal grant to individuals and families were accounted most sacred property, desecration of which was robbery, but now what once was an hereditary right would be looked upon as scandalous graft. Drunkenness once was taken for granted, and with no diminution of public standing or personal respect was practiced by laymen and clergymen alike. But now neither God nor man allows it any more. A thousand things once thought to be right men now repent of in dust and ashes. What God once seemed to condone, we now know that he condemns.

In wide areas of its worst exhibition, therefore, sin means living in the present age upon the ideals and standards of an age gone by. "It was said unto you of old time," the Master repeatedly insists, "but I say unto you." The commandments which thus he supersedes are not precepts obviously bad; they are allowances of conduct that in the times of men's ignorance God winked at. "Thou shalt not kill," as a sufficient law of brotherliness; "Thou shalt not commit adultery," as a sufficient law of purity; "Thou shalt love thy neighbor and hate thine enemy," as a sufficient law of mercy; "An eye for an eye, and a tooth for a tooth," as a sufficient law of justice—these old standards and ideals, now overpassed, Jesus discards. One way to be a sinner in his eyes is to live in his new day as though the old day still were here. Everywhere in the New Testament the characteristic sinners are men who thus refused to go forward with Jesus' living truth, who refused to move on with Paul's universal Gospel. They were men of the closed mind and the backward look. How many folk there are who deserve Proudhon's comment on Metternich! "If he had been present when God began to bring order out of chaos, Metternich would have prayed fervently, 'O God, preserve chaos!'" The pith and marrow of such sin is this: *men lack the insight to perceive and the willingness to follow the forward movement of the living God.*

The practical consequence is clear. If, being in fact a member of a moving humanity with a living God, a man acts as though he were a member of a stationary humanity with a dead God, he inevitably falls out of the forward march of man's moral life. What else were the atrocities of the late war? The burning of Louvain was shameful. Yet consider this story from Joshua: "Joshua drew not back his hand . . . until he had utterly destroyed all the inhabitants of Ai. . . . Behold the smoke of the city ascended up to heaven and they had no power to flee this way or that way. . . . So Joshua burnt Ai, and made it a heap forever, even a desolation" (Josh. 8:26, 20). The needless destruction of the fruit trees of France aroused universal indignation. Consider then this Old Testament record: "They beat down the cities . . . they stopped all the fountains of water, and felled all the good trees; until in Kir-hareseth only they left the stones thereof" (II Kings 3:25). Personal atrocities seemed intolerably barbarous. Yet listen to this story of David: "He brought forth the people that were therein, and put them under saws, and under harrows of iron and under axes of iron, and made them pass through the brickkiln; and thus did he unto all the cities of the children of Ammon" (II Sam. 12:31). How horrible was deliberate cruelty to enemy children! Yet the Hebrew psalmist sings: "Happy shall he be, that taketh and dasheth thy little ones against the rock" (Psalm 137:9). If, then, we indignantly protest against the atrocious conduct of men in modern war, it is because this is twenty centuries after Christ. Conduct which once was thought to be divinely allowed, we now know to be intolerably cruel and devilish.

So does the living God continually force new truths and new ideals upon his children. As General Booth remarked, "You can keep company with God only by running at full speed." Being up to date too often means cheap compliance with a passing fad. It even means refusal to obey truths that being old are ever new, because they never fail. But the perversions of so important a matter as being abreast of the times ought never to cause a Christian to surrender the virtue of it. Imagine a soldier in the trenches who at zero hour decides not to stir. The forward movement has begun but he sits still. Is it, then, so heinous a deed merely to sit still? They *shoot* men for that. So one who stays where he is when the living God has ordered an advance falls under the condemnation of the New Testament. The New Testament throbs with new truths, new hopes, new enterprises, and it called men to its cause who had eyes to see and courage to follow unblazed trails. The true successors of the first apostles

have been men of Livingstone's spirit: "I will go anywhere provided
it be forward."

II

*What the living God does with our minds and our morals he does
with our methods of service.* The spirit and motive of unselfish living
abide, but the machinery of their expression changes. When selfishness fails to conquer a man's generous sentiments, it still may spoil
his usefulness by a belated mind. A soldier at Verdun with bow and
arrows, however brave he be, is about as valuable as no soldier at all.

The urgency of this fact is evident as soon as one remembers the
amazing new powers that modern science has given to men. The
gambler, the murderer, the thief, and the Christian alike have new
tools to work with, which make old methods as obsolete as winnow-
ing by wind. Science has put into the hands of the race such power
as the ancient world never dreamed of; what the race will do with it
is the question on whose answer the hopes of human kind depend.
The one solution of this crucial problem which can relieve the race
from the certainty of ruin is that this new power should be used for
man's service, not for man's destruction.

How perilous the situation is the last terrific years have unmis-
takably revealed. Once science was widely hailed as the savior of the
world. It is reported, however, that Sir Oliver Lodge, lecturing in his
classroom, called the attention of his pupils to the fact that hitherto
science has dealt largely with molecular forces, like steam and electricity, but that now science has its finger tips upon atomic forces,
such as radium. There is enough atomic force, he said, in a mass of
matter no larger than a man's fist to lift the German fleet from the
bottom of the sea and put it on the hill behind Manchester. Then he
paused in his enthusiasm. God forbid, he said, that science now
should cast its harness over the atomic forces! We are not fit to
handle them. Put such a prodigious power into our possession in our
present state and with it we would damn the race.

Such a shift of emphasis from confidence in science to deadly fear
of it is not unjustified. Science has made liquid fire and poison gas,
the submarine and the tank. Science has made guns that at seventy
miles can blast to pieces undefended towns. Science has threatened
to use bacteriology, at first intended to halt epidemics, to cause them
instead. Science has made it possible for a war that started with the

crack of an assassin's pistol at Sarajevo to spread over all the world
and to comprehend humanity in colossal ruin. Science has opened
the door to financial systems by which nations, waging war to the
point of exhaustion, can pledge the credit of many generations yet
unborn. Nobel, the inventor, gave the world dynamite with one hand
and then with the other Nobel, the philanthropist, gave the Peace
Prize to help save the world from the appalling consequence of the
use in war of his invention. The incident is a true parable of our
situation. Modern science presents us with a world headed for perdition unless the spirit of service can take possession of the new
powers which science has conferred.

III

At first this task seems too immense to lay special responsibility
upon the little powers of ordinary folk. But like all large tasks it is
soon reduced to fractions, and every worker for the good of men
can handle part of it. A serviceable man will indeed catch the vision
of a new world in which the increasing powers conferred by science
are set to useful, not destructive tasks. But he will also catch the
vision of his own life mastered by the same spirit. From teaching a
Sunday school class to managing an industry, from tending children
in the home to conducting a missionary enterprise, he will seek to
belt new knowledge into his usefulness. He will look on inefficiency
as sin. He will regard with the same abhorrence visited on all iniquity any willingness to do a good task in less than the best way.
He will hate with perfect hatred the slipshod spirit—

"All along o' doin' things rather-more-or-less."

In home and school, in church and business, in court and legislature, this is a fact upon the recognition of which great issues hang:
usefulness is not a matter of heart alone but of head, not of kind
intention but of efficient skill; slovenliness is wickedness and escapa-
ble ineptitude is treachery; no man's benevolent feeling can cover
from condemnation his avoidable fumbling of a noble task. So says
the Book of Proverbs: "He that is slack in his work is brother to
him that is a destroyer."

One subtle temptation continually assails all Christian service.
Folks suppose that the good will which motives it and the good ends
for which it works will somehow assure its victory. The children of

light, as Jesus said, are tempted to be less wise in their generation than the children of darkness. Outworn methods that we would scorn in business we employ in church. We use the aptest tools, the latest knowledge to make money; we give it away with spasmodic carelessness, as though it were not one of life's most difficult tasks to give money wisely to the help of need. We know efficiency is necessary in self-seeking; we often act as though service were so beautiful in spirit that efficiency could be dispensed with. But God is no friend of fools. We can no more successfully serve him with obsolete ecclesiastical machinery and methods long outgrown than we can carry on modern commerce with dugout canoes or clothe the world from family spinning wheels. We can no more heal the sick and feed the hungry by institutions appropriate to our grandfathers' tasks than we could use oxcarts for locomotives.

Neighborly alms were sufficient in the simple life of a Palestinian village. But he who now restricts his ministry to the poor of a modern city to such haphazard giving as may be called out by his personal discovery of need, is behind the times. Organized philanthropy is indispensable and systematic support of it is a duty. To visit the sick and minister to their healing was a sufficient expression of Christian good will at first, but a man without imagination to see the necessity of hospitals and boards of health and education in hygiene in modern society has a belated mind. To be friendly with fellow-workmen and apprentices in a home shop was adequate brotherliness in days before our modern factories came. But now that employers and employees do not know each other, often have never met each other, live far apart from each other in sympathy and circumstances, and bitterness grows rampant out of the sundered brotherhood, one who does not see the necessity of establishing on a wide scale new methods of democratic cooperation in industry has a mind like Rip Van Winkle's, a generation behind the times. Sectarian Protestantism was once the servant of liberty and men worked through it for great gains, but he who does not see now the necessity for cooperation and unity among Christians, in the face of the world's present needs and tasks, belongs to a past age and is alive after his time. Kindly feeling alone cannot gird a modern man for usefulness. Alert and disciplined intelligence is indispensable to the largest service. To desire to do good is positively dangerous unless one knows what it is good to do.

No one of us can escape the application of this truth to his own service in any realm, however limited. To "take" a Sunday school class is one thing, to teach it is another. To give money is one thing, to help people by giving it is another. To have friends is one thing, to be a master of effective friendliness is another. To be a father or mother, intrusted with a child, is one thing, to be fit to be one is another. In particular, however, our truth is a challenge to all men and women to whom God has given special gifts of leadership. Blessings forever on that youth, endowed with an alert and able mind, who uses his skill to guide bewildered folk, eager to serve but not knowing how, into wise uses of some new power that mankind possesses!

If mankind's intelligence is once deliberately set to this task of using the powers of the new era for serviceable ends, the vistas are as bright with hope as otherwise they are dark with dread. Men thought the age of miracles had passed, but through the knowledge of law a greater age is here. Possibilities that to older generations seemed Utopian now are practicable hopes: humanity can be saved from illiteracy and poverty, war can be abolished, industry can be democratized, and physical and moral scourges that have afflicted the race through all its history can be eliminated. Yellow fever for ages has been the bane and dread of men. Today the five localities on the planet where yellow fever breeds have been plotted out and now are being stalked by scientists as a hunter stalks his game. Surgeon-General Gorgas said that in the end we could make the yellow fever germ as obsolete as the woolly rhinoceros. Hookworm has been sapping the vigor, destroying the ambition, ruining the characters and homes of men for generations. It is a secret, insidious, debilitating disease, whose consequence is listlessness of mind, body, and spirit. One agency took up the problem; found a simple and absolute remedy; proved its case in experimental localities; and today the leading nations of the world are cooperatively attacking and in time can completely overcome an evil that now makes a belt of needless feebleness around the world. Famines, periodic and overwhelming, concerning which no attitude seemed possible save pious resignation, now are known to be utterly needless. Engineering can reclaim useless lands by irrigation; chemistry can save useless soil by fertilization; scientific agriculture can multiply output; means of communication can make one country's products available everywhere on earth.

Nor are the new agencies less useful to the higher ranges of man's life. Better education more widely given, better philanthropy more effectively administered, better government more ably managed, better churches more splendidly useful—such things are within the grasp of our hands if we will take them. And as for the world-wide, Christian cause, Mr. J. Brierley was right: "George Stephenson had as little to do as most men with theology. But his railway locomotive in making the evangelist free, on easy terms with the whole world, has enlarged the religious frontier more than the united labors of shiploads of D.D.'s."

"The moral equivalent of war" has been sought for as though it were difficult to find. Surely not only the moral equivalent of any supposed benefit of war, but the moral cure of war's undoubted horrors and spiritual debaucheries is at hand. To discover and harness for useful tasks the immense powers of our world, to build here in the face of appalling obstacles a decent home for the family of God, is the most arousing task that mankind ever faced. If mankind will but face it in genuine earnest, the stimulus of war will not be missed.

When that leading figure in American philanthropy, Samuel Gridley Howe, left the army of Greece where he had fought for Greek independence and threw himself into a lifelong war against the hardships that oppressed the blind and the insane, he did not cease to be a "Sir Galahad and Good Samaritan" combined. It was this last fight that made Whittier sing of him:

> "Knight of a better era,
> Without reproach or fear,
> Said I not well that Bayards
> And Sidneys still are here?"

IV

In one special realm the perils of a belated mind can be clearly illustrated. Consider the *financial responsibilities* which in an early American settlement a Christian might be expected to assume! They were few and simple. To support his family, to pay taxes, to contribute to the local church, to help his neighbors in their need—whoever did these well was a good Christian and a generous man. If famine raged in India, he did not hear of it. If Turks massacred Armenians, no rumor of it reached his ears. Or if at last the news did come, of what benefit was that? No railroads, no steamship lines, no cables, no world-wide credit system that makes money fly faster than the wind, were at his service. No possibility of world-wide helpfulness was open to him, no responsibility for extensive generosity rested on him.

How many who call themselves Christians live in this new day as though the old day still were here! They, too, support their families, pay taxes, contribute to the local church, and on occasion give to the neediest cases in their town. That is the limit of their financial output. In this modern world they are anachronisms. They are as out of date as horse-cars on New York City's streets. At least a century has passed over their heads without their knowing it. For one of the miracles of our age is the power it puts into the hands of a man with a few dollars to join himself with other men who have a few dollars, and within a few hours to put the pooled resources of all at work anywhere on earth from the center of China to the heart of the Congo. One marvel of this new era is the romance of stewardship.

When an appeal for money is made in church or town or nation, it commonly is regarded as a necessity to be endured or a nuisance to be avoided. Nor is there any wonder that such distaste is associated with financial campaigns, when one considers the frequent tone of their appeal. You *ought* to give; you *ought* to be generous; it is your *duty*—how commonly are we assailed by such injunctions! Yet modern opportunities for money's use are more marvelous and enticing than "Arabian Nights" and more romantic than the folklore of any people. A Christian missionary, Armenian by birth, American by education, was slain by the Kurds on his sickbed in the presence of his wife. His family escaped. Once, no matter how dearly his American friends had loved him, no matter how ardently they had wished for his sake to help his children, they could have done nothing. But in this marvelous era they at once reduce a little of themselves to monetary form, the most portable shape into which human personality can precipitate itself, and in that form they go straightway overseas to Persia and bring back their friend's wife and children to a safe home and a liberal education. One who can see in such an opportunity nothing but duty is blind. Who would not love to play with this new white magic by which a man can put himself at work around the world?

Once in an isolated settlement of the old world of slow communications, a man could hear of cruel need in the antipodes and could go home with nothing but sympathy to offer. Let no man in this modern world express sympathy with any need anywhere on earth unless he *means* it! The acid test can straightway be applied. For we can *do something*, no matter where the need may be. The agencies of human helpfulness now reach in an encompassing network over all the earth. The avenues are open down which our pennies, our dollars, or our millions can walk together in an accumulating multitude to the succor of all mankind. Each of us can take some of his own nerve and sinew reduced in wages to the form of money, and through money, which is a naturalized citizen of all lands and which speaks all languages, can be at work wherever the sun shines. It is a privilege which no one knew before our modern age. It is one of the miracles of science, mastered by the spirit of service, that a man busy at his daily tasks at home can yet be preaching the Gospel in Alaska, healing the sick in Korea, teaching in the schools of Persia, feeding the hungry in India, and building a new civilization at the head waters of the Nile. Consider, then, the shame of one who in such an era is still a spiritual inhabitant of an age gone by! Only a man who with generous, systematic stewardship is taking advantage of the new opportunities is fully abreast of his times.

What is true of opportunity for financial service is true of many new agencies for usefulness which the modern world has given us. Once our fathers living under absolutism could not control at all the processes of government; now a democratic state offers new chances of usefulness through citizenship and new obligations to employ them well. Once our fathers, never having dreamed of such an invention as movable type, had neither chance nor responsibility to use the printed page; now the printing press offers a supremely powerful agency of education and evangelization. Once nations, lacking all vital contacts with one another, could become international neither in their spirit nor in their political arrangements; now nations are woven by countless vital relationships into each other's lives and these accumulating contacts offer the supreme opportunity of all history to bring in the day of international cooperation. On every side new powers and new possibilities are put into our hands. The best hopes of mankind cannot be realized save as these new powers are converted, baptized, Christianized, and harnessed for ministry to human weal. A belated mind, therefore, is fatal to large usefulness.

"New occasions teach new duties; Time makes ancient good uncouth;

They must upward still, and onward, who would keep abreast of
    Truth;
Lo, before us gleam her camp-fires! we ourselves must Pilgrims be,
Launch our Mayflower, and steer boldly through the desperate
    winter sea,
Nor attempt the Future's portal with the Past's blood-rusted key."

CHAPTER X

The Great Obstacle

DAILY READINGS

We are to consider this week the difficulties which the Christian spirit of service faces when it encounters the economic motives and practices common in industry and commerce. There is a strange prejudice in some quarters that Christianity ought not to concern itself with economic questions at all. One would suppose that any system of faith and conduct, if it is to be good for anything, must concern itself with the most absorbing portion of man's life, his toil for sustenance. It certainly is clear that Jesus had more to say about money, its making and its spending, its perils and its uses, than about any other subject whatsoever. Let us inquire, therefore, in our daily readings, what the enormous stakes are which Christianity has in the economic problem.

Tenth Week, First Day

But they that are minded to be rich fall into a temptation and a snare and many foolish and hurtful lusts, such as drown men in destruction and perdition. For the love of money is a root of all kinds of evil: which some reaching after have been led astray from the faith, and have pierced themselves through with many sorrows.

But thou, O man of God, flee these things; and follow after righteousness, godliness, faith, love, patience, meekness.—I Tim. 6:9-11.

No one would deny that Christianity is chiefly interested in the *conquest of sin*. But sin does not exist in general, it exists in concrete, particular forms, and when one traces to their origin the iniquities that are most familiarly ruinous, one discovers how correctly this

passage from First Timothy locates their source. "The master iniquities of our time," says Professor E. A. Ross, "are connected with
money-making." It is futile, therefore, for the Christian individual
or the Christian Church to deal in general with a vague, diffused,
undefined idea of sin, while all the time the concrete sins of the
economic life are ruining men. And it is also futile to attack the
merely personal transgressions of equity in business and avoid dealing with the organization of business itself which so often is the
occasion of them. Consider this passage from St. Augustine's "City
of God":

"That was an apt and true reply which was given to Alexander
the Great by a pirate whom he seized. For when that King had asked
the man how he durst so molest the sea, he answered with bold
pride: 'How darest thou molest the whole world? But because I do
it with a little ship I am called a robber, whilst thou who dost it
with a great fleet art styled Emperor.' "

Surely the Christian cannot so lend himself to discrimination
against minor economic sins in favor of great ones. Whoever sets
himself seriously to be a Christian and to labor for a Christian world,
therefore, must deal with the economic problem, in both its individual and social aspects.

*O Thou, whose commandment is life eternal, we confess that we
have broken Thy Law, in that we have sought our own gain and
good rather than Thy gracious Will, who willest good unto all men.
We have sinned by class injustice, by indifference to the sufferings of
the poor, by want of patriotism, by hypocrisy and secret self-seeking.
But do Thou in Thy mercy hear us. Turn Thou our hearts that we
may truly repent, and utterly abhor the great and manifold evils
which our sins have brought upon the nation. Break down our idols
of pride and wealth. Shatter our self-love. Open our eyes to know in
daily life, in public work, that Thou alone art God. Thee only let us
worship, Thee only let us serve, for His sake, who sought not His
own will but Thine alone.—M. P. G. E.*

Tenth Week, Second Day

Come now, ye rich, weep and howl for your miseries that are
coming upon you. Your riches are corrupted, and your garments

are moth-eaten. Your gold and your silver are rusted; and their rust shall be for a testimony against you, and shall eat your flesh as fire. Ye have laid up your treasure in the last days. Behold, the hire of the laborers who mowed your fields, which is of you kept back by fraud, crieth out: and the cries of them that reaped have entered into the ears of the Lord of Sabaoth. Ye have lived delicately on the earth, and taken your pleasure; ye have nourished your hearts in a day of slaughter.—James 5:1-5.

One has only to read such passages as Matt. 19:24, Luke 6:24, Luke 12:15 f, Luke 16:13 f, to see that James, the brother of our Lord, was true to the tradition which Jesus left, when he spoke these words. One reason why the Christian cannot avoid the economic application of the Gospel is because he is sincerely interested in character; and *wealth, acquired as it often is, is ruinous to the characters of those who win it.* Two per cent of the people in the United States own sixty per cent of the wealth. If by the poor we mean those whose possession consists only of clothing, furniture, and personal belongings to the value of $400 each, then one man in the United States owns as much as 2,500,000 of his fellow-citizens. That is perilous to the commonwealth; but it is also perilous to the rich. When we see a wealthy man, who, honorably fortunate, is as simple in his life and as sensitive in his conscience as when he was a boy, as amiable, approachable, democratic, fraternal, and generous as when his business life began, we have seen one of the most difficult and admirable spiritual victories that a man can win. But consider Henry Ward Beecher's vivid and precise description of the other type, which James also had in mind.

"There are men of wealth in New York, honored, because prosperous, who heap up riches, and hoard them, and live in a magnificent selfishness. They use the whole of society as a cluster to be squeezed into their cup. They are neither active in any enterprise of good, except for their own prosperity, nor generous to their fellows. They build palaces, and fill them sumptuously; but the poor starve and freeze around about them. No struggling creature of the army of the weak ever blesses them. And yet their names are heralded. They walk in specious and spectacular honor. Men flatter them, and fawn upon them. Dying, the newspapers, like so many trumpets in procession, go blaring after them to that grave over which should be inscribed the text of Scripture, 'The name of the wicked shall rot.'"

We pray for our land. Let us not be left unrich in manhood. De-
stroy our ships; destroy our dwellings; but grant that poverty may
not come upon manhood in this nation. Raise up nobler men—men
that shall scorn bribes; men that shall not run greedily to ambition;
men that shall not be devoured by selfishness; men that shall fear
God and love man; men that shall love this nation with a pure and
disinterested love. And so we beseech of Thee that our peace may
stand firm upon integrity, and that righteousness may everywhere
prevail. Amen.—Henry Ward Beecher.

Tenth Week, Third Day

Thus saith Jehovah: For three transgressions of Israel, yea, for
four, I will not turn away the punishment thereof; because they
have sold the righteous for silver, and the needy for a pair of shoes
—they that pant after the dust of the earth on the head of the poor,
and turn aside the way of the meek: and a man and his father go
unto the same maiden, to profane my holy name: and they lay
themselves down beside every altar upon clothes taken in pledge;
and in the house of their God they drink the wine of such as have
been fined.—Amos 2:6-8.

Jehovah will enter into judgment with the elders of his people,
and the princes thereof: It is ye that have eaten up the vineyard;
the spoil of the poor is in your houses: what mean ye that ye crush
my people, and grind the face of the poor? saith the Lord, Jehovah
of hosts.—Isa. 3:14, 15.

The people of the land have used oppression, and exercised robbery; yea, they have vexed the poor and needy, and have oppressed the sojourner wrongfully.—Ezek. 22:29

How can one say that the prophets of God were not dealing with
their business when they were dealing with the problem of poverty?
Poverty is not alone a matter of dollars; it translates itself into *sickness, ruined family life, wayward and untended children, cramped
opportunity, blasted character.* Consider the portentous meaning in
terms of human life of such simple facts as these: in Chicago, in
1914, one person in every twenty-eight was given relief; of every ten
persons who die in New York City, one is buried at public expense in
the Potter's Field; upward of thirty per cent of the city and town
population in England live in extreme poverty; some 10,000,000

people in the United States are habitually below the poverty line. Add also the fact that in Great Britain and the United States the cases of destitution due to misfortune outnumber two to one the cases due to misconduct.[1] Can the Church pass by on the other side of such a situation? Can the Church content itself with giving alms to alleviate poverty when the conditions which cause it are still at work? Theodore Roosevelt once said: "This country will not be a good place for any of us to live in unless we make it a good place for all of us to live in."

We pray for our own Nation, and for all whom we ourselves have set in authority, and for all true social reformers therein, that crying evils may be abolished, and that peace and happiness, truth and justice, true religion and piety may be established in the land for all generations.—W. B. Graham.

Tenth Week, Fourth Day

Whence come wars and whence come fightings among you? come they not hence, even of your pleasures that war in your members? Ye lust, and have not: ye kill, and covet, and cannot obtain: ye fight and war; ye have not, because ye ask not. Ye ask, and receive not, because ye ask amiss, that ye may spend it in your pleasures.— James 4:1-3.

Surely there is no more central interest in Christianity than *the winning of human life to the principle of love and brotherhood.* How, then, can the Christian avoid the economic problem? For the seams and cracks and open ruptures that rend class from class today, and plunge us into endless turmoil and fratricidal strife, all run along economic lines. James is right when he ascribes wars and fightings to covetousness. The very crux of the whole problem of fraternal living lies not in home and church and neighborhood but in the class-conscious strife of employers and employees, in the rivalry of competitive industry, in the avarice of nations for economic advantage. To talk of brotherhood without reference to these crucial questions is to beat the air. Must not the Church, then, take to heart such words as these from Bishop Gore? "This is the first great claim that we make upon the Church today; that it should make a tre-

---

[1] Warner, "American Charities," revised edition, 1908, pp. 50-53.

mendous act of penitence for having failed so long and on so wide a scale to behave as the champion of the oppressed and the weak; for having tolerated what it ought not to have tolerated; for having so often been on the wrong side. And the penitence must lead to reparation while there is yet time, ere the well-merited judgments of God take all weapons of social influence out of our hands."

O God, the Father, Origin of Divinity, good beyond all that is good, fair beyond all that is fair, in whom is calmness, peace, and concord; do Thou make up the dissensions which divide us from each other, and bring us back into an unity of love, which may bear some likeness to Thy sublime Nature. Amen.—Jacobite Liturgy of St. Dionysius.

Tenth Week, Fifth Day

My brethren, hold not the faith of our Lord Jesus Christ, the Lord of glory, with respect of persons. For if there come into your synagogue a man with a gold ring, in fine clothing, and there come in also a poor man in vile clothing; and ye have regard to him that weareth the fine clothing, and say, Sit thou here in a good place; and ye say to the poor man, Stand thou there, or sit under my footstool; do ye not make distinctions among yourselves, and become judges with evil thoughts? Hearken, my beloved brethren; did not God choose them that are poor as to the world to be rich in faith, and heirs of the kingdom which he promised to them that love him? But ye have dishonored the poor man. Do not the rich oppress you, and themselves drag you before the judgment-seats? Do not they blaspheme the honorable name by which ye are called? Howbeit if ye fulfil the royal law, according to the scripture, Thou shalt love thy neighbor as thyself, ye do well: but if ye have respect of persons, ye commit sin, being convicted by the law as transgressors.—James 2:1-9.

With all the failures of which organized Christianity has been guilty, something of this accent of human equality before God has been retained. Where today do we find the acutest economic unrest? In the non-Christian world? Rather in Christendom, and often in those very parts of Christendom where widespread privilege has been greatest. Our economic restlessness does not come because conditions are worse, but because, in general, they are better. We cannot educate the people, build schools, erect libraries, print newspapers, and make as widespread as possible the gains of civilization without awakening such ambition for more education, more comfort, more leisure, more equality, in the whole mass of the people as never stirred men in history before. Edwin Markham's "Man with a Hoe" causes no industrial unrest.

> "Bowed by the weight of centuries he leans
> Upon his hoe and gazes on the ground,
> The emptiness of ages in his face,
> And on his back the burden of the world."

But awaken in his sluggish, sullen breast even the dim suspicion that seeds are slumbering there which, sunned by fairer economic opportunity, would blossom into education, privilege, comfort, equality, and power for him and for his children, and then industrial unrest will come. Spencer was right: "The more things improve, the louder become the exclamations about their badness." Our very economic problem, therefore, is in large part the child of Christianity's desire and hope. It springs from just such vehement championship of the poor as the Lord's brother felt. And multitudes of Christian business men share that spirit and are trying to work it out in industry and commerce. Christianity cannot evade her responsibility. *The problem which she helped to create, she must help to solve.*

Merciful Father, to whom all sons of men are dear, we pray for all that sit in darkness and in the shadow of death, that the Dayspring from on high may visit them; for the poor and oppressed, for those that dwell amid ugliness and squalor, far from loveliness and purity, and for whom the fire-gemmed heavens shine in vain; for those who toil beyond their strength and beyond Thine ordinance, without pleasure in the work of their hands, and without hope of rest; for those who sink back to the beast, and seek to drown all thought and feeling, and for all who are trampled under foot by men. Raise up deliverance for the peoples. Amen.—"A Book of Prayers for Students."

Tenth Week, Sixth Day

Ye are the salt of the earth: but if the salt have lost its savor, wherewith shall it be salted? it is thenceforth good for nothing, but

to be cast out and trodden under foot of men. Ye are the light of
the world. A city set on a hill cannot be hid. Neither do men light a
lamp, and put it under the bushel, but on the stand; and it shineth
unto all that are in the house. Even so let your light shine before
men; that they may see your good works, and glorify your Father
who is in heaven.—Matt. 5:13-16.

These words, usually applied to individuals, have today an unmistakable application to Christendom as a whole. Is she letting her
light shine that the non-Christian world may see her good works?
*Rather the whole program of foreign missions is inextricably tied up
with the present economic and international situation in Christendom,* and our evil deeds often speak louder than any words our missionaries can say. The Church's stake in the economic question is
immediate and vital. The most critical point in her missionary program lies here: the non-Christian world suspects our civilization of
colossal failure and has reason to. The barriers are all down. Cal-
cutta and Pekin know us through and through; the islands of the sea
understand our miserable failure to be brotherly in business and in
statecraft. So an Oriental speaks: "You wonder why Christianity
makes such slow progress among us. I will tell you why. It is because
you are not like your Christ." Until we can make brotherhood work
in industry and international relations we leave a great barrier across
the path of all the heralds of the Cross.

*We beseech Thee to hear us, O God, for all who profess and call
themselves Christians, that they may be led to the right understanding and practice of their holy faith; for all who preach the
Gospel of Jesus Christ; for all missionaries, evangelists, and teachers,
and for all who are seeking and striving in other ways to bless their
fellows, and to build up the Kingdom of God in the world, that they
may be steadfast and faithful, and that their labour may not be in
vain; through Jesus Christ Thy Son our Lord. Amen.*—John Hunter.

Tenth Week, Seventh Day

After this manner therefore pray ye: Our Father who art in
heaven, Hallowed be thy name. Thy kingdom come. Thy will be
done, as in heaven, so on earth. Give us this day our daily bread.

And forgive us our debts, as we also have forgiven our debtors. And
bring us not into temptation, but deliver us from the evil one.—
Matt. 6:9-13.

How often we say that prayer without praying it! At its very beginning the Master put the dominant desire of his life—the Kingdom. And he defined what he meant—no superhuman realm of
disembodied spirits, but God's will done here on earth. But that
transformed earth cannot come without changes. To save the world
without altering it is absurd. Wherever Christianity goes, it transforms conditions; it becomes in any land where its disciples carry it
a "standard of revolution." Would anybody expect polygamy, human sacrifice, infanticide, cannibalism, to persist where Christian
missions go? How then can conditions at home which hurt the children of God be tamely allowed, undisturbed by the antagonism of
the Christian people? *Christianity denies its own nature when it
keeps its hands off any situation which cripples personality.*

Such is the stake which Christianity has in the economic question.
The sins it fights are often born of the economic struggle; the characters it tries to save are often spoiled by excessive wealth or crushed
by excessive poverty; the brotherhood it endeavors to further is prevented by economic strife; the very industrial unrest which must be
dealt with, Christianity itself somehow helped to cause; its world-
wide evangel is hampered by our lamentable economic chaos; and
the hope of the Kingdom is a perpetual challenge to discontent with
conditions which deny it.

*We beseech of Thee that Thou wilt forgive us our selfishness, and
our pride, and our sordidness, and our abandonment of things spiritual, and our inordinate attachment to things carnal and temporal.
Forgive, we beseech of Thee, our unkindness one to another. Forgive
us that in honor we have sought our own selves first, and not others;
that we have not borne one another's burdens, and fulfilled the law
of God Forgive us that we have made ourselves unlovely by our evil
carriage. Forgive us that we have failed to discharge those obligations of love and gratitude which Thy sufferings and Thy death and
Thy resurrection have laid every one of us under. Open the way of
the future for us, that we may walk without stumbling; that we may
live with a higher purpose and better accomplishment; that we may*

*not only be forgiven for past sin, but be cured of sin, and of those
infirmities out of which so many transgressions spring. Amen.—*
Henry Ward Beecher.

COMMENT FOR THE WEEK

I

The *giving* of money clearly is involved in effective modern
service, but the *making* of money is even more closely interlaced
with the problem of a serviceable life. In what sharp contrast with
our acquisitive spirit in business, where men compete for profit and
where one's success so often means another's failure, does our talk
of service stand! We are told to love each other, to desire each the
other's good as though it were his own, to let sympathy, magnanimity, generosity, control our thought and conduct. Then we go out
into the scramble of our commercial life. Just how can the ideal of
service be naturalized in so alien a land as this industrial system of
competing individuals, corporations, economic groups, and greedy
nations, all struggling for profit?

Two Christians may meet in brotherly love in family and neighborhood and wish each other every good. But if one opens a grocery
in their little town next door to the grocery which the other long
has kept, how shall they pray for each other when each man's gain
means the other's loss? "O God"—will the older merchant pray?—
"bless his business; give him customers; open the hearts of our citizens more and more to desire his wares; may each year enlarge his
boundaries and increase his patrons and his profits!" One suspects
that if Saint Francis of Assisi himself, instead of leaving the world
to be a monk, had been a grocer—a much more difficult enterprise—
he could not with earnest zeal have prayed like that. "Thou shalt
not covet," sounds well in the abstract, but it becomes perplexing
when one adds, "Thou shalt not covet thy neighbor's customers."

From so simple a situation through the whole *melée* of our industrial life, how much of our business is a constant and terrific temptation to selfishness! Men are tempted to hire laborers as cheaply as
possible, regardless of the living conditions imposed by the wages
paid, and laborers are tempted to give as slack work as they can
manage for as large pay as they can get. Men are tempted to sell
goods as dearly as possible, regardless of families thrust below the

poverty line by the increasing cost of life's necessities. "I think it is fair to get out of the consumers all you can, consistent with the business proposition"—so testified the head of a great American corporation supplying an article of food without which men cannot live. Men are tempted to knead chalk, alum, and plaster into bread, to make children's candy with terra alba, to put cocaine into popular drinks and chloroform into children's remedies, to preserve milk with formalin, and to sell dried peas and cocoa shells for coffee. And they *do* it, so that in 1906 before the Pure Food Bill was passed the American Secretary of Agriculture reported that thirty per cent of all money paid for food in the United States was paid for adulterated and misbranded goods.

What appalling selfishness is engendered by our competitive struggle after profits! For money's sake men defraud the poor, so that in a single three months in New York City 3,906 falsely adjusted scales and measures were confiscated by inspectors. For money's sake men make life-preservers that will not float; they maintain hovels at high rentals to the ruin of human life; they practice jerry-building to the jeopardy of all subsequent occupants; they fill our business life with petty pilfering and small graft; they gamble in securities in an organized endeavor to get something for nothing; they make journalism yellow with tales of crime and appeals to sex; they take profiteering advantage of war and coin into cash the bloody sacrifices of the world's best youth; they play on the appetite for drugs and stimulants and make commercial gain from the purposed degradation of manhood; they traffic in the bodies of women; they prostitute the drama to ignoble uses and seek eagerly for plays that, as a producer recently declared with appalling candor, "appeal from the waist down." The meanest, most cynical and unscrupulous selfishness that stops at no cruelty and that feels no shame is the fruit of the economic struggle. The New Testament is right: "The love of money is a root of all kinds of evil" (I Tim. 6:10).

We have spoken in these studies of sacrificial conflicts against inveterate abuses, such as political absolutism, legal monopolies, slave systems, the liquor traffic. What, then, is the sinister power which has made these conflicts for a better world so difficult and has made so laggard and uncertain the final victory? Always the selfishness of vested interests has stood across the path of progress. In New York City a northern merchant called out Mr. May, the philanthropist, from an antislavery meeting and said to him: "Mr. May, we are not such fools as not to know that slavery is a great evil; a great wrong. But it was consented to by the founders of our Republic. It was provided for in the Constitution of our Union. A great portion of the property of the Southerners is invested under its sanction; and the business of the North, as well as the South, has become adjusted to it. There are millions upon millions of dollars due from Southerners to the merchants and mechanics of this city alone, the payment of which would be jeopardized by any rupture between the North and the South. We cannot afford, sir, to let you and your associates succeed in your endeavor to overthrow slavery. It is not a matter of principle with us. It is a matter of business necessity. We cannot afford to let you succeed. I have called you out to let you know, and to let your fellow-laborers know, that we do not mean to allow you to succeed. We mean, sir," he said, with increased emphasis—"we mean, sir, to put you Abolitionists down—by fair means if we can, by foul means if we must."

When the interests of property have been imperiled by humane reforms, that tone of voice has been one of the most familiar sounds in history. Why do so many children still work in the shops and factories of rich America? Why is it so bitterly difficult to pass legislation for their relief, or to assure safety appliances in factories, or to gain decent conditions for women in industry? What was the organized source of power that for years bribed legislators, bought up electorates, debauched the judiciary, and exhausted every sinister method known to human ingenuity to stave off all encroachments on the liquor traffic's exploitation of the people? Macaulay said that if the multiplication table had interfered with any vested interests, some people would not have believed it yet.

Nor is this hardness and selfishness of our economic struggle altogether a matter of personal ill will. Men of generous good will are caught in it, and do not know how to extricate themselves. How can a merchant easily pay high wages and give shorter hours to the girls who serve him, when his rival pays low wages and works his laborers long hours? How can a manufacturer in one state welcome legislation that saddles him with the expense of safety appliances, shorter hours, and high wages, when in a neighboring state his rivals are under no restrictions? Just what shall an honest and serviceable business do when it is held up by a legislature with ruinous bills plainly intended for blackmail? What shall an employer do if, when wages increase, shiftless laborers work only half as many days and live as they did before? What shall laborers do if, working faithfully, they find themselves out of employment half the year? *Whether he be employer or employee, the most colossal difficulty which many a man faces when he sets himself to live unselfishly, is presented by the ingrained selfishness of the economic struggle.*

II

All this, in principle, is familiar to anyone who knows the gospels. The preeminent enemy which the Master faced as he proclaimed his evangel of good will was Mammon. He, too, saw rich young men not far from the Kingdom, held back from whole-hearted service by the love of money (Mark 10:17 f). He, too, saw Dives lulled into selfish indolence by great possessions (Luke 16:19 f) ; saw brotherhood cut asunder by covetous desires (Luke 12:13 f) ; saw able business men absorbing all their energies in heaping wealth on wealth in ever enlarging barns (Luke 12:16 f) ; saw grafters even in the temple courts (Mark 11:15). He, too, found his message met by the sneers of "Pharisees, who were lovers of money" (Luke 16:14), and in the circle of his friends he was betrayed by a man with an itching palm.

The Master was not the sponsor of any economic theory. No social panacea may rightly claim the sanction of his name. But he was the teacher and exemplar of the spirit of service, and he found in the economic struggle for money his chief antagonist. He wanted men to possess the heavenly treasures of the Spirit, and they sought with absorbed concern treasures where moth and rust corrupt and thieves break through and steal (Matt. 6:19). He sowed the seed of the Gospel, looking for fruitage in serviceable lives, and the "deceitfulness of riches" choked it (Matt. 13:22). He saw life as a marvelously rich experience, but his passion to share his life with others was balked in those who sordidly thought that their lives consisted in the abundance of the things which they possessed (Luke 12:15). Everywhere he found the issue joined between economic acquisitiveness and useful living, and he stated the issue in clear-cut, uncompromising words: "No servant can serve two masters: for either he will hate the one and love the other; or else he will hold to one, and despise the other. Ye cannot serve God and mammon" (Luke 16:13).

The situation since the Master's day has not in essence greatly changed. What tragedies today befall the characters of our young

men and women! Youth is naturally idealistic; it responds to the
appeal of chivalry; if rightly trained, it feels the lure of knighthood
and desires to ride abroad redressing human wrongs. With such a
spirit of service our best youth go out from our schools and colleges,
and the saddest sight that eyes can see is their gradual disillusionment, their loss of knightly thoughts, their subjugation to mercenary
motives, and at last in how many cases the utter triumph in them of
sordid ambitions!

Many of them long maintain the struggle between the ideals of
sacrificial usefulness and the actualities of business. They live a
bifurcated life. They read the Master's teaching with an approval
which they cannot deny; they see in the economic conflict necessities which they cannot evade; and the two do not agree. Finally,
however, the balance dips one way or the other. Some deliberately
throw over the Christian ethic and become confessedly selfish; some
consciously apply one set of ideals to home and friends, to church
and neighborhood, and another to business, changing gear between
the two, and losing all unity and wholeness from their lives; some
become morally blinded by the continual impact of the economic
struggle, until they seriously think that our merciless competitive
conflicts after profits is not unchristian in the least. The last estate is
the most hopeless. So Bishop Gore cries: "What I am complaining
of is—not that commercial and social selfishness exists in the world,
or even that it appears to dominate in society; but that its profound
antagonism to the spirit of Christ is not recognized—that there is not
among us anything that can be called an adequate conception of
what Christian morality means."

III

In his relationship with the making of money, therefore, lies for
many a man the nub of the problem of a serviceable life. Let it be
frankly said that the problem is fundamentally social; that no man
alone can satisfactorily solve it in his own life until society as a
whole makes economic relationships more decent than they are. In
the meantime, however, some obvious duties are enjoined upon the
individual by Christian principles.

For one thing, *let a man take both his investments and his personal work away from any business that in its main intention is not
useful to the community!* That business and service ever should con-

flict is the more pathetic, because the basic idea of all good business is to serve the people. A fair bargain is far better than charity, for charity involves one man in want served by a superior, while a fair bargain involves two men on an equality, the exchange of whose goods is a mutual benefit. So Ruskin, summing up the functions of the five great intellectual professions which have existed in every civilized country, says: "The Soldier's profession is to defend it; the Pastor's to teach it; the Physician's to keep it in health; the Lawyer's to enforce justice in it; the Merchant's to provide for it." Service is the primary intention of commerce. And the tragedy of our economic conflict lies here: *the very purpose of business is perverted when service which should be first is put last or is lost sight of altogether.* In war we have seen how indispensable to the common weal are farm and shop and factory, railroad and steamship line; in war we appealed for industrial help not alone to avarice but to loyalty, not alone to greed but to patriotism. Has that appeal no standing ground in time of peace? What traitors are in an army, what hypocrites are in the ministry, what shysters are in the law, what quacks are in medicine—perversions and caricatures of their profession's main intention—so are men in business who have lost sight of their function as loyal servants of the common weal in providing for the needs of men. The first duty of a Christian, therefore, is to desert, with his money and his labor, any parasitic, useless business, any traffic that seeks something for nothing, or that makes profit from demoralizing men. A Christian must at least be conscious that he is in a business upon whose presence in some form the happy maintenance of human society depends.

Again, *a Christian must never in any business be a consenting party to the sacrifice of manhood and womanhood for profit.* When Ruskin had exalted the five professions, with the merchant as the climax of them all, he turned to define their obligation to society: "The duty of all these men is, on due occasion, to die for it. 'On due occasion' namely: the Soldier, rather than leave his post in battle; the Physician, rather than leave his post in plague; the Pastor, rather than teach falsehood; the Lawyer, rather than countenance injustice; the Merchant—what is *his* 'due occasion' of death? It is the main question for the Merchant." That question is not difficult for a Christian to answer. The merchant should die rather than willingly make profit that involves the degradation of manhood and womanhood.

Lord Shaftesbury, the great Christian philanthropist, and his allies worked fourteen years to secure a ten-hour bill in England. How widely was he helped by Christian business men, who knew as well as he did that in Lancashire alone, for example, 35,000 children from five to thirteen years of age were working fourteen and fifteen hours a day in the factories to pile up profits for them? Let Lord Shaftesbury's diary answer: "Prepared as I am, I am oftentimes distressed and puzzled by the strange contrasts I find; support from infidels and non-professors; opposition or coldness from religionists or declaimers." "I find that evangelical religionists are not those on whom I can rely. The factory, and every question for what is called 'humanity' receive as much support from the men of the world as from church men, who say they will have nothing to do with it." "Last night pushed the bill through the committee; a feeble and discreditable opposition! 'Sinners' were with me; 'saints' were against me—strange contradiction in human nature." "The clergy here (Manchester) as usual are cowed by capital and power. I find none who cry aloud and spare not; but so it is everywhere." Such records are the disgrace of the Church. No money can be so spent in charity as to atone for such a satanic spirit in its making. A disciple of Jesus must be free from such willing consent to take profit out of human degradation. This does not mean that he must throw away securities in every business whose policies he disapproves; it does mean that, however his private fortune may be affected, he must by every means in his power fight those policies and that he must always be on the side of any movement which promises more decent living to men and women. To put profits before personality is the swiftest and completest way of denying everything that Jesus ever said. Let a man be a pagan and say so, if he so chooses; but let him not call himself a follower of Jesus, while he forgets the spirit of Jesus: "It were well for him if a millstone were hanged about his neck, and he were thrown into the sea, rather than that he should cause one of these little ones to stumble" (Luke 17:2).

IV

To be engaged in a useful business and to be seeking to make the processes of that business contribute not to profits alone but to human welfare, are the simplest elementals of the Christian spirit in industry. The full flower of even these elemental qualities, however, is plainly impossible without putting the idea of service at the very center of one's business life. Consider what that would mean!

The essence of selfishness is to face any human relationship with the main intent of seeing what can be gotten out of it for oneself. What, then, shall we say of the common attitude toward business? That is one human relationship which multitudes of men confessedly face with the major purpose of making profit from it for themselves. Business as often conceived is the driving of a bargain with intent to win.

Another attitude toward life, however, is perfectly familiar, and in certain areas of human enterprise it is expected from all honorable men. Schubert sold his priceless songs for tenpence apiece. But he did not *write* them for tenpence apiece. He wrote them for the love of music and the joy and pride of fine workmanship. Milton sold "Paradise Lost" for ten pounds. But he did not write it for ten pounds. He wrote it for the easing of his spirit, for the love of poetry, and the delight of excellent craftsmanship. Such men take pay for work; but they do not work for pay. Their life is not a bargain but a vocation; it is not a trade but an art. They would say with a great teacher: "Harvard University pays me for doing what I would gladly pay for the privilege of doing if I could only afford it." They feel about their chosen tasks what Stradivari felt about his violins: God

"Could not make
Antonio Stradivari's violins
Without Antonio."

No man's life is fully redeemed to the spirit of Jesus until he has come over into this attitude toward his work. In the Master's figure he must cease being a hireling working for pay and must become a shepherd with a passion for service (John 10:11 f). Note that the shepherd was no musician or poet, no teacher, or builder of exquisite violins. He was doing the hardest of manual work, exposed to all weathers, so humble a toiler that the scribes counted him outside the orthodox pale, since he could not in his occupation keep all the law. Yet this toiler is the Master's figure of a man who glorifies his life work as a vocation and an art, who puts the passion of service into it, who scorns to be a hireling with his eye on payday, skimping his labor and seeking only cash. "You make pretty good hammers here," said a visitor to a workman in a factory. "No, sir," came the swift answer. "We make the best hammers that can be made." There is a man who has caught the spirit of the Master's shepherd. His life is not consumed in driving bargains; he has achieved the professional attitude; he has made a common task into a fine art.

It is evident that in no realm whatsoever is the best work ever done without this spirit. One may write hack music for money, but when Handel in a passion of tears and prayer writes the Halluelujah Chorus, money is forgotten. A soldier may conceivably join the army for pay, but when at Verdun men endure for their country what they never would endure for themselves, something more than money has motived them. Caiaphas might well be High Priest for pay, but the Master's saviorhood had no such motive. How much money do we think would *buy* Luther to go to Worms; or *buy* John Knox to brave the wrath of Mary, Queen of Scots; or *buy* Washington to endure the winter at Valley Forge? Money can do some things; for the sake of it men have sometimes done good work; often they have done devilish work; but for the sake of it *no man ever did his best work.* Money never manned a lifeboat. Money never sent a preacher into his pulpit with a declaration of unpopular but needed truth. Money never gave us railroads or steamships or telephones or telegraphs, for even such things could not have come if beyond the love of money had not risen joy and pride in scientific workmanship. Every discovery of new truth, every advance in social life, all basic industries introduced to supply the needs of men, rest back on lives that loved creative work for its own sake. Wherever one looks, man's life at its best has never been a trade. It has been a vocation.

This is the point of crisis which separates the secular from the sacred. When a minister in a pulpit preaches for pay, is that sacred? It is as secular a deed as the sun shines on. When a woman in the home or a man in business puts into daily life the professional spirit, facing the day's task with the major motive of putting service in rather than taking pay out, is that secular? It is as sacred a sight as God sees. For there are no secular *things;* there are only secular *people;* and secular people work for pay. How scathing is the comment that Gibbon passes on his tutor, who "remembered that he had a salary to receive and forgot that he had a duty to perform." This does not mean that the economic motive is unworthy. It may be one of the most valuable weapons in the human arsenal. Paul says that he who does not provide for his own family is worse than an infidel (I Tim. 5:8). But it does mean that when the economic motive be-

comes predominant, Christian living ceases. However hard the saying may at first appear, one surely cannot read the New Testament
without perceiving that a physician who cares more for his patients'
money than for their health; a lawyer who is more concerned to
secure fees than to secure justice; a statesman whose first love is his
purse and whose second is good government; a teacher who thinks
of his salary before he thinks of his students; a minister who cannot
sincerely say with Paul, "I desire not yours but you"; and a business
man who in his desire for profits submerges his desire to serve the
public, are none of them living Christian lives. The spirit of service
cannot be given the freedom of all man's life except the quarantined
area of his economic relationships. The spirit of service must comprehend and permeate that also. For this is the central heresy, which,
so long as it maintains its hold, condemns our economic life to be
unchristian, and involves us in industrial bitterness: *business is primarily a means of making wealth for individuals.* And this is the
truth, whose recognition and enforcement alone can bring decency:
*business primarily is an essential social service to the whole commu-
nity.*

v

Under present circumstances, however, it is impossible to expect
the general body of workers in our industries to put into their tasks
the spirit of joyful and creative labor. Let a man put himself in their
place and see. Workers on twelve-hour shifts seven days a week;
workers at minutely subdivided tasks repeating a single process ten
hours a day week in week out; workers who never rise above the
poverty line no matter how hard they toil, but to whom life is a
hopeless animal struggle to sustain a meager physical existence—
these are at the bottom of our economic conflict. To expect such
folk to put the professional spirit into their work is mockery.

Moreover, one fundamental fact in our present economic situation is the struggle between organized capital and organized labor,
and in consequence the dominant note in our economic life is not
service but conflict. Here is the description of a master tailor's shop
before the modern machines came in: "His shop was upstairs in his
home. Half a dozen journeymen and a couple of apprentices
squatted cross-legged on tables plying the needle. The master worked
with them and shared their talk. At noon all ate at his table, and he

cut the bread and served the soup to them with due respect to sen-
iority. When he said grace before and after meat all bowed their
heads with him. Downstairs in a tiny store, like a hall bedroom, were
a few bolts of stuff." Into this system of home manufacture came
steam-driven machines, and in their wake great factories. Home
manufacture was forced to the wall. The workers, in despair and
hate, mobbed the first factories in England, and before their attacks
were ended the legal penalty of death was affixed for destroying a
machine. All production was centered then in the factory towns; no
one could compete with them; all power was in the hands of the men
to whom the machines belonged.

The years that followed are among the cruelest in human history.
No one with squeamish sensibilities easily can read the records of the
barbarous oppressions practiced on the workers before there was any
organization among them for self-protection, or any laws to control
wages, conditions of labor, or hours of toil. It is easy now to condemn the evils of organized labor. But if any group of our employers
could themselves be put back into such conditions as the laborers
faced before the days of labor unions, the first thing those employers
would do would be to combine in leagues for mutual defense.

Our industrial life, therefore, has fallen inevitably into the two-
group system: organized capital and organized labor. The old brotherhood of toil is broken. The employers and employees are far apart.
However much individuals may feel good will, they find themselves
arrayed against each other in economic groups from which they cannot extricate themselves. Our industry has become a tragic conflict,
in which cooperation is swamped in class consciousness. And so
much is human nature alike under all jackets that it is with difficulty
that one can discern where the more selfishness lies, with capital or
with labor, when either gains the power for self-aggrandizement.

In this intolerable situation only a blind man can recommend the
endeavor to turn back the clock to the old days before laborers were
organized at all. Probably the most important movements now afoot
in the economic world are experiments where employers and employees are trying out methods of democratic cooperation. *How,
without impairing productiveness while the process of change is
going on, can recognized channels be established in industry, by
which the whole body of workers can have a fair and satisfying opportunity to help determine the conditions under which they live and
work?*—that significant question must find reply. A hopeful fact is

that scores of experiments are being tried in the endeavor to secure the answer. For the spirit of service cannot control industry, until from out this jungle of broken brotherhood the path is found that leads toward regularly established methods of industrial cooperation.

Moreover, behind these immediate and clamorous questions lie others more elemental still. Our present economic order is an organized denial of the spirit of service, because it involves the right of individuals to own and to exploit for private profit all the natural resources of the earth, and thereby to control the fate of multitudes of people, dependent on those natural resources for the means of their labor and the maintenance of their lives. The extension of private property to mean not simply the ownership of what we use, but the ownership of what other men must use or die, has given to a small group in the commonwealth more control over the destinies of their fellows than was often exercised by emperors in the ancient world. The Christianizing of our life involves the righteous solution of such critical problems at the basis of our economic order.

Until such questions are answered, even the *idea* of applying Jesus' principles of service to the conduct of industry will seem to some utterly unreal. When enforced religion is the established order, it is hard to think that voluntary religion will work; when feudalism is universally accepted, democracy looks Utopian; when judicial torture is agreed on by all as the motive for true testimony in the courts, truth obtained by voluntary evidence seems a dream; when the economic system is built on selfishness, to motive it by service seems sentimental. This, then, is the conclusion of the matter. The triumph of the spirit of Christian service in our economic relationships involves something more than the individual's desire to be in a useful business, to make industry help human welfare as well as create profit, and to put the professional spirit into his work. It involves profound changes in our economic system. Christians will differ, as other men will, about the nature of these changes and the methods by which they should be achieved. But that reforms are critically demanded to bring our industrial life under the sway of cooperative methods, he who takes in earnest Jesus Christ's rightful mastery of all man's life can hardly doubt. And such a man will seek, at any cost to his own profit, to bring those changes in.

CHAPTER XI

The Motive of Gratitude

DAILY READINGS

Our study has concerned itself with the principles and methods of the service which we ourselves are called upon to render. We have not yet faced the considerable fact that a great deal of serving was done before we were born; that our own lives are the children of sacrifice beyond our power to estimate or to repay. Let a man meditate upon the cost of all the blessings he enjoys, let him gratefully recall the burdens borne, the blood poured out for common benedictions which he shares, and he will be the readier to make repayment in service to the race. Consider in the daily readings the frequent experiences in which this backward look of gratitude would steady and strengthen us.

Eleventh Week, First Day

Say not ye, There are yet four months, and then cometh the harvest? behold, I say unto you, Lift up your eyes, and look on the fields, that they are white already unto harvest. He that reapeth receiveth wages, and gathereth fruit unto life eternal; that he that soweth and he that reapeth may rejoice together. For herein is the saying true, One soweth, and another reapeth. I sent you to reap that whereon ye have not labored: others have labored, and ye are entered into their labor.—John 4:35-38.

In service, as in every other activity, days come when monotony makes our tasks seem stale and tasteless. The bane of commonplaceness falls upon our work. Martineau wrote: "God has so arranged the chronometry of our spirits that there shall be a thousand silent moments between the striking hours." Many a useful life succumbs to fag, that never would have given in to opposition. Let a man, then, look back! What accumulated labor, obscure, patient, and wearisome, has made possible the privileges into the possession of which we were born! Civilization has grown like coral islands from the imperceptible contributions of innumerable sacrifices. In 1864, when Lee's army was invading Pennsylvania, a citizen of Philadelphia telegraphed General Halleck at Washington to know if he could be of any service. He received this grim reply: "We have five times as many generals as we want, but we are greatly in need of privates. Any one volunteering in that capacity will be thankfully received." We recall the names of the generals who have led the forward march of man. Think today of the privates, of the weariness of their marching, the monotony of their endurance, the patience of their obscure carrying on, to which we are illimitably indebted. Cannot we then add our quota of enduring labor for the common good?

Our Father, unto Thee, in the light of our Saviour's blessed life, we would lift our souls. We thank Thee for that true Light shining in our world with still increasing brightness. We thank Thee for all who have walked therein, and especially for those near to us and dear, in whose lives we have seen this excellent glory and beauty. Make us glad in all who have faithfully lived; make us glad in all who have peacefully died. Lift us into light, and love, and purity, and blessedness, and give us at last our portion with those who have trusted in Thee and sought, in small things as in great, in things temporal and things eternal, to do Thy holy Will. Amen.—Rufus Ellis.

Eleventh Week, Second Day

For it hath been signified unto me concerning you, my brethren, by them that are of the household of Chloe, that there are contentions among you. Now this I mean, that each one of you saith, I am of Paul; and I of Apollos; and I of Cephas; and I of Christ. Is Christ divided? was Paul crucified for you? or were ye baptized into the name of Paul? I thank God that I baptized none of you, save Crispus and Gaius; lest any man should say that ye were baptized into my name.—I Cor. 1:11-15.

Paul had poured out his labor on the Corinthian church, and here, in dissension, they were forgetting their indebtedness to him, were bestowing the credit of their founding and the loyalty of their allegiance on Cephas or Apollos. Let none suppose that this was easy for Paul to bear. He smarted under this lack of recognition. He knew that he was not being justly treated. Few servants of any cause can escape altogether such hours as Paul must have faced when Chloe told him the unhappy news from Corinth. We all like to be recognized and accorded due credit, and *we all are tempted to quit service when we are slighted.* Let a man, then, look back! What if all the unrecognized, unrewarded soldiers of the common good, whose beneficiaries we are, had left their posts because another received the credit that was their due? We ourselves are the offspring of that kind of devotion which Paul put into his work. He did not demand pay on Saturday night or ask for all the recognition he deserved. Cannot we, then, contribute our share of that self-forgetfulness without which the world could not go on?

O Almighty God, who hast knit together Thine elect in one communion and fellowship, in the mystical body of Thy Son, Christ our Lord: Grant us grace so to follow Thy blessed saints in all virtuous and godly living, that we may come to those unspeakable joys, which Thou hast prepared for them that unfeignedly love Thee; through Jesus Christ our Lord. Amen.—Book of Common Prayer, 1549.

Eleventh Week, Third Day

And what shall I more say? for the time will fail me if I tell of Gideon, Barak, Samson, Jephthah; of David and Samuel and the prophets: who through faith subdued kingdoms, wrought righteousness, obtained promises, stopped the mouths of lions, quenched the power of fire, escaped the edge of the sword, from weakness were made strong, waxed mighty in war, turned to flight armies of aliens. Women received their dead by a resurrection: and others were tortured, not accepting their deliverance; that they might obtain a better resurrection: and others had trial of mockings and scourgings, yea, moreover of bonds and imprisonment: they were stoned, they were sawn asunder, they were tempted, they were slain with the sword: they went about in sheepskins, in goatskins; being destitute, afflicted, ill-treated (of whom the world was not worthy), wandering in deserts and mountains and caves, and the holes of the earth.—Heb. 11:32-38.

Such a passage as this should always be read by those who *in their service are meeting with active opposition*. Many a servant of good causes in his community, who seriously proposes the abatement of some social nuisance or moral plague, is surprised at the hornets' nest of antagonism he arouses. Said General Booth in an impatient hour: "The day has gone when the priest and Levite are content to pass by the wounded man. They must needs stop now, turn back, and punch the head of any good Samaritan who dares to come to the rescue." If in such circumstances a man is tempted to be conquered by disgust, let him look back! Of what stuff have the men and women been, who refused to get on with the world but proposed to get the world on? The fire of their resolution was no flickering candle to be blown out by man's hostility; it was fanned rather to a stronger blaze by the antagonistic wind. Beneficiaries as we are of such courageous service, can we not render our share of it when the need comes? Moreover, "the memory of one good fight for freedom or justice gives a thrilling sense of worth for a lifetime."

Almighty and everlasting God, who adornest the sacred body of Thy Church by the confessions of holy Martyrs; grant us, we pray Thee, that both by their doctrines and their pious example, we may follow after what is pleasing in Thy sight; through Jesus Christ our Lord. Amen.—Leonine Sacramentary.

Eleventh Week, Fourth Day

For this cause left I thee in Crete, that thou shouldest set in order the things that were wanting, and appoint elders in every city, as I gave thee charge. . . . For there are many unruly men, vain talkers and deceivers, specially they of the circumcision, whose mouths must be stopped; men who overthrow whole houses, teaching things which they ought not, for filthy lucre's sake. One of themselves, a prophet of their own, said,
Cretans are always liars, evil beasts, idle gluttons.
This testimony is true.—Titus 1:5, 10-13.

What a remarkable reason for setting a man at work in Crete! The people there are bestial, idle liars—therefore work for them! They are gluttonous, sordid, scandalous—therefore, live among them! Surely, before he was through with Paul's commission, Titus must have faced the temptation to be thoroughly out of patience

with the folk for whom he toiled. Nor can any serious servant of his
fellows escape this trial. People are so often contemptible; their sly
deceits, their hard ingratitude, their characters as weak as rotted
cloth that punctures at the touch, fill us with loathing. We are
tempted to accept the motto which John Hay, with genial cynicism,
has suggested, "Love your neighbor, but be careful of your neighborhood." Yet, before a man utterly surrenders to this easy doctrine,
let him look back! If the Christian missionaries that evangelized our
barbarous forefathers had lacked Titus's spirit when he went to
Crete, where would our civilization now have been? The entire
background of our lives from the Cross of Christ to our parents'
patience with our wayward youth is compact with the *ministry of
love to unloveliness.* Have we no gratitude that will lead us to repay
a little on our immeasurable debt?

*Almighty and everlasting God, who dost enkindle the flame of
Thy love in the hearts of the Saints, grant to our minds the same
faith and power of love; that as we rejoice in their triumphs, we may
profit by their examples; through Jesus Christ our Lord. Amen.*—
Gothic Missal.

Eleventh Week, Fifth Day

The godly man is perished out of the earth, and there is none
upright among men: they all lie in wait for blood; they hunt every
man his brother with a net. Their hands are upon that which is evil
to do it diligently; the prince asketh, and the judge is ready for a
reward; and the great man, he uttereth the evil desire of his soul:
thus they weave it together. The best of them is as a brier; the most
upright is worse than a thorn hedge: the day of thy watchmen,
even thy visitation, is come; now shall be their perplexity. Trust
ye not in a neighbor; put ye not confidence in a friend; keep the
doors of thy mouth from her that lieth in thy bosom. For the son
dishonoreth the father, the daughter riseth up against her mother,
the daughter-in-law against her mother-in-law; a man's enemies
are the men of his own house.

But as for me, I will look unto Jehovah; I will wait for the God
of my salvation: my God will hear me.—Micah 7:2-7.

The Bible is not an optimist's paradise. The men of Scripture face
black outlooks, meet discouraging situations, recognize frankly the

appalling nature of human sin and its consequences. Nor can any servant of mankind in any age go on, wide-eyed to life's forbidding facts, without encountering the temptation to despondency.

"The time is out of joint: O cursed spite
That ever I was born to set it right!"

Yet, consider that all the great victories of the past have been won in the face of just such difficulties. Henry Ward Beecher said once in his pulpit: "Twenty years ago in my most extravagant mood, I could not have dared to say to Christ, 'Let me live to see slavery destroyed'; and yet I have lived to see it destroyed. One such coronation, one such epoch lived through, I should be indeed most unreasonable to ask to live through any more such victories. . . . I shall die before I see commerce and industry fairly regenerated. Some of you will live to see the beginnings of it. But I foresee it. I preach it. My word will not die when I am dead. The seed has sprouted and you cannot unsprout it." *Children as we are of such unconquerable faith and sacrifice, can we not pay our quota in to the world's salvation?*

From being satisfied with myself, save me, good Lord. Burn into me the sight of the Cities of Dreadful Night and the City of Righteousness. Make me ever to hunger and thirst after righteousness. As I walk in mean streets, as I am importuned by beggars, as I talk with my friends, let impatience with the world make me patient to serve Thee in any way, however lowly; let discontent with modern life make me content to bear some part of the sorrows of the world. O Christ our Saviour, Man of Sorrows and King of Glory, ever leading us from darkness to light, from evil to goodness, ever calling us and recalling us from earth to heaven, let me count all things but loss that I may be found in Thee, and be numbered among those who follow Thee whithersoever Thou goest. Amen.—"Prayers for the City of God."

Eleventh Week, Sixth Day

But know this, that in the last days grievous times shall come. For men shall be lovers of self, lovers of money, boastful, haughty, railers, disobedient to parents, unthankful, unholy, without natural

affection, implacable, slanderers, without self-control, fierce, no lovers of good, traitors, headstrong, puffed up, lovers of pleasure rather than lovers of God; holding a form of godliness, but having denied the power thereof: from these also turn away. For of these are they that creep into houses, and take captive silly women laden with sins, led away by divers lusts, ever learning, and never able to come to the knowledge of the truth. And even as Jannes and Jambres withstood Moses, so do these also withstand the truth; men corrupted in mind, reprobate concerning the faith. But they shall proceed no further: for their folly shall be evident unto all men, as theirs also came to be.—II Tim. 3:1-9.

The prevalence of selfishness oppresses the apostle's spirit. How familiar that mood is! The world seems to us, in our despondent moods, to be degenerating rapidly. We say in our haste that all men are not only liars, but are "lovers of pleasure rather than lovers of God." Professor Gilbert Murray of Oxford tells us that one of the oldest documents known to men—a cuneiform fragment from the lowest, most ancient stratum of the ruins of Babylon—begins with these words, "Alas! alas! times are not what they were!" When this familiar mood is on us, let us look back! What magnificent battles have been fought by folk whose service seemed swamped in the world's selfishness! Through what dismaying times, when all slick, swift schemes for tidying up the world went to pieces, have men, committed to unselfishness, gone on, depressed but not beaten! They ended even their dark visions of human sin on the major note of hope, as the Apostle does in our passage. They have said with Rupert Brooke,

> "Now God be thanked,
> Who hath matched us with His hour."

All our blessings have cost that indomitable spirit. Are we not under obligation to display our share of it in our own generation?

O Thou Lord of all worlds, we bless Thy Name for all those who have entered into their rest, and reached the Promised Land, where Thou art seen face to face. Give us grace to follow in their footsteps, as they followed in the footsteps of Thy Holy Son. Encourage our wavering hearts by their example, and help us to see in them the memorials of Thy redeeming grace, and pledges of the heavenly might in which the weak are made strong. Keep alive in us the memory of those dear to ourselves, whom Thou hast called out of this world, and make it powerful to subdue within us every vile and unworthy thought. Grant that every remembrance which turns our hearts from things seen to things unseen, may lead us always upwards to Thee, till we, too, come to the eternal rest which Thou hast prepared for Thy people; through Jesus Christ our Lord. Amen.— F. J. A. Hort.

Eleventh Week, Seventh Day

When a man looks back from any position of difficulty and stress in which his service lands him, he always sees behind him men who bore more of the same burden, suffered more of the same ill, overcame more of the same obstacle. He is unpayably indebted for his blessings, to sacrifices greater than any he can make.

Therefore let us also, seeing we are compassed about with so great a cloud of witnesses, lay aside every weight, and the sin which doth so easily beset us, and let us run with patience the race that is set before us, looking unto Jesus the author and perfecter of our faith, who for the joy that was set before him endured the cross, despising shame, and hath sat down at the right hand of the throne of God. For consider him that hath endured such gain-saying of sinners against himself, that ye wax not weary, fainting in your souls.—Heb. 12:1-3.

The fathers who have sacrificed before us may well surround us like a crowd of spectators to watch our contest, for we have in our hands the spoiling or the fulfilment of their hard-won gains. It is idle to suppose that civilization's gains cannot be lost. History is the narrative of one civilization after another that began with promise, rose to its climax, and, failing to learn the lessons of righteousness, fell on ruin. God does not guarantee the perpetuity of our blessings; "romantic belief in some ameliorative drift" is a fool's paradise. Only vigilance, devotion, self-sacrifice, righteousness, obedience to the law of God, can assure us the retention of present gains and the achievement of new advances. All that we have was bought and paid for by unselfishness. Can we not do for others, not simply as we would be done by, but as we have been done by?

O my God, O my Love, let Thy unwearied and tender love to me make my love unwearied and tender to my neighbour, and zealous to procure, promote, and preserve his health, and safety, and happiness, and life, that he may be the better able to serve and to love Thee. Amen.—Bishop Ken.

COMMENT FOR THE WEEK

I

Behind the manifest differences between selfish and serviceable lives, there lies a contrast, deep though often hidden, between the ideas of life from which selfishness and service spring. Compare two contemporaries like Napoleon Bonaparte and William Wilberforce. While the colossus was busy bestriding the world, Wilberforce was busy killing the African slave trade. The story of his tireless labors against the villainous abomination is one of the most thrilling tales in history. Rich in fortune, frail in health, beset by bitter antagonism, he waged a philanthropic war that knew no truce and would accept no armistice. On the day when victory came and the slave trade of the British Empire finally was doomed, Sir Samuel Romilly, amid the cheers of the House of Commons, compared the thoughts of Wilberforce as he went to rest with the thoughts of Napoleon across the Channel, then at the climax of his power. The very tombs of the two still advertise the contrast: one symbolic of imperial pomp and pride, the other celebrating the life which "removed from England the guilt of the African slave trade." If one seeks the dominating ideas of life which controlled two such characters, how evident they are! Napoleon looked on life as an excellent place for self-aggrandizement; Wilberforce, as an excellent opportunity for self-bestowal. Napoleon assumed that the world owed him all that he could get; Wilberforce assumed that he owed the world all that he could give. Napoleon's principle was that humanity was under infinite obligation to him; Wilberforce's principle was that he was under infinite obligation to humanity.

Only this second motive is adequate to support such a life of service as we have been considering. But is it true? In what sense are we so under unpayable obligation to mankind that we should pour life out in sacrificial usefulness, and when we have done all, should say,

"We are unprofitable servants, we have done that which it was our duty to do"?

II

Plenty of people plainly do not feel under any such indebtedness. They stroll into life and settle down in it, as though all its blessings had been dropped by accident and had cost nothing. They pick life up and spend it carelessly, as a tramp picks up a chance coin lost upon the street, with no gratitude to the one who earned it and with no sense of honorable obligation in its use. They take the liberties, the civic privileges, the cultural gains, the spiritual inheritance of the civilization in which at so late a date they have arrived, and they appropriate it all as though it were their own. They are like citizens who never have seen any flag except a bright new flag, unspoiled by battle. They lack the sobering effect that comes when a man sees a battle-flag, rent and torn by shot and shell and slit by saber strokes— a flag whose soiled dishevelment symbolizes the sacrifice which made the bright new flag a possibility.

How often one wishes that these flippant, easy-going batteners upon the privileges of their generation could be made seriously to face the sacrifices of their sires! While the Great War was on, Professor Gilbert Murray wrote: "As for me personally, there is one thought that is always with me—the thought that other men are dying for me, better men, younger, with more hope in their lives, many of whom I have taught and loved. The orthodox Christian will be familiar with the thought of One who loved you, dying for you. I would like to say that now I seem to be familiar with the feeling that something innocent, something great, something that loved me, is dying and is dying daily for me." Shall men feel that once about their own contemporaries, and forget its constant truth about their sires? From the Stone Age until now, lives beyond our power to repay have been preparing for us physical comforts, civic security, spiritual enlightenment and liberty, cultural privilege and Christian faith. What do we suppose all this has cost? One of the most ennobling insights that can come to any man is the perception that no blessing's trail can be traced far back without running upon blood, that at the end of every road down which a benediction comes there stands a cross.

We take our *modern conveniences* for granted until we chance upon some comment like this from Roger Bacon, dreaming in the thirteenth century: "Machines for navigating are possible without rowers, so that great ships suited to rivers and oceans and guided by one man may be borne with greater speed than as if they were full of men rowing. Likewise cars might be made, so that without a draft animal they could be moved with incredible celerity. And flying machines are possible so that a man may sit in the middle turning some device by which artificial wings may beat the air in the manner of a flying bird." What a lavish expenditure of sacrificial thought and energy from that day to this, to give us the most commonplace conveniences of modern life!

We take our *educational systems* for granted, until we run by chance upon such a word as this from Governor Berkeley of the Colony of Virginia in 1670: "I thank God there are no free schools, nor printing, and I hope we shall not have them these hundred years; for learning has brought disobedience and heresy and sects into the world, and printing has divulged them and libels against the best government. God keep us from both!" Who can measure the sacrificial devotion that has been required from that day to this to give schools to all the people?

We take for granted our *national security and our inherited ideals of civic life,* until some special anniversary like the Tercentenary of the Pilgrims reminds us of our unfathomable indebtedness. In 1607, thirteen years before the Mayflower came, a settlement of English commercial men was founded at Popham Beach in Maine. It lasted but a single winter. For one winter only did they bear the bitter cold, the loneliness of separation from their homes, the fear of hostile Indians. They had come for money, and all the money that they could get was not worth what they endured. But there was that other settlement that loneliness and bitter cold and hunger and fear of hostile savages could not dismay. Historians say that at Popham Beach they came for money and it was not worth while; but the Pilgrims and the Puritans remained, because they came for conscience's sake and God's. Consider those rememberable words of John Robinson and Elder Brewster: "We are knite togeather, as a body, in a most strict and sacred bond and covenante of the Lord, of the violation whereof we make great conscience, and by vertue whereof we do hould ourselves straitly tied to all care of each others good and of ye whole. . . . It is not with us as with other men; whom small things can discourage, and small discontentments cause to wish themselves at home again." Not a blessing does the Anglo-Saxon race enjoy today, that has not been baptized with the blood and tears of men like that.

How easily also do we take for granted the *innumerable blessings that have permeated our lives because the Christian Gospel has been for sixty generations at work among us!* The English Book of Common Prayer can now be cheaply purchased, easily used, and peacefully enjoyed. We assume it as a possession of the Christian world, put freely at anyone's disposal. Dean Stanley, however, calls our attention to the strange tautologies which the book contains: "assemble and meet together," "acknowledge and confess," "humble and lowly," "goodness and mercy." Why this curious reduplication of ideas? Because "assemble," "confess," "humble," and "mercy" are Norman French, and "meet together," "acknowledge," "lowly," and "goodness" are Anglo-Saxon. Imbedded in the very structure of the book are the relics of an old struggle, where with blood and strife two races were trying to live together on the Isle of Britain and one Church was striving to put her arms about them both. Here is a true parable of every Christian blessing that Christendom enjoys. The signs of sacrifice are on them all; their trail is red with blood; they come to us every one like Paul to the Corinthians, bearing in his body "the marks of the Lord Jesus." Common convenience, cultural opportunity, national inheritance, spiritual privilege—they are not to be taken for granted. They should awaken the depths of gratitude in every recipient. They have all been bought and paid for with other blood than ours, and with sacrificial toil that we never can repay.

III

Such a grateful consciousness of the cost which other generations and other men have paid for privileges which we commonly enjoy, cannot be left a passive sentiment expressed alone in words. For these men of olden times launched enterprises which they could not bring to a conclusion. They pushed as far as their finger tips could further them causes upon which they had set their hearts; but at the last they had to trust the generations which should come after them to bring those causes to successful culmination. *If we fail, they fail!* They fail as soldiers do who have fought well and fallen, but who have no successors now to press on over their dead bodies and complete the charge which they were making. They fail as builders do, who lay broad the foundations of their temple, but leave behind them children who forget their fathers' plans and neglect the shrine which the fathers had begun.

In Europe there are cathedrals that took as long as six centuries in building. What dreams dawned upon the minds of those who planned them at their start! What ideals may well have thronged the thoughts of those who, midway in their construction, wrought here a graceful spire or there a buttress! But at every stage in the building all the past depended upon the present. The generation then alive could leave to ruin and neglect, or bring to culmination, the things the fathers had conceived. Any sensitive man at work upon the structure during the six centuries of its building, may well have heard his forefathers pleading: Lo, how great a thing we planned! And now the responsibilty for its furtherance falls on you; fail us not!

> "Our fathers in a wondrous age,
> Ere yet the earth was small,
> Insured to us an heritage,
> And doubted not at all
> That we, the children of their heart,
> Which then did beat so high,
> In later time should play like part
> For our posterity. . . .
> Dear-bought and clear, a thousand year
> Our fathers' title runs.
> Make we likewise their sacrifice,
> Defrauding not our sons!"

Sacrificial service, therefore, is not a matter of generosity alone; it is a matter of honor. To be selfish is to be an ingrate. The unserviceable man is taking with full hands blessings that cost toil and tears and blood, and is expending them all upon himself. His lack of generosity is fundamentally lack of gratitude.

IV

To this sentiment of gratitude the New Testament makes its characteristic appeal for service. The distinguishing quality of the

Christian motive for unselfishness lies here: *we are expected to live sacrificial lives, because we ourselves already are the beneficiaries of sacrificial living beyond our power to equal or repay.* Now, gratitude, however homely its occasion or simple its expression, is in itself an engaging quality. Capacity to appreciate benefits received and thankfully to recall them is inseparable from fine-grained character. When races are discovered with no word to convey gratitude, no phrase for even the simple "Thank you," and with no apparent feeling that would call for such a phrase, we know that they are in the abysmal pit of human character. But both depth and delicacy of nature are revealed when in human relationships men are serviceably grateful to one another, or when they interpret their religious life as Benjamin Franklin did in his daily morning prayer: "Accept my kind offices to Thy other children as the only return in my power for Thy continual favors to me."

To this grace the New Testament makes its habitual appeal. We should love others because God first loved us (I John 4:19); we should forgive our enemies because we have been forgiven (Luke 6:36); we should lay down our lives for the brethren because Christ first laid down his life for us (I John 3:16); we should love even our enemies because God's impartial care has included us all, just and unjust, good and evil (Matt. 5:45); we should be kind one to another, tenderhearted, forgiving each other, even as God also in Christ forgave us (Eph. 4:32); the law of our life should be, "Freely ye have received, freely give" (Matt. 10:8). Continually in the New Testament one lifts his eyes from an appeal for generous service to see in the background prior service, still more generous, long since rendered us. The Gospel insists that we are under an unpayable debt of gratitude which all our self-denying service never can discharge.

Consider in terms of our personal experience how many things there are for which we never bargained and for which we cannot pay! They are not for sale. They belong to that area of life—the New Testament calls it "grace"—where we receive blessings which we did not earn, are given free gifts of which we must be as worthy as we can.

The beauty of nature is a free gift. We paid no installment of service down, in return for which God so gloriously furnished the house in which we live. Sunrise and sunset, snow-capped mountains and the ancient sea, elm trees and fringed gentians, white birch trees against green backgrounds, the surf on a windy day, the grass,

"the handkerchief of the Lord,
A scented gift and remembrancer designedly dropt,
Bearing the owner's name someway in the corners,
That we may see and remark, and say, *Whose?*"

—all this is a free bestowal to be gratefully taken and worthily used.

The great spirits who have preceded us and through whom God has shined, like the sun through an eastern window, to our spiritual enlightenment, are a free gift. We can purchase the letter to the Ephesians for a few pence, but we cannot pay for Paul. A volume of Phillips Brooks's sermons is for sale, but nothing we can do could earn for us the presence in our world of such a soul as his. We can pay for the printing of Browning's poems, but what shall we give in exchange for the poems themselves or for the personal life from which they flow? A few dollars will buy a seat at the concert, but we can never pay for Bach's Passion music. Such blessings are not for sale; we cannot bargain for them; they are given us straightway when we are born, and we grow up, if we are wise, to be glad that they are in our world and to use them worthily.

Our most beautiful human relationships are a free gift. The first fact in our childhood was not service rendered but service received. We did not pay in advance for the motherhood that bore us and the love that nourished us; all this was poured out freely; we were the unconscious recipients of unselfish love that we had never earned. Home life is thus built on the honor system, where children are first of all served with uncalculating devotion and then are expected in return to live as gratitude will prompt. In some relationships we may work first and be paid afterward; in a home we are paid first with lavish love and afterward make our return in thankfulness. Moreover, all fine friendship and true love are free bestowals. One cannot buy them. They do not belong to the realm of the bargain counter; they belong to the realm of grace; and he who is blessed in possessing them, if he have an understanding heart, is humbly thankful for an unspeakable gift.

Whether we look, therefore, at the social life of man, with its large gains for which our sires poured out their sacrifice, or at our own personal experience, the whole background of our existence is com-

pact with free bestowals for which we cannot pay. To be sure, life
is not *all* grace; with other realms of experience differing from grace
or conflicting with it our daily lives must deal. *Injustice* is here; we
sometimes suffer ills that we do not deserve. *Just punishment* is here;
fair retribution sometimes is meted out upon our ill deserts. *Just
reward* is here; sometimes we are paid as we deserve for meritorious
work. But around these other realms and interpenetrating them is
the realm of grace, and the tone of a man's life depends largely upon
where among these four realms his major emphasis falls. If he
stresses life's injustice, he grows bitter. If he is too much impressed
by life's stern punishments, he grows hard. If he relishes too much
life's just rewards, he grows self-satisfied and proud. A man of fine
quality is of another spirit altogether. He regards himself as the
fortunate recipient of countless blessings which he never earned. He
knows that he is in debt beyond his capacity to pay, and that therefore, so far from the world owing him a living, he owes the world a
life. While some are greedily trying to get what they deserve, he is
trying to deserve what already has been given him. He is gracious,
because he sees his life in terms of grace.

v

If such a spirit is conceivable in one who is not consciously a
Christian, what ought we to expect from one who has entered into
saving fellowship with Jesus Christ? For the realm of grace belongs
peculiarly to our Lord. He is its representative and master. Grace
had been in the world before he came, but as a slender stream flows
out at last into its main channel, deep and broad, and takes its name
from the place of its debouching, so grace flowed out at last into
human life through the ministry of Jesus, and from that day to this
its name has been, "the grace of our Lord Jesus Christ."

He knew injustice; upon his brow the crown of thorns was pressed.
Just punishment he understood, and warned men that the last farthing must be paid (Matt. 5:26). Just reward he believed in, and
promised it to all who wrought righteousness. But the characteristic
of his life which determines the flavor of his spirit is the constant
presence in his thought of God's immeasurable grace. A love that
surrounds us before we are born, broods over our unconsciousness,
seeks us in our waywardness, and welcomes us home again as a
father greets his long-lost son from a far country, is nothing which

anyone can earn. A love which freely forgives when by the very
nature of forgiveness the recipient does not deserve it, has no claim
upon it, has merited its opposite, is pure grace. A love that opens
before us vistas of expectation where

"All we have willed or hoped or dreamed of good shall exist;
    Not its semblance, but itself,"

is clear grace. The Fourth Gospel describes him truly: He was "full
of grace" (John 1:14).

Above all, his disciples poignantly have felt that the vicarious
sacrifice of his life and death, by which all his teaching was set afire
in a conflagration that has lighted up the world, involves us in a
debt which we can never pay. Sinners cannot themselves bear all
the consequences of their own iniquity. Some consequences fall in
punishment upon the evil-doers; some fall in unsought tragedy upon
the innocent; some are voluntarily assumed by saviorhood when it
seeks the reclamation of the sinners. This is the law of grace which
runs through all of life, like the scarlet thread through the ropes of
the British Navy which shows that they are the property of the
Crown. This is the law that Christ exalted and made glorious, when
for us men and our salvation he endured in life and death his Cross
of vicarious saviorhood.

If, therefore, a man is indeed a Christian; if around his life he sees
the generous bestowal of ancestral sacrifice, and in his daily experience feels the benediction of free gifts for which he never paid; and
if still deeper he has been blessed by the love of God which Christ
revealed, forgiven by his mercy, enlarged and liberated by his hopes,
and so knows himself to be beyond computation the beneficiary of
the Cross, honor demands of him nothing less than such a life of
sacrificial service as the New Testament exalts. The essence of paganism is to see life as a huge grab bag, somehow mysteriously put
here, from which the strongest hands may snatch the most. The
heart of Christianity is to see life overshadowed by the Cross; to
stand humble and grateful in the presence of immeasurable grace;
to know that we have already been served beyond our possibilty to
make return. The inevitable consequence of such an outlook on life
is tireless, self-denying usefulness, without condescension, for we are
hopelessly in debt ourselves, without pride, for we have nothing to

give which we did not first of all receive. Our spirit is Joyce Kilmer's when he went out to fight and to die in France:

> "Lord, Thou didst suffer more for me
> Than all the hosts of land and sea.
> So let me render back again
> This millionth of Thy gift. Amen."

CHAPTER XII

Victorious Personality

DAILY READINGS

Granted that service to our fellows is both our obligation and privilege, what has religion to do with it? Might not a plea for service be made from which all mention of God had been elided, and in which alike the motive, exercise, and issue of helpfulness were confined to human relationships? Such questions are frequent in our generation. Mystical experience of fellowship with God and practical service to humankind do not seem to involve each other. According to temperament some are tempted to divorce service from a cherished religious experience, or to divorce religion from a zealous desire to serve.

Twelfth Week, First Day

We know that we have passed out of death into life, because we love the brethren. He that loveth not abideth in death. Whosoever hateth his brother is a murderer: and ye know that no murderer hath eternal life abiding in him. Hereby know we love, because he laid down his life for us: and we ought to lay down our lives for the brethren. But who so hath the world's goods, and beholdeth his brother in need, and shutteth up his compassion from him, how doth the love of God abide in him? My little children, let us not love in word, neither with the tongue; but in deed and truth.— I John 3:14-18.

The love of God for us, our love for God, and our love for our brethren are in John's thought perfectly mingled. As old John Scotus Erigena put it: "We are not bidden to love God with one love, and our neighbour with another; neither are we instructed to cleave to the Creator with one part of our love, and to creation with another part; but in one and the same undivided love should we embrace both God and our neighbour." The difficulty which many folk have in seeing the need for God in a serviceable life is that they *miss utterly this vital idea of God as a present, permeating Spirit of Love,* the immediate source of all the love there is. Their God is an isolated individual a long way off; he is not a present Spirit in whom "we live and move and have our being." Say "God" to them, and their thought shoots up into the interstellar spaces; it leaps back into the pre-nebular aeons; it does not go down into the fertile places of the spirit, here and now, where, as Jesus said, living waters rise. We do actually deal daily with two kinds of existence: one material, the other spiritual. The central question of all life, then, is this: which of these two represents and expresses the eternal and creative Power? *To believe in God is to believe that our spirits, rather than our bodies, express Eternal Reality.* To believe in God is to believe that all that is best in us is the Eternal in us, and that when we deal with righteousness and love we are actually dealing with God, for "God *is* love."

God is ever ready, but we are ever unready; God is nigh to us, but we are far from Him; God is within, we are without; God is at home, we are strangers. The prophet says: "God leadeth the righteous by a narrow path into a broad highway, till they come into a wide and open place"; that is, unto the true freedom of that spirit which hath become one spirit with God. God help us to follow Him, that He may bring us unto Himself. Amen.—John Tauler (1290-1361).

Twelfth Week, Second Day

Take heed, brethren, lest haply there shall be in any one of you an evil heart of unbelief, in falling away from the living God: but exhort one another day by day, so long as it is called To-day; lest any one of you be hardened by the deceitfulness of sin: for we are become partakers of Christ, if we hold fast the beginning of our confidence firm unto the end.—Heb. 3:12-14.

Evidently this writer did not think that faith in God or the lack of it was a small matter; clearly he felt the large concerns of Christian integrity and usefulness to be at stake. Nor has our modern naturalism with its insistence that our bodies, not our spirits, are the spokesmen of ultimate, creative power, done anything to mitigate the New Testament's serious estimate of unbelief. One naturalist has given us a candid picture of the universe in which he lives: "In the visible world the Milky Way is a tiny fragment. Within this fragment the solar system is an infinitesimal speck, and of this speck our planet is a microscopic dot. On this dot tiny lumps of impure carbon and water crawl about for a few years, until they dissolve into the elements of which they are compounded." On such a world-view, an individual, supported by the social and religious influences of his own and previous generations, may live a practically useful life. But suppose that all men at last shared this world-view, that no man held any other, that this was the universally accepted philosophy of life. *Just how much enduring, sacrificial service for men's salvation and the hope of social righteousness would persist on the earth?*

O Lord, our Light and our Salvation, banish the night of gloom and ignorance, and grant to those in doubt the illumination of truth and of knowledge; that their hope may be firmly set in Thee, and the assaults of malicious foes may be brought to naught. Establish their confidence upon a rock of stone, that, surely grounded in the faith of Christ, they may be built up in love to their highest perfection. Amen.—"A Book of Prayers for Students."

Twelfth Week, Third Day

Beloved, let us love one another: for love is of God; and every one that loveth is begotten of God, and knoweth God. He that loveth not knoweth not God; for God is love. Herein was the love of God manifested in us, that God hath sent his only begotten Son into the world that we might live through him. Herein is love, not that we loved God, but that he loved us, and sent his Son to be the propitiation of our sins. Beloved, if God so loved us, we also ought to love one another. No man hath beheld God at any time: if we love one another, God abideth in us, and his love is perfected in us: hereby we know that we abide in him and he in us, because he hath given us of his Spirit.—I John 4:7-13.

John here expresses one of the immediate consequences of believing in God. He is assured that all the love in human life is begotten of God, that it has an eternal source and backing, that it is not thin, surface water which by chance has gathered in human lives but that it has behind it infinite reservoirs and ahead of it infinite destinies. So one of Cromwell's men said, *"It was a great instruction that the best courages are but beams of the Almighty."* Granted such a faith, the self-denying servant of his fellows is sustained, as a sentry is, who knows that around his humble and often monotonous obedience are the encompassing movement of a great army and the supporting plan of a wise commander. A real Christian is not endeavoring somehow to save a world fundamentally unsavable. He is endeavoring to make his love an open channel down which the Love that is eternal may flow into human life.

Grant us, we beseech Thee, Almighty and most Merciful God, fervently to desire, wisely to search out, and perfectly to fulfil, all that is well-pleasing unto Thee this day. Order Thou our worldly condition to the glory of Thy Name; and, of all that Thou requirest us to do, grant us the knowledge, the desire, and the ability, that we may so fulfil it as we ought; and may our path to Thee, we pray, be safe, straightforward, and perfect to the end. Give us, O Lord, a steadfast heart, which no unworthy affection may drag downwards; give us an unconquered heart, which no tribulation can wear out; give us an upright heart, which no unworthy purpose may tempt aside. Bestow upon us also, O Lord our God, understanding to know Thee, diligence to seek Thee, wisdom to find Thee, and a faithfulness that may finally embrace Thee; through Jesus Christ our Lord. Amen.—Thomas Aquinas (1225-1274).

Twelfth Week, Fourth Day

And Jesus answered and said, O faithless and perverse generation, how long shall I be with you? how long shall I bear with you? bring him hither to me. And Jesus rebuked him; and the demon went out of him: and the boy was cured from that hour.

Then came the disciples to Jesus apart, and said, Why could not we cast it out? And he saith unto them, Because of your little faith: for verily I say unto you, If ye have faith as a grain of mustard seed, ye shall say unto this mountain, Remove hence to yonder place; and it shall remove; and nothing shall be impossible unto you.—Matt. 17:17-20.

Faith in God is not simply, as we have said, a high philosophy of life, a savior from the hopelessness of unbelief, and a sustaining motive for patient service. *It is also a source of power for positive achievement.* How often does the anxious servant of human weal face mountains that must be removed! Especially in mature years, when with unveiled eyes we long have looked on human life, its sin, its waywardness, its dull unwillingness even to wish a better day, its resurgent evils that ruinously flame up like dead volcanoes come to life again, it is not easy to believe in great possibilities for the race. But with faith in God this conviction always is involved: *what ought to be done, can be done.* If one believe really in God—not in a theoretical analysis of deity but in a basic Fact which makes the universe moral through and through—then he may be sure that *ought* and *can* are twins. To say that what ought to be done cannot be done is a brief but complete confession of atheism; a man who says that does not believe in God.

O Lord, in these difficult times, when there is a seeming opposition of knowledge and faith, and an accumulation of facts beyond the power of the human mind to conceive; and good men of all religions, more and more, meet in Thee; and the strife between classes in society, and between good and evil in our own souls, is not less than of old; and the love of pleasure and the desires of the flesh are always coming in between us and Thee; and we cannot rise above these things to see the light of Heaven, but are tossed upon a sea of troubles—we pray Thee be our guide and strength and light, that, looking up to Thee always, we may behold the rock on which we stand, and be confident in the word which Thou hast spoken. Amen.—Benjamin Jowett.

Twelfth Week, Fifth Day

Then cometh the end, when he shall deliver up the kingdom to God, even the Father; when he shall have abolished all rule and all authority and power. For he must reign, till he hath put all his enemies under his feet. The last enemy that shall be abolished is death. For, He put all things in subjection under his feet. But when he saith, All things are put in subjection, it is evident that he is excepted who did subject all things unto him. And when all things have been subjected unto him, then shall the Son also himself be

subjected to him that did subject all things unto him, that God may
be all in all.—I Cor. 15:24-28.

The need for a vital faith in God is further seen in such an expression of *hope in final victory* as Paul here presents. On the naturalistic
basis alone there is neither hope nor possibility of any crowning
triumph of righteousness. On the naturalistic basis alone generation
after generation will pour out toil and sacrifice, until at last the sun
will grow cold, and the vitality of the physical universe—which to
the naturalist philosopher is the only universe there is—will fail. Like
an ice-floe from the northern seas, drifting south and melting as it
drifts, our habitable earth will shrink. And like polar bears upon
that melting floe, hopelessly watching the wasting of their home,
humanity will see its inevitable end approach, until it is finally
engulfed and lost. That is the only expectation which naturalism
can suggest or ever has suggested. But faith in God involves confidence in ultimate victory, in this world or in another or in both.
What inspiration to service this means! Any service is worth while.
"He is able to keep that which I have committed unto him against
that day" (II Tim. 1:12).

*O Eternal God, the Father of all mankind, in whom we live and
move and have our being: Have mercy on the whole human race.
Pity their ignorance, their foolishness, their weakness, their sin. Set
up an ensign for the nations, O Lord, and bring them to Thy glorious rest. Let the earth be filled with the knowledge of the Lord as
the waters cover the sea. Hasten Thy Kingdom, O Lord, and bring
in everlasting righteousness, for the honor of Thy Son, our Lord and
Saviour Jesus Christ. Amen.*—"Prayers for the City of God."

Twelfth Week, Sixth Day

For ye, brethren, were called for freedom; only use not your freedom for an occasion to the flesh, but through love be servants one
to another.—Gal. 5:13.
Let love be without hypocrisy. Abhor that which is evil; cleave to
that which is good. In love of the brethren be tenderly affectioned
one to another; in honor preferring one another.—Rom. 12:9, 10.
The Lord make you to increase and abound in love one toward
another, and toward all men, even as we also do toward you.—
I Thess. 3:12.

But concerning love of the brethren ye have no need that one
write unto you: for ye yourselves are taught of God to love one
another.—I Thess. 4:9.

Seeing ye have purified your souls in your obedience to the truth
unto unfeigned love of the brethren, love one another from the
heart fervently.—I Peter 1:22.

He that loveth his brother abideth in the light, and there is no
occasion of stumbling in him.—I John 2:10.

Consider how continuous is the emphasis on serviceable love in
the New Testament! But no one can tear such verses loose from
their entanglement with faith in God and immortality. These folk
who love one another in that first century Church are all intent on
strengthening one another's faith and deepening one another's spiritual experience. One reason for this indivisible relationship of love
and faith is that to the writers of the New Testament the supreme
service which love could render to another was the quickening and
deepening of faith. People need bread, health, homes; a multitude
of practical ministries the New Testament is concerned about; but
above all else people need God, and to make him real, to illumine
the path to him by godly living, to win to Christian trust and spiritual victory an unbelieving man—that, in the eyes of the New Testament, is the supreme service. The Master ministered to men by every
avenue of need he could discover; but his supreme ministry lies in
his revelation of God, for in that he met the deepest need of man.
Men are hungry for this bestowal of faith and confidence upon their
spiritual lives. Said Tennyson on his eightieth birthday: "I do not
know what I have done that so many people should feel grateful to
me, except that I have always kept my faith in immortality." To
keep Christian faith, to be assured of its truth, to make it in life
convincing and challenging, and to win people to see it and accept
it—that is service at its climax.

*O Thou God of infinite mercy and compassion, in whose hands
are all the hearts of the sons of men, look, we beseech Thee, graciously upon the darkened souls of the multitudes who know not
Thee. Enlighten them with the saving knowledge of the truth. Let
the beams of Thy Gospel break forth upon them, and bring them
to a sound belief in Thee, God manifested in flesh. Bring in the
fulness of the Gentiles; gather together the outcasts of Israel, and*

make Thy Name known over all the earth. Grant this, through Jesus Christ. Amen.—Bishop Hall (1574-1656).

Twelfth Week, Seventh Day

What then shall we say to these things? If God is for us, who is against us? He that spared not his own Son, but delivered him up for us all, how shall he not also with him freely give us all things? Who shall lay anything to the charge of God's elect? It is God that justifieth; who is he that condemneth? It is Christ Jesus that died, yea rather, that was raised from the dead, who is at the right hand of God, who also maketh intercession for us. Who shall separate us from the love of Christ? shall tribulation, or anguish, or persecution, or famine, or nakedness, or peril, or sword? Even as it is written,

> For thy sake we are killed all the day long;
> We were accounted as sheep for the slaughter.

Nay, in all these things we are more than conquerors through him that loved us. For I am persuaded, that neither death, nor life, nor angels, nor principalities, nor things present, nor things to come, nor powers, nor height, nor depth, nor any other creature, shall be able to separate us from the love of God, which is in Christ Jesus our Lord.—Rom. 8:31-39.

What a triumphant personality Paul was! And what a source of triumphant personality have thousands like Paul found in the faith and fellowship of him who said: "Be of good cheer; I have overcome the world." When one asks what religion has to do with service, this answer is plain—*the most useful gift which anyone can bring to the world is a triumphant life,* and the sources of that lie deep in a spiritual experience of God. The fundamental failure of mankind is spiritual; the basic need of man is inward life, abundant, undiscourageable, victorious.

> "It takes a soul
> To move a body: it takes a high-souled man,
> To move the masses—even to a cleaner stye;
> It takes the ideal, to blow a hair's breadth off
> The dust of the actual."

To give people things may leave them much as they were before; but to have personality to bestow, radiant, triumphant, contagious— that not only changes circumstances, it changes *men*.

Religious faith supplies to service elements not easily dispensable: an idealistic interpretation of life, salvation from the deadening hopelessness of unbelief, a sustaining motive for patient service, dynamic power for achievement, reasonable basis for expecting victory, a spiritual message necessary to meet man's deepest need, and resources to make possible triumphant personality.

O Faithful Lord, grant to us, we pray Thee, faithful hearts devoted to Thee, and to the service of all men for Thy sake. Fill us with pure love of Thee, keep us steadfast in this love, give us faith that worketh by love, and preserve us faithful unto death; through Jesus Christ our Lord. Amen.—Christina G. Rossetti.

COMMENT FOR THE WEEK

I

Throughout our study we have been dealing with many ministries of practical helpfulness in which a Christian spirit ought rightfully to overflow. But the most serviceable gift which any man can give the world is a radiant and inwardly victorious personality. The long missionary journeys of Francis Xavier, his tireless labors, his inexhaustible devotion, his fearlessness of the face of mortal clay, have all been celebrated as they deserve to be. But one gains an insight into Xavier's quality which no record of outward ministry can give when he reads the words of a contemporary: "Sometimes it happened that if any of the brothers were sad, the way they took to become happy was to go and look at him." Such service, springing not so much from what a man does as from what he is, is the richest contribution which anyone can make to life.

This consideration at once gives pause to that glib and superficial readiness with which too many people propose for themselves a life of helpfulness. "Ach, man," they say in Goethe's words, "you need only blow on your hands!" Granted a little good will and energy, they think, and anyone who wishes can be useful. But not even such simple ministries as the Master named in his parable of the judgment (Matt. 25:31-46) can in such a spirit be well rendered. To feed the hungry, to clothe the naked, and to give drink to the thirsty are outward deeds, which by a thrust of will can be performed. But how deeply and permanently one will *help* people by these ministries depends on invisible accompaniments which are not to be had by blowing on one's hands. The same outward gift may leave the recipient in one case angry and humiliated, in another cold and thankless, in another comforted and inspired. "When I have attempted to give myself to others by services," said Emerson, "it proved an intellectual trick—no more. They eat your service like apples and leave you out. But love them and they feel *you*, and delight in you all the time." Not till the humblest ministry is thus made spiritually significant by the personality behind it, is full-orbed service rendered.

> "Not what we give, but what we share,
> For the gift without the giver is bare;
> Who gives himself with his alms feeds three,
> Himself, his hungering neighbor, and me."

If this be true even of such external deeds as supplying food, drink, and clothing, what shall be said of the Master's next example of helpfulness? "I was sick and ye came unto me." Some strong, successful friend, with years of promising activity ahead of him, suddenly breaks down in health. His capacity to work is exhausted; his plans have crashed in ruin about his head; and you, aware of that, go up to help him "carry on." Is that a ministry to be lightly turned off? Rather you stand, humiliated and afraid, on your friend's doorsill. Yesterday you may have been self-complacent, but today you are miserable over your own weakness and futility. God in heaven, you pray, give me a stronger faith, a richer spirit! My friend needs me at my best and what have I to give?

Nothing so humbles a man, so reveals to him the poverty of his own spirit, so throws him back on God for a renewed and enriched life, as the serious attempt to be of use to other people. Christ introduces us to a life of service, and then in recoil a life of service sends us back to Christ and to the God whom he reveals for those full, spiritual reservoirs from which alone life-giving service flows. "Young man," said Tolstoi to an eager, youthful reformer, "you sweat too much blood for the world; sweat some for *yourself* first. . . . If you want to make the world better you have to *be* the best you can. . . .

You cannot bring the Kingdom of God into the world until you bring it into your own heart first."

Anyone who is endeavoring to catch the spirit of the most serviceable life that ever ministered to men cannot avoid the fact that quality of personality is the supreme contribution which the world needs, without which any other gift is of minor worth. The Master's care for the poor and sick, his practical service to the physical needs of men, are examples not to be surpassed of tireless interest in the concrete, homely wants of man's daily life. But all these services have had permanent significance for mankind and the bestower of them has taken possession of the realm of service, as its acknowledged exemplar and master, just because all these concrete services flowed from a personality rich with those spiritual goods without which men cannot live.

The ultimate secret of the Master's greatness in service the Fourth Gospel gives us in an illuminating passage: "Jesus, knowing that the Father had given all things into his hands, and that he came forth from God, and goeth unto God, riseth from supper, and layeth aside his garments; and he took a towel and girded himself. Then he poureth water into the basin and began to wash the disciples' feet" (John 13:3-5). What an extraordinary preparation for a very humble act of service! Aware of illimitable spiritual wealth, he took basin and towel and like a household slave washed his disciples' feet. One's first impression is that an immense disparity exists between the Master's lofty consciousness and his lowly deed. One's second impression is that we recall that lowly deed these twenty centuries afterwards, see it still as a symbol of self-forgetful service, flooded with such rememberable dignity that we are always humbled and chastened by its recollection, just because of the lofty heights of personality from which it flowed. The two parts of that passage do belong together. It was the personality behind the deed that made the deed unforgettable. The window of that humble service was very small, but what a radiant sun was shining through it to make it glorious forever!

When, therefore, we have said all that may be said of the Christian's obligation to serve his fellows in every ministry that their most lowly needs require, we must stress this central service which lies behind and gives abiding value to all other ministries whatsoever. Above all else men need contact with personalities who infectiously re-create faith and courage, and inspire confidence in God and man.

Above all else the disheartened spirits of ordinary folk, "laggard, fearsome, and thin-ranked," need the rallying impact of men whose vision and faith make them unafraid. A youth, now a professor at Harvard University, once sought Phillips Brooks for an interview on a problem that had long perplexed him. With careful thought he phrased his question that he might surely ask it right. When the long anticipated day arrived he spent a radiant hour with Phillips Brooks. He came out from it transfigured, life glorious again; until at last as he went up Beacon Street toward home, it dawned on him that he had clean forgotten to ask Phillips Brooks that question. "But," he says, "I did not care. I had found out that what I needed was not the solution of a special problem, but the contagion of a triumphant spirit." That is still the supreme need of the world. To supply that need is the richest gift that any man can bestow.

II

Not only does the ultimate significance of personal service thus depend upon quality of personality; the final efficiency of *social service* also springs from the same fountain. We have rightly emphasized the importance to the normal and wholesome life of man of social and economic readjustments. But such readjustments cannot in the first instance be obtained, nor once secured can they be preserved, unless they have their natural source in an inward, spiritual life, whose appropriate expressions they are. Of anything that happens in the social life of man, however vast its range or external its circumstance, the words of the prophet are true: "I will bring evil upon this people, even the fruit of their thoughts" (Jer. 6:19).

What, for example, is the ultimate source of the catastrophe from whose aftermath this generation cannot escape? Politicians will explain the trouble, doubtless with some truth, in diplomatic maladjustments. Economists will explain the War's source, doubtless truthfully, as due to economic maladjustments. But to prophetic insight such explanations are as incomplete as though a man in New Orleans should account for the Mississippi River by saying that it came from Memphis, or a man in Memphis should explain it by saying that St. Louis was its source. They speak truly enough so far as they go, but they have not traced the river back to its ultimate origin. It really rises from many springs far up in the Rockies. So, high up among the mountains of our human life, a prophetic spirit sees, innumerable and obscure, the inner thoughts of multitudes of folk, the quality of their spirits, the emphasis of their desires, from which, as from many fountains blending, flow down the resultant destinies of humankind. No matter how vast the public consequence with which he deals, he traces back the creative source of it to these springs in the habitual thinking of the people.

Behind this generation's cataclysm one sees clearly the group of old ideas, inveterately held, which brought on the dire disaster. That war is necessary, inextricably woven into the fabric of international relationships; that the ethic of good will and cooperation is applicable to individuals but not to states; that economic supremacy can be achieved by organized violence; that nations must always go on raising vast armies, building vast armaments, teaching all their youth to kill, and laying greedy hands on each new invention to make gregarious death more swift and horrible; that war is not only inevitable but desirable, a valuable tonic to man's moral life—such are the ideas out of which our catastrophe has come. And if repeatedly such disasters are not to fall upon the world, something more than new arrangements of diplomatic and economic affairs must be achieved. There must be a widespread, deep-seated, popular repentance of the old *ideas* and a resolute renunciation of them. In international affairs as well as in personal character, out of the heart are the issues of life (Prov. 4:23).

So, to a man of insight, the noisy, angry busyness of the world, with its economic upheavals and its crashing armies, often seems illusion, through which as through a transparent veil one looks into the reality behind. And this is the reality: the minds of men and women like inward looms, where the tirelessly moving shuttles of our habitual thinking weave the texture of our human destinies.

The ultimate service, therefore, without which any other ministries are little worth, is spiritual. It consists in the spreading of information, in the teaching of truth, in the inspiration of faith, in the contagious bestowal of clean hearts and right spirits. Lacking such service, all confidence in the mere manipulation of outward circumstances is living in a fool's paradise. An American believes in democracy. Yet many nations, having constitutions like his own, still are the unstable victims of continual revolution. It is not so much the constitution that saves the country as it is the quality of manhood that makes the constitution work. An American believes in the abolition of the liquor traffic. Yet the Turks have lived under a regime where the liquor traffic is forbidden, from the days of the prophet until now, and by that fact alone have not been saved to greatness of personal and national character. An internationalist believes in a league of nations. But he should not forget that such a league will be the most extensive experiment in cooperation ever tried; that it will put an unprecedented strain upon tolerance, patience, good will, and faith; that such forty-story buildings cannot be erected safely on three-story foundations. An industrial reformer believes in more leisure for the workingmen. But he should recall that there has been leisure in plenty in the South Sea Islands for many generations, with little to do save to pluck fruit and to eat it in the shade, but that no great consequence for human weal ever came from such spare time. Whether for employer or employee, it is one thing to achieve outward leisure; it is another thing to achieve that quality of character which will make good use of it. We may well be concerned lest, enthusiastic for outward reforms, we in the end achieve them— and get *nothing*. For outward reforms have permanence only when they proceed from, are sustained by, and issue in personality redeemed to wisdom and truth, to God and godliness.

Napoleon, so the story runs, was once told that French letters were showing signs of decay under his regime, and that a renaissance of creative literature was needed. "So!" said the Emperor. "I will speak to the Minister of the Interior about it." Creative literature from a department of state! "King Lear," or the "Ode to the West Wind," or "Intimations of Immortality" by order of the Minister of the Interior! Yet one may as reasonably expect that, as to expect creative character from the mere manipulation of outward circumstance. Creative character comes from the deep fountains of spiritual life; changed circumstance gives it free room for utterance. The deepest service that one man can do for others, therefore, is to minister to the spiritual sources of life, inwardly to change their minds, to make great faiths real and great ideals convincing, to establish for them vital contacts with the spiritual world, to bring them into transforming fellowship with Jesus Christ.

III

Not only are personal and social service thus dependent for their final efficiency upon the quality of man's inward life, but *the persistence of service itself*, in any form whatever, rests back at last upon that indispensable foundation. The streets are full of people who started out to be of use. They, too, had a youth when knighthood was in flower, but they have fallen now into disillusioned uselessness. Like automobiles with good self-starters they were off and away with fleet eagerness to serve the world, but they have petered out in a sandy stretch or have gone dead on a high hill. The Master's thumb-nail sketch in the Parable of the Builder fits them exactly: "This man began to build but was not able to finish" (Luke 14:30).

This aspect of the problem of a serviceable life is one of the most serious that men face now, as it was when Jesus was on earth. He was not always met by callous selfishness, that grossly rebuffed his appeal and scorned his teaching. Plenty of people were swept off their feet by his presence, were stirred by swift and eager emotion at his words, but how much of this enthusiasm turned out to be bubbling effervescence! It had no substance in it, no abiding motives to give it permanence. Like seed in shallow soil, as he pictured it, "there was no deepness of root." So to this day the life of Jesus is too alluring, the ideals of Jesus too challenging, the first chivalrous endeavors in unselfishness too rewarding, not to lead many folk to accept gladly the life which he proposes. But the course of true service does not run smooth. People whom we try to help, turn out to be obstinate, ungrateful, incorrigible. They return evil for good. They cling to the very conditions from which we try to save them. The most gracious spirit is at times tempted to cry with Keats: "I admire human nature, but I do not like men." To one who has centered his hopes on social causes, how laggard their progress often seems, how roundabout and hard bestead is the wilderness journey to the Promised Land! It has been said of Alpine peaks that they pass through three stages: first, "absolutely inaccessible"; second, "a very dangerous climb"; third, "a pleasant summer excursion." But how long do the heights of social reformation have to wait before they thus are climbed and conquered!

The upshot of it is that of all who start to live lives of Christian service, one suspects that only a small proportion carry through. Launchings are a gala sight. Amid cheers and music the ship, gay with color, takes to the sea. But every old salt knows that launching is not the test of a ship. When northeasters howl and billows roll mast high, will she beat up against the tempest and make port when other ships go down? Such is the severe strain to which man's wickedness, ignorance, thanklessness, his sluggishness, blindness, apathy, subject a life of service. *The final resource of a serviceable man must be his own inwardly victorious spirit, sustained by motives which wear well, by unsmothered faiths, and by hopes which refuse to grow dim.* Only a personality so equipped can easily see through to a triumphant close a life of sustained and sacrificial ministry.

IV

With the ultimate efficiency and the abiding power of personal and social service thus depending upon inward spiritual resources, it is plain that not only does Christianity overflow in usefulness, but usefulness has need of all those sustaining and life-giving Christian faiths by which spiritual victory is gained in the souls of men. The final tragedy in human life is not physical poverty but whipped spirits, and whipped spirits are found on avenues as well as alleys, in palaces as well as hovels, in universities as well as barrooms. Men are beaten in spirit by the hugeness of the physical universe, until they think of it as a vast, pitiless machine, without spiritual origin, meaning, purpose, or destiny. Men are beaten by trouble until, maimed at the very center of their lives, they crawl through existence without God and without hope. Men are beaten in spirit by sin, and, like dogs that return to lick the hand that flogged them, these bewitched souls come back again and again to the transgressions that are their ruin. Men are beaten in spirit by hopelessness, until they look out on the social life of man with no enthusiasm for any cause and with no expectation of any betterment.

Service to these victims of spiritual disillusionment, infidelity, and hopelessness cannot be rendered by man's fingers only. No *thing* that can be given greatly helps. Only spirits who are themselves victorious can minister to these deepest needs of men. Alice Freeman Palmer, second president of Wellesley College, was once reproved because she did not do more public lecturing; to which, out of her passion for personal service, she replied: "It is people that count. You want to put yourself into people; they touch other people; these, others still, and so you go on working forever." We easily applaud that program of service by personal contagion. But we may well inquire what richness of personality we possess that the world should greatly care whether or not we put our *selves* into people. How many who eagerly give themselves, have selves to give, so poor in quality, that for all their busyness the world is none the richer! The Master looked on service as too deep and inward an enterprise lightly to be undertaken. *"For their sakes,"* he said, *"I sanctify myself."*

Sir Bartle Frere was coming to visit a Scotch home. The master of the household, sending a servant to meet him, sought for some description by which the visitor might easily be recognized. "When the train comes in," he said at last to the servant, "you will see *a tall gentleman, helping somebody."* That, in parable, is the Christian ideal. Over these sixty generations one Figure has towered, from the fascination and dominance of whose personality mankind never can escape. Height and helpfulness in him were perfectly combined. And the world has come to recognize his spirit, living again on earth, whenever there appears spiritual altitude blending with lowly service—a tall gentleman, helping somebody.

The issue of this line of thought, however, is not a life which seeks *first* to be right and *then* to go out to serve. Victorious personality and practical service cannot be so chronologically arranged. They grow together, are mutually influential, are indispensable each to the other's health and wholeness. As one reads the New Testament he becomes aware that the Epistle to the Hebrews (6:4, 5) gives a true description of the fully Christian life of the first generation, and that the climax of this description is the gist of the matter: those first Christians had "tasted . . . the powers of the age to come." They believed in a new day of righteousness to appear upon the earth, when God's long-maturing plans would come to glorious fulfilment. That coming age they loved, to its ideals they were devoted, for it they would die. They were patriots for a day not yet arrived.

One outstanding distinction, therefore, between Christians and non-Christians in the first generation lay here: like Demas, non-Christians "loved this present age" (II Tim. 4:10), with all its unconquered evil, while the followers of Jesus were working and waiting for the age to come. If one would be a Christian, then, he must in this sense be a revolutionist: he must have his heart set on a new order of humanity where godliness, righteousness, and brotherhood shall have superseded the reign of bitterness and wrath. He must believe in, pray for, and labor toward the coming of God's Kingdom in the world. This is the central passion of a fully Christian life, its guiding star, its regulating standard.

If that supreme patriotism for a better world, divinely ordered, "rooted and grounded in love," once does take intelligent possession

of a human life, impressive consequences are certain: personal penitence for sin that hinders the Kingdom's coming, personal desire for
inward life worthy of the Kingdom's ideals, personal entrance into
secrets of spiritual power by which alone the Kingdom's coming is
assured, personal devotion to every good cause by which the day of
Christian triumph is hastened. Victorious personality is not the fruit
of cloistered piety. It is the accompaniment of full devotion to God's
Kingdom:

> "I ask no heaven till earth be Thine;
> No glory crown while work of mine
> Remaineth here.
> When earth shall shine among the stars,
> Her sins wiped out, her captives free,
> Her voice a music unto Thee,
> For crown, more work give Thou to me.
> Lord, here am I!"

SCRIPTURE PASSAGES
USED IN THE DAILY READINGS

RUTH 1:14-18 (V-6).

ECCLESIASTES 1:12-18 (IX-3).

ISAIAH 1:11-17 (I-2); 2:2-4 (VIII-6); 3:14, 15 (X-3); 19:23-25 (IX-4); 62:1-5 (VIII-5).

JEREMIAH 7:3-11 (I-5).

EZEKIEL 22:29 (X-3); 33:30-32 (I-6); 34:1-10 (VIII-7).

HOSEA 6:4-6 (I-4).

AMOS 2:6-8 (X-3); 5:21-24 (I-3).

MICAH 6:6-8 (I-1); 7:2-7 (XI-5).

MATTHEW 5:13 (II-5); 5:13-16 (X-6); 5:21, 22 (VI-3); 5:23, 24 (II-2); 5:29, 30 (V-1); 5:43-45 (VI-7); 6:9-13 (X-7); 7:3-5 (VII-3); 8:1-4 (VIII-2); 8:18-20 (VII-5); 11:7-11 (VII-6); 12:43-45 (II-6); 13:44-46 (V-2); 16:21-25 (V-7); 17:17-20 (XII-4); 18:2-6 (VI-5); 18:10-14 (VI-6); 20:20-28 (VII-7); 21:12, 13 (VI-4); 22:34-40 (VI-1); 23:5-12 (III-5); 23:15-19, 23, 24 (I-7); 25:34-40 (VIII-3).

MARK 5:1-5 (II-3); 9:50 (II-5); 10:13-16 (VIII-1); 10:23-27 (III-6).

LUKE 4:16-21 (II-1); 5:10, 11, 27, 28 (V-5); 6:31 (VI-1); 8:11-15 (II-7); 10:30-37 (II-4); 12:16-21 (III-3); 15:1-7 (VIII-4); 16:19-26 (III-2); 18:9-14 (III-7); 19:8-10 (V-4); 21:1-4 (V-3).

JOHN 4:35-38 (XI-1); 8:3-11 (VI-2); 10:9, 10 (IV-7); 14:25-27 (IV-4); 15:9-11 (IV-4); 15:12-15 (IV-1).

ROMANS 1:8-12 (IV-3); 6:12, 13 (IX-6); 8:31-39 (XII-7); 12:3-5 (VII-4); 12:9, 10 (XII-6).

I CORINTHIANS 1:11-15 (XI-2); 3:6-9 (IX-2); 15:24-28 (XII-5).

II CORINTHIANS 8:1-5 (IX-5).

GALATIANS 5:13 (XII-6); 6:2, 3 (VII-4).

EPHESIANS 3:14-19 (IV-5).

PHILIPPIANS 2:1-4 (VII-2); 3:13-19 (IX-7); 4:10-13 (III-1)

I THESSALONIANS 3:12 (XII-6); 4:9 (XII-6).

II THESSALONIANS 3:7-13 (IV-2); 3:11, 12 (VII-1).

I TIMOTHY 6:9-11 (X-1); 6:17-19 (III-4).
II TIMOTHY 3:1-9 (XI-6); 4:6-8 (IV-6).
TITUS 1:5, 10-13 (XI-4).
HEBREWS 3:12-14 (XII-2); 11:32-38 (XI-3); 12:1-3 (XI-7).
JAMES 1:27 (IX-1); 2:1-9 (X-5); 4:1-3 (X-4); 5:1-5 (X-2).
I PETER 1:22 (XII-6); 4:15, 16 (VII-1).
I JOHN 2:10 (XII-6); 3:14-18 (XII-1); 3:17, 18 (IX-1); 4:7-13
    (XII-3).

SOURCES OF PRAYERS
USED IN THE DAILY READINGS

AQUINAS, THOMAS—XII-3.

BEECHER, HENRY WARD—VI-2; VI-6; X-2; X-7. "The Original Plymouth Pulpit," vol. III.

BERSIER, EUGENE—VIII-3. "A Chain of Prayer Across the Ages," S. F. Fox.

BOOK OF COMMON PRAYER—III-7; XI-2.

BOOK OF PRAYERS FOR STUDENTS—II-6; III-3; V-5; VI-7; VII-4; IX-6; X-5; XII-2.

BRENT, BISHOP CHARLES R.—VII-6. "Prayers for Today," Samuel McComb.

BROUGH, DR.—VIII-2; VIII-4. "Prayers for the City of God," Gilbert Clive Binyon.

CHRISTIAN PRAYERS—III-1.

CHURCH GUILD—V-6. "A Chain of Prayer Across the Ages," S. F. Fox.

DEARMER, PERCY—VIII-6, "Prayers for the City of God," Gilbert Clive Binyon.

ELLIS, RUFUS—XI-1. "A Chain of Prayer Across the Ages," S. F. Fox.

FRENCH CORONATION ORDER—I-1. "Prayers for the City of God," Gilbert Clive Binyon.

GELASIAN SACRAMENTARY—II-1. "A Chain of Prayer Across the Ages," S. F. Fox.

GOTHIC MISSAL—XI-4. "A Chain of Prayer Across the Ages," S. F. Fox.

GRAHAM, W. B.—X-3. "Prayers for the City of God," Gilbert Clive Binyon.

GRINDAL, ARCHBISHOP—VI-4. "The Communion of Prayer," William Boyd Carpenter.

HALL, BISHOP—XII-6. "A Chain of Prayer Across the Ages," S. F. Fox.

HERFORD, BISHOP VERNON—II-3. "Prayers for the City of God," Gilbert Clive Binyon.

HOLLAND, H. SCOTT—V-7. "Prayers for the City of God," Gilbert Clive Binyon.

HORT, F. J. A.—XI-6. "A Chain of Prayer Across the Ages," S. F. Fox.

HUNTER, JOHN—I-4. "Prayers for the City of God," Gilbert Clive Binyon; IX-1, X-6. "A Chain of Prayer Across the Ages," S. F. Fox.

JACOBITE LITURGY OF ST. DIONYSIUS—X-4. "Prayers for the City of God," Gilbert Clive Binyon.

JOWETT, BENJAMIN—XII-4.

JOWETT, JOHN HENRY—V-1. "The Communion of Prayer," William Boyd Carpenter.

KEMPIS, THOMAS À—III-5; VII-1. "The Communion of Prayer," William Boyd Carpenter.

KEN, BISHOP—V-4; XI-7. "Prayers for the City of God," Gilbert Clive Binyon.

KINGSLEY, CHARLES—I-3; III-6; VII-7. "Prayers for the City of God," Gilbert Clive Binyon.

KNIGHT, W. ANGUS—IV-4. "Prayers for Today," Samuel McComb.

LEONINE SACRAMENTARY—XI-3. "A Chain of Prayer Across the Ages," S. F. Fox.

McCOMB, SAMUEL—I-5; IV-1; IX-4. "Prayers for Today."

MACLAREN, ALEXANDER—I-2, "Pulpit Prayers."

MACLEOD, NORMAN—III-4; VII-2. "The Communion of Prayer," William Boyd Carpenter.

MARTINEAU, JAMES—II-5. "A Book of Prayers for Students"; V-2. "A Chain of Prayer Across the Ages," S. F. Fox.

MATHESON, GEORGE—IV-3. "Prayers for Today," Samuel McComb.

MILLER, GEORGE A.—IV-6; VI-3. "Prayers for Today," Samuel Mc-Comb.

M. P. G. E.—X-1. "Prayers for the City of God," Gilbert Clive Binyon.

NASH, HENRY S.—IV-7.

PRAYERS FOR THE CITY OF GOD—VI-1; VIII-5; XI-5; XII-5. Gilbert Clive Binyon.

QUEEN ELIZABETH'S PRAYER BOOK—II-4.

RAUSCHENBUSCH, WALTER—IV-2; VI-5; VIII-1; VIII-7; IX-2; IX-3. "Prayers of the Social Awakening."

RIDDING, BISHOP—I-6.

ROSSETTI, CHRISTINA G.—IV-5. "Prayers, Ancient and Modern," Mary W. Tileston; XII-7. "A Chain of Prayer Across the Ages," S. F. Fox.

ST. AUGUSTINE—V-3. "A Chain of Prayer Across the Ages," S. F. Fox.

TAULER, JOHN—XII-1. "The Communion of Prayer," William Boyd Carpenter.

TILLOTSON, JOHN—VII-5. "A Chain of Prayer Across the Ages," S. F. Fox.

WESTCOTT, BISHOP—II-2; III-2; VII-3.

WESLEY, JOHN—II-7.

WILLIAMS, ROWLAND—IX-7. "A Chain of Prayer Across the Ages," S. F. Fox.